KAPLAN EDUCATIONAL
FOUNDATION

# Your 2018 Guide to College Transfer

## 90 SCHOOL PROFILES

Nancy Lee Sánchez

*Author:* Nancy Lee Sánchez

*Developmental Editor:* Mike Tague
*Research Editors:* Rhoda Tamakloe, Renika Montgomery
*Production Editor:* Dominique Polfliet
*Designer:* Joanna Graham
*Publishing Coordinator:* Jessica Yee
*Copyeditor:* Laurel Haines
*Typesetter:* Pamela Beaulieu

This publication is designed to provide accurate and authoritative information in regard to the subject matter covered. It is sold with the understanding that the publisher is not engaged in rendering medical, legal, accounting, or other professional services. If legal advice or other expert assistance is required, the services of a competent professional should be sought.

*100% of the proceeds from the sale of this book will go to the Kaplan Educational Foundation, a 501(c)3 public charity.*

Published by Kaplan Publishing, a division of Kaplan, Inc.
750 Third Avenue
New York, NY 10017

ISBN: 978-1-5062-3391-8
10 9 8 7 6 5 4 3 2 1

# TABLE OF CONTENTS

# DEDICATION

This book became a reality thanks to a community of individuals committed to making college degrees more accessible.

To Mike Tague, for your guidance and support in seeing this project through at every phase, Rhoda Tamakloe, for your partnership and brilliance in all that you do, Ayania Wellington, for keeping us on track and holding down the fort, and Deborah Shames, for leading the transfer admissions process and never giving up on our students.

To our lead researcher, Renika Montgomery, for taking ownership of the research and being relentless in your pursuit of data. And to the research team: Shandel Burke, Jessenia Preciado, Iracema Sanchez, Rebecca Levy, Norbesida Bagabila, Raquel Melendez, Carlos Velez, Ninotska Love, and Ethan Levy.

To the Kaplan Publishing team, Maureen McMahon, and Mark Harrad, for your expertise and focus.

To our committed board of directors: Jane Rosenberg, Rebecca Campoverde, Karen P. Ross, Harold Elish, and Ernest Bervell Mensah, and especially to the chairman of the board, Melissa Mack, for your leadership, vision, and unwavering support of our mission. I also want to thank Jennifer Benn, my predecessor. It was Jennifer's own dream to make sure that our Scholars reached high, far, and wide and that they should be thoroughly supported. I am ever grateful for your belief in our Scholars and me.

To Jonathan Grayer, the founder of the Kaplan Educational Foundation, who was convinced that given the opportunity, resources, and preparation, our Scholars would thrive as leaders.

To our long-standing supporters in Kaplan, Inc.'s leadership, including Andy Rosen, John Polstein, and the many, many employees who volunteer and give so much, both personally and professionally.

To Don Graham, who from the very beginning believed in our work and knew that our mission was worth the investment and hard work.

To our champions at the community colleges of the City University of New York and four-year colleges, who are committed to diversity and access for transfer students on the non-traditional path. I will always be grateful to you and to our "thought partners," including Phi Theta Kappa and the National Institute for the Study of Transfer Students, who from the very beginning shared your expertise and knowledge to help us succeed.

Finally, this book is dedicated to our Kaplan Leadership Scholars, for the trust, bravery, and resilience you have demonstrated over the last 11 years. Despite many barriers, you have focused on the endless possibilities of your goals. In doing so, you have opened the doors for so many. Your big dreams spread hope and strength in our communities. Thank you.

And thank you to my mother, Adela Badillo, who showed me that life is best lived in pursuit of dreams and gave me a compass that demanded I follow integrity, kindness, curiosity, and knowledge. To my brothers and sisters, you sacrificed so much for me, your baby sister. Los amo.

## ABOUT THE KAPLAN EDUCATIONAL FOUNDATION

The Kaplan Educational Foundation is a 501(c)3 public charity initially established with the support of a generous endowment funded by Kaplan, Inc. executives. In 2006, the Kaplan Educational Foundation launched the Kaplan Leadership Program (KLP). It is a highly comprehensive program designed to provide financial aid, academic support, leadership skills development, and cultural enrichment. The program's unique and trailblazing model is filling a gap among an often overlooked population of students: low-income, high-potential, underrepresented community college students. KLP Scholars are attending highly competitive four-year schools while program alumni have graduated with honors, landed notable positions in their fields of interest, and earned degrees from highly selective graduate schools.

## ABOUT THE AUTHOR

**Nancy Lee Sánchez**, M.A., is the executive director for the Kaplan Educational Foundation. As the founding director for academic advisement and student development, Sánchez was responsible for the design and implementation of the Kaplan Leadership Program model.

Sánchez has over 18 years of expertise providing greater access to higher education, improving the college experience, and supporting leadership among low-income, underrepresented, and non-traditional students through collaborative partnerships and services that directly target factors affecting degree-attainment gaps.

Sánchez's own educational journey started at Kingsborough Community College, where she earned her associate's degree in early childhood education. She went on to earn a bachelor's degree in education from Long Island University and a master's in sociology from Brooklyn College. As a 2014 National Hispanic Executive Leadership Fellow, Sánchez completed Harvard University's John F. Kennedy School of Government's Executive Leadership Program and the Leadership Development Program at the Center for Creative Leadership. Born in Las Piedras, Puerto Rico, Sánchez currently resides in Brooklyn.

**K**

# FOREWORD

As the executive director of the Kaplan Educational Foundation (KEF), I recognize that I live in a college admissions bubble. That is, for more than a decade, I have seen our Kaplan Leadership Scholars transfer from community colleges to highly selective institutions. I have seen them graduate with competitive resumes including challenging internships, culturally diverse study-abroad programs, and extracurriculars that illustrate the wide range of interests that reside in most of us. Unfortunately, that's not the norm.

At KEF, we ardently believe that any student who has excelled at their current community college should be supported to meet their highest transfer admissions potential and take advantage of opportunities like our Scholars have. Our goal with this guide is to make such opportunities possible for more students.

You will find the schools we've listed in this guide are some of the most selective four-year colleges and universities across the United States. There's a reason for this. They usually have the most financial, academic, and experiential resources, all of which make it possible for students to thrive and develop the hard and soft skills necessary to excel in their fields.

But the students in our program are not your typical college students. They come from low-income backgrounds and historically underrepresented groups, with many being the first generation in their families to attend college. Even the most talented students from these backgrounds face difficulties getting into selective schools. Without the support of their community colleges, the resources to submit strong applications, and the four-year colleges' commitment to consider, accept, fund, and support them, many of these students fall outside of the college admissions bubble I mentioned.

To help students bridge the gap between community colleges and selective schools, we need them to be informed consumers of education. We also need top colleges to value their contributions and make a commitment to their transition, with the same resources freshmen have, such as informative orientations, opportunities to study abroad, options to perform research, and the ability to live on campus if they desire.

I can speak from experience about growing up without the resources to bridge the gap. For close to 10 years at Kingsborough Community College in Brooklyn, I had the honor to serve community college students in multiple roles, including in the study-abroad program and Bilingual College Discovery Program, a college access program for students with low English and/or math proficiency. Kingsborough was where I had earned my own associate's degree and where I developed an understanding of the many challenges that students like me and our future Scholars face even today. While completing my own associate's degree in early childhood education, I spent many hours with fellow students commuting to and from Brooklyn, our multiple jobs, and our far-flung living spaces.

Kingsborough was the first place where my opinions, reactions to the world around me, and critical thinking skills were taken seriously. It was where my dreams and aspirations changed from being just part of an internal conversation with myself to part of a wider dialogue with my community. Before community college, I had no real adult relationships based on interests other than my family and our household expenses. I was put on a secretarial track in high school, so I was never asked whether I'd take the SAT or what colleges I planned to apply to. Instead, I was told that my fast typing skills would surely get me a job as a secretary. With my high-school years geared toward finding a job, not getting a college degree, I was like so many people around me who were stuck in low-paying jobs that failed to engage their intellectual abilities and depleted their dreams.

As a young Puerto Rican living in New York City, I was moved by many of the problems facing the city, from crime to the poor public school education I had received to the fact that health care services were scarce. At the same time, I did not understand how I could help fix these problems. I lived a very disempowered life, and my connection to the community, country, and world was extremely narrow. When I was at Kingsborough, for the first time I saw people in my community studying abroad, discussing current events in detail, taking internships, and even receiving feedback on their performance in class and in their fieldwork. With the horizon broadening ahead of me, I realized I could not only obtain a college degree, but also be a valued contributor to any institution I chose to join.

Coming to the realization that I could achieve my dreams and work on systemic problems facing my community and beyond was a bit shocking for me. For many people like me, college appeared to be a dead end. Some of us, like my brother, started college but didn't complete. Others saw going to college as a vacation that you couldn't afford to take. The fact is that going to a school that fits your needs and supports your goals is the best way to become the best at what you do.

It's frightening to me that this was not made obvious to me and my classmates. That's why when I first read the mission of the Kaplan Educational Foundation, it read like poetry. When I met with Jennifer Benn, the foundation's then executive director, we agreed it was not a lack of ability, but a lack of opportunity that was holding these students back. Connections between two-year and four-year schools were missing. Information and resources for students were too hard to find or nonexistent. And to create true leaders, we couldn't just throw money at the problem. Instead, we created a system where brilliant students had roundtable discussions among themselves, their tutors, and other mentors who challenged them to become even better students. We talked to people who had children and asked them what kind of support they'd need to succeed. For our immigrant students, we realized we needed to explain the language of transfer—from explaining what a wait list was to getting them to differentiate between undergraduate and graduate courses. Making it possible for students to set foot on campus was also key. Seeing is believing. Over the past decade, I've seen students who were already exceptional truly blossom into leaders.

While not all schools are equal when it comes to transfer, I'm happy to say more and more are starting to understand the value of accepting and supporting transfer students. At the Kaplan Educational Foundation, we help our students map out the pathways to selective institutions. We work with them to eliminate barriers of every kind so they can have greater domain over their own financial future, happiness, and self-satisfaction. In turn, they go on to help solve some of society's most pressing issues. And you can too. I hope this guide helps you get there.

# CHAPTER ONE

# Why Transfer Changes Lives

Transfer changes lives. Not just for individual students, not just for their families, and not even just for their communities. Transfer is an essential part of the American dream that helps students reach their fullest potential and give back to the greater good. It's no surprise that Barack Obama, Warren Buffett, Jim Lehrer, Steven Spielberg, and Eileen Collins were all transfer students. We can all agree that transfer students have changed the world.

In 2006, the Kaplan Educational Foundation launched the Kaplan Leadership Program through an endowment established by Kaplan, Inc. executives. We planned to be the "Rhodes Scholarship" program for community college students who wanted to transfer to competitive four-year colleges. Impacting a small group of low-income, high-potential students in a big way, we aimed to develop them into global leaders.

Our mission reflects our heritage. Stanley Kaplan started his business by tutoring immigrant students who wanted access to top universities. While they lacked the pedigree typically associated with students of prestigious schools, standardized tests enabled them to demonstrate their merit, opening doors to better futures.

Still, at our founding over a decade ago, we discovered that many selective four-year colleges had not given serious consideration or developed solid recruitment or retention plans to accept and graduate transfer students from community colleges. The Jack Kent Cooke Foundation had opened the door to conversations with admissions staff around the country by funding important research and access programs. The time was right for us to dive in headfirst, bringing talented community college students from diverse backgrounds to these elite colleges. We worked with community college students and staff to develop the students' study skills, close the gaps in their education, guide them through the transfer process, and submit outstanding transfer applications. We invited key people at four-year institutions to meet Kaplan Leadership Scholars and get to know them in person. We took our students on college campus tours so they could see for themselves what it meant to study and live at these institutions. The direct approach yielded serious results. Over the past decade, the same schools that once asked us, "Do you know how hard it is to get into this school?" are now saying, "We need more students like yours."

Selective schools are beginning to recognize that transfer students, especially those that persevered and excelled at community colleges, have much to offer their campuses. They understand the fact that a student seeking to leave one college and continue at another is not displaying weakness, but determination. As schools look to identify students with intellectual curiosity and prowess, socioeconomic diversity, and a passion for learning, they quickly notice that transfer students bring with them a proven record of all of these traits. Most importantly, they see that these students can be change agents as long as we help them expand their goals from "I'm going to take two jobs" to "I'm going to help fix income inequality." Educational opportunities take transfer students from survivors to dreamers and make them among the best people to tackle systemic issues.

We're excited to broaden our mission with the publication of this guide, created to help students prepare and successfully transfer to the college of their choice. It's meant to give students the tools to go on to be the very best in their field, no matter how they began their postsecondary education. We hope it helps discredit the myth that these students can't succeed at top colleges or afford them. And we hope it helps them take advantage of transfer opportunities to change their lives, their communities, and the world.

# A NOTE FOR STUDENTS

You're reading this guide because you're thinking about taking the next step on your educational journey. As you consider your future, try to take a step back from your immediate goals and consider the big picture. How can you become a better student and a better thinker? How can you have more time to dedicate to your goals and passions, and how can you become the very best at what you do?

There is a famous quote by Benjamin Elijah Mays, mentor to Dr. Martin Luther King, Jr.: "Whatever you do, strive to do it so well that no man living and no man dead and no man yet to be born could do it any better." While many transfer students consider themselves to be in "survival mode," at the Kaplan Educational Foundation, we encourage our scholars to look beyond getting a degree just to get a job. Becoming the very best at what you do is the real goal, and highly selective institutions are often the best places to do that. Using this guide, you can start to identify the schools that are the best fit for you, offer you the most support, and give you the tools you need to dream big.

If you're worried that top schools aren't looking for people like you, don't be. Our students have transferred from community colleges into some of the top schools in the country: Brown, Stanford, Amherst, Occidental, Syracuse, and many others. And anyone can be a transfer student. Whether you're looking to transfer from a community college to a four-year school, switching from your current four-year school to one that's a better fit, or continuing your education after having taken time off, this guide is for you. In fact, 37 percent of college students transfer at least once within six years.[1] So you're in good company!

Let's be honest: you may have legitimate concerns about your ability to reach your goals at your current college. Or you may be at an amazing school right now but recognize there are others that match your specific needs better. That's OK; sometimes going to your first school helps you figure out what you really need from your college experience. Whatever your situation, the advice and School Profiles you'll find in this guide will help you find the right place to continue down your educational path and become a leader in your chosen field. You'll find that transfer can be a stepping stone for those who want to aim higher, take on leadership positions, and reach their goals.

If you take one thing away from this guide, let it be this: you can apply to these schools, and you can succeed at them. In fact, they're looking for you.

---

1   Source: National Student Clearinghouse Research Center

## A NOTE FOR COMMUNITY COLLEGES

There are many factors that make community college a logical start to a postsecondary education. Cost and geographic proximity lead many students, especially low-income students, to start their college journey at the door of the local community college. But for many of these students, getting an associate's degree from their community college is not the final destination. In fact, more than 80 percent of first-time community college students aspire to a bachelor's degree, though only 33 percent actually transfer to a four-year institution within six years.[2] There is an enormous amount of potential caught in the gap between community colleges and four-year schools.

To bridge the gap that so many community college students need help crossing, we've been advocating for creating a "culture of transfer." The fact is, transfer requires extensive planning and preparation, ideally starting as soon as possible at the community college level. Creating a true culture of transfer entails building the kinds of support systems that well-off students often take for granted, like admissions counseling, a better explanation of transferable credits, extra tutoring, and help navigating the application and financial aid processes. While those systems are difficult to build and fund, we hope this book helps point the way in terms of the kinds of information transfer students are looking for.

If you have a solid transfer program in place, you already know that it can help attract dedicated students with a strong sense of purpose. From our experience working closely with the City University of New York, we've seen that students who are motivated enough to transfer will do well at the colleges they start out at and become credits to the reputation of their community colleges.

At the end of the day, successful transfer students provide the opportunity to show how powerful community college education is, as well as how many talented students come through community college systems. We know you are very proud of these students, and we encourage you to use this guide to help them get to the next level.

## A NOTE FOR SELECTIVE SCHOOLS

Top schools often struggle to find diverse students. In fact, at 38 US colleges, including 5 in the Ivy League, more students came from the top 1 percent of the income scale than from the entire bottom 60 percent.[3] Transfer education can be a vital source of diversity for all kinds of schools, especially selective schools. Diversity of all kinds—socioeconomic, racial, cultural, ethnic, religious—is paramount for any school that wants to remain a beacon for top achievers and offer its students perspectives from many walks of life.

For over a decade, our Kaplan Scholars have thrived at elite colleges throughout the US, with a graduation rate of 92 percent. Bear in mind that our Scholars all come from low-income and underrepresented backgrounds, and many are non-traditional-age students, single parents, and the sole source of income for their families. Yet the graduation rate for the general US student population of first-time, full-time students who start their undergraduate careers at four-year institutions is just 59 percent.[4] Clearly, investing in transfer students yields results. In addition, most only spend two to three years at their transfer schools, meaning those schools do not bear financial aid costs for their pre-transfer years.

---

2   Source: Community College Research Center
3   Source: The Equality of Opportunity Project
4   Source: National Center for Education Statistics

Princeton recently made the value of transfer students clear when it announced it would resume accepting these students after three decades of barring them from admissions. As its strategic plan states, "Experience at other universities shows that transfer programs can provide a vehicle to attract students with diverse backgrounds and experiences, such as qualified military veterans and students from low-income backgrounds, including some who might begin their careers at community colleges."[5]

Over the past decade, we've worked closely with selective schools that have already proven this point: Stanford University, Brown University, Amherst College, New York University, Mount Holyoke College, Smith College, and more. In this guide, we've highlighted programs and resources at these and other selective schools designed for non-traditional and transfer students. Many now offer advisors specifically for transfer students, orientation days that focus on transfer needs, and housing for transfer students with families, among other helpful programs and resources.

We hope to see more of these transfer-friendly programs in the future as four-year schools continue to recruit and mentor transfer students through to the end of their studies. This book helps define where schools are in this process so we can make students aware of their options and the support services in place to help them transfer. If you are from a school struggling to find diverse students who will thrive and give back to their alma maters, go to community colleges and recruit them!

---

5   Source: Princeton University Strategic Framework

# CHAPTER TWO

# How to Use This Guide

## AS A STUDENT

The purpose of this book is to identify which schools are best for you based on your individual needs and goals. This guide also provides you with the tools to present your best transfer application to schools that match well with your interests, skills, and career ambitions. Your education is an important investment, so it's crucial to make informed decisions about the next step in your pursuit of higher education.

- Start by learning the lingo. While you may know many of the terms in the glossary (**The Language of Transfer**), these terms often have a different meaning and apply differently to you as a transfer student. Learning the language of transfer will help you ask better questions and ultimately guide you toward applying to the best schools for you, so take a look at the glossary before diving into the guide if you need a refresher.

- **Chapter Three: The Myths of Transfer** is designed to help you keep an open mind about transfer. We provide a myth-busting section because there is a lot of misinformation about the college transfer process. Give yourself the opportunity to consider all of your options by clearing your mind of these common misconceptions about transfer.

- Pay close attention to **Chapter Four: How to Be a Transfer Star**. Through our work on the Kaplan Leadership Program, we have collaborated closely with college admissions offices to learn what they are looking for in a college transfer applicant. This section outlines your transfer timeline, provides advice on maximizing transfer credits to save time and money, and provides advice on tackling each part of the transfer application. You will also find ways to reduce the cost of applications in order to maximize your transfer school pool.

- You may be convinced that the cost of attendance is limiting your transfer options. **Chapter Five: Financial Aid for Transfer** will guide you through the complex financial aid application process for transfer students. When applying to colleges with access to more financial aid, you often need to fill out additional applications beyond the FAFSA. Take note of the information in this section if you are looking to maximize your financial aid packages.

- Last but certainly not least, take time to review the **School Profiles**. This is where you will get to know each school, determine which ones meet your transfer goals, and understand what they can offer a student like you. Emphasis is placed on each school's desired transfer student profile, transfer admissions and financial aid policies, and overall environment.

*Note:* Military students, students with families, and undocumented or DACA students often have special needs. If you are in one of these groups, you'll find information in the School Profiles to help you understand which schools can offer you the best resources for your unique situation.

## AS A COMMUNITY COLLEGE TRANSFER ADVISOR

This book addresses both the needs of community college students who originally enrolled with the plan of completing only an associate's degree as well as those who wanted to collect credits with the aim of transferring. It is fair to say that we should encourage both groups to consider transfer and complete a bachelor's degree. While students who earn an associate's degree have higher salaries after graduation in the short term, earning a bachelor's degree provides higher long-term earning potential.[6] For low-income, first-generation, and non-traditional students, who often find community college to be the best and most convenient option, finding the best transfer school can determine that student's ability to complete a bachelor's degree.

The 90 transfer School Profiles provided here are a good indication of the many choices your students have, and we recommend that you familiarize students with the options and resources available to them beyond their community or local college. We hope you'll take a fresh look at the transfer process, as we have seen significant changes over the past decade that have made schools previously inaccessible to community colleges more accessible. At KEF, we have seen a wave of interest in community college students, as these schools have come to understand that community college students often bring with them a spirit of perseverance, an interesting cultural and social perspective, and a passion to be change agents.

We encourage you to build relationships with these 90 schools and let them know about your talented students. We also recommend that you identify students who are looking to transfer and seek to start the transfer conversation as early as recruitment. Position your community college as a bridge to four-year institutions.

## AS A FOUR-YEAR ADVISOR OR ADMINISTRATOR

Whether you accept 5 or 100 transfer students per academic year, we encourage you to evaluate your ability to meet the needs of potential transfer students, transfer applicants, and your transfer population. Move beyond the number you've accepted to how you're serving the transfer population and making the college experience for them as fulfilling as that of students who entered as freshmen.

How easy are you making it for transfer students to evaluate your school and apply? If it is harder for a transfer student to apply to your school than it is for a freshman student, take the time to review your website and the resources you provide online, on the phone, or in person. Consider how the information you provide could be packaged better so students can better evaluate you as a transfer school, feel valued by your college community, and have a seamless transition that minimizes transfer shock. If you want to accept students from the best pool of transfer students, just as you do with high-school graduates, you'll need to provide the best resources tailored for this group.

Being a great transfer school is not just about how many students you accept. It's about what you provide when you do accept them. For example, do you offer orientation for transfer students, and how extensive is it? Do you have financial aid, housing, and other resources that transfer students often need to succeed? Again, creating the best experience for transfer students will allow you to recruit the best in the nation.

---

6   Source: Center on Education and the Workforce, Georgetown University

If your college is featured in the School Profiles section, we encourage you to review your profile and really consider if your transfer admissions policies are geared toward matching your goals for socioeconomic, experiential, racial, ethnic, and other forms of diversity. Look at how you compare to other schools in addressing the financial and academic needs of transfer populations.

## AS A HIGH-SCHOOL GUIDANCE COUNSELOR OR COLLEGE ACCESS ADVISOR

If you are a guidance or college counselor at a high school, college-access office, or community-based organization, think about what percentage of your students will start their higher education journey by enrolling in a community college. For many of your students, the decision to attend a community college comes as a result of their need to stay close to home, the reduced cost of attendance, a lack of preparedness to attend a four-year college, or a combination of these factors. And many students who start their college education at four-year colleges find that their first college may not be a good fit as they gain greater insight into their preferred majors, career interests, and academic and socioemotional strengths and weaknesses.

Do not wait to have a discussion about transfer until the student is accepted or enrolled at a college. Transfer admissions should be discussed as early as possible when you talk about their potential college trajectories. Transfer is not a failure. As such, it should be presented as an opportunity for students as they complete their associate's degree and pursue a good four-year fit or if they are considering changing their academic goals and aren't able to pursue their education as they would like.

As you help your student apply to and enroll at their desired college, include workshops and conversations focused on why and when transfer may be appropriate to secure a degree. Talk about the skills necessary to be successful in the long term. Utilize the "language of transfer" in your discussions to make sure your student is evaluating schools for their ability to support degree completion. Help them understand that there is a strong likelihood they may change their major during the first two years of college education, and if they do, they should consider transfer if their first college doesn't meet their needs.

If you believe that you have students of great promise who were undermatched in their college applications and enrolled in a college that doesn't meet their academic potential, a deliberate and well-executed transfer admissions plan can offer them the opportunity to be admitted to selective schools that best match their capabilities. Undermatching of freshmen, especially first-generation and historically underrepresented students from low-income backgrounds, often occurs because a high school or local organization doesn't have the resources to fully develop the admissions profile of a student. This can happen due to a lack of adequate ACT/SAT preparation, rigorous or Advanced Placement courses, individualized college counseling, or extracurricular or leadership opportunities. First-generation students who lack a support network for the college search and admissions process may not possess the information or language to even consider a selective college, let alone submit a competitive application.

This guide can be used as an inspirational resource for students to see a realistic and achievable path with concrete steps and actions to achieve admissions at a dream college. With your help and the information here, they can open the doors to schools that were closed when they originally applied, or that they never even sought to open.

# CHAPTER THREE

# The Myths of Transfer

A lot of students aren't sure transfer is for them. They think they aren't wanted by top schools, can't afford them, or can't make the most of them due to their personal or family situations. We're here to tell you that none of that is true! All of these challenges can be overcome. We hope dispelling these "myths of transfer" will help you and other transfer students understand how some of the top colleges in the country have systems in place to recruit and support students like you.

## YOUR PERSONAL SITUATION

**"Top colleges don't want transfer students."**

The fact is, selective colleges around the nation such as Smith, Mount Holyoke, Amherst, Brown, and others have consistently admitted transfer students. Although the numbers of admitted transfer students may range from year to year, many top schools are using transfer admissions as a way to expand the diversity of their student body. Transfer students are also valued for their relatively high retention and completion rates. And as you can see in the School Profiles later in this guide, many selective schools even have special programs, orientation sessions, advisors, and financial aid opportunities specifically for transfer students, as they understand their needs are different from those of freshman students.

**"I'm too old/I've been out of school for too long."**

There's no such thing as being too old to earn a college degree! There are many options for students like you. Programs for transfer students usually take into account that older students may not want to live with freshman, may prefer to live with graduate students, or in some cases would like housing that is specifically geared toward non-traditional-age students and their families. When they review your application, you are often being evaluated not only on academic experiences, but also your life experiences. Although leadership and extracurriculars are highly important in the admissions process, you may be surprised to learn that schools often consider your involvement with family, work, and local organizations like your church or community centers. Military experience is appreciated by many schools, as are other forms of specialized training.

**"I am a caregiver at home. My parent/kid takes up all my time."**

Family obligations and responsibilities, especially the care of dependents, may seem to obstruct your plans for transfer. However, it takes a lot of maturity and commitment to take care of a loved one, whether it is a parent, child, or other person in need, and schools recognize this. Your biggest hurdle is not what you've been responsible for in the past, it's whether you will be able to find the resources and focus to take on a full course load at your prospective transfer school. We have found that, for students who have family responsibilities but wish to attend college full-time, having a conversation with your family and finding resources locally to make sure they are taken care of is an important first step. If you're responsible for children, keep in mind that some of the schools in this guide provide family housing or will help you find local housing. We've marked some of the best schools for non-traditional students so you can easily find them.

### "I went to high school outside of the United States."

As long as the institutions you went to are accredited, your high-school records and/or college credits earned outside of the United States are likely to be accepted and put through the same review process as credentials earned in the country. Each school has its own policy on the number of credits it will accept in the transfer process and has the right to request official documentation (and determine what "official" is). A certified copy with appropriate translation often fulfills the requirements of these schools. We have found that if you communicate with the admissions office and show them what you already have on file, the school will usually advise you on how to find the proper documentation. Do not let a missing diploma or transcript keep you from applying for transfer! While it may be costly to get official records sent directly from certain countries, in many cases schools may be able to accept a certified (unofficial) copy of those records.

### "I'm a DACA/undocumented student."

Many Deferred Action for Childhood Arrivals (DACA) students today have questions about their status as it pertains to long-term study in the United States. However, many four-year schools are committed to accepting and funding DACA and undocumented students. It's also important to note that some of these schools are prepared to fund and even extend their 100 percent financial aid policies regardless of immigration status. This means DACA and undocumented students can qualify for merit and need-based aid regardless of immigration status. On our School Profiles, we've marked some of the best schools for DACA/undocumented students.

### "I am afraid to move to a faraway school even though it has a great program for me."

If you are living in the United States, it is important to recognize that top colleges exist in all parts of the country. Considering a school in a city other than yours, or even clear across the country, may seem like a challenge. But finding the school that can nurture your strengths and address your needs (academic, financial, and social) may require you to step out of your geographical comfort zone. For example, if you are interested in a specific type of engineering program but also thrive in small classrooms where you can make close relationships with your professors, that combination may only be available at a few schools. And you may find that the school that will give you the best financial aid package is located in a small town in a different state. Trying to fit into a school that doesn't address your needs only because of geographic location can limit your potential.

### "I don't have the help/resources to complete the difficult transfer process."

Once you set a goal in life, rallying people around you to help you fulfill that goal is the mark of a successful leader. Your current college should be the first place for you to find people that can help you submit a strong transfer application. Please see Chapter Four: How to Be a Transfer Star for tips on how to work with your writing center, faculty, and advisors to complete your applications, get strong letters of recommendation, interview, and succeed in the overall transfer process.

**"I don't want to go to a school that I've never visited."**

If you've been accepted, many schools are likely to invite you to Accepted Students Day, when you'll get the chance to spend some time on campus, meet faculty, and get to know the school. For students that don't have the funds to visit, some schools will work with you to help cover some transportation fees and provide food and board during your stay. We don't recommend that any student commits to attending a school that they've never been to in person.

## YOUR FINANCIAL SITUATION

**"I can't afford the application fees."**

Good news: although transfer admissions application fees are typically around $50–75 per school, which can present a challenge for many students, you can often get these fees waived simply by requesting a waiver and/or having someone who knows your financial situation request one on your behalf. This process does not require you to write paragraphs upon paragraphs about why you need the fee waived. Instead, you usually only need to submit a letter consisting of a few sentences asking for a waiver. Don't let the sticker price keep you from applying!

**"Housing is not available for non-traditional students."**

When applying for financial aid, schools take into account the costs of room and board, which can become part of your financial aid package. And there are a few ways that schools can facilitate housing for non-traditional students. They may have set aside housing specifically for non-traditional students. They may not distinguish between traditional and non-traditional students in housing. Or they may allow you to live in graduate housing, which is usually where older students live and tends to be apartment-style. If you decide to live in off-campus housing, your financial aid package may be designed by the school to take this into account.

**"I can't consider private schools because I can't afford them."**

If you look at the average costs of private schools, they often appear to cost much more than state colleges or other publicly funded schools. Thankfully, many of these schools have a commitment to meet the needs of all students they accept, regardless of income or financial status. In addition, many private schools set aside funding to make sure that students' financial situations do not prevent them from enrolling.

To figure out what loans you may need to take out or what costs you will actually have to pay out of pocket, you can work with the school's financial aid office to ensure they understand your situation.

In many instances, it may actually be less expensive to attend a private school than a state or city school because the latter schools sometimes struggle to find funding to grant merit or need-based aid to their students. Do not assume that because a school costs $70,000 per year, you will actually be responsible for all of that cost. More and more top colleges have committed themselves to providing merit and need-based aid that will help you afford tuition, fees, housing, and more.

**"Interviewing is required/recommended, and I can't afford to visit the school."**

Schools offer a variety of ways to reduce the costs of interviewing. Some schools offer funding to low-income students to cover transportation to the school. For overnight visits, students may be able to stay overnight with a student host. You can also request meal vouchers that can be used for meals in the dining halls. Many schools also offer phone or video conference interviews, as well as interviews with alumni who may live near you.

# YOUR ACADEMIC SITUATION

### "I need to take the SAT/ACT."

Most college admissions departments will not give strong consideration to transfer students' standardized test scores, especially if they have already attended college. They are more likely to look at your academic performance at your current or previous college to determine your fit for their programs. Some schools will require you to submit test scores if you've taken these tests recently (length of time varying by school), but you will not be required to take the tests if you haven't already.

Our School Profiles provide each school's policies on standardized test scores, but you should consult with your prospective transfer schools to ensure you have met their requirements. At the Kaplan Educational Foundation, we provide Kaplan Test Prep services for all of our students, as we have found that very good standardized scores can give further insight into a student's academic potential.[7] Still, as these tests were designed to predict freshman-year performance, it is truly much more important to have a strong academic record at your pre-transfer college.

### "I did terribly in high school."

Students who got poor grades, had poor attendance records, did not take rigorous courses in high school, or even dropped out may find that their high-school records do not demonstrate their full academic potential—or even worse, highlight their weaknesses. This can also apply to students who passed all their classes and graduated, but did not excel.

If any of these situations sound like yours, but you've been attending college and have accumulated credits in courses that demonstrate college-level competency in writing and math and ability to take rigorous courses, your high-school performance will have less of an impact on admissions decisions.

You will have the opportunity in your application to provide a few sentences addressing your high-school performance. Always be honest in explaining why you didn't do as well as you could have, as well as what you've done since then that demonstrates your academic abilities.

### "I have a GED or High-School Equivalency diploma."

Having a High-School Equivalency (HSE) diploma, often known as a GED, should not deter anyone from applying to a selective institution. As long as you can explain the circumstances that led to you getting an HSE diploma, and pair it with a strong college transcript, you can expect admissions officers to focus on your college performance. The fact is that people drop out of high school for many reasons, and often those reasons are not academic.

Oftentimes, having a High-School Equivalency diploma will also require you to submit high-school transcripts. See the previous myth (above) for more details.

---

7    The Kaplan Educational Foundation is an independent 501(c)3 nonprofit public charity initially established and supported by an endowment funded by Kaplan, Inc. executives. Kaplan, Inc. and its employees continue to provide financial, in-kind, and volunteer support to KEF and our Kaplan Scholars.

**"My credits will not transfer."**

Each school has its own policy in terms of transfer credits, but they'll evaluate them on a person-by-person basis with you. Having a syllabus for all of your past classes is going to be significant as you negotiate transfer credits and how they are allocated to your credit requirements. You must report all of your higher education credits from any school that you've attended. Some schools may be able to work with you even if you've taken the courses too long ago for them to transfer.

# EXPLORING YOUR OPTIONS

**"I would never consider a women's college."**

Women's colleges were created to provide access for women in higher education at a time when established colleges and universities would not admit them. As a result, women's colleges have developed curricula and academic environments in which women are able to develop the leadership skills to become the very best in their chosen fields. These schools are particularly good at meeting the needs of women and often have made it part of their mission to serve non-traditional-age women who are returning to college, as well as students with families. As you'll see in the School Profiles, these colleges come in a variety of sizes, but for the most part they are relatively small liberal arts colleges. They have become magnets for companies that are looking to address gender inequalities. The stereotypes of a women's college as a place where there are no men around, or as an institution that keeps you locked up, or as a home to women who only think one way are all untrue. The reality is that these colleges seek to build diversity of all kinds on campus, from diversity of thought to diversity of skin color, and everything in between. Within the "Seven Sisters" schools (traditionally women's colleges) and other women's colleges, you will find programs designed to recruit transfer students like you.

**"I'm not sure an HBCU is right for me."**

Historically black colleges and universities (HBCUs) were founded as educational sanctuaries. They have helped countless African American students who were barred from attending other institutions get excellent educations, and they continue to provide close-knit communities where people with similar interests and cultural experiences can thrive. Students choose to attend HBCUs for many reasons. For example, you may feel that your current college does not offer you exposure to classes or extracurriculars that focus on the African American experience. Even worse, you may feel isolated as a minority at your current school or feel that your classmates and professors do not understand you or care to support your educational journey. Being around students and instructors who share your cultural experience can help you make the most of your education. HBCUs excel at helping their students become leaders by providing them with top-notch educations. Furthermore, there is a great deal of diversity within these schools as well. Our students who have attended HBCUs have told us that they've discovered different perspectives, stories, and approaches that they did not know existed in their own communities. And within the HBCU world, there are schools of differing sizes and atmospheres that are strong in different fields of study.

# CHAPTER FOUR

# How to Be a Transfer Star

To create the best possible transfer application and make the most of your new school, you'll need to be prepared. Using the knowledge we've gained over the past decade getting students from disadvantaged backgrounds into the top schools in the country, we've put together some tips, insights, and plans that you can use to make the most of transfer.

## SETTING YOUR TRANSFER TIMELINE

As you think about transfer, it can help to identify concrete steps to take at each stage of your educational career. Here are our recommendations for what you should focus on during your path to transfer. While it's never too late to start thinking about transfer, getting ahead of the game will make your life much easier!

### Contemplating Enrolling in College

Whether you are in high school, are completing your GED, or are ready to transfer from your current college, you should prepare yourself to build a strong transcript, student profile, and understanding of how college and admissions work.

- **Prep for entrance exams required by some colleges.** For example, the City University of New York requires students to take an entrance exam in math, writing, and reading.
- **Get the support of your family, friends, employers, and others.** Let them know you plan to attend college and that there will be a time commitment needed for you to do well.
- **Visit colleges and become well versed in the language of transfer.** Terminology about college admissions, college requirements, and financial aid is very important. Ask to speak with admissions advisors to discuss degree options, academic interests, strengths, and areas for improvement.
- **Avoid remedial courses, if possible.** These do not count toward your degree requirements and may prevent you from taking credit-bearing courses, and therefore may delay graduation. If you must take remedial courses, look for specialized or immersive remediation programs that will help you complete remediation faster.
- **Enroll in suitable coursework.** Courses that can easily be applied to multiple majors and transfer to another school will help you the most as you prepare to transfer.
- **Explore out-of-classroom activities.** These will help to build your leadership profile.

- **Apply for special programs that may offer you additional support services.** Some colleges offer accelerated enrollment programs that may guarantee enrollment in courses or offer additional tutoring, specialized advisement, tailored courses for group needs, and additional financial support such as travel allowance, book vouchers, child-care services, etc.
- **Understand requirements around standardized exams such as the ACT and SAT.** While keeping in mind that many schools do not require test scores from transfer students, obtaining high scores can further strengthen your application. See the Standardized Tests section that follows for more info.

## First Year at Pre-Transfer College (0–30 Credits)

Your first goal in college is to build a network that will help you excel at your pre-transfer school and develop a strong profile for transfer admission.

- **Become familiar with the academic calendar of your college.** This will guide many registration policies and deadlines and help you understand your responsibilities. Be aware you will have a limited amount of time to add or drop a course and that there are deadlines by which you will owe a certain percentage of tuition and fees to the school.
- **Get to know your college resources.** These may include your financial aid office, registrar's office, and medical and mental health services. Do not wait until you need help to start understanding your resources.
- **Meet with faculty.** Get to know professors who teach your classes and those who teach classes in the major(s) you are interested in. Let them know what your goals are, and make them aware of any concerns you may have or aspirations for the course.
- **Make sure you know your advisors.** Key people at your college may include financial aid advisors, degree or academic advisors, and overall leadership advisors. If you are not assigned an advisor, identify a person that will meet with you consistently to address your questions or follow up with you to make sure you are thriving. You should know their name, title, schedule, email address, phone, and location on campus.
- **Assess what extracurricular activities best support your interests or help you explore the world around you.** Attend club meetings, get to know the leaders and members of clubs, and give yourself the opportunity to learn from social interactions beyond the classroom.
- **Establish a study schedule and join study groups whenever possible.** Getting support from your peers will help keep you on track and involved with coursework and social life.
- **Assess personal and financial responsibilities.** Set realistic expectations for yourself and your family while in school. Have a plan to address any changes in your ability to provide financial support or care for your household.
- **Maintain records of your course syllabi.** You may need to show them to a transfer school to get credits appropriately transferred.
- **Get to know people in your field.** If you are interested in a particular field of study or career, aim to work, intern, or volunteer with people in that field to help determine if you're on the right track.

## Second Year at Pre-Transfer College (30–60 credits)

At the point when you have 30 or more credits, you'll have completed enough courses for your transfer school to evaluate you academically, and you'll also have had enough time to build connections with faculty and campus leaders through your participation in class, coursework, and extracurriculars.

- **Focus on accumulating (transferable) courses toward your degree.** Always keep in mind transferability. If you are unsure about your major or area of concentration, it's best to take a liberal arts and/or general studies track that will allow you flexibility once you decide your major.

- **Continue to explore fields you are interested in.** You can do this in a variety of ways, from work and internships to volunteer opportunities and networking.

- **Enroll in classes that demonstrate you can take advanced courses.** Making consistent academic progress is key. If you have any doubts about your ability to take advanced courses, speak with your academic advisor or the faculty teaching those courses.

- **Make sure your transcript reflects college-level proficiency.** At a minimum, this includes strong college-level math (pre-calculus) and English reading and writing skills (two semesters of English).

- **Identify transfer schools that match your goals.** If you are unclear about your major or career prospects, don't panic! Your undergraduate education should allow you to develop skills that will help you succeed in a variety of fields. Make a list of general fields of study that interest you (some examples: health care, education, business, social justice, or law) and research the different concentrations or specialties available in each field. This will allow you to narrow down your choices based on which schools excel in these areas.

- **Get to know transfer advisors.** Check with your school to determine if there is a transfer office or transfer specialist who can help you in the transfer process. You may also speak to faculty members or your advisors to help you identify transfer schools.

- **Start reaching out to transfer schools.** Sign up for open houses, local events, and on-campus events geared toward transfer admissions. Most colleges have at least one person in their admissions office that focuses on transfer applicants. Make sure you know their name, title, email, and phone number. Let them know that you are considering applying for transfer. Be ready to share your transcript, resume, and extracurricular/leadership profile to provide context and demonstrate your seriousness in applying to that school.

- **Set a budget.** You will need to cover or get assistance in covering transfer application fees, transcript costs, postage, school visits, and other fees. See the Reducing the Costs of Applying section later in this chapter for more information.

- **Schedule school visits and a timeline to work on your applications.** Because you will be writing multiple essays (per school), you will need a support network to review and help you revise your writing. Do not wait to get help!

- **Set a plan and timeline to collect documentation.** Letters of recommendation, college reports, transcripts, high school records, translations, and other forms will not collect and file themselves!

- **Deal with Incomplete or Withdraw grades.** If for any reason, you have received a grade of Incomplete (I) or Withdraw (W) in any of your courses to this point, work with your college to fulfill Incomplete courses and find ways to explain Withdraw grades.

## Transfer Application

It's time to apply! You have more options and more resources available to you than you might think, so make sure you give yourself time to discover the many different paths you can take to pursue your bachelor's degree and to find the support you need to get it.

- **Identify a list of at least 10 potential transfer schools.** Make sure you consider reach, target, and safety schools that you can see yourself attending.
- **Be first in line for financial aid.** Submit applications to your final schools at least two to three weeks before the deadlines.
- **Set a schedule for interviews.** See the Acing Your Interviews section later in this chapter for tips on how to excel during the interview process.
- **Prove your financial need to schools.** Schools will need to determine how much financial aid they can provide and let you know how much, if anything, you are required to pay. To do this, the school will look at your entire financial picture, which in some instances requires information and verifying documentation from parents/guardians, spouse, siblings, or extended family members. Their cooperation is key in getting you the documentation in a timely manner. Please consult the list of documents provided in Chapter Five: Financial Aid for Transfer, and share it with anyone that you think may have to provide you with income and assets information.
- **Follow up on your application status.** Do not assume your application has been received and accurately attributed to your file. You do not want your application to be kept in the incomplete file simply because a school is missing one document or a document you submitted doesn't satisfy their requirements. Follow up once a week until you receive word that your application is complete. Some schools may use an online portal, which typically gives a detailed record of the status of your application. When following up, be sure to provide your name and the semester you are applying for, and explain that you are a transfer admissions applicant. If you already have a contact person, ask to speak to that person and follow up with an email thanking them and confirming what you discussed. This makes it easier for both sides to maintain records and allows you to confirm that the communication was received and noted. If you do not have a contact person in the admissions or financial aid office, ask if there is a person assigned to your application and if you can speak to or email that person.
- **Establish contact with faculty at transfer schools.** There are many reasons to do so:
  - » Faculty are usually the best experts on a particular major, subject, field of study, or overall department. Taking the opportunity to speak to a biology professor who conducts research in an area that interests you, for example, can give you an idea of the academic environment at their school and what to expect as a student.
  - » Faculty members are usually eager to meet prospective students and share insights into the school, as they want to work with the best students and with those who have a clear understanding of what their expectations are.
  - » If you are exploring a particular major/field of study, but you have limited exposure, a faculty member can provide you with honest and detailed information regarding the opportunities and possible limitations of the program.

## Transfer Decision and Enrollment

Congratulations! You have now submitted your admissions and financial aid applications and confirmed that all required documentation and information has been received, making it possible for the schools to make their admissions and financial aid decisions.

- **Confirm each school's decision deadline.** Do not depend on the dates that may be online or listed on the Common App. Unfortunately, some of the dates offered apply more to freshmen applicants. Keep in mind that transfer admissions decisions for some schools depend on the number of freshmen that were accepted and the spots that are left. The number of transfer applicants offered admission may also depend on the number of "beds" available, which is determined in part by students studying abroad or taking a semester or year off from college, as well as students that have dropped out, been dismissed, or transferred to other colleges. Admissions officers may set a goal to admit 20 students for the fall semester, for example, but find that they can only offer admissions to 15 (or vice versa).

- **Confirm your financial aid package and credit evaluation.** If you have been accepted to a school, be sure to follow up with the admissions office and ask when you will get financial aid and credit evaluation information and how you can move the process along. You should not make a decision to attend unless you have a financial aid package and at least some assessment of your credits.

- **Attend Accepted Students Day.** Your school should let you know of accepted student activities, including school visit days when they will do their very best to help you assess their institution and make a decision. These usually include opportunities for you and your family to meet faculty and staff, as well as some members of the student body. You will find that some schools have special programming for students with unique needs or from specific populations (non-traditional-age students, certain majors, first generation, etc.). Although these events are geared toward putting the school in the best light possible, admissions representatives and school staff want you to make the best decision, so these events are usually very good about answering your questions honestly. You may want to take some members of your family or network with you to familiarize them with the different factors affecting your decision, and this can help them understand how they can support you.

- **Ask for an extension to your acceptance deadline (if needed).** When accepted, the admissions officer will provide you with a deadline by which you must accept or decline their offer. If you feel you cannot make a decision because you are waiting to hear from other schools, ask for an extension and explain why. Make sure you offer a date that accommodates the decision dates from your other prospective colleges. Some schools may frown upon this, so make sure to have an honest conversation with the admissions office. If you aren't able to decide by the deadline because you have not received a financial aid package or transcript evaluation, schools will likely understand and offer you an extension. Try to get something in writing via email confirming any extension. Keep in mind that some schools will not extend the deadline. This is a tough situation, and in some instances, if the school is at the very top of your list, you may want to submit a deposit.

- **Work with schools to get the maximum number of credits transferred.** If you believe that your transcript evaluation doesn't appropriately accept your credits, you have limited time to address this with the admissions office and the people that evaluate credits. Some colleges have the registrar's office evaluate credits, but some may also work with individual departments or majors. If some credits are not accepted or appropriately attributed to your prospective degree, you should reach out to the college and address your individual issues.

Make sure you have the course descriptions for the classes you have taken and copies of their syllabi. If you do not have copies of the relevant syllabi, contact your current college and ask for them.

- **Look for exemptions from language requirements.** If your prospective college has a language requirement (usually a one- or two-year language requirement and/or demonstrated proficiency), ask if you can test to be exempt from it. If you choose to take a language other than English, which we strongly recommend, having the exemption will give you more time and less pressure in pursuing your goal. Often, an unfulfilled language requirement at the time of transfer can swallow up many credit hours and delay graduation. Look for exemptions whenever possible, but simultaneously look to develop further proficiency in another language through course enrollment, study abroad, internships, clubs, and other extracurricular activities.

- **Verify financial aid information.** Your school may want to verify all information before coming up with an aid package for you. Each school will have very specific requests for documentation in order to assess your financial needs and confirm household income and assets. Schools may change their financial aid offering if they find through the process of verification that they under/overestimated their package for you. Be sure to follow up to confirm that your financial aid information has been verified.

- **Evaluate your housing options.** Housing options on most campuses are limited. The sooner you decide to attend the school, the sooner you are considered for housing. Where, how, and with whom you will live at your transfer school will certainly contribute to your experience. Do not always assume that having a single apartment or room is the best option. Having a roommate may help you get to know the school better and build strong bonds. You may not necessarily become best friends forever with your roommate, but that person can certainly be an important part of your network. Having a roommate may also allow you to experience and learn from any cultural differences that might exist between the two of you, which can enrich your life.

- **Investigate special housing arrangements, if applicable.** If a school has a housing requirement that demands that all students live on campus for a certain amount of time, ask if it applies to transfer students. If so, you will likely be guaranteed housing. However, some schools that guarantee housing may not guarantee it for students in special programs. We have found that older students may want to take advantage of graduate housing, where older students can live alone or bring their families to live with them. Please keep in mind that graduate housing is usually more costly. If living off campus, your financial aid package can be adjusted, as this kind of housing can sometimes be the most expensive option.

- **Submit immunization records.** These will be needed in order to be considered for on-campus housing. You may be able to submit documentation from a doctor for some exemptions, but you will need to communicate with the school early on. Make sure you have your immunization records from your current college and doctor and that you verify your transfer school's requirements.

- **Have honest discussions with your friends, family, and network about what's next.** Your college journey, especially if you are moving out of your home to attend a school in a different city or state, will likely affect the relationships you have with your family, friends, and overall network. The sooner you communicate your transfer plans, the better. Share the short- and long-term benefits of your decision, as well as any changes or sacrifices everyone will have to make. For example, you may no longer be available to care for a loved one, or you simply may not be seeing people as often. We have found that people are more likely to rally around you or be honest about their limitations to help you once you are open and honest with them. However, do not expect that people will immediately support or accept your decision. It may take time, and you may also need time yourself to be okay with the responses you get. Do not forget to communicate your plans with your current school and the faculty and staff that have been a part of your journey. They may be great resources as you continue your education, and you may still be able to count on their advice and cheerleading.

# BREAKING DOWN YOUR TRANSFER APPLICATION AND ESSAYS

First things first: you can not rush through your application. Applying to each school will likely take you days of work to get all of the information and documents requested. For many schools, applying for transfer requires you to complete multiple forms where you will provide personal data, academic records, references or recommendations, and essays. Rushing through this process may result in an incomplete picture of who you are and a missed opportunity to impress an admissions committee.

But don't get discouraged! At the Kaplan Educational Foundation, our students apply to between 7 to 10 schools, all while going to school and sometimes working as well, and they've proven they're up to the task. Here are some tips for keeping things together:

- Know the deadlines for all of your schools. Check the Setting Your Transfer Timeline section above for more details, and check the School Profiles for specific dates.

- Assemble a group of people who can review your applications, especially your essays. These people should know you and your accomplishments, and it helps if some of them know about the admissions process. See the Building Your Board of Directors section later in this chapter for more on that.

The first step in completing your transfer application is determining which kind of application (Common App vs. school-specific) and forms are required. In addition to the information in the School Profiles in this guide, you can look online or contact the admissions office or special programs office at your prospective schools to find out what they require.

Many private colleges use the Common App as part of the transfer admissions process. If your school uses the Common App, good news: they are looking to improve the way that transfer and non-traditional students apply in 2018.

Keep in mind that even if your school uses the Common App, there may be additional required forms specific to the school, especially for students applying to transfer programs. Many state and city school systems have their own application processes that are not served by the Common App.

## Personal Statement

Most schools require a personal statement or essay that serves as an introduction to who you are, your interests in and out of the classroom, your goals, and how you approach those goals. For transfer students, the personal statement is a good place for you to share with the admissions committee how you arrived at your decision to transfer and how your personal, academic, and professional journey thus far make you a competitive candidate for admission.

Your personal statement essay should accomplish the following:

- Provide a narrative for understanding your application as a whole (without simply repeating what is in your transcript, resume, and other parts of the app)
- Demonstrate your ability to write eloquently

- Paint a clear picture of your strengths, how you develop them, and what makes you unique
- Explain how you address challenges with examples of your resiliency, problem-solving skills, and follow-through to resolutions
- Show how you perceive, value, and build communities around you, including at your current college, job, church, or other organizations
- Demonstrate how you have evolved through your college education so far and how you are going to continue to evolve at your transfer school

Your personal statement should NOT:

- Repeat information that can be found in other parts of your application without contextualizing it further
- Criticize or critique your current college. If you aren't happy with your current college, focus on what you've learned about yourself rather than what's wrong with the school.
- Brag about your achievements. While you want to share examples of what makes you a strong candidate, your personal statement should not be a list of accomplishments that are separated from what those accomplishments have added to the greater good.
- Focus on gaining sympathy. Writing from a negative perspective about challenges or tragedies you may have faced is not advised. You can, however, talk about challenges from the point of view of illustrating your resilience and how you've managed those challenges.

For many schools that use the Common App, you can submit one personal statement that covers multiple schools. The Common App personal statement prompt, as listed in the 2017 application, is as follows:

Please provide a statement that addresses your reasons for transferring and the objectives you hope to achieve. (250–650 words)

Please note that, because your Common App statement can go to multiple schools, this is not the place to talk about why you want to go a specific school. You will have to address that in the supplemental essays that ask why you want to transfer to a specific school or pursue a specific major.

The Common App's personal statement prompt is a good guide even for non-Common App personal statements, as it helps schools understand why you want to transfer and what you want to do once you transfer, both short- and long-term.

Let's break down the first part of the Common App prompt. You may have multiple reasons for transferring, and it is OK to offer more than one in your personal statement if you take the time to explain those reasons using examples that depict your journey. Here are some general reasons why students seek to transfer that may apply to you:

- To further your commitment to becoming the best in your field
- To develop your skills and expertise in a deeper way
- To make the change to becoming a full-time student who can fully engage with earning your degree
- To follow up on your realization that you are capable of getting a four-year degree
- To reengage with your studies after taking some time off from school

You should be able to articulate that you have made an informed decision about transfer that comes out of your own personal goals, not just because a family member told you to or an employer requires it. Although those things may have inspired you to transfer, your essay should dig deeper into why you think that this is the best decision and why the school should accept you into their community.

The second part of the Common App prompt deals with your objectives. You should not just focus on career or major objectives. These are usually evident in other required application questions. The college experience is about much more than your major or type of degree, so your objectives should demonstrate that what you're looking to achieve goes beyond the classroom. For example:

- If you want to focus on a particular major or field of study, how did you arrive at this decision and what do you hope your contributions will be in that field?
- What skills, experiences, and deeper understanding do you hope to develop at your transfer school?
- How do you plan to utilize your degree to resolve local, national, or international issues?

## Academic Challenges

If you have had poor academic performance or faced challenges that did not allow you to complete a semester, schools will want to know the reasons why you were not able to perform as expected. You should look to explain any of the following:

- D or F grades in general. If you received these due to reasons other than your grasp of the material, such as an Incomplete grade that turned into an F, you should make sure that you mention this. At the same time, you should take responsibility for what you could have done differently and discuss how you will treat any similar situations going forward.
- C grades, if they represent a departure from your usual performance or are in areas that you are interested in pursuing at your transfer school.
- Withdraw (W) grades. Schools will want to understand the circumstances that led you to withdraw from any course. It's important to take responsibility, not blame others, and fairly represent how you came to a decision to withdraw and what you learned from the experience. For example, if you withdrew because you could not work out hours to attend class with your employer, you should explain how in the future you will try to confirm your schedule earlier.
- Incomplete (I) grades. If you are sending your transcript at the point when the work for an Incomplete grade has not been turned in, provide a timeline for when the grade will be completed. If possible, request a note from your professor showing what grade you have accomplished in the course so far. If you have turned in all the work and are waiting for an administrative grade in your transcript, work with the registrar's office and professor to make the change as soon as possible. Keep in mind that this may take weeks or even months. Make sure to provide an explanation as to why you could not complete the work for your class and your plan to fulfill it.

## Reasons for Transfer to a Specific School

This type of essay asks you why you are interested in transferring to a specific school. For example, Brown University asks its transfer students the following question:

"Please tell us more about your interest in transferring. Why does Brown appeal to you as a college option? Who or what has influenced your decision to apply? (300 word limit)"

You should demonstrate in these kinds of essays that you know enough about the school to determine that it matches your goals and interests. Although you may be attracted to the climate, location, or prestige of a school, your analysis should show greater depth. Distinct characteristics about the school, like strong programs in your desired field or resources for military students, are much more compelling. If the school has an open curriculum, for example, and you believe that having the flexibility to take courses in multiple areas will give you the skills necessary to achieve the goals you set forth in your personal statement, you should explain why this is a good match for you.

Your essay should confirm to the admissions committee that who you are, your interests, and your goals will find fulfillment at their school. You can best do this by referencing specific academic, extracurricular, and career development activities that helped you come to the decision to apply to the school and how you can contribute there.

## Intellectual or Creative Analysis

Another kind of essay asks you to demonstrate your analytical, reasoning, and/or creative skills. For example, Amherst College asks its transfer students to respond to one of four quotations from Amherst faculty, leadership, or alumni:

"Please respond to one of the following quotations in an essay of not more than 300 words. It is not necessary to research, read, or refer to the texts from which these quotations are taken; we are looking for original, personal responses to these short excerpts rather than book reviews or book reports. Remember that your essay should be personal in nature and not simply an argumentative essay."

**Prompt 1:** "Rigorous reasoning is crucial in mathematics, and insight plays an important secondary role these days. In the natural sciences, I would say that the order of these two virtues is reversed. Rigor is, of course, very important. But the most important value is insight—insight into the workings of the world. It may be because there is another guarantor of correctness in the sciences, namely, the empirical evidence from observation and experiments."
*Kannan Jagannathan, Professor of Physics, Amherst College*

**Prompt 2:** "Translation is the art of bridging cultures. It's about interpreting the essence of a text, transporting its rhythms and becoming intimate with its meaning...Translation, however, doesn't only occur across languages: mentally putting any idea into words is an act of translation; so is composing a symphony, doing business in the global market, understanding the roots of terrorism. No citizen, especially today, can exist in isolation— that is, untranslated."
*Ilan Stavans, Professor of Latin American and Latino Culture, Amherst College, Robert Croll '16 and Cedric Duquene '15, from "Interpreting Terras Irradient,"* Amherst Magazine, *Spring 2015*

**Prompt 3:** "Creating an environment that allows students to build lasting friendships, including those that cut across seemingly entrenched societal and political boundaries... requires candor about the inevitable tensions, as well as about the wonderful opportunities, that diversity and inclusiveness create."
*Carolyn "Biddy" Martin, President of Amherst College, Letter to Amherst College Alumni and Families, December 28, 2015*

**Prompt 4:** "Difficulty need not foreshadow despair or defeat. Rather, achievement can be all the more satisfying because of obstacles surmounted."
*Attributed to William Hastie, Amherst Class of 1925, the first African American to serve as a judge for the United States Court of Appeals*

For these kinds of essays, schools want to go beyond your reading comprehension skills and understand how you approach a more high-level, analytical process. While you must demonstrate that you understand the passage or prompt, your ability to use creative problem-solving or complex reasoning is what they're really looking for. Provide a well-thought-out opinion and support it with evidence.

If you look closely at the Amherst example, you'll see that your answer should also have a "personal" component. Many schools will ask you to do the same. To put a personal twist on your answer, think deeply about the people and ideas you've learned about that have inspired you. These should be people, experiences, works of art, or philosophies that truly changed how you think about the world and how you can contribute to it. This is not the time to write a biography of that person or provide a summary of a book. Instead, pick an example of how these things have impacted you and how you will use them in pursuit of your short- and long-term goals.

## Reviewing Your Essays and Getting Help

First things first: do not feel that you are cheating if someone is helping you. Over the course of your education, you will come to understand that collaboration at every stage of the academic process, from brainstorming to revising drafts to submitting work, is crucial. This is especially true when you realize that completing essays can take hours or even days of work.

Use the support system you've developed to brainstorm ideas and provide helpful criticism. It's very useful to include people who know your journey and can help you relate it, but remember that people who think your writing is perfect or are afraid to give you real feedback are not the best people to work with. You may need to involve multiple people depending upon their different strengths.

If you are currently attending college, visit your school's writing center for expert help. Other places to turn include your transfer office or a trusted professor. And if you've already written an essay for other purposes, such as a scholarship application, you can use this as a starting point.

One of the most important things to remember is to help your support network help you. Make sure the people you are working with understand your goals, fields of interest, the colleges you are applying to, and how you got to where you are.

## Transcripts

You must supply transcripts from all schools you have attended, even if you did not receive a grade. Omitting a college you have attended can result in your application being rejected. Even if you withdrew from a college, make sure you supply a transcript from that school.

Keep in mind you must have a cleared bill at each school, as they will likely not release transcripts if you have even a $5 late fee from the school library. If you are unable to pay your fees, or believe the fees are being charged to you in error, you should work with the bursar and the administrative offices to try to come to a resolution.

If you are currently attending college, the deadline for your transfer application will likely come midsemester, meaning you will probably have to send your transcript multiple times. Because delivery of transcripts may sometimes take up to three weeks, we recommend you put in a request immediately at the end of the semester you are currently attending.

For example, if you are applying for Fall 2019, the deadlines for your transfer school will likely be in January or February 2019. You will first have to send your transcript in December with Fall 2018 grades. Then, if you are taking Intersession or Spring 2019 classes, you will have to send a transcript again at the end of those semesters as well.

If you still have a semester left to complete at your current school, it's important that the transcript you're sending lists the courses you are registered for in the subsequent semester. So if you haven't registered for your next semester yet, go ahead and do it before asking for your transcript. This way, the information will appear on the transcript and help the admissions committee understand the progression of your academic abilities. The more courses they see, the better they'll be able to evaluate you.

If you have attended college outside of the US, your transfer schools will have their own policies about whether they need an official document or can accept a copy. Because this can be a lengthy process, we recommend that you submit a copy with an explanation that you have also asked for an official version. If your non-US school is hard to reach or get an official copy from, make that known to your transfer school and work with them directly to come to a resolution.

## Midsemester Report

If you are currently attending college, you will also have to submit midsemester reports. These let schools know how you are performing in your current classes. Please keep in mind that schools can rescind your acceptance if your performance is poor.

To get a midsemester report, download the form from the Common App website and have your professors sign it. If it's still early in the semester, they may be able to share the grade you've received so far, but they may also write that they cannot evaluate you at this time.

When the form is complete, upload it to the Common App site.

## Transfer College Report

The transfer college report, also known as a dean's report, confirms that you are in good standing or whether you have any honor code violations on your permanent record. It is usually signed by a school official within the dean of students or registrar's office, so check with your pre-transfer school to establish who can sign it for you.

This is not required by all transfer schools. To get the report to those that do, keep in mind you may have to go through the step of submitting a FERPA[8] form confirming to your pre-transfer schools that they can release information to your transfer schools.

When you receive this document, you can upload it to the Common App site.

---

8   FERPA (Family Educational Rights and Privacy Act of 1974) is federal legislation in the United States that protects the privacy of students' personally identifiable information.

## ACING YOUR INTERVIEWS

Many schools will require or recommend interviews. In some cases, these may be offered near you or by video conference with an alumnus of the school and/or an admissions representative, which will save you the costs of traveling for an on-campus interview. For schools that don't offer these flexible options, be sure to plan well in advance, as there is a small window for interviewing on campus at each school.

Even if interviewing is not required, just recommended, it is a very good way to strengthen your application, as it offers opportunities for the school to get to know you personally and lets you showcase who you are beyond the application you submitted. Interviews are a great forum for expressing your strong interest in the school and getting to know the school by asking questions.

You should prepare for the interview by practicing with someone familiar with the interview process, doing your research on the school ahead of time, and having a convincing argument for why you're a good fit for the school and what you'll bring to the student body.

Here are a few more tips for getting the most out of your interviews:

- Be ready to discuss your extracurricular activities and how you have solved problems. Schools like to hear examples of how you've problem-solved and managed difficult situations.

- Do not repeat verbatim everything you wrote in your application. This is a time for you to expand, share other interests, and show what makes you a passionate and curious learner.

- Be a good listener and make sure you understand the questions being asked. Understand that some interviewers may not have specific questions for you and may be relying on your questions to drive the conversation.

- Keep in mind that most selective schools are looking for people with strong communication skills. Do not be concerned if you have an accent. Be proud of it! Make sure you are using complete sentences and correct subject-verb agreement.

- As a transfer student, you should have a lot to say about what you've learned about yourself and your community during your academic journey, but don't be afraid to also share how you've resolved problems at work and how your family, friends, and social circles have contributed to your life and goals.

- The interview process is not the place for you to complain about your current college or offer criticism. You are best served by presenting examples of situations where you demonstrated your role as an active thinker or engaged member of your community, not simply a critic. Keep it positive!

Interviews are a dialogue between you and the interviewer. Be ready with at least five questions, and do not waste your opportunity to ask questions with "filler questions" that can be easily answered by going to a school's website. Here are some good examples of questions you may ask:

- What do you look for in your transfer students from an academic perspective?

- How soon will I know how many credits will be accepted and how they will apply to my degree?

- What are the kinds of contributions that transfer students make to your campus?

- What are some of the challenges transfer students face here, and what is the school doing to resolve them?

- Are there any transfer-specific resources or clubs on campus?
- My research shows you offer transfer orientation. What happens during that process?
- Based on my number of credits, will I be able to study abroad?
- Is there a residency requirement for me as a transfer student?
- Can you tell me about housing availability for transfer students? What are your specific policies?
- [Question for alumni] Can you tell me about one thing you got out of going to this school that you wouldn't have gotten anywhere else?
- What are some things you would change about this school? What are some things you would always want to stay the same?
- What is your advice for me as a transfer student to transition smoothly at this school?

You should be prepared to answer questions about who you are, your goals, how you overcome challenges, and what you will contribute to the college community. For example, you may be asked:

- Can you tell me a little bit about yourself?
  - » You can briefly talk about where you're from in terms of geography and personal history, but your focus should be on painting a picture of the role you play at your current college or in your community.
- Why are you interested in transfer?
  - » Focus on specific examples demonstrating that your goals match what the school has to offer.
  - » Do not provide negative critiques about your current college. Instead, focus on what you've learned that has helped you realize that transfer is the next step.
- What are you planning to major in?
  - » You should be able to explain that you've explored enough at your current college or through your work experiences to make informed decisions about your major.
  - » Don't focus on one specific major unless you're absolutely certain. You'll want to demonstrate that you are open to advice that will help you pursue your goals and to the opportunities open to you as a transfer student.
- How will you overcome challenges along your educational journey?
  - » Interviewers may ask specific questions about things they see as roadblocks for you, such as family issues or attending school far from home.
  - » Be prepared to show you've thought about your challenges and have addressed them, or have a solid plan to address them. You want to convey that, if accepted, you will be able to complete your degree.

## GETTING GREAT LETTERS OF RECOMMENDATION

Here's some advice on how to request letters of recommendation in support of your transfer applications.

### Academic Letters of Recommendation

Most schools require one or two letters of recommendation from professors. These are called academic recommendations and can only be submitted by professors whose classes you have taken. These should provide a picture of how you perform in the classroom. Do not make the mistake of having a faculty member who has taught you write about your performance outside of the classroom without also writing about your in-class performance.

Your letter of recommendation will have a great deal of weight with transfer admissions offices if it illustrates your relationships with fellow classmates, intellectual curiosity, problem-solving skills, academic strengths, and areas for you to develop. Your transcript only offers a grade. Letters provide a narrative by which your professor can compare you to students they've had. If a professor notes that you are one of the strongest students they've ever met, it gives greater context than an A or B grade ever could.

Always remember that the first step to getting a strong letter of recommendation is building great relationships with your professors. This process usually develops out of your participation and performance in a course. It can also be strengthened by discussing your academic interests and career goals or by seeking the professor's insights outside of class to expand upon what you learned in class. Don't expect a strong letter of recommendation if you have never put in the time to build a strong relationship first.

If you've taken some time off from school or otherwise lost touch with professors, it is even more important that you go to them with very specific examples of your abilities. It is also important to include a narrative of what you experienced in their course, as they may not clearly remember on their own. Share some of your coursework, presentations, group work, notes, and a narrative about your participation in their class to help them write you a good letter.

Before you ask a professor for an academic letter of recommendation, ask yourself the following questions to make sure you'll be able to get what you need:

- Does this professor know me well, and can they speak to my abilities? Can they paint a positive picture of my academic skills and development, teamwork, and participation?
- Can I ask them for this favor in person, whether during office hours or by appointment? An in-person request is usually better received than a request via email and can help you provide context and communicate the importance of your request.
- Have I given them enough time to write a letter? (Your professors are busy, so giving them at least three weeks to prepare a letter is the polite way to go about this.)
- Have I shared the information they need to write a good letter?

If you answered yes to all of these questions, you're all set for a good academic letter of recommendation!

We have found that most faculty are very happy to hear their students want to continue their studies and are eager to help you. Just make sure you give them the help they need to write you a good letter. And don't be upset or offended if a professor tells you they can't write in great detail about your performance. Many receive requests from multiple students or have personal or professional commitments that may make it difficult to write a good letter in a short amount of time. If they can't help you, it's OK for you to move on and find someone who can. If they can help, make sure to send them a handwritten thank-you note for their work on your behalf!

## Additional Letter of Recommendation

In addition to your academic letters, you may also submit a more general letter that attests to your leadership and performance outside of the classroom. This can speak to your extracurricular activities, your performance at a job, your character, or any other aspect that you think would help give the transfer admissions office a good sense of your potential.

As with your academic letters, make sure you have a conversation ahead of time with the person writing it to share how you feel they can best evaluate you. The best letters of recommendation provide examples, so when you make your request, remind them of accomplishments they've observed and ask them to speak to your problem-solving, stress and time management, communication, and people skills.

**What to Share with the Writer of a Letter of Recommendation**

- Cover letter explaining your request for a letter of recommendation, when it's due, and exactly how to submit it
- For an academic letter:
  » Details on what course you took with them, and when
  » Transcript or written copy of what grades you got in their course
  » Coursework (papers, projects, exams, presentations) you completed for their class
  » Any examples from class that you'd like them to focus on
- For a nonacademic letter:
  » Description and dates of when you worked/volunteered with them
  » Any accomplishments or features you would like them to focus on
- Your resume
- The list of schools you are considering

# MAKING THE MOST OF STANDARDIZED TESTS

For non-traditional students and transfer students with at least 30 college credits, standardized test scores carry less weight in the admissions process than they do for students going straight from high school to college. As these tests are typically designed for and taken by high-school students, many colleges do not require standardized test scores in transfer admissions.

If a school you want to attend has a standardized test requirement and you are a non-traditional-age student, you should contact them to find out if the requirement can be waived. If they deny your waiver request and you are convinced that this is the school for you, you should consider some kind of test preparation.

Keep in mind that good test prep takes many hours of studying and practice, so you should consider how taking time out of your schedule for it will affect your other activities. We always advise our scholars to focus on course performance and learning rather than preparing to take a test that may be required for only some schools on your list. In some instances, our scholars have prepared for and taken standardized tests, including the SAT II subject area tests, to demonstrate a strength in a particular area that relates to their intended major, like biology or history.

If you decide you need to take standardized tests, remember that many people take them multiple times, sometimes preparing as early as ninth grade. To compete at top schools, give strong consideration to enrolling in a test prep course, either online or in-person. Test preparation can have a considerable cost, but there are also free and low-cost options available that can help you improve your scores.

In making your decision about standardized tests, don't forget that there are costs to take the test and costs to submit your scores. Please refer to the Reducing the Costs of Applying section later in this chapter for more information.

In the School Profiles section, we've provided SAT and ACT ranges for each school. These are heavily based on what they are looking for in their high-school population and should not deter you from applying. They should, however, give you an idea of how academically competitive the admissions process is for each school.

Here are some details on each test. Refer to the official website for each test for the dates on which they are offered, their rules, and their requirements.

### SAT

- Designed to measure what students learned in high school to determine their academic readiness for college.
- 3 hours long (plus 50 minutes for the optional essay section).
- Scores range from 400–1600, combining test results from two 800-point sections (evidence-based reading and writing, and math).

### ACT

- Designed to measure what students learned in high school to determine their academic readiness for college.
- 3 hours long (plus 40 minutes for the optional essay section).
- Scores range from 1–36, combining scores from four skill areas: English, math, reading, and science.

### TOEFL

- Designed to measure the English language ability of non-native speakers.
- Most colleges are looking for high proficiency, as classes are conducted primarily in English.
- While there are other English proficiency tests, we have found that the TOEFL satisfies the requirements of most schools.
- Scores range from 0–120, combining results from reading, listening, speaking, and writing sections.

### SAT II

- There are 20 different tests in five general areas: English, history, languages, mathematics, and science. They test your knowledge of these subjects on a high-school level.
- Each test is an hour long, is multiple-choice, and is scored on a 200–800 scale.
- You can take up to three SAT II subject tests per test date, but cannot take the SAT and an SAT II test on the same day.

# REDUCING THE COSTS OF APPLYING

In order to reduce the cost of applying for transfer, you will need to work with all the institutions involved in the processing and issuing of documents.

| Document | What You Need to Know | Fee Amount | Institution Issuing | How to Avoid or Reduce the Cost |
|---|---|---|---|---|
| Transfer admissions application (Common App) | The cost per transfer admissions application, as established by each school you are applying to. | $0–100, although most schools fall in the $40–60 range. See school profiles for individual fees. | The Common Application, the organization that administers the Common App. Most of the admissions applications in our guide are processed by the Common App. Not all colleges are on the Common App. | Request a fee waiver through the Common App. You may request a fee waiver for the reasons listed below, but if these do not apply to you and you cannot afford the fees, you should still write a request with a brief statement explaining your circumstances. Most schools will grant you the waiver if a school official, advisor, financial aid officer or community leader writes a letter in support of your request. Here are the automatic fee waiver situations: You have received or are eligible to receive an ACT or SAT testing fee waiver. You are enrolled in or eligible to participate in the Federal Free or Reduced Price Lunch program (FRPL). Your annual family income falls within the Income Eligibility Guidelines set by the USDA Food and Nutrition Service. You are enrolled in a federal, state, or local program that aids students from low-income families (e.g., TRIO programs such as Upward Bound). Your family receives public assistance. You live in federally subsidized public housing, live in a foster home, or are homeless. You are a ward of the state or an orphan. |
| Transfer admissions application (non-Common App) | Many public and private institutions process their own applications and establish their own fees. Some schools may also have separate application requirements for special programs, such as those for non-traditional students. | Each school establishes their own fees and require-ments for applications. Some schools may not charge a fee, but for many they range between $40 and $60. | The school you are applying to. Applications will be online, and supplements for special programs may be located on the specific program's website. | The school may incorporate a fee waiver request into the application itself and/or have a separate form to request one. Please note the Common App fee waiver situations above, for which many non-Common App institutions will also issue a fee waiver. If none of these apply to you, write a request and ask a school official (such as an advisor, counselor, or financial aid officer) to write a brief statement explaining that you cannot afford the fee. Letters do not have to be addressed to each individual school. It is okay if you have the letter addressed to "Admissions Officer" and make multiple copies. Paper or electronic copies are OK, unless specified by your prospective college. |

| Document | What You Need to Know | Fee Amount | Institution Issuing | How to Avoid or Reduce the Cost |
|---|---|---|---|---|
| High-school transcripts | Some schools will require you to submit high-school transcripts regardless of when you graduated or how many credits you have earned. | The cost may vary, with some schools not charging for any or for a certain number of transcripts. Some schools use third-party providers that charge fees. | Transcripts can be issued by your high school or a supervising board or centralized organization that governs the school. In some cases, the high school may use a third party. Your school will be able to provide you with this information. | Some colleges may be willing to accept an unofficial copy if a school official certifies it to be unaltered. This is common when the high school has closed, you graduated a long time ago, and/or you attended school outside of the United States. Contact the prospective college directly to see if they will accept this. Contact your high school to find out any transcript costs. If there is a fee and you cannot afford it, ask if there is a way that the fee can be waived. If the high school utilizes a third-party provider, ask if they can issue the transcript directly to you instead to avoid the fee. |
| GED or High-School Equivalency (HSE) transcript and/or diploma | The transcript will have the individual scores for science, social studies, mathematics, and language arts (including reading and writing). A composite score is also provided. | Fees are charged for individual transcripts and usually range between $10–15. When ordering a transcript, you will be asked if you would like a transcript and/or the diploma or certificate. There is usually an additional fee for the diploma/ certificate. | The high-school equivalency program you attended (if applicable). | Research whether your college needs an official copy or if you can submit a copy of your original. In some cases, colleges are willing to take a copy. We have found that colleges are usually willing to work with you, but you must communicate with them early on, as official documentation may take a few weeks to arrive. If you are afraid you will miss the admissions deadline, let the college know you have requested an official version, and ask if it can evaluate you using a copy. If accepted with a copy version, you may still need to bring the original to an admissions official if the college wants an official copy in its records. |

| Document | What You Need to Know | Fee Amount | Institution Issuing | How to Avoid or Reduce the Cost |
|---|---|---|---|---|
| College transcripts | Official transcripts for any postsecondary school you have attended.<br><br>An official college transcript can be mailed directly to your school, or you may pick up a copy in a sealed envelope. | Schools have varying fees, with some schools not charging and others charging in the range of $9–12. There may be additional fees if the request is processed by a third-party service, such as National Clearing House. | You must provide official transcripts for each postsecondary, credit-granting institution that you have attended.<br><br>Even if you did not earn any credits because you withdrew or took remedial courses, you still must submit your transcripts. | A college will usually not release a transcript if you owe it any money. In some instances, you may have a hold because of an unreturned library book, a late fee, or an outstanding tuition bill.<br><br>You will have to work with your current school to clear any outstanding debt and get access to your transcripts. If you aren't able to pay the whole amount you owe, try working with your bursar's office or dean of students to work out a payment plan and get your records released.<br><br>The cost of these fees usually doubles because you typically have to send transcripts twice if you have credits in progress. You will be asked to submit transcripts (1) at the time of application and (2) once you have completed or earned the credits that were in progress at the time you submitted the first transcript.<br><br>Before you start your application process, make sure you check with any institution you've attended and are cleared to get transcripts issued by the school.<br><br>If you aren't able to pay for your transcripts, it is important that you talk to a school official, such as the person that handles outgoing transfer advisement or a dean of students. Do not let this fee keep you from applying. |
| English translations (for international students) | If your official high-school or college records are written in a language other than English, you will need to submit an official and certified translation. You will need at least one copy of your officially translated document along with the original. | The costs for translations differ according to the service provider that you are working with. | There are many translation services, but it is important that the service provider you use has a good reputation for accuracy. You may want to consult with a local school or your current college to find out if it recommends any providers. | You may not need to submit official translation documents to each individual prospective school. You may be able to provide copies of the documents.<br><br>However, some of your prospective schools may want copies of translations to be certified by a school official and/or public notary.<br><br>The cost of having multiple official copies of your translation may become steep. Therefore, ask the service provider to give you a cost for each additional copy. It should be considerably less than the original translation. |

| Document | What You Need to Know | Fee Amount | Institution Issuing | How to Avoid or Reduce the Cost |
|---|---|---|---|---|
| CSS Profile | The CSS Profile form is a financial aid application used by many colleges to collect the documents that determine the amount of institutional aid they will provide to your financial aid package. | $16 per school, with a $9 fee up front. | The College Board provides the CSS Profile. | There is no official process to waive the CSS Profile for transfer students at this time.<br><br>However, we have found that some prospective schools that use the CSS Profile to determine financial need may waive the application altogether and allow you to complete their own internal form.<br><br>Non-traditional students who find it extremely difficult to complete the CSS Profile because they are not able to provide the necessary information should reach out to prospective schools and find out if the form can be waived. |

| Document | What You Need to Know | Fee Amount | Institution Issuing | How to Avoid or Reduce the Cost |
|---|---|---|---|---|
| Standardized tests | SAT—college admissions exam | $60 with essay, $42 without. Free to report scores to four schools, $12 per school after the first four. | The College Board administers the SAT test. | Each school establishes its own policies regarding standardized testing. The cost of sending scores to schools can be high, and in the event that you are required to submit scores, you will want to do some test prep, which may also add costs. |
| | ACT—college admissions exam | $58.50 with essay, $42.50 without. Free to report scores to four schools, $12 per school after the first four. | The ACT organization administers the ACT test. | Reducing costs in this area requires you to understand if your scores will play a significant role and add value to your application. For many schools, test scores play a minimal role in their assessment of transfer students. For example, some schools do not require standardized test scores from students that have more than 30 credits or students that completed high school more than two years prior to applying. Other schools require you to submit scores if you took the tests, but don't expect you to take them if you haven't already. |
| | SAT II—subject tests focused on specific topics in sciences and humanities. Specific programs may require SAT IIs, especially STEM majors. | $26 to register for a test date. You can take up to three subject tests per date at $21 each. Free to report scores to four schools, $12 per school after the first four. | The College Board administers the SAT II tests. | If you are applying to a school that requires test scores and you have not taken the test, you should give strong consideration as to how to best prepare, as well as when and how many times you will take the test. Consider all costs before deciding if you want to apply to that school, as you may be better served by applying to other colleges. After all, you will find that many highly competitive colleges do not require any type of testing for transfer students. |
| | TOEFL (Test of English as a Foreign Language)—measures the English-language ability of non-native speakers wishing to enroll in English-speaking universities. | Fees vary depending upon which country you take the test in. Free to report scores to four schools, $20 per school after the first four. | ETS administers the TOEFL. | |

| Document | What You Need to Know | Fee Amount | Institution Issuing | How to Avoid or Reduce the Cost |
|---|---|---|---|---|
| Enrollment deposit fee | Deposits secure a spot for you and set the ball rolling to secure housing, registration, and full enrollment. Deposits are usually non-refundable. | Varies | You should only issue a deposit to the school you are committing to attend. Avoid issuing multiple deposits. | The good news: You have been accepted! The bad news: Your college is asking for a deposit to let you enroll. For low-income students, some schools or special programs will automatically waive your deposit, but in some instances, you may have to ask for this. Reach out to your admissions office contact and let them know that you do not have the funds but would like to commit. Keep in mind that even if they waive the fee, you are making a commitment to attend. Keep in mind that some schools will not issue a waiver. |
| Housing deposit fee | If you want to live on campus, you may be asked to make a deposit to start the process of applying for housing. Not all schools have housing deposits. | Varies | The school you have committed to attend, if you plan to live in one of their housing facilities. | Like your enrollment deposit fee, your housing deposit may be waived if you aren't able to pay. If you are certain you want to live on campus, ask the admissions and/or residential office if this deposit can be waived. |
| Immunization fees | Requirements are based on the rules in place in the state that the school is located in. Some schools may have additional requirements or processes for waiving them. | Varies by health care provider and health insurance. | A health provider or health office at your current college. | If you're already at a pre-transfer college, you will likely be up-to-date in your immunization records, since your current college would have required proof of immunization. You should submit the same records you submitted to your pre-transfer school to your prospective school. The prospective school may provide you a form to complete or ask you to submit documentation from your health provider or health office at your current school. If you must get immunized, check with your health insurance to determine if they cover the cost of immunization. Keep in mind that depending on your age, immunization may not be covered. There are some organizations that offer low-cost immunization, but many have age restrictions. You can call the department of health for your city or state to get low- or no-cost resources, but you may want to start by calling your own doctor to find out if they offer it and if your insurance covers it. Please keep in mind that you may not be able to register for courses or housing if you do not complete medical requirements. Students on sports teams may have additional requirements. |

# PICKING A MAJOR WITH CREDITS THAT WILL TRANSFER

What am I going to do "when I grow up"? How can I get a job with my degree? These are the questions that many of us have as we consider college. These questions do not disappear the minute you enroll in your first class. In fact, we've found that these questions recur consistently in our educational pursuits. In those moments, when the answer is unclear or seems nonexistent, don't panic. A good education is often grounded in reassessing goals and figuring out how to achieve them.

Many students tell us they just want to pick a major that will get them a good job. Instead, we push them to become the best in their field and to work on identifying the path to get there. Demonstrating mastery of communications, technical, problem-solving, analytical, and teamwork skills will be more important to people interviewing you for a job than your major. Even if you have a high GPA in a complex major, a lack of experience and demonstrated impact beyond the classroom might reduce your chances of landing the job you want.

## Timing

You have time to declare your major. There is no need to rush into making a decision. You should look to declare a major somewhere between acquiring 45 and 70 credits, which means that even as a transfer student with a solid associate's degree (60 credits), you can still change your mind and graduate within two or three years. That said, it's never a bad idea to look ahead and find opportunities to get exposed to fields that catch your interest during your first year of college.

## Choosing Flexible and Rigorous Courses

The most transferable and flexible associate's degree is a liberal arts and sciences degree. Your courses will be mostly introductory behavioral, social, and physical sciences along with English, math, history, and the humanities. These courses are offered at most institutions and are likely to be general education requirements for most bachelor's degrees.

If you are interested in transferring to a selective institution, you want to be able to demonstrate that you can compete academically and will be able to contribute to the classroom. The best way to do this is to have a range of rigorous courses in the liberal arts and sciences. Taking courses that are noted as writing-intensive or honors courses shows you are willing to challenge yourself academically and gives greater insight into your ability to manage a heavy load of course materials.

Finally, make sure you are also exploring your passions and interests. Do not be afraid to take art courses, for example. Art courses have their own rigor and can demonstrate that you are a multidimensional learner. The same is true for health courses, which some students perceive as "weaker." The fact is that being well-rounded and having an interest in your health and that of others will demonstrate your zest for learning and balance.

## Changing Your Major

For many students, not having a major that they are certain about can be a great cause of anxiety. Understanding that a great percentage of students change their major at least once (and many change their major more than once) can help ease this anxiety. In fact, approximately 80 percent of students change their majors before they graduate.[9] There are many reasons for this, but here are some we've seen as our Scholars go through our program:

---

9   Source: National Center for Education Statistics

- Some students find that their initial interest leads to a new one. For example, students pursuing medical school often begin in nursing or biology, but some decide to focus on the health of a particular group, leading them to an anthropology degree.

- Some students find their credits won't transfer. For example, if you are interested in pursuing a prelaw track, you may find out your paralegal courses won't transfer. In order to pursue your career goals, you can major in other areas that may not necessarily be directly connected to the career you want to pursue.

- Some students simply find out that they dislike their initial major after doing some fieldwork or delving deeper into the subject matter. They may simultaneously find out that they enjoy another major that they've learned a great deal about and developed a stronger connection to.

## Specific Majors

### STEM

For STEM (Science, Technology, Engineering, and Math) majors, it is important to demonstrate reading and writing proficiency. Many four-year colleges, especially those with strong research programs, will expect a great deal of discussion, group work, writing, and strong communication skills that will allow you to excel in and out of a lab. Mathematical and scientific analysis goes beyond formulas and lab work and involves looking at how math and science actually apply to the greater world. Schools want to know you can understand the subject matter in great detail so you can solve real-world problems.

### Medicine

If you are interested in applying to medical school after completing your bachelor's degree, you need to complete premedical requirements before transferring. These may vary slightly between schools but generally include one year of biology with lab, one year of general chemistry with lab, one year of organic chemistry with lab, one year of physics with lab, and one year of English.

You are not required to major in a science to gain admission to medical school and should pursue a degree in a field that interests you. Studies in the humanities can complement your pursuit of a medical degree. Medical doctors are practitioners that need to be effective communicators who understand the impact of culture, environment, and economic trends on the health and well-being of their patients. Science is only one piece of the puzzle. When picking a major, look for classes that will transfer. Associate's degree programs in the medical sciences do not necessarily transfer well to bachelor's degree programs.

Students who do not complete premedical requirements during their undergraduate years can either take the classes after graduation or enroll in a postbaccalaureate program designed to help nonscience degree holders complete the requirements and apply to medical school.

### Law

Law schools look for strong, persuasive communicators (written and verbal), analytical minds, and the ability to understand very complicated ideas. If you are seriously considering law school after completing your bachelor's degree, meet with law-school students and people with law degrees, visit law schools, and look for internships in the field. Many four-year colleges have prelaw programs with advisors that specialize in prelaw admissions and how to prepare for law school. Often, these advisors can connect you to law schools that can further advise you on what they're looking for and what you should aim for on your LSAT. Some prelaw programs also offer low-cost or free test preparation or can refer you to test prep resources.

Please note that there is no one law-specific major. And remember that having a law degree doesn't necessarily mean you will work exclusively in litigation. If you are interested in law school, try to identify the reasons why you are interested in becoming an attorney and what type of advocacy, policies, fields, communities, or laws interest you. Then, consider the classes, subjects, and majors that would best prepare you to develop your skills in those areas.

### Engineering

If you declare engineering to be your major in your first or second year, you may have taken some engineering courses already. However, most college courses taken early in college fall in the liberal arts and sciences, like Intro to Chemistry or Intro to Calculus, so if you haven't yet taken many engineering courses, don't worry.

A strong and proven record in math and science (including, for example, physics and calculus I and II) can help establish the level of interest and foundational skills that transfer schools are looking for in prospective engineering majors. Fieldwork (internships, research, extracurriculars) and a strong background in general science courses can confirm for schools that you will be able to keep up as an engineering student. Some engineering departments may have specific requirements or guidelines, so be sure to check ahead of time.

## Credit Evaluation

Most schools will accept up to 60–70 credits, but keep in mind that some of those credits will be accepted as electives if they cannot be applied to any specific degree requirements. Usually, a credit is considered an elective if there is no equivalent at the transfer school. The good news is that schools can work with you in reviewing the course credit and reclassifying it if you are able to prove that it meets a certain degree requirement. You can do this by providing course materials including course syllabi, assignments, and course descriptions.

If you are enrolled in an associate's degree program in an applied science or a career-focused track, you may lose those major-specific credits when you transfer. A career-focused associate's degree does have a great deal of value to help you secure employment in your desired field without a bachelor's degree, and it can play a significant role in your ability to meet your financial responsibilities. But if you plan on transferring, and time and financial resources allow it, you should seek to complement your enrollment with as many liberal arts courses as possible, as most of these credits will transfer.

## Remain Open

Prospective colleges are not always looking for a transfer student who is certain about what they will pursue if accepted, especially if the student is unable to fully articulate or demonstrate from their previous record that they have had enough academic exposure and experiences to make a final decision about their major. If this is the case for you, it's best to communicate (in your transfer application and in person) the general fields you are interested in (health care, education, government, etc.) and the kinds of work you may want to do. Work with your pre-transfer advisor to figure out which majors, minors, and concentrations could apply so you have a skill set after graduation that allows you to go into those fields with some flexibility.

Do not try to prove to a school (or to yourself) that one particular major is the only path to your chosen field if you truly do not want to declare that major. For example, some students think a history or political science major is the only path for them to pursue a career in government. The fact is, other majors can help them approach policy-making from different perspectives. Think about where your interests lie, and be open to majors that you may not have initially considered.

## DEVELOPING A LEADERSHIP PROFILE

As part of your admissions assessment, schools will look closely at how you engage with your community and the individuals around you. What's really important here is quality over quantity. The depth of your contributions is more important than being a member of multiple clubs or activities where you haven't shown leadership or brought about change.

To build a strong leadership profile, keep in mind the differences between being a passive member of an organization, an active member, and a leader. You don't have to be a leader in all of the organizations you participate in, but you should seek to develop your leadership profile by taking on some challenges. As you consider how you will get involved, consider these different levels of participation:

| Passive Member | Active Member | Leader |
|---|---|---|
| • Joins an organization<br>• Regularly attends meetings | • Organizes some events<br>• Participates in decision-making | • Sets the agenda<br>• Carries the mission forward<br>• Sets systems in place for new leaders<br>• Ensures members are engaged and well informed |

Don't think of leadership as a way to fill out a checklist for a college app. Instead, look at it as a way to develop the following attributes that will serve you over the course of your life and help admissions officers confirm you are a good fit for their community:

- Engaged in self-development
- Well-rounded in and out of the classroom
- Action-oriented
- Involved with a network of like-minded people
- Committed to your passions
- Able to contribute to a common cause

All of these positive aspects of leadership will help you build a transfer application that truly stands out. Here are some questions to ask yourself as you decide what kinds of activities to pursue:

- Will you have the opportunity to engage in an area of interest you are passionate about (personally, academically, creatively, or professionally) and enjoy?
- Will you be able to meet the responsibilities of the position, and what adjustments will you have to make in order to fulfill your duties?
- Is this the type of organization where you can leave behind a legacy or accomplishments with long-term benefits?
- Will you work closely with other members and be able to help in decision-making?

- Are you going to be able to expand your social network by getting to know people you can have fun with and learn from?
- What are the opportunities for you to learn something new while also sharing your expertise or skill set?
- How does this organization tie in to your overall goals?

One of the most important organizations to consider joining is Phi Theta Kappa (PTK), an international honor society for two-year colleges that has provided development opportunities, scholarships, and other support for over 3.2 million members since it was founded in 1918.

In the School Profiles section of this guide, you'll see that PTK has formed partnerships with many colleges and universities to offer over $37 million in transfer scholarships to its members. The average member receives a transfer scholarship of $2,500 per year. Some chapters of PTK have GPA requirements or require an additional application, so be sure to review the information in the School Profiles.

PTK also offers its members job search assistance—including letters of recommendation, professional development plans, and leadership development programs—and a community of students, advisors, and mentors that support you as you pursue the academic and extracurricular activities that will make you a star candidate for transfer admissions.

You can visit www.ptk.org for more information about PTK membership.

## BUILDING YOUR PERSONAL "BOARD OF DIRECTORS"

At the Kaplan Educational Foundation, our scholars are asked to build a board of directors, or a group of individuals to advise them in making important decisions. These should be talented people with different skills who you can consistently count on for guidance, support, critique, and motivation.

Pursuing your education will require you to make complex and sometimes difficult decisions. Self-reliance and independence are valuable traits, but seeking help with hard choices will increase your success over time and help you grow.

When you consider transfer schools, you'll find that the ability to seek advice and build strong relationships with people who can help you make sound decisions is highly valued. The most successful leaders have both strong personal drive and a network of trusted advisors. Many people throw the term *networking* around, and you have probably heard it's important to network. But identifying, seeking out, and engaging people is not passive. It demands that you clearly communicate who you are, what you're trying to achieve, how your success will contribute to them, and why they should want to be a part of your board of directors.

As you pursue your degree and becoming the very best in your field, we recommend you engage people with the following attributes:

- Up-to-date and involved in their area of expertise
- Familiar with you and your goals
- Committed to your success
- Trustworthy and honest in their advice
- Open-minded and good listeners
- Resourceful in coming up with problem-solving options for and with you

Your board of directors should be comprehensive. Look to your family and friends, past and current employers, teachers and professors, fellow students, spiritual leaders, experts in your desired field, and people current in college admissions to build your board.

Be ready to accept advice, weigh different options and perspectives, and follow through. Your board of directors may disengage from you if they see that you don't value their well-thought-out advice. You don't have to agree with everything they say, but oftentimes the best decisions are made by synthesizing the different kinds of information and advice you receive.

Your board of directors can become lifelong allies, friends, and mentors. They will be there for you at your toughest moments in life and help you celebrate the happiest times. The best way to thank them is to pay it forward by eventually becoming someone else's board member and helping them pursue their own dreams.

# CHAPTER FIVE

# Financial Aid for Transfer

Your financial aid application provides a picture of your financial situation for the schools you apply to and helps them determine how they can help you afford them. For these reasons, it's one of the most important parts of the entire transfer admissions process!

## UNDERSTANDING THE BASICS

Your main goal in applying for financial aid is to get the most financial support possible, so it's essential to approach the process by understanding how college education can be afforded. Assessing how much you and/or your parents are willing and able to contribute is one piece of the puzzle, but the real key to affording college is submitting an accurate and thorough financial aid application. Rather than worrying about the total cost of any given school, which can be intimidating at first, your focus should remain on how much financial aid each school can afford to give you.

Here are the first few things you should do to start the financial aid application process and get the best financial aid packages:

1. **Review the glossary at the back of the book.** The explanations about some of the financial aid terms will give you a grasp of the basics you'll need to make sense of the process.
2. **Realize that the "sticker price" of a school is not the real price.** Looking at the overall costs of attending selective schools can seem daunting, but don't let that define your transfer college search.

For example, the School Profiles in this guide show that the annual cost of attendance for some private schools can be as high as $72,000. However, many of the schools listed have made a commitment to fulfill 100 percent of their accepted students' financial need, or have other programs in place to address need, so the actual cost you will be responsible for is much lower. Make sure you know the answers to the following questions about the schools you're applying to:

- Does this school have a commitment to meet 100 percent need for students, including transfer students?
- Does this school have special programs to address the particular living and financial needs that will make my attendance at the school possible, such as housing for families or services for veterans?
- Does this school limit the amount of loans students have to take out, or do they not consider loans at all in their financial aid awards?
- If this school provides me with a considerable financial aid award packet that includes loans, will I be open to taking on debt? If so, how much am I comfortable taking on?

- Will this school accept the credits I've already taken so I don't have to take similar courses and pay for them all over again?
- When considering my school options, will I have to work in order to attend school? Or would I be willing and able to stop working and focus on my studies?

Looking at these questions can yield some surprising results. In fact, some schools that appeared to be out of your financial reach can end up costing you less money after they've packaged you for financial aid. For example, here are some school sticker prices compared to what they'd actually cost you to attend, according to the US Department of Education's College Scorecard:

| School Name | Type of School | Cost of Attendance* | Average Cost for a Family Income of $0–$30,000 | Average Cost for a Family Income of $30,001–$48,000 | Average Cost for a Family Income of $48,001–$75,000 |
|---|---|---|---|---|---|
| Brown University | Selective private research university | $67,439 | $3,186 | $7,129 | $10,700 |
| Amherst University | Selective private liberal arts college | $73,250 | $3,700 | $4,840 | $10,759 |
| Muhlenberg College | Less selective private school | $50,830 | $18,765 | $18,285 | $22,140 |
| State University of New York at New Paltz | State | $24,300 | $8,551 | $12,014 | $18,151 |
| City University of New York— City College | City | $20,536 | $4,537 | $6,340 | $10,364 |

The Scorecard is a great resource because it helps you estimate the average annual net price (meaning the average price after school, state, or federal aid) for students eligible for federal financial aid. You can use it to get a better idea of the true cost of attendance for your prospective transfer schools.

At the Kaplan Educational Foundation, we urge our scholars to always consider that institutional aid (financial aid granted by the institution you are attending) is usually the most generous, comprehensive, and renewable type of aid. Schools with generous endowments and a commitment to fulfilling 100 percent need for their students can be the most affordable choices.

As you can see, you may have many financial options to weigh. That's why it's so important to give schools accurate information so you can receive back from them relevant financial aid packages and make informed decisions based on what they offer you.

---

*Cost of attendance information comes from school websites.
 Average cost per income bracket comes from College Scorecard.

3. **Remember that financial aid forms were mostly created for traditional students.** Don't be discouraged or get caught up in how many of the questions don't seem to apply to you. Remain focused on finalizing your application.

4. **Think strategically about how you will draw a picture of your financial circumstances.** Your main goal is to help your schools assess how much aid you will need, how much the federal government or state can provide you, how much aid the schools should provide themselves, and how much you and your parents are responsible for. The rest of this chapter will outline exactly what you need to do.

# WORKING ON YOUR FINANCIAL AID APPLICATION

Now that you've got a handle on the basics, let's dive into the specifics of the financial aid forms you'll have to complete, whose information you should provide, and what documents you will need as backup.

### What Financial Aid Application Forms Will I Need to Complete?

Identifying the forms you'll need to fill out will require you to have at least a preliminary list of schools, as each school may require a different combination of these forms:

### FAFSA

The Free Application for Federal Student Aid is the first place to start for many students, regardless of whether you qualify for federal aid or not. In addition to its primary function of determining how much federal student aid you are eligible for, the FAFSA also provides a thorough picture of your and your parents' income and assets for your schools. For more information, visit fafsa.ed.gov.

### State Financial Aid

Each US state has its own grant and student aid programs. When completing the FAFSA, you will be given the opportunity to provide your financial information to the state higher education agencies where your schools are located. State aid can be provided through several different programs per state, and many of these have residency requirements, so do your research to understand what you may be eligible for. The National Association of Student Financial Aid Administrators portal is a great resource to find the state aid programs in your prospective schools' states. Please note that you may be able to attend a school outside of your state and still be eligible for in-state tuition rates if your state takes part in tuition exchange programs, which provide students with access to discounted rates and do not generally require the FAFSA. You can research programs you may be eligible for on the National Association of Student Financial Aid Administrators State and Regional Tuition Exchange portal. For more information, visit www.nasfaa.org/State_Financial_Aid_Programs.

*Warning! You do not have to pay a fee to complete the FAFSA or state financial aid forms. Beware of any service with fees to file these forms. Although there are financial aid experts that charge for their services, we urge you to work with your current college or school staff instead, or use the online free services provided by the federal government at studentaid.ed.gov.*

### CSS Profile

The CSS/Financial Aid Profile is an application distributed by the College Board for college students to apply for financial aid. The CSS Profile is much more thorough in its consideration of income than the FAFSA and expands into student and parental assets. In addition, while for the FAFSA you may only provide information from your custodial parent, the CSS Profile may require you to also include income and asset information from a noncustodial parent.

We've seen that our scholars can typically complete the FAFSA in 20 minutes but may take over an hour to complete the CSS Profile, so be sure to budget time for it. The CSS Profile typically takes into consideration union, retirement, life insurance policies, stock holdings, business ownership, and other assets, but schools may add even more specific questions, down to the make and model of cars you own. You may also be asked about your religious affiliation in order to be considered for faith-based scholarships.

While you may feel many of the questions regarding assets may not apply to you or your parents, you can use this opportunity to provide a very thorough picture of your financial situation and demonstrate the extent of your financial need. If you have special circumstances and feel the information you are being asked to provide doesn't really reflect your financial circumstances, you should contact the financial aid office of the school you are applying to and seek their advice, or at least make them aware of your situation. You will also have the opportunity to explain your financial picture more accurately in the Special Circumstances section of the CSS Profile, which provides you a space to make your case.

Here are some examples of special circumstances:

- If your income for the year you are being asked to report is considerably higher than your current income and doesn't reflect your financial circumstances, you can explain how you have lost or reduced employment. You can ask schools to consider your current income and expenses instead.
- If your household composition has changed due to events like divorce, birth of a child, adoption, or a death in your family, you can explain how this impacts your financial situation.
- If you have extraordinary expenses that take a considerable toll on your assets or income, you can provide proof, like medical bills.

Here's one final money- and time-saving tip: some special programs will waive the CSS Profile altogether. If you are applying through a special program, please contact that program first before registering at that school or paying to submit the CSS Profile there.

*Warning! There is a fee to file the CSS Profile. For the 2017–2018 scholastic year, the application fee is $25 to submit to a single school and $16 per additional college. These fees stack up very quickly, so check with each of your schools, especially if you are applying via special programs, as sometimes you may be able to avoid filing.*

### Institutional Forms

Some colleges will require you to complete their own institutional forms for financial aid.

Many schools that use the CSS Profile also use IDOC (Institutional Documentation Service), another service of the College Board, to collect families' federal tax returns and other documents. IDOC provides a platform for you to submit all required documents, but it also will, in most cases, note that you must submit a college-specific form or document.

If you are applying to admissions through a special program, do not rely on IDOC to provide you with a complete list of documents needed. Consult the school's special program website or admissions first, and if you aren't clear, contact the school.

For schools that do not utilize the CSS Profile and/or IDOC, you will need to follow up with the school directly to determine if there are any additional forms to complete.

## Whose Information Will I Need to Provide?

### On the FAFSA

For the FAFSA, your dependency status determines if you have to provide parental income information. If you're a dependent student, you will report your and your parents' information. If you're an independent student, you report only your own information (and your spouse's if you are married). If any of the following statements apply to you, you're considered to be an independent student and are exempt from providing parental information on the FAFSA:

- You were born before January 1, 1995.
- You are married, or you are separated but not divorced.
- At the beginning of the 2018–2019 school year, you will be working on a master's or doctorate program.
- You are currently serving on active duty in the US armed forces for purposes other than training. (If you are a National Guard or Reserves enlistee, you are on active duty for other than state or training purposes.)
- You are a veteran of the US armed forces.
- You now have or will have children who will receive more than half of their support from you between July 1, 2018, and June 30, 2019.
- You have dependents (other than your children or spouse) who live with you and who receive more than half of their support from you, now and through June 30, 2019.
- At any time since you turned age 13, both your parents were deceased, you were in foster care, or you were a dependent or ward of the court.
- A court in your state of legal residence has determined that you are an emancipated minor or that someone other than your parent or stepparent has legal guardianship of you. (This applies if you are now an adult but were in legal guardianship or were an emancipated minor immediately before you reached the age of being an adult in your state. It does not apply if the court papers say "custody" rather than "guardianship.")
- At any time on or after July 1, 2017, you were determined to be an unaccompanied youth who was homeless or were self-supporting and at risk of being homeless, as determined by (a) your high-school or district homeless liaison, (b) the director of an emergency shelter or transitional housing program funded by the US Department of Housing and Urban Development, or (c) the director of a runaway or homeless youth basic center or transitional living program.

### On the CSS Profile

The process of determining whose financial information you will provide for the CSS Profile is more complicated. This is for two reasons. First, each school that requires the CSS Profile will have its own policy for determining dependency status. Second, the CSS Profile's questions change depending upon how you answer its initial questions, unlike the FAFSA, which always asks for the same information.

Here are some additional tips for completing the CSS Profile:

- Don't give up. This may get complicated, but being patient and collaborating with the schools you are applying to will help you cross the finish line. Communicating with each school's financial aid advisors is usually the most direct way to ensure you are providing the information needed to determine your financial aid need and academic merit.

- In order to complete the CSS Profile, you will first fill out a registration form that asks questions about your household composition and requires you to list the colleges you are applying to. Your responses here are the most important of all because they determine how the CSS Profile's questions are customized for you. Make sure you answer these correctly so you don't get tripped up later in the process by questions that don't apply to you or your family.

- In some instances, schools that demand parental information may still reconsider your and your parents' contributions if you can verify your independent status or the unwillingness or inability of your parents to contribute.

- If you are unable to provide information regarding your parents or feel that providing parental income information is irrelevant to your financial circumstances, you should contact the individual schools to determine what information you need to send them and how they can better assess your financial situation with any other documentation you can provide.

- You may find that although on the FAFSA you were considered independent and did not have to provide any parental information, the CSS Profile may still have questions regarding your parental (custodial/noncustodial) income and assets.

### What Documents Will I Need to Complete My Forms and Verify My Financial Aid?

You are collecting documents for two reasons. First, to complete your financial aid forms accurately, and later, to verify the information you are providing.

Use this checklist to assemble your documents to apply for 2018–2019 academic year financial aid:

| Documents and Materials | Description | Student | Parent | Noncustodial Parent |
|---|---|---|---|---|
| Student Aid Report (SAR) | You will receive this after filling out the FAFSA. It is helpful to have on hand as it contains much of the information you'll need for other forms. | | N/A | N/A |
| CSS Profile ID and password | Make sure you create an account with the College Board and keep your ID and password information handy. | | N/A | N/A |
| Federal Student Aid ID (FSA ID) | The FSA ID and password will allow you to file the FAFSA electronically and access the IRS File Retrieval Tool, which makes it possible to transfer data from federal tax returns. | | N/A | N/A |
| Copies of institutional financial aid forms for special programs, including veterans and non-traditional programs | Some schools use specific financial aid forms for special programs. Please check with individual schools, especially if you are applying as a veteran, non-traditional, DACA, or undocumented student. | | N/A | N/A |

| Documents and Materials | Description | Student | Parent | Noncustodial Parent |
|---|---|---|---|---|
| 2016 federal tax forms (with all schedules and attachments) | Have complete copies of federal forms with attachments and schedules. Note that usually you are only required to submit the first 1–2 signed pages of federal 1040 forms. | | | |
| 2016 W-2s, 1099s | Have all copies of W-2 and 1099 forms issued by employers or contract holders. | | | |
| 2017 federal tax forms (with all schedules and W-2s) | You will likely be asked to submit income information and filing information for 2017. If you are filing before January 1, 2018, you will not have official copies of your federal tax forms. You should be able to provide estimates utilizing W-2s, 1099s, pay stubs, and other personal records noting earnings/income for the year. | | | |
| 2017 W-2s and 1099s | As copies of W-2s and 1099s may not be available at the time that you are filing the application, make sure you have them for the verification process. | | | |
| 2016 state tax forms (with all schedules and W-2s) | When filing for state aid, you will also have to submit state tax forms and some accompanying documentation. | | | |
| 2017 state tax forms (with all schedules and W-2s) | Forms may not be available at the time of filing for financial aid. You should still aim to file as early as possible and have them available. | | | |
| Non-tax filers (W-2s and 1099s) | If you are not required to file taxes, you can use your own personal or employer records for earnings along with W-2s or 1099s for contractual work. Please note that if you are required to file, but plan not to, some colleges may still request tax filings. | | | |

| Documents and Materials | Description | Student | Parent | Noncustodial Parent |
|---|---|---|---|---|
| Non-tax filers (statement of income and confirmation from the IRS) | If you are not required to file taxes, some colleges may request proof from the IRS that you are not required to file. You may also be asked for W-2s, 1099s, and a statement of income noting your earnings. | | | |
| Proof of citizenship or US permanent residency | US birth certificate, US passport, naturalization papers, non-US passport with visa stamp, or permanent residency card. | | | |
| Social Security number | You will need a Social Security number to file for FAFSA. Some undocumented students with DACA status may apply for a Social Security number. See the section below on DACA students for more info. | | | |
| Driver's license | If you have a driver's license, you will provide the ID number assigned. | | N/A | N/A |
| Untaxed income from the past year (for example: Social Security, Temporary Assistance For Needy Families (TANF), veterans' benefits, welfare, etc. | Have a summary of funds received for 2016 and 2017. You may estimate the total amount, but plan to have an official document for your records and verification. | | | |
| Most recent bank statements | You will be asked for the amount of funds in the bank at the time of filing. | | | |
| Mortgage information | Mortgage information will also include the value of your home and how much is owed. | | | |

| Documents and Materials | Description | Student | Parent | Noncustodial Parent |
|---|---|---|---|---|
| Other assets, which may include life insurance, investments, retirement, etc. | Please note that some assets or portions of some assets will not be considered in the financial aid formula. Check with your financial aid advisor to determine what must be reported. The Expected Family Contribution formula is published each year by the US Department of Education. It can be very complicated, but you can find out more about what assets are protected. | | | |
| Financial aid award letters for current school | How much financial aid you are receiving for the current academic year. These are required for anyone in your or your parents' household. | | | |
| Cost of attendance for each school | Educational enrollment and costs for household members included in the CSS Profile for anyone in your and your parents' household (school, cost of education, financial aid received, name of school, location). | | | |
| Automobile information | Make and model of cars owned. | | | |
| Employment information | Position, company, dates of employment, and unemployment. | | | |
| Scholarship awards | Have copies or records of any scholarship awards you have received. | | N/A | N/A |
| Financial aid award letter for 2017–2018 | Your financial aid award letter for the current year will provide you with clear information about your financial aid awards issued during the year. | | N/A | N/A |

| Documents and Materials | Description | Student | Parent | Noncustodial Parent |
|---|---|---|---|---|
| CSS Profile summary | After you complete your CSS Profile, you will get a summary of the form and information about what documents you will need to submit to each school. The summary also will note which schools utilize IDOC for document submission. | | N/A | N/A |

Here are some additional tips for collecting your documents:

- Make copies of all documents and keep them secured in hard copy and in electronic format for uploading.
- When submitting information about other people, make sure you have all the documents you need and inform them that you will be submitting their information. If possible, coordinate with them so that you can call them if needed when you are sitting down to complete your financial aid forms.
- For the CSS Profile, you will need to provide information many people keep private, such as age, educational background, and information about assets like savings accounts or retirement funds. Explaining why you are asking for the information may help you get their cooperation.
- You will also need to provide information about your current educational costs and financial aid you are receiving. Collect this information from your online school portal (if available), or contact your bursar or financial aid office.
- Make sure that the Social Security numbers and names of everyone on your application match what is on their official Social Security card. The same is true for any immigration or naturalization information.

## VERIFYING YOUR INFORMATION

It is important to note that although your financial aid application may be processed before the institutions you apply to can confirm all of your information, to actually receive funding you may later be asked to submit proof of US and state residency, citizenship, age, income, assets, debt, and more. This process is called verification.

- If you complete the FAFSA, the Student Aid Report you receive after completing the FAFSA will inform you if you have been selected for verification.
- If you complete the CSS Profile, the verification process can be fulfilled through your submission of documents on IDOC.
- If any of your schools do not use the CSS Profile, you will have to reach out to them individually to confirm you are in the clear.

The amount of governmental or institutional financial aid you will receive may increase or decrease considerably once the school verifies your documents. This is why it is very important that you accurately represent your financial information in the first place.

For any information you provide with oversight from the US government, such as Social Security, US permanent residency, immigration status, citizenship, or income reported to the IRS and state agencies, please understand that FAFSA will verify the information and base the amount they issue on this.

Not all students are selected for verification, but we have found that you should at least be prepared to submit the documentation. You do not want any surprises at the time of enrollment, like finding out that your financial aid package is decreasing after a last-minute verification. Avoid this by being proactive.

# EXPLORING OPTIONS FOR MILITARY AND DACA/UNDOCUMENTED STUDENTS

Colleges often have special financial aid programs or policies for military students or DACA/undocumented students. If you fall into these categories, you'll want to make sure you understand how financial aid works for you.

### What Financial Aid Programs Am I Eligible for as a Military Student?

When researching schools, you should ask about the additional resources available for veterans, as you may be eligible for additional school funding. You may need to submit documentation regarding your service (e.g., DD14) to the registrar to be considered for additional financial aid. We have found that many colleges have designated faculty and staff that have expertise and are assigned to work in the admissions and financial aid process for veterans.

The Post-9/11 GI Bill[10] is offered as an education benefit for individuals who served in active duty after September 10, 2001. You may be eligible for this benefit if you served a minimum of 90 aggregate days on active duty after September 10, 2001, or received an honorable discharge for a service-connected disability after serving 30 continuous days following September 10, 2001. If you are the child of a member of the armed forces who died in the line of duty on or after September 11, 2001, you may be eligible to receive the Post-9/11 GI benefits under the Marine Gunnery John David Fry Scholarship program. The educational benefits may include the following: tuition and fee payment on your behalf, a monthly housing allowance, and an annual books and supplies stipend of up to $1,000. As of August 1, 2017, individuals eligible for 100 percent maximum benefit for the Post-9/11 GI Bill will receive all tuition and fee payments for in-state public schools and up to $22,805.34 per academic year toward tuition and fees at private colleges and universities.

The Yellow Ribbon Program,[11] a provision of the law that created the Post-9/11 GI Bill, allows approved degree-granting institutions to partially or fully fund tuition, fees, and expenses that exceed the maximum benefit payouts for the Post-9/11 GI Bill. The Yellow Ribbon Program is only available for veterans who are eligible for the 100 percent Post-9/11 GI benefit. You can visit www.benefits.va.gov/gibill/yellow_ribbon.asp to determine whether a school participates in the program. Keep in mind that the school's agreement may limit the number of students that can participate in the program; availability may be on a first come, first served basis; and your participation may not be automatically renewed each year. This program only covers required tuition and fees. Room and board and study abroad (unless it counts as a degree requirement) cannot be covered by this funding.

---

10   Source: http://benefits.va.gov/GIBILL/resources/benefits_resources/rates/ch33/ch33rates080117.asp
11   Source: www.benefits.va.gov/GIBILL/docs/factsheets/Yellow%20Ribbon%20Program.pdf

### What Financial Aid Programs Am I Eligible for as an Undocumented or DACA Student?

Students seeking to enroll in an accredited college in the US who lack documented immigrant status may still qualify for financial aid from certain educational institutions. Many schools have a commitment to fulfilling 100 percent of demonstrated financial need regardless of immigration status. Please note that policies around DACA/undocumented students are subject to rapid change, so the information provided here is current at the time of this writing. Any significant updates you should know about will be posted on www.yourguidetocollegetransfer.org.

### Undocumented Students

Undocumented students, sometimes referred to as "DREAMers" from the DREAM Act legislation introduced to Congress, are students living in the United States who are not US citizens, US nationals, or eligible noncitizens (including US permanent residents, individuals with refugee, asylum granted, indefinite parole, humanitarian parole, or Cuban-Haitian entrant status; citizens of the Republic of Palau, the Republic of the Marshall Islands, or the Federated States of Micronesia).

Since 2001, over 20 states have adopted policies that allow undocumented students who attended and graduated from in-state high schools to qualify for in-state tuition costs. Many institutions have also established scholarship funds to support these students. Undocumented students without a Social Security number will not be able to fill out the FAFSA. If you are an undocumented student, you should check the admissions and financial aid policies for undocumented applicants, taking care to inquire specifically about undocumented transfer applicants. While undocumented students are not eligible for federal financial aid, there are schools still willing to meet 100 percent demonstrated need. Check the School Profiles in this guide to find out which schools offer undocumented students financial aid.

### DACA Students

Deferred Action for Childhood Arrivals (DACA) students are a subgroup of undocumented students who have applied for their status through the US Citizenship and Immigration Services (USCIS). DACA status may be granted a period of deferral of deportation and a work authorization by USCIS, with the possibility for renewal under certain circumstances.

To obtain DACA status, applicants must meet several criteria and provide backup documentation; more information on the process can be found on the USCIS website. DACA students are often able to obtain work authorization. DACA students who have secured work authorization may be eligible to apply for a Social Security number (SSN). To learn more about applying for an SSN as an individual with DACA status, please visit the Social Security website, where you will find a PDF document at https://www.ssa.gov/pubs/deferred_action.pdf.

DACA students with SSNs can complete the FAFSA to assist schools in determining financial need, but should pay close attention to the following[12]:

- Check with your financial aid counselor to determine if completing the FAFSA is the way to apply for state and college aid for each of your schools. We recommend not filling out the FAFSA unless your school requires it, and if so, only filling out a paper version.
- Your parents' citizenship status is not a question on the form and will not affect your eligibility for submitting the FAFSA.
- You will not need your parents' Social Security numbers, as their citizenship status is not a factor. Enter 000-00-0000 when the FAFSA asks for their Social Security numbers.

---

12   Source: https://studentaid.ed.gov/sa/sites/default/files/financial-aid-and-undocumented-students.pdf

- You must answer the question about being a US citizen with "No, I am not a citizen or eligible noncitizen."
- For the question about legal residence, you should select the state of your local permanent legal residence. Contact your financial aid counselor for additional information on legal state residence requirements. You should follow the same considerations for the question about your parents' legal residence.

TheDream.US, a national organization that currently partners with 76 colleges in 14 states and Washington, D.C., committed to accepting and supporting DREAMers, provides scholarships and guidance for DREAMer high school and community college students.

# School Profiles

The schools selected for inclusion here rank among the best in the nation. They include:

- All of the Ivy League schools
- The top 15 national universities (as ranked by US News)
- The top 10 liberal arts colleges (as ranked by US News)
- The top 15 state colleges and universities (as ranked by US News)
- The Seven Sisters (historically top women's colleges)
- Top historically black colleges and universities (as ranked by US News)

In addition, schools that the Foundation has worked with or identified as having a special dedication to the success of transfer students are profiled.

As you study the school profiles to evaluate which schools are the best fit for you, be sure to look for transfer-friendly schools by paying attention to whether they offer these resources:

- Transfer admissions orientation events
- Admissions staff dedicated to transfer admissions
- 100 percent financial need for transfer students or other policies to minimize debt
- Study-abroad options for transfer students
- Housing options for transfer students

Don't spend as much time focusing on the following attributes:

- Overall cost, which can be decreased significantly by financial aid
- Number of transfer students accepted, which is less important than if a school has the resources above showing it is dedicated to transfer students
- Standardized test scores, as these are less relevant for transfer students, where the focus is on a rigorous transcript, whether you've taken recommended courses (college-level English, math, etc.), and a strong GPA

On some of the profiles, you'll see we've put badges to mark which schools have friendly policies and strong resources for military students, non-traditional students and students with families, and DACA or undocumented students. Here's a quick explanation of the criteria we used to choose which schools earned badges.

## VETERAN-FRIENDLY SCHOOLS

Schools with this badge meet some or all of the following criteria:

- Private schools that take part in the Yellow Ribbon Program (see Chapter 5: Financial Aid for Transfer for more detail on the program).
- Public schools that go above and beyond fulfilling the GI Bill. For example, a school that has a veterans affairs office or staff assigned to veterans services.
- Military schools that are focused on training servicemen and servicewomen. Keep in mind that gaining admission to these schools as a transfer student may be more difficult than accessing them as a freshman because of their unique policies.
- Dedicate recruitment and admissions staff to veterans or have admissions staff who work closely with veterans affairs offices.
- Have specific scholarships or grants earmarked for veterans.
- Provide veterans and their families with appropriate on-campus housing or resources for finding off-campus housing.

## NON-TRADITIONAL AND FAMILY-FRIENDLY SCHOOLS

Schools with this badge meet some or all of the following criteria:

- Have established programs supporting non-traditional students from the point of admission to the completion of their degrees.
- Provide on-campus housing for families or graduate housing for non-traditional-age undergraduate students.
- Provide year-round housing, making it possible for students to have consistent living arrangements.
- Maintain policies for reduced credit load in recognition of family responsibilities.
- Have continuing education programs for non-traditional students with family obligations and provide financial aid.
- Accept and recognize non-traditional students and families as an important part of the mission and fabric of their school.

## DACA/UNDOCUMENTED-FRIENDLY SCHOOLS

Please note that policies around DACA/undocumented students are subject to rapid change, so the information provided here is current at the time of this writing.

Schools with this badge meet some or all of the following criteria:

- Do not consider the immigration status of students at point of admission.
- Have clear DACA/undocumented policies and/or staff who specialize in addressing the concerns and challenges of these students.
- Agree to meet 100 percent financial need for DACA/undocumented students.
- Apply national financial aid guidelines to DACA/undocumented students even if they admit them through their international admissions processes.

# AMERICAN UNIVERSITY

**Location:** Washington, D.C.

**Website:** www.american.edu

**Endowment:** $580 million

**Type of School:** Private/Co-ed, Research University

**# of Undergraduate Students:** 7,909

**# of Graduate Students:** 5,291

**Average Class Size:** 23.3

**School Mission (in their own words):** The place of American University among major universities with first-rate faculties and academic programs grounded in the arts and sciences is secured by its enduring commitment to uncompromising quality in the education of its students. But its distinctive feature, unique in higher education, is its capacity as a national and international university to turn ideas into action and action into service. It does this by emphasizing the arts and sciences, then connecting them to the issues of contemporary public affairs writ large, notably in the areas of government, communication, business, law, and international service.

Recognized for its emphasis on personalized teaching and experiential education, the university provides for the direct involvement of faculty and students in the institutions and culture of the most important capital city in the world. Since its founding by an Act of Congress in 1893 as a private, independent, coeducational institution, under the auspices of The United Methodist Church, American University has been a national and international university. This is reflected in the scope of its teaching and research programs and the diversity of its faculty, staff, alumni, trustees, and student body, today representing over 135 countries.

The university actively encourages a commitment to public service, inclusive participation in university governance, equity and equal access, and an appreciation of diverse cultures and viewpoints. Its commitment to social justice, its ability to respond to the needs of a changing world while retaining its core values, and its capacity to turn to educational advantage the resources of the nation's capital are hallmarks of the institution.

## Admissions

**Admissions office mailing address:** 4400 Massachusetts Ave NW, Washington DC 20016

**Admissions office phone:** (202) 885-6000

**Admissions office email:** admissions@american.edu

**# of transfer applications:** Fall 2016 admissions: 1,404. Spring 2017 admissions: No information provided.

**# of transfer students accepted:** Fall 2016: 819. Spring 2017: No information provided.

**Transfer student acceptance rate (2016–2017 academic year):** 53%

**Freshman applications received in Fall 2016:** 19,325

**Freshman applications accepted in Fall 2016:** 5,008

**Acceptance rate for 2016–2017 freshmen:** 25.8%

## Transfer Admissions Process

**Transfer policy (in their own words):** Students who wish to be considered for transfer admission must be in good academic and social standing at all previously attended schools. Competitive transfer applicants have a GPA of at least 2.5/4.0 at their current institution. The following AU academic units have specific minimum GPA requirements:

- Kogod School of Business: 2.75
- School of Communication: 2.50
- School of Education: 2.70
- School of International Service: 3.00
- School of Public Affairs: 2.50

**Transfer admissions contact person:** Jessica Turgeon, Assistant Director of Admissions

**Transfer admissions contact info:** jturgeon@american.edu

**Offers transfer-focused admissions events:** Yes. Also an orientation called Eagle Summit. Consists of a 1-day or 2-day program, as well as transfer success series: www.american.edu/ocl/orientation/TSS.cfm.

**Transfer application deadline:** Fall 2018 deadline is 7/1/18 (3/1/18 is the deadline to be considered for financial aid). Spring 2019 deadline is 11/1/18.

**Acceptances announced to transfer applicants:** Fall 2018/ Spring 2019: You will be notified of your admission decision on a rolling basis approximately 4–6 weeks after all admission materials have been received. Notification of your financial aid award (if applicable) will be sent at a later date.

**Transfer application on Common App:** Yes. Common App fee: $70 (fee waiver available).

**SAT/ACT required for transfer applicants:** No

**High-school records requirements:** If you have less than 24 semester hours, have your high school send AU an official copy of your final high-school transcript.

**High-school records requirements for applicants who completed outside the US:** Academic records with official transcripts and certified English translations, if applicable, for each postsecondary institution attended

**Submission requirements for transfer applicants who completed high-school equivalency test:** Official copy of GED or HISET required.

**College transcript requirements:** Official transcript(s) or mark sheets enclosed in a sealed envelope from all colleges or universities attended should be sent to AU. Make sure that your full legal name and date of birth are on the transcripts.

**Interviews available for transfer applicants:** No

**Additional requirements for transfers seeking admissions to business school:** Yes. 2.75 GPA minimum.

## Costs & Financial Aid

**FAFSA code:** 1434

**CSS Profile code:** 5007

**Are internal school financial aid forms required?** No

**Financial aid deadlines for transfer applicants:**
Fall 2018: 3/1/18. Spring 2019: 3/1/18.

**Costs for the 2017–2018 year:** Tuition & Fees: $46,615. Room & Board: $14,702.

**Financial aid for transfer students:** Yes

**Guarantees meeting 100% need for transfer students:** No

**Need-based aid for transfer students:** Yes

**Merit-based financial aid for transfer students:**
Yes—Phi Theta Kappa scholarship. Phi Theta Kappa membership required.

**Phi Theta Kappa Scholarship:** Yes, $10,000 per year. Renewable for up to 8 semesters. See www.american.edu/financialaid/transferscholarships.cfm for details.

**Reduced or zero tuition fees for low-income students:** No

**Includes loans in financial aid packages:** Yes

**% of all undergraduates qualifying for Pell Grants:**
17% (2014–2015)

**% of all undergraduates receiving financial aid:**
63% (2014–2015)

**Average financial aid award for all undergraduate students:**
$27,623 (2014–2015)

## Academics

**GPA range for transfer students accepted in 2016–2017:**
2.5–4.0

**SAT ranges for all students admitted in 2016:** Critical Reading: 590–690. Mathematics: 580–670. Writing: 570–670.

**ACT composite score range for all students admitted in 2016:**
27–32

**Type of curriculum:** Gen. Ed. requirements

**Type of academic year:** Semester

**Advisors specifically for transfer students:** Yes

**Credit policy (in their own words):** Courses eligible for transfer upon matriculation to AU must have a recorded grade of C or above. Courses with a grade of "P" or Pass are eligible for transfer, providing that the grade of "P" is the equivalent of a C or above. Only credits for courses taken at another institution are recorded on the AU transcript and will count toward the total number of credits needed for graduation if the grade is a 2.0 or above on a 4.0 scale. Grades for transfer courses are not computed in the cumulative grade point average. Courses taken on the quarter system will receive the standard .67 credit per credit-hour of study (i.e., a 3 credit course at a quarter school will merit 2 credits here). Transfer courses must have the same number of credit hours as an AU course in order to be considered "equivalent."

**Max number of transfer credits accepted:** 75 credits

**Residency requirement for transfer students:** Yes. At least 45 of the last 60 credit hours must be completed in residence at American University.

**Study abroad available for transfer students:** Yes. Must fulfill the residency requirement.

**Free tutoring for all students:** The Peer Tutoring Lab offers free one-to-one, face-to-face tutoring in selected classes. For classes not covered by the lab, students can use the Referral System (this service has a modest fee).

**Writing center for all students:** Yes

**Career support/access to internships and resume prep for all students:** Yes

**Additional resources specifically designated for transfer and/or non-traditional students:** Yes. Orientation, Transition & Retention conducts orientation programs for both fall and spring transfer students. Fall transfer students are invited to select from 2 options for orientation. They can participate in a 2-day intensive orientation program in July or a 1-day nuts and bolts program in August. Spring transfers are invited to a 2-day orientation in January.

**Transfer Articulation Equivalency:** www.american.edu/provost/registrar/transfer/index.cfm

## Housing

**Available for transfer students:** Yes

**Available for non-traditional students:** Yes

**Guaranteed for transfer students:** No. Housing is offered to transfer students on a space available basis, but is not guaranteed. Preference is given to transfer students who are admitted with 36 or fewer credits and who have submitted an enrollment deposit and housing application by July 1.

**Non-traditional students can reside in housing year-round:**
No information provided.

**Family housing available:** Yes

## Non-Traditional Admissions

**Name of program:** Guaranteed Admission Agreements Program

**Program description:** A Guaranteed Admission Agreement is an arrangement between a 2-year institution and a 4-year institution to provide a clear pathway of transfer for academically talented students. These agreements are also known as 2+2 agreements, as it is intended that the student will complete 2 years at a community college and 2 years at a 4-year institution, and earn a bachelor's degree. Students who meet the qualifications for admission at AU and who adhere to the requirements of the agreement will essentially be guaranteed admission with junior standing.

Students matriculating to AU under this agreement are guaranteed that all 60 credits earned through their associate's degree will transfer toward their AU degree.

Completion of an associate's degree will satisfy the AU General Education requirements; students come to AU as an upper division student, having met the lower division requirements.

Students with a cumulative GPA of 3.5 or above on a 4.0 scale at the time of admission will qualify for priority registration.

Once a student has signed a Letter of Intent, they may start working with an AU academic advisor in the discipline in which they intend to study. This allows the student to tailor their courses at the community college to prepare them for study at AU.

**Program deadline:** 2/1/18

**Program admission requirements:** Upon completion of 15 credit hours (and no more than 45 credit hours) at the community college, students may submit a Letter of Intent by October 1 the year prior to transfer. The students must:

- Have a cumulative GPA of at least 3.0 based on a 4.0 scale, at the time of admission
- Adhere to the student conduct codes of both the community college and American University
- Meet AU's university mathematics requirement and writing requirement for transfer students
- Complete an associate's degree while remaining continuously enrolled at the 2-year institution
- Submit an application and transcripts by February 1 for Fall admission
- Apply for financial aid with the Office of Financial Aid by February 1 for Fall admission

GAAP applies to the following community colleges:

- Daytona State College Agreement
- Green River Community College
- Howard Community College
- Miami Dade College
- Montgomery College
- Northern Virginia Community College
- Tidewater Community College

**Program website:** www.american.edu/admissions/transfer/GAA.cfm

## Military/Veteran Students

**Military/veteran admissions policy (in their own words):** At AU, we're extremely proud of our veteran, active-duty/reserve service member and military dependent students. We thank you for your service, and we're excited that you've chosen AU for your academic career. You've invested in us; now we want to invest in you and your experience here. Feel free to explore the site, give us a call, or stop in to see us about whatever your need may be.

**Status considered in admissions:** No

**Special admissions process:** No. American University will consider up to a maximum of 30 credits for transfer from a combination of military coursework that the American Council on Education (ACE) has deemed appropriate for academic credit.

Transfer credit for work completed at a regionally accredited institution, such as the Community College of the Air Force or the American Military University, may be included in the overall cumulative total of 75 transfer credits.

For additional information on military credits, please contact the appropriate admissions representative.

Last names A–M:

> Jeremy Lowe
> Associate Director of Admissions
> American University
> Phone: (202) 885-6012
> lowe@american.edu

Last names N–Z:

> Kayla Black
> Assistant Director of Admissions
> American University
> Phone: (202) 885-6052
> sajjadie@american.edu

**Special financial aid:** Yes. The Yellow Ribbon Program.

**Specific programs/policies to address needs:** Yes

## DACA/Undocumented Students

**DACA and undocumented admissions policy (in their own words):** Since its founding, AU has been a place that welcomes students and faculty from around the world and has dedicated itself to advancing international service. Consistent with these inclusive values, students who are undocumented (with or without DACA) are welcome to apply to AU.

Citizenship is not, and has never been, a condition for admission to American University. All candidates for admission are evaluated on the basis of their academic strength and fit with the university.

**Admitted:** Yes (DACA and undocumented)

**Status considered in admissions:** No

**Eligible for institutional financial aid:** Merit awards only. No need-based financial aid is available. Transfer students who are members of Phi Theta Kappa are eligible for scholarships up to $10,000. Students must identify themselves as PTK members on the admissions application and provide a PTK advisor letter of recommendation.

# Hamissou Samari

**John F. Kennedy School of Government, Harvard University, C'12**
Master's Degree in Public Administration

**American University, C'09**
Bachelor's Degree in International Affairs, with Honors

**Borough of Manhattan Community College, C'07**
Associate's Degree in Liberal Arts & Sciences

**Current Employment:** Senior Program Officer, Millennium Challenge Corporation

**Bio:** A Togolese native and active member of society, Hamissou has embarked on a career in international development that focuses on reducing poverty through economic growth and addressing challenges and constraints to growth in the developing world. This includes policy reform, livelihood strengthening, access to energy and water, and other factors of production. He is focusing his career on monitoring and evaluating development projects, helping track projects' progress and results, and evaluating the long-term impacts of investments.

*"For me, the American University Honors Program's rigor was a major stepping stone toward a more challenging graduate program at Harvard, giving me the unique opportunity to take honors-tailored classes with some of the most engaging classmates, as well as complete some of the most meaningful and career-shaping internships in the nation's capital.*

*As a premier academic institution in the field of international studies, with world-class professors and researchers, American challenged my preconceived assumptions and perceptions on global issues and taught me to think outside the box and see things from others' perspectives. In short, it shaped me into a more global citizen. But above all, the opportunity that American's Honors Program afforded me to take classes with graduate-level students was a confidence booster, as it prepared me for my master's program just one year after graduation. Indeed, I came to AU as a non-traditional student with little experience in the US college education system and limited English-language capabilities, yet I left AU assured of my ability to challenge stereotypes, my desire to overcome self-imposed doubts, and my potential to achieve higher. And so I did."*

## Leadership Activities

- Fellow, Public Policy and International Affairs, University of Michigan
- Public Policy Intern, White House Commission on Remembrance
- Volunteer, AmeriCorps
- Member, Phi Theta Kappa International Honor Society of Community Colleges

# AMHERST COLLEGE

**Location:** Amherst, Massachusetts

**Website:** www.amherst.edu

**Endowment:** $2.032 billion

**Type of School:** Private/Co-ed, Liberal Arts

**# of Undergraduate Students:** 1,849

**# of Graduate Students:** 0

**Average Class Size:** 19

**School Mission (in their own words):** Amherst College educates men and women of exceptional potential from all backgrounds so that they may seek, value, and advance knowledge, engage the world around them, and lead principled lives of consequence. Amherst brings together the most promising students, whatever their financial need, in order to promote diversity of experience and ideas within a purposefully small residential community. Working with faculty, staff, and administrators dedicated to intellectual freedom and the highest standards of instruction in the liberal arts, Amherst undergraduates assume substantial responsibility for undertaking inquiry and for shaping their education within and beyond the curriculum. Amherst College is committed to learning through close colloquy and to expanding the realm of knowledge through scholarly research and artistic creation at the highest level. Its graduates link learning with leadership—in service to the College, to their communities, and to the world beyond.

## Admissions

**Admissions office mailing address:** 220 S Pleasant St, Amherst MA 01002

**Admissions office phone:** (413) 542-2328

**Admissions office email:** admission@amherst.edu

**# of transfer applications:** Fall 2016 admissions: 403. Spring 2017 admissions: 94.

**# of transfer students accepted:** Fall 2016: 25. Spring 2017: 14.

**Transfer student acceptance rate (2016–2017 academic year):** 7.8%

**Freshman applications received in Fall 2016:** 8,406

**Freshman applications accepted in Fall 2016:** 1,161

**Acceptance rate for 2016–2017 freshmen:** 14%

## Transfer Admissions Process

**Transfer policy (in their own words):** You are eligible for transfer admission to Amherst if you have completed a minimum of 32 transferrable credits while enrolled in a liberal arts curriculum at a college or university. To be competitive, you should have at least an A– average in your college courses. We do not accept applications from individuals who have already earned a bachelor's degree. Nor do we accept transfer applications from students who have completed college coursework as part of any program of early graduation from secondary school or other accelerated completion of secondary school. (Such students should apply as first-year applicants.)

For more important information on transfer eligibility and transfer of credit, please read our Transferring to Amherst information sheet: www.amherst.edu/media/view/613327.

**Transfer admissions contact person:** Alexandra Hurd, Associate Dean of Admission

**Transfer admissions contact info:** ashurd@amherst.edu

**Offers transfer-focused admissions events:** Yes—Community College Transfer Open House. An open house offered each fall for prospective students applying from community colleges.

**Transfer application deadline:** Fall 2018 deadline is 3/1/18. Spring 2019 deadline is 11/1/18.

**Acceptances announced to transfer applicants:** Fall 2018 on 3/15/18. Spring 2019 on 12/15/18.

**Transfer application on Common App:** Yes. Common App fee: $60.

**Separate application or in addition to the Common App:** No. The Common App and Coalition App can both be used for transfer admissions.

**Fee for separate transfer application:** $60 like the Common App

**Waiver available for separate transfer application fee:** Yes

**SAT/ACT required for transfer applicants:** No, but highly recommended

**High-school records requirements:** Amherst does not require the secondary school "Final Report" form, only the secondary school transcript.

**High-school records requirements for applicants who completed outside the US:** Official transcript

**Submission requirements for transfer applicants who completed high-school equivalency test:** Submit results of their equivalency test as well as a high-school transcript, if possible

**College transcript requirements:** College transcripts (from all postsecondary institutions at which you have completed college coursework)

**Interviews available for transfer applicants:** No

**Additional requirements for transfers seeking admissions to arts major:** Yes. Students with exceptional accomplishments or talents in the arts may submit related material for review by Amherst faculty through SlideRoom, where you will find additional, Amherst-specific instructions for each category of submission—music, theater, dance, and visual art. Prior to submission on SlideRoom, you should review our Special Information for Arts Supplement Submission. Please do not send originals to us, as we cannot return to you any material submitted.

## Costs & Financial Aid

**FAFSA code:** 22115

**CSS Profile code:** 3003

**Are internal school financial aid forms required?** No

**Financial aid deadlines for transfer applicants:**
Fall 2018: 3/1/18. Spring 2019: 11/1/18.

**Costs for the 2017–2018 year:** Tuition & Fees: Comprehensive fee (all room, board, tuition, fees, books, personal expense budget, travel budget, etc.) is $67,620 for the 2017–2018 academic year. Room & Board: Included in the comprehensive fee.

**Financial aid for transfer students:** Yes

**Guarantees meeting 100% need for transfer students:** Yes

**Need-based aid for transfer students:** Yes. If admitted, you will receive financial aid equal to your financial need through a combination of scholarships and a work opportunity. Your demonstrated need is met in full; there is no "gap" (unmet need) in our aid awards.

**Merit-based financial aid for transfer students:** No

**Phi Theta Kappa Scholarship:** No

**Reduced or zero tuition fees for low-income students:** No

**Includes loans in financial aid packages:** No

**% of all undergraduates receiving financial aid:** 55% (2016–2017)

**% of all undergraduates qualifying for Pell Grants:** 23% (2014–2015)

**Average financial aid award for all undergraduate students:** $51,775 (2016–2017)

**Enrollment deposit can be waived for low-income students:** Yes, in some cases

## Academics

**GPA range for transfer students accepted in 2016–2017:** 3.5–4.0

**SAT ranges for all students admitted in 2016:** Critical Reading: 700–800. Mathematics: 690–780. Writing: 690–780.

**ACT composite score range for all students admitted in 2016:** 31–34

**Type of curriculum:** Open curriculum. Amherst has no distribution requirements and no core curriculum. Instead, students choose the courses that matter most to them. Our open curriculum ensures that each classroom is filled with inquisitive, fully engaged students committed to the topic at hand.

**Type of academic year:** Semester

**Advisors specifically for transfer students:** Yes

**Credit policy (in their own words):** Credit is granted only for courses in the Liberal Arts.

Credit is not awarded for the following: online courses; courses in business, criminal justice, engineering, speech and communication, computer application, journalism, or other pre-professional training courses; math courses below the level of calculus; Advanced Placement, International Baccalaureate, or collegiate coursework completed during secondary school or in lieu of a traditional high-school experience; however, some Amherst departments will allow students to forego introductory-level courses in areas in which they have already completed rigorous work.

**Max number of transfer credits accepted:** 64 credits

**Residency requirement for transfer students:** Yes. Students who transfer to Amherst must fulfill the 2-year, 4-semester residency requirement in order to receive a degree.

**Study abroad available for transfer students:** Yes. Students must be sure to fulfill our 2-year residency requirement.

**Free tutoring for all students:** Yes

**Writing center for all students:** Yes

**Career support/access to internships and resume prep for all students:** Yes

## Housing

**Available for transfer students:** Yes

**Available for non-traditional students:** Yes

**Guaranteed for transfer students:** Yes

**Non-traditional students can reside in housing year-round:** N/A

**Family housing available:** No

## Non-Traditional Admissions

**Non-traditional student policy (in their own words):** While Amherst welcomes traditional- and non-traditional-aged applicants to apply, all applicants must be capable of enrolling as full-time students in the successive years needed to complete their degree. Due to the structure of our residential community, we do not have resources to house families on or off campus. Students are not required to live on campus and may independently arrange living accommodations off campus.

## Military/Veteran Students

**Military/veteran admissions policy (in their own words):**
In general, US veterans follow the same first-year or transfer application process as other applicants do. There are, however, some exceptions to the general process that apply selectively to US veteran applicants:

- Active duty US veteran applicants: Ordinarily, applicants for admission to Amherst College are required to submit 2 academic evaluations from former instructors. However, if you are currently engaged in active duty in the US military and you are consequently experiencing difficulty obtaining 2 academic evaluations for your application, please contact Alexandra Hurd, Associate Dean of Admission, to discuss possible alternatives.

- US veteran applicants for transfer admission: Ordinarily, the submission of standardized test results is optional for transfer applicants. However, if you are a US veteran and you have not been enrolled for the past 5 years in academic coursework eligible for transfer credit, you are strongly advised to submit standardized testing. Recommended testing includes: SAT (Essay Section recommended) or ACT (Writing Test recommended).

**Application fee waiver:** The college is proud to offer an application fee waiver to any veteran interested in applying through our Quick Pass fee waiver.

**Status considered in admissions:** Yes

**Special admissions process:** No

**Special financial aid:** Yes. As part of our commitment, Amherst College participates in the US Department of Veterans Affairs Yellow Ribbon Program. For qualifying admitted students, Amherst does not cap Yellow Ribbon spaces and offers an uncapped maximum school contribution per student. Should you fully qualify for the Yellow Ribbon Program, your tuition at Amherst will be 100% free. Amherst is able to support unlimited Yellow Ribbon funding through the generous donations to endowed scholarship funds designated for veteran students.

**Specific programs/policies to address needs:** Last year, the Supreme Court ruled that schools must open their campuses without restrictions to military recruiters if the schools wish to receive federal funding—funding that helps support the first-class scholarship and research taking place at Amherst every day. As a result, Amherst is open to military recruiters without precondition. They will also sign formal agreements with the Reserve Officers' Training Corps (ROTC) at UMass to ensure that their students may participate in its programs. Amherst does not wish to hold the college apart from the armed forces, but rather to honor those who defend our nation.

## DACA/Undocumented Students

**DACA and undocumented admissions policy (in their own words):** Amherst seeks to enroll an intellectually talented and diverse student body and therefore welcomes first-year and transfer applications from all interested students—US citizens or non-US citizens, living domestically or abroad, including undocumented students and students granted Deferred Action for Childhood Arrivals (DACA) status.

**Admitted:** Yes (DACA and undocumented)

**Status considered in admissions:** No

**Special admissions process:** No

**Eligible for institutional financial aid:** Yes. Amherst is committed to meeting 100% of the full demonstrated financial need of every admitted student, regardless of citizenship or immigration status. Our financial aid packages for non-US citizens include on-campus employment and institutional grant aid, without loan. In circumstances where students are unable to fulfill work expectations, Amherst may replace the employment contribution with loan. To apply for financial aid, undocumented and DACA students must submit the College Board Profile and federal tax returns or income verification, as requested by our Office of Financial Aid.

**Specific programs/policies to address needs:** No

# BARD COLLEGE

**Location:** Annandale-on-Hudson, New York

**Website:** www.bard.edu

**Endowment:** $267 million

**Type of School:** Private/Co-ed, Liberal Arts

**# of Undergraduate Students:** 2,290 (2015–2016)

**# of Graduate Students:** 200

**Average Class Size:** 10–20 students

**School Mission (in their own words):** Bard College seeks to inspire curiosity, a love of learning, idealism, and a commitment to the link between higher education and civic participation. The undergraduate curriculum is designed to address central questions facing new generations, and reshapes traditional disciplines into multidisciplinary fields and programs. Students pursue a rigorous course of study reflecting varied traditions of scholarship, research, speculation, and artistic expression. They engage philosophies of human existence, theories of human behavior and society, the making of art, and the study of science, nature, and history.

Bard's approach to learning focuses on the individual and is structured around small group seminars to encourage thoughtful discourse. Faculty are active in their fields and stress the connection between life inside and outside of the classroom. They strive to foster critical inquiry, intellectual ambition, and creativity.

Bard acts at the intersection of education and civil society. Through its undergraduate college, its distinctive graduate programs, its commitment to the fine and performing arts, and its network of international dual-degree partnerships, early colleges, prison education initiatives, and public engagement programs, Bard offers unique opportunities for students and faculty to study, experience, and realize the principle that higher-education institutions can and should operate in the public interest.

## Admissions

**Admissions office mailing address:** 30 Campus Rd, Annandale-on-Hudson NY 12504

**Admissions office phone:** (845) 758-7472

**Admissions office email:** admission@bard.edu

**# of transfer applications:** Fall 2016 admissions: 339. Spring 2017 admissions: No information provided.

**# of transfer students accepted:** Fall 2016: 212 (2015–2016). Spring 2017: No information provided.

**Transfer student acceptance rate (2016–2017 academic year):** 63%

**Freshman applications received in Fall 2016:** 6,820

**Freshman applications accepted in Fall 2016:** 2,318

**Acceptance rate for 2016–2017 freshmen:** 33%

## Transfer Admissions Process

**Transfer policy (in their own words):** A transfer student is defined as one who has officially matriculated into a degree program (associate's or bachelor's) at an accredited junior college, college, or university and completed at least 1 semester at that institution. Candidates who have taken college classes without being admitted into an institution's degree program are considered incoming first-year students, not transfer students. Transfer students who are 25 years or older should apply directly to Bard's Returning to College Program (RCP).

**Transfer admissions contact person:** Timand Bates, Assistant Dean of Students or Center for Student Life & Advising

**Transfer admissions contact info:** tbates@bard.edu

**Offers transfer-focused admissions events:** Yes

**Transfer application deadline:** Fall 2018 deadline is 3/1/18. Spring 2019 deadline is 11/1/18.

**Acceptances announced to transfer applicants:** Fall 2018 in mid-April 2018. Spring 2019 on 12/1/18.

**Transfer application on Common App:** Yes. Common App fee: $0.

**Separate application or in addition to the Common App:** No

**SAT/ACT required for transfer applicants:** No

**High-school records requirements:** A high-school transcript is required unless the candidate will have completed an associate's degree by the time of matriculation at Bard.

**High-school records requirements for applicants who completed outside the US:** A high-school transcript is required unless the candidate will have completed an associate's degree by the time of matriculation at Bard.

**Submission requirements for transfer applicants who completed high-school equivalency test:** Bard Entrance Examination

**College transcript requirements:** Official college transcript and college report

**Interviews available for transfer applicants:** Yes. Recommended but not required.

**Additional requirements for transfers seeking admissions to arts major:** Yes. Artistic supplements (portfolios) are required for transfer candidates seeking admission to the Written Arts or Photography programs. Written Portfolio: At least 10 but no more than 20 pages of written work (hard copy only). Photography Portfolio: At least 20 prints—traditional color or silver prints. Digital prints, websites, and/or CDs are not acceptable.

## Costs & Financial Aid

**FAFSA code:** 2671

**CSS Profile code:** 2037

**Are internal school financial aid forms required?** No

**Financial aid deadlines for transfer applicants:** Fall 2018: 2/15/18. Spring 2019: 12/1/18.

**Costs for the 2017–2018 year:** Tuition & Fees: $52,226. Room & Board: $15,066.

**Financial aid for transfer students:** Yes

**Guarantees meeting 100% need for transfer students:** No

**Need-based aid for transfer students:** Yes. Bard has a need-aware admission policy.

**Merit-based financial aid for transfer students:** No

**Phi Theta Kappa Scholarship:** No

**Reduced or zero tuition fees for low-income students:** No

**Includes loans in financial aid packages:** Yes

**% of all undergraduates receiving financial aid:** 69%

**% of all undergraduates qualifying for Pell Grants:** 21% (2014–2015)

**Average financial aid award for all undergraduate students:** $47,737

**Funding available for low-income students to visit:** Yes

**Enrollment deposit can be waived for low-income students:** Yes

## Academics

**GPA range for transfer students accepted in 2016–2017:** 3.5–4.0

**SAT ranges for all students admitted in 2016:** Critical Reading: 590–700. Mathematics: 550–670. Writing: 590–690.

**ACT composite score range for all students admitted in 2016:** Median: 29

**Type of curriculum:** Gen. Ed. requirements. The pillars of the Bard education are the structure of the first year, including First-Year Seminar; the program- and concentration-based approach to study; moderation; the concept of distribution by modes of thought; and the Senior Project.

**Type of academic year:** Semester

**Advisors specifically for transfer students:** Yes

**Credit policy (in their own words):** A student transferring from an accredited institution usually receives full credit for work completed with a grade of C or better in courses appropriate to the Bard curriculum. Specifically, no transfer credit will be given for courses that are dissimilar from those offered at Bard. For example, "fashion design" per se is not offered at Bard, therefore the Registrar's Office would not grant transfer credit for a fashion design class. Also, credits will not transfer from online or distance learning classes, nor will they transfer from college algebra or lower-level math courses. Regardless

of course credit eligibility, a maximum of 64 transfer credits can be granted.

**Max number of transfer credits accepted:** 64

**Residency requirement for transfer students:** Yes. Transfer students must complete a minimum of 64 credits at Bard, for a total of 128, in order to receive a Bard degree.

**Study abroad available for transfer students:** Yes. Must fulfill residency requirements as well.

**Free tutoring for all students:** Yes

**Writing center for all students:** Yes

**Career support/access to internships and resume prep for all students:** Yes

**% of undergraduate students hired within 6 months of graduation:** No information provided.

**Additional resources specifically designated for transfer and/or non-traditional students:** No

## Housing

**Available for transfer students:** Yes

**Available for non-traditional students:** Yes

**Guaranteed for transfer students:** No

**Non-traditional students can reside in housing year round:** No information provided.

**Family housing available:** No

## Non-Traditional Admissions

**Non-traditional student policy (in their own words):** A cornerstone of Bard College's mission is a commitment to the transformative nature of a liberal arts education and the role of the liberally educated student in a democratic society. This power to transform extends to students beyond traditional college age and, for this reason, the College has historically been committed to its programs that serve this population, specifically the Returning to College Program (RCP).

**Name of program:** Returning to College Program

**Program description:** The Returning to College Program resists the separation of adult degree students and regular undergraduates. The program is founded on the premise that returning students benefit from participating in the regular undergraduate curriculum, taking their places at the seminar table, the lab bench, and barre, and learning from and with their younger colleagues. Within the liberal arts curriculum at Bard, students in the RCP will engage in a rigorous encounter with their courses of study. It is through this process of engagement that the liberal arts enrich our lives and empower us to effect change in the world, and this is true for adult learners no less than their traditionally aged peers.

In most cases, RCP students should expect to spend at least two years, or four semesters, at Bard. Transfer credits are evaluated by the registrar after the first year of study. All RCP students must moderate into their major area of study and then complete a Senior Project in order to receive a Bard degree. Please note that the RCP does not accommodate those who are seeking to earn a second bachelor's degree. Also, on-campus housing is not available for RCP students.

**Program deadline:** Rolling basis

**Program admission requirements:** Individuals who are 25 years of age or older and have successfully completed at least 1 year of college work (as determined by the registrar of the College) may apply to Bard through the RCP as transfer students. Please note, however, those who have already earned a bachelor's degree are ineligible for this program. RCP students are eligible for financial aid if they register for 12 or more credits in 1 semester. The FAFSA, CSS Profile, and a copy of the most current tax return must be submitted to the Financial Aid Office. If an RCP student registers for fewer than 12 credits in a given semester, the cost is calculated on a per-credit basis and no financial aid is available. In general, all transfer forms and supplements are applicable for RCP students. However, while we prefer recommendation letters from college instructors, we recognize that this may not be possible for RCP candidates; therefore, personal or employment recommendations are accepted. In addition to the application forms listed on the transfer student webpage, RCP candidates are required to:

1. Clearly specify in the "additional information" section of the Common Application that they are applying to the Returning to College Program (RCP)
2. Include a cover letter summarizing employment and academic history
3. Complete a personal interview with an admission counselor

**Program website:** www.bard.edu/admission/returntocollege

**Program contact person:** Greg Armbruster, Senior Associate Director of Admission/Director of Transfer Admission

**Program contact info:** (845) 758-7472 or (845) 758-7091, garmbrus@bard.edu

**Name of program:** Bard Educational Opportunity Program (BEOP)

**Program description:** Bard College is proud to offer 3 distinct Educational Opportunity Program scholarships: HEOP for New York State residents, BOP for residents of all 50 states, and the ECO scholarship for Bard Early College students. HEOP and BOP scholarships provide Bard College with the funds to help meet the cost of a scholar's education. Qualifying students are also eligible for state, federal, work-study, and other institutional financial aid awards. New York State residents are required to apply for the state's Tuition Assistance Program (TAP) and the federal Pell Grant. All students are expected to make a small contribution to the cost of their education from family savings or summer earnings and to assume a small loan.

**Program deadline:** N/A

**Program admission requirements:**

Arthur O. Eve HEOP Scholarship:

There are 3 qualifications a student must meet for admission into HEOP:

- The student must be a resident of New York State.
- A student is eligible if he or she is not admissible under Bard's regular admission guidelines due to an under-resourced academic background. This standard changes each year as Bard adapts to the national standards of each year's high school graduating class.
- A student is eligible if he or she meets the financial criteria for economic disadvantage set by the New York State Education Department (NYSED).

Bard Opportunity Program Scholarship (BOP):

In order to be considered for a Bard Opportunity Program (BOP) Scholarship, a student must:

- Be a US citizen or US permanent resident.
- Be a high-school graduate by June 30 of the school year in which you will begin at Bard College.
- Have a high-school grade point average (GPA) of at least 85/100 or 3.0/4.0.
- Demonstrate significant financial need. To qualify for the BOP Scholars program, families must apply for financial aid and meet estimated earning guidelines.

**Program website:** www.bard.edu/beop/about

**Program contact person:** Jane E. Duffstein, Director, BEOP

**Program contact info:** (845) 758-7492, duffy@bard.edu

## Military/Veteran Students

No specific policies or programs available.

## DACA/Undocumented Students

**DACA and undocumented admissions policy (in their own words):** Bard upholds a mission of inclusion and diversity, and we welcome all students, regardless of citizenship status or national origin to apply to the College. This includes students who are undocumented and students who hold DACA (Deferred Action for Childhood Arrivals) status.

The application process for DACA or undocumented students does not differ from the application process for any student living in the United States. Our admission process is confidential and holistic, and we encourage students to use their application as an opportunity to share their lived experience with the admission committee. For more information, please refer to and utilize the requirements and deadlines for domestic first-year or transfer applicants. If you have any further questions about applying, please contact admission@bard.edu.

While federal financial aid protocols impact undocumented students, DACA or undocumented students may apply for Bard College institutional financial aid using either the CSS Profile or the International Student Application for Financial

Aid. Links to both forms and more information about financial aid application deadlines can be found on the financial aid website. Questions regarding financial aid can be directed to finaid@bard.edu.

**Admitted:** Yes

**Status considered in admissions:** No

**Special admissions process:** No

**Eligible for institutional financial aid:** Yes. DACA or undocumented students may apply for Bard College institutional financial aid using either the CSS Profile or the International Student Application for Financial Aid. Most students living in the US find that the International Student Aid Application does not fit them well and choose to complete the CSS Profile instead. The Office of Financial Aid encourages each student to review both forms and complete whatever form seems most relevant to their individual circumstance. Both forms allow the student to provide additional narrative explaining any unique circumstances.

**Specific programs/policies to address needs:** No

# BARNARD COLLEGE

**Location:** New York, New York

**Website:** https://barnard.edu

**Endowment:** $286.8 million

**Type of School:** Private/Single-Sex, Liberal Arts

**# of Undergraduate Students:** 2,574

**# of Graduate Students:** N/A

**Average Class Size:** 10–19

**School Mission (in their own words):** Barnard College aims to provide the highest quality liberal arts education to promising and high-achieving young women, offering the unparalleled advantages of an outstanding residential college in partnership with a major research university. With a dedicated faculty of scholars distinguished in their respective fields, Barnard is a community of accessible teachers and engaged students who participate together in intellectual risk-taking and discovery. Barnard students develop the intellectual resources to take advantage of opportunities as new fields, new ideas, and new technologies emerge. They graduate prepared to lead lives that are professionally satisfying and successful, personally fulfilling, and enriched by love of learning.

As a college for women, Barnard embraces its responsibility to address issues of gender in all of their complexity and urgency and to help students achieve the personal strength that will enable them to meet the challenges they will encounter throughout their lives. Located in the cosmopolitan urban environment of New York City, and committed to diversity in its student body, faculty, and staff, Barnard prepares its graduates to flourish in different cultural surroundings in an increasingly interconnected world.

The Barnard community thrives on high expectations. By setting rigorous academic standards and giving students the support they need to meet those standards, Barnard enables them to discover their own capabilities. Living and learning in this unique environment, Barnard students become agile, resilient, responsible, and creative, prepared to lead and serve their society.

## Admissions

**Admissions office mailing address:** 3009 Broadway, New York NY 10027

**Admissions office phone:** (212) 854-2014

**Admissions office email:** admissions@barnard.edu

**# of transfer applications:** Fall 2016 admissions: 658. Spring 2017 admissions: No information provided.

**# of transfer students accepted:** Fall 2016: 155. Spring 2017: No information provided.

**Transfer student acceptance rate (2016–2017 academic year):** 23.7%

**Freshman applications received in Fall 2016:** 7,071

**Freshman applications accepted in Fall 2016:** 1,184

**Acceptance rate for 2016–2017 freshmen:** 32%

## Transfer Admissions Process

**Transfer policy (in their own words):** For transfer students entering with 24 or more points, the Bachelor of Arts degree requires the satisfactory completion of 121 points of academic work (a minimum of 60 points taken at Barnard) and 1 term of physical education (1 point). Transfer students must complete at least 60 points and 2 years (4 semesters) full-time in residence at Barnard to receive the degree. As part of these requirements, students must fulfill the General Education and Major Requirements described below. A complete listing of courses which satisfy the General Education requirements will be posted by July on the registrar's page on the Barnard website: barnard.edu/registrar. For more information on Bard's transfer policies, visit https://admissions.barnard.edu/apply-barnard/transfer-and-visiting.

**Transfer admissions contact person:** Brittany Dávila, Associate Director of Admissions Coordinator of Multicultural Recruitment, Coordinator of Transfer Application Review

**Transfer admissions contact info:** bdavila@barnard.edu

**Offers transfer-focused admissions events:** No

**Transfer application deadline:** Fall 2018 deadline is 3/15/18. Spring 2019 deadline is 11/1/18.

**Acceptances announced to transfer applicants:** Fall 2018 on 5/15/18. Spring 2019 on 12/1/18.

**Transfer application on Common App:** Yes. Common App fee: $75 (fee waiver available).

**SAT/ACT required for transfer applicants:** Yes

**High-school records requirements:** Official final high-school transcript or official GED results

**High-school records requirements for applicants who completed outside the US:** Transcripts must be sent from schools themselves. Students with transcripts or official documents not issued in English need to provide certified English translations along with the official documents.

**Submission requirements for transfer applicants who completed high-school equivalency test:** Official GED results

**College transcript requirements:** Official transcripts from all colleges and universities attended

**Interviews available for transfer applicants:** No

## Costs & Financial Aid

**FAFSA code:** 2708

**CSS Profile code:** 2038

**Are internal school financial aid forms required?** No

**Financial aid deadlines for transfer applicants:** Fall 2018: 3/15/18. Spring 2019: No clear deadline because Spring transfer students do not qualify for institutional aid. To qualify for federal aid, students are recommended to submit the FAFSA form around November.

**Costs for the 2017–2018 year:** Tuition & Fees: $50,882. Room & Board: $16,100 (based on multiple occupancy room).

**Financial aid for transfer students:** Yes (with the exception of students who transfer in the Spring)

**Guarantees meeting 100% need for transfer students:** No. Barnard is need-aware for transfer students and has limited funds available for them.

**Need-based aid for transfer students:** It does, but the school is need-aware.

**Merit-based financial aid for transfer students:** No

**Phi Theta Kappa Scholarship:** No

**Reduced or zero tuition fees for low-income students:** No

**Includes loans in financial aid packages:** Yes

**% of all undergraduates receiving financial aid:** 50% (2015)

**% of all undergraduates qualifying for Pell Grants:** No information provided.

**Average financial aid award for all undergraduate students:** $49,012

**Funding available for low-income students to visit:** Yes

**Enrollment deposit can be waived for low-income students:** Yes

## Academics

**GPA range for transfer students accepted in 2016–2017:** 3.69

**SAT ranges for all students admitted in 2016:** Critical Reading: 630–730. Mathematics: 620–710. Writing: 650–730.

**ACT composite score range for all students admitted in 2016:** 28–32

**Type of curriculum:** Gen. Ed. requirements

**Type of academic year:** Semester

**Advisors specifically for transfer students:** Yes

**Credit policy (in their own words):** For transfer students entering with 24 or more points, the Bachelor of Arts degree requires the satisfactory completion of 121 points of academic work (a minimum of 60 points taken at Barnard) and 1 term of physical education (1 point). Transfer students must complete at least 60 points and 2 years (4 semesters) full-time in residence at Barnard to receive the degree. As part of these requirements, students must fulfill the General Education and Major Requirements.

**Max number of transfer credits accepted:** 60

**Residency requirement for transfer students:** Yes. To receive the A.B. degree at Barnard, a transfer student must be enrolled at Barnard (Morningside Heights, Reid Hall, Kyoto, Beijing, or the Berlin Consortium) for at least 4 full-time regular academic terms during which she must complete at least 60 points, including at least 6 courses in the major field (and 3 in the minor field, if a minor is elected). Additional major (and minor) courses, as well as general education requirements, may be satisfied by transfer courses.

**Study abroad available for transfer students:** Yes. Must fulfill the residency requirements.

**Free tutoring for all students:** Yes

**Writing center for all students:** Yes

**Career support/access to internships and resume prep for all students:** Yes

**% of undergraduate students hired within 6 months of graduation:** No information provided.

**Additional resources specifically designated for transfer and/or non-traditional students:** N/A

## Housing

**Available for transfer students:** Yes, but it is limited.

**Available for non-traditional students:** No

**Guaranteed for transfer students:** No

**Non-traditional students can reside in housing year-round:** N/A

**Family housing available:** No

## Military/Veteran Students

No specific policies or programs available.

## DACA/Undocumented Students

**DACA and undocumented admissions policy (in their own words):** Undocumented students receive the same consideration for admission as any other application for admission to Barnard College. If applying for financial aid, undocumented students follow the same financial aid procedures outlined for international citizens. If admitted, we follow the same procedures Barnard uses to grant need-based aid to international citizens. However, if a student's parents file a US federal income tax return, the family should complete a CSS Profile Application instead of the College Board International Student Financial Aid Application.

**Admitted:** Yes

**Status considered in admissions:** No

**Special admissions process:** No

**Eligible for institutional financial aid:** Yes. They must demonstrate need.

**Specific programs/policies to address needs:** N/A

# BATES COLLEGE

**Location:** Lewiston, Maine

**Website:** www.bates.edu

**Endowment:** $251 million

**Type of School:** Private/Co-ed, Liberal Arts

**# of Undergraduate Students:** 1,780

**# of Graduate Students:** 0

**Average Class Size:** 2–9

**School Mission (in their own words):** Since 1855, Bates College has been dedicated to the emancipating potential of the liberal arts. Bates educates the whole person through creative and rigorous scholarship in a collaborative residential community. With ardor and devotion—Amore ac Studio—we engage the transformative power of our differences, cultivating intellectual discovery and informed civic action. Preparing leaders sustained by a love of learning and a commitment to responsible stewardship of the wider world, Bates is a college for coming times.

## Admissions

**Admissions office mailing address:** 2 Andrews Rd, Lewiston ME 04240

**Admissions office phone:** (855) 228-3755

**Admissions office email:** admissions@bates.edu

**# of transfer applications:** Fall 2016 admissions: 170. Spring 2017 admissions: 0.

**# of transfer students accepted:** Fall 2016: 0. Spring 2017: 0.

**Transfer student acceptance rate (2016–2017 academic year):** 0

**Freshman applications received in Fall 2016:** 5,356

**Freshman applications accepted in Fall 2016:** 1,213

**Acceptance rate for 2016–2017 freshmen:** 22.6%

## Transfer Admissions Process

**Transfer policy (in their own words):** Bates transfers most of your liberal arts and science courses that are similar to Bates courses in content, rigor, and length and have been taken at accredited institutions. A grade of at least a C is required for course credit to transfer to Bates.

**Offers transfer-focused admissions events:** Yes

**Transfer application deadline:** Fall 2018 deadline is 3/1/18.

**Acceptances announced to transfer applicants:** Fall 2018 on 5/15/18.

**Transfer application on Common App:** Yes. Common App fee: $60 (fee waiver available).

**SAT/ACT required for transfer applicants:** No

**High-school records requirements:** Final high-school official transcript should be sent directly from the high school and bear its official seal.

**High-school records requirements for applicants who completed outside the US:** Official transcript

**Submission requirements for transfer applicants who completed high-school equivalency test:** Official GED results

**College transcript requirements:** One copy of your official college transcript. This should be sent directly from the Office of the Registrar and bear the college or university seal.

If you've attended more than one college or university, we need an official transcript from each institution. Your application won't be reviewed until we receive a copy of your official transcript from each institution you've attended.

**Interviews available for transfer applicants:** No

## Costs & Financial Aid

**FAFSA code:** 2036

**CSS Profile code:** 3076

**Are internal school financial aid forms required?** Yes

**Financial aid deadlines for transfer applicants:** Fall 2018: 3/1/18. Spring 2019: 11/1/18.

**Costs for the 2017–2018 year:** Tuition & Fees: $50,310. Room & Board: $14,190.

**Financial aid for transfer students:** Yes

**Guarantees meeting 100% need for transfer students:** Bates College meets the demonstrated need of every admitted student.

**Need-based aid for transfer students:** Yes

**Merit-based financial aid for transfer students:** No

**Phi Theta Kappa Scholarship:** No

**Reduced or zero tuition fees for low-income students:** No information provided.

**Includes loans in financial aid packages:** Yes

**% of all undergraduates receiving financial aid:** 49%

**% of all undergraduates qualifying for Pell Grants:** 11% (2014–2015)

**Average financial aid award for all undergraduate students:** Grants/scholarship aid: $37,942

**Funding available for low-income students to visit:** No information provided.

**Enrollment deposit can be waived for low-income students:** No information provided.

## Academics

**GPA range for transfer students accepted in 2016–2017:** 3.86 average

**SAT ranges for all students admitted in 2016:** Critical Reading: 570–690. Mathematics: 580–700. Writing: 580–690.

**ACT composite score range for all students admitted in 2016:** 27–32

**Type of curriculum:** Gen. Ed. requirements

**Type of academic year:** Semester

**Advisors specifically for transfer students:** No

**Credit policy (in their own words):** Transfer students must earn a minimum of 16 Bates course credits, not including Short Term credits. They may transfer a maximum of 2 non-Bates course credits earned after matriculating at Bates. The registrar and the department or program chair are responsible for the overall evaluation of non-Bates credit, subject to established policies. Exceptions to the established policies may only be granted by the Committee on Academic Standing.

**Max number of transfer credits accepted:** 32

**Residency requirement for transfer students:** Yes. For students entering in the fall of 2015 and thereafter, degree candidates matriculating as first-year students, either in the fall or winter semester, must earn at least 28 Bates course credits or approved program credits, not including Short Term credits. Students may earn a maximum of 4 approved-program credits per semester and may apply a maximum of 8 toward their Bates degree. Transfer students must earn a minimum of 16 Bates course credits, not including Short Term credits. They may transfer a maximum of 2 non-Bates course credits earned after matriculating at Bates. All degree candidates must earn a minimum of 16 Bates credits. Degree candidates matriculating as first-year students, either in the fall or winter semester, must earn a minimum of 24 Bates course credits or approved program credits.

**Study abroad available for transfer students:** Yes. Must fulfill residency requirements.

**Free tutoring for all students:** Yes

**Writing center for all students:** Yes

**Career support/access to internships and resume prep for all students:** Yes

**% of undergraduate students hired within 6 months of graduation:** 99% (reflects students that are hired and continue on to graduate school within 6 months)

**Additional resources specifically designated for transfer and/or non-traditional students:** No

## Housing

**Available for transfer students:** Yes

**Available for non-traditional students:** Yes

**Guaranteed for transfer students:** Yes

## Non-Traditional Admissions

No specific policies or programs available.

## Military/Veteran Students

**Special financial aid:** Bates participates in the Yellow Ribbon Program for Veterans. Bates provides a matching school contribution of $14,500 for 10 students annually, and funds are awarded on a first come, first served basis determined by the date of receipt of all completed application requirements.

## DACA/Undocumented Students

**DACA and undocumented admissions policy (in their own words):** The Office of Admission will consider undocumented and DACA students as domestic applicants, and their applications will be evaluated accordingly. Undocumented and DACA students will follow the same application process as those of domestic first-year or transfer applicants, and are welcome to share relevant narratives unique to their circumstances. As with all students, Bates will meet 100% of demonstrated financial need for those admitted to the college, regardless of citizenship or immigration status. The financial aid package will consist of grant aid and on-campus employment, for those who qualify.

To apply for financial aid, undocumented and DACA students must submit the College Board Profile and provide federal tax returns or other income verification to Student Financial Services. Visit www.bates.edu/financial-services/financial-aid/first-year-applicants to learn more about Bates's DACA policy.

**Admitted:** Yes

**Status considered in admissions:** No

**Eligible for institutional financial aid:** Yes. To apply for financial aid, undocumented and DACA students must submit the College Board Profile and provide federal tax returns or other income verification to Student Financial Services.

# BOSTON COLLEGE

**Location:** Chestnut Hill, Massachusetts

**Website:** www.bc.edu

**Endowment:** $2.064 billion

**Type of School:** Private/Co-ed, Research University

**# of Undergraduate Students:** 405

**# of Graduate Students:** 14,256

**Average Class Size:** 10–19

**School Mission (in their own words):** Strengthened by more than a century and a half of dedication to academic excellence, Boston College commits itself to the highest standards of teaching and research in undergraduate, graduate, and professional programs and to the pursuit of a just society through its own accomplishments, the work of its faculty and staff, and the achievements of its graduates. It seeks both to advance its place among the nation's finest universities and to bring to the company of its distinguished peers and to contemporary society the richness of the Catholic intellectual ideal of a mutually illuminating relationship between religious faith and free intellectual inquiry.

Boston College draws inspiration for its academic societal mission from its distinctive religious tradition. As a Catholic and Jesuit university, it is rooted in a worldview that encounters God in all creation and through all human activity, especially in the search for truth in every discipline, in the desire to learn, and in the call to live justly together. In this spirit, the University regards the contribution of different religious traditions and value systems as essential to the fullness of its intellectual life and to the continuous development of its distinctive intellectual heritage.

## Admissions

**Admissions office mailing address:** 140 Commonwealth Ave, Chestnut Hill MA 02467

**Admissions office phone:** (617) 552-3100

**Admissions office email:** transfer@bc.edu

**# of transfer applications:** Fall 2016 admissions: 1,411. Spring 2017 admissions: No information provided.

**# of transfer students accepted:** Fall 2016: 369. Spring 2017: No information provided.

**Transfer student acceptance rate (2016–2017 academic year):** 26%

**Freshman applications received in Fall 2016:** 28,956

**Freshman applications accepted in Fall 2016:** 9,107

**Acceptance rate for 2016–2017 freshmen:** 31.4%

## Transfer Admissions Process

**Transfer policy (in their own words):** The transfer admission process at Boston College is highly selective. A minimum college GPA of a 3.0 is required to submit a transfer application. Increased competition in recent cycles has resulted in a mean grade point average of 3.6 among admitted students. Students most successful in our process also have strong high-school records and standardized test scores.

Students who hold a high-school diploma or General Education Diploma and have completed 9 or more transferable credits at a regionally accredited college or university may apply for transfer admission. To read more, visit www.bc.edu/admission/undergrad/process/transfer/requirements.html.

**Transfer admissions contact person:** Kelly Bellavance, Associate Director

**Transfer admissions contact info:** kelly.montrym@bc.edu

**Offers transfer-focused admissions events:** Yes

**Transfer application deadline:** Fall 2018 deadline is 3/15/18. Spring 2019 deadline is 11/1/18.

**Acceptances announced to transfer applicants:** Fall 2018 on or by 5/20/18. Spring 2019 on or by 12/15/18.

**Transfer application on Common App:** Yes. Common App fee: $75 (fee waiver available).

**SAT/ACT required for transfer applicants:** Yes, SAT or ACT. However, if more than 5 years have passed since an applicant's graduation from high school, the standardized testing requirement can be waived.

**High-school records requirements:** Official high-school transcript

**High-school records requirements for applicants who completed outside the US:** If you attend a secondary school outside the US, we require you submit a TOEFL or IELTS score. Minimum scores of 100 on the IBT or 7.5 on the IELTS are recommended.

**Submission requirements for transfer applicants who completed high-school equivalency test:** Certificate of GED from institution

**College transcript requirements:** Official transcripts of all courses taken in all semesters at other colleges or universities

**Interviews available for transfer applicants:** No

**Additional requirements for transfers seeking admissions to business school:** Yes. The Carroll School of Management (CSOM) is accredited by AACSB International (Association of Advanced Collegiate Schools of Business). Students from institutions that do not hold the same professional accreditation may transfer only Accounting I and II, Macro and Micro Economic Principles, Business Law I, Statistics I, and Computer Science credits. Students in the Carroll School of Management must also meet a foreign language requirement. The Admission Committee looks for candidates with strong math backgrounds when considering applicants to the CSOM.

**Additional requirements for transfers seeking admissions to other majors:** Application to these programs of study is only open to students who are applying to begin their sophomore year. Applicants who have completed more than 1 year (2 semesters) of full-time study at another institution cannot apply for the Pre-Medical/Pre-Dental/Pre-Veterinary program of study at Boston College.

Because our Pre-Medical/Pre-Dental/Pre-Veterinary Committee requires that at least half of the required courses for entrance to medical school (2 biology, 4 chemistry, 2 physics, 2 math, and 2 English) be taken at Boston College, students who have been enrolled elsewhere for more than 1 year will have completed too much coursework to be considered for our program.

Candidates for the Connell School of Nursing should have completed Anatomy and Physiology I and II, General Chemistry with lab, and Statistics before enrolling as a sophomore in the Connell School of Nursing.

Transferred courses may be used to fulfill Boston College Core Requirements, the pre-nursing sciences, and up to 3 electives.

Nursing students may only enroll in the fall semester (March application) and must enter as sophomores. Lynch School of Education students complement their certification with an interdisciplinary major in the College of Arts & Sciences.

Students seeking double majors may be required to spend an extra semester to complete student teaching and state certification requirements in both fields.

Students transferring from programs of study that did not specialize in education may lose time toward graduation because of course prerequisites and practicum requirements in the Lynch School of Education.

## Costs & Financial Aid

**FAFSA code:** 2128

**CSS Profile code:** 3083

**Are internal school financial aid forms required?** No

**Financial aid deadlines for transfer applicants:** Fall 2018: 4/15/18. Spring 2019: 11/17/18.

**Costs for the 2017–2018 year:** Tuition & Fees: $53,901. Room & Board: $14,142.

**Financial aid for transfer students:** Yes

**Guarantees meeting 100% need for transfer students:** Yes

**Need-based aid for transfer students:** Yes. Boston College is also committed to meeting the full, demonstrated institutional need of students who are US citizens or US permanent residents. Demonstrated financial need is the difference between the estimated cost of attendance for the academic year and the estimated family contribution as determined by the review of your financial aid application. Our Net Price Calculator may be helpful in estimating your expected family contribution.

**Merit-based financial aid for transfer students:** No

**Phi Theta Kappa Scholarship:** No

**Reduced or zero tuition fees for low-income students:** No

**Includes loans in financial aid packages:** Yes

**% of all undergraduates receiving financial aid:** 66% (2016)

**% of all undergraduates qualifying for Pell Grants:** 13% (2015–2016)

**Average financial aid award for all undergraduate students:** $39,942

**Funding available for low-income students to visit:** No information provided.

**Enrollment deposit can be waived for low-income students:** No information provided.

## Academics

**GPA range for transfer students accepted in 2016–2017:** 3.0–4.0, 3.6 average

**SAT ranges for all students admitted in 2016:** Critical Reading: 620–720. Mathematics: 640–740. Writing: 640–730.

**ACT composite score range for all students admitted in 2016:** 30–33

**Type of curriculum:** Gen. Ed. requirements

**Type of academic year:** Semester

**Advisors specifically for transfer students:** No

**Credit policy (in their own words):** Boston College's transfer credit policies are established by the deans and faculty of each undergraduate division. Course evaluations are completed by the Office of Transfer Admission. Any questions regarding the evaluation of courses, either before or after enrollment, should be directed to the Office of Transfer Admission. At Boston College, transfer credit is established on a course-by-course basis. Of the credit hours required for graduation, a maximum of 60 credits may be transferred from another college or university. Graduation terms are determined by the number of transferred credits. Transferable courses must have been completed at regionally accredited colleges or universities and must be similar in content, depth, and breadth to courses taught at Boston College. In addition, a minimum grade of C must have been earned. The unit of credit at Boston College is the semester hour. Most courses earn 3 semester hours of credit; lab sciences usually earn 4 semester hours of credit.

**Max number of transfer credits accepted:** 60

**Residency requirement for transfer students:** Yes. Students must spend 4 semesters in the full-time day program and complete a minimum of 60 credit hours at Boston College in order to be eligible for the degree. Courses taken in the Woods College of Advancing Studies or during the Summer Session may not be applied toward the 4-semester minimum residency requirement.

**Study abroad available for transfer students:** Yes. Must fulfill the residency requirements.

**Free tutoring for all students:** Yes

**Writing center for all students:** Yes

**Career support/access to internships and resume prep for all students:** Yes

**% of undergraduate students hired within 6 months of graduation:** No information provided.

**Additional resources specifically designated for transfer and/or non-traditional students:** No

## Housing

**Available for transfer students:** Yes

**Available for non-traditional students:** Yes

**Guaranteed for transfer students:** Yes. In recent years, most transfer students entering in September have been guaranteed 1 year of campus housing, while those students entering in January have been guaranteed 1 semester of campus housing.

**Non-traditional students can reside in housing year-round:** N/A

**Family housing available:** Yes

## Non-Traditional Admissions

**Non-traditional student policy (in their own words):** Same requirements as transfer students.

## Military/Veteran Students

**Military/veteran admissions policy (in their own words):** Same requirements as transfer students.

**Status considered in admissions:** No

**Special admissions process:** No

**Special financial aid:** Yes. The Yellow Ribbon Program.

**Specific programs/policies to address needs:** Boston College acts as a liaison with the Veterans Administration for students who may qualify to receive veterans' education benefits. Eligible students should apply through the United States Department of Veterans Affairs in order to obtain a Certificate of Eligibility. Once the Certificate of Eligibility has been received, the student should contact the VA Certifying Official in the Office of Student Services. The Certifying Official will then certify the student's enrollment information to the Regional Processing Office (RPO). The RPO will process payment of benefits directly to the student. For more information, please contact Linda Malenfant, VA Certifying Official at linda.malenfant@bc.edu or (800) 294-0294.

## DACA/Undocumented Students

No DACA/undocumented student policies or programs available.

# BOWDOIN COLLEGE

**Location:** Brunswick, Maine

**Website:** www.bowdoin.edu

**Endowment:** $1.34 billion

**Type of School:** Private/Co-ed, Liberal Arts

**# of Undergraduate Students:** 1,806

**# of Graduate Students:** 0

**Average Class size:** 10–19

**School Mission (in their own words):** It is the mission of the College to engage students of uncommon promise in an intense full-time education of their minds, exploration of their creative faculties, and development of their social and leadership abilities, in a four-year course of study and residence that concludes with a baccalaureate degree in the liberal arts.

Two guiding ideas suffuse Bowdoin's mission. The first, from the College of the 18th and 19th centuries, defines education in terms of a social vision. "Literary institutions are founded and endowed for the common good, and not for the private advantage of those who resort to them . . . but that their mental powers may be cultivated and improved for the benefit of society" (President Joseph McKeen's inaugural address, 1802); "To lose yourself in generous enthusiasms and cooperate with others for common ends: this is the offer of the College" (President William DeWitt Hyde, 1903). The second idea stresses the formation of a complete individual for a world in flux: there is an intrinsic value in a liberal arts education of breadth and depth, beyond the acquisition of specific knowledge, that will enable a thinking person "to be at home in all lands and all ages" (President Hyde).

At the root of this mission is selection. First, and regardless of their wealth, Bowdoin selects men and women of varied gifts; diverse social, geographic, and racial backgrounds; and exceptional qualities of mind and character. Developed in association with one another, these gifts will enable them to become leaders in many fields of endeavor. Second, it recruits faculty members of high intellectual ability and scholarly accomplishment who have a passion for education both of undergraduates and of themselves, as lifelong creators and pursuers of knowledge.

## Admissions

**Admissions office mailing address:** 6000 College Station, Brunswick ME 04011

**Admissions office phone:** (207) 725-3100

**Admissions office email:** admissions@bowdoin.edu

**# of transfer applications:** Fall 2016 admissions: 175. Spring 2017 admissions: N/A.

**# of transfer students accepted:** Fall 2016: 6. Spring 2017: N/A.

**Transfer student acceptance rate (2016–2017 academic year):** 3.4%

**Freshman applications received in Fall 2016:** 6,799

**Freshman applications accepted in Fall 2016:** 1,009

**Acceptance rate for 2016–2017 freshmen:** 14.3%

## Transfer Admissions Process

**Transfer policy (in their own words):** Although Bowdoin sets no cutoff guidelines, successful candidates usually submit college work of honors quality: B work or better or a GPA of no lower than 3.0.

**Transfer admissions contact person:** E. Whitney Soule, Dean of Admissions and Financial Aid (Manhattan)

**Transfer admissions contact info:** esoule@bowdoin.edu

**Offers transfer-focused admissions events:** Yes

**Transfer application deadline:** Fall 2018 deadline is 3/1/18. Spring 2019 deadline is 3/1/18.

**Acceptances announced to transfer applicants:** Fall 2018 in early May 2018. Spring 2019 in early May 2018.

**Transfer application on Common App:** Yes. Common App fee: 0. Bowdoin automatically waives the application fee for the Common Application and Coalition Application for students applying for financial aid and first-generation-to-college students (neither parent graduated from a 4-year college or university).

**SAT/ACT required for transfer applicants:** No, test optional

**High-school records requirements:** A high-school diploma or its recognized equivalent is required before enrolling at Bowdoin College. If student matriculates at Bowdoin, the application and transcript become part of his or her permanent record.

**High-school records requirements for applicants who completed outside the US:** Requires an official transcript of academic work in the language in which it was prepared and a certified translation into English of the transcript.

**Submission requirements for transfer applicants who completed high-school equivalency test:** GED is not accepted.

**College transcript requirements:** Official transcript and information concerning candidate's school offerings and environment. Midyear report or official school transcript at midyear.

**Interviews available for transfer applicants:** Yes, but not required. A personal interview is encouraged for transfer applicants, but not required. On campus or Skype.

**Additional requirements for transfers seeking admissions to arts major:** Yes. Art supplement. While the Bowdoin Arts Supplement is not a required element of your application, it is an optional way for you to demonstrate your sustained dedication to the arts. Your submission will be reviewed by the appropriate faculty in the Music, Visual Arts, and/or Theater and Dance departments, and commentary will be submitted to Admissions Office on your behalf. Must submit admissions application first. Due March 1.

## Costs & Financial Aid

**FAFSA code:** 2038

**CSS Profile code:** 3089

**Are internal school financial aid forms required?** No information provided.

**Financial aid deadlines for transfer applicants:** Fall 2018: 3/1/18. Spring 2019: No spring applicants.

**Costs for the 2017–2018 year:** Tuition & Fees: $49,900. Room & Board: $13,600.

**Financial aid for transfer students:** Yes, limited aid is available.

**Guarantees meeting 100% need for transfer students:** No

**Need-based aid for transfer students:** All financial aid at Bowdoin is based upon financial need. Financial aid is occasionally available for transfer students, but is often limited by the commitment the College has made to assist already enrolled and incoming first-year students. The competition among transfer candidates for financial aid, therefore, is usually quite intense. All financial aid at Bowdoin is based upon financial need. Bowdoin offers no special scholarships based solely on academic, athletic, or artistic achievement. Bowdoin has no financial aid for international transfer candidates.

**Merit-based financial aid for transfer students:** No

**Phi Theta Kappa Scholarship:** No

**Reduced or zero tuition fees for low-income students:** No

**Includes loans in financial aid packages:** Yes

**% of all undergraduates receiving financial aid:** 46%

**% of all undergraduates qualifying for Pell Grants:** 14% (2014–2015)

**Average financial aid award for all undergraduate students:** $44,112

**Funding available for low-income students to visit:** No information provided.

**Enrollment deposit can be waived for low-income students:** No information provided.

## Academics

**GPA range for transfer students accepted in 2016–2017:** 3.0–4.0

**SAT ranges for all students admitted in 2016:** Critical Reading: 650–750. Mathematics: 640–760. Writing: 650–760.

**ACT composite score range for all students admitted in 2016:** 30–34

**Type of curriculum:** Gen. Ed. requirements. Students complete at least 1 full-credit course in each of 5 distribution areas

along with a first-year seminar in their first 2 years of study, declaring a major in spring of the sophomore year. For graduation, students complete a minimum of 32 courses, leaving ample room for exploration in the curriculum.

**Type of academic year:** Semester

**Advisors specifically for transfer students:** No

**Credit policy:** 1 Bowdoin course is considered equal to 4 semester hours or 6 quarter hours. Therefore, courses taken elsewhere that are worth less than 4 semester hours or 6 quarter hours will transfer as less than 1.00 credit. See the Application for Transfer of Credit form for more details and examples. While some exceptions may occur, no course taken elsewhere will be worth more than 1.00 Bowdoin credit. Thus, students will not receive "extra" credit for courses that have accompanying laboratory credits.

**Max number of transfer credits accepted:** The maximum number of credits that may be transferred are 16. You must complete a minimum of 16 credits at Bowdoin to earn your bachelor's degree.

**Residency requirement for transfer students:** Yes. You must spend 4 semesters and successfully pass 16 full-credit courses or the equivalent, in residence, at least 2 semesters of which have been during the junior and senior years. No student will ordinarily be permitted to remain at Bowdoin for more than 9 semesters of full-time work.

**Study abroad available for transfer students:** Yes. Must fulfill residency requirements.

**Free tutoring for all students:** Yes

**Writing center for all students:** Yes

**Career support/access to internships and resume prep for all students:** Yes

**% of undergraduate students hired within 6 months of graduation:** No information provided.

**Additional resources specifically designated for transfer and/or non-traditional students:** N/A

## Housing

**Available for transfer students:** Yes

**Available for non-traditional students:** Yes

**Guaranteed for transfer students:** No

## Non-Traditional Admissions

No specific policies or programs available.

## Military/Veteran Students

**Military/veteran admissions policy (in their own words):** The degree programs of Bowdoin College meet the standards set by the Maine State Approving Agency for Veterans Education Programs for persons eligible for benefits (GI Bill) from the US Department of Veterans Affairs. Students who request veterans' educational assistance are required to have all previous postsecondary experience evaluated for possible transfer credit in order to be eligible for benefits. Bowdoin participates in the Yellow Ribbon program. For more information, contact the Student Aid Office.

**Status considered in admissions:** No

**Special financial aid:** Yes. The Yellow Ribbon Program.

**Specific programs/policies to address needs:** N/A

## DACA/Undocumented Students

**DACA and undocumented admissions policy (in their own words):** Undocumented or DACA students should follow the same application process for all first-year or transfer domestic students. As with all domestic applicants, students will be evaluated within the context of their high school. In order to accurately assess each applicant, we encourage all students to share any information pertaining to their unique experiences to the selection committee.

**Admitted:** Yes

**Status considered in admissions:** No

**Eligible for institutional financial aid:** Yes. Parental citizenship status will NOT affect your financial aid eligibility at Bowdoin since aid is determined solely by financial need. Undocumented students with employment authorization may be able to find on- and off-campus employment.

**Specific programs/policies to address needs:** No

# BROWN UNIVERSITY

**Location:** Providence, Rhode Island

**Website:** www.brown.edu

**Endowment:** $3.2 billion

**Type of School:** Private/Co-ed, Research University

**# of Undergraduate Students:** 6,652

**# of Graduate Students:** 2,806

**Average Class Size:** 2–9

**School Mission (in their own words):** The mission of Brown University is to serve the community, the nation, and the world by discovering, communicating, and preserving knowledge and understanding in a spirit of free inquiry, and by educating and preparing students to discharge the offices of life with usefulness and reputation. We do this through a partnership of students and teachers in a unified community known as a university-college.

## Admissions

**Admissions office mailing address:** Office of College Admission, PO Box 1876, Providence RI 02912

**Admissions office phone:** (401) 863-2378

**Admissions office email:** admission@brown.edu

**# of transfer applications:** Fall 2016 admissions: 1,832. Spring 2017 admissions: No information provided.

**# of transfer students accepted:** Fall 2016: 96. Spring 2017: No information provided.

**Transfer student acceptance rate (2016–2017 academic year):** 8.29%

**Freshman applications received in Fall 2016:** 32,390

**Freshman applications accepted in Fall 2016:** 2,875

**Acceptance rate for 2016–2017 freshmen:** 9.29%

## Transfer Admissions Process

**Transfer policy (in their own words):** Applicants who submit transfer applications to Brown in the Spring of 2017 will only be eligible to apply if they will have completed at least 1 year of full-time college enrollment before September 2017.

University rules stipulate that anyone admitted as a transfer must be enrolled full-time at Brown for at least 4 semesters prior to earning their undergraduate degree. For this reason, we discourage transfer applications from students who will have accrued more than 4 semesters of college work prior to their enrollment at Brown. Students who have already completed a bachelor's degree at another college are ineligible to apply as transfers.

Applicants from British universities must have completed a year or more of their undergraduate education prior to applying. We will make exceptions to this rule for applicants from British universities that provide graded fall-semester transcripts for their students.

**Transfer admissions contact person:** Maitrayee Bhattacharyya, Associate Dean for Diversity and Inclusion

**Transfer admissions contact info:** maitrayee_bhattacharyya@ brown.edu

**Offers transfer-focused admissions events:** Yes

**Transfer application deadline:** Fall 2018 deadline is 3/1/18. Spring 2019 deadline is 3/1/18.

**Acceptances announced to transfer applicants:** Fall 2018 in mid-May 2018. Spring 2019 in mid-May 2018.

**Transfer application on Common App:** Yes. Common App fee: $75 (fee waiver available).

**SAT/ACT required for transfer applicants:** Yes. SAT or ACT (required for all domestic and international applicants, except for domestic applicants applying from domestic community colleges).

**High-school records requirements:** Official copy of high-school transcript

**High-school records requirements for applicants who completed outside the US:** Official copy of high-school transcript

**Submission requirements for transfer applicants who completed high-school equivalency test:** Official GED results required.

**College transcript requirements:** Official copy of your current college transcript—including grades from your Fall 2016 semester work and a list of your current course enrollments

**Interviews available for transfer applicants:** No

## Costs & Financial Aid

**FAFSA code:** 3401

**CSS Profile code:** 3189

**Are internal school financial aid forms required?** No

**Financial aid deadlines for transfer applicants:** Fall 2018: 3/1/18. Spring 2019: 3/1/18.

**Costs for the 2017–2018 year:** Tuition & Fees: $53,419. Room and Board: $14,020.

**Financial aid for transfer students:** Yes

**Guarantees meeting 100% need for transfer students:** Yes

**Need-based aid for transfer students:** Yes. Brown's transfer admission process is need-aware, meaning that an applicant's ability to pay for tuition, room, and board is factored in when we make an admission decision. Brown guarantees to meet the full demonstrated need (as determined by the Office of Financial Aid) of all its admitted students. If you are a transfer applicant who may need financial aid at some point during your Brown career, you must submit a financial aid application when you first apply. Admitted transfer applicants who did not apply for aid in their original transfer application are not eligible to apply for financial aid at any point later in their time at Brown.

**Merit-based financial aid for transfer students:** No

**Phi Theta Kappa Scholarship:** No

**Reduced or zero tuition fees for low-income students:** No

**Includes loans in financial aid packages:** Yes. Students with family earnings above $100,000 have moderate loans dependent on family total income level.

**% of all undergraduates receiving financial aid:** 49%

**% of all undergraduates qualifying for Pell Grants:** 16%

**Average financial aid award for all undergraduate students:** 48,420

**Funding available for low-income students to visit:** No information provided.

**Enrollment deposit can be waived for low-income students:** There is no enrollment deposit.

## Academics

**GPA range for transfer students accepted in 2016–2017:** 3.8–4.0

**SAT ranges for all students admitted in 2016:** Critical Reading: 680–780. Mathematics: 690–790. Writing: 690–780.

**ACT composite score range for all students admitted in 2016:** 31–34

**Recommended extracurricular engagement:** We look for applicants with long-term commitment to extracurricular activities who we expect will involve themselves in similar pursuits at Brown. We actively try to admit students from a variety of perspectives and backgrounds to make Brown's undergraduate student body a thorough reflection of the diversity of identity and perspective that exists in the nation and in the world.

**Type of curriculum:** Open Curriculum. At Brown, rather than specifying these areas, we challenge you to develop your own core. Our open curriculum ensures you great freedom in directing the course of your education, but it also expects you to remain open to people, ideas, and experiences that may be entirely new.

**Type of academic year:** Semester

**Advisors specifically for transfer students:** Yes

**Credit policy (in their own words):** Generally speaking, most liberal arts courses taken at other colleges and universities are transferable to Brown. More specifically, Brown will transfer credit for courses at other colleges that are similar to courses offered in our own curriculum. If you are wondering which of your classes will be transferable, you should peruse Brown's online Course Search to see if the University offers a similar course. Brown will not award transfer credit for

correspondence courses, online courses, courses taken during summer programs, or courses that were taken as part of a dual enrollment curriculum. Brown also will not award transfer credit for AP test scores.

**Max number of transfer credits accepted:** 15 courses (1 course = 4 semester hours)

**Residency requirement for transfer students:** Yes. Minimum of 15 credits at Brown University to earn a bachelor's degree at Brown.

**Study abroad available for transfer students:** Yes. Must fulfill the residency requirements.

**Free tutoring for all students:** Yes

**Writing center for all students:** Yes

**Career support/access to internships and resume prep for all students:** Yes

**% of undergraduate students hired within 6 months of graduation:** No information provided.

**Additional resources specifically designated for transfer and/or non-traditional students:** Yes. RUE students have dedicated advising through the Office of the Dean of the College. Upon declaring a concentration, each RUE student is also assigned a concentration advisor from that department. RUE students take advantage of the full range of other advising at Brown, including the CareerLAB and preprofessional advising for those interested in careers in medicine, law, and business. There is also a First-Generation College and Low-Income Student Center available.

## Housing

**Available for transfer students:** Yes

**Available for non-traditional students:** Yes

**Guaranteed for transfer students:** No

**Non-traditional students can reside in housing year-round:** No information provided.

**Family housing available:** No

## Non-Traditional Admissions

**Non-traditional student policy (in their own words):** Applicants who have earned a high-school diploma or equivalent and have been out of high school for 6 or more years by the time of proposed enrollment at Brown. Veterans may request a waiver of the 6 years out of high school requirement, to be considered on a case-by-case basis.

**Name of program:** Resumed Undergraduate Education (RUE)

**Program description:** The Resumed Undergraduate Education Program is a small, highly competitive program ideal for students who interrupted or delayed their formal education due to family commitments, financial concerns, health issues, military service, employment opportunities, or simply a compelling need to explore other paths.

RUE students take the same rigorous courses, earn the same bachelor's degree (A.B. or Sc.B.), and have access to the full range of opportunities as other Brown students. RUE students take advantage of the flexibility of Brown's open curriculum and may pursue any academic concentration. RUE students typically pursue 3–4 courses per semester. Requests for reduced course load are considered on a case-by-case basis.

**Program deadline:** 3/1/18

**Program admission requirements:** A completed RUE application form, available only on our website
(See link below.)

- A current resume.
- A nonrefundable application fee of $75 or a fee waiver
- Official academic transcripts sent to us directly from your secondary school(s) and college(s), if any.
- At least 1 academic recommendation (2 preferred), from a professor, teacher, or academic counselor, if possible.
- Additional recommendations from employers, military commanding officers, religious leaders, or others who can speak to your experience and talents are welcomed but not required.
- Standardized test scores, including those from the SAT, ACT, or TOEFL, are not required, but are considered if submitted.

Please have both academic and nonacademic recommenders complete, and sign the RUE Recommendation Form (note they may attach a letter in response to the questions), and send the recommendation directly to the Office of College Admission, Attention RUE, Box 1876, Brown University, Providence, RI 02912, or fax to (401) 863-9300.

Individuals who have earned a previous bachelor's degree or have substantially more than 2 years of full-time college experience are not eligible for the program.

Applicants with little or no college experience are considered RUE first-year applicants; those with 1–2 years of college credits are considered RUE transfer applicants.

**Program website:** www.brown.edu/admission/undergraduate/ apply/resumed-undergraduate-education-applicants

## Military/Veteran Students

**Military/veteran admissions policy (in their own words):** Brown values the extraordinary talents, experiences, and diversity that veterans bring to campus. In recognition of their service, Brown commits to waiving the application fee and guaranteeing to offer a phone interview to all US military service members and veterans who complete an undergraduate application. Depending upon your background, you may apply in 1 of 3 ways—as a first-year applicant, a transfer applicant, or a RUE applicant.

**Status considered in admissions:** No

**Special admissions process:** No

**Special financial aid:** Yes. The Yellow Ribbon Program.

**Specific programs/policies to address needs:** Yes

## DACA/Undocumented Students

**DACA and undocumented admissions policy (in their own words):** Undocumented and DACA-status applicants will be considered under the University's need-blind admission policy, and Brown will meet 100% of each student's demonstrated financial need upon matriculation.

**Admitted:** Yes

**Status considered in admissions:** No

**Special admissions process:** No

**Eligible for institutional financial aid:** Yes. Beginning with the class entering in Fall 2017, if a first-time, first-year student with undocumented or DACA status is admitted to Brown and is determined to have financial need, Brown will award the student with Brown financial aid funds to meet their demonstrated need. These funds could include University need-based scholarship and campus employment (DACA students only).

**Specific programs/policies to address needs:** Resources include guidance and support through a faculty advisor, services offered through the new First-Generation College and Low-Income Student Center, the elimination of the distinction between domestic applicants and undocumented and DACA-status students in the admission process, and a pledge to continue to meet 100% of these students' demonstrated financial need at Brown.

# Godwin Boaful

**Brown University, C'15**
Bachelor's Degree in Health and Human Biology

**Bronx Community College, C'13**
Associate's Degree in Liberal Arts

**Current Employment:** Medical Student

**Bio:** Born and raised in Ghana, Godwin's professional goal is to help advance health care and preventive care in developing countries. As a medical doctor, Godwin would like to eradicate the spread of contagious illnesses by ensuring that health professionals work with communities to see that everyone is educated on how to prevent and properly treat waterborne illnesses.

*"Brown University played an instrumental role in my professional trajectory. My experiences as a Brunonian reinforced my resolve to pursue medicine. The collaborative academic atmosphere that Brown promotes encouraged me to explore its innate breadth of opportunities, which ultimately allowed me to refine my skill of coordinating ideas with peers across disciplines as well as forge lasting connections. Moreover, the liberty afforded by the open curriculum assisted me immensely in developing depth in my chosen concentration of Health and Human Biology.*

*Similarly, Brown University is unparalleled with respect to its dedication to non-traditional students. In addition to its unique Resumed Undergraduate Education (RUE) program, which is for students who had to interrupt or delay their education, Brown has world-class administrators who cater to the needs of non-traditional students. One of these exceptional staff members is Dean Bhattacharyya, who was always willing to help me succeed. The same is true for other RUE students and Edemir Castano, a fellow RUE and Kaplan Scholar. If given a chance to do it all over again, I would still elect to become a Brunonian."*

## Leadership Activities

- Member, Phi Theta Kappa International Honor Society of Community Colleges
- Mavis Hawthorne Scholarship for Campus Leadership and Involvement
- Robert L. Clarke Scholarship for Excellence in Chemistry
- Event Logistics Volunteer, African Solution Network
- Math Tutor, Bronx Community College
- Vice President, Math and Computer Science Club, Bronx Community College
- Researcher, Department of Energy, Brookhaven National Laboratory
- Black Student Union, Brown University
- Intern, Advocacy, NYPIRG (New York Public Interest Research Group)
- Tutor, Upward Bound Program
- Volunteer, New York Cares
- Inter-organizational Liaison, Toastmasters
- Peer Counselor, Dean's Office, Brown University
- Cancer Resource Representative, Rhode Island Hospital Cancer Center

# BRYN MAWR COLLEGE

**Location:** Bryn Mawr, Pennsylvania

**Website:** www.brynmawr.edu

**Endowment:** $804 million

**Type of School:** Private/Single-Sex, Liberal Arts

**# of Undergraduate Students:** 1,381

**# of Graduate Students:** 327

**Average Class Size:** Student faculty ratio is 8:1. Around 50% of classes have less than 20 students, typically around 17.

**School Mission (in their own words):** The mission of Bryn Mawr College is to provide a rigorous education and to encourage the pursuit of knowledge as preparation for life and work. Bryn Mawr teaches and values critical, creative, and independent habits of thought and expression in an undergraduate liberal arts curriculum for women and in coeducational graduate programs in arts and sciences and social work and social research. Bryn Mawr seeks to sustain a community diverse in nature and democratic in practice, for we believe that only through considering many perspectives do we gain a deeper understanding of each other and the world.

Since its founding in 1885, the College has maintained its character as a small residential community, which fosters close working relationships between faculty and students. The faculty of teacher/scholars emphasizes learning through conversation and collaboration, primary reading, original research, and experimentation. Our cooperative relationship with Haverford College enlarges the academic opportunities for students and their social community. Our active ties to Swarthmore College and the University of Pennsylvania and the proximity of the city of Philadelphia further extend the opportunities available at Bryn Mawr.

Living and working together in a community based on mutual respect, personal integrity, and the standards of a social and academic Honor Code, each generation of students experiments with creating and sustaining a self-governing society within the College. The academic and co-curricular experiences fostered by Bryn Mawr, both on campus and in the College's wider setting, encourage students to be responsible citizens who provide service to and leadership for an increasingly interdependent world.

## Admissions

**Admissions office mailing address:** 101 N Merion Ave, Bryn Mawr PA 19010

**Admissions office phone:** (610) 526-5152

**Admissions office email:** admissions@brynmawr.edu

**# of transfer applications:** Fall 2016 admissions: 129

**# of transfer students accepted:** Fall 2016: Approx. 17

**Transfer student acceptance rate (2016–2017 academic year):** 13.2%

**Freshman applications received in Fall 2016:** 3,012

**Freshman applications accepted in Fall 2016:** 1,203

**Acceptance rate for 2016–2017 freshmen:** 40%

## Transfer Admissions Process

**Transfer policy (in their own words):** Eligible students must have a high-school diploma or equivalent and must have completed a minimum of 1 semester of college work. College credits earned from general education courses in the arts, humanities, social sciences, and natural sciences may be eligible for transfer. Full-time enrollment is required for transfer students, and financial aid is available.

**Transfer admissions contact person:** Amanda Barwise, Senior Assistant Director of Admissions

**Transfer admissions contact info:** abarwise@brynmawr.edu

**Offers transfer-focused admissions events:** Yes

**Transfer application deadline:** Fall 2018 deadline is 3/1/18.

**Acceptances announced to transfer applicants:** Fall 2018: Usually the beginning of May.

**Transfer application on Common App:** Yes. Common App fee: Waived when submitted online.

**SAT/ACT required for transfer applicants:** No for US citizens or residents. Yes for other applicants.

**High-school records requirements:** Official copy of high-school transcript or a GED transcript equivalent

**High-school records requirements for applicants who completed outside the US:** Official high-school transcripts and certified translations

**Submission requirements for transfer applicants who completed high-school equivalency test:** A GED transcript equivalent is required.

**College transcript requirements:** Transfer students should submit official transcripts for all college work completed.

**Interviews available for transfer applicants:** Yes. Strongly recommended. On campus and online (Skype).

## Costs & Financial Aid

**FAFSA code:** 3237

**CSS Profile code:** 2049

**Are internal school financial aid forms required?** No

**Financial aid deadlines for transfer applicants:** Fall 2018: 3/1/18

**Costs for the 2017–2018 year:** Tuition & Fees: $66,860. Room & Board: $15,910.

**Financial aid for transfer students:** Yes

**Guarantees meeting 100% need for transfer students:** Yes, but Bryn Mawr College is need sensitive. This means that the amount of aid a student requests of the College may affect the admissions decision. This is because Bryn Mawr has a limited pool of resources, yet is also committed to meeting full demonstrated need for all admitted students. Once admissibility is determined, funds are distributed until the financial aid budget has been depleted. If there are places remaining in the class, a student's request for aid may determine if she is admitted or not.

**Need-based aid for transfer students:** Yes

**Merit-based financial aid for transfer students:** Yes

**Phi Theta Kappa Scholarship:** No

**Reduced or zero tuition fees for low-income students:** No

**Includes loans in financial aid packages:** Yes

**% of all undergraduates receiving financial aid:** 77%

**% of all undergraduates qualifying for Pell Grants:** N/A

**Average financial aid award for all undergraduate students:** $46,357

**Funding available for low-income students to visit:** Yes

**Enrollment deposit can be waived for low-income students:** Yes

## Academics

**GPA range for transfer students accepted in 2016–2017:** No information provided.

**SAT ranges for all students admitted in 2016:** No information provided.

**ACT composite score range for all students admitted in 2016:** No information provided.

**Type of curriculum:** Gen. Ed. requirements

**Type of academic year:** Semester

**Advisors specifically for transfer students:** Yes

**Credit policy:** Credit for work completed before matriculating at Bryn Mawr will be calculated as described in the General Guidelines above. Ordinarily, the residency requirement means that transfer students will be required to earn all their remaining credits in residence. Students who bring in 8 credits or fewer will normally be expected to earn a minimum of 24 in residence. Those who bring in 9 to 16 credits will normally be expected to complete their remaining credits in residence.

**Max number of transfer credits accepted:** 16 units

**Residency requirement for transfer students:** Yes. Bryn Mawr's residency requirement states that students must complete 24 units during semesters registered at Bryn Mawr, either during the regular academic year or during the College's summer sessions.

**Study abroad available for transfer students:** Yes. Transfers admitted as sophomores will require the permission of the Special Cases Committee to undertake study abroad. The student will be expected to demonstrate a compelling educational rationale for including study abroad in her major work plan.

**Free tutoring for all students:** Yes

**Writing center for all students:** Yes

**Career support/access to internships and resume prep for all students:** Yes

**% of undergraduate students hired within 6 months of graduation:** No information provided.

**Additional resources specifically designated for transfer and/or non-traditional students:** Yes. Transfer and non-traditional students have access to any and all resources that are available to undergraduate students. In addition, Bryn Mawr has an Assistant Dean & Program Coordinator, Community College Connection who works specifically with transfer students. Please contact Christina Rose at cmrose@brynmawr.edu or (610) 526-5375 for more information.

## Housing

**Available for transfer students:** Yes

**Available for non-traditional students:** Not as much because non-traditional students usually live off campus

**Guaranteed for transfer students:** No

**Non-traditional students can reside in housing year-round:** N/A

**Family housing available:** No

## Non-Traditional Admissions

**Non-traditional student policy (in their own words):** Students who are 24 years and older who did not complete their college education immediately after high school are considered non-traditional students. They can attend school full- or part-time through the McBride Scholars program. They must have completed high school in order to apply and are eligible for financial aid.

**Name of program:** McBride Scholar Program

**Program description:** The Katharine E. McBride Scholars are women over the age of 24 who are in the process of beginning or completing their college education. McBride Scholars participate in all the same classes and programs as traditionally aged students, but also have access to additional advising if needed as they transition into undergraduate education. McBride Scholars are eligible to apply for financial aid.

**Program deadline:** 3/1/18

**Program admission requirements:** Must submit Common App, Bryn Mawr writing supplement, official transcripts for all colleges/universities attended, 2 professor evaluations, and high-school or GED-equivalent transcript.

**Program website:** www.brynmawr.edu/admissions/mcbride-scholars

**Program contact person:** Marissa Turchi, Associate Dean of Admissions

**Program contact info:** (610) 526-5151, mturchi@brynmawr.edu

## Military/Veteran Students

**Military/veteran admissions policy (in their own words):** The Yellow Ribbon GI Education Enhancement Program is a provision of the Post-9/11 Veterans Educational Assistance Act of 2008. All VA benefits, including housing allowances and book stipends sent directly to the student will be considered resources before Bryn Mawr Grant eligibility is calculated. For more information, visit www.gibill.va.gov/benefits/post_911_gibill/yellow_ribbon_program.

**Status considered in admissions:** No

**Special admissions process:** No

**Special financial aid:** Yes. The Yellow Ribbon Program.

**Specific programs/policies to address needs:** No information provided.

## DACA/Undocumented Students

**DACA and undocumented admissions policy (in their own words):** All of our academic programs will continue to consider applicants who are undocumented immigrants in the same way they consider US citizens and permanent residents, and will not discriminate on the basis of immigration status.

The College will continue its practice of not releasing information about students' citizenship or immigration status (including information regarding students' visas and Green Cards), unless presented with a subpoena or similar legal requirement. As is currently the case, Campus Safety will not be involved with enforcing federal immigration laws, including Green Card and visa issues, nor will it inquire about or record a student's immigration status when interacting with students. Law enforcement officials seeking to come on campus are expected to check in first with Campus Safety and present a warrant or other enforceable legal instrument. The College does not use E-Verify to verify a student's (or staff member's) eligibility to work at the College.

The College will continue to welcome applicants and to support students of all nationalities and religions.

**Admitted:** Yes

**Status considered in admissions:** No

**Special admissions process:** No

**Eligible for institutional financial aid:** Yes. We will continue to meet full, demonstrated financial need for all students, including undocumented and international students, enrolled at Bryn Mawr. To read more, visit www.brynmawr.edu/global/us-immigration-policy-information.

**Specific programs/policies to address needs:** Yes. DACA and undocumented students have access to speak with advisors who will understand their situation and can help them navigate and find resources that could be useful.

# CALIFORNIA INSTITUTE OF TECHNOLOGY

**Location:** Pasadena, California

**Website:** www.caltech.edu

**Endowment:** $2.107 billion

**Type of School:** Private/Co-ed, Research University

**# of Undergraduate Students:** 983 (2014–2015)

**# of Graduate Students:** 1,226 (2014–2015)

**Average Class Size:** 10–19

**School Mission (in their own words):** The mission of the California Institute of Technology is to expand human knowledge and benefit society through research integrated with education. We investigate the most challenging, fundamental problems in science and technology in a singularly collegial, interdisciplinary atmosphere, while educating outstanding students to become creative members of society.

## Admissions

**Admissions office mailing address:** 1200 E California Blvd, Pasadena CA 91125

**Admissions office phone:** (626) 395-6341

**Admissions office email:** ugadmissions@caltech.edu

**# of transfer applications:** Fall 2016 admissions: 169. Spring 2017 admissions: 0.

**# of transfer students accepted:** Fall 2016: 3. Spring 2017: 0.

**Transfer student acceptance rate (2016–2017 academic year):** 1.8%

**Freshman applications received in Fall 2016:** 6,855

**Freshman applications accepted in Fall 2016:** 179

**Acceptance rate for 2016–2017 freshmen:** 8.1%

## Transfer Admissions Process

**Transfer policy (in their own words):** Caltech does not have a preference between the Common Application or the Coalition Application. We advise that you use the best platform for your application process. $75 application fee. Every transfer student must complete the Caltech math and physics examinations after submitting an application to Caltech.

**Transfer admissions contact person:** Jann Lacoss, Associate Director

**Transfer admissions contact info:** jlacoss@caltech.edu

**Offers transfer-focused admissions events:** No

**Transfer application deadline:** Fall 2018 deadline is 2/15/18.

**Acceptances announced to transfer applicants:** Fall 2018 on 5/1/18.

**Transfer application on Common App:** Yes. Common App fee: $75.

**SAT/ACT required for transfer applicants:** No

**High-school records requirements:** Official transcripts from the last secondary school

**High-school records requirements for applicants who completed outside the US:** Official transcripts from the last secondary school

**Submission requirements for transfer applicants who completed high-school equivalency test:** Official GED results

**College transcript requirements:** Official transcripts from all colleges and universities attended

**Interviews available for transfer applicants:** No

**Additional requirements for transfers seeking admissions to engineering major:** Yes. All transfer-student applicants are required to take a Caltech Transfer Entrance Examination in both mathematics and physics.

## Costs & Financial Aid

**FAFSA code:** 1131

**CSS Profile code:** 4034

**Are internal school financial aid forms required?** Call to enquire.

**Financial aid deadlines for transfer applicants:** Fall 2018: 3/1/18.

**Costs for the 2017–2018 year:** Tuition & Fees: $49,908. Room & Board: 14,796.

**Financial aid for transfer students:** Yes

**Guarantees meeting 100% need for transfer students:** No

**Need-based aid for transfer students:** Yes

**Merit-based financial aid for transfer students:** No

**Phi Theta Kappa Scholarship:** No

**Reduced or zero tuition fees for low-income students:** No

**Includes loans in financial aid packages:** Yes

**% of all undergraduates receiving financial aid:** 59%

**% of all undergraduates qualifying for Pell Grants:** 16% (2014–2015)

**Average financial aid award for all undergraduate students:** $41,669 (2014–2015)

**Funding available for low-income students to visit:** No information provided.

**Enrollment deposit can be waived for low-income students:** No deposit required.

## Academics

**GPA range for transfer students accepted in 2016–2017:** 3.8–4.0

**SAT ranges for all students admitted in 2016:** Critical Reading: 740–800. Mathematics: 770–800. Writing: 730–800.

**ACT composite score range for all students admitted in 2016:** 34–36

**Recommended completed level of math for transfer applicants:** Calculus

**Recommended courses transfer applicants interested in STEM should complete before transfer:** 1 year of physics, 1 year of chemistry; must take physics and math entrance exam.

**Type of curriculum:** Gen. Ed. requirements

**Type of academic year:** Semester

**Advisors specifically for transfer students:** No information provided.

**Credit policy (in their own words):** The courses for which you will receive credit as an enrolling transfer student will be determined at the time of your enrollment. Caltech faculty will review your achievements on an individual basis and will take into consideration how you performed on your placement examinations. It is not possible, therefore, to determine in advance which, if any, courses taken at your previous institution will earn you credit, and which, if any, will not.

**Max number of transfer credits accepted:** The courses for which you will receive credit as an enrolling transfer student will be determined at the time of your enrollment. Caltech faculty will review your achievements on an individual basis and will take into consideration how you perform.

**Residency requirement for transfer students:** Yes. 216 credits must be completed at Caltech.

**Study abroad available for transfer students:** Yes. Must fulfill the residency requirements.

**Free tutoring for all students:** Yes

**Writing center for all students:** Yes

**Career support/access to internships and resume prep for all students:** Yes.

**% of undergraduate students hired within 6 months of graduation:** No information provided.

**Additional resources specifically designated for transfer and/or non-traditional students:** No

## Housing

**Available for transfer students:** Yes.

**Available for non-traditional students:** Yes

**Guaranteed for transfer students:** No

**Non-traditional students can reside in housing year-round:** No

**Family housing available:** Yes

## Non-Traditional Admissions

No non-traditional programs or policies available.

## Military/Veteran Students

**Veterans' policy (in their own words):** In support of United States military service members, veterans, and their family members, Caltech provides leave for military training and active duty. In addition, the Institute accepts GI Bill benefits for eligible students and participates in the supplementary Yellow Ribbon Program.

**Status considered in admissions:** No

**Special admissions process:** No

**Special financial aid:** Yes. The Yellow Ribbon Program.

**Specific programs/policies to address needs:** No information provided.

## DACA/Undocumented Students

No DACA/undocumented student policies or programs available.

# CARLETON COLLEGE

**Location:** Northfield, Minnesota
**Website:** www.carleton.edu
**Endowment:** $738.1 million
**Type of School:** Private/Co-ed, Liberal Arts
**# of Undergraduate Students:** 2,105
**# of Graduate Students:** 0
**Average Class Size:** 16

**School Mission (in their own words):** The mission of Carleton College is to provide an exceptional undergraduate liberal arts education. In pursuit of this mission, the College is devoted to academic excellence, distinguished by the creative interplay of teaching, learning, and scholarship, and dedicated to our diverse residential community and extensive international engagements.

## Admissions

**Admissions office mailing address:** 1 N College St, Northfield MN 55057
**Admissions office phone:** (507) 222-4190
**Admissions office email:** admissions@carleton.edu
**# of transfer applications:** Fall 2016 admissions: 197
**# of transfer students accepted:** Fall 2016: 0
**Transfer student acceptance rate (2016–2017 academic year):** 0
**Freshman applications received in Fall 2016:** 6,485
**Freshman applications accepted in Fall 2016:** 1,467
**Acceptance rate for 2016–2017 freshmen:** 23%

## Transfer Admissions Process

**Transfer policy (in their own words):** Transfer applications can be done through the Common Application, and they differ only slightly from those of prospective freshman. These differences are:

- Your personal essay should provide some insight into why you are looking to transfer and why Carleton is a good match for you.
- Your recommendations should be recent. If you have only completed 1 semester of college, it is reasonable to include 2 high-school recommenders. If, however, you have completed more than 1 year, we advise that at least 1 recommendation be from a recent professor.
- You should include both high-school and college transcripts.
- Students wishing to apply for the fall term should submit applications prior to March 31 and will be notified of the Admissions Committee's decision before May 15. All transfer applicants are expected to submit results from the College Board's SAT I or the American College Test. To qualify for the Carleton degree, students must spend at least 2 years in residence including the senior year.

**Transfer admissions contact person:** Rhemi Abrams-Fuller, Coordinator of Multicultural Programs/Senior Assistant Dean of Admissions
**Transfer admissions contact info:** rfuller@carleton.edu

**Offers transfer-focused admissions events:** No
**Transfer application deadline:** Fall 2018 deadline is 03/31/18.
**Acceptances announced to transfer applicants:** Fall 2018 on 5/15/18.
**Transfer application on Common App:** Yes. Common App fee: There's no fee for students applying online.
**Separate application or in addition to the Common App:** No, but the Coalition and Questbridge applications are also available.
**SAT/ACT required for transfer applicants:** Yes
**High-school records requirements:** Official high-school transcript
**High-school records requirements for applicants who completed outside the US:** Must complete a SEVIS transfer form.
**Submission requirements for transfer applicants who completed high-school equivalency test:** N/A
**College transcript requirements:** Official college transcript from all colleges attended
**Interviews available for transfer applicants:** Yes. Optional interviews can be held on campus, off campus, or by alumni.
**Additional requirements for transfers seeking admissions to arts major:** No. Arts supplements in music, theater, dance, the visual arts, and film are allowed. These samples are forwarded by the admissions office to the appropriate professors on campus, who then provide review for the admissions committee. However, these portfolios are not required for participation and/or majoring in the arts at Carleton, and all students are welcome to submit materials, regardless of their plans once at Carleton.

After applying to Carleton, you'll gain access to the applicant status page, where you'll share examples of your work. You can upload your portfolio of work, all the way at the bottom of the page, under Portfolio.

Please note the following guidelines, when applicable:

- All arts: Include contrasting examples of expression and technique.
- Visual art: Submit no more than 20 images.
- Video and audio samples: No more than 3–5 minutes long.

## Costs & Financial Aid

**FAFSA code:** 2340

**CSS Profile code:** 6081

**Are internal school financial aid forms required?** N/A

**Financial aid deadlines for transfer applicants:** Fall 2018: 3/31/18. Spring 2019: No spring applicants.

**Costs for the 2017–2018 year:** Tuition & Fees: $50,874. Room & Board: $13,197.

**Financial aid for transfer students:** Yes

**Guarantees meeting 100% need for transfer students:** Yes

**Need-based aid for transfer students:** Yes

**Merit-based financial aid for transfer students:** No

**Phi Theta Kappa Scholarship:** No

**Reduced or zero tuition fees for low-income students:** Yes

**Includes loans in financial aid packages:** Yes

**% of all undergraduates receiving financial aid:** 56%

**% of all undergraduates qualifying for Pell Grants:** 13%

**Average financial aid award for all undergraduate students:** $45,763

**Funding available for low-income students to visit:** Yes

**Enrollment deposit can be waived for low-income students:** Yes

## Academics

**GPA range for transfer students accepted in 2016–2017:** No information provided.

**SAT ranges for all students admitted in 2016:** Critical Reading: 660–770. Mathematics: 660–770. Writing: 850–750.

**ACT composite score range for all students admitted in 2016:** 30–33

**Type of curriculum:** Gen. Ed. requirements

**Type of academic year:** Quarter

**Advisors specifically for transfer students:** No information provided.

**Credit policy (in their own words):** Carleton transfers credit from other institutions only in rare situations. An official transcript from the issuing institution must be received by the Office of the Registrar before any academic work done elsewhere may be accepted for Carleton credit. An official transcript is one that has been authenticated by the issuing institution, usually by applying the official seal to the copy of the academic record along with a facsimile of the signature of the registrar or recorder or by recognized authentication delivery methods in the case of electronic transcripts. The transcript must be mailed directly to Carleton College Office of the Registrar by the issuing institution.

A matriculated student may apply toward the Carleton degree a total of 54 credits earned while off campus (Carleton faculty-led off-campus seminars are excluded from the 54-credit maximum) unless, as in the case of certain transfer students, this would result in a total number of transfer credits exceeding the 102 overall maximum.

**Max number of transfer credits accepted:** 102

**Residency requirement for transfer students:** Yes. Students must spend at least 2 years (6 terms) in residence, including the senior year (last 3 terms).

**Study abroad available for transfer students:** Yes. Must fulfill residency requirements.

**Free tutoring for all students:** Yes

**Writing center for all students:** Yes

**Career support/access to internships and resume prep for all students:** Yes

**% of undergraduate students hired within 6 months of graduation:** No information provided.

**Additional resources specifically designated for transfer and/or non-traditional students:** No

## Housing

**Available for transfer students:** Yes

**Available for non-traditional students:** Yes

**Guaranteed for transfer students:** Yes

**Non-traditional students can reside in housing year-round:** No

**Family housing available:** No

## Non-Traditional Admissions

No non-traditional student policies or programs available.

## Military/Veteran Students

No military/veteran student policies or programs available.

## DACA/Undocumented Students

**DACA and undocumented admissions policy (in their own words):** Undocumented students should follow the same admissions application procedures as US citizens and permanent residents who attend high school in the US. Because of our limited financial resources, we must consider these undocumented students among all international applicants applying for aid. Undocumented students are eligible for Carleton-based grants and loans. Students with DACA status are considered among all other legal permanent residents and US citizens.

**Admitted:** Yes, both

**Status considered in admissions:** Yes

**Special admissions process:** No

**Eligible for institutional financial aid:** Yes. DACA students are treated the same as domestic financial aid applicants, meeting 100% need. Undocumented students, without DACA status, are considered among all international applicants when applying for aid.

**Specific programs/policies to address needs:** No

# CITY UNIVERSITY OF NEW YORK

**Location:** New York, New York

**Website:** www.cuny.edu

**Endowment:** Each CUNY school has its own endowment amount.

**Type of School:** Public, Liberal Arts

**# of Undergraduate Students:** 146,661 for senior colleges and 96,865 for community colleges

**# of Graduate Students:** 29,431

**Average Class Size:** Varies by school.

**School Mission (in their own words):** The mission of The City University of New York, embodied in state education law, Article 125, Section 6201, as the finding and intent of the New York State Legislature, states in part:

"The Legislature intends that The City University of New York should be maintained as an independent system of higher education governed by its own Board of Trustees responsible for the governance, maintenance and development of both senior and community college units of The City University.

"The University must remain responsive to the needs of its urban setting and maintain its close articulation between senior and community college units. Where possible, governance and operation of senior and community colleges should be jointly conducted or conducted by similar procedures to maintain the University as an integrated system and to facilitate articulation between units.

"The Legislature's intent is that The City University be supported as an independent and integrated system of higher education on the assumption that the University will continue to maintain and expand its commitment to academic excellence and to the provision of equal access and opportunity for students, faculty and staff from all ethnic and racial groups and from both sexes. The City University is of vital importance as a vehicle for the upward mobility of the disadvantaged in the City of New York. The pioneering efforts of the SEEK and College Discovery programs must not be diminished as a result of greater state financial responsibility.

"Only the strongest commitment to the special needs of an urban constituency justifies the Legislature's support of an independent and unique structure for the University. Activities at the City University campuses must be undertaken in a spirit which recognizes and responds to the imperative need for affirmative action and the positive desire to have City University personnel reflect the diverse communities which comprise the people of the city and state of New York."

## Admissions

**Admissions office mailing address:** 217 E 42 St, New York NY 10017

**Admissions office phone:** (212) 997-2869

**Admissions office email:** admissions@cuny.edu

**# of transfer applications:** Fall 2016 admissions: 0. Spring 2017 admissions: Not provided.

**# of transfer students accepted:** Fall 2016: Depends on each CUNY school: www2.cuny.edu/wp-content/uploads/sites/4/page-assets/admissions/undergraduate/counselor/Admission-Profile-Transfer.pdf. Spring 2017: Not provided.

**Transfer student acceptance rate (2016–2017 academic year):** Varies by school.

**Freshman applications received in Fall 2016:** Varies by school.

**Freshman applications accepted in Fall 2016:** Varies by school.

**Acceptance rate for 2016–2017 freshmen:** Varies by school.

## Transfer Admissions Process

**Transfer policy (in their own words):** Applicants to our 4-year colleges must have completed at least 1 college-level course in Mathematics and English with a grade of C or better, or must demonstrate college-level readiness based on SAT, ACT, AP, IB, or New York Regents test scores.

Your entire college/postsecondary school academic history, including grades earned from courses taken more than once, will be used to determine a grade point average (GPA). If more than 1 college/postsecondary school was attended, your GPA will be determined through a combined calculation of all attempted coursework.

Your high-school/secondary school record will be considered if you have completed fewer than 30 college credits.

As we consider each applicant, we also look beyond the classroom. Extracurricular accomplishments, special talents, awards in particular fields, and academic achievements in light of life experiences and special circumstances are weighed to determine a student's potential for success at CUNY.

**Transfer admissions contact person:** Varies by college.

**Transfer admissions contact info:** Varies by college.

**Offers transfer-focused admissions events:** Yes, many CUNY schools offer their own transfer events.

**Transfer application deadline:** Fall 2018 deadline is 2/1/18. Spring 2019 deadline is 9/15/18.

**Acceptances announced to transfer applicants:** Fall 2018 on rolling basis beginning mid-February to July 1. Spring 2019 on rolling basis beginning mid-October to December 15.

**Transfer application on Common App:** No. Common App fee: N/A.

**Separate application or in addition to the Common App:** Yes

**Fee for separate transfer application:** Yes, $70

**Waiver available for separate transfer application fee:** Must demonstrate financial need.

**SAT/ACT required for transfer applicants:** Varies by school. All students entering the CUNY system must sit for the CUNY Assessment Test.

**High-school records requirements:** Must submit official sealed transcripts.

**High-school records requirements for applicants who completed outside the US:** Generally, CUNY schools require official transcripts to be submitted along with official translations if necessary.

**Submission requirements for transfer applicants who completed high-school equivalency test:** Must submit official GED certificate.

**College transcript requirements:** Previous institutions must send official transcripts.

**Interviews available for transfer applicants:** Varies by school.

**Additional requirements for transfers seeking admissions to business school:** Varies by school.

**Additional requirements for transfers seeking admissions to arts major:** Varies by school.

**Additional requirements for transfers seeking admissions to engineering major:** Varies by school.

## Costs & Financial Aid

**FAFSA code:** Each CUNY school has its own FAFSA code.

**CSS Profile code:** N/A

**Are internal school financial aid forms required?** Varies by school.

**Financial aid deadlines for transfer applicants:** Fall 2018: Varies by school. Spring 2019: Varies by school.

**Costs for the 2017–2018 year:** Tuition & Fees: Varies by school. Room & Board: Varies by school.

**Financial aid for transfer students:** Yes

**Guarantees meeting 100% need for transfer students:** Varies by school.

**Need-based aid for transfer students:** Yes. Must demonstrate need.

**Merit-based financial aid for transfer students:** Yes. Varies by school.

**Phi Theta Kappa Scholarship:** Yes

**Reduced or zero tuition fees for low-income students:** No

**Includes loans in financial aid packages:** Yes

**% of all undergraduates receiving financial aid:** Varies by school.

**% of all undergraduates qualifying for Pell Grants:** More than 58% of CUNY's full-time undergraduate population.

**Average financial aid award for all undergraduate students:** Varies by school.

**Funding available for low-income students to visit:** No

**Enrollment deposit can be waived for low-income students:** Yes

## Academics

**GPA range for transfer students accepted in 2016–2017:** Varies by school.

**SAT ranges for all students admitted in 2016:** Varies by school.

**ACT composite score range for all students admitted in 2016:** Varies by school.

**Recommended completed level of math for transfer applicants:** Varies by school.

**Recommended completed level of English for transfer applicants:** Varies by school.

**Recommended courses transfer applicants should have on transcripts:** Varies by school.

**Recommended courses transfer applicants interested in STEM should complete before transfer:** Varies by school.

**Type of curriculum:** Gen. Ed. requirements

**Type of academic year:** Semester

**Advisors specifically for transfer students:** Yes

**Credit policy:** Varies by school and program. Please contact each school directly.

**Max number of transfer credits accepted:** Generally, a maximum of 60 credits.

**Residency requirement for transfer students:** Students must complete at least 32 credits.

**Study abroad available for transfer students:** Yes. Varies by school.

**Free tutoring for all students:** Yes

**Writing center for all students:** Yes

**Career support/access to internships and resume prep for all students:** Yes

**% of undergraduate students hired within 6 months of graduation:** Varies by school.

**Additional resources specifically designated for transfer and/or non-traditional students:** Yes. Most of the schools usually have advisors that work specifically with non-traditional students.

## Housing

**Available for transfer students:** Yes

**Available for non-traditional students:** Yes

**Guaranteed for transfer students:** No

**Non-traditional students can reside in housing year-round:** N/A

**Family housing available:** No

## Non-Traditional Admissions

**Non-traditional student policy (in their own words):** Adult learners often balance the demands of higher education with work and family responsibilities. The University values this important, growing group of students age 25 and over, and offers programs and services designed to support them. Visit www2.cuny.edu/academics/current-initiatives/adult-learners-at-cuny to learn more about CUNY adult learners. Specific policies and programs vary by school.

## Military/Veteran Students

**Military/veteran admissions policy (in their own words):** As a veteran applicant, it is important that you first find out what information will be needed to apply to the college and program of your choice. We recommend that you download and complete either the Freshman Admission Application Worksheet or Transfer Admission Application Worksheet along with the Admission Application Worksheet for Veterans. Applicants who only have military training should apply for freshman admission. Visit www2.cuny.edu/admissions/undergraduate/prepare to learn more.

**Status considered in admissions:** No

**Special admissions process:** No

**Special financial aid:** Yes. Must meet Department of Veteran Affairs' service requirements.

**Specific programs/policies to address needs:** Students may be eligible for Veterans' Work-Study benefits. In order to be eligible, students must be receiving at least 3/4-time veterans benefits. CUNY also works with NYC Serves, which is New York City's first coordinated network of public, private, and nonprofit organizations working together to serve veterans and their families. Besides this, CUNY works with American Corporate Partners (ACP), which helps post-9/11 veterans achieve their career goals through a free national mentorship program.

## DACA/Undocumented Students

**DACA and undocumented admissions policy (in their own words):** Students who have received part or all of their secondary/high-school education outside the US must carefully review the CUNY application requirements. Undocumented immigrants are welcome to apply to CUNY and should follow the same steps for admission as any other applicant.

**Admitted:** Yes

**Status considered in admissions:** No

**Special admissions process:** No

**Eligible for institutional financial aid:** Yes. Must demonstrate financial need.

**Specific programs/policies to address needs:** Yes. CUNY offers the program called The Dream.US, which helps DACA students obtain scholarships of up to $25,000. Also, each CUNY school has its own resources for these students.

# CLAFLIN UNIVERSITY

**Location:** Orangeburg, South Carolina

**Website:** www.claflin.edu

**Endowment:** $25.3 million (2015)

**Type of School:** Private/Co-ed, Liberal Arts

**# of Undergraduate Students:** 1,851

**# of Graduate Students:** 74

**School Mission (in their own words):** Claflin University is a comprehensive institution of higher education affiliated with the United Methodist Church. A historically black university founded in 1869, Claflin is committed to providing students with access to exemplary educational opportunities in its undergraduate, graduate, and continuing education programs. Claflin seeks to foster a rich community comprised of students, faculty, staff, and administrators who work to nurture and develop the skills and character needed for engaged citizenship and visionary and effective leadership.

In our undergraduate programs, Claflin provides students with the essential foundation of a liberal arts education. Emphasizing critical and analytic thinking, independent research, and oral and written communication skills, the University invites students to use disciplined study to explore and confront the substantive challenges facing the global society. Claflin's graduate programs provide opportunities for advanced students to increase their specialization in particular fields of study oriented toward professional enhancement and academic growth. Our continuing education programs provide students with expanded avenues for professional development and personal fulfillment.

## Admissions

**Admissions office mailing address:** 400 Magnolia St, Orangeburg SC 29115

**Admissions office phone:** (800) 922-1276

**Admissions office email:** admissions@claflin.edu

**Acceptance rate for 2016–2017 freshmen:** 41%

## Transfer Admissions Process

**Transfer policy (in their own words):** To be considered for admission as a transfer student, you must have attended a postsecondary institution but not yet received your bachelor's degree. This does not include high-school students who are enrolled in college-level coursework. See www.claflin.edu/admissions-aid/how-to-apply/transfer for more information.

**Transfer admissions contact person:** Ebony R. James, Admissions Transfer Counselor/Recruiter

**Transfer admissions contact info:** ebony.james@claflin.edu

**Offers transfer-focused admissions events:** No

**Transfer application deadline:** Fall 2018 deadline is 4/15/18. Spring 2019 deadline is 10/15/18.

**Acceptances announced to transfer applicants:** Fall 2018 in May 2018 or rolling basis. Spring 2019 in November 2018 or rolling basis.

**Transfer application on Common App:** No. Common App fee: N/A.

**Separate application or in addition to the Common App:** Yes

**Fee for separate transfer application:** Yes, $30

**Waiver available for separate transfer application fee:** No information provided.

**SAT/ACT required for transfer applicants:** Yes

**High-school records requirements:** An official high-school transcript must be submitted along with high-school grade point average and rank in graduating class.

**High-school records requirements for applicants who completed outside the US:** You must submit official certificates and/or final secondary school records, university transcripts, and mark sheets with official translations if the document is in another language.

**Submission requirements for transfer applicants who completed high-school equivalency test:** Official records

**College transcript requirements:** Official transcript(s) from ALL colleges and universities previously attended in order to complete the decision-making process

**Interviews available for transfer applicants:** No

## Costs & Financial Aid

**FAFSA code:** 3424

**CSS Profile code:** 0

**Are internal school financial aid forms required?** Yes

**Financial aid deadlines for transfer applicants:** Fall 2018: 4/15/18. Spring 2019: 10/15/18.

**Costs for the 2017–2018 year:** Tuition & Fees: Tuition: $15,840 ($7,920 a semester), fees $320. Room & Board: $4,556 (2016–2017).

**Financial aid for transfer students:** Yes

**Guarantees meeting 100% need for transfer students:** No

**Need-based aid for transfer students:** Yes

**Merit-based financial aid for transfer students:** No

**Phi Theta Kappa Scholarship:** No

**Reduced or zero tuition fees for low-income students:** No

**Includes loans in financial aid packages:** Yes

**% of all undergraduates receiving financial aid:** 99%

**% of all undergraduates qualifying for Pell Grants:** 81%

**Average financial aid award for all undergraduate students:** $15,587

**Funding available for low-income students to visit:** No

**Enrollment deposit can be waived for low-income students:** No information provided.

## Academics

**GPA range for transfer students accepted in 2016–2017:** 2.8–4.0

**SAT ranges for all students admitted in 2016:** Critical Reading: 410–490. Mathematics: 400–480. Writing: No information provided.

**ACT composite score range for all students admitted in 2016:** 15–19

**Type of curriculum:** Gen. Ed. requirements

**Type of academic year:** Semester

**Advisors specifically for transfer students:** Yes

**Credit policy (in their own words):** Be prepared to submit course descriptions from the official catalog of the institution(s) from which credits are to be transferred. Students transferring from nonaccredited institutions are temporarily categorized as unclassified students.

**Max number of transfer credits accepted:** No more than 60 semester credit hours may be transferred from 2-year institutions.

**Residency requirement for transfer students:** Yes. Must complete at least half of their credits at Claflin.

**Study abroad available for transfer students:** Yes

**Free tutoring for all students:** Yes

**Writing center for all students:** Yes

**Career support/access to internships and resume prep for all students:** Yes

**% of undergraduate students hired within 6 months of graduation:** No information provided.

**Additional resources specifically designated for transfer and/or non-traditional students:** No

## Housing

**Available for transfer students:** Yes

**Available for non-traditional students:** Yes

**Guaranteed for transfer students:** No

**Non-traditional students can reside in housing year-round:** No information provided.

**Family housing available:** No

## Non-Traditional Admissions

**Non-traditional student policy:** N/A

**Name of program:** Accelerated Degree Program

**Program description:** Claflin's Accelerated Degree Program allows transfer students to complete certain programs within 18 months if they have passed all of the core courses in their major and met all of the general education requirements to graduate.

**Program deadline:** For more information on Claflin's professional and continuing studies department and programs offered in Orangeburg, Fort Jackson-Columbia, or online, call (803) 535-5575 or email crichburg@claflin.edu.

**Program admission requirements:** Contact the university at (803) 535-5575 or email crichburg@claflin.edu.

**Program website:** www.claflin.edu/news-events/news/2015/06/19/professional-and-continuing-studies-offers-accelerated-degree-programs-for-non-traditional-students

**Program contact person:** Dr. Cindye Richburg, Executive Director of the Center of Professional and Continuing Studies

**Program contact info:** (803) 535-5575, crichburg@claflin.edu

## Military/Veteran Students

**Military/veteran admissions policy (in their own words):** The goal of the Office of Veterans Affairs at Claflin University is to assist veterans in pursuing their educational, vocational, or professional objectives. The Office of Student Financial Aid serves as a liaison between enrolled veterans, dependents of veteran students, and the US Department of Veterans Affairs. Our goal is to better serve our veterans and to offer availability, accuracy, and excellent service in relation to veteran educational benefits, certifying enrollments for the Department of Veterans Affairs, and monitoring students' degree plans and academic progress. To learn more about specific benefits for new, transfer, and continuing military students, visit www.claflin.edu/docs/default-source/admissions/Financial-Aid/office-of-veterans-affairs-(pdf).pdf?sfvrsn=0.

**Status considered in admissions:** No

**Special admissions process:** Yes. Military and veteran students are encouraged to fill out the Veterans Affairs application via the Department of Veterans Affairs website.

**Special financial aid:** Yes, if they fill out the Veterans Affairs application. Military members must meet the service requirements stated by the Department of Defense and Department of Veteran Affairs. 425/credit hour regular tuition; 345/credit hour active duty military rate. Claflin also participates in the Yellow Ribbon Program.

**Specific programs/policies to address needs:** Claflin University offers Air Force and Army ROTC programs through a cross enrollment agreement with South Carolina State University and the University of South Carolina.

## DACA/Undocumented Students

No DACA/undocumented student policies or programs available.

# CLAREMONT MCKENNA COLLEGE

**Location:** Claremont, California

**Website:** www.cmc.edu

**Endowment:** $709.1 million

**Type of School:** Private/Co-ed, Liberal Arts

**# of Undergraduate Students:** 1,347

**# of Graduate Students:** 0

**Average Class Size:** 19

**School Mission (in their own words):** Claremont McKenna College is a highly selective, independent, coeducational, residential undergraduate liberal arts college. Its mission, within the mutually supportive framework of The Claremont Colleges, is to educate its students for thoughtful and productive lives and responsible leadership in business, government, and the professions, and to support faculty and student scholarship that contributes to intellectual vitality and the understanding of public policy issues. The College pursues this mission by providing a liberal arts education that emphasizes economics and political science, a professoriate that is dedicated to effective undergraduate teaching, a close student-teacher relationship that fosters critical inquiry, an active residential and intellectual environment that promotes responsible citizenship, and a program of research institutes and scholarly support that makes possible a faculty of teacher-scholars.

*Crescit cum commercio civitas.*

"Civilization prospers with commerce."

## Admissions

**Admissions office mailing address:** 888 Columbia Ave, Claremont CA 91711

**Admissions office phone:** (909) 621-8088

**Admissions office email:** admission@cmc.edu

**# of transfer applications:** Fall 2016 admissions: 426. Spring 2017 admissions: No information provided.

**# of transfer students accepted:** Fall 2016: 29. Spring 2017: No information provided.

**Transfer student acceptance rate (2016–2017 academic year):** 6.8%

**Freshman applications received in Fall 2016:** 6,342

**Freshman applications accepted in Fall 2016:** 599

**Acceptance rate for 2016–2017 freshmen:** 9.4%

## Transfer Admissions Process

**Transfer policy (in their own words):** There is no minimum GPA required for admission. Nor is there any GPA which will guarantee admission. However, we recommend that applicants have a college GPA of at least 3.3. The Admission Committee also considers factors such as course selection, reasons for transfer, recommendations, extracurricular involvement, writing ability, and personal circumstances. Interviews are available for students who have questions about the admission process. A grade lower than a C will not earn transfer credit at CMC.

**Transfer admissions contact person:** Jennifer Sandoval-Dancs, Assistant Vice President and Director of Admission

**Transfer admissions contact info:** jsandoval@cmc.edu

**Offers transfer-focused admissions events:** No

**Transfer application deadline:** Fall 2018 deadline is 4/1/18. Spring 2019 deadline is 11/1/18.

**Acceptances announced to transfer applicants:** Fall 2018 on 5/15/18. Spring 2019 on 12/15/18.

**Transfer application on Common App:** Yes. Common App fee: $70.

**SAT/ACT required for transfer applicants:** Yes, but only for transfer students coming from 4-year colleges/universities.

**High-school records requirements:** Must submit official high-school transcripts from all secondary schools attended.

**High-school records requirements for applicants who completed outside the US:** All transfer applicants must submit their official high-school transcripts as well as any national exam results (e.g., GSCE O- and A-Levels, International Baccalaureate, Abitur, etc.). Official exam scores must be submitted on an official high-school transcript.

**Submission requirements for transfer applicants who completed high-school equivalency test:** Must come from the institution, with official translation if not in English.

**College transcript requirements:** Institutions must submit official transcripts.

**Interviews available for transfer applicants:** Yes. Highly Recommended. On campus (admissions officer, alumni) and off campus (alumni).

## Costs & Financial Aid

**FAFSA code:** 1170

**CSS Profile code:** 4054

**Are internal school financial aid forms required?** Yes

**Financial aid deadlines for transfer applicants:** Fall 2018: 3/1/18. Spring 2019: 11/1/18.

**Costs for the 2017–2018 year:** Tuition & Fees: $50,945. Total expenses with Room & Board: On campus: $69,385. Off campus: $68,795. Off campus w/family: $61,397.

**Financial aid for transfer students:** Admission at CMC is need-blind for transfer applicants who are US citizens or permanent residents. However, CMC may be need-sensitive when admitting transfer students from the waiting list.

**Guarantees meeting 100% need for transfer students:** Yes, if they're US citizens or residents.

**Need-based aid for transfer students:** Yes. In order to qualify for need-based financial aid, you must show financial need.

**Merit-based financial aid for transfer students:** No

**Phi Theta Kappa Scholarship:** No

**Reduced or zero tuition fees for low-income students:** No

**Includes loans in financial aid packages:** Yes

**% of all undergraduates receiving financial aid:** 49%

**% of all undergraduates qualifying for Pell Grants:** No information provided.

**Average financial aid award for all undergraduate students:** $48,623

**Funding available for low-income students to visit:** Yes, but it is limited.

**Enrollment deposit can be waived for low-income students:** Yes

## Academics

**GPA range for transfer students accepted in 2016–2017:** We recommend that applicants have a college GPA of at least 3.3. Most successful applicants to CMC have earned a 3.5 or higher.

**SAT ranges for all students admitted in 2016:** Critical Reading: 650–740. Mathematics: 670–750. Writing: 670–750.

**ACT composite score range for all students admitted in 2016:** 31–33

**Recommended completed level of math for transfer applicants:** Calculus

**Type of curriculum:** Gen Ed. requirements

**Type of academic year:** Semester

**Advisors specifically for transfer students:** No

**Credit policy (in their own words):** Each course at CMC is equivalent to 4 semester units or 6 quarter units, and students need to have completed 32 courses in order to graduate. There are general education requirements that must be completed as well as specific requirements for the major.

In order for a course to transfer to CMC from another college, there must be an equivalent course offered at CMC or one of the other Claremont Colleges. Courses with grades of C– and below will not be transferable. When talking to an admissions officer or the registrar, be sure to ask about credit you received at your current college for AP or IB tests. The policy for accepting these scores may be different at CMC.

CMC does not accept CLEP credits, online or web-based courses, or distance learning courses. There may be additional restrictions on other non-traditional courses or courses taken in a non-traditional setting (such as military service). Please consult the registrar regarding the specifics of your situation.

**Max number of transfer credits accepted:** 16 courses

**Residency requirement for transfer students:** Yes. CMC requires 32 courses for a Bachelor of Arts degree, and 16 courses must be completed while at CMC. Students must spend at least 2 years, including the senior year, and successfully complete at least 16 courses while in residence at CMC in order to earn the bachelor of arts degree. "In residence" is defined as being registered as a full-time student (at least 3 full courses per semester) at CMC or in one of its sanctioned programs.

**Study abroad available for transfer students:** Yes, but only if they transferred in as sophomores or second-semester sophomores.

**Free tutoring for all students:** Yes

**Writing center for all students:** Yes

**Career support/access to internships and resume prep for all students:** Yes

**% of undergraduate students hired within 6 months of graduation:** No information provided.

**Additional resources specifically designated for transfer and/or non-traditional students:** No

## Housing

**Available for transfer students:** Yes

**Available for non-traditional students:** Yes, but very limited.

**Guaranteed for transfer students:** No

**Non-traditional students can reside in housing year-round:** Yes

**Family housing available:** No

## Non-Traditional Admissions

No non-traditional student policies or programs available.

## Military/Veteran Students

**Military/veteran admissions policy (in their own words):** Claremont McKenna College is a member of the Yellow Ribbon Program of the US Department of Veteran Affairs. Veterans should follow the same application procedure as other applicants for admission to CMC. In addition, veterans are welcome to provide additional materials to supplement their applications, such as further explanation of their educational records and/or supplementary essays addressing their military experience and how it has influenced their readiness and desire for further education. Veterans should note that under the Yellow Ribbon Program, the maximum CMC contribution amount per student, per year, is $15,000. Candidates who are veterans of the armed services should submit a copy of their honorable separation papers with their credentials. Veterans who have served at least 2 years may be eligible for elective credit toward graduation. For further information, contact the Admissions Office or the Registrar.

**Status considered in admissions:** No

**Special admissions process:** Yes. In compliance with the Code of Federal Regulations, CFR §21.4253, CMC requires veterans and other eligible persons to submit transcripts and a DD-214 (honorable separation papers), together with other appropriate documents, to the registrar for evaluation and, as appropriate, granting of credit for prior training upon commitment to the College. If such documents are not received within 2 semesters, the students will not be certified for further benefits.

**Special financial aid:** Yes. The Yellow Ribbon Program.

**Specific programs/policies to address needs:** Army ROTC program

## DACA/Undocumented Students

**DACA and undocumented admissions policy (in their own words):** Through the California DREAM Act, undocumented students without SSNs who have completed the DREAM application are allowed to apply for and receive state-administered financial aid, university grants, and Cal Grants. It is important to note that only a limited amount of funding is available. To learn more, visit https://dream.csac.ca.gov.

**Admitted:** Yes

**Status considered in admissions:** No

**Special admissions process:** Yes. In addition to applying through the Common App, these students must fill out the California Dream Act application.

**Eligible for institutional financial aid:** Yes. Average institutional financial aid for Fall 2016: $39,045.

**Specific programs/policies to address needs:** No, but there is a diversity inclusion center that can offer support to these students.

# CLARK UNIVERSITY

**Location:** Worcester, Massachusetts

**Website:** www.clarku.edu

**Endowment:** $371.9 million

**Type of School:** Private/Co-ed, Research University

**# of Undergraduate Students:** 2,227 (Fall 2016)

**# of Graduate Students:** 976 (Fall 2016)

**Average Class Size:** 21

**School Mission (in their own words):** Clark University's mission is to educate undergraduate and graduate students to be imaginative and contributing citizens of the world, and to advance the frontiers of knowledge and understanding through rigorous scholarship and creative effort.

The University seeks to prepare students to meet the challenges of a complex and rapidly changing society. In students and faculty, Clark fosters a commitment to excellence in studying traditional academic disciplines, as well as innovation in exploring questions that cross disciplinary boundaries. The free pursuit of inquiry and the free exchange of ideas are central to that commitment.

The focus of Clark's academic program is a liberal-arts education enriched by interactions among undergraduate students, graduate students, and faculty, and is closely linked to a select number of professional programs. Clark also serves students who wish to continue formal education throughout their lives.

The intellectual and personal growth of students is enhanced by a wide variety of educational programs and extracurricular activities. Clark believes that intellectual growth must be accompanied by the development of values, the cultivation of responsible independence, and the appreciation of a range of perspectives.

Clark's academic community has long been distinguished by the pursuit of scientific inquiry and humanistic studies, enlivened by a concern for significant social issues. Among many other scholarly endeavors, Clark contributes to understanding human development, assessing relationships between people and the environment, and managing risk in a technological society.

Clark is dedicated to being a dynamic community of learners able to thrive in today's increasingly interrelated societies. The University maintains a national and international character, attracting high-caliber students and faculty from all quarters of the globe. As a university residing in an urban context, Clark also strives to address the needs and opportunities of contemporary urban life.

Clark's intimate academic setting and tradition of "elbow teaching" provide many opportunities for students to pursue knowledge through participation. High expectations, as well as easy access to the scholar-teacher faculty, encourage students to become autonomous learners.

Clark's international and interdisciplinary orientation is combined with a tradition of strong self-direction among students and faculty. These attributes enhance the University's ability to contribute to the development of new modes of thought and to the advancement of society through the creation and transmission of knowledge.

## Admissions

**Admissions office mailing address:** 950 Main St, Worcester MA 01610

**Admissions office phone:** (508) 793-7431

**Admissions office email:** transferadmissions@clarku.edu

**# of transfer applications:** Fall 2016 admissions: 200. Spring 2017 admissions: 73.

**# of transfer students accepted:** Fall 2016: 89. Spring 2017: 29.

**Transfer student acceptance rate (2016–2017 academic year):** 43.2%

**Freshman applications received in Fall 2016:** 7,914

**Freshman applications accepted in Fall 2016:** 4,331

**Acceptance rate for 2016–2017 freshmen:** 54%

## Transfer Admissions Process

**Transfer policy (in their own words):** Emphasis is placed on your college work (as represented by grades and recommendations) and some of your high-school record if you've completed less than 1 full year of college (equivalent to 8 Clark units, which is typically 8 courses). Test scores are considered if you choose to submit them, but they are not required. Typically, transfer students with a college grade point average of 3.0 or higher are successful at Clark University.

**Transfer admissions contact person:** Lexi Alm, Assistant Director of Admissions and Transfer Coordinator

**Transfer admissions contact info:** aalm@clarku.edu

**Offers transfer-focused admissions events:** No information provided.

**Transfer application deadline:** Fall 2018 deadline is 5/1/18. Spring 2019 deadline is 11/1/18.

**Acceptances announced to transfer applicants:** Fall 2018: 2–4 weeks after complete application has been received. Spring 2019: 2–3 weeks after complete application has been received.

**Transfer application on Common App:** Yes. Common App fee: $60.

**SAT/ACT required for transfer applicants:** No, it's optional.

**High-school records requirements:** Must submit official final secondary school transcript.

**High-school records requirements for applicants who completed outside the US:** Must submit official transcript along with certified translation if it's written in another language.

**Submission requirements for transfer applicants who completed high-school equivalency test:** Must submit official certification.

**College transcript requirements:** Must submit official college transcripts from all institutions attended.

**Interviews available for transfer applicants:** No

## Costs & Financial Aid

**FAFSA code:** 2139

**CSS Profile code:** 3279

**Are internal school financial aid forms required?** Yes, depending on your situation.

**Financial aid deadline for Fall 2018 transfer applicants:** Fall 2018: 5/15/18. Spring 2019: 11/15/18.

**Costs for the 2017–2018 year:** Tuition & Fees: $43,150. Room & Board: varies by room type $5,200-$7,100.

**Financial aid for transfer students:** Yes

**Guarantees meeting 100% need for transfer students:** No

**Need-based aid for transfer students:** Yes. To be considered for need-based aid, you must complete a financial aid application and demonstrate need.

**Merit-based financial aid for transfer students:** Yes. Top consideration for Clark's merit scholarships goes to admitted students who have excelled in secondary school and college and whose academic achievement and personal qualities indicate they will perform at the highest level when they enroll at the University.

**Phi Theta Kappa Scholarship:** Yes, $12,000. Details at www2.clarku.edu/financial-aid/scholarships/transfer-scholarships.cfm.

**Reduced or zero tuition fees for low-income students:** No

**Includes loans in financial aid packages:** Yes

**% of all undergraduates receiving financial aid:** 89% as of Fall 2016

**% of all undergraduates qualifying for Pell Grants:** Approximately 20%

**Average financial aid award for all undergraduate students:** $35,774

**Funding available for low-income students to visit:** Yes, they have done it for the last 3 years but it is not guaranteed. Usually on a case-by-case basis. Usually based on scholarship (trainer scholarship) and open houses.

**Enrollment deposit can be waived for low-income students:** Yes, but it is on a case-by-case basis. Student must explain why it is needed, or sometimes students pay some now and the rest later.

## Academics

**GPA range for transfer students accepted in 2016–2017:** Typically, transfer students with a college grade point average of 3.0 or higher are successful at Clark University.

**SAT ranges for all students admitted in 2016:** Critical Reading: 619. Mathematics: 621. Writing: 620.

**ACT composite score range for all students admitted in 2016:** 28

**Type of curriculum:** Other. Liberal Education and Effective Practice (LEEP) is Clark's bold effort to advance liberal education. It intentionally links a deep and integrated undergraduate curriculum with opportunities to put knowledge into practice in order to prepare our students for remarkable careers and purposeful, accomplished lives.

**Type of academic year:** Semester

**Advisors specifically for transfer students:** Yes

**Credit policy:** No transfer grades below C will be accepted.

**Max number of transfer credits accepted:** 64 credits or 16 units

**Residency requirement for transfer students:** Yes. They must spend 4 semesters at Clark.

**Study abroad available for transfer students:** Yes. Must fulfill residency requirements.

**Free tutoring for all students:** Yes

**Writing center for all students:** Yes

**Career support/access to internships and resume prep for all students:** Yes

**% of undergraduate students hired within 6 months of graduation:** 85% of grad class got back to them with this info. 97% of students are employed full-time in their field of study or are in grad school.

**Additional resources specifically designated for transfer and/or non-traditional students:** There are specific advisors who work with transfer and military students who are considered non-traditional. Besides this, there's also the School of Professional Studies, which caters to non-traditional students.

## Housing

**Available for transfer students:** Yes

**Available for non-traditional students:** They can live on campus if they desire to, but usually these students choose to live off campus.

**Guaranteed for transfer students:** Yes

**Non-traditional students can reside in housing year-round:** No

**Family housing available:** No

## Non-Traditional Admissions

**Non-traditional student policy (in their own words):**
Demonstrating the ability to handle college-level work is one of the factors our Admissions Committee will consider when evaluating your application. If you don't have recent college experience, we suggest enrolling in courses at a community college before applying to Clark.

## Military/Veteran Students

**Military/veteran admissions policy:** N/A

**Status considered in admissions:** No

**Special admissions process:** Yes. Aside from filling out the regular application, these students should register with the Dept. of Veteran Affairs.

**Special financial aid:** Yes. The Yellow Ribbon Program.

**Specific programs/policies to address needs:** No information provided.

## DACA/Undocumented Students

**DACA and undocumented admissions policy (in their own words):** Clark welcomes all applicants regardless of citizenship status. Undocumented students, with or without Deferred Action for Childhood Arrivals (DACA), are treated the same as other US citizens or permanent residents in Clark's admissions process. To learn more, visit www2.clarku.edu/offices/oia/resources/documents/InformforUndocumentedStudents.pdf.

**Admitted:** Yes

**Status considered in admissions:** No

**Special admissions process:** No

**Eligible for institutional financial aid:** Yes. Must complete CSS Profile and submit parents' income tax return if available.

**Specific programs/policies to address needs:** Clark University takes the privacy rights of all members of our community very seriously. We protect all nonpublic information regarding our students to the maximum extent that the law allows. To ensure that we fully protect the rights of undocumented students at Clark University, we will develop a written protocol to be followed by University employees receiving such requests for information. If DACA is ended, our students will face additional challenges in financing their education. For example, DACA provides students with work authorization. Should DACA lapse or be ended, Clark University will provide additional financial support to assist our DACA students in completing their education. In addition, if students have questions about their rights and immigration status, students should contact Patty Doherty, Director of International Students and Scholars Office. The Office of Multicultural and First Generation Student Support offers social and academic support to these students. Also, students can participate in identity-based community groups that meet regularly.

# Lavar Thomas

**Clark University, C'13**
Bachelor's Degree in Political Science, cum laude

**Kingsborough Community College, C'11**
Associate's Degree in Liberal Arts

**Current Employment:** Community Involvement Coordinator, United States Environmental Protection Agency

**Bio:** Born to Guyanese parents and raised in New York City, Lavar is passionate about providing mentorship to students in underserved communities. His ultimate goal is to establish a leadership organization that targets youth and addresses issues within minority employment, financial literacy, and public policy.

*"Clark University's motto, 'Challenge Convention, Change Our World,' was one that struck me as an incoming transfer student. I believe Clark cultivates a community of students and faculty who are passionate about social change and seek to make a difference. As a community college transfer student, I knew such a community would help cultivate my gifts as a student, but more importantly as a leader. Transferring from community college to a four-year institution was a significant challenge. While adjusting to the academic rigor as a transfer, I found my voice in advocating for other students within the transfer community who may have had difficulty in their transition and lacked support. It was through this experience I learned the power of resourcefulness, actualizing a vision bigger than myself, advocacy, and service.*

*Those four things served me well as a United States Peace Corps volunteer in Rwanda. It all started with a conversation in my political science advisor's office at Clark. She shared with me her experience as a Peace Corps volunteer. What impressed me was how the work embodied the sentiments of Clark's motto. As a college senior, she had faced the pressures of pursuing graduate school immediately because it was the popular thing to do. Her decision to challenge that convention by volunteering two years of her life teaching English in Jordan, where she became fluent in Arabic and encountered her passion for Middle Eastern politics, made an indelible impression on me. I knew I wanted to gain a global experience while serving a community and growing as an individual. I believe the Clark experience planted a seed in me that would germinate and position me to be a global game changer."*

## Leadership Activities

- Volunteer, Peace Corps, Rwanda, 2014–2016
- Inductee, Phi Theta Kappa International Honor Society of Community Colleges
- Presidential Scholar, Kingsborough Community College
- Honors Club, Kingsborough Community College
- Salzburg Global Seminar Scholar, Kingsborough Community College
- Dr. Rachelle Goldsmith Honors Award, Kingsborough Community College
- Research Assistant, Kingsborough Institute for Civic Connections
- Research Assistant, City of Worcester Division of Public Health
- Ralph Bunche Scholar, American Political Science Association
- Leader of the Week, Gryphon and Pleiades Honor Society, Clark University
- Student Ambassador, Clark University
- Co-Founder, Transfer Students Association, Clark University
- Financial Chair, Millennium Leadership Conference, Clark University
- Mentor, Connections Pre-Orientation Program, Clark University
- Member, RIA Community Advisory Board, Harvard Medical School
- Presenter, 2012 National Association of Ethnic Studies, New Orleans, LA

# CLARKSON UNIVERSITY

**Location:** Potsdam, New York

**Website:** www.clarkson.edu

**Endowment:** $186.1 million

**Type of School:** Private/Co-ed, Research University

**# of Undergraduate Students:** 3,268

**# of Graduate Students:** 1,116

**Average Class Size:** 19

**School Mission (in their own words):** Clarkson University is an independent, nationally recognized technological university whose faculty of teacher-scholars aspires to offer superior instruction and engage in high-quality research and scholarship in engineering, business, science, health, and liberal arts. Our primary mission is to educate talented and motivated men and women to become successful professionals through quality pre-collegiate, undergraduate, graduate, and professional continuing education programs, with particular emphasis on the undergraduate experience. Our community and campus settings enhance the quality of student life and afford students access to and interaction with their faculty. We value the diversity of our University community, and we strive to attune ourselves and our programs to our global, pluralistic society. We share the belief that humane and environmentally sound economic and social development derive from the expansion, diffusion, and application of knowledge.

## Admissions

**Admissions office mailing address:** 8 Clarkson Ave, Potsdam NY 13699

**Admissions office phone:** (800) 527-6577, (315) 268-2125 (transfer students)

**Admissions office email:** admission@clarkson.edu, tradmission@clarkson.edu (transfer students)

**# of transfer applications:** Fall 2016 admissions: 276. Spring 2017 admissions: N/A.

**# of transfer students accepted:** Fall 2016: 200. Spring 2017: N/A.

**Transfer student acceptance rate (2016–2017 academic year):** 72.4%

**Freshman applications received in Fall 2016:** 7,066

**Freshman applications accepted in Fall 2016:** 4,820

**Acceptance rate for 2016–2017 freshmen:** 68%

## Transfer Admissions Process

**Transfer policy (in their own words):** We look for the same qualities in our transfer students as traditional first-year applicants: strong academic records, persuasive recommendations, and a spark that sets you apart. We highly recommend that all transfer applicants visit Clarkson and participate in an admission interview.

**Transfer admissions contact person:** Patrick Smalling '09, Associate Dean of Transfer Admission

**Transfer admissions contact info:** psmalling@clarkson.edu

**Offers transfer-focused admissions events:** No

**Transfer application deadline:** Fall 2018 deadline is 7/1/18. Spring 2019 deadline is 12/1/18.

**Acceptances announced to transfer applicants:** Fall 2018 on rolling basis. Spring 2019 on rolling basis.

**Transfer application on Common App:** No. Common App fee: N/A.

**Separate application or in addition to the Common App:** Yes

**Fee for separate transfer application:** Yes

**Waiver available for separate transfer application fee:** The application fee for all transfer applicants is waived up front. If you are offered admission and decide to attend Clarkson, we add the $50 application fee onto your $300 enrollment deposit (for a total of $350). Students who apply online or who interview with us either on or off campus, will have the $50 application fee waived altogether.

**SAT/ACT required for transfer applicants:** Yes, but only if you have earned fewer than 24 hours of credit at your current college or university.

**High-school records requirements:** If you have earned less than 24 hours of credit at your current college or university, you will also need to supply the following information: official high-school record.

**High-school records requirements for applicants who completed outside the US:** Institution must send official transcript.

**Submission requirements for transfer applicants who completed high-school equivalency test:** Must submit official transcripts with official translation if written in another language.

**College transcript requirements:** Official transcripts from each college or university you have attended (please include course descriptions if attending a college or university outside New York State)

**Interviews available for transfer applicants:** Yes. Optional, but are strongly recommended. Offers one-on-one interviews with a transfer admission representative when student visits campus.

## Costs & Financial Aid

**FAFSA code:** 2699

**CSS Profile code:** 0

**Are internal school financial aid forms required?** No

**Financial aid deadlines for transfer applicants:** Fall 2018: 4/15/2018 is the preferred deadline, but the latest the application can be submitted is 7/1/18. Spring 2019: 12/1/18.

**Costs for the 2017–2018 year:** Tuition & Fees: $46,132. Total expenses with Room & Board: On campus: $64,018. Off campus: $59,886. Off campus w/family: $50,508.

**Financial aid for transfer students:** Yes

**Guarantees meeting 100% need for transfer students:** No

**Need-based aid for transfer students:** Yes. Must fill out FAFSA and demonstrate need.

**Merit-based financial aid for transfer students:** Yes. Must demonstrate academic excellence.

**Phi Theta Kappa Scholarship:** Yes, $8,000. Details available at www.clarkson.edu/admissions/undergrad_admissions/costs/transfer_aid.html.

**Reduced or zero tuition fees for low-income students:** No

**Includes loans in financial aid packages:** Yes

**% of all undergraduates receiving financial aid:** No information provided.

**% of all undergraduates qualifying for Pell Grants:** No information provided.

**Average financial aid award for all undergraduate students:** $41,810

**Funding available for low-income students to visit:** Yes, but mostly what they cover is the expenses while the student is on campus. For example, they'll provide meal tickets and will house them.

**Enrollment deposit can be waived for low-income students:** Yes

## Academics

**GPA range for transfer students accepted in 2016–2017:** We look for a cumulative GPA of 2.75. Most students who transfer to Clarkson have a GPA of 3.0 or higher.

**SAT ranges for all students admitted in 2016:** Critical Reading: 570. Mathematics: 612. Writing: 535.

**ACT composite score range for all students admitted in 2016:** 27

**Type of curriculum:** Gen. Ed. requirements

**Type of academic year:** Semester

**Advisors specifically for transfer students:** Yes

**Credit policy (in their own words):** If you are offered transfer admission to Clarkson, we will send your transcript(s) and course descriptions to your academic department at Clarkson for an official evaluation. The faculty evaluator will compare the courses you have taken, or will have taken by the time you enroll, to the required courses in your Clarkson degree program. A grade of C or better must be achieved for a course to transfer. We will only transfer in those courses which meet a requirement in your degree program.

**Max number of transfer credits accepted:** 60

**Residency requirement for transfer students:** Yes. A student entering as a first-semester freshman must have been in residence for at least 4 semesters, including the final undergraduate semester. Or, if entering with advanced standing, a student must have completed at least half the remaining upper-level undergraduate work in residence at Clarkson.

**Study abroad available for transfer students:** Yes, if they entered as a second-year student

**Free tutoring for all students:** Yes

**Writing center for all students:** Yes

**Career support/access to internships and resume prep for all students:** Yes

**% of undergraduate students hired within 6 months of graduation:** No information provided.

**Additional resources specifically designated for transfer and/or non-traditional students:** There are advisors that work with transfer students.

## Housing

**Available for transfer students:** Yes

**Available for non-traditional students:** Yes

**Guaranteed for transfer students:** Yes

**Non-traditional students can reside in housing year-round:** No information provided.

**Family housing available:** Yes

## Non-Traditional Admissions

No non-traditional student policies or programs available.

## Military/Veteran Students

**Status considered in admissions:** No

**Special admissions process:** No

**Special financial aid:** Yes. The Yellow Ribbon Program.

**Specific programs/policies to address needs:** Besides being able to be part of the Yellow Ribbon Program, students can also continue with their military career by joining the ROTC. Clarkson University is proud to be 1 of 272 Army ROTC programs nationwide and 1 of 6 Air Force ROTC programs in NY State. Clarkson has a long history of honoring the military and supporting our vets.

## DACA/Undocumented Students

No DACA and undocumented student policies or programs available.

**Admitted:** Yes

# Leonardo Minier

**University of Michigan, C'16**
Master's Degree in Mechanical Engineering with a focus in Automotive Engineering

**Clarkson University, C'15**
Bachelor's Degree in Mechanical Engineering with a minor in Mathematics

**Bronx Community College, C'12**
Associate's Degree in Engineering Science

**Current Employment:** Vehicle Control Plan Engineer, Chrysler Automobile Company

**Bio:** Born in the Dominican Republic, Leonardo is passionate about repairing and customizing vehicles and would like to utilize his engineering skills to make motorcycles safer and more accessible in the United States, especially in urban centers, due to their high mobility and low fuel usage.

*"Transferring to Clarkson University allowed me to expand my perspective on the world by introducing me to an entirely different environment and culture than New York City. Clarkson challenged me academically and pushed me to accomplish things I'd never thought of by surrounding me with intelligent students who later became my competition. Knowing who my competitors were, I had to find a way to keep up, and Clarkson provided several resources from which I could receive help, like the C-STEP program.*

*Clarkson's C-STEP program encouraged me to pursue a master's degree in engineering and provided me with resources to prepare for and apply to grad school. The staff of C-STEP were very comforting and showed a great interest in my achievements and goals. I encourage any future and current students at Clarkson to participate in C-STEP; I guarantee they will not regret it. My best times and happiest moments at Clarkson University were with them!"*

## Leadership Activities

- Vice President, Phi Theta Kappa International Honor Society of Community Colleges
- Member, Tau Alpha Phi, National Honor Society for Engineering and Technology
- Site Group Leader, Supported Children's Advocacy Network
- Physics & Math Tutor, Research Foundation, City University of New York
- Manufacturing Engineering Co-op, The Raymond Corporation
- Math & Science Tutor, GED Preparation
- Thermodynamics Tutor, Clarkson University
- Researcher, Louis Stokes Alliance for Minority Participation (LSAMP), Brookhaven National Laboratory
- SPEED Team, Formula SAE, Clarkson University
- Peer Leader, RAPP (Relationship Abuse Prevention Program)
- Buick Achievers Scholarship
- National Science Foundation Scholarship, BCC

# COLLEGE OF WILLIAM AND MARY

**Location:** Williamsburg, Virginia

**Website:** www.wm.edu

**Endowment:** $803.7 million

**Type of School:** Public/Co-ed, Research University

**# of Undergraduate Students:** 6,276

**# of Graduate Students:** 2,341

**Average Class Size:** 19

**School Mission (in their own words):** The College of William & Mary, a public university in Williamsburg, Virginia, is the second-oldest institution of higher learning in the United States. Established in 1693 by British royal charter, William & Mary is proud of its role as the Alma Mater of generations of American patriots, leaders, and public servants. Now, in its fourth century, it continues this tradition of excellence by combining the best features of an undergraduate college with the opportunities offered by a modern research university. Its moderate size, dedicated faculty, and distinctive history give William & Mary a unique character among public institutions and create a learning environment that fosters close interaction among students and teachers.

The university's predominantly residential undergraduate program provides a broad liberal education in a stimulating academic environment enhanced by a talented and diverse student body. This nationally acclaimed undergraduate program is integrated with selected graduate and professional programs in 5 faculties—Arts and Sciences, Business, Education, Law, and Marine Science. Masters and doctoral programs in the humanities, the sciences, the social sciences, business, education, and law provide a wide variety of intellectual opportunities for students at both graduate and undergraduate levels.

At William & Mary, teaching, research, and public service are linked through programs designed to preserve, transmit, and expand knowledge. Effective teaching imparts knowledge and encourages the intellectual development of both student and teacher. Quality research supports the educational program by introducing students to the challenge and excitement of original discovery, and is a source of the knowledge and understanding needed for a better society. The university recognizes its special responsibility to the citizens of Virginia through public and community service to the Commonwealth as well as to national and international communities. Teaching, research, and public service are all integral parts of the mission of William & Mary.

## Admissions

**Admissions office mailing address:** Sadler Center, 200 Stadium Dr, Williamsburg VA 23185

**Admissions office phone:** (757) 221-4223

**Admissions office email:** admission@wm.edu

**# of transfer applications:** Fall 2016 admissions: 887. Spring 2017 admissions: No information provided.

**# of transfer students accepted:** Fall 2016: 364. Spring 2017: No information provided.

**Transfer student acceptance rate (2016–2017 academic year):** 41%

**Freshman applications received in Fall 2016:** 14,382

**Freshman applications accepted in Fall 2016:** 5,253

**Acceptance rate for 2016–2017 freshmen:** 35.4%

## Transfer Admissions Process

**Transfer policy:** N/A

**Transfer admissions contact person:** Whitney Pitschke, Senior Assistant Dean of Admission/Director of Transfer Admission

**Transfer admissions contact info:** wmlink@wm.edu, whitney@wm.edu

**Offers transfer-focused admissions events:** No

**Transfer application deadline:** Fall 2018 deadline is 3/1/18. Spring 2019 deadline is 11/1/18.

**Acceptances announced to transfer applicants:** Fall 2018 on 5/1/18. Spring 2019 on 12/10/18.

**Transfer application on Common App:** Yes. Common App fee: $70.

**SAT/ACT required for transfer applicants:** Yes, but only if the student has completed less than a full year of college coursework

**High-school records requirements:** Must submit official high-school transcript.

**High-school records requirements for applicants who completed outside the US:** Must submit official transcript.

**Submission requirements for transfer applicants who completed high-school equivalency test:** Official GED certificate must be submitted.

**College transcript requirements:** Official transcripts from all colleges and universities attended.

**Interviews available for transfer applicants:** No

**Additional requirements for transfers seeking admissions to business school:** Yes. The School of Business admits a total of 225 students to the business major program each year (180 in the fall semester and 45 in the spring semester). Students must have a 2.5 GPA to apply to the majors program; however, meeting this minimum benchmark does not guarantee admission. In addition, prospective majors must completely obtain junior standing (54 credits) and complete the following prerequisite courses prior to their first semester in the School of Business:

- Principles of Accounting (BUAD 203)
- Introductory Microeconomics (ECON 101)
- Introductory Macroeconomics (ECON 102)
- Introductory Calculus (MATH 108, MATH 111, MATH 112, MATH 131, or MATH 132)
- Introductory Statistics (BUAD 231, MATH 106, ECON 307, PSYC 301, SOCL 353, MATH 351, or KINE 394)

**Additional requirements for transfers seeking admissions to arts major:** Yes. If you possess a skill/talent in the creative or performing arts and are interested in continued study or application in that area at the college level, you may submit a sample of your work for review by our faculty for music, art, photography, theatre, or dance.

## Costs & Financial Aid

**FAFSA code:** 3705

**CSS Profile code:** 5115

**Are internal school financial aid forms required?** No

**Financial aid deadlines for transfer applicants:** Fall 2018: 3/1/18. Spring 2019: 11/15/18.

**Costs for the 2017–2018 year:** Tuition & Fees: Tuition in-state: $16,370, fees: $5,674. Tuition out-of-state: $37,425, fees: $6,245. Room & Board: $11,799 for both in-state and out-of-state.

**Financial aid for transfer students:** Yes

**Guarantees meeting 100% need for transfer students:** No

**Need-based aid for transfer students:** Yes

**Merit-based financial aid for transfer students:** No

**Phi Theta Kappa Scholarship:** No

**Reduced or zero tuition fees for low-income students:** No

**Includes loans in financial aid packages:** Yes

**% of all undergraduates receiving financial aid:** 33%

**% of all undergraduates qualifying for Pell Grants:** No information provided.

**Average financial aid award for all undergraduate students:** $21,243

**Funding available for low-income students to visit:** No

**Enrollment deposit can be waived for low-income students:** Yes

## Academics

**GPA range for transfer students accepted in 2016–2017:** 3.5 and above

**SAT ranges for all students admitted in 2016:** Critical Reading: 630–730. Mathematics: 620–740. Writing: 620–720.

**ACT composite score range for all students admitted in 2016:** 28–33

**Recommended courses transfer applicants should have on transcripts:** Mathematics and quantitative reasoning; natural sciences (with the associated laboratory); social sciences; world cultures and history; literature and history of the arts; creative and performing arts; philosophical, religious, and social thought

**Recommended courses transfer applicants interested in STEM should complete before transfer:** Physics, calculus, general biology, general chemistry

**Recommended extracurricular engagement:** None in particular, but the school would like to see that the student was involved in the previous institution.

**Type of curriculum:** Gen. Ed. requirements

**Type of academic year:** Semester

**Advisors specifically for transfer students:** Yes

**Credit policy (in their own words):** Transfer credit evaluations at William & Mary are based on a careful review of course descriptions for all of the courses completed by the transfer student at the prior institution. The Transfer Services Coordinator (TSC) in the Office of the University Registrar, (757) 221-2823, shepherds this process. In accordance with guidelines established by each department, the TSC considers course level, prerequisites, and other information to determine transferability. The TSC may consult the departmental Transfer Credit Evaluators (TCE) for some courses. Transfer Credit Evaluators are faculty members with extensive knowledge of the departmental curriculum and requirements.

Note that grades do not transfer; only credits are awarded for prior college work or examination scores. All credits earned through transfer will show a grade of "T," which does not figure into the W&M grade point average.

**Max number of transfer credits accepted:** While there is no limit to the number of credits that may be transferred, William & Mary requires that at least 60 credit hours, including the last 2 full-time semesters and a minimum of 15 credits in the major and a minimum of 9 credits in the minor, be earned in residence at the College.

**Residency requirement for transfer students:** Yes. No degree will be granted by the College until the undergraduate applicant has completed a minimum of 60 credit hours in residence at the College. This period must include the last 2 full-time semesters in which credits counted toward the degree are earned. A minimum of 15 credit hours in the major and 9 credit hours in the minor must be taken in residence at the College.

**Study abroad available for transfer students:** Yes. Must fulfill residency requirements.

**Free tutoring for all students:** Yes

**Writing center for all students:** Yes

**Career support/access to internships and resume prep for all students:** Yes

**% of undergraduate students hired within 6 months of graduation:** No information provided.

**Additional resources specifically designated for transfer and/or non-traditional students:** Yes. There are specific advisors that work with transfer and non-traditional students.

## Housing

**Available for transfer students:** Yes

**Available for non-traditional students:** Yes

**Guaranteed for transfer students:** Yes

**Non-traditional students can reside in housing year-round:** Yes, if the students live in the Ludwell Apartments. Ludwell is adjacent to the Mason School of Business. Residents have a short five minute walk to New Campus, while Old Campus is accessible by the bus system, which departs/arrives every 30 minutes.

**Family housing available:** Yes, at the Ludwell Apartments.

## Non-Traditional Admissions

**Non-traditional student policy:** N/A

**Name of program:** FlexTrack

**Program description:** FlexTrack is a program for non-traditional students with significant time constraints outside of the classroom—family commitments, full-time employment, etc. Because FlexTrack students can take anywhere between 3 to 18 credits per semester, they are the only students on campus that can be classified as part-time undergraduates (taking fewer than 12 credits). Many FlexTrack students, however, do take a full course load (taking 12 credits or more). It all depends on how William & Mary fits into your life. This program is meant to be flexible, after all! Allows students to take classes part-time around their schedules.

**Program deadline:** No information provided.

**Program admission requirements:** Your application for admission should indicate your desire to enroll as a FlexTrack student. Questions can be directed to the Office of Undergraduate Admission.

**Program website:** www.wm.edu/offices/deanofstudents/academicpolicies/flextrackfaqs/index.php

**Program contact person:** N/A

**Program contact info:** N/A

## Military/Veteran Students

**Military/veteran admissions policy:** Same as undergraduate application.

**Status considered in admissions:** No

**Special admissions process:** No

**Special financial aid:** Yes. The Yellow Ribbon Program.

**Specific programs/policies to address needs:** Armed Forces Tuition Assistance (TA) is a benefit paid to eligible members of the Army, Navy, Marines, Air Force, and Coast Guard. Congress has given each service the ability to pay up to 100% for the tuition expenses of its members. Certification for educational benefits is a service provided by the Office of the Registrar. We assist students with the processing of Department of Veterans Affairs (VA) forms for educational benefits, provide guidance about specific procedural requirements, and submit enrollment certifications for each semester to VA. It is the student's responsibility to decide which benefit is most appropriate for her or him based on individual circumstances and then apply to VA (VONApp) in order to use the benefits. In addition, there's a ROTC program that students can join in order to continue their military education/career.

## DACA/Undocumented Students

**DACA and undocumented admissions policy (in their own words):** DACA students are enrolled at William & Mary under guidelines approved by Virginia's Attorney General. They are important members of the William & Mary community, belong here, and should be allowed to finish their W&M educations. It is important that they know we support them.

**Admitted:** Yes

**Status considered in admissions:** No

**Special admissions process:** No

**Eligible for institutional financial aid:** Yes. Must demonstrate need. Contact the financial aid office for more information.

**Specific programs/policies to address needs:** In collaboration with faculty, staff, and departments across the university, the Reves Center provides support and advocacy for DACA students at W&M. Reves Center works closely with the law firm McCandlish Holton of Richmond to provide support and assistance to DACA students on campus, including:

- Workshops/information sessions for DACA students (free)
- Answering individual questions (free)
- Comprehensive consultations and/or representation of individual students (reduced fee)

# COLORADO COLLEGE

**Location:** Colorado Springs, Colorado
**Website:** www.coloradocollege.edu
**Endowment:** $683.2 million
**Type of School:** Private/Co-ed, Liberal Arts
**# of Undergraduate Students:** 2,101
**# of Graduate Students:** 13
**Average Class Size:** 16

**School Mission (in their own words):** At Colorado College our goal is to provide the finest liberal arts education in the country. Drawing upon the adventurous spirit of the Rocky Mountain West, we challenge students, one course at a time, to develop those habits of intellect and imagination that will prepare them for learning and leadership throughout their lives.

## Admissions

**Admissions office mailing address:** 14 E Cache La Poudre St, Colorado Springs CO 80903
**Admissions office phone:** (719) 389-6344
**Admissions office email:** admission@coloradocollege.edu
**# of transfer applications:** Fall 2016 admissions: 572. Spring 2017 admissions: No information provided.
**# of transfer students accepted:** Fall 2016: 55. Spring 2017: No information provided.
**Transfer student acceptance rate (2016–2017 academic year):** 9.6%
**Freshman applications received in Fall 2016:** 7,894
**Freshman applications accepted in Fall 2016:** 1,262
**Acceptance rate for 2016–2017 freshmen:** 16%

## Transfer Admissions Process

**Transfer policy:** N/A
**Transfer admissions contact person:** William Schiffelbein, Assistant Director
**Transfer admissions contact Info:** william.schiffelbein@ coloradocollege.edu, (719) 389-7994
**Offers transfer-focused admissions events:** Yes
**Transfer application deadline:** Fall 2018 deadline is 3/1/18. Spring 2019 deadline is 11/7/18.
**Acceptances announced to transfer applicants:** Fall 2018 in late April. Spring 2019 in early December.
**Transfer application on Common App:** Yes. Common App fee: $60.
**SAT/ACT required for transfer applicants:** Yes, but only if they were required for entry to the student's current college/ university
**High-school records requirements:** Must submit official final high-school transcript.
**High-school records requirements for applicants who completed outside the US:** Must submit official transcript with a translation if written in a different language.

**Submission requirements for transfer applicants who completed high-school equivalency test:** Official GED scores must be submitted.
**College transcript requirements:** Must submit official transfer college transcript (from college registrar).
**Interviews available for transfer applicants:** Yes. Optional, but recommended. On campus and off campus (off-campus interviews are done with alumni).
**Additional requirements for transfers seeking admissions to arts major:** Yes. Students interested in the arts can submit an optional art supplement in visual art, music, dance, theater, creative writing, or film. Art supplements will be included in a student's application for consideration as part of our holistic review process.

## Costs & Financial Aid

**FAFSA code:** 1347
**CSS Profile code:** 4072
**Are internal school financial aid forms required?** No
**Financial aid deadlines for transfer applicants:** Fall 2018: 3/1/18. Spring 2019: 11/15/18.
**Costs for the 2017–2018 year:** Tuition: $52,380. Fees: $438. Room & Board: $12,256.
**Financial aid for transfer students:** Yes
**Guarantees meeting 100% need for transfer students:** Yes
**Need-based aid for transfer students:** Yes
**Merit-based financial aid for transfer students:** No
**Phi Theta Kappa Scholarship:** No
**Reduced or zero tuition fees for low-income students:** No
**Includes loans in financial aid packages:** Yes
**% of all undergraduates receiving financial aid:** 35%
**% of all undergraduates qualifying for Pell Grants:** No information provided.
**Average financial aid award for all undergraduate students:** $46,024
**Funding available for low-income students to visit:** Yes
**Enrollment deposit can be waived for low-income students:** Yes

## Academics

**GPA range for transfer students accepted in 2016–2017:** No information provided.

**SAT ranges for all students admitted in 2016:** Critical Reading: 610–730. Mathematics: 620–720. Writing: 620–710.

**ACT composite score range for all students admitted in 2016:** 28–32

**Recommended extracurricular engagement:** While there is no ideal extracurricular profile for a Colorado College applicant, we appreciate students who have cultivated nonacademic pursuits that complement their classroom achievements. Generally speaking, we are looking for sustained commitment to a few interests (possibly achieving leadership positions within those activities) rather than sporadic participation in various pursuits each year.

**Type of curriculum:** Gen. Ed. requirements

**Type of academic year:** Semester

**Advisors specifically for transfer students:** Yes

**Credit policy (in their own words):** Colorado College does accept transfer credit for previous work done by a student. The following is a set of guidelines used in the transfer and awarding of academic credit from an accredited institution or approved program:

- To earn credit at Colorado College, all transfer credit must come from a regionally accredited, degree-granting college or university (including community colleges) or a program pre-approved by the Office of International & Off-Campus Programs for off-campus study and exchanges.
- Students who have completed work at other colleges and who wish to have this work credited toward a CC degree must have official transcripts from those colleges sent directly to the registrar at Colorado College. Course descriptions/syllabi for each course may also be requested.
- Students who wish to complete a semester abroad or study away as domestic exchange students must receive approval from the Office of International & Off-Campus Programs, department chairs or program directors, and the Registrar's Office for all coursework prior to enrolling.
- A letter grade of C– or higher is required to earn transfer credit. D+ and below will not earn transfer credit at Colorado College. Courses for which a Pass or Satisfactory was earned at another college will earn credit at Colorado College ONLY if the college can provide verification that the student passed with a letter grade of C– or higher.
- Courses must be substantially similar to Colorado College courses and cannot duplicate, overlap, or regress from previous work.
- One Colorado College unit is equivalent to 4 semester hours, or 6 quarter hours.

**Max number of transfer credits accepted:** 16 units

**Residency requirement for transfer students:** Yes. All students must complete 32 units of credit to qualify for a Colorado College B.A. degree. As described below, a specified number of the 32 units must be taken in residence, here at Colorado College, or through Colorado College programs and exchanges, including the ACM semester programs, detailed elsewhere in this catalog.

The following rule applies to the academic residence requirement: transfer students are required to complete a minimum of 16 units at Colorado College or Colorado College programs and exchanges, including the ACM semester programs.

**Study abroad available for transfer students:** Yes. Must fulfill the residency requirements.

**Free tutoring for all students:** Yes

**Writing center for all students:** Yes

**Career support/access to internships and resume prep for all students:** Yes

**% of undergraduate students hired within 6 months of graduation:** 86% of 2010 graduates responding to survey questions on employment reported having been employed, and 91% of 2011 graduates were found to be employed.

**Additional resources specifically designated for transfer and/or non-traditional students:** Yes. The CC Transfer Mentor Program aims to actively engage incoming transfers in the CC community through peer-led support in the realms of academic, social, and extracurricular activities.

## Housing

**Available for transfer students:** Yes

**Available for non-traditional students:** Yes

**Guaranteed for transfer students:** Yes

**Non-traditional students can reside in housing year-round:** No

**Family housing available:** No

## Non-Traditional Admissions

**Non-traditional student policy (in their own words):** Colorado College has always evaluated candidates for admission on an individual basis. In recent years, we have been asked about our policies regarding homeschooling, narrative transcripts, portfolio assessment, and other non-traditional approaches to a standard high-school transcript. Students presenting non-traditional transcripts are still a very small percentage of our applicant pool, but they are not disadvantaged in the admission process. Since Colorado College does not require an official high-school diploma or GED for admission consideration, we have had students apply after 3 years of high school and we have had students with some combination of high-school record and other kinds of assessments. More recently, applicants have included homeschooled students and those enrolled in alternative school programs.

With our individual assessment of all students, we look at 4 things. Those 4 things are: academic information, application information, recommendations, and tests scores. To learn more: www.coloradocollege.edu/admission/application/firstyear/nontraditional.

## Military/Veteran Students

**Military/veteran admissions policy (in their own words):** Beginning with the 2013–2014 academic year, Colorado College agreed to participate in the Yellow Ribbon Program. Eligible students are expected to complete our Application for Veteran Education Benefits and the Statement of Understanding and submit to the certifying official in the Registrar's Office.

New students will be accepted on a first come, first served basis or placed on a waitlist, if necessary. Only admitted students' applications will be accepted or placed on the waitlist.

Colorado College offers 9 undergraduates $7,000 matched by the VA's contribution of $7,000 (total of $14,000) and 6 graduate students $5,000 matched by the VA's contribution of $5,000 (total $10,000). The Yellow Ribbon benefit is in addition to the VA education benefit of $21,970.46 for the academic year, 2016–2017.

**Status considered in admissions:** No

**Special admissions process:** No

**Special financial aid:** Yes. The Yellow Ribbon Program.

**Specific programs/policies to address needs:** No information provided.

## DACA/Undocumented Students

**DACA and undocumented admissions policy (in their own words):** At Colorado College, all applicants, regardless of citizenship, will be considered for admission. Admission is highly competitive, with a 16% overall admit rate for the class of 2020. We guarantee to meet full demonstrated need of every admitted student. In the case of DACA and undocumented students, this is accomplished using private grant aid from the college.

For more information about funding and support for DACA and undocumented students in the US, please visit the NASFA Tip Sheet for Undocumented Students.

Please contact Cari Hanrahan, Senior Assistant Director of Admission, with questions at cari.hanrahan@coloradocollege.edu.

We will be posting more information on how to submit the application, how to list your citizenship status, and how to apply for financial aid in the near future.

**Admitted:** Yes

**Status considered in admissions:** No

**Special admissions process:** No

**Eligible for institutional financial aid:** Yes. DACA students who are interested in applying for financial aid at CC should complete a College Board CSS/Financial Aid Profile form. They should submit signed copies of parents' and student's federal income tax returns (including all pages, schedules, and forms) and parents' and student's W-2 forms to the Financial Aid Office.

**Specific programs/policies to address needs:** Yes. The Butler Center is the hub of diversity, inclusion, intercultural exchange, equity, and empowerment for the Colorado College community. These students are encouraged to connect with The Butler Center and its programming while at CC.

# COLUMBIA UNIVERSITY

**Location:** New York, New York

**Website:** www.columbia.edu

**Endowment:** $9.6 billion

**Type of School:** Private/Co-ed, Research University

**# of Undergraduate Students:** 8,712

**# of Graduate Students:** 22,605

**Average Class Size:** No standard number. Core curriculum courses are capped at 22 students.

**School Mission (in their own words):** Columbia University is one of the world's most important centers of research and at the same time a distinctive and distinguished learning environment for undergraduates and graduate students in many scholarly and professional fields. The University recognizes the importance of its location in New York City and seeks to link its research and teaching to the vast resources of a great metropolis. It seeks to attract a diverse and international faculty and student body, to support research and teaching on global issues, and to create academic relationships with many countries and regions. It expects all areas of the university to advance knowledge and learning at the highest level and to convey the products of its efforts to the world.

## Admissions

**Admissions office mailing Address:** 212 Hamilton Hall, Mail Code 2807, New York NY 10027

**Admissions office phone:** (212) 854-2522

**Admissions office email:** ugrad-transfer@columbia.edu

**# of transfer applications:** Fall 2016 admissions: 2,444

**# of transfer students accepted:** Fall 2016: 204

**Transfer student acceptance rate (2016–2017 academic year):** 8.4%

**Freshman applications received in Fall 2016:** 36,292

**Freshman applications accepted in Fall 2016:** 2,279

**Acceptance rate for 2016–2017 freshmen:** 6.3%

## Transfer Admissions Process

**Transfer policy (in their own words):** Columbia College and Columbia Engineering are the undergraduate divisions of Columbia University; both serve full-time students only. Potential applicants to Columbia College who have taken a break of more than a full year in their educations after high school (with the exception of those who must complete national military service) or those who wish to attend part-time for personal or professional reasons should consider instead Columbia University School of General Studies. Potential applicants to Columbia Engineering should proceed with this transfer application regardless of any break in schooling. To be eligible to enroll as a transfer student at Columbia, you must have completed, or be registered for, 24 points of credit (the equivalent of 1 year of full-time study) at another institution, as well as have earned a high-school diploma or equivalent (by the application deadline). Candidates with more than 4 semesters of college coursework elsewhere are not encouraged to apply. Columbia's academic requirements and institutional policies make completion of all graduation requirements in a reasonable and timely fashion unlikely. International students should read our International Transfer Students section.

If you left high school without receiving a diploma in order to attend an early college program, you are not eligible for transfer admission and must apply as a first-year student by the appropriate Early Decision or Regular Decision deadline. You will not be eligible to receive credit for such accelerated programs except for credit earned through standardized examinations (e.g., AP and IB exams); such credit will be limited to 16 points, the equivalent of 1 full semester at Columbia.

**Transfer admissions contact person:** N/A

**Transfer admissions contact info:** N/A

**Offers transfer-focused admissions events:** Yes

**Transfer application deadline:** Fall 2018 deadline is 3/1/18.

**Acceptances announced to transfer applicants:** Fall 2018 on 5/15/18.

**Transfer application on Common App:** Yes. Common App fee: $85.

**SAT/ACT required for transfer applicants:** Yes

**High-school records requirements:** An official high-school transcript from all schools attended and the Common Application Secondary School Final Report

**High-school records requirements for applicants who completed outside the US:** Any documents that are part of your application file and not in English, such as transcripts or recommendations, need to be officially translated into English and submitted along with the original documents.

**Submission requirements for transfer applicants who completed high-school equivalency test:** A GED or TASC credential with a passing score may be submitted.

**College transcript requirements:** Official transcripts from all colleges and universities attended

**Interviews available for transfer applicants:** No

**Additional requirements for transfers seeking admissions to engineering major:** No. If you are applying to the Fu Foundation School of Engineering and Applied Science (Columbia Engineering), we would certainly hope to see strong math and science preparation (calculus, chemistry, physics, etc.). Columbia Engineering recommends that prospective transfers follow a course of study similar to our First Year-Sophomore program.

## Costs & Financial Aid

**FAFSA code:** 2707

**CSS Profile code:** 2116

**Are internal school financial aid forms required?** No

**Financial aid deadline for transfer applicants:** Fall 2018: 3/1/18

**Costs for the 2017–2018 year:** Tuition & Fees: $55,056. Room & Board: $13,244.

**Financial aid for transfer students:** Yes

**Guarantees meeting 100% need for transfer students:** Yes

**Need-based aid for transfer students:** Yes. All transfer applicants who are citizens or permanent residents of the US or students granted refugee visas by the US are read in a need-blind manner. Foreign students applying for aid must understand that such aid is awarded on an extremely limited basis. Columbia meets 100% of demonstrated financial need for admitted transfer students, and Columbia does not give any scholarships for academic, athletic, or artistic merit.

**Merit-based financial aid for transfer students:** No

**Phi Theta Kappa Scholarship:** Yes, for the School of General Studies. $6,000–$8,000. Renewable. Details available at https://gs.columbia.edu/special-scholarships.

**Reduced or zero tuition fees for low-income students:** No

**Includes loans in financial aid packages:** No

**% of all undergraduates receiving financial aid:** 50%

**% of all undergraduates qualifying for Pell Grants:** 16%

**Average financial aid award for all undergraduate students:** $47,490

**Funding available for low-income students to visit:** No information provided.

**Enrollment deposit can be waived for low-income students:** No information provided.

## Academics

**GPA range for transfer students accepted in 2016–2017:** 3.5

**SAT ranges for all students admitted in 2016:** Critical Reading: 730–790. Mathematics: 720–800. Writing: No information provided.

**ACT composite score range for all students admitted in 2016:** 31–35

**Recommended extracurricular engagement:** We encourage you to convey the breadth and depth of your extracurricular pursuits within the Activities section of your admission application, including the full name of each organization in which you participate and, if appropriate, a brief description of your involvement.

**Type of curriculum:** Gen. Ed. requirement

**Type of academic year:** Semester

**Advisors specifically for transfer students:** Yes

**Credit policy (in their own words):** At least 124 points are required for graduation from Columbia College; at least 128 are required for graduation from Columbia Engineering. Since Columbia requires that a minimum of 60 points toward the degree be earned at Columbia, you may not enter with more than 64 points in Columbia College or with more than 68 points in Columbia Engineering. Up to 16 points granted on the basis of Advanced Placement, International Baccalaureate, or other standardized examinations will count toward the 64/68 point maximum (official score reports are required). Note that Columbia University does not grant credit for any college courses that you took before graduating from high school.

**Max number of transfer credits accepted:** 64 credits for Columbia College; 68 credits for Columbia Engineering

**Residency requirement for transfer students:** Yes. 60–68.

**Study abroad available for transfer students:** Yes. Your ability to study abroad depends quite a bit on your class standing when you enter Columbia and your remaining degree requirements. If you enter Columbia as a sophomore, the possibility of studying abroad is greater. If you enter Columbia as a junior, it is unlikely that you will be able to study abroad. Regardless of your class standing, this is a conversation you should have with your academic adviser as soon as possible.

**Free tutoring for all students:** Yes

**Writing center for all students:** Yes

**Career support/access to internships and resume prep for all students:** Yes

**% of undergraduate students hired within 6 months of graduation:** No information provided.

**Additional resources specifically designated for transfer and/or non-traditional students:** Yes. Transfer students will enjoy a number of transfer-specific academic and social programs, including brunches, student panels, advising sessions, and joint outings in the city with Barnard and Columbia transfer students. Your orientation group of 10–12 students will consist only of transfer, Combined Plan, and visiting students. In addition, most social events during orientation are open to transfers, as well as first-year students. You will receive transfer orientation highlights in the packet sent to you in the summer.

## Housing

**Available for transfer students:** Yes

**Available for non-traditional students:** Yes

**Guaranteed for transfer students:** Yes

**Non-traditional students can reside in housing year-round:** Yes

**Family housing available:** Yes

## Non-Traditional Admissions

**Non-traditional student policy (in their own words):** General Studies (GS) identifies non-traditional students as those who have had at least a 1-year break in their educational history since high school, those who have a compelling reason to attend part-time or those who are taking a non-traditional academic path through one of GS's joint/dual degree programs. It is important to note that whether a student has a 1-year break or a 10-year break, most students who choose GS usually see themselves as being more mature and independent than traditional students.

**Name of program:** School of General Studies

**Program description:** Columbia University School of General Studies (GS) is the undergraduate college created specifically for students with non-traditional backgrounds who, after a break of a year or more in their educational paths, are now seeking a rigorous, traditional, Ivy League education. Most students at GS, for personal or professional reasons, have interrupted their education, have never attended college, or are only able to attend part-time.

Whether you've taken time off for personal reasons, parenthood, travel, or your career, the School of General Studies—Columbia University's college for returning and non-traditional students—makes it possible for you to complete your degree at one of the finest institutions in the country. In fact, Columbia is the only Ivy League university with a freestanding college in which non-traditional undergraduates are fully integrated into the undergraduate curriculum.

Because the average age of GS students is 27, they usually have 8 to 10 more years of experience in life than traditional college students. That means that diversity at Columbia is not only measured by ethnicity and gender, but also by experience and maturity—a maturity we find leads to great academic success. At GS, you'll join a community of students who after graduation go on to pursue advanced degrees and lead stimulating professional lives. What defines our students as non-traditional is that GS students have taken breaks of 1 year or more in their educational paths. Despite these differences, GS students take the same courses as all other Columbia undergraduates, are taught by the same professors in the same classes, and are fully integrated into Columbia's undergraduate curriculum.

**Program deadline:** Early action: March 1

**Regular decision:** June 1

**Program admission requirements:**

- Application
- Official high-school transcripts, secondary school records, or GED/TASC test results. Applicants with a GED or TASC and 2 or more years of high school will need to submit their high-school transcripts.
- Official transcripts from all colleges or universities attended
- Official test scores (SAT, ACT, or General Studies Admissions Examination if the SAT/ACT scores are more than 8 years old for native English speakers/those whose secondary education was in English; TOEFL, IELTS, or the Duolingo English Test for non-native English speakers/those whose secondary instruction was in another language other than English)
- One typed, double-spaced essay of approximately 1,500–2,000 words. See the Application for Admission for essay question.
- Two letters of recommendation from academic and/or professional sources
- A nonrefundable application fee of $80 in the form of a check or money order payable to Columbia University. Applicants using the online application may use a credit card to pay the $80 fee.

## New Student Scholarship Application

**Program website:** https://gs.columbia.edu

**Program contact person:** Matthew Rotstein, Director of Admissions

**Program contact info:** (212) 854-2772, mr2185@columbia.edu

## Military/Veteran Students

**Military/veteran admissions policy (in their own words):** GS is a proud participant of the US Department of Veterans Affairs' Yellow Ribbon Program. The scope of benefits provided by the Post 9/11 GI Bill and the Yellow Ribbon Program helps make a traditional Columbia education accessible to eligible veterans, regardless of socioeconomic status, who wish to pursue a rigorous undergraduate degree program.

**Status considered in admissions:** Yes

**Special admissions process:** Yes. Veterans should apply to the Columbia School of General Studies.

**Special financial aid:** Yes. The Yellow Ribbon Program.

**Specific programs/policies to address needs:** MilVets, student veterans association

## Veterans Liaison

Time off for active duty: Any student who is a member of the National Guard or other reserve component of the armed forces of the United States or of the state-organized militia and is called or ordered to active duty will be granted a military leave of absence for the period of active duty and for 1 year thereafter.

Upon return from military leave of absence, the student will be restored to the educational status attained prior to being called or ordered to such duty without loss of academic credits earned, scholarships or grants awarded, or tuition or other fees paid prior to the commencement of active duty. The University will credit any tuition or fees paid for the period of the military leave of absence to the next enrollment period or will refund the tuition and fees paid to the student, at the student's option.

## DACA/Undocumented Students

**DACA and undocumented admissions policy (in their own words):** Columbia University is one of the most diverse college campuses nationwide, with a long history of civic engagement, activism, and access. With one of the most generous financial aid programs in the nation, Columbia University is committed to removing barriers to college access.

Columbia's admissions application process is largely the same for all students regardless of their citizenship or country of residence.

Undocumented students are eligible for the same need-blind admissions policy as US citizens, permanent residents, and eligible non-citizens, which means we evaluate admissions applications without regard to financial need.

Columbia University is committed to meeting 100% of the demonstrated financial need of all students admitted as first-years or transfer students pursuing their first degree, regardless of citizenship status. International students, including undocumented students, are not eligible to receive federal and state financial aid, so Columbia meets their full need entirely from institutional resources.

**Admitted:** Yes

**Status considered in admissions:** No

**Special admissions process:** No

**Eligible for institutional financial aid:** Yes. Undocumented students are eligible for the same need-blind admissions policy as US citizens, permanent residents, and eligible non-citizens, which means we evaluate admissions applications without regard to financial need.

International students, including undocumented students, are not eligible to receive federal and state financial aid, so Columbia meets their full need entirely from institutional resources.

**Specific programs/policies to address needs:** If the Deferred Action for Childhood Arrival (DACA) policy is terminated or substantially curtailed and students with DACA status lose the right to work, the University pledges to expand the financial aid and other support we make available to undocumented students, regardless of their immigration status.

# CONNECTICUT COLLEGE

**Location:** New London, Connecticut
**Website:** www.conncoll.edu
**Endowment:** $283 million (2015)
**Type of School:** Private/Co-ed, Liberal Arts
**# of Undergraduate Students:** 1,865
**# of Graduate Students:** 0

**Average Class Size:** 18
**School Mission (in their own words):** Connecticut College educates students to put the liberal arts into action as citizens in a global society.

## Admissions

**Admissions office mailing Address:** 270 Mohegan Ave, New London CT 06320

**Admissions office phone:** (860) 439-2200

**Admissions office email:** admission@conncoll.edu

**# of transfer applications:** Fall 2016 admissions: 143. Spring 2017 admissions: No information provided.

**# of transfer students accepted:** Fall 2016: 63. Spring 2017: No information provided.

**Transfer student acceptance rate (2016–2017 academic year):** 44.1%

**Freshman applications received in Fall 2016:** 5,879

**Freshman applications accepted in Fall 2016:** 2,065

**Acceptance rate for 2016–2017 freshmen:** 35%

## Transfer Admissions Process

**Transfer policy (in their own words):** To be considered for transfer admission, you must complete at least 1 semester at an accredited college or university, and it is recommended that you maintain a minimum 3.0 GPA. Financial aid is available for transfer applicants, but very limited aid is available for foreign citizens.

**Transfer admissions contact person:** Deb Wright, Director of Admissions and Transfer Admissions

**Transfer admissions contact info:** deborah.wright@conncoll.edu

**Offers transfer-focused admissions events:** Yes

**Transfer application deadline:** Fall 2018 deadline is 4/1/18. Spring 2019 deadline is 11/1/18.

**Acceptances announced to transfer applicants:** Fall 2018 in mid-May. Spring 2019 in December.

**Transfer application on Common App:** Yes. Common App fee: $60.

**SAT/ACT required for transfer applicants:** No

**High-school records requirements:** Official final high-school transcript

**High-school records requirements for applicants who completed outside the US:** An official record of secondary (or higher secondary) school work with all courses and grades, including results (or probable results) of final examinations. An explanation of the grading system used by your school should be provided on the International Supplement.

**Submission requirements for transfer applicants who completed high-school equivalency test:** Official GED scores required.

**College transcript requirements:** Official transcript(s) of all college work to date

**Interviews available for transfer applicants:** Yes. Optional, but highly recommended. On campus with an admissions advisor or off campus with either a traveling admissions counselor or an alumnus.

## Costs & Financial Aid

**FAFSA code:** 1379

**CSS Profile code:** 3284

**Are internal school financial aid forms required?** No

**Financial aid deadlines for transfer applicants:** Fall 2018: 3/31/18. Spring 2019: 11/1/18.

**Costs for the 2017–2018 year:** Tuition & Fees: The comprehensive fee for 2016–17 is $65,000. This covers tuition, room and board, lab fees, studio fees, special programs, some course-related travel, study away, and even music lessons. Room & Board: Included in the comprehensive fee.

**Financial aid for transfer students:** Yes

**Guarantees meeting 100% need for transfer students:** Yes

**Need-based aid for transfer students:** Yes

**Merit-based financial aid for transfer students:** No

**Phi Theta Kappa Scholarship:** No

**Reduced or zero tuition fees for low-income students:** No

**Includes loans in financial aid packages:** Yes

**% of all undergraduates receiving financial aid:** 54%

**% of all undergraduates qualifying for Pell Grants:** No information provided.

**Average financial aid award for all undergraduate students:** $38,709

**Funding available for low-income students to visit:** No information provided.

**Enrollment deposit can be waived for low-income students:** No information provided.

## Academics

**GPA range for transfer students accepted in 2016–2017:** No information provided.

**SAT ranges for all students admitted in 2016:** Critical Reading: 690–740. Mathematics: 680–720. Writing: 690–730.

**ACT composite score range for all students admitted in 2016:** 31–33

**Type of curriculum:** Gen. Ed. requirements

**Type of academic year:** Semester

**Advisors specifically for transfer students:** Yes

**Credit policy (in their own words):** College-level courses completed prior to matriculation at Connecticut College may be transferable, subject to an evaluation conducted by the Office of the Registrar. First-year and transfer applicants are required to submit transcripts for all coursework to the Office of Admission as part of the application process. Transfer students, in most cases, will receive their transfer credit determination upon admission. First-year students who believe they have transfer-eligible coursework for which credit was not awarded should contact the Office of the Registrar to request its review. Further questions about transfer admission should be directed to the Office of Admission.

Online courses taken prior to matriculation are not eligible for transfer.

Transfer credit may be awarded for courses taken prior to matriculation if, upon review by the Registrar's Office, they are found to have an approximate counterpart in the Connecticut College curriculum and were completed with grades of C or better.

Courses taken prior to enrollment at the College, including prior to secondary school graduation, must meet all of the following criteria:

- Completed on a college campus
- Completed in a class with matriculated college students
- Were not used to satisfy any high-school graduation requirements

**Max number of transfer credits accepted:** 64 credits

**Residency requirement for transfer students:** Yes. Must complete at least 64 credits toward the degree at Connecticut College.

**Study abroad available for transfer students:** Yes. Must fulfill residency requirements.

**Free tutoring for all students:** Yes

**Writing center for all students:** Yes

**Career support/access to internships and resume prep for all students:** Yes

**% of undergraduate students hired within 6 months of graduation:** 96%

**Additional resources specifically designated for transfer and/or non-traditional students:** No

## Housing

**Available for transfer students:** Yes

**Available for non-traditional students:** No

**Guaranteed for transfer students:** Yes

**Non-traditional students can reside in housing year-round:** N/A

**Family housing available:** No

## Non-Traditional Admissions

**Non-traditional student policy (In their own words):** The Return to College (RTC) program is open to adult learners, 25 years or older, whose undergraduate education was interrupted and who now propose to finish a bachelor of arts degree by enrolling in 12 or fewer credits per semester, instead of the traditional 16. All applicants must have successfully completed at least 1 year of college level work or the equivalent.

**Name of program:** The Return to College Program

**Program description:** RTC students are helped by specific advisors who guide them throughout their time at the college. The students also have the option to take fewer than 16 credits.

**Program deadline:** The deadline for Fall semester is 4/1/18, with a notification by mid-May. The deadline for Spring semester is 12/1/18, with notification by mid-December.

**Program admission requirements:** Students who are US citizens 25 years or older, whose undergraduate education was interrupted and who now propose to finish a bachelor of arts degree

**Program website:** www.conncoll.edu/academics/graduate-study-non-traditional-programs/return-to-college-rtc

**Program contact person:** Cynthia Goheen, Associate Director of Admission and Coordinator of Transfer Admission

**Program contact info:** (860) 439-2200, cynthia.goheen@conncoll.edu

## Military/Veteran Students

**Military/veteran admissions policy (in their own words):** Connecticut College values the perspectives and contributions of those who have served our country in the military. We welcome applications from veterans who may wish to finish a bachelor of arts degree through our Return to College program. Veterans with questions should email Cynthia Goheen at cynthia.goheen@conncoll.edu.

**Status considered in admissions:** No

**Special admissions process:** Yes. Students are recommended to apply through the RTC program.

**Special financial aid:** Yes. The Yellow Ribbon Program.

**Specific programs/policies to address needs:** The RTC program is open to adult learners 25 years or older, whose undergraduate education was interrupted and who now propose to finish a bachelor of arts degree by enrolling in 12 or fewer credits per semester, instead of the traditional 16.

## DACA/Undocumented Students

**DACA and undocumented admissions policy (in their own words):** N/A

**Admitted:** Yes

**Status considered in admissions:** No

**Special admissions process:** No

**Eligible for institutional financial aid:** Yes. Limited need-based aid is available.

**Specific programs/policies to address needs:** Yes. Bridget Moore, the Associate Director of Admission and Coordinator of International Admission, works with these students and provides guidance.

# CORNELL UNIVERSITY

**Location:** Ithaca, New York

**Website:** www.cornell.edu

**Endowment:** $5.758 billion

**Type of School:** Private/Co-ed, Research University

**# of Undergraduate Students:** 14,566

**# of Graduate Students:** 7,753

**Average Class Size:** Under 30 students; varies at a large scale.

**School Mission (in their own words):** Learning. Discovery. Engagement. Cornell is a private Ivy League university and the land-grant university for New York State. Cornell's mission is to discover, preserve, and disseminate knowledge; produce creative work; and promote a culture of broad inquiry throughout and beyond the Cornell community. Cornell also aims, through public service, to enhance the lives and livelihoods of our students, the people of New York, and others around the world.

## Admissions

**Admissions office mailing address:** 144 East Ave, Ithaca NY 14853

**Admissions office phone:** (607) 255-5241

**Admissions office email:** admissions@cornell.edu

**# of transfer applications:** Fall 2016 admissions: 4,248. Spring 2017 admissions: No information provided.

**# of transfer students accepted:** Fall 2016: 831. Spring 2017: No information provided.

**Transfer student acceptance rate (2016–2017 academic year):** 19.5%

**Freshman applications received in Fall 2016:** 44,965

**Freshman applications accepted in Fall 2016:** 6,337

**Acceptance rate for 2016–2017 freshmen:** 14%

## Transfer Admissions Process

**Transfer policy (in their own words):** You must apply to Cornell as a transfer student if you've graduated from high school and have earned 12 or more credits at another college or university since then. If you are enrolled as a full-time student at another institution, you are also considered a transfer applicant.

**Transfer admissions contact person:** N/A

**Transfer admissions contact info:** transfer@cornell.edu

**Offers transfer-focused admissions events:** Yes

**Transfer application deadline:** Fall 2018 deadline is 3/15/18. Spring 2019 deadline is 10/15/18.

**Acceptances announced to transfer applicants:** Fall 2018 in May–June. Spring 2019 in November.

**Transfer application on Common App:** Yes. Common App fee: $80.

**SAT/ACT required for transfer applicants:** If you have previously taken the SAT or ACT, you should have an official score report sent to Cornell by the testing agency. It is not necessary to take the SAT or ACT if you have not previously done so.

**SAT II scores required for transfer applicants:** Yes

**High-school record requirements:** Official high school transcript

**High-school records requirements for applicants who completed outside the US:** We want to review at least 3 years of secondary school records that list subjects you studied and marks received for each subject. State or national tests or other external exams taken should be included also.

**Submission requirements for transfer applicants who completed high-school equivalency test:** Official GED report

**College transcript requirements:** Official transcripts from all colleges and universities attended

**Interviews available for transfer applicants:** Yes, for some of the schools. Required for some of Cornell's schools. The programs that do require or offer an interview are:

- College of Architecture, Art, and Planning—an interview is required for architecture applicants and is strongly recommended for fine arts applicants.
- School of Hotel Administration—offers an interview.

**Additional requirements for transfers seeking admissions to business school:** School of Hotel Administration: Although we do not specify transfer course requirements, we recommend transfer applicants complete the following:

- Chemistry with a lab component taken in either high school or college
- Three years of 1 foreign language in high school and/or college
- Math or quantitative courses, including a minimum of pre-calculus in high school or college
- A broad range of general education and introductory business courses in economics, writing, and accounting
- Hospitality-related work experience

**Additional requirements for transfers seeking admissions to arts major:** Yes. Architecture, Art, and Planning.

**Architecture:** Applicants to the B.Arch. program may submit their portfolio either online via Cornell AAP SlideRoom (preferred) or in hard copy. The content of the portfolio remains the same regardless of the format of submission. Samples of freehand drawing are required. In addition to drawings, please include a variety of work from media such as painting, sculpture, graphics, art photography, woodworking, ceramics, or any other visual media that demonstrate interest, experience, and aptitude in creative and graphic areas.

Please submit 15–20 items and present the material in a neat, well-organized manner.

**Art:** Applicants must submit their portfolios online at Cornell AAP SlideRoom. The portfolio should consist of high-quality images of 18–20 pieces of work, including at least 4 examples of freehand observational drawing. The portfolio should contain examples of work from at least 3 of the department's studio practice areas: drawing, digital media, painting, photography, print media, and sculpture. Applicants should choose the media that best reflects their highest level of skill and conceptual development. While there is no requirement that any particular subject or style of work be included in the portfolio, the faculty admissions committee would like to see a selection of work that has been made both independently and in school or workshop settings.

**Additional requirements for transfers seeking admissions to engineering major:** Yes. Specific courses for each major can be found here: www.engineering.cornell.edu/admissions/undergraduate/transfer/requirements.cfm.

**Additional requirements for transfers seeking admissions to other major:** Yes, required coursework for the majors in the College of Agriculture and Life Sciences can be found here: https://admissions.cals.cornell.edu/apply/transfer/requirements. Required coursework for the College of Human Ecology can be found here: www.human.cornell.edu/admissions/upload/Transfer-Coursework-requirements-2018.pdf.

Required coursework for the School of Industrial and Labor Relations can be found here: www.ilr.cornell.edu/sites/ilr.cornell.edu/files/Curriculum%20Requirements_0.pdf.

## Costs & Financial Aid

**FAFSA code:** 2711

**CSS Profile code:** 2098

**Are internal school financial aid forms required?** No

**Financial aid deadlines for transfer applicants:** Fall 2018: 2/15/18. Spring 2019: 10/15/18.

**Costs for the 2017–2018 year:** Tuition & Fees: $52,853. Room & Board: $14,330.

**Financial aid for transfer students:** Yes

**Guarantees meeting 100% need for transfer students:** Yes

**Need-based aid for transfer students:** Yes

**Merit-based financial aid for transfer students:** No, Cornell does not offer merit-based aid to any undergraduate student.

**Phi Theta Kappa Scholarship:** No

**Reduced or zero tuition fees for low-income students:** No

**Includes loans in financial aid packages:** Yes

**% of all undergraduates receiving financial aid:** Nearly 50%

**% of all undergraduates qualifying for Pell Grants:** No information provided.

**Average financial aid award for all undergraduate students:** $39,787—average need-based scholarship/grant award.

**Funding available for low-income students to visit:** No information provided.

**Enrollment deposit can be waived for low-income students:** No information provided.

## Academics

**GPA range for transfer students accepted in 2016–2017:** Most successful applicants will have a 3.0 or better; there is no range or average.

**SAT ranges for all students admitted in 2016:** Critical Reading: 650–750. Mathematics: 680–780. Writing: 650–750.

**ACT composite score range for all students admitted in 2016:** 31–34

**Recommended completed level of math for transfer applicants:** Mathematics courses at the level of calculus or above normally transfer if they are equivalent to Cornell courses.

**Recommended completed level of English for transfer applicants:** Almost all freshmen in the College of Arts and Sciences take a first-year writing seminar during their first semester at Cornell. There are high standards for these courses—visit the Writing Program website to learn how courses taken elsewhere might transfer.

**Recommended courses transfer applicants should have on transcripts:** The recommended courses vary by which school you would like to be a part of. Here's a link that explains the recommended courses for each school: https://admissions.cornell.edu/sites/admissions.cornell.edu/files/2017%20Transfer%20Requirements.pdf.

**Recommended courses transfer applicants interested in STEM should complete before transfer:** The recommended courses depend on which science major the student would like to study. In order to get more information, a student should visit the specific website of their preferred major or call the department.

**Type of curriculum:** Gen. Ed. requirements

**Type of academic year:** Semester

**Advisors specifically for transfer students:** Yes. During the admissions process, Reba McCutcheon.

**Credit Policy (in their own words):** The number of transferrable credits depends upon the college, but in general the following applies: The Registrar's Office manages the transfer credit process in coordination with the Directors of Undergraduate Studies in the College. Transfer students are required to complete all degree requirements with at least 60 credits of coursework from Cornell University. Thus, a maximum of 60 hours in transfer credit, for courses with a grade of C– or above may be allowed from other accredited colleges or universities.

Cornell University does not accept credit for courses sponsored by colleges but taught in high school to high-school students, even if the college provides a transcript of such work.

Students must submit an official transcript from all institutions in which transfer credit is being requested. Courses with a grade of C– or above will be considered for transfer.

A syllabus for each course containing the information below should be submitted for review:

- Syllabus must cover 80% of the material covered in the Cornell course.
- Syllabus must use a standard textbook equivalent to that used in a Cornell course.
- Syllabus must include examinations, writing, projects, or other submitted work, produced individually or collectively, that is roughly as extensive as that required in the equivalent Cornell course.
- Syllabus must indicate roughly equivalent meeting hours as are required in the equivalent Cornell course.
- Transfer credit may be awarded for Freshmen Writing Seminar requirements. These courses may be reviewed by the Knight Institute at the request of the registrar.

**Max number of transfer credits accepted:** Depends upon the college: 60–70

**Residency requirement for transfer students:** Yes. Depends on the college. In general, students must spend 4–6 semesters at Cornell earning at least half the required credits for their major.

**Study abroad available for transfer students:** Yes. Must fulfill the residency requirements.

**Free tutoring for all students:** Yes

**Writing center for all students:** Yes

**Career support/access to internships and resume prep for all students:** Yes

**% of undergraduate students hired within 6 months of graduation:** 61%

**Additional resources specifically designated for transfer and/or non-traditional students:** Yes. The office of Academic Diversity and Inclusion offers tutoring, peer support, and academic support to non-traditional students.

## Housing

**Available for transfer students:** Yes

**Available for non-traditional students:** Yes

**Guaranteed for transfer students:** No

**Non-traditional students can reside in housing year-round:** Yes

**Family housing available:** Yes

## Non-Traditional Admissions

No non-traditional student policies or programs available.

## Military/Veteran Students

**Military/veteran admissions policy (in their own words):** Cornell has a proud military history dating back to 1862 and the Morrill Land Grant Act requiring every land grant institution to include military training in its curriculum. As the land grant university of New York State, Cornell has offered instruction in military science from the university's inception. We are proud of our students who have graduated from Cornell and gone on to serve in the military, and we are proud of our veterans who have made the choice to attend Cornell after they have served our country. Today, Cornell is home to 57 veteran students and over 400 veterans that work or study at Cornell. For questions about admissions, please contact veteranadmission@cornell.edu.

**Status considered in admissions:** No

**Special admissions process:** No

**Special financial aid:** Yes. The Yellow Ribbon Program.

**Specific programs/policies to address needs:** Cornell Undergraduate Veterans Association, Cornell ROTC, Cornell Military Science Program, VetsGuide, Entrepreneurship Bootcamp for Veterans with Disabilities (https://admissions.cornell.edu/learn/veterans-cornell)

## DACA/Undocumented Students

**DACA and undocumented admissions policy (in their own words):** Beginning in Fall 2016, undergraduate students who hold DACA status granted by the federal government will be considered domestic students by Cornell University for purposes of admissions and financial aid, and thus are eligible for need-blind admissions and need-based financial aid like any US citizen or permanent resident. To read more, visit https://admissions.cornell.edu/news/daca-students.

**Admitted:** Yes

**Status considered in admissions:** No—DACA students are considered domestic students.

**Special admissions process:** No

**Eligible for institutional financial aid:** Yes—DACA students only. Cornell is need-aware for undocumented students. While federal and state financial aid (including grants, loans, and federal work-study) is not available for DACA students, Cornell University provides institutional financial aid in place of federal/state grants and loans; summer savings and academic-year work may be included in the financial aid package, and DACA students are expected to obtain federal work authorization as part of their federal DACA status. Undergraduate students with DACA status will be charged nonresident tuition. Cornell offers need-based financial aid to US citizens, permanent residents, and students with DACA status, and has a very limited amount of need-based aid for international and undocumented students without DACA status.

**Specific programs/policies to address needs:** Yes. The Office of Academic Diversity Initiatives offers resources and support for these students, which include peer support and social events, tutoring, and a resource library (https://oadi.cornell.edu/programs/student-success-programs/cdsjp/non-traditional-student-resources/undocumented-students-at-cornell.html).

# DARTMOUTH COLLEGE

**Location:** Hanover, New Hampshire

**Website:** dartmouth.edu

**Endowment:** $4.5 billion

**Type of School:** Private/Co-ed, Research University

**# of Undergraduate Students:** 4,310

**# of Graduate Students:** 2,099

**Average Class Size:** Varies (depends on class level and majors)

**School Mission (in their own words):** Dartmouth College educates the most promising students and prepares them for a lifetime of learning and of responsible leadership, through a faculty dedicated to teaching and the creation of knowledge.

## Admissions

**Admissions office mailing address:** 6016 McNutt Hall, Hanover NH 03755

**Admissions office phone:** (603) 646-2875

**Admissions office email:** Contact link: www.dartmouth.edu/admissions/actions/contact.html

**# of transfer applications:** Fall 2016 admissions: 685

**# of transfer students accepted:** Fall 2016: 32

**Transfer student acceptance rate (2016–2017 academic year):** 4.6%

**Freshman applications received in Fall 2016:** 20,675

**Freshman applications accepted in Fall 2016:** 2,190

**Acceptance rate for 2016–2017 freshmen:** 10.6%

## Transfer Admissions Process

**Transfer Policy (in their own words):** Students who have taken college coursework that is counting toward their high-school graduation must apply for first-year admission. This includes students pursuing an associate's degree while finishing high school.

Students who have completed high school and have matriculated at a college, even if they have attended for 1 term or less, must apply for transfer admission.

Students who have completed 2 years or less of college coursework at the time of application are eligible to apply as transfer students. Students who have previously earned a bachelor's degree are not eligible for transfer or first-year admission to Dartmouth.

Students who are not currently enrolled in school, or whose education has been interrupted, may apply as transfers and often use the "Additional Information" portion of the application to provide background on their experiences and their educational path.

An applicant's year of graduation or the number of credits completed within the guidelines stated above will not have an impact on the outcome of an application. Because Dartmouth enrolls such a small number of new transfer students each year, the Admissions Committee does not need to balance the numbers of students entering as new sophomores or juniors.

**Transfer admissions contact person:** N/A

**Transfer admissions contact info:** N/A

**Offers transfer-focused admissions events:** No

**Transfer application deadline:** Fall 2018 deadline is 3/1/18.

**Acceptances announced to transfer applicants:** Fall 2018 on 5/15/18.

**Transfer application on Common App:** Yes. Common App fee: $90, but if paying the application fee would cause unusual financial hardship for you or your family, you may be eligible for a waiver.

**SAT/ACT required for transfer applicants:** Yes, but a testing waiver is available. If you have not taken the required tests or if sitting for these exams would be a hardship, you may request a testing waiver by contacting Janet MacElman at janet.l.macelman@dartmouth.edu.

**SAT II scores required for transfer applicants:** No, but Dartmouth recommends submitting 2 SAT II Subject Tests.

**High-school records requirements:** Official high-school transcript

**High-school records requirements for applicants who completed outside the US:** Official high-school transcript and final report

**Submission requirements for transfer applicants who completed high-school equivalency test:** Official GED results

**College transcript requirements:** College official's report with college transcript

**Interviews available for transfer applicants:** No

## Costs & Financial Aid

**FAFSA code:** 2573

**CSS Profile code:** 3351

**Are internal school financial aid forms required?** No

**Financial aid deadlines for transfer applicants:** Fall 2018: 3/1/18. Spring 2019: N/A.

**Costs for the 2017–2018 year:** Tuition & Fees: Tuition: $51,468, fees: $1,482. Room & Board: $15,159.

**Financial aid for transfer students:** Yes

**Guarantees meeting 100% need for transfer students:** We guarantee to meet 100% of demonstrated need. Help may come from a combination of federal aid, student loans, and Dartmouth scholarships.

**Need-based aid for transfer students:** Dartmouth Scholarships are need-based and are given without expectation of repayment. Amounts range from $1,000 to over $50,000, depending on determination of your eligibility.

**Merit-based financial aid for transfer students:** No

**Phi Theta Kappa Scholarship:** No

**Reduced or zero tuition fees for low-income students:** No

**Includes loans in financial aid packages:** Yes

**% of all undergraduates receiving financial aid:** 44%

**% of all undergraduates qualifying for Pell Grants:** No information provided.

**Average financial aid award for all undergraduate students:** $47,833

**Funding available for low-income students to visit:** Yes, there is a program called Dartmouth Bound.

**Enrollment deposit can be waived for low-income students:** No deposit required.

## Academics

**GPA range for transfer students accepted in 2016–2017:** No information provided.

**SAT ranges for all students admitted in 2016:** Critical Reading: 670–780. Mathematics: 680–780. Writing: 680–790.

**ACT composite score range for all students admitted in 2016:** 30–34

**Type of curriculum:** Gen. Ed. requirements

**Type of academic year:** Quarter

**Advisors specifically for transfer students:** No

**Credit policy (in their own words):** Please be reminded that not all previously earned college credit will necessarily be applied toward the Dartmouth degree. Evaluation of transfer student transcripts and individual syllabi for each college course previously taken determines total credits awarded and the minimum number of terms of enrollment that will be necessary to complete Dartmouth degree requirements.

Students transferring to Dartmouth after their first or second years at other institutions will be allowed a maximum of 17 credits. They should be aware that depending on the number of credits approved for transfer, they may need to be in residence longer than they might have expected in order to complete their Dartmouth requirements. This may not be able to be determined until after you have arrived on campus in September.

**Max number of transfer credits accepted:** 17 courses and advanced placement credits

**Residency requirement for transfer students:** Yes. Transfer students must be in residence a minimum of 6 R-terms (typically 18 credits), but may need as many as 8 or 9 R-terms (24–27 credits).

With the exception of international students on an F-1 visa, those transfer students who enter as sophomores (up to 9 credits) are required to be in residence the summer after their sophomore year.

Students who transfer after their second year are encouraged to be in residence this same summer.

All students are also required to be in residence in the fall, winter, and spring terms of their senior year.

**Study abroad available for transfer students:** Yes. Must fulfill the residency requirements.

**Free tutoring for all students:** No. Expenses incurred by tutees who receive financial aid from the college or are on a varsity athlete team will be covered by the College. However, tutees NOT on financial aid or on a varsity team are expected to pay their tutors independently.

**Writing center for all students:** Yes

**Career support/access to internships and resume prep for all students:** Yes

**% of undergraduate students hired within 6 months of graduation:** No information provided.

**Additional resources specifically designated for transfer and/or non-traditional students:** No

## Housing

**Available for transfer students:** Yes

**Available for non-traditional students:** Yes

**Guaranteed for transfer students:** Dartmouth College houses transfer and exchange students in all of its upper-class clusters. The majority of students arriving at Dartmouth are assigned to double and triple rooms while a few are assigned to single rooms.

**Non-traditional students can reside in housing year-round:** No (unless they sign up for summer courses)

**Family housing available:** Not for undergraduates, but if necessary, you can contact housing and try to arrange something.

## Non-Traditional Admissions

No non-traditional student policies or programs available.

## Military/Veteran Students

**Military/veteran admissions policy (in their own words):** Veterans often come to Dartmouth with unique knowledge and experience that enhance our academically motivated and diverse student body. At Dartmouth, your access to professors and resources, the flexibility to take advantage of all opportunities, and the global engagement of our community will forge a valuable educational experience. And we are not the only ones who think so. Dartmouth was selected as a Top School in the 2016 Military Advance Education & Transition Guide to Colleges and Universities. Dartmouth is partnering with the Posse Program to welcome highly qualified veteran students to the university, guaranteeing free tuition even if the GI Bill and other government funding runs out.

**Status considered in admissions:** No

**Special admissions process:** No. If you have been enrolled in university-level coursework during your service, you may consider applying to Dartmouth as a transfer applicant. Some veterans take college courses after they exit the service, and then apply as transfer applicants.

Please note that the Dartmouth faculty evaluates each individual course taken by every enrolling student before awarding credit; therefore, it can be difficult to predict how many courses taken at another college or university will count toward a Dartmouth degree.

**Special financial aid:** Yes. The Yellow Ribbon Program.

**Specific programs/policies to address needs:** Dartmouth Undergraduate Veterans Association, Dartmouth College Army ROTC, Dartmouth Graduate Veterans Association, and Dartmouth Uniformed Service Alumni (DUSA). 2- to 4-year ROTC scholarships at Dartmouth are based on merit, not financial need. The school provides full tuition or room and board, and an allowance for living expenses.

## DACA/Undocumented Students

**DACA and undocumented admissions policy (in their own words):** Undocumented and Deferred Action for Childhood Arrivals (DACA) students apply the same way that US citizens and permanent residents do.

You will not be considered an international applicant if you live in the US.

Citizenship or financial status will not affect your application outcome.

You do not need a Social Security number to use the Common Application; that field can be left blank.

If your family situation seems complicated, please contact us so we can help you through the application process.

**Admitted:** Yes

**Status considered in admissions:** No

**Special admissions process:** No

**Eligible for institutional financial aid:** Yes. We will meet 100% of your demonstrated need, using Dartmouth's financial aid.

**Specific programs/policies to address needs:** Yes. When you come to Dartmouth, we will support you.

CoFIRED—Dartmouth Coalition for Immigration Reform, Equality and DREAMers

OVIS—Dartmouth Office of Visa and Immigration Service

# DAVIDSON COLLEGE

**Location:** Davidson, North Carolina

**Website:** www.davidson.edu

**Endowment:** $697.2 million

**Type of School:** Private/Co-ed, Liberal Arts

**# of Undergraduate Students:** 1,796

**# of Graduate Students:** 0

**Average Class Size:** 15

**School Mission (in their own words):** Davidson College is an institution of higher learning established in 1837 by Presbyterians of North Carolina. Since its founding, the ties that bind the college to its Presbyterian heritage, including the historic understanding of Christian faith called the Reformed Tradition, have remained close and strong. The college is committed to continuing this vital relationship.

The primary purpose of Davidson College is to assist students in developing humane instincts and disciplined and creative minds for lives of leadership and service. In fulfilling its purpose, Davidson has chosen to be a liberal arts college, to maintain itself as a residential community of scholars, to emphasize the teaching responsibility of all professors, and to ensure the opportunity for personal relationships between students and teachers. Further, Davidson believes it is vital that all students in every class know and study under mature and scholarly teachers who are able and eager to provide for each of them stimulation, instruction, and guidance.

The Christian tradition to which Davidson remains committed recognizes God as the source of all truth, and believes that Jesus Christ is the revelation of that God, a God bound by no church or creed. The loyalty of the college thus extends beyond the Christian community to the whole of humanity and necessarily includes openness to and respect for the world's various religious traditions. Davidson dedicates itself to the quest for truth and encourages teachers and students to explore the whole of reality, whether physical or spiritual, with unlimited employment of their intellectual powers. At Davidson, faith and reason work together in mutual respect and benefit toward growth in learning, understanding, and wisdom.

As a college that welcomes students, faculty, and staff from a variety of nationalities, ethnic groups, and traditions, Davidson values diversity, recognizing the dignity and worth of every person. Therefore, Davidson provides a range of opportunities for worship, civil debate, and teaching that enrich mind and spirit. Further, Davidson challenges students to engage in service to prepare themselves for lives of growth and giving.

Davidson seeks students of good character and high academic ability, irrespective of economic circumstances, who share its values and show promise for usefulness to society. In the selection of faculty, the college seeks men and women who respect the purpose of the college, who are outstanding intellectually, who have the best training available in their fields of study, and whose interest in students and teaching is unfeigned and profound. The Trustees commit to being faithful stewards of the traditions of the college. They are charged with governing under the Constitution and By-laws and with providing the financial resources necessary for adequate student aid and appropriate facilities and programs, including furnishing the faculty with the time and opportunity for creative scholarship fundamental to the best teaching.

As a liberal arts college, Davidson emphasizes those studies, disciplines, and activities that are mentally, spiritually, and physically liberating. Thus, the college concentrates upon the study of history, literature and languages, philosophy and religion, music, drama and the visual arts, the natural and social sciences, and mathematics. The college encourages student engagement with other cultures through domestic and international studies. The college also requires physical education, provides for competitive athletics, and encourages a variety of social, cultural, and service activities. While Davidson prepares many of its students for graduate and professional study, it intends to teach all students to think clearly, to make relevant and valid judgments, to discriminate among values, and to communicate freely with others in the realm of ideas.

Davidson holds a priceless heritage bequeathed by those who have dedicated their lives and their possessions for its welfare. To it much has been entrusted, and of it much is required.

## Admissions

**Admissions office mailing address:** 405 N Main St, Davidson NC 28035

**Admissions office phone:** (800) 768-0380

**Admissions office email:** admission@davidson.edu

**# of transfer applications:** Fall 2016 admissions: 129. Spring 2017 admissions: 50.

**# of transfer students accepted:** Fall 2016: 22. Spring 2017: 3.

**Transfer student acceptance rate (2016–2017 academic year):** 14%

**Freshman applications received in Fall 2016:** 5,618

**Freshman applications accepted in Fall 2016:** 1,130

**Acceptance rate for 2016–2017 freshmen:** 20.1%

## Transfer Admissions Process

**Transfer policy (in their own words):** Students will have successfully completed at least 1 full year of acceptable college coursework upon enrolling at Davidson College. Students must plan to be enrolled at Davidson for at least 2 academic years (16 courses).

**Transfer admissions contact person:** David Kraus, Senior Associate Dean/Director of Admission

**Transfer admissions contact info:** dakraus@davidson.edu

**Offers transfer-focused admissions events:** No

**Transfer application deadline:** Fall 2018 deadline is 3/15/18. Spring 2019 deadline is 11/1/18.

**Acceptances announced to transfer applicants:** Fall 2018 in late April. Spring 2019 in late November.

**Transfer application on Common App:** Yes. Common App fee: $50.

**SAT/ACT required for transfer applicants:** Yes

**High-school records requirements:** Official high-school transcript

**High-school records requirements for applicants who completed outside the US:** Official high-school transcript

**Submission requirements for transfer applicants who completed high-school equivalency test:** High-school diploma required. GED is not accepted.

**College transcript requirements:** Official transcripts from all colleges and universities attended

**Interviews available for transfer applicants:** No

**Additional requirements for transfers seeking admissions to arts major:** Yes. Art students usually send a portfolio for review.

## Costs & Financial Aid

**FAFSA code:** 2918

**CSS Profile code:** 5150

**Are internal school financial aid forms required?** No

**Financial aid deadlines for transfer applicants:** Fall 2018: 3/15/18. Spring 2019: 11/1/18.

**Costs for the 2017–2018 year:** Tuition & Fees: $49,949. Room & Board: $13,954

**Financial aid for transfer students:** Yes

**Guarantees meeting 100% need for transfer students:** Yes

**Need-based aid for transfer students:** Yes

**Merit-based financial aid for transfer students:** No

**Phi Theta Kappa Scholarship:** No

**Reduced or zero tuition fees for low-income students:** No

**Includes loans in financial aid packages:** No. Through the Davidson Trust, we meet 100% of your calculated financial need entirely through grants and student employment. Our financial aid packages do not include a loan component, but you have the option of borrowing educational loans as a matter of personal choice.

**% of all undergraduates receiving financial aid:** 70%

**% of all undergraduates qualifying for Pell Grants:** No information provided.

**Average financial aid award for all undergraduate students:** $45,001

**Funding available for low-income students to visit:** No information provided.

**Enrollment deposit can be waived for low-income students:** Yes

## Academics

**GPA range for transfer students accepted in 2016–2017:** No information provided.

**SAT ranges for all students admitted in 2016:** Critical Reading: 630–720. Mathematics: 620–720. Writing: 620–720.

**ACT composite score range for all students admitted in 2016:** 28–33

**Recommended completed level of math for transfer applicants:** Calculus

**Recommended completed level of English for transfer applicants:** 4 years of high-school English is required.

**Type of curriculum:** Gen. Ed. requirements

**Type of academic year:** Semester

**Advisors specifically for transfer students:** No, students are assigned to an advisor who will guide students through their years at Davidson.

**Credit policy (in their own words):** Davidson College accepts credits from other colleges and universities based upon equivalency in terms of level, content, quality, comparability, and program relevance to a liberal arts curriculum. The following conditions must typically be met. The college or university must be accredited for a "liberal arts and general program" or have similar accreditation abroad. A maximum of 2 online/hybrid courses may be transferred. The courses must involve ongoing interaction with instructors and not be independent, self-paced modules.

The courses are consistent with the academic objectives of a liberal arts curriculum and the mission of Davidson College. Credit by examination (except AP/IB) are not transferable.

Authority for approving transfer credit rests with the registrar, who also may determine whether a course satisfies a non-major graduation requirement. Authority for determining whether a transfer credit will count toward a major, a minor, or an interdisciplinary minor rests with the appropriate chair. The course must be completed with a grade of C– or better. "Pass" grades (or similar) are accepted only if the transcript indicates that the grade represents work of C– or better. We do not transfer more than 4 courses in a semester or 2 in a summer, though in a few special cases approved in advance,

3 in a summer may be permissible. In general: 3–5 semester hours yield 1 Davidson credit, 6–9 hours yield 2, and 10–13 hours yield 3.

**Max number of transfer credits accepted:** 16

**Residency requirement for transfer students:** Yes. Transfer students should have completed at least half the remaining upper-level undergraduate work at the college.

**Study abroad available for transfer students:** Yes. Must fulfill the residency requirements.

**Free tutoring for all students:** Yes

**Writing center for all students:** Yes

**Career support/access to internships and resume prep for all students:** Yes

**% of undergraduate students hired within 6 months of graduation:** No information provided.

**Additional resources specifically designated for transfer and/or non-traditional students:** No

## Housing

**Available for transfer students:** Yes

**Available for non-traditional students:** Yes

**Guaranteed for transfer students:** Yes

**Non-traditional students can reside in housing year-round:** No

**Family housing available:** No

## Non-Traditional Admissions

**Non-traditional student policy (in their own words):** You may be considered a non-traditional student if you are transferring from another college, homeschooled, seeking early admission, or visiting from another college. Special steps may be required during your application process. The requirements for this type of non-traditional applicant may vary on a case-by-case basis. You may contact Director of Admission Dave Kraus at (704) 894-2969 to discuss your situation.

## Military/Veteran Students

**Military/veteran admissions policy (in their own words):** Davidson College participates in the Yellow Ribbon GI Education Enhancement Program (Yellow Ribbon Program). Eligible students who have accepted their admission to the college should notify the Registrar's Office of their eligibility and interest in participating. Participation is limited to 8 students and awarded on a first come, first served basis.

**Status considered in admissions:** No

**Special admissions process:** No

**Special financial aid:** Yes. Davidson College participates in the Yellow Ribbon Program.

**Specific programs/policies to address needs:** No information provided.

## DACA/Undocumented Students

**DACA and undocumented admissions policy (in their own words):** Davidson College continues to expand its resources and expertise in supporting the development and education of undocumented students and students with DACA status. We encourage interested applicants to apply for admission regardless of their immigration status and for admitted students to explore the following resources (see specific programs and resources below).

**Admitted:** Yes

**Status considered in admissions:** No

**Special admissions process:** No

**Eligible for institutional financial aid:** Yes, the college strives to remove social and financial barriers that may otherwise exclude students from historically underrepresented populations, such as undocumented/DACA students. Must demonstrate financial need.

**Specific programs/policies to address needs:** Yes. Undocumented/DACA students are strongly encouraged to participate in STRIDE (Students Together Reaching for Individual Development and Education) or First Scholars, pre-orientation programs for diverse and underrepresented student populations. These programs expand students' networks with peers, faculty, and staff. Students who have identified themselves as African American, Asian American, Native American, Latino/Hispanic, or multicultural will receive an automatic invitation upon matriculation. Participation is voluntary, and there are no fees associated with registration. Travel grants and financial assistance are also available.

### PEER MENTORING & SOCIAL SUPPORT

If you are unable to attend the pre-orientation portion of STRIDE, you may still participate in the STRIDE mentoring and academic support component once classes begin. Students seeking more specialized support and the opportunity to connect with other undocumented students on campus may also reach out to Tae-Sun Kim (takim@davidson.edu), director of multicultural affairs and campus advisor for undocumented students.

### PRE-MAJOR ADVISING

Students will be matched with pre-major advisors that are sensitive to, and trained about, the special needs unique to undocumented/DACA students. Disclosing your status is optional. If you have any concerns about your pre-major advising, you may contact Leslie Marsicano (lemarsicano@davidson.edu), associate dean for academic administration.

### STUDY ABROAD

Study abroad may be an option for students enrolled in DACA. Davidson students may study abroad as early as the summer after their first year. Study abroad requires planning ahead, and we encourage you to meet with a study abroad counselor during your first year to begin planning for this option.

# DUKE UNIVERSITY

**Location:** Durham, North Carolina

**Website:** www.duke.edu

**Endowment:** $6.8 billion

**Type of School:** Private/Co-ed, Research University

**# of Undergraduate Students:** 6,609

**# of Graduate Students:** 9,319

**Average Class Size:** More than 73% of classes have fewer than 20 students.

**School Mission (in their own words):** James B. Duke's founding Indenture of Duke University directed the members of the University to "provide real leadership in the educational world" by choosing individuals of "outstanding character, ability, and vision" to serve as its officers, trustees, and faculty; by carefully selecting students of "character, determination, and application"; and by pursuing those areas of teaching and scholarship that would "most help to develop our resources, increase our wisdom, and promote human happiness."

To these ends, the mission of Duke University is to provide a superior liberal education to undergraduate students, attending not only to their intellectual growth but also to their development as adults committed to high ethical standards and full participation as leaders in their communities; to prepare future members of the learned professions for lives of skilled and ethical service by providing excellent graduate and professional education; to advance the frontiers of knowledge and contribute boldly to the international community of scholarship; to promote an intellectual environment built on a commitment to free and open inquiry; to help those who suffer, cure disease, and promote health through sophisticated medical research and thoughtful patient care; to provide wide ranging educational opportunities, on and beyond our campuses, for traditional students, active professionals, and lifelong learners using the power of information technologies; and to promote a deep appreciation for the range of human difference and potential, a sense of the obligations and rewards of citizenship, and a commitment to learning, freedom, and truth.

By pursuing these objectives with vision and integrity, Duke University seeks to engage the mind, elevate the spirit, and stimulate the best effort of all who are associated with the University; to contribute in diverse ways to the local community, the state, the nation, and the world; and to attain and maintain a place of real leadership in all that we do.

## Admissions

**Admissions office mailing address:** 2138 Campus Dr, PO Box 90586, Durham NC 27708

**Admissions office phone:** (919) 684-3214

**Admissions office email:** undergrad-admissions@duke.edu

**# of transfer applications:** Fall 2016 admissions: 1,085

**# of transfer students accepted:** Fall 2016: 52

**Transfer student acceptance rate (2016–2017 academic year):** 8.9%

**Freshman applications received in Fall 2016:** 31,671

**Freshman applications accepted in Fall 2016:** 3,430

**Acceptance rate for 2016–2017 freshmen:** 10.8%

## Transfer Admissions Process

**Transfer policy (in their own words):** We welcome your interest in transferring to Duke. Every fall, approximately 30 students transfer into either the Trinity College of Arts & Sciences or the Pratt School of Engineering. Most will enroll as sophomores, although the selection committee will also admit a small number of juniors.

While transfer students are new to the Duke community, they bring with them the same characteristics of talent and engagement as the rest of their undergraduate peers. Transfer students add a tremendous amount to campus life—all while pursuing their unique intellectual interests at one of America's leading universities.

## Eligibility

Please consult the following guidelines to determine your eligibility to transfer to Duke:

- If you have attended any college or university in the past 4 years and will have successfully completed at least 1 full year of transferable college work by the August in which you hope to enroll, you qualify to apply to Duke as a transfer applicant.

- All transferable college work should be completed at an accredited degree-granting institution. College work completed at a vocational, technical, performance, or professional program will not be considered.

- If you are a high-school student in an "early college" or dual-enrollment program who will earn an associate's degree while finishing high school, you should apply as a first-year applicant.

- If you have already completed an undergraduate (bachelor's) degree at a 4-year college, you cannot be considered for transfer admission.

- Unfortunately, you may not apply for transfer to Duke as a part-time student. Instead, we encourage you to contact Duke Continuing Studies for information on taking courses on a nondegree basis.

- The admissions committee seeks applicants who can provide evidence of academic preparation within the past 4 years. If you have not recently attended high school or college, we strongly encourage you to do so prior to applying for transfer, either through Duke Continuing Studies or an accredited degree-granting institution in your local area.

**Transfer admissions contact person:** Madeline Barrow, Admissions Officer (Transfer Students)

**Transfer admissions contact info:** madeline.barrow@duke.edu

**Offers transfer-focused admissions events:** No

**Transfer application deadline:** Fall 2018 deadline is 3/15/18.

**Acceptances announced to transfer applicants:** Fall 2018 on 5/15/18.

**Transfer application on Common App:** Yes. Common App fee: $85.

**SAT/ACT required for transfer applicants:** No

**High-school records requirements:** Neither a high-school diploma nor a GED is required to apply for transfer to Duke. However, applicants should be aware that a candidate's academic record is a very important part of the application.

**High-school records requirements for applicants who completed outside the US:** Neither a high-school diploma nor a GED is required to apply for transfer to Duke. However, applicants should be aware that a candidate's academic record is a very important part of the application.

**Submission requirements for transfer applicants who completed high-school equivalency test:** Neither a high-school diploma nor a GED is required to apply for transfer to Duke. However, applicants should be aware that a candidate's academic record is a very important part of the application.

**College transcript requirements:** College transcripts are required.

**Interviews available for transfer applicants:** No

**Additional requirements for transfers seeking admissions to arts major:** Optional. If you have exceptional talent in dance, theater, art, music, photography, or film/video/digital media, you may submit supplementary material to be evaluated by an appropriate faculty member. You may begin to submit artistic materials on February 15.

**Additional requirements for transfers seeking admissions to engineering major:** Yes. We anticipate that engineering majors will have the math and science background that would allow them to graduate from Duke within the usual 2 years for rising juniors or 3 years for rising sophomores.

## Costs & Financial Aid

**FAFSA code:** 2920

**CSS Profile code:** 5156

**Are internal school financial aid forms required?** No

**Financial aid deadline for transfer applicants:** Fall 2018: 3/20/18

**Costs for the 2017–2018 year:** Tuition & Fees: $53,744. Room & Board: $15,500.

**Financial aid for transfer students:** Yes. To that end, Duke admits transfer applicants who are US citizens and permanent residents without regard to financial circumstance or aid eligibility and meets 100% of each admitted student's demonstrated need throughout their undergraduate education.

**Guarantees meeting 100% need for transfer students:** Yes

**Need-based aid for transfer students:** Yes. Must demonstrate need.

**Merit-based financial aid for transfer students:** No

**Phi Theta Kappa Scholarship:** No

**Reduced or zero tuition fees for low-income students:** No

**Includes loans in financial aid packages:** Yes, but Duke tries to include the least amount of loans as possible.

**% of all undergraduates receiving financial aid:** 55%

**% of all undergraduates qualifying for Pell Grants:** N/A

**Average financial aid award for all undergraduate students:** $50,312

**Funding available for low-income students to visit:** No

**Enrollment deposit can be waived for low-income students:** Yes

## Academics

**GPA range for transfer students accepted in 2016–2017:** 3.7

**SAT ranges for all students admitted in 2016:** Critical Reading: 680–770. Mathematics: 770–800. Writing: 680–780.

**ACT composite score range for all students admitted in 2016:** 31–34

**Recommended completed level of math for transfer applicants:** Calculus

**Recommended completed level of English for transfer applicants:** English Composition

**Recommended courses transfer applicants interested in STEM should complete before transfer:** We require coursework in calculus and strongly recommend physics.

**Type of curriculum:** Gen. Ed. requirements

**Type of academic year:** Semester

**Advisors specifically for transfer students:** No

**Credit policy (in their own words):** Duke will grant credit for no more than 2 years of coursework completed elsewhere, regardless of the number of credits a student has previously earned. In order to earn a Duke degree, a transfer student must spend at least 2 years at Duke. We do not offer a preliminary credit evaluation to applicants prior to the release of admissions decisions. Instead, credit evaluations are completed upon matriculation by an academic dean.

**Max number of transfer credits accepted:** 17

**Residency requirement for transfer students:** Yes. The Board of Trustees mandates that all undergraduates live on campus for 3 years. As an extension of this practice, transfer students are required to live on campus for 2 years. Exceptions to the housing requirement include: transfer students who enter as juniors may request to live on campus for only 1 year. Non-traditional transfer students (married students, military veterans, and those students older than most undergraduates) may request the housing requirement be waived entirely.

**Study abroad available for transfer students:** Yes. Must fulfill the residency requirements.

**Free tutoring for all students:** Yes. The Peer Tutoring Program (PTP) offers up to 12 hours of free tutoring each semester to Duke undergraduates who are enrolled in select introductory-level courses. Not all courses are offered for tutoring.

**Writing center for all students:** Yes

**Career support/access to internships and resume prep for all students:** Yes

**% of undergraduate students hired within 6 months of graduation:** No information provided.

**Additional resources specifically designated for transfer and/or non-traditional students:** No

## Housing

**Available for transfer students:** Yes

**Available for non-traditional students:** Yes

**Guaranteed for transfer students:** Yes

**Non-traditional students can reside in housing year-round:** No

**Family housing available:** Yes, through the apartment housing on campus.

## Non-Traditional Admissions

**Non-traditional student policy (in their own words):** Non-traditional students are welcome to apply to Duke as they bring a unique perspective that is not often found in our more traditional undergraduate population. You must have been enrolled in college at some point during the last 4 years.

## Military/Veteran Students

**Military/veteran admissions policy (in their own words):** Duke is proud to have you join our community of students, faculty, and staff. The Division of Student Affairs is available to assist in your transition and experience. To support your transition, we have brought together many resources from throughout the Duke and Durham community. We hope that you will take advantage of the available resources and let us know how we may assist and support your needs.

**Status considered in admissions:** No. Duke University honors the men and women who have served in the military, and has a proud history of association with the military.

**Special admissions process:** No

**Special financial aid:** Yes. Must meet service requirements of the Department of Veterans Affairs for the Yellow Ribbon Program.

**Specific programs/policies to address needs:** DukeVets (student organization), Fuqua Armed Forces (student organization), ROTC Programs: Army, Navy, Air Force, DukeReach

## DACA/Undocumented Students

**DACA and undocumented admissions policy (in their own words):** We welcome applications from undocumented and DACA students. You apply in the same way US citizens and permanent residents do, and your application will be considered the same way US citizens and permanent residents are, by the regional admissions officer responsible for where you attend high school.

When you apply, you should be honest about your current citizenship status. You do not need a Social Security number to use the Common Application or Coalition Application; that field can be left blank.

**Admitted:** Yes

**Status considered in admissions:** No

**Special admissions process:** No

**Eligible for institutional financial aid:** Yes, Duke University views its financial aid program as an investment in students and their futures. That's why we are committed to meeting 100% of the demonstrated need for each admitted student. Beginning with the class entering in the fall of 2017, Duke will meet 100% of the demonstrated financial need for undocumented students (both DACA and undocumented) admitted to the University. Financial aid packages will include institutional need-based scholarship funds. DACA students will also be eligible for Duke work-study funding for on-campus employment.

**Specific programs/policies to address needs:** No information provided.

# EMERSON COLLEGE

**Location:** Boston, Massachusetts
**Website:** www.emerson.edu
**Endowment:** No information provided.
**Type of School:** Private/Co-ed, Research University
**# of Undergraduate Students:** 3,783
**# of Graduate Students:** 641

**Average Class Size:** No information provided.

**School Mission (in their own words):** Emerson College educates students to assume positions of leadership in communication and the arts and to advance scholarship and creative work that brings innovation, depth, and diversity to these disciplines.

## Admissions

**Admissions office mailing address:** 120 Boylston St, Boston MA 02116

**Admissions office phone:** (617) 824-8600

**Admissions office email:** admission@emerson.edu

**# of transfer applications:** Fall 2016 admissions: 0. Spring 2017 admissions: 195.

**# of transfer students accepted:** Fall 2017: 510. Spring 2017: 110.

**Transfer student acceptance rate (2016–2017 academic year):** 65%

**Freshman applications received in Fall 2016:** 9,149

**Freshman applications accepted in Fall 2016:** 4,397

**Acceptance rate for 2016–2017 freshmen:** 48%

## Transfer Admissions Process

**Transfer policy (in their own words):** At Emerson, we define a transfer student as anyone with a high-school diploma or GED (General Equivalency Diploma) who has matriculated full-time at another college or enrolled part-time for 3 or more college courses (9 or more college credits). Students with college credits earned prior to high-school graduation (e.g., dual enrollment) are considered first-year applicants.

**Transfer admissions contact person:** Lisa Yaeger, Associate Director, Transfer Coordinator

**Transfer admissions contact info:** lisa_yaeger@emerson.edu

**Offers transfer-focused admissions events:** Yes, transfer-focused info sessions

**Transfer application deadline:** Fall 2018 deadline is 3/15/18. Spring 2019 deadline is 11/1/18.

**Acceptances announced to transfer applicants:** Fall 2018 on rolling basis. Spring 2019 on rolling basis.

**Transfer application on Common App:** Yes. Common App fee: $65.

**Separate application or in addition to the Common App:** Yes. Emerson application.

**Fee for separate transfer application:** Yes

**Waiver available for separate transfer application fee:** Must demonstrate financial need.

**SAT/ACT required for transfer applicants:** Optional

**High-school records requirements:** An official, final high-school transcript or GED indicating your date of graduation is required.

**High-school records requirements for applicants who completed outside the US:** Must submit official transcript.

**Submission requirements for transfer applicants who completed high-school equivalency test:** An official, final high-school transcript or GED indicating your date of graduation is required.

**College transcript requirements:** An official transcript is required from each college or university you have attended. For your current institution, make sure the transcript indicates courses in progress.

**Interviews available for transfer applicants:** No

**Additional requirements for transfers seeking admissions to business school:** No. Business of Creative Enterprises major is not available to transfer applicants at this time.

**Additional requirements for transfers seeking admissions to arts major:** Yes. Additional application materials are required for applicants to Performing Arts programs and recommended for Media Arts Production applicants. The Department of Performing Arts only accepts transfer applications for the fall term. You will be able to submit a creative sample via the Application Portal after submitting your application.

## Costs & Financial Aid

**FAFSA code:** 2146

**CSS Profile code:** 3367

**Are internal school financial aid forms required?** No

**Financial aid deadlines for transfer applicants:** Fall 2018: 4/4/18. Spring 2019: 11/15/18.

**Costs for the 2017–2018 year:** Tuition & Fees: $44,032. Room & Board: $17,492 for single rooms, $16,992 for double rooms.

**Financial aid for transfer students:** Yes

**Guarantees meeting 100% need for transfer students:** No

**Need-based aid for transfer students:** Yes. To apply for need-based aid, you must be a US citizen or US permanent resident. Financial aid funding is based on several factors including, but not limited to: meeting financial aid deadlines, demonstrated financial need, enrollment status, living arrangements, and satisfactory academic progress.

**Merit-based financial aid for transfer students:** Yes. To be considered for merit-based aid, you should have a distinguished academic record or demonstrate leadership or outstanding potential either in your school or community.

**Phi Theta Kappa Scholarship:** Yes, $4,000. Renewable. Details available at www.emerson.edu/undergraduate-admission/tuition-financial-aid/scholarships.

**Reduced or zero tuition fees for low-income students:** No

**Includes loans in financial aid packages:** Yes

**% of all undergraduates receiving financial aid:** 62%

**% of all undergraduates qualifying for Pell Grants:** 17%

**Average financial aid award for all undergraduate students:** $21,848

**Funding available for low-income students to visit:** No

**Enrollment deposit can be waived for low-income students:** Yes, student may ask for enrollment extension and 2 weeks will be provided. Afterward, admissions counselor can discuss if applicant qualifies for a waiver.

## Academics

**GPA range for transfer students accepted in 2016–2017:** 2.5–4.0

**SAT ranges for all students admitted in 2016:** Critical Reading: 580–680. Mathematics: 540–650. Writing: 570–670.

**ACT composite score range for all students admitted in 2016:** 25–30

**Type of curriculum:** Gen. Ed. requirements

**Type of academic year:** Semester

**Advisors specifically for transfer students:** Yes

**Credit policy (in their own words):** To receive transfer credit, current students must have an official transcript sent directly from the institution to the Emerson Registrar's Office. Newly admitted students must have their official transcript(s) sent to the Admission Office, which will disseminate the information to the Registrar's Office when appropriate.

The Registrar's Office will review the transcript to determine liberal arts equivalency and elective credits.

Major course equivalency will be determined by the academic department, either by the department chair or undergraduate coordinator. It is advised that students keep course descriptions and syllabi, in case additional information is necessary to determine course equivalency.

Transfer credit is granted for comparable coursework completed at accredited 2- and 4-year institutions with a grade of C or better.

Students with junior or senior status who have not reached their credit transfer limit may only request transfer credit for courses taken at a 4-year, baccalaureate degree–granting institution.

Quarter hour and trimester hour credits will be reduced to semester hour credits.

**Max number of transfer credits accepted:** Students transferring into Emerson College from another institution may transfer in a maximum of 80 pre-matriculation credits, with no more than 64 of those credits from a junior or community college and no more than 32 credits from exams (e.g., AP, IB, CLEP). Post-matriculation transfer students will be limited to a maximum of 64 transfer credits, including those credits transferred in pre-matriculation.

**Residency requirement for transfer students:** Yes. Transfer students are required to complete a minimum of 48 credits at Emerson, of which at least 20 credits must be in their major. In addition, they are required to earn their final 16 credits at the College.

**Study abroad available for transfer students:** Yes. Must fulfill the residency requirements.

**Free tutoring for all students:** Yes

**Writing center for all students:** Yes

**Career support/access to internships and resume prep for all students:** Yes

**% of undergraduate students hired within 6 months of graduation:** No information provided.

**Additional resources specifically designated for transfer and/or non-traditional students:** No

## Housing

**Available for transfer students:** Yes, but it is very limited.

**Available for non-traditional students:** No

**Guaranteed for transfer students:** No

**Non-traditional students can reside in housing year-round:** N/A

**Family housing available:** No

## Non-Traditional Admissions

**Non-traditional student policy (in their own words):**
A non-traditional transfer student is anyone who has been out of high school for a minimum of 3 years prior to beginning college and/or returning to college after an extended absence. If there are any gaps present with your educational history, we will ask you to account for them within your transfer writing supplement.

## Military/Veteran Students

**Military/veteran admissions policy (in their own words):** Students that are 100% eligible for Chapter 33 Post-9/11 benefits are eligible to receive money via the Yellow Ribbon Program. Yellow Ribbon funds can only be granted to a student once all Chapter 33 Post-9/11 funds have been exhausted for the academic year. In most cases, a student will only receive Yellow Ribbon funds in the spring semester.

**Status considered in admissions:** No

**Special admissions process:** No

**Special financial aid:** Yes. Students must meet the Department of Veteran Affairs service requirements.

**Specific programs/policies to address needs:** Yes. The Veterans Affairs and Resources Office.

## DACA/Undocumented Students

**DACA and undocumented admissions policy (in their own words):** We consider you an international student if you do not have US citizenship, dual-US citizenship, or permanent residency.

**Admitted:** Yes

**Status considered in admissions:** No

**Special admissions process:** No

**Eligible for institutional financial aid:** Yes, but it's decided on an individual basis. Also eligible for merit-based aid. Must demonstrate financial need.

**Specific programs/policies to address needs:** No

# Andrew Santiago

**Emerson College, C'11**
Bachelor's Degree in Visual Media Arts, concentrating in Writing for Film & TV

**Borough of Manhattan Community College, C'09**
Associate's Degree in Liberal Arts & Sciences

**Current Employment:** Editor, Mitú

**Bio:** As a proud Nuyorican, Andrew would like to write for television and feature films to share his love for comedy and satire and his passion for life. He is especially interested in sharing his own story and observations growing up in Brooklyn, highlighting the unique experiences of trying to make it in the face of great adversity through a comedic lens.

*"Before entering the Kaplan Leadership Program, I was a GED recipient and community college student, and my career limitations felt extremely real. In the film and television industry, connections are everything. Who you know can actually get you in the door, and so many times, my Emerson College education has been the secret password to get by the bouncer of life.*

*'Oh really, Emerson?' is the 'You don't say?' of the film and TV world. Emerson alum are known as some of the hardest-working people in the industry. It's the stamp of approval before I even walk in the door. And any leg up that you can get in this tough industry is worth having. It's also amazing that the school has gotten even more reputable in the years since I've graduated, expanding their campus, increasing their programs, becoming more and more known for comedy, and rising on the lists of 'top film schools,' 'top communication schools,' and most importantly for me, 'top comedy schools.'"*

## Leadership Activities

- Out-in-Two Scholar, BMCC
- Member, Phi Theta Kappa International Honor Society of Community Colleges
- Supervisor, Center for Family Life Beacon at PS1
- Correspondent, "Common Agenda," Emerson College Channel
- Resident Assistant, Emerson College
- Development Intern, Comedy Central—Emerson Los Angeles Program
- Development Intern, Powerhouse Productions
- Development Intern, Original Media
- Winner, Nickelodeon Writer Script Review (Austin Film Festival)
- Vice President, Amigos

# EMORY UNIVERSITY

**Location:** Atlanta, Georgia

**Website:** www.college.emory.edu

**Endowment:** $6.402 billion

**Type of School:** Private/Co-ed, Liberal Arts

**# of Undergraduate Students:** 6,867

**# of Graduate Students:** 6,921

**Average Class Size:** 5–25

**School Mission (in their own words):** The scholarly mission of Emory College involves research and creativity, teaching, and service. As an institution dedicated to intellectual discovery and creativity, Emory College is charged both with generating new knowledge and with inventing new ways of understanding what is already known. Faculty, administrators, and students cooperate to expand the boundaries of the known through research, experimentation, creation, performance, and publishing the results of their efforts for the general advancement of learning and the betterment of the human prospect.

As a teaching institution, Emory College imparts to its students the kinds of knowledge that traditionally compose a broad liberal education: practical skills in critical thinking, persuasive writing, mathematics and computation, and a foreign language; a basic familiarity with modes of inquiry proper to natural science and mathematics, to the social sciences, and to the arts and humanities; and a mature command of at least one discipline or field of concentration.

Through instruction that aims to be the symbiotic complement of research, Emory College prepares its graduates to live an active life of the mind, aware of their responsibilities to assume a part in the intellectual leadership of the nation.

As an institution responsive to the various communities of which it is a member, Emory College acknowledges a commitment to service in its local community, in the national and international academic community, and in the nation as a whole.

Each aspect of this threefold mission must be carried forward in an atmosphere of intellectual and moral integrity, one of habitual regard for the ethical dimensions of research, creativity, teaching, and service.

## Admissions

**Admissions office mailing address:** 550 Asbury Cir, Atlanta GA 30322

**Admissions office phone:** (404) 727-6036

**Admissions office email:** admission@emory.edu

**# of transfer applications:** Fall 2016 admissions: 912. Spring 2017 admissions: No information provided.

**# of transfer students accepted:** Fall 2016: 260. Spring 2017: No information provided.

**Transfer student acceptance rate (2016–2017 academic year):** 28.5%

**Freshman applications received in Fall 2016:** 19,924

**Freshman applications accepted in Fall 2016:** 5,020

**Acceptance rate for 2016–2017 freshmen:** 25.1%

## Transfer Admissions Process

**Transfer policy (in their own words):** Emory University considers you a transfer student if you have completed 1 year as a full-time student (or are in the second semester of your first complete year as a full-time student) in a degree-seeking program at another 2-year or 4-year college or university after completing high school (dual-enrollment credit does not count).

**Transfer admissions contact person:** Scott Allen, Senior Associate Dean of Admission and Director of International Recruitment

**Transfer admissions contact info:** scott.allen@emory.edu

**Offers transfer-focused admissions events:** Yes

**Transfer application deadline:** Fall 2018 deadline is 3/15/18. Spring 2019 deadline is 10/15/18.

**Acceptances announced to transfer applicants:** Fall 2018 on 4/30/18. Spring 2019 usually on 11/15/18.

**Transfer application on Common App:** Yes. Common App fee: $75. Waiver available.

**SAT/ACT required for transfer applicants:** Yes, if student has less than 2 semesters

**High-school records requirements:** Official high-school transcripts

**High-school records requirements for applicants who completed outside the US:** Official TOEFL scores are required for all international applicants, and the institution should send the official transcript.

**Submission requirements for transfer applicants who completed high-school equivalency test:** While Emory recognizes the completion of GED programs and service to our country, students will need to complete 28 hours at an accredited college or university before they will be eligible to apply to Emory as a transfer student.

**College transcript requirements:** Official transcript(s) from all colleges and universities attended (including summer coursework)

**Interviews available for transfer applicants:** No

**Additional requirements for transfers seeking admissions to business school:** Yes. You will be required to spend at least 1 academic year at Emory College before being eligible to apply to the Goizueta Business School, and the admission to the program requires a strong academic performance and involvement at Emory, not just at your previous school.

**Additional requirements for transfers seeking admissions to arts major:** Emory University values that many of our applicants are artistically talented and want to showcase those talents for the Admission Committee. Applicants should fully present their achievements on their application. The submission of arts supplements is by request only. It's important to note that a request for arts supplements (or lack thereof) is not an indication of a student's final admission decision.

**Additional requirements for transfers seeking admissions to engineering major:** Yes, with Georgia Tech. Choose an engineering major(s) approved by the Georgia Institute of Technology for the Dual Degree Program. You must:

- Register your intent to pursue the Dual Degree Program
- Complete your General Education Requirements (GERs) at Emory
- Complete your major courses and a minimum of 100 credit hours at Emory
- You must have both an overall GPA and math and science GPA above a 3.0

**Additional requirements for transfers seeking admissions to other major:** Yes, nursing. Students interested in the School of Nursing (SON) should be aware of the following when applying as a transfer student:

Review the prerequisites for applying for a bachelor of science in nursing. If you have completed these requirements by the time you would like to start at Emory, you should apply directly to the SON. If you have not completed these prerequisites, you should apply to Emory College.

Required Prerequisites:

- CHEM 150 Structure and Properties with lab
- BIOL 141 Foundations of Modern Biology I with lab
- MATH 107 Intro to Probability and Statistics OR QTM 100 Intro to Stat Inference
- NRSG 201 Human Anatomy and Physiology I (+)
- NRSG 202 Human Anatomy and Physiology II (+)
- NRSG 200 Human Growth and Development (+)
- Additional coursework totaling 60 credit hours

## Costs & Financial Aid

**FAFSA code:** 1564

**CSS Profile code:** 5187

**Are internal school financial aid forms required?** Yes

**Financial aid deadlines for transfer applicants:** Fall 2018: 3/15/18. Spring 2019: 11/1/18.

**Costs for the 2017–2018 year:** Tuition & Fees: $47,954. Room & Board: $13,486.

**Financial aid for transfer students:** Yes

**Guarantees meeting 100% need for transfer students:** Yes

**Need-based aid for transfer students:** Yes

**Merit-based financial aid for transfer students:** No

**Phi Theta Kappa Scholarship:** No

**Reduced or zero tuition fees for low-income students:** No

**Includes loans in financial aid packages:** Yes

**% of all undergraduates receiving financial aid:** 64% in forms of grants and scholarships

**% of all undergraduates qualifying for Pell Grants:** No information provided.

**Average financial aid award for all undergraduate students:** $35,348

**Funding available for low-income students to visit:** No information provided.

**Enrollment deposit can be waived for low-income students:** Yes

## Academics

**GPA range for transfer students accepted in 2016–2017:** 3.3–4.0

**SAT ranges for all students admitted in 2016:** Critical Reading: 620–720. Mathematics: 560–770. Writing: 640–730.

**ACT composite score range for all students admitted in 2016:** 29–33

**Type of curriculum:** Gen. Ed. requirements

**Type of academic year:** Semester

**Advisors specifically for transfer students:** No

**Credit policy (in their own words):** A minimum of 28 credit hours is required, not including AP, IB, or dual enrollment credit. A transfer student is required to complete 2 years (4 semesters) of coursework at Emory University; for that reason, a transfer student may only transfer up to 64 semester hours of college credit to Emory University.

**Max number of transfer credits accepted:** 64 credits for both 2- and 4-year schools

**Residency requirement for transfer students:** 28 credit minimum. 64 credits must be completed at the school to obtain a bachelor's degree.

**Study abroad available for transfer students:** Yes. Must fulfill the residency requirements.

**Free tutoring for all students:** Yes

**Writing center for all students:** Yes

**Career support/access to internships and resume prep for all students:** Yes

**% of undergraduate students hired within 6 months of graduation:** 36% full-time employment

**Additional resources specifically designated for transfer and/or non-traditional students:** No

## Housing

**Available for transfer students:** Yes

**Available for non-traditional students:** No information provided.

**Guaranteed for transfer students:** No

**Non-traditional students can reside in housing year-round:** No information provided.

**Family housing available:** No information provided.

## Non-Traditional Admissions

**Non-traditional student policy (in their own words):** Non-traditional students are frequently defined as students outside the usual college age range of 18–22. Since Emory focuses on the traditional residential university experience, it is recommended that non-traditional students take that fact into consideration when applying. It is recommended that non-traditional students consider continuing education programs instead: www.ece.emory.edu.

**Program contact person:** Michael Toney, Director of Orientation

**Program contact info:** (404) 727-9236, michael.toney@emory.edu

## Military/Veteran Students

**Military/veteran admissions policy (in their own words):** Emory University invested over 1 million dollars in financial aid to students who are veterans of the US military through the Yellow Ribbon Program. The Yellow Ribbon Program is a provision of the Post-9/11 Veterans Educational Assistance Act of 2008. This program allows degree-granting institutions of higher learning in the US to voluntarily enter into an agreement with the VA to fund tuition expenses that exceed the annual VA tuition and fees benefit. All of Emory's 9 schools have chosen to participate.

**Status considered in admissions:** No

**Special admissions process:** No

**Special financial aid:** Yes. The Yellow Ribbon Program.

**Specific programs/policies to address needs:** Emory's Veterans Program offers veterans of the wars in Iraq and Afghanistan and their family members a variety of expert support resources. The program is focused on helping people in the Southeastern United States get help for PTSD and TBI. As part of Warrior Care Network, Emory's Veterans Program offers innovative 2- to 3-week intensive outpatient programs that will provide individualized care that is tailored to each wounded veteran and family member.

## DACA/Undocumented Students

**DACA and undocumented admissions policy (in their own words):** Our current undocumented student policy is only for students applying as first-year students. Unfortunately, transfer students are not eligible.

# FLORIDA A&M UNIVERSITY

**Location:** Tallahassee, Florida

**Website:** www.famu.edu

**Endowment:** $113.1 million

**Type of School:** Public/Co-ed, Research University

**# of Undergraduate Students:** 7,769

**# of Graduate Students:** 1,850

**Average Class Size:** No information provided.

**School Mission (in their own words):** Florida Agricultural and Mechanical University (FAMU) is an 1890 land-grant institution dedicated to the advancement of knowledge, resolution of complex issues, and the empowerment of citizens and communities. The University provides a student-centered environment consistent with its core values. The faculty is committed to educating students at the undergraduate, graduate, doctoral, and professional levels, preparing graduates to apply their knowledge, critical thinking skills, and creativity in their service to society. FAMU's distinction as a doctoral/research institution will continue to provide mechanisms to address emerging issues through local and global partnerships. Expanding upon the University's land-grant status, it will enhance the lives of constituents through innovative research, engaging cooperative extension, and public service. While the University continues its historic mission of educating African Americans, FAMU embraces persons of all races, ethnic origins, and nationalities as lifelong members of the university community.

## Admissions

**Admissions office mailing address:** 1601 S Martin Luther King Jr Blvd, Tallahassee FL 32301

**Admissions office phone:** (850) 599-3796

**Admissions office email:** ugrdadmissions@famu.edu

**# of transfer applications:** Fall 2016 admissions: 1,539. Spring 2017 admissions: No information provided.

**# of transfer students accepted:** Fall 2016: 735. Spring 2017: No information provided.

**Transfer student acceptance rate (2016–2017 academic year):** 47.7%

**Freshman applications received in Fall 2016:** 6,988

**Freshman applications accepted in Fall 2016:** 2,174

**Acceptance rate for 2016–2017 freshmen:** 31%

## Transfer Admissions Process

**Transfer policy (in their own words):** A transfer applicant is an undergraduate student with at least 12 transferable semester credit hours (not remedial) earned following graduation from high school. All Florida State College graduates who have completed a university-parallel program and an associate of arts degree will receive priority consideration for transfer admission.

**Transfer admissions contact person:** Crystal Flowers, Transfer Student Coordinator

**Transfer admissions contact info:** crystal.flowers@famu.edu

**Offers transfer-focused admissions events:** Yes

**Transfer application deadline:** Fall 2018 deadline is 5/1/18. Spring 2019 deadline is 11/1/18.

**Acceptances announced to transfer applicants:** Fall 2018 on rolling basis. Spring 2019 on rolling basis.

**Transfer application on Common App:** No. Common App fee: N/A.

**Separate application or in addition to the Common App:** Yes

**Fee for separate transfer application:** Yes, $35

**Waiver available for separate transfer application fee:** First-Time-in-College Florida residents

**SAT/ACT required for transfer applicants:** Yes, but only for freshmen/sophomore transfers with less than 30 semester hours. Official scores must be sent to FAMU directly from the testing agency.

**High-school records requirements:** Submit all high-school transcripts (transfer applicants with less than 30 transferable semester credit hours). Official transcripts can be sent to FAMU in two ways: paper transcript received by FAMU in a sealed envelope or electronic transcripts sent from the institution.

**High-school records requirements for applicants who completed outside the US:** Original transcripts from all institutions must be submitted from the foreign institutions directly to the Office of Admissions. To determine academic eligibility for admissions, academic credentials must be: (a) translated into English and (b) evaluated course by course by an evaluation service.

**Submission requirements for transfer applicants who completed high-school equivalency test:** Official GED results required.

**College transcript requirements:** Official transcripts for all colleges and universities attended

**Interviews available for transfer applicants:** Specific academic programs may request an on-campus interview with an admissions counselor.

**Additional requirements for transfers seeking admissions to engineering major:** Yes. Achieve a grade of C or better, from any institution attended, in First Year Engineering Laboratory, Calculus I, Calculus II, General Chemistry I, and General Physics I to be admitted to an engineering major. Intended chemical engineering students shall replace General Physics I with General Chemistry II. A single repeated attempt in only 1 of the 5 courses listed above with no more than 1 grade of C– is allowed. Transfer students may receive an exemption from First-Year Engineering Laboratory if they have completed all of the other courses listed above prior to their matriculation to the College. Students should contact the College of Engineering if they feel they qualify for an exemption.

## Costs & Financial Aid

**FAFSA code:** 1480

**CSS Profile code:** 0

**Are internal school financial aid forms required?** No

**Financial aid deadlines for transfer applicants:** Fall 2018: 3/1/18. Spring 2019: 11/1/18.

**Costs for the 2017–2018 year:** Tuition & Fees (differential fees included): In-state on-campus: $22,419. In-state off-campus: $22,871. Out-of-state on-campus: $34,356. Out-of-state off-campus: $34,817. Room & Board: Costs depend on type of housing and on the time of year.

**Financial aid for transfer students:** Yes

**Guarantees meeting 100% need for transfer students:** No

**Need-based aid for transfer students:** Yes

**Merit-based financial aid for transfer students:** No

**Phi Theta Kappa Scholarship:** Yes, $4,000. Renewable. Additional application and 3.5 GPA required.

**Reduced or zero tuition fees for low-income students:** No

**Includes loans in financial aid packages:** Yes

**% of all undergraduates receiving financial aid:** 76%

**% of all undergraduates qualifying for Pell Grants:** No information provided.

**Average financial aid award for all undergraduate students:** $13,113, excluding loans

**Funding available for low-income students to visit:** No

**Enrollment deposit can be waived for low-income students:** No

## Academics

**GPA range for transfer students accepted in 2016–2017:** Minimum GPA: 2.5

**SAT ranges for all students admitted in 2016:** Critical Reading: 420–540. Mathematics: 420–530. Writing: 400–510.

**ACT composite score range for all students admitted in 2016:** 18–23

**Recommended courses transfer applicants interested in STEM should complete before transfer:** Achieve a grade of C or better, from any institution attended, in First Year Engineering Laboratory, Calculus I, Calculus II, General Chemistry I, and General Physics I to be admitted to an engineering major. Intended chemical engineering students shall replace General Physics I with General Chemistry II. A single repeated attempt

in only 1 of the 5 courses listed above with no more than 1 grade of C– is allowed.

**Type of curriculum:** Gen. Ed. requirements

**Type of academic year:** Semester

**Advisors specifically for transfer students:** Yes

**Credit policy (in their own words):** Credits are transferred based on the following: the institution from which the student wishes to transfer is regionally accredited (credit can be transferred from a non-regionally accredited institution that participates in the Florida Statewide Course Numbering System, per Florida Statute); the overall GPA is at least 2.00 on a 4.00 scale on the transfer transcript; the grades of individual courses to be transferred are C or better, or S or P; college credits earned by high-school or college students on the basis of the College Entrance Examination Board's College Level Examination Program (CLEP) subject examination, College Board Advanced Placement Program examination (AP), Advanced International Certificate of Education examination (AICE), International Baccalaureate examination (IB), and other examinations shall be accepted for transfer provided the scores attained by the student on these examinations meet the standards determined by the Articulation Coordinating Committee (ACC) Credit-by-Exam Equivalencies as adopted by the Board of Governors (www.fldoe.org/articulation). FAMU will award credit for specific courses for which competency has been demonstrated by successful scores on any of the examinations listed above unless the award of credit duplicates credit already awarded. Students may be exempt from courses based on the award of credit if competencies have been so demonstrated.

**Max number of transfer credits accepted:** 64

**Residency requirement for transfer students:** Yes

**Study abroad available for transfer students:** Yes. Must fulfill residency requirements.

**Free tutoring for all students:** Yes

**Writing center for all students:** Yes

**Career support/access to internships and resume prep for all students:** Yes

**% of undergraduate students hired within 6 months of graduation:** No

**Additional resources specifically designated for transfer and/or non-traditional students:** N/A

## Housing

**Available for transfer students:** Yes

**Available for non-traditional students:** No

**Guaranteed for transfer students:** No

**Non-traditional students can reside in housing year-round:** N/A

**Family housing available:** No

## Non-Traditional Admissions

No non-traditional student policies or programs available.

## Military Students

**Special admissions process:** No

**Special financial aid:** Yes. Please contact financial aid for more information.

## DACA/Undocumented Students

No DACA and undocumented student policies or programs available.

# FRANKLIN & MARSHALL COLLEGE

**Location:** Lancaster, Pennsylvania

**Website:** www.fandm.edu

**Endowment:** $339.2 million

**Type of School:** Private/Co-ed, Liberal Arts

**# of Undergraduate Students:** 2,255

**# of Graduate Students:** 0

**Average Class Size:** 18

**School Mission (in their own words):** Franklin & Marshall College is a residential college dedicated to excellence in undergraduate liberal education. Its aims are to inspire in young people of high promise and diverse backgrounds a genuine and enduring love for learning; to teach them to read, write, and think critically; to instill in them the capacity for both independent and collaborative action; and to educate them to explore and understand the natural, social, and cultural worlds in which they live. In so doing, the College seeks to foster in its students qualities of intellect, creativity, and character that they may live fulfilling lives and contribute meaningfully to their occupations, their communities, and their world.

## Admissions

**Admissions office mailing address:** 415 Harrisburg Ave, Lancaster PA 17603

**Admissions office phone:** (717) 358-3951

**Admissions office email:** admission@fandm.edu

**# of transfer applications:** Fall 2016 admissions: 151. Spring 2017 admissions: 33.

**# of transfer students accepted:** Fall 2016: 48. Spring 2017: 6.

**Transfer student acceptance rate (2016–2017 academic year):** 30%

**Freshman applications received in Fall 2016:** 6,954

**Freshman applications accepted in Fall 2016:** 2,529

**Acceptance rate for 2016–2017 freshmen:** 36%

## Transfer Admissions Process

**Transfer policy (in their own words):** The Admission Committee looks for the following when reviewing transfer candidates: successful completion of college-level coursework in a challenging college curriculum, faculty endorsements, high-school record, and overall potential for future academic success. A GPA of at least 3.0 (on a 4.0 scale) is recommended.

In addition to academic considerations, the Admission Committee takes note of a student's engagement in student or community life. The committee is interested in quality of participation, level of commitment, special talents, honors received, and leadership roles held.

**Transfer admissions contact person:** Cathy Rintz, Transfer Admission Counselor

**Transfer admissions contact info:** cathy.rintz@fandm.edu

**Offers transfer-focused admissions events:** No

**Transfer application deadline:** Fall 2018 deadline is 4/15/18. Spring 2019 deadline is 11/15/18.

**Acceptances announced to transfer applicants:** Fall 2018 on 5/15/18. Spring 2019 on 12/15/18.

**Transfer application on Common App:** Yes. Common App fee: $60.

**SAT/ACT required for transfer applicants:** You may choose to submit either SAT I or ACT results. F&M also offers a Standardized Test Option, which allows applicants to submit 2 graded college-level writing samples in place of standardized test scores.

**High-school records requirements:** The Secondary School Final Report is *optional* at F&M, as long as we receive an official high-school transcript with date of graduation.

**High-school records requirements for applicants who completed outside the US:** Franklin & Marshall College requires students who have earned postsecondary credit at institutions outside of the US and Canada to verify their credentials through a credential verification agency. The International Credit Evaluation requirement is waived for those who have completed all postsecondary coursework at institutions located in the US or Canada.

**Submission requirements for transfer applicants who completed high-school equivalency test:** An official copy of HiSET or GED completion

**College transcript requirements:** We require official transcripts for all college-level courses completed.

**Interviews available for transfer applicants:** Yes. Optional. On-campus or Skype.

**Additional requirements for transfers seeking admissions to arts major:** Yes. The Art Department welcomes samples of your artistic work in any medium. Art talent samples should include between 6 to 20 works (no less, no more), preferably submitted as a PDF file to your F&M application portal.

**Additional requirements for transfers seeking admissions to engineering major:** Yes. Students should have completed some calculus courses along with basic chemistry if it applies to their engineering major.

## Costs & Financial Aid

**FAFSA code:** 3265

**CSS Profile code:** 2261

**Are internal school financial aid forms required?** No

**Financial aid deadlines for transfer applicants:** Fall 2018: 4/15/18. Spring 2019: 11/15/18

**Costs for the 2017–2018 year:** Tuition & Fees: $54,280. Room & Board: $8,714.

**Financial aid for transfer students:** Yes

**Guarantees meeting 100% need for transfer students:** For admitted domestic US transfer applicants, Franklin & Marshall College will meet 100% of institutionally determined financial aid need throughout the duration of full-time study.

**Need-based aid for transfer students:** Yes. Financial aid is available to admitted domestic US applicants. Financial aid is not available for international transfer applicants.

**Merit-based financial aid for transfer students:** No

**Phi Theta Kappa Scholarship:** No

**Reduced or zero tuition fees for low-income students:** No

**Includes loans in financial aid packages:** Yes

**% of all undergraduates receiving financial aid:** 63%

**% of all undergraduates qualifying for Pell Grants:** 21%

**Average financial aid award for all undergraduate students:** $35,494

**Funding available for low-income students to visit:** No

**Enrollment deposit can be waived for low-income students:** No

## Academics

**GPA range for transfer students accepted in 2016–2017:** 2.7–4.0

**SAT ranges for all students admitted in 2016:** Critical Reading: 570–680. Mathematics: 630–730. Writing: N/A—score is not separated this way.

**ACT composite score range for all students admitted in 2016:** 28–31

**Type of curriculum:** Gen. Ed. requirements. The CONNECTION curriculum has 3 phases: Introduction, Exploration, and Concentration. Together with electives, these phases offer appropriate balance between structure and choice to allow the construction of an individualized educational experience.

**Type of academic year:** Semester

**Advisors specifically for transfer students:** Admitted transfer students schedule academic advising sessions prior to arriving on campus. Like all students, once transfer students formally select a major, they are assigned a permanent academic advisor within that department.

**Credit policy (in their own words):** Coursework completed at other colleges may satisfy requirements in most areas of the Franklin & Marshall curriculum (major requirements, distribution requirements, exploration, and electives), depending upon the nature of that coursework. Credit evaluation is based on both the number of credit hours earned and the grades earned. A course will be evaluated only if the earned grade is C– or better. In general, no transfer credit is granted for the following type of courses: technical, physical education, secretarial, engineering, drafting, military science, or any courses from non-regionally accredited institutions. Additionally, most education courses, communications courses, and vocal or instrumental lesson credits are not awarded Franklin & Marshall course credit.

**Max number of transfer credits accepted:** 16

**Residency requirement for transfer students:** Yes. To qualify for a Franklin & Marshall degree, transfer students must successfully complete at least 16 course credits at the campus. This minimum course requirement is equivalent to 4 full-time semesters with 4 courses per semester.

**Study abroad available for transfer students:** Yes. Must fulfill residency requirements.

**Free tutoring for all students:** Yes

**Writing center for all students:** Yes

**Career support/access to internships and resume prep for all students:** Yes

**% of undergraduate students hired within 6 months of graduation:** 90%

**Additional resources specifically designated for transfer and/or non-traditional students:** No

## Housing

**Available for transfer students:** Yes. F&M is a residential college, and we strongly believe that a rich residential experience is vital to the life of the College. F&M provides housing to transfer students appropriate to their incoming status and age.

**Available for non-traditional students:** Yes

**Guaranteed for transfer students:** Yes

**Non-traditional students can reside in housing year-round:** Yes

**Family housing available:** No

## Non-Traditional Admissions

No non-traditional student policies or programs available.

## Military/Veteran Students

**Military/veteran admissions policy (in their own words):**
Students who receive Veterans Benefits will have those
funds applied to their financial aid package at F&M. Provided
that total funds from all sources (Veterans Benefits and
awarded aid from the federal government, the State, the
College, and private organizations) do not exceed the total
cost of annual attendance, the funds themselves will neither
displace already awarded aid, nor will the funds impact
the family's demonstrated need or the family's calculated
expected family contribution; i.e., receipt of Veterans Benefits
will not adversely affect a student's financial aid package.
This applies to dependent students of veterans and veteran
students.

**Status considered in admissions:** Yes

**Special admissions process:** No

**Special financial aid:** Yes. The Yellow Ribbon Program.

**Specific programs/policies to address needs:** No information
provided.

## DACA/Undocumented Students

**DACA and undocumented admissions policy:** No policy
provided.

**Admitted:** Yes

**Status considered in admissions:** Yes

**Special admissions process:** No

**Eligible for institutional financial aid:** Yes. F&M meets 100%
of demonstrated need for all admitted transfer applicants.
This includes DACA/undocumented students. In lieu of the
FAFSA, DACA/undocumented students must submit either
the CSS College Profile or the F&M International Financial Aid
Form.

**Specific programs/policies to address needs:** Yes. F&M has a
peer cohort of undocumented students who are supported by
a faculty advisor.

# GEORGETOWN UNIVERSITY

**Location:** Washington, D.C.

**Website:** www.georgetown.edu

**Endowment:** $1.484 billion

**Type of School:** Private/Co-ed, Research University

**# of Undergraduate Students:** 7,562

**# of Graduate Students:** 10,897

**Average Class Size:** Student faculty ratio 10:1

**School Mission (in their own words):** Georgetown is a Catholic and Jesuit student-centered research university.

Established in 1789 in the spirit of the new republic, the university was founded on the principle that serious and sustained discourse among people of different faiths, cultures, and beliefs promotes intellectual, ethical, and spiritual understanding. We embody this principle in the diversity of our students, faculty, and staff; our commitment to justice and the common good; our intellectual openness and our international character.

An academic community dedicated to creating and communicating knowledge, Georgetown provides excellent undergraduate, graduate, and professional education in the Jesuit tradition for the glory of God and the well-being of humankind. Georgetown educates women and men to be reflective lifelong learners, to be responsible and active participants in civic life, and to live generously in service to others.

## Admissions

**Admissions office mailing address:** 3700 O St NW, Washington DC 20057

**Admissions office phone:** (202) 687-3600

**Admissions office email:** guadmiss@georgetown.edu

**# of transfer applications:** Fall 2016 admissions: 2,136. Spring 2017 admissions: N/A.

**# of transfer students accepted:** Fall 2016: 263. Spring 2017: N/A.

**Transfer student acceptance rate (2016–2017 academic year):** 12.31%

**Freshman applications received in Fall 2016:** 19,997

**Freshman applications accepted in Fall 2016:** 3,369

**Acceptance rate for 2016–2017 freshmen:** 16.85%

## Transfer Admissions Process

**Transfer policy (in their own words):** Typically, a cumulative B+ average or higher is recommended for transfer admission consideration.

Georgetown admits transfer students who have attended community colleges or 4-year colleges and universities. Transfer applicants must have graduated from high school or earned a high-school diploma equivalent, and should have completed at least 1 full-time semester of at least 12 transferable credits, or the equivalent, on the college level but no more than 4 full-time semesters. High-school students currently enrolled in a dual enrollment program, earning both high-school and college credit toward their high-school graduation requirements, must submit the first-year application.

Transfer applicants are only admitted for the fall semester. Transfer applicants must provide official college/university transcripts from all previous institutions, as well as a completed Dean's Report, Professor's Report, and Secondary School Report that includes the final high-school transcript.

Transfer applicants are required to provide either an SAT or ACT exam as part of the application process, unless the candidate has been out of high school for 5 or more years prior to the date of intended matriculation at Georgetown.

Transfer applicants are strongly encouraged to apply online. While PDF copies of the Georgetown Transfer Application and Georgetown Transfer Application Supplement are available, submission of an online application greatly facilitates file completion and timely review.

**Transfer admissions contact info:** transferadmissions@georgetown.edu

**Transfer application deadline:** Fall 2018: 3/1/18

**Acceptances announced to transfer applicants:** Fall 2018 on 6/1/18.

**Transfer application on Common App:** No. Separate application from Common App: Yes. Online (recommended) or paper.

**Fee for separate transfer application:** Yes, $75

**Waiver available for separate transfer application fee:** The Admissions Office accepts fee waiver requests submitted from guidance counselors using the official NACAC Application Fee Waiver form. Guidance counselors may also submit a written letter or email on behalf of the student, indicating that the fee would present a financial hardship for the student (in lieu of the official NACAC form) on behalf of the student. Students requesting a fee waiver may apply by emailing a completed application fee waiver form to feewaiver@georgetown.edu.

**SAT/ACT required for transfer applicants:** Yes. SAT or ACT. Testing requirement is waived only for applicants who graduated from high school 5 or more years prior to intended matriculation at Georgetown.

**High-school records requirements:** Must submit a secondary school report and include an official high-school transcript.

**High-school records requirements for applicants who completed outside the US:** Same as US citizen requirements

**Submission requirements for transfer applicants who completed high-school equivalency test:** GED documentation should be submitted by mail or as an attachment to their Georgetown Transfer Application Supplement. A high-school transcript, albeit incomplete, is still requested to complete all transfer application files.

**College transcript requirements:** Transfer applicants must provide official college/university transcripts from all previous institutions, as well as a completed Dean's Report and Professor's Report.

**Interviews available for transfer applicants:** Alumni interviews are not guaranteed for transfer applicants. If a volunteer alumni interviewer is available in your area, you will be contacted by email.

**Additional requirements for transfers seeking admissions to arts major:** Yes/optional. Art portfolios/supplements must be submitted on a disk with up to 20 images. Images must be in jpg format (72 dpi and no larger than 400k bytes), not in PowerPoint presentations. Other forms of art portfolios, such as photographs of artwork or original artwork, will not be accepted. The disk should be submitted in a protective case to the undergraduate admissions office with a label indicating the student's name.

**Additional requirements for transfers seeking admissions to engineering major:**

- Calculus I
- Calculus II
- General Chemistry I
- Microeconomics
- Computer Science I

## Costs & Financial Aid

**FAFSA code:** 1445

**CSS Profile code:** 5244

**Are internal school financial aid forms required?** No

**Financial aid deadlines for transfer applicants:** Fall 2018: 3/1/18. Spring 2019: N/A.

**Costs for the 2017–2018 year:** Tuition & Fees: $51,720. Room & Board: $15,434 first-year, $16,036 continuing.

**Financial aid for transfer students:** Yes

**Guarantees meeting 100% need for transfer students:** Yes

**Need-based aid for transfer students:** Yes. Demonstrated need (CSS/Financial Aid Profile tax returns).

**Merit-based financial aid for transfer students:** No

**Phi Theta Kappa Scholarship:** Yes, at the School of Continuing Studies. Half tuition. Renewable. Details available at https://scs.georgetown.edu/admissions/scholarships/#9.

**Includes loans in financial aid packages:** Yes

**% of all undergraduates receiving financial aid:** 36.95% (2015–2016)

**Average financial aid award for all undergraduate students:** $42,314 (2015–2016)

**Enrollment deposit can be waived for low-income students:** Yes

## Academics

**GPA range for transfer students accepted in 2016–2017:** Average transfer GPA is 3.8/4.0.

**SAT ranges for all students admitted in 2016:** Critical Reading: 660–750 (Fall 2015 common data set). Mathematics: 660–750 (Fall 2015 common data set). Writing: 660–750 (Fall 2015 common data set).

**ACT composite score range for all students admitted in 2016:** 30–34 (Fall 2015 common data set)

**Recommended completed level of math for transfer applicants:** 2 semesters of single variable calculus in high school or college

**Type of curriculum:** Gen. Ed. requirements

**Type of academic year:** Semester

**Advisors specifically for transfer students:** No

**Credit policy:** Credit awarded from other institutions are subject to the following limitations:

- Credit for required courses will be given if the course is similar to the one required at Georgetown.
- Credit for electives will be given if the course is similar to courses offered at Georgetown. Credit for courses not offered at Georgetown will be considered on an individual basis.
- Grades earned must be at least one level above minimum passing level (e.g., C). Passing grades on a Pass/Fail system are acceptable if defined as C or better.
- The maximum number of transferable credits is one-half of the total required for the degree (60 credits). All transfer students must enroll as full-time students. They must spend a minimum of 4 full semesters in residence at Georgetown to earn a degree. Summer sessions and study abroad programs will not count toward fulfilling the residency requirement.

**Max number of transfer credits accepted:** 60

**Residency requirement for transfer students:** Yes. Students must spend a minimum of 4 full semesters and earn 60 credits in residency at Georgetown to earn a degree. Students over 22 years old can be exempt from living on campus.

**Study abroad available for transfer students:** Yes, must meet residency requirements.

**Free tutoring for all students:** Yes

**Writing center for all students:** Yes

**Career support/access to internships and resume prep for all students:** Yes. Career support is for undergrads, graduates, and alumni who graduated within 2 years.

**% of undergraduate students hired within 6 months of graduation:** 72.7%

**Additional resources specifically designated for transfer and/or non-traditional students:** No

## Housing

**Available for transfer students:** Yes

**Available for non-traditional students:** Yes

**Guaranteed for transfer students:** Yes

**Non-traditional students can reside in housing year-round:** Yes (Apply for winter and summer housing.)

**Family housing available:** No

## Non-Traditional Admissions

No non-traditional student policies or programs listed.

## Military/Veteran Students

**Military/veteran admissions policy (in their own words):** Active military and veterans applying for transfer admission must have earned at least 12 credits at a 2-year or 4-year institution prior to transferring to Georgetown. If a minimum of 12 credits have not been earned by time of application, applicants should submit the first-year student application. Note that a Dean's Report is a required piece of the application. For the Professor's Report, Georgetown will accept a recommendation from a military superior if it is not possible to submit a letter from a professor. For additional information about campus resources for veterans, please visit www.georgetown.edu/campus-life/offices-resources/veterans.

**Status considered in admissions:** No

**Special financial aid:** Yes. The Yellow Ribbon Program.

**Specific programs/policies to address needs:** Georgetown University Student Veterans Association (GUSVA), McDonough Military Association (MMA), Military Medicine Interest Group (MMIG), Military Law Society (MLS), HOYA Battalion ROTC

## DACA/Undocumented Students

**DACA and undocumented admissions policy (in their own words):** Georgetown welcomes and supports students of all backgrounds without regard to their immigration status. We welcome all interested individuals to apply, and we do not require students to provide proof of citizenship. Georgetown is proud of its need-blind/meet-full-need policy regarding all of its undergraduate students. Consistent with that commitment, although federal aid programs are not available to undocumented students, Georgetown provides institutional aid to all undergraduate students who qualify for need-based aid, without regard to immigration status.

**Admitted:** Yes

**Status considered in admissions:** No

**Eligible for institutional financial aid:** Yes. If you have a valid Social Security number, complete the most current FAFSA application at https://fafsa.gov. If you do not have a valid Social Security number, complete the most current CSS Profile at www.collegeboard.org (make sure you complete the domestic version and not the international version). If you are DACA eligible, please indicate that in the "notes" section of the CSS Profile. If your parents have filed or are planning on filing a 2016 tax return, please upload that document (including all schedules and W-2s) to the IDOC system at www.collegeboard.org. One of our financial aid counselors will contact you regarding your financial aid application. However, if your financial aid package does not come within a few days of your offer of admission—or if you have any questions about this process—please contact our office at http://finaid.georgetown.edu.

**Specific programs/policies to address needs:** Yes.

Hoyas for Immigrant Rights & Georgetown Solidarity Committee: work toward a campus that is a safe and open space for all members of the Georgetown community. We foster informed and respectful dialogue about immigration and immigrant rights. We form a network of individuals committed to action and advocacy.

Email: hoyasforimmigrantrights@gmail.com.
Facebook: facebook.com/HoyasforImmigrantRights.

Georgetown Solidarity Committee: dedicated to workers' rights and social justice issues both on campus and in the greater community. Since its founding in 1996, Georgetown Solidarity Committee has continued its fight for workers' rights, particularly alongside our campus workers. GSC also supports and engages with other student allies in support of their campaigns to build a better campus and local community.

Email: gschoyas@gmail.com or solidaritycommittee@georgetown.edu

Facebook: facebook.com/georgetownsolidarity

# GEORGIA INSTITUTE OF TECHNOLOGY

**Location:** Atlanta, Georgia

**Website:** www.gatech.edu

**Endowment:** $1.844 billion

**Type of School:** Public/Co-ed, Research University

**# of Undergraduate Students:** 15,489

**# of Graduate Students:** 11,350

**Average Class Size:** Information not provided.

**School Mission (in their words):** Technological change is fundamental to the advancement of the human condition. The Georgia Tech community—students, staff, faculty, and alumni—will realize our motto of "Progress and Service" through effectiveness and innovation in teaching and learning, our research advances, and entrepreneurship in all sectors of society. We will be leaders in improving the human condition in Georgia, the United States, and around the globe.

## Admissions

**Admissions office mailing address:** North Ave NW, Atlanta GA 30332

**Admissions office phone:** (404) 894-4154

**Admissions office email:** admission@gatech.edu

**# of transfer applications:** Fall 2016 admissions: 1,770. Spring 2017 admissions: Not available.

**# of transfer students accepted:** Fall 2016: 685. Spring 2017: Not available.

**Transfer student acceptance rate (2016–2017 academic year):** 38.7%

**Freshman applications received in Fall 2016:** 30,528

**Freshman applications accepted in Fall 2016:** 7,868

**Acceptance rate for 2016–2017 freshmen:** 25.77%

## Transfer Admissions Process

**Transfer policy (in their own words):** An eligible transfer applicant is a degree-seeking student who has completed a minimum of 30 semester or 45 quarter credit hours transferable to Georgia Tech. This includes students who have earned college credit through Move On When Ready (MOWR), dual enrollment, early college, or examination (AP or IB). A transfer student may not enroll in the same year as the student's high-school graduation. For example, if a student graduates high school in May 2017, he or she will not be eligible to enroll as a transfer student until 2018 or later.

Non-native speakers of English who seek transfer from a non-US institution must complete 2 college-level English composition courses to satisfy the English proficiency requirement at Georgia Tech.

The minimum GPA requirement is 3.3 on a 4.0 grade scale for College of Computing and College of Engineering applicants. The minimum GPA requirement is 3.0 on a 4.0 grade scale for College of Design, College of Sciences, Ivan Allen College of Liberal Arts, and Scheller College of Business applicants.

**Transfer admissions contact person:** Alexandra Thackston, Senior Admission Counselor (degree-seeking transfer applicants)

**Transfer admissions contact info:** alexandra.thackston@admission.gatech.edu, (404) 385-1900

**Offers transfer-focused admissions events:** Yes

**Transfer application deadline:** Fall 2018 deadline is 3/1/18. Spring 2019 deadline is 9/15/18.

**Acceptances announced to transfer applicants:** Fall 2018 on 6/15/18. Spring 2019 on 11/1/18.

**Transfer application on Common App:** No

**Separate application or in addition to the Common App:** Yes

**Fee for separate transfer application:** Yes, $75

**Waiver available for separate transfer application fee:** Contact Admissions for more information.

**SAT/ACT required for transfer applicants:** No

**High-school records requirements:** Official copy of high-school transcript

**High-school records requirements for applicants who completed outside the US:** Must be sent to a professional foreign credential evaluation agency (WES or Josef Silny & Associates) for a course-by-course and GPA evaluation.

**Submission requirements for transfer applicants who completed high-school equivalency test:** No information provided.

**College transcript requirements:** Official transcripts for all colleges and universities attended

**Interviews available for transfer applicants:** Yes, optional for most transfer applicants but required for non-native English speakers. On campus.

**Additional requirements for transfers seeking admissions to engineering major:** Minimum GPA of 3.3/4.0, Calculus I & II, 1 semester of linear algebra, 2 semesters of calculus-based physics with lab, 2 semesters of chemistry with lab, 1 year of biology with lab.

**Additional requirements for transfers seeking admissions to other majors:** Additional requirements can be found here: http://admission.gatech.edu/images/pdf/Transfer_Requirements_May_2017.pdf.

## Costs & Financial Aid

**FAFSA code:** 1569

**CSS Profile code:** 5248

**Are internal school financial aid forms required?** Yes (GTAPP)

**Financial aid deadlines for transfer applicants:**
Fall 2018: 1/31/18. Spring 2019: 9/15/18.

**Costs for the 2017–2018 year:** Tuition & Fees: In-state: $12,212. Out-of-state: $32,404. Room & Board: $13,640.

**Financial aid for transfer students:** Yes

**Guarantees meeting 100% need for transfer students:** No

**Need-based aid for transfer students:** Yes

**Merit-based financial aid for transfer students:** Yes.
To be considered for scholarships awarded by the Office of Scholarships and Financial Aid, you must complete a financial aid application (FAFSA) and the Georgia Tech Application for Scholarships and Financial Aid each year.

**Phi Theta Kappa Scholarship:** No

**Includes loans in financial aid packages:** Yes

**% of all undergraduates receiving financial aid:**
No information provided.

**% of all undergraduates qualifying for Pell Grants:**
No information provided.

**Average financial aid award for all undergraduate students:** $15,687

**Funding available for low-income students to visit:** No

**Enrollment deposit can be waived for low-income students:**
No information provided.

## Academics

**GPA range for transfer students accepted in 2016–2017:**
3.0 for Georgia residents, 3.6 for out-of-state.

**SAT ranges for all students admitted in 2016:** Critical Reading: 630–730. Mathematics: 680–770. Writing: 640–730.

**ACT composite score range for all students admitted in 2016:** 30–33

**Recommended completed level of math for transfer applicants:** Calculus I

**Recommended completed level of English for transfer applicants:** 1 year of college English

**Recommended courses transfer applicants should have on transcripts:** Please see this chart: http://admission.gatech.edu/images/pdf/Transfer_Requirements_May_2017.pdf.

**Recommended courses transfer applicants interested in STEM should complete before transfer:** Calculus I & II, 2 semesters of chemistry with lab, 2 semesters of calculus-based physics with lab, 2 semesters of biology with lab

**Recommended extracurricular engagement:** No information provided.

**Type of curriculum:** Gen. Ed. requirements

**Type of academic year:** Semester

**Advisors specifically for transfer students:** No information provided.

**Credit policy (in their own words):** The basic policy regarding the acceptance of courses by transfer is to allow credit for courses completed with satisfactory grades (C or better) at other accredited colleges and universities in the US and Canada, provided the courses correspond in time and content to courses offered at Georgia Tech. The Institute will not accept credit for courses successfully completed at another institution but previously taken at Georgia Tech unless the final grade received at Georgia Tech is a W. The student must request and file an official transcript of transfer courses before the Institute can award credit. Coursework completed at colleges and universities outside the United States and Canada will be evaluated on a case-by-case basis. Credit may be awarded for AP and SAT II test scores. Transfer credit is not calculated in the Georgia Tech GPA. 122 credits are required for graduation.

**Max number of transfer credits accepted:** Contact the Registrar's Office.

**Residency requirement for transfer students:** Yes.
Must complete at least 36 credit hours at GA Tech.

**Study abroad available for transfer students:** Yes.
Must complete 36 credit hours at GA Tech.

**Free tutoring for all students:** Yes

**Writing center for all students:** Yes

**Career support/access to internships and resume prep for all students:** Yes.

**% of undergraduate students hired within 6 months of graduation:** No information provided.

**Additional resources specifically designated for transfer and/or non-traditional students:** Yes

## Housing

**Available for transfer students:** Yes

**Available for non-traditional students:** No

**Guaranteed for transfer students:** No

**Non-traditional students can reside in housing year-round:** No

**Family housing available:** Yes

## Non-Traditional Admissions

**Non-traditional student policy:** No specific non-traditional policy available.

**Name of program:** Regent's Engineering Pathway Program (REPP)

**Program description:** REPP students attend a participating REPP institution for 2 years and then attend Georgia Tech for 2 years within one of the College of Engineering's undergraduate degree programs. Upon completion of the engineering program, students receive a bachelor's degree at Georgia Tech. The Regent's Engineering Transfer Program (RETP) was established in 1986 by the University System of Georgia (USG) to promote engineering education in Georgia. The USG recently revised the RETP and created the Regent's Engineering Pathway Program (REPP) to serve more students in Georgia who have an interest in an engineering degree.

REPP promotes all engineering education programs in the state of Georgia: Georgia Institute of Technology, Georgia Southern University, Kennesaw State University, Mercer University, and the University of Georgia.

Students may apply to 1 or more engineering education programs after completion of curriculum requirements. Admission and curriculum requirements vary by institution.

Select the appropriate option below for Georgia Tech REPP requirements, and contact a REPP partner institution for more information.

**Program deadline:** 3/1/18

**Program admission requirements:** Complete REPP institution and Georgia Tech admission requirements.

Successful completion of course requirements by engineering major.

Achieve the minimum grade point average (GPA) requirements by the document deadline.

Complete at least 30 credit hours of course requirements of engineering major at a REPP institution by the document deadline.

Have no more than 2 math or lab science course requirements in progress at the document deadline (spring and summer term applicants only).

Georgia Tech will request a recommendation from the REPP coordinator at the participating REPP institution.

**Program website:** http://admission.gatech.edu/transfer/repp

**Name of program:** Arts & Sciences Pathway Program

**Program description:** Beginning in 2016, freshman applicants who are Georgia residents and are not offered admission within the College of Design, Ivan Allen College of Liberal Arts, and College of Sciences may be given the opportunity to apply as a transfer student through the Arts & Sciences Pathway Program.

The Arts & Sciences Transfer Pathway offer is valid for the fall semester 1 year after beginning full-time college studies. Students choosing to stay at another institution beyond 1 year of matriculation or who are unable to complete the requirements below will need to apply and be reviewed in our regular, competitive transfer applicant pool.

**Program deadline:** 3/1/18

**Program admission requirements:** After graduating from high school, complete a minimum of 30 transferable semester hours (or 45 quarter hours) at a fully accredited college in the US. Completed coursework should align with the degree requirements of the intended major at Georgia Tech.

Complete course requirements by major prior to the established fall document deadline.

Establish both a cumulative GPA of 3.3 or higher and a combined math/lab science GPA of 3.3 or higher. The cumulative GPA includes all courses taken at all colleges and/or universities attended. The math/lab science GPA includes a combination of mathematics courses at the calculus level and higher along with all natural science courses, including both lecture and laboratory components.

Apply for transfer admission for the Fall 2018 term by published application deadlines, and submit all official transcript(s) showing completion of the above criteria by the corresponding document deadline.

Note: Applicants to Music Technology must submit a portfolio for review by faculty as part of their application. Approval of the portfolio is also required for admission to this program. If your portfolio is not approved and you meet all other criteria of the Arts & Sciences Transfer Pathway, you will have the opportunity to enroll at Georgia Tech in your secondary major.

Applicants may change their major when applying for the Arts & Sciences Pathway Program as long it is a major within the Colleges of Design, Liberal Arts, or Sciences.

**Program website:** http://admission.gatech.edu/georgia-tech-arts-sciences-pathway-program.

## Military/Veteran Students

**Military/veteran admissions policy (in their own words):** The Veterans Pathway Program. This program is uniquely designed to assist military veterans who have completed active duty within the past 5 years and are interested in pursuing a non-Engineering major at Georgia Tech. Applicants interested in transferring to Georgia Tech for a major within our College of Engineering are encouraged to explore our REPP program.

**Status considered in admissions:** Yes

**Special admissions process:** Veterans Pathway Admission Criteria:

- Have completed active duty military service in the US armed forces within the past 5 years. Please see the veteran definition as outlined by the US Department of Education.
- After graduating from high school, complete a minimum of 30 transferable semester hours (or 45 quarter hours) at an accredited college in the US. (Dual enrollment courses, AP/IB, or other applicable placement credit will not be counted toward this 30+ hour requirement).
- Complete all required courses based on your intended major prior to the established document deadline.
- Establish a cumulative GPA of 3.3 or higher and a combined math/science GPA of 3.3 or higher. The cumulative GPA includes all courses taken at all colleges and/or universities attended. The math/science GPA includes a combination of all mathematics courses at the calculus level and higher along with all natural science courses, including both lecture and laboratory components.

**Special financial aid:** Yes. The Yellow Ribbon Program.

**Specific programs/policies to address needs:** The Georgia Tech Veterans Resource Center has a listing of all the resources available to veterans: www.veterans.gatech.edu.

## DACA/Undocumented Students

**DACA and undocumented admissions policy (in their own words):** In accordance with University System of Georgia policy, students admitted to Georgia Tech must verify their lawful presence in the United States prior to enrollment. Students in Deferred Action status do not qualify for enrollment based on USG policy.

# HAMPTON UNIVERSITY

**Location:** Hampton, Virginia

**Website:** www.hamptonu.edu

**Endowment:** $253.8 million

**Type of School:** Private/Co-ed, Liberal Arts

**# of Undergraduate Students:** 3,836

**# of Graduate Students:** 810

**Average Class Size:** Student-faculty ratio: 9:1

**School Mission (in their own words):** Hampton University is a comprehensive institution of higher education, dedicated to the promotion of learning, building of character, and preparation of promising students for positions of leadership and service. Its curriculum emphasis is scientific and professional with a strong liberal arts undergirding. In carrying out its mission, the University requires that everything that it does be of the highest quality.

A historically black institution, Hampton University is committed to multiculturalism. The University serves students from diverse national, cultural, and economic backgrounds. From its beginnings to the present, the institution has enrolled students from 5 continents—North America, South America, Africa, Asia, and Europe—and many countries including Gabon, Kenya, Ghana, Japan, China, Armenia, Great Britain, and Russia, as well as the Hawaiian and Caribbean Islands and numerous American Indian nations.

## Admissions

**Admissions office mailing address:** 100 E Queen St, Hampton VA 23668

**Admissions office phone:** (757) 727-5328

**Admissions office email:** http://admissions.hamptonu.edu/contact

**# of transfer applications:** No information provided.

**# of transfer students accepted:** No information provided.

**Transfer student acceptance rate (2016–2017 academic year):** No information provided.

**Freshman applications received in Fall 2016:** No information provided.

**Freshman applications accepted in Fall 2016:** 1,278

**Acceptance rate for 2016–2017 freshmen:** No information provided.

## Transfer Admissions Process

**Transfer policy (in their own words):** Students who have satisfactorily completed at least 15 semester hours at an accredited institution may be admitted to regular standing with such advanced standing as their previous records may warrant. Requirements for advanced standing are as follows: If a student is suspended from another college, but eligible to return, he or she may be considered for enrollment at Hampton University after the lapse of at least 1 semester or the term of suspension, whichever is longer. The University has the right, based upon the student's record, to revise the academic classification given such students at entrance. Students who have earned a cumulative 2.5 cumulative grade point average in all college courses receive the highest consideration for admission.

**Transfer admissions contact person:** Angela Nixon Boyd, Dean of Admissions

**Transfer admissions contact info:** angela.boyd@hampton.edu

**Offers transfer-focused admissions events:** No

**Transfer application deadline:** Fall 2018 deadline is 3/1/18. Spring 2019 deadline is 11/1/18.

**Acceptances announced to transfer applicants:** Fall 2018 on rolling basis, 3–4 weeks after receipt of materials. Spring 2019 on rolling basis, 3–4 weeks after receipt of materials.

**Transfer application on Common App:** No

**Separate application or in addition to the Common App:** Yes. Online application.

**Fee for separate transfer application:** Yes, $35

**Waiver available for separate transfer application fee:** No

**SAT/ACT required for transfer applicants:** Only if applicant has fewer than 30 credit hours. Non-US citizens must submit TOEFL scores.

**High-school records requirements:** Official high-school transcript required for students with less than 30 credit hours.

**High-school records requirements for applicants who completed outside the US:** Official high-school transcript required for students with less than 30 credit hours.

**Submission requirements for transfer applicants who completed high-school equivalency test:** Official certificate must be submitted.

**College transcript requirements:** Official transcripts from all colleges and universities attended

**Interviews available for transfer applicants:** An on-campus interview may be required at the discretion of the Dean of Admission.

**Additional requirements for transfers seeking admissions to other major:** The Department of Architecture may request a portfolio. Doctor of Pharmacy 6-year program requires 2.75 minimum GPA, on-campus interview, general and organic chemistry, calculus, biology, English, speech, social science, and history prerequisites.

## Costs & Financial Aid

**FAFSA code:** 3714

**CSS Profile code:** N/A

**Are internal school financial aid forms required?** Yes

**Financial aid deadlines for transfer applicants:** Fall 2018: 2/15/18. Spring 2019: 2/15/18 (priority processing date).

**Costs for the 2017–2018 year:** Tuition & Fees: $22,630. Room & Board: $11,668.

**Financial aid for transfer students:** Yes

**Guarantees meeting 100% need for transfer students:** No

**Need-based aid for transfer students:** Yes

**Merit-based financial aid for transfer students:** No

**Phi Theta Kappa Scholarship:** No

**Reduced or zero tuition fees for low-income students:** No

**Includes loans in financial aid packages:** Yes

**Funding available for low-income students to visit:** No

**Enrollment deposit can be waived for low-income students:** No

## Academics

**GPA range for transfer students accepted in 2016–2017:** 2.5–4.0

**SAT ranges for all students admitted in 2016:** Critical Reading: 470–540. Mathematics: 470–550. Writing: 300–400.

**ACT composite score range for all students admitted in 2016:** 20–24

**Type of curriculum:** Gen. Ed. requirements

**Type of academic year:** Semester

**Advisors specifically for transfer students:** No

**Credit policy (in their own words):** The Office of Admission and the academic departments are responsible for evaluating credits earned from other educational institutions. The Office of Admission reviews all general education coursework. Other courses will be evaluated by an academic advisor within your major course of study.

**Max number of transfer credits accepted:** Max 60 credits from a 2-year school/90 credit max from a 4-year school

**Residency requirement for transfer students:** Yes. Students seeking a degree from Hampton University must complete a minimum of 30 academic credit hours at Hampton University.

**Study abroad available for transfer students:** Yes. Must fulfill residency requirements.

**Free tutoring for all students:** Yes

**Writing center for all students:** Yes

**Career support/access to internships and resume prep for all students:** Yes

**% of undergraduate students hired within 6 months of graduation:** No information provided.

**Additional resources specifically designated for transfer and/or non-traditional students:** No information provided.

## Housing

**Available for transfer students:** Yes

**Available for non-traditional students:** Yes

**Guaranteed for transfer students:** No

**Non-traditional students can reside in housing year-round:** No

**Family housing available:** No

## Non-Traditional Admissions

**Non-traditional student policy (in their own words):** The University College at Hampton University allows students to earn certificates, associate's, or bachelor's degrees quickly and at an affordable price, without sacrificing the quality of their education. The College's programs have been carefully developed to meet the needs of busy professionals who are juggling heavy workloads, family life, and community commitments.

**Name of program:** Continuing Education and Professional Services (CEPS)

**Program description:** Continuing Education and Professional Studies (CEPS), located at Hampton University in Virginia, serves working adults, ages 21 and over. CEPS allows students to earn certificates, associate's, and bachelor's degrees, through traditional and accelerated learning programs at an affordable price, without sacrificing educational quality. CEPS's adult education and evening programs (accredited by SACS Commission on Colleges) are carefully developed to meet the needs of busy professionals who are juggling heavy workloads, family life, and community commitments. By providing a stimulating learning environment, small classes, instructors who are professionals in their fields, and a year-round calendar consisting of 5 9-week sessions, CEPS is well suited for all requiring a flexible and affordable option for continuing education.

**Program deadline:** No information provided.

**Program admission requirements:** All applicants desiring admission to the University College at Hampton must have obtained a high-school diploma or GED equivalent and be at least 21 years of age or emancipated. Application requirements: non-refundable application fee of $35, official high-school transcript verifying graduation and date graduated or proof of completion of GED and date completed, and a 250–300 word essay on "Why I Want to Attend College." A short writing sample is required as part of the admissions process. Official transcripts from all former colleges/universities/military with a GPA of 2.0 or better at the previous college. Transcripts must reflect all undergraduate courses completed as of date of application. Active duty and retired military personnel must present the appropriate military transcript.

**Program website:** http://universitycollege.hamptonu.edu/
page/Continuing-Education-and-Professional-Studies-CEPS

**Program contact info:** (757) 727-5773, ucadmissions@
hamptonu.edu

## Military/Veteran Students

**Status considered in admissions:** No

**Special admissions process:** No

**Special financial aid:** Yes. The Yellow Ribbon Program.

**Specific programs/policies to address needs:**
Servicemembers Opportunity Colleges (SOC)

The Division of Continuing Studies and Hampton U Online are
proud members of the Servicemembers Opportunity Colleges
(SOC) consortium and are thus pledged to implement
military-friendly policies and procedures related to student
services and admission. In addition, Hampton U Online works
to ensure transparency of all military-related information
regarding our degree programs, policies, and procedures.

As a SOC consortium member, Hampton U Online guarantees
the following:

- Students are required to take no more than 30% of their
  degree requirements with Hampton U Online.
- No final year or final semester residency requirement.
- Transfer credit is maximized for military experience.
- Credit is awarded for nationally recognized tests, such as
  College-Level Examination Program (CLEP), General and
  Subject Examinations, and DANTES Subject Standardized
  Tests (DSST).
- Hampton U Online supports our military students by
  adhering to the SOC Military Students Bill of Rights.

## DACA/Undocumented Students

No DACA/undocumented student policy or programs
available.

# HARVARD UNIVERSITY

**Location:** Cambridge, Massachusetts

**Website:** www.harvard.edu

**Endowment:** $34.54 billion

**Type of School:** Private/Co-ed, Research University

**# of Undergraduate Students:** 6,700

**# of Graduate Students:** 14,500

**Average Class Size:** 10–13

**School Mission (in their own words):** The mission of Harvard College is to educate the citizens and citizen-leaders for our society. We do this through our commitment to the transformative power of a liberal arts and sciences education.

Beginning in the classroom with exposure to new ideas, new ways of understanding, and new ways of knowing, students embark on a journey of intellectual transformation. Through a diverse living environment, where students live with people who are studying different topics, who come from different walks of life and have evolving identities, intellectual transformation is deepened and conditions for social transformation are created. From this we hope that students will begin to fashion their lives by gaining a sense of what they want to do with their gifts and talents, assessing their values and interests, and learning how they can best serve the world.

## Admissions

**Admissions office mailing address:** Massachusetts Hall, Cambridge MA 02138

**Admissions office phone:** (617) 495-1551

**Admissions office email:** None provided.

**# of transfer applications:** Fall 2015 admissions: 1,432

**# of transfer students accepted:** Fall 2015: 13

**Transfer student acceptance rate (2015–2016 academic year):** 0.91%

**Freshman applications received in Fall 2016:** 39,041

**Freshman applications accepted in Fall 2016:** 2,106

**Acceptance rate for 2016–2017 freshmen:** 5.39%

## Transfer Admissions Process

**Transfer policy (in their own words):** To be eligible to transfer, you must have completed at least 1 continuous academic year in a full-time degree program at 1 college and not have completed more than 2 years total in college. You must complete at least 2 full years of study at Harvard. Once a student has completed more than 2 years total of college at another institution, regardless of courses taken, that student is no longer eligible for transfer admission.

**Transfer admissions contact person:** Mary Hogan, Assistant Director of Admission

**Transfer admissions contact info:** college@fas.harvard.edu

**Offers transfer-focused admissions events:** No

**Transfer application deadline:** Fall 2018 deadline is 3/1/18. Harvard only accepts transfer students in the fall.

**Acceptances announced to transfer applicants:** Fall 2018 on 6/15/18. Spring 2019: N/A.

**Transfer application on Common App:** Yes. Common App fee: $75, waiver is available.

**SAT/ACT required for transfer applicants:** Yes, ACT with writing or old SAT or new SAT with writing

**SAT II scores required for transfer applicants:** Optional, but 2 SAT II subject tests are strongly recommended.

**High-school records requirements:** Official high-school transcript

**High-school records requirements for applicants who completed outside the US:** Official high-school transcript required. TOEFL is required (if you did not attend high school in the US or an English-language high school).

**Submission requirements for transfer applicants who completed high-school equivalency test:** Official high-school transcript

**College transcript requirements:** Official transcripts from all schools attended

**Interviews available for transfer applicants:** On campus, at the admissions committee's request

## Costs & Financial Aid

**FAFSA code:** 2155

**CSS Profile code:** 3434

**Are internal school financial aid forms required?** No

**Financial aid deadlines for transfer applicants:** Fall 2018: 3/1/18. Spring 2019: Fall admission only.

**Costs for the 2017–2018 year:** Tuition & Fees: $47,074. Room & Board: $15,951.

**Financial aid for transfer students:** Yes

**Guarantees meeting 100% need for transfer students:** Yes

**Need-based aid for transfer students:** Yes

**Merit-based financial aid for transfer students:** No merit-based aid offered.

**Phi Theta Kappa Scholarship:** Yes, but only the Harvard Extension School. Tuition for 3 courses. Renewable. Details available at www.extension.harvard.edu.

**Reduced or zero tuition fees for low-income students:** Yes, sites/extension.harvard.edu/files/atoms/files/ext_ptk.pdf. Families with total income less than $65,000 are not expected to contribute. Families with incomes between $65,000 and $150,000 will contribute from 0–10%.

**Includes loans in financial aid packages:** Yes

**% of all undergraduates receiving financial aid:** 70%

**Average financial aid award for all undergraduate students:** $47,475 (2015 common data set)

**Funding available for low-income students to visit:** Yes

**Enrollment deposit can be waived for low-income students:** Yes

## Academics

**GPA range for transfer students accepted in 2016–2017:** N/A

**SAT ranges for all students admitted in 2016:** Critical Reading: 700–800. Mathematics: 700–800. Writing: 710–790.

**ACT composite score range for all students admitted in 2016:** 32–35

**Recommended courses transfer applicants should have on transcripts:** Students are eligible to transfer only from a liberal arts curriculum that is similar to Harvard's. Candidates whose education has been in a vocational, professional, technical, online, extension, or performance program will not ordinarily qualify for transfer admission.

**Recommended extracurricular engagement:** Student should show they have challenged themselves in leadership roles.

**Type of curriculum:** Gen. Ed. requirements

**Type of academic year:** Semester

**Advisors specifically for transfer students:** Yes

**Credit policy (in their own words):** You will be allowed to transfer in a maximum of 16 semester-long courses—the equivalent of 2 full years of academic work—providing you the opportunity to take the remaining half of the courses required for your A.B. or S.B. degree at Harvard. Applicants must have completed at least 1 full academic year of undergraduate study at 1 college, but not more than 2 full academic years of study with earned grades of C (or the equivalent) or better.

**Max number of transfer credits accepted:** You will be allowed to transfer in a maximum of 16 semester-long courses—the equivalent of 2 full years of academic work.

**Residency requirement for transfer students:** Yes. Must take the remaining half of the courses required for your A.B. or S.B. degree at Harvard.

**Study abroad available for transfer students:** Yes. Must fulfill the residency requirements. Students who receive Harvard grant assistance are eligible to transfer their financial aid to an approved term-time study abroad program.

**Free tutoring for all students:** Yes

**Writing center for all students:** Yes

**Career support/access to internships and resume prep for all students:** Yes

**% of undergraduate students hired within 6 months of graduation:** 66.7%

**Additional resources specifically designated for transfer and/or non-traditional students:** No

## Housing

**Available for transfer students:** Yes

**Available for non-traditional students:** No information provided.

**Guaranteed for transfer students:** Yes, for all 4-year students.

**Non-traditional students can reside in housing year-round:** No information provided.

**Family housing available:** Harvard College does not offer undergraduate housing in the houses or dorms to married undergraduates and/or undergraduates with families. However, students who are married and/or have children may be eligible for Harvard-affiliated housing.

## Non-Traditional Admissions

**Name of program:** Harvard Extension School

**Program description:** We are Harvard—extended to the world for every type of adult learner. Our students come to us from every time zone, every culture and career background, every age from 18 to 89.

They have one thing in common: the motivation to take the next challenging step in their lives. They find that challenge here, where our academic standards are high and our resources extensive. As 1 of 12 degree-granting institutions at Harvard University, we teach to the largest and most eclectic student body. We offer undergraduate degrees, graduate degrees, graduate certificates, and 800 courses that meet: in the evening in Harvard Square, online weekly, featuring video lectures or live web conferences, and online with an intensive learning weekend on the Harvard campus.

We place student success at the heart of everything we do. Whatever your goal, we want to support your progress. With our open enrollment policy, any adult student with the motivation to enroll is welcome in our courses. Prove yourself in our classes, and you can earn your way into a Harvard degree program. An education flexible enough to fit your schedule, while also tailored to meet your goals and achievable at a reasonable cost. On average, tuition ranges from $1,400 to $2,550 for our 4-credit courses, and degree-seeking students may apply for financial aid.

We rarely ask if classroom or online learning is better. Instead, we experiment with multiple models to provide greater access to world-class teaching and help you find that style of learning that works best for you. Harvard professors teach many of our courses, and they do so for the engaging dialogue that comes from the diversity of life experiences in our students, who juggle carpools and careers and competing life interests to come prepared for discussion.

We are a fully accredited Harvard school. Our degrees and certificates are adorned with the Harvard University insignia. They carry the weight of that lineage. Our graduates walk at University commencement and become members of the Harvard Alumni Association.

**Program admission requirements:** Earn Your Way In. Most of our degree programs have a unique admission process. Before you apply, you start your coursework, taking 3 admission courses to demonstrate your ability to succeed at Harvard. Earn at least a B in each, and you qualify for admission.

**Program website:** www.extension.harvard.edu

## Military/Veteran Students

**Status considered in admissions:** Yes

**Special admissions process:** No

**Special financial aid:** Yes. The Yellow Ribbon Program.

**Specific programs/policies to address needs:** Military applicants are allowed to defer acceptance for 2 years.

## DACA/Undocumented Students

**DACA and undocumented admissions policy (in their own words):** Harvard University aims to fulfill its promise of excellence in research and teaching by attracting and welcoming into the community individuals of exceptional talent.

The University does not make citizenship status a condition for admission to any of Harvard's Schools. With the admissions decision comes a commitment to every person who has been admitted, regardless of immigration status. As President Faust has recently noted, we are all Harvard. Each School oversees its own admissions process and qualified, interested undocumented applicants should be in touch with the admissions offices in the Schools they are interested in applying to. Please see the Admissions tab on the website for links to information about the Schools's admissions policies and procedures.

Please be in touch via email at undocumented@harvard.edu with comments, suggestions, or concerns.

**Admitted:** Yes

**Status considered in admissions:** No

**Special admissions process:** No

**Eligible for institutional financial aid:** Yes. Need to file the CSS Profile or a paper submission that requires Financial Statement from Students from Foreign Countries, as well as wage or income tax return.

**Specific programs/policies to address needs:** Yes. Act on a Dream, which is a student support program. Students are also sent to Harvard's law school to attend seminars and info sessions that have to do with DACA and immigration laws.

The Office for Equity, Diversity, and Inclusion maintains a listing of DACA resources.

# HARVEY MUDD COLLEGE

**Location:** Claremont, California
**Website:** www.hmc.edu
**Endowment:** $272.6 million
**Type of School:** Private/Co-ed, Liberal Arts
**# of Undergraduate Students:** 829
**# of Graduate Students:** 0
**Average Class Size:** 20 students or fewer

**School Mission (in their own words):** Harvey Mudd College seeks to educate engineers, scientists, and mathematicians well versed in all of these areas and in the humanities and the social sciences so that they may assume leadership in their fields with a clear understanding of the impact of their work on society.

## Admissions

**Admissions office mailing address:** 301 Platt Blvd, Claremont CA 91711

**Admissions office phone:** (909) 621-8011

**Admissions office email:** admission@hmc.edu

**# of transfer applications:** Fall 2016 admissions: 89

**# of transfer students accepted:** Fall 2016: 4

**Transfer student acceptance rate (2016–2017 academic year):** 4.5%

**Freshman applications received in Fall 2016:** 4,180

**Freshman applications accepted in Fall 2016:** 538

**Acceptance rate for 2016–2017 freshmen:** 12.87%

## Transfer Admissions Process

**Transfer policy (in their own words):** Prospective students are eligible to apply as transfer students if they will have completed 2 or more terms of academic work (in good standing) at a recognized institution of higher learning by the academic term for which they apply. The transfer application process is highly selective, with fewer than 5 applicants given admission each year. Note: Transfer students are only accepted in the fall.

**Transfer admissions contact person:** Peter Osgood, Director of Admission

**Transfer admissions contact info:** posgood@hmc.edu, (909) 621-8011

**Offers transfer-focused admissions events:** No

**Transfer application deadline:** Fall 2018 deadline is 4/1/18.

**Acceptances announced to transfer applicants:** Fall 2018 on 5/15/18.

**Transfer application on Common App:** Yes. Common App fee: $70.

**SAT/ACT required for transfer applicants:** Only if taken within the past 5 years. If you have not taken them, you are not required to sit for the exams.

**SAT II scores required for transfer applicants:** Only if taken within the past 5 years. If you have not taken them, you are not required to sit for the exam.

**High-school records requirements:** Final report and official transcripts from all high schools attended

**High-school records requirements for applicants who completed outside the US:** Final report and official transcripts from all high schools attended with certified translations, as applicable

**Submission requirements for transfer applicants who completed high-school equivalency test:** Final Report and an official final high-school transcript

**College transcript requirements:** Official transcripts from all colleges attended

**Interviews available for transfer applicants:** Yes, optional

**Additional requirements for transfers seeking admissions to engineering major:** Yes. In order for a student to be considered, the student must have taken: entire physics sequence, entire calculus sequence, mechanics, electricity, magnetism, quantum physics, and a few other courses depending on the type of engineering major.

## Costs & Financial Aid

**FAFSA code:** 1171

**CSS Profile code:** 4341

**Are internal school financial aid forms required?** No

**Financial aid deadlines for transfer applicants:** Fall 2018: 1/5/18. Spring 2019: N/A.

**Costs for the 2017–2018 year:** Tuition & Fees: $52,916. Room & Board: $17,051.

**Financial aid for transfer students:** Yes

**Guarantees meeting 100% need for transfer students:** Yes

**Need-based aid for transfer students:** Yes

**Merit-based financial aid for transfer students:** No

**Phi Theta Kappa Scholarship:** No

**Includes loans in financial aid packages:** Yes

**% of all undergraduates receiving financial aid:** 75%

**% of all undergraduates qualifying for Pell Grants:** 12%

**Average financial aid award for all undergraduate students:** $36,774

**Funding available for low-income students to visit:** Yes

**Enrollment deposit can be waived for low-income students:** Yes

## Academics

**GPA range for transfer students accepted in 2016–2017:** 3.5–4.0

**SAT ranges for all students admitted in 2016:** Critical Reading: 670–760. Mathematics: 730–800. Writing: 680–760.

**ACT composite score range for all students admitted in 2016:** 32–35

**Recommended completed level of math for transfer applicants:** 1 year of Calculus I & II

**Recommended completed level of English for transfer applicants:** 2 semesters of writing-intensive courses

**Recommended courses transfer applicants should have on transcripts:** Basic computer science courses, every type of calculus, linear algebra and differential equations, probability theory, and at least 2 writing-intensive courses

**Recommended courses transfer applicants interested in STEM should complete before transfer:** 2 semesters with lab of physics, biology, and chemistry; 1 year of calculus

**Type of curriculum:** Gen. Ed. requirements

**Type of academic year:** Semester

**Advisors specifically for transfer students:** No

**Credit policy (in their own words):** The Harvey Mudd College registrar provides an estimate of credit status to admitted transfer students a few days after they receive their official letters of admission. Official placement decisions are made by our faculty during Orientation in the fall. Keep in mind that transfer students may be expected to take some placement examinations. Please contact us for your specific questions about transferring credits.

**Max number of transfer credits accepted:** 64 credit maximum from 2- and 4-year schools

**Residency requirement for transfer students:** 64 minimum credit must be earned at HMC to earn bachelor's degree.

**Study abroad available for transfer students:** Yes. Must fulfill residency requirement.

**Free tutoring for all students:** Yes

**Writing center for all students:** Yes

**Career support/access to internships and resume prep for all students:** Yes

**% of undergraduate students hired within 6 months of graduation:** Almost all—typically 97%

**Additional resources specifically designated for transfer and/or non-traditional students:** No

## Housing

**Available for transfer students:** Yes

**Available for non-traditional students:** Yes, but very limited

**Guaranteed for transfer students:** Yes

**Non-traditional students can reside in housing year-round:** Summer housing is available on campus for students that are participating in a summer programs or research at Harvey Mudd College.

**Family housing available:** No

## Non-Traditional Admissions

No non-traditional student policies or programs available.

## Military/Veteran Students

No military/veteran student policies or programs available.

## DACA/Undocumented Students

**DACA and undocumented admissions policy:** DACA and undocumented students are not eligible to apply as transfers.

# HAVERFORD COLLEGE

**Location:** Haverford, Pennsylvania
**Website:** www.haverford.edu
**Endowment:** $495 million
**Type of School:** Private/Co-ed, Liberal Arts
**# of Undergraduate Students:** 1,268
**# of Graduate Students:** 0
**Average Class Size:** 14

**School Mission (in their own words):** Haverford College is committed to providing a liberal arts education in the broadest sense. This education, based on a rich academic curriculum at its core, is distinguished by a commitment to excellence and a concern for individual growth. Haverford has chosen to remain small and to foster close student/faculty relationships to achieve these objectives.

Haverford strives to be a college in which integrity, honesty, and concern for others are dominant forces. The College does not have as many formal rules or as much formal supervision as most other colleges; rather, it offers an opportunity for students to govern their affairs and conduct themselves with respect and concern for others. Each student is expected to adhere to the Honor Code as it is adopted each year by the Students' Association.

Haverford College, while a nonsectarian institution, has Quaker origins that inform many aspects of the life of the College. They help to make Haverford the special college that it is, where the excellence of its academic program is deepened by its spiritual, moral, and ethical dimensions. These show most clearly in the close relationship among members of the campus community, in the emphasis on integrity, in the interaction of the individual and the community, and in the College's concern for the uses to which its students put their expanding knowledge.

## Admissions

**Admissions office mailing address:** 370 Lancaster Ave, Haverford PA 19041
**Admissions office phone:** (610) 896-1350
**Admissions office email:** admission@haverford.edu
**# of transfer applications:** Fall 2016 admissions: 151. Spring 2017 admissions: N/A.
**# of transfer students accepted:** Fall 2016: 22. Spring 2017: N/A.
**Transfer student acceptance rate (2016–2017 academic year):** 14.56%
**Freshman applications received in Fall 2016:** 4,066
**Freshman applications accepted in Fall 2016:** 870
**Acceptance rate for 2016–2017 freshmen:** 21.39%

## Transfer Admissions Process

**Transfer policy (in their own words):** A student is eligible for transfer admission to Haverford if at least 1 year has been completed as a full-time student at a college or university by the time of enrollment at Haverford. (Students who have completed 1 year of full-time university study must apply as transfer students; they may not apply as first-year students.)

Transfer students must enroll as full-time students and must spend a minimum of 2 years at Haverford. The College only awards the bachelor of arts or bachelor of science degree, and does not accept applications from students who have already earned a bachelor's degree.

**Transfer admissions contact person:** Janela Harris, Assistant Director of Admission
**Transfer admissions contact info:** jaharris@haverford.edu

**Offers transfer-focused admissions events:** No
**Transfer application deadline:** Fall 2018 deadline is 3/31/18. Spring 2019: N/A.
**Acceptances announced to transfer applicants:** Fall 2018 on 5/15/18. Spring 2019: N/A
**Transfer application on Common App:** Yes. Common App fee: $65 (waivable).
**SAT/ACT required for transfer applicants:** Yes
**High-school records requirements:** Official high-school transcript
**High-school records requirements for applicants who completed outside the US:** High-school transcripts should be mailed to the Admission Office by institution, with certified translations as applicable.
**Submission requirements for transfer applicants who completed high-school equivalency test:** Official GED certificate
**College transcript requirements:** Official college transcripts from all schools attended
**Interviews available for transfer applicants:** No
**Additional requirements for transfers seeking admissions to arts major:** Optional. You can include a portfolio.

## Costs & Financial Aid

**FAFSA code:** 3274
**CSS Profile code:** 2289
**Are internal school financial aid forms required?** Yes
**Financial aid deadlines for transfer applicants:** Fall 2018: 3/1/18. Spring 2019: N/A.

**Costs for the 2017–2018 year:** Tuition & Fees: $51,024. Room and Board: $15,466.

**Financial aid for transfer students:** Yes

**Guarantees meeting 100% need for transfer students:** Yes

**Need-based aid for transfer students:** Yes

**Merit-based financial aid for transfer students:** No

**Phi Theta Kappa Scholarship:** No

**Reduced or zero tuition fees for low-income students:** No

**Includes loans in financial aid packages:** Yes, for families with income above $60,000, $1,500–$3,000 per year.

**% of all undergraduates receiving financial aid:** 56%

**Average financial aid award for all undergraduate students:** $40,404

**Funding available for low-income students to visit:** Yes

**Enrollment deposit can be waived for low-income students:** Contact admissions directly.

## Academics

**GPA range for transfer students accepted in 2016–2017:** 3.0–4.0

**SAT ranges for all students admitted in 2016:** Critical Reading: 660–760. Mathematics: 660–760. Writing: 670–770.

**ACT composite score range for all students admitted in 2016:** 31–34

**Recommended extracurricular engagement:** Student should demonstrate leadership and involvement in their previous schools.

**Type of curriculum:** Gen. Ed. requirements

**Type of academic year:** Semester

**Advisors specifically for transfer students:** No

**Credit policy (in their own words):** The registrar will review your college transcripts, and a credit analysis will be sent to you with your letter of admission. 4 semester hours or 6 quarter hours are equivalent to 1 Haverford credit. There are 3 primary requirements for transferring credit from another college: You must have received, at minimum, a C or its equivalent in the course. The course can't have been used to satisfy a high-school graduation requirement (e.g., a fourth year of English). The course must be substantially similar to coursework taught at Haverford. For example, while courses in engineering, business, journalism, criminal justice, or any other strictly preprofessional program can be quite rigorous, Haverford doesn't offer courses in these areas so credit will not be transferred. Math courses below the level of calculus don't receive credit either. Occasionally, the registrar may contact you for clarification of a course description.

**Max number of transfer credits accepted:** 64 credit maximum from 2- and 4-year schools

**Residency requirement for transfer students:** Yes. Students who have had more than 4 semesters of full-time college or university work must still fulfill our 2-year residency requirement by completing 4 full-time semesters at Haverford. Please note that studying abroad for a semester or a year would not count toward that requirement.

For transfer students to meet degree requirements, a minimum of 16 course credits and 4 semesters must be taken at Haverford (or our cooperating institutions: Bryn Mawr College, Swarthmore College, or the University of Pennsylvania, exclusive of summer study).

**Study abroad available for transfer students:** Yes, but only if the student entered the college as a sophomore. Students who have had more than 4 semesters of full-time college or university work must still fulfill our 2-year residency requirement by completing 4 full-time semesters at Haverford. Please note that studying abroad for a semester or a year would not count toward that requirement.

**Free tutoring for all students:** Yes

**Writing center for all students:** Yes

**Career support/access to internships and resume prep for all students:** Yes

**% of undergraduate students hired within 6 months of graduation:** 86%

**Additional resources specifically designated for transfer and/or non-traditional students:** No

## Housing

**Available for transfer students:** Yes

**Available for non-traditional students:** No

**Guaranteed for transfer students:** Yes

**Non-traditional students can reside in housing year-round:** No

**Family housing available:** No

## Non-Traditional Admissions

No non-traditional student policies or programs available.

## Military/Veteran Students

No military student policies or programs available.

## DACA/Undocumented Students

DACA and undocumented students are considered as international students. If admitted, Haverford will meet 100% of demonstrated need. However, international students are not accepted as transfers.

# HOWARD UNIVERSITY

**Location:** Washington, D.C.

**Website:** www2.howard.edu

**Endowment:** $685.8 million

**Type of School:** Private/Co-ed, Liberal Arts

**# of Undergraduate Students:** 6,883 (2015)

**# of Graduate Students:** 3,119 (2015)

**Average Class Size:** 9–29

**School Mission (in their own words):** Howard University, a culturally diverse, comprehensive, research intensive, and historically Black private university, provides an educational experience of exceptional quality at the undergraduate, graduate, and professional levels to students of high academic standing and potential, with particular emphasis upon educational opportunities for Black students. Moreover, the University is dedicated to attracting and sustaining a cadre of faculty who are, through their teaching, research, and service, committed to the development of distinguished, historically aware, and compassionate graduates and to the discovery of solutions to human problems in the United States and throughout the world. With an abiding interest in both domestic and international affairs, the University is committed to continuing to produce leaders for America and the global community.

## Admissions

**Admissions office mailing address:** 2400 Sixth St NW, Washington DC 20059

**Admissions office phone:** (202) 806-2763

**Admissions office email:** admission@howard.edu

**Transfer student acceptance rate (2016–2017 academic year):** Information not provided.

**Acceptance rate for 2016–2017 freshmen:** Information not provided.

## Transfer Admissions Process

**Transfer policy (in their own words):** Each year, we welcome hundreds of talented transfer students from institutions throughout the nation and the world. Admission criteria vary among Howard University's schools and colleges. As a transfer applicant, you must meet the following minimum requirements for admission consideration: at least 15 transferable credit hours from a regionally accredited postsecondary institution, a 2.5 cumulative GPA, and a passing grade of C or better in both a college-level English and college-level math course.

**Transfer admissions contact person:** Hugh Durham, Admissions Representative/Recruitment Officer

**Transfer admissions contact info:** hugh.durham@howard.edu

**Offers transfer-focused admissions events:** N/A

**Transfer application deadline:** Fall 2018 deadline is in late July. Spring 2019 deadline N/A.

**Acceptances announced to transfer applicants:** Fall 2018 TBA. Spring 2019 TBA.

**Transfer application on Common App:** Yes. Common App fee: $45 waiver is available.

**SAT/ACT required for transfer applicants:** Yes

**SAT II scores required for transfer applicants:** No, but recommended

**High-school records requirements:** Official transcript may be requested for admission.

**High-school records requirements for applicants who completed outside the US:** Applicants whose native language is not English must submit evidence of having scored 500 or above on the Test of English as a Foreign Language (TOEFL). Admission requirements for international applicants are the same as for residents.

**Submission requirements for transfer applicants who completed high-school equivalency test:** No information available.

**College transcript requirements:** College transcripts from all institutions attended

**Interviews available for transfer applicants:** Optional

**Additional requirements for transfers seeking admissions to business school:** 30 credit hours, 3.0 GPA, C or better in Applied Calculus or Calculus I

## Costs & Financial Aid

**FAFSA code:** 1448

**CSS Profile code:** 5248

**Are internal school financial aid forms required?** No information available.

**Financial aid deadlines for transfer applicants:** Fall 2018: 2/15/18. Spring 2019: Usually falls on 11/1.

**Costs for the 2017–2018 year:** Tuition & Fees: $24,908. Room & Board: $13,280.

**Financial aid for transfer students:** Yes

**Guarantees meeting 100% need for transfer students:** No

**Need-based aid for transfer students:** Yes

**Merit-based financial aid for transfer students:** To be eligible for consideration, prospective transfer applicants must have at least 30 transferable credit hours at the time of admission and at least a 3.25 GPA from their transferring institution. The Transfer Scholarship is a one-time award of $10,000 only offered in the fall semester.

**Phi Theta Kappa Scholarship:** No

**Reduced or zero tuition fees for low-income students:** No

**Includes loans in financial aid packages:** Yes

**% of all undergraduates receiving financial aid:** 68%

**Average financial aid award for all undergraduate students:** $21,952

**Funding available for low-income students to visit:** No

**Enrollment deposit can be waived for low-income students:** No

## Academics

**GPA range for transfer students accepted in 2016–2017:** 2.5–4.0 for admission, 3.0–4.0 for the school of business

**SAT ranges for all students admitted in 2016:** Critical Reading: 500–610. Mathematics: 490–610. Writing: 500–600.

**ACT composite score range for all students admitted in 2016:** 21–27

**Recommended extracurricular engagement:** Demonstrate community engagement.

**Type of curriculum:** Gen. Ed. requirements

**Type of academic year:** Semester

**Advisors specifically for transfer students:** No

**Credit policy (in their own words):** Howard University accepts academic courses from regionally accredited colleges and universities as transfer credits. For a new student entering Howard University, and upon receipt of the student's official transcript(s), transfer credits will be evaluated by using the following criteria: Transfer courses must be of comparable content, academic level, and scope to the curricular offerings at Howard University. Credit hour(s) assignment to transfer courses will be semester credit hours. If the originating institution is other than the semester system, the appropriate conversion of credit hour(s) will be carried out by the Office of Enrollment Management. Students must have earned a grade of C or higher in academic courses in order for the courses to be transferred to Howard University. Review articulation agreements here: www2.howard.edu/sites/default/files/HUArticulationAgreement.pdf.

**Max number of transfer credits accepted:** 60 credits maximum from an accredited institution

**Residency requirement for transfer students:** 30 minimum credits must be completed at the school.

**Study abroad available for transfer students:** Yes. Must fulfill residency requirements.

**Free tutoring for all students:** Yes, general education courses. If you need subject-specific support, please speak with a faculty member.

**Writing center for all students:** Yes

**Career support/access to internships and resume prep for all students:** Yes, for current students and alumni

**Additional resources specifically designated for transfer and/or non-traditional students:** None provided.

## Housing

**Available for transfer students:** Yes

**Available for non-traditional students:** Not provided.

**Guaranteed for transfer students:** No

**Non-traditional students can reside in housing year-round:** Yes, off campus

**Family housing available:** Yes, off campus

## Non-Traditional Admissions

No non-traditional student policy or programs available.

## Military Students

**Military/veteran admissions policy (in their own words):** Howard University is approved by the District of Columbia State Approving Agency for the enrollment of veterans, service personnel, and dependents of deceased or disabled veterans who are eligible for educational benefits under the GI Bill. With the exception of VA-approved disabled veterans, all beneficiaries of educational benefits from the Veterans Administration are personally responsible for the payment of their bills to the University. These individuals should be financially prepared to pay tuition and fees at the time of registration each semester and to meet all living expenses until VA educational allowances (checks) are received (approximately 60 days). Services and/or assistance to GI Bill students studying at Howard University are available through this office.

**Status considered in admissions:** No

**Special admissions process:** No

**Special financial aid:** Yes. The Yellow Ribbon Program.

**Specific programs/policies to address needs:** Veterans Affairs through Special Student Services Office

## DACA/Undocumented Students

No DACA/undocumented student policy or programs available.

# JOHNS HOPKINS UNIVERSITY

**Location:** Baltimore, Maryland
**Website:** www.jhu.edu
**Endowment:** $3.381 billion
**Type of School:** Private/Co-ed, Research University
**# of Undergraduate Students:** 5,420
**# of Graduate Students:** 2,194
**Average Class Size:** 2–19

**School Mission (in their own words):** To educate its students and cultivate their capacity for lifelong learning, to foster independent and original research, and to bring the benefits of discovery to the world.

## Admissions

**Admissions office mailing address:** Mason Hall, 3400 N Charles St, Baltimore MD 21218
**Admissions office phone:** (410) 516-8171
**Admissions office email:** gotojhu@jhu.edu
**# of transfer applications:** Fall 2014 admissions: 1,071
**# of transfer students accepted:** Fall 2014: 40
**Transfer student acceptance rate (2014–2015 academic year):** 3.7%
**Freshman applications received in Fall 2016:** 27,094
**Freshman applications accepted in Fall 2016:** 3,234
**Acceptance rate for 2016–2017 freshmen:** 12%

## Transfer Admissions Process

**Transfer policy (in their own words):** Johns Hopkins welcomes transfer students from 2- and 4-year colleges and universities into the sophomore and junior classes in the fall semester only. Johns Hopkins University does not accept transfers for the spring, summer, or winter semesters. Transfer admission at Hopkins is not available for students who have already completed an undergraduate degree or equivalent from another institution.

**Transfer admissions contact person:** Ellen Kim, Dean of Undergraduate Admissions (Assistant: Susan Muller)
**Transfer admissions contact info:** susan.muller@jhu.edu
**Transfer application deadline:** Fall 2018 deadline is 3/1/18.
**Acceptances announced to transfer applicants:** Fall 2018 on 5/15/18.
**Transfer application on Common App:** Yes, with supplement. Common App fee: $70 waiver available.
**SAT/ACT required for transfer applicants:** No
**High-school records requirements:** Official high-school transcript
**High-school records requirements for applicants who completed outside the US:** You must submit an official record of academic performance for the equivalent of 9th, 10th, and 11th grades under the US system. All official documents must be accompanied by a verified English translation if the original document is not in English. Include any certificates, diplomas, or examination results marking the completion of secondary education or preparation for higher education (i.e., O- or A-Level or IB exam results). If you have exam results to send and are given only one official copy, you must send attested photocopies of the results to us. Your school official or guidance counselor can attest the copies. Notarized copies are not acceptable.

**Submission requirements for transfer applicants who completed high-school equivalency test:** Official GED results
**College transcript requirements:** Official transcripts from all colleges and universities attended
**Interviews available for transfer applicants:** No

## Costs & Financial Aid

**FAFSA code:** 2077
**CSS Profile code:** 5332
**Are internal school financial aid forms required?** No
**Financial aid deadlines for transfer applicants:** Fall 2018: 4/1/18. Spring 2019: N/A.
**Costs for the 2017–2018 year:** Tuition & Fees: $50,410. Room & Board: $14,976.
**Financial aid for transfer students:** Yes
**Guarantees meeting 100% need for transfer students:** Yes
**Need-based aid for transfer students:** Yes
**Merit-based financial aid for transfer students:** No
**Phi Theta Kappa Scholarship:** No
**Reduced or zero tuition fees for low-income students:** No
**Includes loans in financial aid packages:** Yes
**% of all undergraduates receiving financial aid:** 46%
**Average financial aid award for all undergraduate students:** $38,000
**Funding available for low-income students to visit:** No
**Enrollment deposit can be waived for low-income students:** Contact the admissions office.

## Academics

**GPA range for transfer students accepted in 2016–2017:** 3.0–4.0

**SAT ranges for all students admitted in 2016:** Critical Reading: 670–750. Mathematics: 690–780. Writing: 670–770.

**ACT composite score range for all students admitted in 2016:** 32–34

**Type of curriculum:** Gen. Ed. requirements

**Type of academic year:** Semester, 4-1-4

**Advisors specifically for transfer students:** No information provided.

**Credit policy (in their own words):** If you were accepted as a transfer student, you may assume that at least part of your previously completed college work is eligible to be transferred. We accept credit from many 2-year and 4-year institutions issuing associate's and bachelor's degrees in the liberal arts, natural and physical sciences, mathematics, and engineering, subject to review of each individual course.

To be eligible for transfer credit, an approved course must be taken for a grade at an approved college and completed with a grade of C or better. Ungraded or pass/fail courses taken prior to matriculation, if approved, may receive credit if the host school states in writing that the mark represents a grade of C or better. Credit for approved courses taken at a community college (an institution that issues primarily 2-year degrees) will be transferred only if taken prior to matriculation at Johns Hopkins. A maximum of 6 credits may be granted for courses that are in curriculum areas not covered by the programs of the Johns Hopkins School of Arts and Sciences and the School of Engineering.

**Max number of transfer credits accepted:** Up to 60 credits

**Residency requirement for transfer students:** Yes. Students who enter the university as transfer students must complete at least 60 credits at JHU. Transfer students must be in residence for at least 2 of their final 4 semesters, including the final semester prior to graduation. Transfer students are required to complete 60 credits at Johns Hopkins. Arts and Sciences transfer students are allowed to initially transfer up to 60 credits. Engineering transfer students are allowed to initially transfer a higher number if necessary. Read more at https://apply.jhu.edu/apply/transfer-students.

**Study abroad available for transfer students:** Yes. Must fulfill the residency requirements. All transfer students must complete at least 4 full-time semesters in residence at JHU. Study-abroad programs offered during fall and spring semesters do not count toward this 4-semester requirement. Transfer students must be in residence for at least 2 of their final 4 semesters, including the final semester prior to graduation.

**Free tutoring for all students:** Yes

**Writing center for all students:** Yes

**Career support/access to internships and resume prep for all students:** Yes

**Additional resources specifically designated for transfer and/or non-traditional students:** Yes, transfer orientation

## Housing

**Available for transfer students:** Yes, on-campus housing required if entering as a sophomore. Must live off-campus if entering as a junior.

**Available for non-traditional students:** No

**Guaranteed for transfer students:** No

**Non-traditional students can reside in housing year-round:** No

**Family housing available:** No

## Non-Traditional Admissions

No non-traditional student policy or programs available.

## Military/Veteran Students

**Military/veteran admissions policy (in their own words):** On behalf of the University, we take this opportunity to thank you for your service to our country and for choosing Johns Hopkins University to fulfill your educational goals. We sincerely hope that your experience with our institution is a rewarding one. Johns Hopkins is approved by the Maryland Higher Education Commission for the training of veterans, service members, eligible spouses, and dependents under the provisions of the various federal laws pertaining to Department of Veterans Affairs educational benefits.

**Status considered in admissions:** No

**Special financial aid:** Yes. The Yellow Ribbon Program. Read for more details: https://studentaffairs.jhu.edu/registrar/veterans/yellow-ribbon-program.

**Specific programs/policies to address needs:** No information provided.

## DACA/Undocumented Students

**DACA/undocumented students policy (in their own words):** Students who are not US citizens, permanent residents, or other eligible non-citizens (status of refugee, asylum, humanitarian parole, Cuban-Haitian entrant) are considered international students and are not eligible for federal financial assistance, but may apply for Hopkins funding. Students who hold F1, F2, J1, J2, or G series visas are not eligible for federal financial assistance, but may apply for Hopkins funding.

Hopkins offers need-based scholarships to undergraduate international students. Approximately 10% of the incoming international freshmen received need-based scholarships. The average scholarship is $25,000, but individual amounts can be more or less, depending on the financial need of the student.

**Admitted:** Yes

**Status considered in admissions:** Yes, must apply as international.

**Special admissions process:** Follow the international student application.

**Eligible for institutional financial aid:** Yes

# KENYON COLLEGE

**Location:** Gambier, Ohio

**Website:** www.kenyon.edu

**Endowment:** $208.9 million

**Type of School:** Private/Co-ed, Liberal Arts

**# of Undergraduate Students:** 1,707

**# of Graduate Students:** 0

**Average Class Size:** 9–39

**School Mission (in their own words):** As an undergraduate institution, Kenyon focuses upon those studies that are essential to the intellectual and moral development of its students. The curriculum is not defined by the interests of graduate or professional schools, but by the faculty's understanding of what contributes to liberal education. The faculty's first investment is in Kenyon's students. The College continues to think of its students as partners in inquiry, and seeks those who are earnestly committed to learning. In the future, Kenyon will continue to test its academic program and modes of teaching and learning against the needs of its students, seeking to bring each person to full realization of individual educational potential.

## Admissions

**Admissions office mailing address:** 103 College Rd, Gambier OH 43022

**Admissions office phone:** (800) 848-2468

**Admissions office email:** admissions@kenyon.edu

**# of transfer applications:** Fall 2016 admissions: 268

**# of transfer students accepted:** Fall 2016: 84

**Transfer student acceptance rate (2016–2017 academic year):** 31.3%

**Freshman applications received in Fall 2016:** 6,403

**Freshman applications accepted in Fall 2016:** 1,702

**Acceptance rate for 2016–2017 freshmen:** 26.58%

## Transfer Admissions Process

**Transfer policy (in their own words):** Kenyon welcomes students who apply for admission after beginning undergraduate study at another institution. The admissions staff recognizes that not all students are comfortable with their initial college choice and that academic and career goals often change during the college years. For this reason, the College accepts a limited number of transfer students each year, depending on their class year and the availability of living accommodations.

Students who wish to transfer to Kenyon should present secondary-school and college records that reflect an ability to do work of the quality expected at the College. In most cases, successful transfer applicants present grades of B or better in their current courses.

Read more at www.kenyon.edu/admissions-aid/how-to-apply/transfer-students.

**Transfer admissions contact person:** Jay Bonham, Associate Director of Admissions, Transfer Coordinator

**Transfer admissions contact info:** bonham1@kenyon.edu

**Offers transfer-focused admissions events:** N/A

**Transfer application deadline:** Fall 2018 deadline is 4/1/18.

**Acceptances announced to transfer applicants:** Fall 2018 in late April.

**Transfer application on Common App:** Yes. Common App fee: No fee.

**SAT/ACT required for transfer applicants:** Yes

**High-school records requirements:** Official high-school transcript

**High-school records requirements for applicants who completed outside the US:** They follow the same application requirements as domestic students, but they would need to submit the TOEFL as part of the school's testing policy.

**Submission requirements for transfer applicants who completed high-school equivalency test:** Official GED scores must be submitted.

**College transcript requirements:** Official transcripts from all colleges and universities attended

**Interviews available for transfer applicants:** Yes. Optional. On campus; alumni.

## Costs & Financial Aid

**FAFSA code:** 3065

**CSS Profile code:** 1370

**Are internal school financial aid forms required?** No

**Financial aid deadlines for transfer applicants:** Fall 2018: 4/15/18. Spring 2019: N/A.

**Costs for the 2017–2018 year:** Tuition & Fees: $51,200. Room & Board: $12,130.

**Financial aid for transfer students:** Yes

**Guarantees meeting 100% need for transfer students:** Yes

**Need-based aid for transfer students:** Yes

**Merit-based financial aid for transfer students:** No

**Phi Theta Kappa Scholarship:** No

**Reduced or zero tuition fees for low-income students:** No

**Includes loans in financial aid packages:** Yes

**% of all undergraduates receiving financial aid:** 43%

**% of all undergraduates qualifying for Pell Grants:**
No information provided.

**Average financial aid award for all undergraduate students:**
No information provided.

**Funding available for low-income students to visit:**
No information provided.

**Enrollment deposit can be waived for low-income students:**
No

## Academics

**GPA range for transfer students accepted in 2016–2017:**
3.0–4.0

**SAT ranges for all students admitted in 2016:** Critical Reading:
630–730. Mathematics: 610–710. Writing: 630–730.

**ACT composite score range for all students admitted in 2016:**
28–32

**Advisors specifically for transfer students:** No

**Credit policy (in their own words):** Credit from courses
taken at other institutions of higher education may be
transferred to Kenyon (i.e., counted as meeting a part of the
College's degree requirements) if the following conditions
are met: (1) advance approval is obtained (forms available
from the Registrar's Office); approval sought retroactively
requires a petition; (2) an official transcript is sent directly
to the Kenyon registrar from the credit-granting institution;
(3) courses are taken for letter grades and the grades earned
are C– or above; (4) the other institution is fully accredited
by a recognized accrediting agency, or the Committee on
Academic Standards has specifically approved the program
for off-campus study purposes; and (5) the subject matter
of the courses is liberal arts in nature. Grades for transfer
credit are recorded on the student's record as TR except off-
campus study courses. These grades do not affect a student's
grade point average, except for certain portions of Kenyon
programs—see the section explaining off-campus study.

The registrar determines whether the above criteria are met,
the amount of credit that is transferable, and the distribution
requirements that are fulfilled. Credit is accepted in transfer
to the College on a pro rata basis: 1 Kenyon unit equals 8
semester hours or 12 quarter hours of credit. Kenyon will
not accept transfer credit for which transfer credit would
be granted more than 1 year after the completion of the
coursework (except in the case of a student admitted to
Kenyon as a transfer student). Test scores must be received
no later than December of a student's sophomore year to
have the credit applied to the student record.

Read more at www.kenyon.edu/directories/offices-services/
registrar/course-catalog-2/administrative-matters/transfer-
credits-and-special-programs.

**Max number of transfer credits accepted:** 64 credits from
either a 2- or 4-year school

**Residency requirement for transfer students:** Yes. A minimum
of 4 semesters, including the senior year, must be completed
at Kenyon College, on the Gambier campus.

**Study abroad available for transfer students:** Yes. Must meet
the residency requirements.

**Free tutoring for all students:** Yes

**Writing center for all students:** Yes

**Career support/access to internships and resume prep for
all students:** Yes

## Housing

**Available for transfer students:** Yes

**Available for non-traditional students:** Yes

**Guaranteed for transfer students:** No

**Non-traditional students can reside in housing year-round:**
While Kenyon will assist students who need to work on
campus during campus breaks, Kenyon can't guarantee that
the student will live in the same room. However, during the
academic year, the student will live in the same room.

**Family housing available:** No

## Non-Traditional Admissions

No non-traditional student policies or programs available.

## Military/Veteran Students

**Military/veteran admissions policy (in their own words):**
Military/veteran students follow the same admissions
application as traditional students.

In addition, all Kenyon students are expected to maintain
a GPA of at least 2.0 (a C average) and to accumulate units
of credit at a rate of 4.0 per year of attendance. Those who
receive benefits through the Department of Veterans Affairs
who fall below this standard for 2 consecutive semesters
must be reported by the College to the Department of
Veterans Affairs.

Read more at www.kenyon.edu/directories/offices-services/
registrar/other-resources/veterans-administration.

**Status considered in admissions:** Yes

**Special admissions process:** No

**Special financial aid:** Yes. The Yellow Ribbon Program.

**Specific programs/policies to address needs:** None provided.

## DACA/Undocumented Students

**DACA and undocumented admissions policy (in their own
words):** DACA and undocumented students are considered
international students for both the admissions and the
financial aid application process. Non-US citizens use the
same application as US citizens: the Common Application.
In addition, if admitted, Kenyon meets 100% of a candidate's
demonstrated financial need for all 4 years. Students who are
neither US citizens nor permanent residents who wish to be
considered for financial aid at any time during their 4 years
at Kenyon should apply at the same time that they apply for
admission.

Since Kenyon is not need-blind in the admission of non-US citizens, financial need may be a factor in the evaluation process for admission. Therefore, those admitted without financial aid subsequently would not be eligible to receive Kenyon funding during their years at the college except under the most extreme circumstances (i.e., death of a wage-earning parent, natural disaster, etc.).

Read more at www.kenyon.edu/admissions-aid/how-to-apply/international-students.

**Admitted:** Yes

**Status considered in admissions:** Yes. DACA/undocumented students are considered international students, and Kenyon is need-aware for them.

**Special admissions process:** No

**Eligible for institutional financial aid:** Yes. Kenyon meets 100% need of all admitted students.

**Specific programs/policies to address needs:** No information provided.

# LAWRENCE UNIVERSITY

**Location:** Appleton, Wisconsin

**Website:** www.lawrence.edu

**Endowment:** $275.4 million (2015)

**Type of School:** Private/Co-ed, Liberal Arts

**# of Undergraduate Students:** 1,532

**# of Graduate Students:** 0

**Average Class Size:** 10–19

**School Mission (in their own words):** Lawrence University of Wisconsin, through its undergraduate residential college and Conservatory of Music, educates students in the liberal arts and sciences. The university is devoted to excellence and integrity in all of its activities and committed to the development of intellect and talent, the pursuit of knowledge and understanding, the cultivation of sound judgment, and respect for the perspectives of others. Lawrence prepares students for lives of achievement, responsible and meaningful citizenship, lifelong learning, and personal fulfillment. As a diverse learning community of scholars and artists, we actively foster a transformative process that emphasizes engaged learning, supported by an environment of rich educational opportunities in a residential campus setting.

## Admissions

**Admissions office mailing address:** 711 E Boldt Way, Appleton WI 54911

**Admissions office phone:** (800) 227-0982

**Admissions office email:** admissions@lawrence.edu

**# of transfer applications:** Fall 2016 admissions: 118

**# of transfer students accepted:** Fall 2016: 67

**Transfer student acceptance rate (2016–2017 academic year):** 56.77%

**Freshman applications received in Fall 2016:** 3,579

**Freshman applications accepted in Fall 2016:** 2,254

**Acceptance rate for 2016–2017 freshmen:** 62.97%

## Transfer Admissions Process

**Transfer policy:** Lawrence welcomes transfer applications from students who have graduated from high school or have a GED/HSED and are attending or have attended other colleges or universities. As an institution that prizes individuality and values diversity, Lawrence knows that transfer students often bring with them new or different perspectives that enrich not only their own educational experiences but those of other students.

Read more at www.lawrence.edu/admissions/transfer.

**Transfer admissions contact person:** Liliana Guevara, Transfer Admissions Counselor

**Transfer admissions contact info:** liliana.guevara@lawrence.edu

**Offers transfer-focused admissions events:** No

**Transfer application deadline:** Fall 2018: 4/1/18. Winter 2019: 11/1/18. Spring 2019: 2/1/19.

**Acceptances announced to transfer applicants:** Fall 2018: 4/15/18. Winter 2019: 11/15/18. Spring 2019: 2/15/19.

**Transfer application on Common App:** Yes. Common App fee: No.

**SAT/ACT required for transfer applicants:** No

**High-school records requirements:** Official high-school transcript

**High-school records requirements for applicants who completed outside the US:** Secondary-school report, official high-school transcript, certified translated copies, if applicable

**Submission requirements for transfer applicants who completed high-school equivalency test:** Official GED scores

**College transcript requirements:** Official transcripts for all colleges and universities attended

**Interviews available for transfer applicants:** Yes. Optional, but recommended. On campus; alumni; Skype.

## Costs & Financial Aid

**FAFSA code:** 3856

**CSS Profile code:** 1398

**Are internal school financial aid forms required?** No

**Financial aid deadlines for transfer applicants:** Fall 2018: 4/1/18. Winter 2019: 11/1/18. Spring 2019: 2/1/19.

**Costs for the 2017–2018 year:** Tuition & Fees: $44,844. Room & Board: $9,654.

**Financial aid for transfer students:** Yes

**Guarantees meeting 100% need for transfer students:** No

**Need-based aid for transfer students:** Yes

**Merit-based financial aid for transfer students:** Yes. Merit-based scholarships are based on your application for admission.

**Phi Theta Kappa Scholarship:** Yes, $2,300. Not renewable. 2.75 GPA required.

**Reduced or zero tuition fees for low-income students:** No

**Includes loans in financial aid packages:** Yes

**% of all undergraduates receiving financial aid:** 62%

**% of all undergraduates qualifying for Pell Grants:** No information provided.

**Average financial aid award for all undergraduate students:** $29,622

**Funding available for low-income students to visit:** No

**Enrollment deposit can be waived for low-income students:** No information provided.

## Academics

**GPA range for transfer students accepted in 2016–2017:** No information provided.

**SAT ranges for all students admitted in 2016:** Critical Reading: 560–690. Mathematics: 610–730. Writing: 580–690.

**ACT composite score range for all students admitted in 2016:** 26–32

**Type of curriculum:** Gen. Ed. requirements

**Type of academic year:** Quarter

**Advisors specifically for transfer students:** No

**Credit policy (in their own words):** Lawrence awards credit for courses taken at accredited colleges and universities, provided you have earned a grade of C– or better and that the course is similar in content and length to a Lawrence course. You can use transfer credit to fulfill Lawrence general education requirements, except for the writing and speaking general education requirements. Individual departments will determine if transfer credit fulfills major requirements.

If you are transferring credit from an institution outside the United States, please submit your transcripts/documents to Education Credential Evaluators, Inc. for evaluation. (You will be responsible for any fees incurred.) Lawrence's registrar will use your evaluation report in awarding transfer credit.

At Lawrence, a standard course is valued at 6 units. A normal course load for a Lawrence trimester is 3 standard courses (18 units). For purposes of transcript evaluation, 6 units at Lawrence may be considered the equivalent of 3.3 semester hours or 5 quarter hours at other institutions. A 6-unit Lawrence course that includes extra class or laboratory sessions is the equivalent in content to courses valued at 5 semester hours or 8 quarter hours at some other institutions.

Read more at www.lawrence.edu/admissions/transfer/node/2349.

**Max number of transfer credits accepted:** 108

**Residency requirement for transfer students:** Yes. To qualify for a Lawrence University Bachelor of Arts or Bachelor of Music degree, you must have a minimum of 6 terms (2 years) in residence at Lawrence or on LU-affiliated programs and earn 108 units (approximately 18 courses). 9 terms in residence and 162 units are required for the 5-year B.A. and B.Mus. double-degree program. Enrollment in courses held on campus, at Lawrence off-campus study programs, ACM programs, and other special arrangements under Lawrence sponsorship contribute toward fulfilling the residency requirement.

**Study abroad available for transfer students:** Yes. Participation in all programs requires Lawrence approval and acceptance by the program sponsor or institution.

**Free tutoring for all students:** Yes

**Writing center for all students:** Yes

**Career support/access to internships and resume prep for all students:** Yes

**% of undergraduate students hired within 6 months of graduation:** No information provided.

**Additional resources specifically designated for transfer and/or non-traditional students:** No

## Housing

**Available for transfer students:** Yes

**Available for non-traditional students:** No

**Guaranteed for transfer students:** Yes

**Family housing available:** No

## Non-Traditional Admissions

No non-traditional student policy or programs available.

## Military/Veteran Students

**Military/veteran admissions policy (in their own words):** Military/veteran students do not need to follow a separate admissions process than that of traditional students. In addition, Lawrence participates in the Yellow Ribbon Program.

Read more at www.lawrence.edu/admissions/apply/veterans-admissions.

**Status considered in admissions:** No

**Special financial aid:** Yes. The Yellow Ribbon Program.

**Specific programs/policies to address needs:** We have an admissions officer dedicated to veterans' admissions support; feel free to contact her anytime: Jennifer England, Senior Associate Director of Admissions, (920) 832-6840 or jennifer.england@lawrence.edu.

## DACA/Undocumented Students

**DACA and undocumented admissions policy (in their own words):** Undocumented students are awarded financial aid in similar fashion to US citizens in regard to Lawrence University scholarships and grants.

If your first language is English, you are welcome but not required to submit your ACT or SAT results.

If you have been in the United States and have enrolled in an academic program in which your instruction has been entirely in English for more than 8 years, you are welcome but not required to submit your standardized test results.

If you have been in the United States and have enrolled in an academic program in which your instruction has been entirely in English for less than 8 years, please submit 1 of the following: TOEFL, ACT, SAT, IELTS, or A-Level scores. Read more at www.lawrence.edu/admissions/international.

**Admitted:** Yes

**Status considered in admissions:** No

**Special admissions process:** No

**Eligible for institutional financial aid:** Yes. Please submit the following: CSS Profile, parent 2015 tax return (if applicable), parent W-2 Form (if applicable).

Note: Lawrence does not receive documents through the College Board IDOC service. Tax documents should be emailed, faxed, or mailed directly to the Financial Aid Office.

**Specific programs/policies to address needs:** Yes. The Office of Diversity and Inclusion at Lawrence University facilitates the institutional mission of the development of intellect and talent, the pursuit of knowledge and understanding, the cultivation of sound judgment, and respect for the perspectives of others in several critical ways. Specifically, it provides information, policies, and programs that enable the prevention and redress of discrimination, as well as the promotion of intergroup collaboration, empathy, and cultural competence on the part of students, faculty, staff, alumni, and community partners. Ultimately, the office works to create an environment in which all of the University community can reach their unique potential.

# Ariela Rosa

**Lawrence University, C'15**
Bachelor's Degree in Anthropology and Gender Studies

**Bronx Community College, C'13**
Associate's Degree in Liberal Arts, concentration in Media Studies

**Current Employment:** Assistant Director of Corporate, Foundation, and Sponsored Research Support, Lawrence University

**Bio:** A Bronx native, Ariela cares deeply about issues of poverty, homelessness, and food insecurity. She hopes to one day use her skills as a writer to shed light on these issues and advocate for people in her home borough.

*"I give Lawrence a lot of credit for the ways they accommodated me, a married student determined to bring my husband along for the ride. When I visited, Lawrence not only set up the usual activities, but also included Angel, who got to do all of those same things. They took the time to find out Angel was a chef and set up a meeting with the head of their dining services. They explained to him what kinds of work he could expect to find in this area, and after I decided to go to Lawrence, Angel landed a job with their dining service. In addition to a world-class education, Lawrence made it as easy as possible for me and Angel to settle in, live in a safe and comfortable place, and find the employment we needed to sustain ourselves. All of this allowed me to focus on my education without worrying about the basics, and no other school I applied to, even the ones used to working with married students, went so far above and beyond. It would have been much more difficult for me to obtain my degree without the assistance and care provided by Lawrence and Kaplan, and I am very grateful.*

*In addition, while Lawrence University does not offer family housing, they provided off-campus apartment housing for me and Angel. The rent was quite low, and this arrangement made the transition from New York City to Appleton much easier for me and Angel. Though I was an off-campus student, I always felt like part of the university."*

## Leadership Activities

- Salutatorian, Bronx Community College
- Peer Mentor, First Year Seminar, Bronx Community College
- President's List, Bronx Community College
- Dean's List, Bronx Community College
- Peter J. Rondinone Screenwriting Award, Bronx Community College
- BCC Film & Video Production Award for Excellence in Filmmaking
- Volunteer Interviewer, Covenant House
- Trevor Space Administrative Volunteer, The Trevor Project

# MACALESTER COLLEGE

**Location:** St. Paul, Minnesota

**Website:** www.macalester.edu

**Endowment:** $700.2 million

**Type of School:** Private/Co-ed, Liberal Arts

**# of Undergraduate Students:** 2,146

**# of Graduate Students:** N/A

**Average Class Size:** 17

**School Mission (in their own words):** Macalester is committed to being a preeminent liberal arts college with an educational program known for its high standards for scholarship and its special emphasis on internationalism, multiculturalism, and service to society.

## Admissions

**Admissions office mailing address:** 1600 Grand Ave, St Paul MN 55105

**Admissions office phone:** (651) 696-6357

**Admissions office email:** admissions@macalester.edu

**# of transfer applications:** Fall 2016 admissions: 113

**# of transfer students accepted:** Fall 2016: 40

**Transfer student acceptance rate (2016–2017 academic year):** 35.39%

**Freshman applications received in Fall 2016:** 5,946

**Freshman applications accepted in Fall 2016:** 2,206

**Acceptance rate for 2016–2017 freshmen:** 37.1%

## Transfer Admissions Process

**Transfer policy (in their own words):** Only a student who has been enrolled at another college or university as a full-time, degree-seeking student may apply as a transfer student. A student taking college courses while still in high school must apply as a first-year student.

**Transfer admissions contact person:** Lorne Robinson, Dean of Admissions and Financial Aid

**Transfer admissions contact info:** admissions@macalester.edu, (651) 696-6357

**Offers transfer-focused admissions events:** No

**Transfer application deadline:** Fall 2018 deadline is 4/15/18. Spring 2019 deadline is 10/29/18.

**Acceptances announced to transfer applicants:** Fall 2018 on 5/15/18. Spring 2019 on 11/19/18.

**Transfer application on Common App:** Yes. Common App fee: $40.

**SAT/ACT required for transfer applicants:** Yes, also TOEFL or IELTS (unless English is the first language or primary language of instruction)

**High-school records requirements:** Official high-school transcript

**High-school records requirements for applicants who completed outside the US:** Request that your secondary school send Macalester an official final transcript of your classes and transcript grades beginning with 9th grade. If you attended more than 1 high school, check to make sure all years are included on the most recent transcript.

**Submission requirements for transfer applicants who completed high-school equivalency test:** Official GED scores

**College transcript requirements:** Official transcripts from all colleges and universities attended

**Interviews available for transfer applicants:** Yes. Optional. On campus; alumni.

**Additional requirements for transfers seeking admissions to arts major:** Optional. Students who have made a substantial commitment to the arts (in the areas of fine arts, music, theater, or dance) are welcome to submit samples via the Macalester Application Portal. Information to access the portal is provided after submitting your application.

## Costs & Financial Aid

**FAFSA code:** 2358

**CSS Profile code:** 6390

**Are internal school financial aid forms required?** No

**Financial aid deadlines for transfer applicants:** Fall 2018: 1/15/18. Spring 2019: 10/29/18.

**Costs for the 2017–2018 year:** Tuition & Fees: $52,464. Room & Board: $52,464.

**Financial aid for transfer students:** Yes

**Guarantees meeting 100% need for transfer students:** Yes

**Need-based aid for transfer students:** Yes

**Merit-based financial aid for transfer students:** No

**Phi Theta Kappa Scholarship:** No

**Reduced or zero tuition fees for low-income students:** No

**Includes loans in financial aid packages:** Yes

**% of all undergraduates receiving financial aid:** 67%

**Average financial aid award for all undergraduate students:** $44,085

**Funding available for low-income students to visit:** No

**Enrollment deposit can be waived for low-income students:** Contact admissions office.

## Academics

**GPA range for transfer students accepted in 2016–2017:** 3.33–4.0

**SAT ranges for all students admitted in 2016:** Critical Reading: 630–740. Mathematics: 630–750. Writing: 650–740.

**ACT composite score range for all students admitted in 2016:** 29–33

**Type of curriculum:** Gen. Ed. requirements

**Type of academic year:** Semester

**Advisors specifically for transfer students:** Yes

**Credit policy (in their own words):** You may transfer up to 64 credit hours to Macalester. In order to receive a Macalester degree, you must complete 2 full years of coursework (64 credit hours) at Macalester. To have your credits evaluated for transfer, email a transcript with a request for an evaluation to registrar@macalester.edu or mail an official transcript to: Registrar's Office, 1600 Grand Ave, St Paul MN 55105.

**Max number of transfer credits accepted:** A maximum of 64 credits will be accepted from either a 2- or 4-year school.

**Residency requirement for transfer students:** Yes. At least 4 semesters spent in residency. At least 1 of these must be in the senior year. Participation in off-campus study programs does not count toward satisfaction of this requirement.

**Study abroad available for transfer students:** Yes. At least 4 semesters spent in residency. At least 1 of these must be in the senior year. Participation in off-campus study programs does not count toward satisfaction of this requirement.

**Free tutoring for all students:** Yes

**Writing center for all students:** Yes

**Career support/access to internships and resume prep for all students:** Yes

**% of undergraduate students hired within 6 months of graduation:** No information provided.

**Additional resources specifically designated for transfer and/or non-traditional students:** No

## Housing

**Available for transfer students:** Yes

**Available for non-traditional students:** No information provided.

**Guaranteed for transfer students:** No

**Non-traditional students can reside in housing year-round:** No information provided.

**Family housing available:** No

## Non-Traditional Admissions

No non-traditional student policy or programs available.

## Military/Veteran Students

No military/veteran student policy or programs available.

## DACA/Undocumented Students

**DACA and undocumented admissions policy (in their own words):** In deciding which applicants will be offered admission, we carefully review each student's high-school record. We look for evidence that the applicant has taken a rigorous curriculum, performed at a very high level, and will contribute to the campus community in other ways. Because our ability to offer admission to undocumented students who need financial assistance is severely limited, competition for space in the class is extremely high.

Read more at www.macalester.edu/admissions/apply/undocumented.

**Admitted:** Yes

**Status considered in admissions:** Yes

**Special admissions process:** After you have submitted the Common Application, email admissions@macalester.edu to identify yourself as an undocumented student applying to Macalester.

**Eligible for institutional financial aid:** The College meets 100% of demonstrated financial need for all admitted students. Admitted undocumented students who are not permitted by law to work in the US would receive additional student loans to replace the amount typically earned through student work-study. To apply for financial assistance, undocumented candidates must complete the CSS Profile. Undocumented students residing in Minnesota may be eligible to receive state grant funds because of the MN Dream Act (also known as the Prosperity Act).

**Specific programs/policies to address needs:** Contact for undocumented applicants: Philana Tenhoff, Associate Director of Admissions, ptenhoff@macalester.edu, (651) 696-6258.

# MASSACHUSETTS INSTITUTE OF TECHNOLOGY

**Location:** Cambridge, Massachusetts
**Website:** web.mit.edu
**Endowment:** $13.18 billion
**Type of School:** Private/Co-ed, Research University
**# of Undergraduate Students:** 4,524
**# of Graduate Students:** 6,852
**Average Class Size:** 2–9 students

**School Mission (in their own words):** The mission of the Massachusetts Institute of Technology is to advance knowledge and educate students in science, technology, and other areas of scholarship that will best serve the nation and the world in the 21st century. We are also driven to bring knowledge to bear on the world's great challenges.

## Admissions

**Admissions office mailing address:** 77 Massachusetts Ave, Cambridge MA 02139

**Admissions office phone:** (617) 253-3400

**Admissions office email:** admissions@mit.edu

**# of transfer applications:** Fall 2015 admissions: 490

**# of transfer students accepted:** Fall 2015: 22

**Transfer student acceptance rate (2015–2016 academic year):** 4.5%

**Freshman applications received in Fall 2016:** 19,020

**Freshman applications accepted in Fall 2016:** 1,511

**Acceptance rate for 2016–2017 freshmen:** 7.9%

## Transfer Admissions Process

**Transfer policy (in their own words):** If you have completed 2 or more terms with high academic standing at an accredited college, university, technical institute, or community college, you may apply to MIT for transfer. However, we cannot accept applications from students who at the time of entry to MIT will have finished less than 1 year or more than 2 1/2 years of college. (A transfer student must be in residence at MIT for 3 terms matriculating as a full-time student to earn an MIT degree.) Read more at http://mitadmissions.org/apply/transfer/before.

**Offers transfer-focused admissions events:** No

**Transfer application deadline:** Fall 2018 deadline is 2/5/18. Spring 2019 deadline is 11/15/18.

**Acceptances announced to transfer applicants:** Fall 2018 in early May 2018. Spring 2019 in mid-December 2018.

**Transfer application on Common App:** No. Common App fee: N/A.

**Separate application or in addition to the Common App:** Yes

**Fee for separate transfer application:** Yes, $75

**Waiver available for separate transfer application fee:** Yes. SlideRoom submission explaining hardship.

**SAT/ACT required for transfer applicants:** Yes

**SAT II scores required for transfer applicants:** Yes

**High-school records requirements:** Official high-school transcript

**High-school records requirements for applicants who completed outside the US:** If you went to high school in another country and cannot have your transcripts sent by the school, you may include a copy of your grades with your application.

**Submission requirements for transfer applicants who completed high-school equivalency test:** Official GED scores

**College transcript requirements:** Official transcripts from all colleges and universities attended

**Interviews available for transfer applicants:** No

**Additional requirements for transfers seeking admissions to engineering major:** Yes. Applicants should have 1 year of calculus (or higher level of math, whichever meets your ability level) and calculus-based physics.

## Costs & Financial Aid

**FAFSA code:** 2178

**CSS Profile code:** 3514

**Are internal school financial aid forms required?** Yes

**Financial aid deadlines for transfer applicants:** Fall 2018: 2/15/18. Spring 2019: 11/15/18.

**Costs for the 2017–2018 year:** Tuition & Fees: $58,820. Room & Board: $14,210.

**Financial aid for transfer students:** Yes

**Guarantees meeting 100% need for transfer students:** Yes

**Need-based aid for transfer students:** Yes

**Merit-based financial aid for transfer students:** No

**Phi Theta Kappa Scholarship:** No

**Reduced or zero tuition fees for low-income students:** No

**Includes loans in financial aid packages:** Yes

**% of all undergraduates receiving financial aid:** 91% (2015)

**% of all undergraduates qualifying for Pell Grants:** 17%

**Average financial aid award for all undergraduate students:** $45,419 (need-based), $41,547 (net financial aid)

**Funding available for low-income students to visit:** No

**Enrollment deposit can be waived for low-income students:** MIT does not require an enrollment deposit.

## Academics

**GPA range for transfer students accepted in 2016–2017:** 3.5–4.0

**SAT ranges for all students admitted in 2016:** Critical Reading: 710–800. Mathematics: 760–800. Writing: 700–790.

**ACT composite score range for all students admitted in 2016:** 33–35

**Recommended completed level of math for transfer applicants:** At the very least, you should have 1 year of calculus (or higher level of math, whichever meets your ability level).

**Recommended courses transfer applicants should have on transcripts:** At the very least, you should have 1 year of calculus (or higher level of math, whichever meets your ability level) and calculus-based physics.

**Recommended courses transfer applicants interested in STEM should complete before transfer:** At the very least, you should have 1 year of calculus (or higher level of math, whichever meets your ability level) and calculus-based physics. It is rare that an applicant is admitted without calculus and physics at the college level. MIT prefers that students take these subjects: calculus, physics, chemistry, and biology.

**Recommended extracurricular engagement:** Community involvement, sports, etc.

**Type of curriculum:** Gen. Ed. requirements

**Type of academic year:** Semester, J term

**Advisors specifically for transfer students:** No

**Credit policy (in their own words):** Undergraduates must make certain they will complete the requirements of 180 to 198 units (depending upon major) in addition to the 17-subject General Institute Requirements. Read more at http://web.mit.edu/registrar/graduation/ugrad_requirements.html.

MIT will grant credit for some of the courses you passed at your previous college or university. In addition, you may have done college-level study while in high school. Some of that study is also eligible for MIT credit and/or placement, depending on the setting and your achievement as measured by test scores or grades.

Read more at http://web.mit.edu/firstyear/transfer/credit.

**Max number of transfer credits accepted:** Contact the Registrar's Office.

**Residency requirement for transfer students:** A transfer student must be in residence at MIT for 3 terms matriculating as a full-time student to earn an MIT degree. In order to apply, applicant must have a minimum of 2 semesters of college, but not more than 5 semesters, at the time they would enroll. Transfer credit is assessed by each academic department on a course-by-course basis. Enrolling transfer students are required to complete at least 3 semesters at MIT to earn a bachelor's degree. For entry in the spring semester, only

US citizens and permanent residents may apply. Applicants who are not US citizens or permanent residents must apply for entry in the fall semester.

**Study abroad available for transfer students:** Yes. Must complete residency requirements.

**Free tutoring for all students:** Yes

**Writing center for all students:** Yes

**Career support/access to internships and resume prep for all students:** Yes

**% of undergraduate students hired within 6 months of graduation:** No information provided.

**Additional resources specifically designated for transfer and/or non-traditional students:** No

## Housing

**Available for transfer students:** Yes

**Available for non-traditional students:** Yes

**Guaranteed for transfer students:** Yes

**Non-traditional students can reside in housing year-round:** No

**Family housing available:** Yes

## Non-Traditional Admissions

**Non-traditional student policy (in their own words):** There are many applicants to MIT from many types of backgrounds, and while we consider them all in their context, we need to know some common information about them.

So even though you've been away from high school for a while, we would expect to see the results of your standardized tests, transcript, evaluations from teachers, and other supportive materials that would assist us in getting to know you. Obviously, the greater the distance from your high-school studies, the more creative you'll have to be in submitting evaluations and supportive documentation.

We recommend that non-traditional applicants take some college courses at a community college or in a nondegree program prior to applying to brush up on their classroom experience and get some fresh teacher evaluations. Evaluations/recommendations from your employers, mentors, and training situations can provide useful information, especially if teacher evaluations are difficult to obtain. The decision about what letters of support to send for review is left up to the individual non-traditional applicant to suit their unique circumstances.

## Military/Veteran Students

**Military/veteran admissions policy (in their own words):** MIT participates in the Yellow Ribbon Program through a few graduate programs, but not undergraduate studies. MIT offers need-blind admissions for all undergraduate students, so if you are accepted for undergraduate study, we will make sure that you can afford to come to MIT. Please don't let the cost of an MIT education deter you from applying. Information specific to veterans is available on the Student Financial Services site: https://sfs.mit.edu/undergraduate-financial-aid/types-of-aid/veterans-benefits.

If you were academically a high-achieving high-school student before entering the service and have not completed any college-level coursework, you may apply for freshman admission.

If you have completed 2 or more terms with high academic standing at an accredited college, university, technical institute, or community college, you are not eligible for freshman admission and must apply to MIT for transfer admission.

MIT does not offer any online degree programs, but if you are interested in learning while still completing your service anywhere in the world, we offer thousands of options through edX, MITx, and OpenCourseWare.

**Status considered in admissions:** No

**Special admissions process:** No

**Special financial aid:** No

**Specific programs/policies to address needs:** No

## DACA/Undocumented Students

**DACA and undocumented admissions policy (in their own words):** In the MIT freshman admissions process, you are considered an international applicant if you are not a US citizen or a US permanent resident (Green Card holder). Applicants awaiting Green Cards are considered to have non-US citizen/non-US permanent resident status. Undocumented applicants should list their country of citizenship when applying. An applicant's citizenship, or lack of documentation, will not have any impact on their chances of admission at MIT or the availability of full need-based financial aid.

**Admitted:** Yes

**Status considered in admissions:** No

**Special admissions process:** No

**Eligible for institutional financial aid:** Yes. Although undocumented students are not eligible for federal financial aid, MIT ensures that they meet their full financial need.

**Specific programs/policies to address needs:** No

# MIDDLEBURY COLLEGE

**Location:** Middlebury, Vermont

**Website:** www.middlebury.edu

**Endowment:** $1 billion

**Type of School:** Private/Co-ed, Liberal Arts

**# of Undergraduate Students:** 2,450

**# of Graduate Students:** 0

**Average Class Size:** 18

**School Mission (in their own word):** At Middlebury College, we challenge students to participate fully in a vibrant and diverse academic community. The College's Vermont location offers an inspirational setting for learning and reflection, reinforcing our commitment to integrating environmental stewardship into both our curriculum and our practices on campus. Yet the College also reaches far beyond the Green Mountains, offering a rich array of undergraduate and graduate programs that connect our community to other places, countries, and cultures. We strive to engage students' capacity for rigorous analysis and independent thought within a wide range of disciplines and endeavors, and to cultivate the intellectual, creative, physical, ethical, and social qualities essential for leadership in a rapidly changing global community. Through the pursuit of knowledge unconstrained by national or disciplinary boundaries, students who come to Middlebury learn to engage the world.

## Admissions

**Admissions office mailing address:** 14 Old Chapel Rd, Middlebury VT 05753

**Admissions office phone:** (802) 443-3000

**Admissions office email:** admissions@middlebury.edu

**# of transfer applications:** Fall 2015 admissions: 318

**# of transfer students accepted:** Fall 2015: 39

**Transfer student acceptance rate (2015–2016 academic year):** 12.3%

**Freshman applications received in Fall 2016:** 8,820

**Freshman applications accepted in Fall 2016:** 1,668

**Acceptance rate for 2016–2017 freshmen:** 18.9%

## Transfer Admissions Process

**Transfer policy (in their own words):** Applicants who have been or are currently enrolled as full-time degree seeking students at another college or university must apply as transfer students. The majority of transfer students are admitted as sophomores or first-semester juniors, and preference is given to those students who have completed at least a full year of college work upon entry. The high-school record is weighed heavily, and candidates must be in good standing at their current college with at least a B average. If your college does not give grades, written faculty appraisals must be submitted.

Read more at www.middlebury.edu/admissions/apply/transfer.

**Transfer admissions contact person:** Greg Buckles, Dean of Admission

**Transfer admissions contact info:** deanofadmissions@middlebury.edu, (802) 443-5415

**Offers transfer-focused admissions events:** Yes

**Transfer application deadline:** Fall 2018 deadline is 3/1/18. Spring 2019 deadline is 11/1/18.

**Acceptances announced to transfer applicants:** Fall 2018 in mid-May. Spring 2019 in mid-December.

**Transfer application on Common App:** Yes. Common App fee: $65.

**SAT/ACT required for transfer applicants:** Yes

**High-school records requirements:** Official high-school transcript and final report

**High-school records requirements for applicants who completed outside the US:** Applicants for whom English is not their first language are required to demonstrate their proficiency in English. Middlebury will consider either the TOEFL or the results from other standardized tests, including SAT I Verbal, ACT, IELTS, CPE, and MELAB.

**Submission requirements for transfer applicants who completed high-school equivalency test:** Official GED certificate

**College transcript requirements:** Official college transcript

**Interviews available for transfer applicants:** No

## Costs & Financial Aid

**FAFSA code:** 3691

**CSS Profile code:** 3526

**Are internal school financial aid forms required?** No

**Financial aid deadlines for transfer applicants:** Fall 2018: 3/1/18. Spring 2019: 11/15/18.

**Costs for the 2017–2018 year:** Tuition & Fees: $52,496. Room & Board: $14,968.

**Anticipated costs for the 2018–2019 year:** No information provided.

**Financial aid for transfer students:** Yes

**Guarantees meeting 100% need for transfer students:** Yes

**Need-based aid for transfer students:** Yes

**Merit-based financial aid for transfer students:** No

**Phi Theta Kappa Scholarship:** No

**Reduced or zero tuition fees for low-income students:** No

**Includes loans in financial aid packages:** Yes

**% of all undergraduates receiving financial aid:** 44%

**% of all undergraduates qualifying for Pell Grants:** 15%

**Average financial aid award for all undergraduate students:** $43,154

**Funding available for low-income students to visit:** No

**Enrollment deposit can be waived for low-income students:** Contact the admissions office.

## Academics

**GPA range for transfer students accepted in 2016–2017:** No information provided.

**SAT ranges for all students admitted in 2015:** Critical Reading: 630–750. Mathematics: 640–750. Writing: 650–760.

**ACT composite score range for all students admitted in 2016:** 30–34

**Type of curriculum:** Gen. Ed. requirements

**Type of academic year:** Semester

**Advisors specifically for transfer students:** Yes

**Credit policy (in their own words):** Candidates for the bachelor of arts degree must complete 36 credits. At least 18 of these credits must be Middlebury credits. No more than 6 credits with a D grade may be applied to degree requirements.

Read more at www.middlebury.edu/about/handbook/academics/Degree_Requirements.

An estimate of the number of transferable credits will be provided during the first week or 2 after the student arrives on campus. A final evaluation of credit transfer will only be possible after a complete evaluation by appropriate department chairs, but will be completed before the end of the student's first semester at Middlebury.

**Max number of transfer credits accepted:** 18

**Residency requirement for transfer students:** Yes. Traditionally, transfer students are admitted only to the sophomore year and to the first term of junior year and must plan to complete at least 2 years' work (18 courses) at Middlebury. An estimate of the time required for graduation will be given upon matriculation, but final transcript evaluation may not take place until after a student completes a semester at Middlebury.

**Study abroad available for transfer students:** Yes. Middlebury students must apply for preapproval to study abroad. Credits earned at Middlebury Language Schools or at the Middlebury Schools Abroad will count in the 18-course residency requirement, and the grades will count in the undergraduate grade point average.

**Free tutoring for all students:** Yes

**Writing center for all students:** Yes

**Career support/access to internships and resume prep for all students:** Yes

**% of undergraduate students hired within 6 months of graduation:** No information provided.

**Additional resources specifically designated for transfer and/or non-traditional students:** No

## Housing

**Available for transfer students:** Yes

**Available for non-traditional students:** Yes

**Guaranteed for transfer students:** Yes

**Non-traditional students can reside in housing year-round:** No

**Family housing available:** No

## Non-Traditional Admissions

No non-traditional student policy or programs available.

## Military/Veteran Students

No military/veteran admissions policy available.

**Status considered in admissions:** No

**Special financial aid:** Yes. The Yellow Ribbon Program.

**Specific programs/policies to address needs:** ROTC Program

## DACA/Undocumented Students

**DACA and undocumented admissions policy (in their own words):** If you are an undocumented or DACA student, please follow the same application process as any other student. We evaluate applications from undocumented prospective students under our need-blind admissions policy with a commitment to meet full demonstrated financial need. Admissions contact is Nicole Curvin, ncurvin@middlebury.edu, (802)443-5481. Read more at www.middlebury.edu/admissions/apply/for-undocumented-students.

**Admitted:** Yes

**Status considered in admissions:** No

**Special admissions process:** No

**Eligible for institutional financial aid:** Yes. Middlebury meets 100% of demonstrated financial need for all of our admitted students, regardless of country of citizenship or immigration status. To apply for financial aid, please complete the CSS Profile by the deadlines indicated on our website. You do not need to submit the FAFSA to apply for financial aid.

Your Student Financial Services Office contact is Jackie Davies, jdavies@middlebury.edu.

**Specific programs/policies to address needs:** Middlebury supports undocumented and DACA-designated students throughout their time at the College. Miguel Fernández, Middlebury's Chief Diversity Officer, serves as the point person for current undocumented and DACA students (fernande@middlebury.edu, (802) 443-5792). International Student & Scholar Services (ISSS) has posted DACA Resources on their webpage as a reference for our community.

# MOREHOUSE COLLEGE

**Location:** Atlanta, Georgia

**Website:** www.morehouse.edu

**Endowment:** $130 million

**Type of School:** Private/Single-Sex Male, Liberal Arts

**# of Undergraduate Students:** 2,439

**# of Graduate Students:** 0

**Average Class Size:** No information provided.

**School Mission (in their own words):** The mission of Morehouse College is to develop men with disciplined minds to lead lives of leadership and service by emphasizing the intellectual and character development of its students and by assuming a special responsibility for teaching the history and culture of black people.

## Admissions

**Admissions office mailing address:** 830 Westview Dr SW, Atlanta GA 30314

**Admissions office phone:** (844) 512-6672

**Admissions office email:** N/A

**# of transfer applications:** Fall 2015 admissions: 226. Spring 2016 admissions: 249.

**# of transfer students accepted:** Fall 2015: 124. Spring 2016: 50.

**Transfer student acceptance rate (2015–2016 academic year):** 36.63%

**Freshman applications received in Fall 2015:** 2,288

**Freshman applications accepted in Fall 2015:** 1,738

**Acceptance rate for 2015–2016 freshmen:** 76%

## Transfer Admissions Process

**Transfer policy (in their own words):** Students from accredited colleges may apply for transfer standing if they have completed the equivalent of 26 semester hours of college work. We look for transfer students who have demonstrated a desire to want to fully engage the faculty and student body of the College academically and socially. Your essay should stand out and reflect the level of writing that faculty would expect of a first- or second-year college student. The student needs to have 2 letters of recommendation, 1 from a faculty member and 1 from an administrator of the last college attended. Students who have previously applied to, or who have been enrolled at Morehouse, should make that fact known when contacting the Admissions Office. Students must also complete and submit the Dean of Students Certification Form for each and every school they have attended regardless of the length of time attended. This form must be sent to the Office of Admissions directly from the institution completing the form. No admissions decision will be made without the submission of the Dean of Students Certification Form.

Read more at www.morehouse.edu/admissions/requirements/transfer.html.

**Transfer admissions contact person:** Tony Belser, Assistant Director of Admissions and Recruitment for Transfer Initiatives

**Transfer admissions contact info:** tony.belser@morehouse.edu, (470) 639-0364

**Offers transfer-focused admissions events:** N/A

**Transfer application deadline:** Fall 2018 deadline is 2/1/18. Spring 2019 deadline is 11/1/18.

**Acceptances announced to transfer applicants:** Fall 2018 on 3/15/18. Spring 2019 on 12/15/18.

**Transfer application on Common App:** Yes. Common App fee: $50.

**SAT/ACT required for transfer applicants:** No

**High-school records requirements:** None

**High-school records requirements for applicants who completed outside the US:** Official high-school transcript

**Submission requirements for transfer applicants who completed high-school equivalency test:** None

**College transcript requirements:** Official transcripts of all colleges and universities attended

**Interviews available for transfer applicants:** Required. A video interview answering 5 questions.

## Costs & Financial Aid

**FAFSA code:** 1582

**CSS Profile code:** N/A

**Are internal school financial aid forms required?** No

**Financial aid deadlines for transfer applicants:** Fall 2018: 2/15/18. Spring 2019: 2/15/18.

**Costs for the 2017–2018 year:** Tuition & Fees: $27,236. Room & Board: $13,438.

**Financial aid for transfer students:** Yes

**Guarantees meeting 100% need for transfer students:** No

**Need-based aid for transfer students:** Yes

**Merit-based financial aid for transfer students:** No

**Phi Theta Kappa Scholarship:** No

**Reduced or zero tuition fees for low-income students:** No

**Includes loans in financial aid packages:** Yes

**% of all undergraduates receiving financial aid:** 90%

**% of all undergraduates qualifying for Pell Grants:** No information provided.

**Average financial aid award for all undergraduate students:** No information provided.

**Funding available for low-income students to visit:** No

**Enrollment deposit can be waived for low-income students:** No

## Academics

**GPA range for transfer students accepted in 2015–2016:** 2.5

**SAT ranges for all students admitted in 2015:** Critical Reading: 440–550. Mathematics: 430–550. Writing: 410–520.

**ACT composite score range for all students admitted in 2015:** 18–23

**Type of curriculum:** Gen. Ed. requirements

**Type of academic year:** Semester

**Advisors specifically for transfer students:** No

**Credit policy (in their own words):** New students who transfer from another 4-year institution or junior college must submit, in advance for admission, transcripts of all previous work done on the college level. Such transcripts must be sent directly from the institution at which the work was completed. Academic work completed at other schools that is not listed on the admission application will not be accepted for transfer purposes. Read more at www.morehouse.edu/recordsregistration/transfercredit.html.

**Max number of transfer credits accepted:** 60. A maximum of 60 semester hours (or the equivalent) is ordinarily transferable to Morehouse course credit if: (1) the prior college is accredited, (2) a grade of C or better is earned in the course, and (3) the course is comparable to a course offered at Morehouse.

**Residency requirement for transfer students:** Yes. All transfer students must complete a minimum of 60 semester hours at Morehouse. They must also successfully complete a minimum of 120 semester hours of non-repeat courses (exclusive of courses numbered below 100) and complete at least 2 years of coursework (a minimum of 60 semester hours) in residence at the College. Read more at www.morehouse.edu/academics/degree_requirements.

**Study abroad available for transfer students:** Yes. Must meet residency requirements.

**Free tutoring for all students:** Yes

**Writing center for all students:** Yes

**Career support/access to internships and resume prep for all students:** Yes

**% of undergraduate students hired within 6 months of graduation:** No information provided.

**Additional resources specifically designated for transfer and/or non-traditional students:** No information provided.

## Housing

**Available for transfer students:** Yes

**Available for non-traditional students:** No

**Guaranteed for transfer students:** No

**Non-traditional students can reside in housing year-round:** No

**Family housing available:** No

## Non-Traditional Admissions

No non-traditional student policy or programs available.

## Military/Veteran Students

**Military/veteran admissions policy (in their own words):** Military/veteran students follow the same application process as other students.

**Status considered in admissions:** No

**Special financial aid:** No

**Specific programs/policies to address needs:** Veterans Affairs Office

## DACA/Undocumented Students

**DACA and undocumented admissions policy (in their own words):** Morehouse College does not accept DACA/undocumented students.

# Kaire Cowell

**Northeastern University, C'19**
JD Law

**Morehouse College, C'14**
Bachelor's Degree in Economics, cum laude

**LaGuardia Community College, C'10**
Associate's Degree in Accounting

**Bio:** Kaire plans to earn a law degree and use his skills to advocate and secure legal representation for the indigent. He is concerned about the lack of rehabilitative services and the marginalization of men of color, and would like to strengthen communities by empowering everyone to reach their highest potential. Kaire hopes to give back to his community by establishing a nonprofit organization that offers free financial education, legal advice, training, and college admissions information in low-income neighborhoods.

*"Transferring from LaGuardia Community College to Morehouse was a life-changing decision. My experience at Morehouse geared me toward pursuing a career in law.*

*Social responsibility, service, leadership, and moral character were highly stressed in and outside of the classroom. Thanks to my Morehouse education, I began to recognize these attributes in our legal system and as core principles in a career in law."*

## Leadership Activities

- Officer, Phi Theta Kappa International Honor Society of Community Colleges
- Academic Peer Instruction Tutor, LaGuardia Community College
- Dean's List, LaGuardia Community College
- Volunteer, American Civil Liberties Union
- Phi Alpha Delta Law Fraternity, Morehouse College
- Omicron Delta Epsilon International Honors Society for Economics, Morehouse College
- Dean's List, Morehouse College
- Volunteer, Southern Center for Human Rights
- Legal Intern, Anthony McGee Law Group
- Co-Founder & Mentor, College Initiative Peer Mentor Project, Long Island City, NY
- Member, Morehouse Business Association
- Member, Economics Club, Morehouse College
- Researcher, Morehouse College, Economics Department
- Volunteer, Equal Employment Opportunity Commission, Atlanta Field Office

# Bolaji James

**Morehouse College, C'09**
Bachelor's Degree in Economics, with Honors

**New York City College of Technology, C'07**
Associate's Degree in Ophthalmic Dispensing, with Honors

**Current Employment:** Customer Trade Marketing Manager, Reckitt Benckiser

**Bio:** Bolaji, a native Nigerian, wants to utilize his business and leadership skills to play an instrumental role in the development of emerging markets in African nations and Latin America.

*"Because I was born and raised in Nigeria, my experience as an African living in the United States was very different from that of an African American. I didn't fully grasp the consequences of African American history in today's society. Living in the United States exposed me to a new reality, a 'rude awakening' so to speak. So for me, transferring to Morehouse was motivated by more than just academics. It was personal.*

*Morehouse challenged me. Being amongst brilliant minds that looked like me gave me a renewed sense of pride. My favorite school quote reads, 'Morehouse puts a crown above the heads of her students, and dares them to grow tall enough to wear it!' Even though I graduated from Morehouse eight years ago, this quote remains instilled in me. It is what drives me to perform above expectations, both professionally and personally. I wake up every day determined to be tall enough to wear it!"*

## Leadership Activities

- Co-Salutatorian, Morehouse College, C'09
- Member, Phi Beta Kappa, 2009
- Intern, Inroads
- Member, Morehouse Investment Club
- Peer Mentor, Morehouse College
- Mentor and Math Tutor, Atlanta Public School System
- Scholarship Recipient, New York State Society of Opticians Scholarship, 2006

# MOUNT HOLYOKE COLLEGE

**Location:** South Hadley, Massachusetts

**Website:** www.mtholyoke.edu

**Endowment:** $709 million

**Type of School:** Private/Single-Sex Female, Liberal Arts

**# of Undergraduate Students:** 2,189

**# of Graduate Students:** 0

**Average Class Size:** 12% of classes have fewer than 10 students, 68% of classes have fewer than 20 students, 85% of classes have fewer than 30 students.

**School Mission (in their own words):** Mount Holyoke's mission is to provide an intellectually adventurous education in the liberal arts and sciences through academic programs recognized internationally for their excellence and range; to draw students from all backgrounds into an exceptionally diverse and inclusive learning community with a highly accomplished, committed, and responsive faculty and staff; to continue building on the College's historic legacy of leadership in the education of women; and to prepare students, through a liberal education integrating curriculum and careers, for lives of thoughtful, effective, and purposeful engagement in the world.

## Admissions

**Admissions office mailing address:** 50 College St, South Hadley MA 01075

**Admissions office phone:** (413) 538-2023

**Admissions office email:** admission@mtholyoke.edu

**# of transfer applications:** Fall 2016 admissions: 202. Spring 2017 admissions: 31.

**# of transfer students accepted:** Fall 2016: 84. Spring 2017: 16.

**Transfer student acceptance rate (2016–2017 academic year):** 42.9%

**Freshman applications received in Fall 2016:** 3,543

**Freshman applications accepted in Fall 2016:** 1,849

**Acceptance rate for 2016–2017 freshmen:** 52.19%

## Transfer Admissions Process

**Transfer policy (in their own words):** Transfer students add to the rich mix of student experience on campus and to the intellectual and social life of the College. Each year, approximately 50 new transfers enroll at Mount Holyoke.

Eligible candidates for transfer admission include students with strong academic records from 2-year and community colleges, as well as from 4-year colleges and universities.

Transfer applications are read in a manner similar to that of first-year students, but more emphasis is placed on college-level coursework and professors' letters of recommendation. Mount Holyoke welcomes transfer applications and in recent years has experienced a substantial increase in this population. Transfer students have proven to be excellent students and campus leaders at Mount Holyoke.

Read more at www.mtholyoke.edu/sfs/transfer/transfer_app.

**Transfer admissions contact person:** Carolyn Dietel, Director of Frances Perkins Program and Transfer Affairs

**Transfer admissions contact info:** cdietel@mtholyoke.edu, (413) 538-2077

**Offers transfer-focused admissions events:** Yes. 2 per year: November and February.

**Transfer application deadline:** Fall 2018 deadline is 3/1/18. Spring 2019 deadline is 11/1/18.

**Acceptances announced to transfer applicants:** Fall 2018 in mid-April. Spring 2019 on 12/5/18.

**Transfer application on Common App:** Yes. Common App fee: $60.

**SAT/ACT required for transfer applicants:** No

**High-school records requirements:** If the student does not have a high-school diploma, then a GED can be submitted. Ask your secondary-school counselor or guidance office to send us official secondary-school transcripts as well as any written reports of your secondary-school work.

**High-school records requirements for applicants who completed outside the US:** If your secondary-school documents are not in English, you must submit notarized translations along with the original documents.

**Submission requirements for transfer applicants who completed high-school equivalency test:** Must submit the official scores.

**College transcript requirements:** Submit official transcripts of all previous college work.

**Interviews available for transfer applicants:** They're optional but recommended. Required for Frances Perkins applicants. On-campus, off-campus with an alumna, and online/Skype.

## Costs & Financial Aid

**FAFSA code:** 2192

**CSS Profile code:** 3529

**Are internal school financial aid forms required?** No

**Financial aid deadlines for transfer applicants:** Fall 2018: 3/5/18. Spring 2019: 11/5/18.

**Costs for the 2017–2018 year:** Tuition & Fees: $47,940. Room & Board: $14,060.

**Financial aid for transfer students:** Yes

**Guarantees meeting 100% need for transfer students:** Yes

**Need-based aid for transfer students:** Yes

**Merit-based financial aid for transfer students:** Yes

**Phi Theta Kappa Scholarship:** No

**Reduced or zero tuition fees for low-income students:** No

**Includes loans in financial aid packages:** Yes

**% of all undergraduates receiving financial aid:** 76%

**% of all undergraduates qualifying for Pell Grants:** 26%

**Average financial aid award for all undergraduate students:** $41,109

**Funding available for low-income students to visit:** Yes

**Enrollment deposit can be waived for low-income students:** No

## Academics

**GPA range for transfer students accepted in 2016–2017:** 3.3–4.0

**SAT ranges for all students admitted in 2016:** Critical Reading: 610–730. Mathematics: 610–760. Writing: 630–710.

**ACT composite score range for all students admitted in 2016:** 30

**Recommended completed level of math for transfer applicants:** Pre-calculus or calculus

**Recommended courses transfer applicants should have on transcripts:** Applicants should present a variety of liberal arts course credits from the humanities, sciences, and social sciences.

**Recommended courses transfer applicants interested in STEM should complete before transfer:** Depends upon the discipline.

**Recommended extracurricular engagement:** Application review is holistic; students are encouraged to pursue interests and co-curricular passions.

**Type of curriculum:** Gen. Ed. requirements. The College's distribution requirement is designed to acquaint students with a wide range of knowledge and encourage them to explore new areas of interest. At least 68 credits must be earned from coursework outside the major department, across the 3 curricular divisions: humanities, science and mathematics, and social sciences. Mount Holyoke requires a distribution across divisions of knowledge, a language other than English, and a multicultural perspectives course.

**Type of academic year:** Semester

**Advisors specifically for transfer students:** Yes

**Credit policy (in their own words):** Credit is awarded only when official documentation (official transcript, official test score report) is submitted to the registrar from the external institution. No more than 64 credits will be awarded to students for external work, regardless of whether from pre-matriculation study or post-matriculation study abroad, summer study, etc. Transfer credits are granted on a semester credit-for-credit basis (that is, a 3-credit course taken on a semester schedule will be awarded 3 credits at Mount Holyoke College). Credits earned at schools not on the semester calendar will be converted to semester credits (e.g., a quarter credit will be awarded .66 semester credits at Mount Holyoke College).

Read more at www.mtholyoke.edu/admission/transfer/transferring_credit.

**Max number of transfer credits accepted:** 64

**Residency requirement for transfer students:** Yes. You must be registered at Mount Holyoke for a minimum of 4 semesters.

**Study abroad available for transfer students:** Yes. Must meet residency requirements.

**Free tutoring for all students:** Yes

**Writing center for all students:** Yes

**Career support/access to internships and resume prep for all students:** Yes

**% of undergraduate students hired within 6 months of graduation:** N/A

**Additional resources specifically designated for transfer and/or non-traditional students:** Yes. There are academic advisors that specifically work with non-traditional students. Transfer and Frances Perkins scholars are eligible for a funded internship or research opportunity.

## Housing

**Available for transfer students:** Yes

**Available for non-traditional students:** Yes

**Guaranteed for transfer students:** Yes

**Non-traditional students can reside in housing year-round:** Yes. Frances Perkins students are given the option of purchasing year-round housing in Dickinson Hall.

**Family housing available:** No

## Non-Traditional Admissions

**Non-traditional student policy (in their own words):** Non-traditional students are students 25 years and older, veterans, active military, or under 25 years with dependents.

**Name of program:** Frances Perkins Program

**Program description:** The Frances Perkins Program is open to and designed for women 25 years and older who have experienced an interruption in their education, but who now seek the intellectual challenge of completing their 4-year degree at a top liberal arts institution. Veterans, active military, and women who are under 25 with dependents are also eligible to apply. Frances Perkins scholars fulfill the same requirements as do all other Mount Holyoke students, but have the added flexibility of electing either a full- or part-time (2 course) schedule and, if they enter with sophomore or junior standing, are exempt from the first-year seminar requirement. Women who do not meet the minimum age requirement, but have dependents or are veterans, are also eligible to apply for admission through this program. Full tuition scholarship for 25 admitted FP applicants per year and a dedicated office to provide support pre- and post-admission through graduation are available.

**Program deadlines:** Spring 2018: 11/1/18. Fall 2018: 3/1/18.

**Program admission requirements:** A minimum of 40 college credits in liberal arts classes; evidence of academic achievement (e.g., GPA)

**Program website:** www.mtholyoke.edu/fp

**Program contact person:** Carolyn Dietel, Director of Frances Perkins Program and Transfer Affairs

**Program contact info:** (413) 538-2077, cdietel@mtholyoke.edu

**Name of program:** Transfer Admission (for students who are under the age of 25)

**Program description:** Traditional-age transfer students must present a minimum of 16 credits in liberal arts courses. They are supported by the Director of Transfer Admission pre- and post-admission and have all the rights and privileges of any undergraduate student with ongoing support for students who matriculate with advanced standing.

**Program deadline:** Spring 2018: 11/1/18. Fall 2018: 3/1/18.

**Program admission requirements:** Minimum of 16 credits, evidence of academic achievement (i.e., GPA), as well as academic recommendations

**Program website:** www.mtholyoke.edu/admission/transfer

**Program contact person:** Carolyn Dietel, Director of Frances Perkins Program and Transfer Affairs

**Program contact info:** (413) 538-2077, cdietel@mtholyoke.edu

## Military/Veteran Students

**Military/veteran admissions policy (in their own words):** Military/veteran students are strongly encouraged to apply to the Frances Perkins Program. See details of this program above.

Read more at www.mtholyoke.edu/fp.

**Status considered in admissions:** No

**Special admissions process:** Yes. Apply through the Frances Perkins Program.

**Special financial aid:** Yes. The Yellow Ribbon Program.

**Specific programs/policies to address needs:** There is one-on-one counseling on military benefits, and students have the opportunity to participate in a Reserve Officer's Training Corps program at UMASS Amherst.

## DACA/Undocumented Students

**DACA and undocumented admissions policy (in their own words):** DACA/undocumented students do not need to follow a separate admissions application process. In addition, Mount Holyoke College considers undocumented and DACA status students for both merit scholarships and need-based financial aid. (All applicants are automatically considered for merit scholarships with their admission application.)

To apply for need-based financial aid from the College, an applicant who identifies herself as an undocumented or DACA status student should follow the application requirements, with the exception of filing the FAFSA, according to her application plan: first year, transfer, Frances Perkins (non-traditional age), or current student.

An applicant who has not identified herself to Mount Holyoke as an undocumented or DACA status student should complete the financial aid application requirements for International applicants.

We're here to help you throughout the application process and in managing the cost of a Mount Holyoke education. Please contact us with any questions you may have.

Read more at www.mtholyoke.edu/sfs/undocumented-and-daca-students.

**Admitted:** Yes

**Status considered in admissions:** No

**Special admissions process:** No, with the exception of not needing to file FAFSA form

**Eligible for institutional financial aid:** Yes. Must demonstrate need. Average financial aid given to these students for Fall 2016 was $46,389.

**Specific programs/policies to address needs:** Yes. There's the Undocumented Immigrant Alliance, which provides peer support for students. Besides being able to be part of the Undocumented Immigrant Alliance, students can also talk with advisors who have experience and knowledge with DACA laws.

# Anastasia Morton

**Mount Holyoke College, C'13**
Bachelor's Degree in Psychology and Educational Studies

**LaGuardia Community College, C'09**
Associate's Degree in Liberal Arts

**Current Employment:** Program Coordinator, Amherst Region Public School Family Center

**Bio:** Anastasia is passionate about education that empowers disenfranchised youth, teaching them the importance of identity, cultural appreciation, leadership, and self-esteem. As a mother and dynamic member of the Pioneer Valley community, she works to bridge the communication gap between families, school, and government officials, ensuring the creation of youth services that encourage the full development of children.

*"Transferring to Mount Holyoke College helped me overcome my fear of success. While there, I became more aware of the beauty and cultural capital in my struggle. The classes at MHC were in step with my learning style; small classroom sizes and intergroup dialogue made it easier to speak up, letting my journey have voice, power, and influence. The most beneficial thing MHC gave me was understanding the power and value of intergroup dialogue. While in classes, I gained so much from the deep critical discussions and scholarly lectures that I discovered new layers within myself and emerged a stronger leader.*

*As a mom, having the freedom to bring my son to class, and incorporate him into my academic journey at a young age, changed his and my life trajectory forever. Stimulating, family-friendly classes and workshops let me uncover my hidden strengths. Using my newfound confidence, I perfected my abilities in collecting research; communicating; and planning agendas, curricula, and events."*

## Leadership Activities

- 2012 Passport to Leadership Award, Weissman Center for Leadership, Mount Holyoke College
- Scholar, Frances Perkins Program, Mount Holyoke College
- Facilitator, Pioneer Valley Conferences and Seminars
- School Aide, Wadleigh Secondary School, NYC
- Graduate, Accelerated Study in Associate Program (ASAP), LGCC
- Member, Phi Theta Kappa International Honor Society of Community Colleges
- Parent Committee Co-Chair, Leggett Child Care Center, NYC

# NEW YORK UNIVERSITY

**Location:** New York, New York
**Website:** www.nyu.edu
**Endowment:** $3.5 billion
**Type of School:** Private/Co-ed, Research University
**# of Undergraduate Students:** 25,722 (2015–2016)
**# of Graduate Students:** 24,305 (2015–2016)
**Average Class Size:** N/A

**School Mission (in their own words):** New York University's mission is to be a top quality international center of scholarship, teaching, and research. This involves retaining and attracting outstanding faculty who are leaders in their fields, encouraging them to create programs that draw outstanding students, and providing an intellectually rich environment. NYU seeks to take academic and cultural advantage of its location and to embrace diversity among faculty, staff, and students to ensure a wide range of perspectives, including international perspectives, in the educational experience.

## Admissions

**Admissions office mailing address:** 70 Washington Sq S, New York NY 10012

**Admissions office phone:** (212) 998-4550

**Admissions office email:** admissions.ops@nyu.edu

**# of transfer applications:** Fall 2015 admissions: 7,685

**# of transfer students accepted:** Fall 2015: 2,125

**Transfer student acceptance rate (2015–2016 academic year):** 27.7%

**Freshman applications received in Fall 2015:** 57,727

**Freshman applications accepted in Fall 2015:** 18,515

**Acceptance rate for 2016–2017 freshmen:** 32%

## Transfer Admissions Process

**Transfer policy (in their own words):** Transfer students are students that:

> Currently are or have been enrolled in an associate's degree or bachelor's degree program (part-time or full-time) at a college or university anywhere in the world; or have been enrolled in a nondegree conservatory or vocational training program.

**Transfer admissions contact person:** N/A

**Transfer admissions contact info:** admissions.ops@nyu.edu

**Offers transfer-focused admissions events:** Yes, CCTOP visit days.

**Transfer application deadline:** Fall 2018 deadline is 4/1/18. Spring 2019 deadline is 11/1/18.

**Acceptances announced to transfer applicants:** Fall 2018 on rolling basis from April–May. Spring 2019 on rolling basis from November–December.

**Transfer application on Common App:** Yes. Common App fee: $70.

**SAT/ACT required for transfer applicants:** Not if the applicants have completed at least 1 year of college/university study

**High-school records requirements:** Yes. Official transcript required.

**High-school records requirements for applicants who completed outside the US:** Must include an official translation if the document isn't in English.

**Submission requirements for transfer applicants who completed high-school equivalency test:** Official GED results

**College transcript requirements:** Official transcripts from all colleges/universities attended

**Interviews available for transfer applicants:** No

**Additional requirements for transfers seeking admissions to business school:** Yes. Do so for the fall semester only.

If you wish to transfer into the sophomore year at Stern, you should have completed:

- 1 semester of calculus I or higher (NYU's MATH-UA 121 or higher or equivalent)
- 1–2 semesters of writing/composition

If you wish to transfer into the junior year at Stern, you should have completed:

- 1 semester of calculus I or higher (NYU's MATH-UA 121 or higher or equivalent)
- 1–2 semesters of writing/composition
- 1 semester of introductory-level microeconomics (NYU's ECON-UA 2 Introduction to Microeconomics or equivalent)
- 1 semester of statistics and regression (NYU's STAT-UB 103 Statistics for Business Control and Regression/Forecasting Models or equivalent)
- 1 semester of financial accounting (NYU'S ACCT-UB 1 Principles of Financial Accounting or equivalent)

**Additional requirements for transfers seeking admissions to arts major:** Yes. The following programs accept spring transfers:

- Cinema Studies
- Game Design (internal transfers only)
- Performance Studies
- Photography and Imaging (internal transfers only)

The following programs accept fall transfers:

- Cinema Studies
- Dance
- Drama
- Dramatic Writing
- Film and Television (All accepted transfer students to Film and Television must begin their studies over the summer.)
- Game Design
- Performance Studies
- Photography and Imaging
- Recorded Music

**Additional requirements for transfers seeking admissions to engineering major:** Yes. Top applicants have completed at least 1 full-time semester of college coursework and have demonstrated strengths in science, technology, engineering, and higher-level math.

**Additional requirements for transfers seeking admissions to other major:** No information provided.

## Costs & Financial Aid

**FAFSA code:** 2785

**CSS Profile code:** N/A

**Are internal school financial aid forms required?** Yes. TAP for NY state financial aid.

**Financial aid deadlines for transfer applicants:** Fall 2018: 4/1/18. Spring 2019: 11/1/18.

**Costs for the 2017–2018 year:** Tuition & Fees: $49,242. Room & Board: $17,578.

**Financial aid for transfer students:** Yes

**Guarantees meeting 100% need for transfer students:** No

**Need-based aid for transfer students:** Yes, FAFSA

**Merit-based financial aid for transfer students:** No

**Phi Theta Kappa Scholarship:** Yes, $2,500. Renewable. 3.8 GPA required.

**Reduced or zero tuition fees for low-income students:** No

**Includes loans in financial aid packages:** Yes

**% of all undergraduates receiving financial aid:** 48

**% of all undergraduates qualifying for Pell Grants:** 21

**Average financial aid award for all undergraduate students:** 30,000 (for freshmen)

**Funding available for low-income students to visit:** No

**Enrollment deposit can be waived for low-income students:** No

## Academics

**GPA range for transfer students accepted in 2016–2017:** Minimum C GPA

**SAT ranges for all students admitted in 2016:** Critical Reading: 620–720. Mathematics: 630–750. Writing: 630–730.

**ACT composite score range for all students admitted in 2014:** 28–32

**Type of curriculum:** Gen. Ed. requirements

**Type of academic year:** Semester

**Advisors specifically for transfer students:** Yes

**Credit policy (in their own words):** Credit policy depends on the school from NYU that the student attends. If a student would like to learn more about the policies, they will have to research each different school.

**Max number of transfer credits accepted:** 64

**Residency requirement for transfer students:** Yes. Students must complete at least 64 credits at NYU.

**Study abroad available for transfer students:** Yes. Must complete residency requirement.

**Free tutoring for all students:** Yes

**Writing center for all students:** Yes

**Career support/access to internships and resume prep for all students:** Yes

**% of undergraduate students hired within 6 months of graduation:** 86%

**Additional resources specifically designated for transfer and/or non-traditional students:** No

## Housing

**Available for transfer students:** Yes

**Available for non-traditional students:** No

**Guaranteed for transfer students:** No

**Family housing available:** No

## Non-Traditional Admissions

**Non-traditional student policy (in their own words):** Non-traditional students usually apply to the School of Professional Studies/McGhee Division.

The NYU School of Professional Studies admissions committee performs a holistic review of candidates, taking into consideration every component of the application. Please be sure to review the admissions criteria to better familiarize yourself with the admissions process.

As a transfer student, we understand that you want to complete your degree in a cost-effective and timely manner. At the NYU School of Professional Studies, our staff of dedicated advisors meets, one-on-one, with prospective transfer students to determine how many of their credits will transfer and to map out a course of study that makes sense for their academic and career goals. Our generous transfer credit policy allows students to transfer up to half of the credits required to complete a bachelor's degree. In addition, there is no minimum number of credits required to transfer to McGhee.

Read more at http://sps.nyu.edu/admissions/undergraduate/mcghee/apply/transfer-students.html.

**Name of program:** Community College Transfer Opportunity Program (CCTOP)

**Program description:** The CCTOP is a scholarship and assistance program for students transferring from partnership community colleges into NYU Steinhardt. It includes pre-admission advising, application assistance, transfer credit agreements, scholarship aid, and additional resources during your time at NYU Steinhardt.

**Program deadline:** 4/1/18 for fall applicants, 11/1/18 for spring applicants.

**Program admission requirements:** Be enrolled at a participating community college.

Be nominated by a member of the faculty or administration at your community college.

Have 3.0 cumulative GPA at the community college.

Have 48 transferable credits toward an NYU Steinhardt program of study.

Complete the undergraduate admission process, be offered admission to NYU Steinhardt, and enroll full-time in one of its programs of study.

Be a US citizen or permanent resident and eligible to complete the FAFSA form.

**Program website:** http://steinhardt.nyu.edu/cctop

**Program contact person:** Jacqueline McPhillips, Director

**Program contact info:** (212) 998-5139, jmm34@nyu.edu

**Name of program:** NYU School of Professional Services Paul McGhee Division

**Program description:** For more than 8 decades, the NYU School of Professional Studies has provided comprehensive, professionally oriented educational experiences to students from the New York metropolitan area, across the country, and around the globe. The NYU School of Professional Studies McGhee Division for Undergraduate Studies programs integrate the liberal arts and professional studies, providing a comprehensive undergraduate education that is highly valued in competitive job markets. As a student, you will hone your critical thinking and analytical skills, increase your knowledge base, develop your intellect, and acquire the confidence to excel personally and professionally. The Division provides a wide range of study options in the Humanities and in the Social Sciences that include numerous concentrations from which to choose. A new option in Applied Data Analytics and Visualization focuses on the most current and relevant topics in a dynamic field with a wide spectrum of employment opportunities. Programs are also offered in Applied General Studies, Digital Communications and Media, Healthcare Management, Information Systems Management, Leadership and Management Studies, Marketing Analytics, and Real Estate.

**Program deadlines:**

Fall semester:

- Domestic early decision: July 1
- Domestic final date: August 15

Spring semester:

- Domestic early decision: November 1
- Domestic final date: January 15

Summer semester:

- Domestic early decision: April 1
- Domestic final date: May 1

**Program admission requirements:** Personal statement, resume, official transcripts from all colleges/universities attended

**Program website:** www.sps.nyu.edu/about.html

**Program contact person:** Joanne Miller, Associate Director of Admissions

**Program contact info:** (212) 998-7244, joanne.miller@nyu.edu

## Military/Veteran Students

**Military/veteran admissions policy (in their own words):** Military/veteran students are welcome to apply to NYU's School of Professional Studies. Our admissions process is selective, and applicants are evaluated individually, based on their ability to benefit from and contribute to the challenging environment the school offers. We do not have a separate admissions process for those who have served in the US military. We encourage you to learn more about our admissions and application process, and we also invite you to meet with a dedicated admissions officer during our weekly open office hours to learn more about your degree of interest.

Read more at http://sps.nyu.edu/admissions/undergraduate/mcghee/apply/veterans.html.

**Status considered in admissions:** No

**Special admissions process:** No

**Special financial aid:** Yes. The Yellow Ribbon Program.

**Specific programs/policies to address needs:** Student groups, military/veteran specific events, student veterans group

## DACA/Undocumented Students

**DACA and undocumented admissions policy (in their own words):** On November 15, 2016, NYU President Andrew Hamilton sent a message to the NYU community which made clear that undocumented students will continue to be treated exactly as all other students at NYU with regard to housing, privacy, and all other matters.

Read more at www.nyu.edu/students/communities-and-groups/undocumented-students.html.

**Admitted:** Yes

**Status considered in admissions:** No

**Special admissions process:** No

**Eligible for institutional financial aid:** Yes. NYU offers institutional scholarship aid to eligible undocumented students from New York on par with what is offered to US students.

**Specific programs/policies to address needs:** Yes. NYU Immigrant Defense Initiative and NYU Immigrant Rights Clinic. The NYU Immigrant Defense Initiative offers free legal screenings and referrals for NYU students and staff who are undocumented (with or without DACA) or who are otherwise at risk of deportation.

# Martha Rivas

**Saint John's University, C'15**
Master's Degree in School Building Leadership

**New York University, C'09**
Bachelor's Degree in Elementary Education with a concentration in Special Education

**Borough of Manhattan Community College, C'07**
Associate's Degree in Early Childhood Education

**Current Employment:** Center Director, Gulf Coast Community Center Association

**Bio:** An Ecuador native and mother of three, Martha seeks to influence and develop educational policy so that all children, regardless of income, can have access to a quality preschool and elementary education.

*"The Kaplan Educational Foundation provided me with the financial and leadership support needed in order to take full advantage of my time at New York University. NYU offered a rich program, as well as all the resources needed for me to learn and develop as an early childhood educator, while still allowing me to be a full-time mom and professional. The experiences I lived during my undergraduate program shaped me into the kind of leader that children in low-income communities need as an advocate for their services."*

## Leadership Activities

- Participant, NYU's Community College Transfer Opportunity Program
- Student Government Representative, BMCC
- Peer Mentor, BMCC
- Co-Editor, Acentos Latinos, BMCC; helped to launch the school's first Spanish-language magazine
- Tutor, Jumpstart NYC, nonprofit organization devoted to early education

# NORTH CAROLINA A&T UNIVERSITY

**Location:** Greensboro, North Carolina

**Website:** www.ncat.edu

**Endowment:** $48.1 million (as of 2015, per *US News and World Report*)

**Type of School:** Public/Co-ed, Research University

**# of Undergraduate Students:** 9,203

**# of Graduate Students:** 1,522

**Average Class Size:** No information provided.

**School Mission (in their own words):** North Carolina Agricultural and Technical State University is an 1890 land-grant doctoral research university dedicated to learning, discovery, and community engagement. The University provides a wide range of educational opportunities from bachelor's to doctoral degrees in both traditional and online environments. With an emphasis on preeminence in STEM and a commitment to excellence in all its educational, research, and outreach programs, North Carolina A&T fosters a climate of academic competitiveness that prepares students for the global society.

## Admissions

**Admissions office mailing address:** 1601 E Market St, Greensboro NC 27411

**Admissions office phone:** (336) 334-7946

**Admissions office email:** uadmit@ncat.edu

## Transfer Admissions Process

**Transfer policy (in their own words):** The University accepts qualified students by transfer from other accredited colleges. Applications for admission may be considered if the transfer applicant:

- Is in good standing with the last or current postsecondary institution of attendance and is eligible to return to that institution.
- Has a cumulative GPA of at least a 2.0 or higher on a 4.0 scale from the transferring postsecondary institution.

Applications from transfer students cannot be considered until all credentials are received from the high school and all other postsecondary institutions previously attended. In order to be exempt from all new freshman requirements, transfer applicants who have attended a regionally accredited postsecondary institution must have earned 24 transferable semester hours. Transfer for programs in the College of Engineering requires a 2.5 cumulative GPA and completion of Calculus I.

Read more at www.ncat.edu/admissions/undergraduate/how-to-apply/transfer-apply-criteria.html.

**Transfer admissions contact person:** Sydney Agnew-Hayes, Undergraduate Counselor

**Transfer admissions contact info:** uadmit@ncat.edu, (336) 285-4039

**Offers transfer-focused admissions events:** Yes, open houses, A&T day events at NC community colleges

**Transfer application deadline:** Fall 2018 deadline is 6/30/18. Spring 2019 deadline is 12/1/18.

**Acceptances announced to transfer applicants:** Fall 2018 on rolling basis, 4–6 weeks after application submitted. Spring 2019 on rolling basis, 4–6 weeks after application submitted.

**Transfer application on Common App:** No

**Separate application or in addition to the Common App:** Yes

**Fee for separate transfer application:** $55

**Waiver available for separate transfer application fee:** Must apply during NC College Application Week.

**SAT/ACT required for transfer applicants:** Yes. HS graduates who are under 21 at the time of enrollment and who have fewer than 24 transferable hours.

**High-school records requirements:** Official high-school transcript required for all except applicants who have earned an AA/AS from a NC community college.

**High-school records requirements for applicants who completed outside the US:** Same as for transfer applicants, with the additional requirement that you must have your international transcript evaluated by one of the Credential Evaluation Services: WES (World Educational Services), Educational Perspectives, International Education.

**Submission requirements for transfer applicants who completed high-school equivalency test:** Required for all except applicants who have earned an AA/AS from a NC community college.

**College transcript requirements:** Official transcripts from all colleges/universities attended

**Interviews available for transfer applicants:** No

**Additional requirements for transfers seeking admissions to arts major:** Yes. 2.8 or higher GPA.

**Additional requirements for transfers seeking admissions to engineering major:** Yes. 2.5 or higher GPA; students must complete Calculus I with a grade of C or higher.

## Costs & Financial Aid

**FAFSA code:** 2905

**CSS Profile code:** N/A

**Are internal school financial aid forms required?** No

**Financial aid deadlines for transfer applicants:** Fall 2018: 6/30/18. Spring 2019: 12/1/18.

**Costs for the 2015–2016 year:** Tuition & Fees: In-state: $7,669. Out-of-state: $20,459. Room & Board: $9,558.

**Financial aid for transfer students:** Yes

**Guarantees meeting 100% need for transfer students:** No

**Need-based aid for transfer students:** Yes. Fill out FAFSA.

**Merit-based financial aid for transfer students:** Yes. Apply before May 1 to be considered.

**Phi Theta Kappa Scholarship:** No

**Reduced or zero tuition fees for low-income students:** No

**Includes loans in financial aid packages:** Yes

**Funding available for low-income students to visit:** No

**Enrollment deposit can be waived for low-income students:** No

## Academics

**GPA range for transfer students accepted in 2016–2017:** N/A

**SAT ranges for all students admitted in 2016:** No information provided.

**Type of curriculum:** Gen. Ed. requirements

**Type of academic year:** Semester

**Advisors specifically for transfer students:** No

**Credit policy (in their own words):** A total of 120 credits is required to graduate. Transfer credits are accepted only from the regional accrediting agencies listed below:

- Higher Learning Commission (HLC)
- Middle States Commission on Higher Education (MSCHE)
- Southern Association of Colleges and Schools Commission on Colleges (SACS)
- WASC Senior College and University Commission (WASC-SCUC)
- Accrediting Commission of Community and Junior Colleges—Western Association of Schools and Colleges (ACCJC-WASC)
- New England Association of Schools and Colleges—Commission on Institutions of Higher Education (NEASC-CIHE)
- Northwest Commission on Colleges and Universities (NWCCU)

A minimum grade of C is required for all transferable coursework. Accepted courses are entered on students' academic records, but grade points are not calculated on the transferred courses. NC A&T does not accept transfer credit for remedial coursework and coursework where grades of P/F were earned. Advanced Placement (AP), College Level Examination Program (CLEP), International Baccalaureate (IB) Program, and Defense Activity for Non-Traditional Education Support (DANTES) credits may be accepted by NC A&T.

The North Carolina Comprehensive Articulation Agreement (CAA):

> The University of North Carolina System and the North Carolina Community College System have designed the North Carolina Comprehensive Articulation Agreement. The CAA is a statewide agreement governing the transfer of credits between NC community colleges and NC public universities to facilitate the transfer of courses to most 4-year colleges and universities in North Carolina.
>
> To be eligible for transfer credit under the CAA, the transfer student applicant must have successfully completed a course designated as transferable or graduate with an Associate in Arts (A.A.) or Associate in Science (A.S.). NC A&T accepts credits under the guidelines of the North Carolina Comprehensive Articulation Agreement. If a student from a North Carolina Community College System (NCCCS) college believes the terms of the Comprehensive Articulation Agreement (CAA) have not been honored by NC A&T or any of the other University of North Carolina (UNC) institutions to which the student was admitted, the student may invoke the CAA Transfer Credit Appeal Procedure.
>
> An Associate in Applied Science (A.A.S.) degree is not covered under the CAA and courses will be evaluated on a course-by-course basis. Also, all Associate in Arts (A.A.) and Associate in Science (A.S.) degrees earned from out-of-state institutions are not covered under the CAA and courses will be evaluated on a course-by-course basis.

Read more at www.ncat.edu/admissions/transfer-students/transfer-credits.

**Max number of transfer credits accepted:**

- For coursework completed at a 2-year institution, the maximum number of transferable credits is 64.
- For coursework completed at a 4-year institution, the maximum number of transferable credits is 90.
- For coursework completed at both a 2-year and a 4-year institution, the maximum number of transferable credits is 90.

**Residency requirement for transfer students:** At least 30 credits need to be completed at North Carolina A&T.

**Study abroad available for transfer students:** Yes. Must complete residency requirements.

**Free tutoring for all students:** Yes

**Writing center for all students:** Yes

**Career support/access to internships and resume prep for all students:** Yes

**% of undergraduate students hired within 6 months of graduation:** No information provided.

**Additional resources specifically designated for transfer and/or non-traditional students:** No

## Housing

**Available for transfer students:** Yes

**Available for non-traditional students:** No

**Family housing available:** No

## Non-Traditional Admissions

**Non-traditional student policy (in their own words):** Adults and non-traditional students include students who are: returning after an extended absence, veterans, or students 24 years of age or older attending for the first time, married or single, or with other non-traditional circumstances.

These students follow the same application process as traditional students.

Read more at www.ncat.edu/student-affairs/newstudents/new-student-orientation/non-traditional-students.html.

## Military/Veteran Students

**Military/veteran admissions policy (in their own words):** Military/veteran students apply according to the amount of college credits that they hold. This means that if they have not attended another higher education institution, they will be considered freshmen applicants. But if they have been previously enrolled at an accredited institution, they will apply as transfer students.

**Status considered in admissions:** No

**Special admissions process:** No

**Special financial aid:** Yes. The Yellow Ribbon Program.

**Specific programs/policies to address needs:** Office of Veteran and Disability Support Services

## DACA/Undocumented Students

**DACA and undocumented admissions policy (in their own words):** DACA and undocumented students are not eligible to apply as transfers.

# NORTH CAROLINA CENTRAL UNIVERSITY

**Location:** Durham, North Carolina

**Website:** www.nccu.edu

**Endowment:** $29.4 million

**Type of School:** Public/Co-ed, Liberal Arts

**# of Undergraduate Students:** 6,285

**# of Graduate Students:** 1,801

**Average Class Size:** 21

**School Mission (in their own words):** North Carolina Central University, with a strong tradition of teaching, research, and service, prepares students to become global leaders and practitioners who transform communities. Through a nationally recognized law school, highly acclaimed and innovative programs in visual and performing arts, sciences, business, humanities, and education programs, NCCU students are engaged problem solvers. Located in the Research Triangle, the University advances research in the biotechnological, biomedical, informational, computational, behavioral, social, and health sciences. Our students enhance the quality of life of citizens and the economic development of North Carolina, the nation, and the world.

## Admissions

**Admissions office mailing address:** 1801 Fayetteville St, Durham NC 27707

**Admissions office phone:** (919) 530-6180

**Admissions office email:** admissions@nccu.edu

**# of transfer applications:** Fall 2015 admissions: 1,526

**# of transfer students accepted:** Fall 2015: 888

**Transfer student acceptance rate (2015–2016 academic year):** 58.2%

**Freshman applications received in Fall 2015:** 7,651

**Freshman applications accepted in Fall 2015:** 5,040

**Acceptance rate for 2015–2016 freshmen:** 65.9%

## Transfer Admissions Process

**Transfer policy (in their own words):** When an individual transfers to NCCU from another institution, admissions to NCCU as an undergraduate is governed by the following general standards:

- The transfer applicant must not presently be on probation at the last or current school of attendance. Also, the transfer applicant must not have been suspended or expelled from the last or current institution.
- The transfer applicant has a cumulative average of at least a C or better.
- The transfer applicant has attended another college or university and has earned 24 or more transferable credit hours.

Note: If the transfer applicant has attended another college or university, but has earned less than 24 transferable credit hours of specific acceptable credit and is under the age of 21, the transfer applicant must meet all first-year admission requirements (i.e., both MAR and MCR). Read more at www.nccu.edu/admissions/transfer.cfm.

**Transfer admissions contact person:** Dorothy J. Webster, Transfer Services

**Transfer admissions contact info:** dwebster@nccu.edu, (919) 530-5593

**Offers transfer-focused admissions events:** No

**Transfer application deadline:** Fall 2018 deadline is 7/1/18. Spring 2019 deadline is 11/15/18.

**Acceptances announced to transfer applicants:** Fall 2018 on rolling basis. Spring 2019 on rolling basis.

**Transfer application on Common App:** No

**Separate application or in addition to the Common App:** Yes

**Fee for separate transfer application:** $40

**Waiver available for separate transfer application fee:** No

**SAT/ACT required for transfer applicants:** Yes. Required for high-school graduates who are under 21 at the time of enrollment and who have fewer than 24 transferable hours.

**High-school records requirements:** Official high-school transcript required for all except applicants who have earned an A.A./A.S. from an NC community college.

**High-school records requirements for applicants who completed outside the US:** Same as for transfer applicants, with the additional requirement that you must have your international transcript evaluated by one of the following Credential Evaluation Services: WES (World Educational Services), Educational Perspectives, or International Education.

**Submission requirements for transfer applicants who completed high-school equivalency test:** Required for all except applicants who have earned an A.A./A.S. from a NC community college.

**College transcript requirements:** Required for all colleges and universities attended.

**Interviews available for transfer applicants:** No

## Costs & Financial Aid

**FAFSA code:** 2950

**CSS Profile code:** N/A

**Are internal school financial aid forms required?** No

**Financial aid deadlines for transfer applicants:**
Fall 2018: 6/30/18. Spring 2019: 12/1/18.

**Costs for the 2017–2018 year:** Tuition & Fees: In-state: $8,844. Out-of-state: $21,550. Room & Board: $11,950.

**Anticipated costs for the 2018–2019 year:** No information provided.

**Financial aid for transfer students:** Yes

**Guarantees meeting 100% need for transfer students:** No

**Need-based aid for transfer students:** Yes

**Merit-based financial aid for transfer students:** Yes

**Phi Theta Kappa Scholarship:** No

**Reduced or zero tuition fees for low-income students:** No

**Includes loans in financial aid packages:** Yes

**% of all undergraduates receiving financial aid:**
No information provided.

**% of all undergraduates qualifying for Pell Grants:**
No information provided.

**Average financial aid award for all undergraduate students:** No information provided.

**Funding available for low-income students to visit:** No

**Enrollment deposit can be waived for low-income students:** No

## Academics

**GPA range for transfer students accepted in 2016–2017:**
Minimum C GPA (2.0/4.0)

**SAT ranges for all students admitted in 2016:** Critical Reading: 400–470. Mathematics: 400–470. Writing: 380–460.

**ACT composite score range for all students admitted in 2016:** 16–19

**Recommended extracurricular engagement:** Evidence of participating in scholastic, community, and civic organizations, including leadership participation.

**Type of curriculum:** Gen. Ed. requirements

**Type of academic year:** Semester

**Advisors specifically for transfer students:** No

**Credit policy (in their own words):** NCCU accepts all non-remedial credits earned in a degree program at any accredited 4-year institution. As a constituent institution of the University of North Carolina System, NCCU also accepts college transfer work completed at any community college in the state under the terms stipulated in the Comprehensive Articulation Agreement (CAA) between the UNC System and the North Carolina Community College System. NCCU will accept all college transfer courses completed at 2-year institutions with a grade of C or better, up to a maximum of 64 semester hours. Students completing college transfer degrees at accredited institutions will be awarded at least 60 semester hours of credit upon entering NCCU and will be classified as juniors. Credit for courses completed in non-college transfer degree programs such as technical degree programs will be evaluated on a course-by-course basis. No credit is awarded for coursework completed in nondegree programs such as diploma or certificate programs; however, a student can challenge courses through standardized tests such as the College Level Equivalency (CLEP) Exam or departmental exams.

Please be advised that your official transcripts will not be evaluated until you have been admitted to the university.

Read more at www.nccu.edu/futurestudents/transferservices/transferCredits.cfm.

**Max number of transfer credits accepted:** 64

**Residency requirement for transfer students:** Yes. Must complete at least 30 credits at NCCU.

**Study abroad available for transfer students:** Yes. Must meet residency requirements.

**Free tutoring for all students:** Yes

**Writing center for all students:** Yes

**Career support/access to internships and resume prep for all students:** Yes

**% of undergraduate students hired within 6 months of graduation:** No information provided.

**Additional resources specifically designated for transfer and/or non-traditional students:** No

## Housing

**Available for transfer students:** Yes

**Available for non-traditional students:** No

**Guaranteed for transfer students:** No

**Family housing available:** No

## Non-Traditional Admissions

No non-traditional student policies or programs available.

## Military/Veteran Students

**Military/veteran admissions policy (in their own words):** Military/veteran students apply either as freshmen or transfer students depending on the amount of credits that they have earned at an accredited institution.

**Status considered in admissions:** No

**Special admissions process:** No

**Special financial aid:** Yes. The Yellow Ribbon Program.

**Specific programs/policies to address needs:** Yes, to help veterans acclimate to college. Contact veteransaffairs@nccu.edu for details.

## DACA/Undocumented Students

No DACA/undocumented student policies or programs available.

# NORTHWESTERN UNIVERSITY

**Location:** Evanston, Illinois
**Website:** www.northwestern.edu
**Endowment:** $9.8 billion
**Type of School:** Private/Co-ed, Research University
**# of Undergraduate Students:** 9,001
**# of Graduate Students:** 12,641
**Average Class Size:** No information provided.

**School Mission (in their own words):** Northwestern is committed to excellent teaching, innovative research, and the personal and intellectual growth of its students in a diverse academic community.

## Admissions

**Admissions office mailing address:** 633 Clark St, Evanston IL 60208

**Admissions office phone:** (847) 491-7271

**Admissions office email:** ug-admission@northwestern.edu

**# of transfer applications:** Fall 2016 admissions: 1,660. Spring 2017 admissions: N/A.

**# of transfer students accepted:** Fall 2016: 198. Spring 2017: N/A.

**Transfer student acceptance rate (2016–2017 academic year):** 11.9%

**Freshman applications received in Fall 2016:** 35,304

**Freshman applications accepted in Fall 2016:** 3,751

**Acceptance rate for 2016–2017 freshmen:** 10.7%

## Transfer Admissions Process

**Transfer policy (in their own words):** If you enrolled in college study after secondary-school graduation, you must apply as a transfer student. In order to apply as a transfer student, you must have completed 1 full academic year (24 semester hours or 36 quarter hours) at a postsecondary institution. You must be in good standing and eligible to continue studies at your most recent institution.

Learn more at http://admissions.northwestern.edu/faqs/transferring-to-northwestern/index.html.

**Transfer admissions contact info:** transfer@northwestern.edu, (847) 467-1864

**Offers transfer-focused admissions events:** No

**Transfer application deadline:** Fall 2018 deadline is 3/15/18. Spring 2019 deadline: N/A.

**Acceptances announced to transfer applicants:** Fall 2018 on rolling basis. Spring 2019: N/A.

**Transfer application on Common App:** Yes. The "Why Northwestern" question is strongly encouraged. Common App fee: $75 (fee waiver available).

**SAT/ACT required for transfer applicants:** Yes

**High-school records requirements:** Official high-school transcript

**High-school records requirements for applicants who completed outside the US:** Official copies of qualifying tests and transcripts if available

**Submission requirements for transfer applicants who completed high-school equivalency test:** Official GED certificate

**College transcript requirements:** Required for all colleges and universities attended.

**Interviews available for transfer applicants:** No

**Additional requirements for transfers seeking admissions to arts major:** Yes. Portfolio or audition may be required.

## Costs & Financial Aid

**FAFSA code:** 3783

**CSS Profile code:** 1565

**Are internal school financial aid forms required?** No

**Financial aid deadlines for transfer applicants:** Fall 2018: 3/15/18

**Costs for the 2017–2018 year:** Tuition & Fees: $52,678. Room & Board: $16,047.

**Financial aid for transfer students:** Yes

**Guarantees meeting 100% need for transfer students:** Yes

**Need-based aid for transfer students:** Yes

**Merit-based financial aid for transfer students:** Yes

**Phi Theta Kappa Scholarship:** No

**Reduced or zero tuition fees for low-income students:** No

**Includes loans in financial aid packages:** Yes

**% of all undergraduates receiving financial aid:** 62%

**Average financial aid award for all undergraduate students:** $42,850

**Funding available for low-income students to visit:** No

**Enrollment deposit can be waived for low-income students:** Contact admissions office.

## Academics

**GPA range for transfer students accepted in 2016–2017:** Minimum 3.0–4.0

**SAT ranges for all students admitted in 2016:** Critical Reading: 690–760. Mathematics: 710–800. Writing: N/A.

**ACT composite score range for all students admitted in 2016:** 32–34

**Type of curriculum:** Gen. Ed. requirements

**Type of academic year:** Quarter

**Advisors specifically for transfer students:** No

**Credit policy (in their own words):** Transfer students must earn 23 Northwestern credits and spend 6 quarters at Northwestern in order to receive a bachelor's degree. Courses acceptable for credit must be comparable to courses at Northwestern and in comparable University departments (as listed in our course catalog).

The following courses do not transfer:

- Courses completed at an unaccredited college or university
- Physical education or hygiene courses
- No more than 3 applied music courses (except applicants to the Bienen School of Music)
- Courses for which credit was granted by institutional examination rather than course attendance
- Courses worth less than 3 quarter hours or 2 semester hours
- Credit granted through CLEP examinations
- Courses that an applicant has audited, repeated, or failed
- English as a Second Language courses
- Journalism courses (Medill students only)

In nearly all areas, credit will be given for CEEB Advanced Placement Examination scores of 4 or 5, or higher-level International Baccalaureate results of 5 or higher. You must arrange to have your scores sent to Northwestern.

Students in a foreign university degree program receive credit only for examinations administered by that university (i.e., the Vordiplom awarded by German universities at the end of 2 years/4 semesters).

If you are transferring to the Weinberg College of Arts and Sciences with sophomore standing or higher, your foreign language proficiency requirement will be satisfied if you have earned a score of 4 or 5 on an Advanced Placement examination in a foreign language, or a grade of C or better in the final term of a second-year language course at a previous college.

Grades and cumulative grade point averages do not transfer to Northwestern.

Read more at http://admissions.northwestern.edu/faqs/transferring-to-northwestern/index.html.

**Max number of transfer credits accepted:** 48

**Residency requirement for transfer students:** Yes. Must spend at least 6 quarters at Northwestern and earn 23 credits.

**Study abroad available for transfer students:** Yes. Must fulfill residency requirement.

**Free tutoring for all students:** Yes

**Writing center for all students:** Yes

**Career support/access to internships and resume prep for all students:** Yes

**% of undergraduate students hired within 6 months of graduation:** 90%

**Additional resources specifically designated for transfer and/or non-traditional students:** No

## Housing

**Available for transfer students:** Yes

**Available for non-traditional students:** No

**Guaranteed for transfer students:** No

**Family housing available:** No

## Non-Traditional Admissions

**Non-traditional student policy (in their own words):** No specific non-traditional student policy.

**Name of program:** School of Professional Studies

**Program description:** The mission of the School of Professional Studies (SPS) is to provide a superior Northwestern education to outstanding students whose academic pursuits must be balanced with professional or personal commitments. SPS strives to be a national leader in continuing and professional education by providing innovative learning opportunities that serve the lifelong learning needs of its students. Northwestern University School of Professional Studies (SPS) students are part of a unique and distinguished university community. They learn in a supportive, collaborative environment in evening and online courses that enable them to balance their personal and professional lives with the pursuit of learning. Classes are taught by some of the university's most respected and talented teachers—scholars and professionals who value the diversity, energy, and creativity of our students.

**Program deadline:**

- Fall quarter: August 1
- Winter quarter: November 1
- Spring quarter: February 1
- Summer quarter: May 1

**Program admission requirements:**

- Official high-school transcripts and conferred date of completion (or GED report)
- Official transcripts from all previously attended colleges and universities
- A current resume or CV
- Documentation of English proficiency for students whose first language is not English.

**Program website:** http://sps.northwestern.edu/main/about-sps.php

**Program contact info:** (312) 503-2579, studysps@northwestern.edu

## Military/Veteran Students

**Military/veteran admissions policy (in their own words):** Military/veteran students follow the same admissions application process as any other students. The amount of credits that they hold will determine if they will apply as freshmen or as transfer students.

**Status considered in admissions:** Yes

**Special admissions process:** No

**Special financial aid:** Yes. The Yellow Ribbon Program.

**Specific programs/policies to address needs:** Veterans student association and veterans' liaison Charmaine Nicholson: (847) 491-8465, c-nicholson@northwestern.edu

## DACA/Undocumented Students

**DACA and undocumented admissions policy (in their own words):** According to Northwestern, all applicants are considered in the same highly selective admission pool. In addition, Northwestern reviews applications "need blind" for US citizens, US permanent residents, and DACA/undocumented students.

Read more about DACA/undocumented student admissions at http://admissions.northwestern.edu/faqs/undocumented-students.

**Admitted:** Yes

**Status considered in admissions:** No

**Special admissions process:** No

**Eligible for institutional financial aid:** Yes. Undocumented students wishing to apply for financial aid at Northwestern should submit the College Scholarship Service (CSS) Profile application and federal tax returns or a Non-Tax Filer Statement, along with documentation of household income. Additional materials may be requested, as needed. The Financial Aid Committee will use these forms to establish the family contribution and to determine eligibility for Northwestern need-based scholarship assistance.

Northwestern conducts a holistic review of each student's economic situation.

Students do not have to commit to Northwestern without seeing their aid decision as long as they file the appropriate applications in a timely fashion. There are some cases where the families might be expected to make up for federal and state aid.

**Specific programs/policies to address needs:** Student Enrichment Services (SES) coordinates services for DACA students, undocumented students, and students with undocumented family members. The Immigrant Justice Project (https://northwestern.collegiatelink.net/organization/ijp) is a student-run organization led by a coalition of students seeking to learn and advocate for immigrant rights at Northwestern University, in the Chicago Metropolitan area, and for the nation at large. The International Student Association (https://northwestern.collegiatelink.net/organization/isanu) promotes interaction among students from different cultural backgrounds and serves as a platform to engage with global and cultural issues.

# OBERLIN COLLEGE

**Location:** Oberlin, Ohio

**Website:** https://home.oberlin.edu

**Endowment:** $770.3 million

**Type of School:** Private/Co-ed, Liberal Arts

**# of Undergraduate Students:** 2,912

**# of Graduate Students:** 17

**Average Class Size:** 22

**School Mission (in their own words):** Oberlin seeks a disparate and promising student body. Recognizing that diversity broadens perspectives, Oberlin is dedicated to recruiting a culturally, economically, geographically, and racially diverse group of students. Interaction with others of widely different backgrounds and experiences fosters the effective, concerned participation in the larger society so characteristic of Oberlin graduates. Oberlin seeks students who are talented, highly motivated, personally mature, and tolerant of divergent views. The conservatory in particular seeks talented musicians with considerable potential for further growth and development. Performance is central to all of the curricula including music education, history, theory, composition, and technology.

## Admissions

**Admissions office mailing address:** 38 E College St, Oberlin OH 44074

**Admissions office phone:** (800) 622-6243

**Admissions office email:** college.admissions@oberlin.edu

**# of transfer applications:** Fall 2016 admissions: 221. Spring 2017 admissions: 43.

**# of transfer students accepted:** Fall 2016: 48. Spring 2017: 14.

**Transfer student acceptance rate (2016–2017 academic year):** 23%

**Freshman applications received in Fall 2016:** 7,256

**Freshman applications accepted in Fall 2016:** 2,093

**Acceptance rate for 2016–2017 freshmen:** 29%

## Transfer Admissions Process

**Transfer policy (in their own words):** An applicant is considered to be a transfer student if they meet 1 of the following criteria: 1) They have been enrolled in a degree-seeking program, regardless of how many credits have been earned. 2) They have earned more than 30 semester hours of credit without being enrolled in a degree-seeking program. This is determined on a case-by-case basis, so students who fall into this category are encouraged to contact the Office of Admissions to discuss their situations.

Transfer students may apply for either the spring or the fall semester. Oberlin accepts transfer applications from students in their first, second, and third years of college. If you are currently in your first year of study at another college, you may only apply for fall admission. Read more at https://new.oberlin.edu/arts-and-sciences/admissions/transfer-and-visiting-students.

**Transfer admissions contact person:** Kris Surovjak, Associate Director of Undergraduate Admissions

**Transfer admissions contact info:** kristen.surovjak@oberlin.edu, (800) 622-6243

**Transfer application deadline:** Fall 2018 deadline is 3/1/18. Spring 2019 deadline is 11/1/18.

**Acceptances announced to transfer applicants:** Fall 2018 on 4/15/18. Spring 2019 on 12/31/18.

**Transfer application on Common App:** Yes. With Oberlin specific questions. Common App fee: Free for the College of Arts and Sciences, $100 for Oberlin Conservatory of Music.

**Separate application or in addition to the Common App:** No

**SAT/ACT required for transfer applicants:** Yes

**High-school records requirements:** Official high-school transcript

**High-school records requirements for applicants who completed outside the US:** High-school transcript and TOEFL if fewer than 4 years of high school were taught primarily in English.

**Submission requirements for transfer applicants who completed high-school equivalency test:** This is determined on a case-by case-basis. There are many ways to show success in learning.

**College transcript requirements:** Official transcripts for all colleges and universities attended

**Interviews available for transfer applicants:** Optional. On campus or Skype.

## Costs & Financial Aid

**FAFSA code:** 3086

**CSS Profile code:** 1587

**Are internal school financial aid forms required?** No

**Financial aid deadlines for transfer applicants:** Fall 2018: 2/15/18. Spring 2019: 11/15/18.

**Costs for the 2017–2018 year:** Tuition & Fees: $53,510. Room & Board: $14,402.

**Financial aid for transfer students:** Yes

**Guarantees meeting 100% need for transfer students:** Yes

**Need-based aid for transfer students:** Yes. Oberlin meets 100% of demonstrated financial need for all students.

**Merit-based financial aid for transfer students:** Yes. Merit aid is awarded following a holistic review on a case-by-case basis.

**Phi Theta Kappa Scholarship:** No

**Reduced or zero tuition fees for low-income students:** No

**Includes loans in financial aid packages:** Yes

**% of all undergraduates receiving financial aid:** 80%

**% of all undergraduates qualifying for Pell Grants:** 8.9%

**Average financial aid award for all undergraduate students:** $41,836

**Funding available for low-income students to visit:** Yes

**Enrollment deposit can be waived for low-income students:** Yes

## Academics

**GPA range for transfer students accepted in 2016–2017:** 3.0–4.0

**SAT ranges for all students admitted in 2016:** Critical Reading: 630–730. Mathematics: 620–720. Writing: 623–720.

**ACT composite score range for all students admitted in 2016:** 29–33

**Recommended completed level of math for transfer applicants:** Pre-calculus

**Recommended completed level of English for transfer applicants:** 1 semester of college-level English

**Recommended courses transfer applicants should have on transcripts:** We prefer to see a broad range of coursework including: arts and humanities, social and behavioral sciences, and natural sciences and math.

**Recommended courses transfer applicants interested in STEM should complete before transfer:** No information provided.

**Recommended extracurricular engagement:** None specified (seeking a transfer class that represents a variety of talents, viewpoints, and achievements)

**Type of curriculum:** Gen. Ed. requirements. Distribution requirements.

**Type of academic year:** Semester

**Advisors specifically for transfer students:** No

**Credit policy (in their own words):** Within the limits stated below, Oberlin College permits credit earned at other fully accredited colleges and universities to be applied to the requirements for the Oberlin degree provided that the following 2 criteria are satisfied:

- The student has done C-level work or better.
- The coursework falls within the scope of a liberal arts curriculum.

Special regulations apply to work done in music, in foreign countries, or at nondegree-granting institutions.

To read more about credit policy, go to www.oberlin.edu/admissions-and-aid/arts-and-sciences/transfer-and-visiting-applicants.

**Max number of transfer credits accepted:** 64

**Residency requirement for transfer students:** Yes. 64 credits must be earned at Oberlin (2 full years on campus).

**Study abroad available for transfer students:** Yes. Must meet residency requirements.

**Free tutoring for all students:** Yes

**Writing center for all students:** Yes

**Career support/access to internships and resume prep for all students:** Yes

**% of undergraduate students hired within 6 months of graduation:** No information provided.

**Additional resources specifically designated for transfer and/or non-traditional students:** No

## Housing

**Available for transfer students:** Yes

**Available for non-traditional students:** Yes

**Guaranteed for transfer students:** Yes

**Non-traditional students can reside in housing year-round:** No

**Family housing available:** No

## Non-Traditional Admissions

No non-traditional student policies or programs available.

## Military/Veteran Students

**Military/veteran admissions policy (in their own words):** Military/veteran students follow the same application process as traditional students. Depending on the amount of credits that the students hold, it will be decided if they should apply as freshmen or transfer students.

**Status considered in admissions:** Yes

**Special admissions process:** No

**Special financial aid:** Yes. The Yellow Ribbon Program.

**Specific programs/policies to address needs:** No

## DACA/Undocumented Students

**DACA and undocumented admissions policy (in their own words):** Oberlin College considers undocumented students living in the US as domestic candidates for admission. Students who qualify for "deferred action," and have achieved DACA status (Deferred Action for Childhood Arrivals), are particularly encouraged to apply.

Read more important information about DACA/undocumented student admission at www.oberlin.edu/admissions-and-aid/arts-and-sciences/first-year-applicants.

**Admitted:** Yes

**Status considered in admissions:** No

**Special admissions process:** No

**Eligible for institutional financial aid:** Yes. An undocumented student must indicate an interest in applying for need-based and/or merit-based financial aid on the Common Application. If admitted, Oberlin College will meet 100% of every student's demonstrated need with institutional financial aid.

These funds may include need- or merit-based scholarship, campus employment, and if appropriate, a loan.

**Specific programs/policies to address needs:** Yes. Oberlin admits all qualified students regardless of immigration status and meets the full demonstrated financial need of all admitted students. This position reflects Oberlin's long-standing commitment to the importance of a diverse and inclusive educational community and to dismantling barriers to an Oberlin education. Oberlin's historical legacy teaches us that confronting injustice as an educational community is critical to achieving our goal of offering a truly excellent and transformative education.

Oberlin refrains from providing information about our community members' immigration status to government agents or allowing government agents to gain access to our campus, unless required to do so by a court order, subpoena, warrant, or other lawfully authorized directive—a long-standing practice that we will now regard as institutional policy.

Oberlin identifies resources to promote the success of all students—including undocumented students—at Oberlin. Our commitment to meeting the full demonstrated financial need is unwavering. If a student loses work eligibility and work can no longer be part of a financial aid award, we will identify other sources to meet financial need. Where possible, for students who lose driver's licenses or face other challenges as a result of changes in the DACA program, we will make referrals to legal experts, seek to identify transportation assistance, and offer other support that may become necessary.

# OCCIDENTAL COLLEGE

**Location:** Los Angeles, California
**Website:** www.oxy.edu
**Endowment:** $371.7 million
**Type of School:** Private/Co-ed, Liberal Arts
**# of Undergraduate Students:** 2,062
**# of Graduate Students:** 0
**Average Class Size:** 19

**School Mission (in their own words):** The mission of Occidental College is to provide a gifted and diverse group of students with a total educational experience of the highest quality—one that prepares them for leadership in an increasingly complex, interdependent, and pluralistic world.

## Admissions

**Admissions office mailing Address:** 1600 Campus Rd, Los Angeles CA 90041

**Admissions office phone:** (323) 259-2700

**Admissions office email:** admission@oxy.edu

**# of transfer applications:** Fall 2016 admissions: 455. Spring 2017 admissions: N/A.

**# of transfer students accepted:** Fall 2016: 155. Spring 2017: N/A.

**Transfer student acceptance rate (2016–2017 academic year):** 34.1%

**Freshman applications received in Fall 2016:** 6,409

**Freshman applications accepted in Fall 2016:** 2,936

**Acceptance rate for 2016–2017 freshmen:** 45.8%

## Transfer Admissions Process

**Transfer policy (in their own words):** A transfer student must complete at least 1 semester (16 units) of academic courses at an accredited college or university by the time of application AND have completed 2 semesters (32 units) at the point of your anticipated enrollment. Please note that we do not accept first-year spring transfers.

Note: As a transfer, you must spend a minimum of 2 years at Oxy to earn your degree. This means you need to complete 64 of 128 total units at Oxy. Read more at www.oxy.edu/admission-aid/transfer-students/academic-requirements.

**Transfer admissions contact person:** Maricela Martinez, Associate Dean of Admissions

**Transfer admissions contact info:** mlimas@oxy.edu, (323) 259-2700

**Offers transfer-focused admissions events:** N/A

**Transfer application deadline:** Fall 2018 deadline is 4/1/18. Spring 2019 deadline is 11/1/18.

**Acceptances announced to transfer applicants:** Fall 2018 on 5/1/18. Spring 2019 on 12/10/18.

**Transfer application on Common App:** Yes. Common App fee: $65.

**Separate application or in addition to the Common App:** No

**Fee for separate transfer application:** N/A

**Waiver available for separate transfer application fee:** N/A

**SAT/ACT required for transfer applicants:** Yes

**High-school records requirements:** Official high-school transcript

**High-school records requirements for applicants who completed outside the US:** Official secondary-school transcripts

**Submission requirements for transfer applicants who completed high-school equivalency test:** Official copy of GED certificate

**College transcript requirements:** Official college or university transcripts from ALL institutions you have attended

**Interviews available for transfer applicants:** Optional. On campus.

## Costs & Financial Aid

**FAFSA code:** 1249

**CSS Profile code:** 4581

**Are internal school financial aid forms required?** No

**Financial aid deadlines for transfer applicants:** Fall 2018: 3/2/18. Spring 2019: 11/1/18.

**Costs for the 2017–2018 year:** Tuition & Fees: $52,838. Room & Board: $14,968.

**Financial aid for transfer students:** Yes

**Guarantees meeting 100% need for transfer students:** Yes

**Need-based aid for transfer students:** Yes. No information provided.

**Merit-based financial aid for transfer students:** Yes. Merit scholarships are pro-rated for transfer students based on the units accepted for transfer at the time of admission. Merit scholarships are not available to students enrolled in less than 6 units.

**Phi Theta Kappa Scholarship:** No

**Reduced or zero tuition fees for low-income students:** No

**Includes loans in financial aid packages:** Yes

**% of all undergraduates receiving financial aid:** 71%

**% of all undergraduates qualifying for Pell Grants:**
No information provided.

**Average financial aid award for all undergraduate students:**
$35,780

**Funding available for low-income students to visit:** No

**Enrollment deposit can be waived for low-income students:**
No

## Academics

**GPA range for transfer students accepted in 2016–2017:**
At least 3.0

**SAT ranges for all students admitted in 2016:** Critical Reading:
600–700. Mathematics: 600–720. Writing: 610–700.

**ACT composite score range for all students admitted in 2016:**
28–31

**Type of curriculum:** Gen. Ed. requirements

**Type of academic year:** Semester

**Advisors specifically for transfer students:** No

**Credit policy (in their own words):** Transfer students may
meet the core requirements through classes taken before
matriculation at Occidental, or through classes taken at
Occidental, or (as is the case for most transfer students)
through a combination of both. Transfer students must take
the equivalent of 2 Cultural Studies Seminars (8 units or
2 classes), a minimum of 12 additional units or 3 classes
in distribution courses in culture (including pre-1800) and
the fine arts, and 12 units or 3 classes in science and/or
mathematics, including a designated lab science course. They
must also complete the language requirement. Appropriate
equivalents are determined in consultation with the Core
Program Office and the Registrar's Office. Read more at www.
oxy.edu/core-program/courses-requirements.

**Max number of transfer credits accepted:** 64

**Residency requirement for transfer students:** Yes. Must
complete at least 64 credits and spend at least 2 years at
Oxy to get degree.

**Study abroad available for transfer students:** Yes. Eligible
to participate in Oxy-sponsored study-abroad and exchange
programs (which qualify toward your 2-year residency).

**Free tutoring for all students:** Yes

**Writing center for all students:** Yes

**Career support/access to internships and resume prep for
all students:** Yes

**% of undergraduate students hired within 6 months of
graduation:** 85% have employment or are enrolled in graduate
school.

**Additional resources specifically designated for transfer
and/or non-traditional students:** No

## Housing

**Available for transfer students:** Yes

**Available for non-traditional students:** No

**Guaranteed for transfer students:** Yes

**Non-traditional students can reside in housing year-round:**
N/A

**Family housing available:** No

## Non-Traditional Admissions

**Non-traditional student policy (in their own words):**
Non-traditional students follow the same application
process as traditional students. However, Occidental College
understands that the circumstances of these students are
often different than those of traditional students. As a result,
the school offers certain resources for these students such
as their Child Development Center. The CDC is located on the
Occidental campus and is available to children whose parents
are full- or part-time employees of the College. Children of
Occidental students, alumni, and members of the surrounding
community also are eligible.

To learn more about resources for non-traditional students,
go to www.oxy.edu/admission-aid/transfer-students/
transitioning-oxy.

## Military/Veteran Students

**Military/veteran admissions policy (in their own words):**
Veterans may apply as either first-year or transfer students,
depending on the amount of college coursework units
they have completed. For transfers, our college's registrar
will determine how much credit will be awarded for work
completed at other institutions. Please consult the transfer
section of our admission website to determine if you qualify
as a first-year or transfer.

We understand that military service can result in gaps in
educational enrollment. If you have been out of school for
more than 1 year, we recommend that you enroll full-time
in challenging college-level courses prior to submitting an
application. We have compiled a list of recommended class
selections to consider taking before applying to Oxy.

Occidental College exclusively uses the Common Application
for both first-year and transfer admission. Please refer to the
Applying or Transfer Students sections for detailed information
on what documents and exams are required for admission.
We understand that the Common Application may not
completely capture an individual's interests and experiences,
so please be sure to detail any special circumstances in the
additional section of the Common Application.

Read more at www.oxy.edu/admission-aid/apply/page/
veterans-info.

**Status considered in admissions:** No

**Special admissions process:** No.

**Special financial aid:** Yes. The Yellow Ribbon Program.

**Specific programs/policies to address needs:** N/A

## DACA/Undocumented Students

**DACA and undocumented admissions policy (in their own words):** Undocumented and DACA students should complete the Common Application and follow the same application procedures and deadlines as other first-year or transfer applicants. When completing the application, please select the following fields whether or not you have been granted DACA status:

- Select your citizenship status: Other (Non-US)
- List citizenship: Select the country.
- Do you currently hold a valid US visa? I do not hold a currently valid US non-immigration visa.

For more information about the application process for undocumented and DACA students, please contact Maricela Martinez at mlimas@oxy.edu or (323) 259-2700.

Read more at www.oxy.edu/admission-aid/apply/undocumented-daca-students.

**Admitted:** Yes

**Status considered in admissions:** No

**Special admissions process:** Yes. Treated like international students.

**Eligible for institutional financial aid:** Yes. Limited aid is available. CA residents are eligible for institutional aid and CA DREAM Act aid.

**Specific programs/policies to address needs:** No

# PENNSYLVANIA STATE UNIVERSITY—UNIVERSITY PARK

**Location:** University Park, Pennsylvania

**Website:** www.psu.edu

**Endowment:** $3.64 billion (2015, systemwide), $1.81 billion (2015, University Park)

**Type of School:** Public/Co-ed, Research University

**# of Undergraduate Students:** 83,436

**# of Graduate Students:** 14,058

**Average Class Size:** No information provided.

**School Mission (in their own words):** Penn State is a multi-campus public research university that educates students from Pennsylvania, the nation, and the world, and improves the well-being and health of individuals and communities through integrated programs of teaching, research, and service.

## Admissions

**Admissions office mailing address:** 201 Old Main, University Park PA 16802

**Admissions office phone:** (814) 865-5471

**Admissions office email:** admissions@psu.edu

**# of transfer applications:** Fall 2016: 1,990. Spring 2017: N/A.

**# of transfer students accepted:** Fall 2016: 779. Spring 2017: N/A.

**Transfer student acceptance rate (2016–2017 academic year):** 39.1%

**Freshman applications received in Fall 2016:** 52,974

**Freshman applications accepted in Fall 2016:** 29,878

**Acceptance rate for 2016–2017 freshmen:** 56.4%

## Transfer Admissions Process

**Transfer policy (in their own words):** Students transfer to Penn State in a variety of programs at all of our campuses across the state of Pennsylvania. You will be considered a transfer applicant if you are a:

- Student who has earned a high-school diploma or a GED.
- Student who has attempted or will have attempted 18 or more semester hours of college coursework at a regionally accredited college/university before enrolling at Penn State. (Please note: Transfer status is based on credits earned after high-school graduation.)

Read more at http://admissions.psu.edu/info/future/transfer/requirements.

**Transfer admissions contact person:** N/A

**Transfer admissions contact info:** N/A

**Offers transfer-focused admissions events:** No

**Transfer application deadline:** Fall 2018 deadline is 4/15/18. Spring 2019 deadline is 11/1/18.

**Acceptances announced to transfer applicants:** Fall 2018 in late spring, rolling basis. Spring 2019: mid-December, rolling basis.

**Transfer application on Common App:** No

**Separate application or in addition to the Common App:** Yes

**Fee for separate transfer application:** $65

**Waiver available for separate transfer application fee:** Penn State honors College Board and ACT fee waivers, as well as requests from school counselors documenting extreme financial hardship for the applicant. Please email admissions@psu.edu to request a fee waiver.

**SAT/ACT required for transfer applicants:** Not if you have completed more than 1 semester of full-time college coursework after high school.

**High-school records requirements:** High-school/GED transcripts are required for all transfer students except adult learners who have completed 18 or more college credits at a regionally accredited university. High-school transcripts should be sent from the school directly to Penn State.

**High-school records requirements for applicants who completed outside the US:** Secondary records are required for both first-year and transfer international applicants. Transcripts of coursework and grades are required for all years of secondary-school study.

**Submission requirements for transfer applicants who completed high-school equivalency test:** Same as high-school graduates

**College transcript requirements:** Penn State requires transfer applicants to submit official transcripts from all postsecondary institutions where coursework was attempted.

**Interviews available for transfer applicants:** No

**Additional requirements for transfers seeking admissions to business school:** No transfer admission to University Park. Applicants who meet eligibility requirements may apply to start at a Penn State Campus and transition to University Park on completion of entrance to major requirements.

**Additional requirements for transfers seeking admissions to arts major:** Yes. Requires portfolio submission. The portfolio should include 10–12 images of the applicant's work and a statement (500 word max.) to describe one of the artworks.

**Additional requirements for transfers seeking admissions to engineering major:** Yes. Completion of a 4-credit college calculus class prior to transfer.

## Costs & Financial Aid

**FAFSA code:** 3329

**CSS Profile code:** N/A

**Are internal school financial aid forms required?** No

**Financial aid deadlines for transfer applicants:** Fall 2018: 2/15/18. Spring 2019: N/A.

**Costs for the 2017–2018 year:** Tuition & Fees: In-state: $17,900. Out-of-state: $32,382. Room & Board: $11,230.

**Financial aid for transfer students:** Yes

**Guarantees meeting 100% need for transfer students:** No

**Need-based aid for transfer students:** Yes. Submit financial aid forms.

**Merit-based financial aid for transfer students:** Yes

**Phi Theta Kappa Scholarship:** No

**Reduced or zero tuition fees for low-income students:** No

**Includes loans in financial aid packages:** Yes

**% of all undergraduates receiving financial aid:** 73%

**% of all undergraduates qualifying for Pell Grants:** No information provided.

**Average financial aid award for all undergraduate students:** No information provided.

**Funding available for low-income students to visit:** No

**Enrollment deposit can be waived for low-income students:** No

## Academics

**GPA range for transfer students accepted in 2016–2017:** No information provided.

**SAT ranges for all students admitted in 2016:** Critical Reading: 530–630. Mathematics: 560–670. Writing: No information provided.

**ACT Composite Score Range for all students admitted in 2016:** 25–29

**Type of curriculum:** Gen. Ed. requirements

**Type of academic year:** Semester

**Advisors specifically for transfer students:** No

**Credit policy (in their own words):** Penn State requires an official transcript to consider credits for transfer. Upon review of a student's materials during the application review, we will evaluate any official college or university transcripts that are included with the application.

We do not evaluate transcripts before an offer of admission is made.

Coursework successfully completed at other colleges and universities recognized by the 6 regional accrediting associations will be considered for transfer credit.

College-level coursework completed at colleges/universities licensed by state boards of education to award associate degrees or higher, but are not members of one of the 6 regional accrediting associations, may be eligible for credit by validation.

If accepted, students will receive an evaluation of transferable credits. Domestic students will receive the evaluation of credits in the mail with their offer of admission, while international students will receive the evaluation via email.

In addition, to earn a Penn State degree, students transferring credit to Penn State must be aware of the following:

- For a bachelor's degree, 36 of the last 60 credits must be completed at Penn State.
- For an associate's degree, 18 of the last 30 credits must be completed at Penn State.

Read more at http://admissions.psu.edu/info/future/transfer/credit.

**Max number of transfer credits accepted:** 30

**Residency requirement for transfer students:** Yes. Must complete at least 36 credits at Penn State.

**Study abroad available for transfer students:** Yes

**Free tutoring for all students:** Yes

**Writing center for all students:** Yes

**Career support/access to internships and resume prep for all students:** Yes

**% of undergraduate students hired within 6 months of graduation:** No information provided.

**Additional resources specifically designated for transfer and/or non-traditional students:** No

## Housing

**Available for transfer students:** Yes

**Available for non-traditional students:** Yes

**Guaranteed for transfer students:** No

**Non-traditional students can reside in housing year-round:** No

**Family housing available:** Yes

## Non-Traditional Admissions

**Non-traditional student policy (in their own words):**
The following information is from the adult learner's page:

In today's dynamic and competitive marketplace, education has become a lifelong endeavor that is an essential element of career success. Understanding that education improves job performance and enhances marketability, adult learners are enrolling in colleges and universities in record numbers. As an adult student at Penn State, you will not only earn the quality education employers demand, but you will receive the individual attention you deserve.

Penn State understands that while pursuing higher education can be an exciting experience for an adult learner, this experience can also prove to be challenging. To help adult learners make the most of their educational opportunities and achieve academic success, Penn State offers a number of resources unique to the needs of these students. Whether you are just beginning a college career or you are returning to college after several years, Penn State is here to help you achieve your goals.

Note: If an adult learner has attempted 18 or more credits at an accredited institution of higher education, they must apply as transfer students. Learn more about adult learners at http://admissions.psu.edu/info/future/adult.

## Military/Veteran Students

**Military/veteran admissions policy (in their own words):**
If you are interested in starting or continuing your degree at Penn State, we are happy to outline the important next steps you need to take on your path toward becoming a Penn State student. As an actively serving member of the armed services or a veteran, you are classified as an adult learner at Penn State, so please review all of the requirements and information available for that student type as you consider applying to Penn State.

Read more at http://admissions.psu.edu/info/future/adult.

**Status considered in admissions:** No

**Special admissions process:** Yes. Active duty military are considered Adult Learners and must apply as such.

**Special financial aid:** Yes. The Yellow Ribbon Program.

**Specific programs/policies to address needs:** Office of Veterans Programs is specifically geared toward helping military/vets with PSU.

## DACA/Undocumented Students

**DACA and undocumented admissions policy (in their own words):** These students are considered as international students in both the admissions and the financial aid application process. Note: International students do not qualify for both federal and institutional financial aid.

**Admitted:** Yes

**Status considered in admissions:** No

**Special admissions process:** Yes. Must apply as international students.

**Eligible for institutional financial aid:** No

**Specific programs/policies to address needs:** N/A

# POMONA COLLEGE

**Location:** Claremont, California

**Website:** www.pomona.edu

**Endowment:** $1.98 billion

**Type of School:** Private/Co-ed, Liberal Arts

**# of Undergraduate Students:** 1,663

**# of Graduate Students:** 0

**Average Class Size:** 15

**School Mission (in their own words):** Throughout its history, Pomona College has educated men and women of exceptional promise. We gather students, regardless of financial circumstances, into a small residential community that is strongly rooted in Southern California yet global in its orientation. Through close ties among a diverse group of faculty, staff, and classmates, Pomona students are inspired to engage in the probing inquiry and creative learning that enable them to identify and address their intellectual passions. This experience will continue to guide their contributions as the next generation of leaders, scholars, artists, and citizens to fulfill the vision of its founders: to bear their added riches in trust for all.

## Admissions

**Admissions office mailing address:** 333 N College Way, Claremont CA 91711

**Admissions office phone:** (909) 621-8134

**Admissions office email:** admissions@pomona.edu

**# of transfer applications:** Fall 2016 admissions: 250

**# of transfer students accepted:** Fall 2016: 22

**Transfer student acceptance rate (2016–2017 academic year):** 8.8%

**Freshman applications received in Fall 2016:** 8,102

**Freshman applications accepted in Fall 2016:** 765

**Acceptance rate for 2016–2017 freshmen:** 9.4%

## Transfer Admissions Process

**Transfer policy (in their own words):** We value the diversity and breadth of experience that transfer students bring to our academic and social communities. If you will have completed at least one year's full-time college work by the time you expect to enroll at Pomona, you must apply as a transfer applicant. (Please consult our office if you've completed less than 1 academic year at another college.) We do not accept applications from students who have already received a bachelor's degree. Students who have completed college coursework as part of an early college program should apply as first-year applicants.

Read more at www.pomona.edu/admissions/apply/transfer-applicants.

**Transfer admissions contact person:** Christopher Teran, Associate Dean of Admissions

**Transfer admissions contact info:** christopher.teran@pomona.edu, (909) 621-8134

**Offers transfer-focused admissions events:** No

**Transfer application deadline:** Fall 2018 deadline is 2/15/18. Spring 2019 deadline is N/A.

**Acceptances announced to transfer applicants:** Fall 2018 on 4/1/18. Spring 2019: N/A.

**Transfer application on Common App:** Yes, with Pomona specific questions. Common App fee: $70.

**SAT/ACT required for transfer applicants:** Yes

**High-school records requirements:** Official high-school transcript

**High-school records requirements for applicants who completed outside the US:** Official high-school transcript with English translation

**Submission requirements for transfer applicants who completed high-school equivalency test:** Official GED results submission

**College transcript requirements:** Required for all colleges and universities attended.

**Interviews available for transfer applicants:** Optional. On campus; off campus; alumni.

## Costs & Financial Aid

**FAFSA code:** 1173

**CSS Profile code:** 4607

**Are internal school financial aid forms required?** No

**Financial aid deadlines for transfer applicants:** Fall 2018: 3/1/18. Spring 2019: N/A.

**Costs for the 2017–2018 year:** Tuition & Fees: $49,352. Room & Board: $15,605.

**Financial aid for transfer students:** Yes

**Guarantees meeting 100% need for transfer students:** Yes

**Need-based aid for transfer students:** Yes

**Merit-based financial aid for transfer students:** No

**Phi Theta Kappa Scholarship:** No

**Reduced or zero tuition fees for low-income students:** No

**Includes loans in financial aid packages:** All financial aid packages are needs-met without student loans.

**% of all undergraduates receiving financial aid:** No information provided.

**% of all undergraduates qualifying for Pell Grants:**
No information provided.

**Average financial aid award for all undergraduate students:**
No information provided.

**Funding available for low-income students to visit:** No

**Enrollment deposit can be waived for low-income students:**
No

## Academics

**GPA range for transfer students accepted in 2016–2017:** N/A

**SAT ranges for all students admitted in 2016:** Critical Reading: 670–770. Mathematics: 670–770. Writing: 670–770.

**ACT composite score range for all students admitted in 2016:**
31–34

**Type of curriculum:** Gen. Ed. requirements. The College's Breadth of Study requirements provide a window to the vast extent and variety of our accumulated experience and knowledge in the liberal arts. The courses are drawn from broad curricular areas (criticism, analysis, and contextual study of works of the human imagination; social institutions and human behavior; history, values, ethics, and cultural studies; physical and biological sciences; mathematical reasoning; and creation and performance of works of art and literature). No 2 Breadth areas can be fulfilled with courses from the same discipline. Pomona has additional overlay requirements, including a foreign language requirement, a writing intensive requirement, a speaking intensive requirement, and an analyzing difference course requirement. Transfer students can fulfill any of these requirements through transferable course credit if Pomona or one of the other undergraduate Claremont Colleges teaches a similar course.

**Type of academic year:** Semester

**Advisors specifically for transfer students:** No information provided.

**Credit policy (in their own words):** Students must complete the equivalent of at least 32 course credits to graduate, 30 of which must be earned following matriculation as a degree-seeking student at Pomona College, or, for transfer students, at a regionally accredited college or university.

If admitted, transfer applicants will receive a credit evaluation with their offer of admission and will be able to transfer a maximum of 16 credits (this is usually 16 courses). Credits are usually transferrable if: they were earned at a regionally accredited institution, the course grade is a C or better, and Pomona offers an equivalent course.

Read more at http://catalog.pomona.edu/content.php?catoid=21&navoid=4397.

**Max number of transfer credits accepted:** 16

**Residency requirement for transfer students:** Yes. At least 16 credits must be earned at Pomona.

**Study abroad available for transfer students:** Yes. Students earn Pomona credit while abroad. Financial aid also supports a study-abroad experience. Senior year must be enrolled in residence at Pomona (not abroad).

**Free tutoring for all students:** Yes

**Writing center for all students:** Yes

**Career support/access to internships and resume prep for all students:** Yes

**% of undergraduate students hired within 6 months of graduation:** No information provided.

**Additional resources specifically designated for transfer and/or non-traditional students:** No

## Housing

**Available for transfer students:** Yes

**Available for non-traditional students:** Yes

**Guaranteed for transfer students:** Yes

**Non-traditional students can reside in housing year-round:** Yes

**Family housing available:** Yes

## Non-Traditional Admissions

No non-traditional student policies or programs available.

## Military/Veteran Students

**Military/veteran admissions policy (in their own words):** Veterans should follow the same application procedures as other applicants for admission as first-year or transfer students. In addition, veterans are welcome to provide additional supplementary materials with their applications. This might include further explanation of a candidate's educational record and/or a supplementary essay addressing how the candidate's military experience has influenced his or her readiness and desire for further education.

Veterans considering Pomona are strongly encouraged to arrange an interview with an admissions staff member. While not required, such a conversation may help answer important questions about the College and clarify whether Pomona is a good fit. For more information regarding admissions, please email Associate Dean of Admissions Chris Teran or call him at (909) 621-8731.

Read more at www.pomona.edu/admissions/apply/veterans.

**Status considered in admissions:** No

**Special admissions process:** Yes. Military applicants should follow the same procedures as first-year or transfer students. They can provide additional supplementary information with their application about their service, if desired. They are encouraged to interview with an admissions staff member.

**Special financial aid:** Yes. The Yellow Ribbon Program.

# DACA/Undocumented Students

**DACA and undocumented admissions policy (in their own words):** Pomona College seeks to enroll the best students, regardless of citizenship status. We strive to establish a diverse community of individuals who are intellectually talented, and who are eager learners and passionate contributors. In the admissions and financial aid processes, the College fully reviews applications from undocumented and DACAmented students who graduate from a US high school by the same criteria as for all domestic students. Financial need does not affect admission decisions for US citizens or students graduating from a US high school, including those who are undocumented or DACAmented. 100% of need is met for all admitted students.

Read more at www.pomona.edu/admissions/apply/undocumenteddacamented-applicants.

**Admitted:** Yes

**Status considered in admissions:** No

**Special admissions process:** No

**Eligible for institutional financial aid:** Yes 100% need met for all admitted students.

**Specific programs/policies to address needs:** Yes. A strong, student-led IDEAS (Improving Dreams Equality Access and Success) organization at the Claremont Colleges, which can be an excellent support for students in their transition to Pomona.

Confidential emergency grant funding through the Dean of Students Office. Grants cover the fee to apply for DACA if students would like to apply for the first time or would like to apply for a renewal.

A committed group of faculty and staff advisors work to support DREAM students at Pomona.

Study-abroad opportunities, including legal and financial assistance for Advance Parole. Pomona has a growing network of DACAmented students who have recently studied abroad.

# PRINCETON UNIVERSITY

**Location:** Princeton, New Jersey
**Website:** www.princeton.edu
**Endowment:** $22.2 billion
**Type of School:** Private Co-ed, Research University
**# of Undergraduate Students:** 5,277
**# of Graduate Students:** 2,697
**Average Class Size:** No information provided.

**School Mission (in their own words):** Princeton University advances learning through scholarship, research, and teaching of unsurpassed quality, with an emphasis on undergraduate and doctoral education that is distinctive among the world's great universities, and with a pervasive commitment to serve the nation and the world.

## Admissions

**Admissions office mailing address:** 110 W College, Princeton NJ 08544
**Admissions office phone:** (609) 258-3060
**Admissions office email:** uaoffice@princeton.edu
**# of transfer applications:** Fall 2016: 0. Spring 2017: 0.
**# of transfer students accepted:** Fall 2016: 0. Spring 2017: 0.
**Transfer student acceptance rate (2016–2017 academic year):** 0%
**Freshman applications received in Fall 2016:** 29,303
**Freshman applications accepted in Fall 2016:** 1,911
**Acceptance rate for 2016–2017 freshmen:** 6.5%

## Transfer Admissions Process

**Transfer policy (in their own words):** Princeton does not offer transfer admission at this time. Any student who has graduated from secondary school and enrolled as a full-time or part-time degree candidate at any college or university worldwide is considered a transfer applicant and is not eligible for undergraduate admission for Fall 2017. Additionally, any student who has completed a postsecondary degree is not eligible for undergraduate admission or a second undergraduate degree from Princeton. Princeton plans to reinstate its transfer admission process in 2018, at the earliest. We will make a formal announcement about the new process once the program is put into place.

## Costs & Financial Aid

**FAFSA code:** 2627
**CSS Profile code:** N/A
**Are internal school financial aid forms required?** Yes
**Financial aid deadline for Fall 2018 transfer applicants:** Fall 2018: N/A. Spring 2019: N/A.
**Costs for the 2017–2018 year:** Tuition & Fees: $50,650. Room & Board: $15,495.
**% of all undergraduates receiving financial aid:** 60%
**% of all undergraduates qualifying for Pell Grants:** 21%

**Average financial aid award for all undergraduate students:** $48,000
**Funding available for low-income students to visit:** No information provided.
**Enrollment deposit can be waived for low-income students:** N/A

## Academics

**GPA range for transfer students accepted in 2016–2017:** No transfer program until 2018.
**SAT ranges for all students admitted in 2016:** Critical Reading: 690–790. Mathematics: 710–800. Writing: 700–790.
**ACT composite score range for all students admitted in 2016:** 32–35
**Type of curriculum:** Gen. Ed. requirements
**Type of academic year:** Semester
**Free tutoring for all students:** Yes
**Writing center for all students:** Yes
**Career support/access to internships and resume prep for all students:** Yes
**% of undergraduate students hired within 6 months of graduation:** No information provided.
**Additional resources specifically designated for transfer and/or non-traditional students:** N/A

## Housing

**Available for transfer students:** N/A
**Available for non-traditional students:** N/A
**Guaranteed for transfer students:** N/A
**Non-traditional students can reside in housing year-round:** N/A
**Family housing available:** No

## Non-Traditional Admissions

**Non-traditional student policy (in their own words):** Non-traditional students follow the same application process that traditional students follow. In addition, Princeton recognizes that once accepted, these students might need special accommodations, and it will do the best it can to provide them. One of those special accommodations includes separate housing.

## Military/Veteran Students

**Military/veteran admissions policy (in their own words):** Princeton University welcomes students who are veterans and dependents of veterans who are eligible to receive education benefits offered by the Department of Veterans Affairs (DVA). The deputy registrar coordinates enrollment services for these students and is the liaison to the DVA.

Princeton participates fully in the Yellow Ribbon program without limitation on the number of students who are eligible.

In addition, military/veteran students follow the same application process as other students.

Read more at https://registrar.princeton.edu/student-services/veterans.

**Status considered in admissions:** Yes

**Special admissions process:** Yes. Princeton University welcomes students who are veterans and dependents of veterans who are eligible to receive education benefits offered by the Department of Veterans Affairs (DVA). The deputy registrar coordinates enrollment services for these students and is the liaison to the DVA.

**Special financial aid:** Yes. The Yellow Ribbon Program.

**Specific programs/policies to address needs:** N/A

## DACA/Undocumented Students

**DACA and undocumented admissions policy (in their own words):** These students follow the same application process as US citizens. They are also evaluated in the same way as US citizen students for both the admissions and the financial aid application process.

**Admitted:** Yes

**Status considered in admissions:** No

**Special admissions process:** No

**Eligible for institutional financial aid:** Yes. University's need-based financial aid program equally applies to all applicants.

**Specific programs/policies to address needs:** N/A

# PURDUE UNIVERSITY

**Location:** West Lafayette, Indiana

**Website:** www.purdue.edu

**Endowment:** $2.26 billion

**Type of School:** Public Research University

**# of Undergraduate Students:** 30,043

**# of Graduate Students:** 10,408

**Average Class Size:** 31

**School Mission (in their own words):** The mission of Purdue University is to serve the citizens of Indiana, the United States, and the world through discovery that expands the realm of knowledge, learning through dissemination and preservation of knowledge, and engagement through exchange of knowledge.

---

## Admissions

**Admissions office mailing address:** Schleman Hall of Student Services, 475 Stadium Mall Dr, West Lafayette IN 47907-2050

**Admissions office phone:** (765) 494-1776

**Admissions office email:** admissions@purdue.edu

**# of transfer applications:** Fall 2016 admissions: 2,996

**# of transfer students accepted:** Fall 2016: 1,233

**Transfer student acceptance rate (2016–2017 academic year):** 41.2%

**Freshman applications received in Fall 2016:** 48,775

**Freshman applications accepted in Fall 2016:** 27,226

**Acceptance rate for 2016–2017 freshmen:** 55.8%

## Transfer Admissions Process

**Transfer policy (in their own words):** Before applying, transfer students must have at least 12 graded credit hours of college-level coursework (not remedial) and be registered to complete at least 12 more. Depending on the strength of your academic credentials, before making its final decision, the admissions committee may wait to see final grades for any coursework that was in progress when you submitted your application.

Who is eligible to transfer?

- Students are eligible to transfer if they will have at least 24 credits of transferable postsecondary work upon entrance to Purdue.
- Transfer students may enroll at sophomore or junior standing.

If you have been out of high school for at least 5 years and your high-school record is significantly deficient (poor grades and/or missing many of Purdue's high-school course requirements), you may use Purdue's community college roadmap to prepare for admission to Purdue as a college transfer student: www.admissions.purdue.edu/apply/collegeroadmap.php

**Transfer admissions contact person:** Peg Wier, Associate Director, Transfer Specialist

**Transfer admissions contact info:** pjmwier@purdue.edu, (765) 494-1271

**Offers transfer-focused admissions events:** Yes

**Transfer application deadline:** Summer 2018 deadline is 4/1/18.

Fall 2018 deadline is 7/1/18 (exceptions: vet tech deadline is 2/1/18; computer science and nursing deadlines are 5/1/18).

Spring 2019 deadline is 11/1/18.

**Acceptances announced to transfer applicants:** Rolling basis—12 weeks after receipt of all documentation.

**Transfer application on Common App:** Yes. Common App fee: $60.

**SAT/ACT required for transfer applicants:** Yes. SAT or ACT is required unless you have at least 24 graded credit hours of college-level coursework (not remedial) or have been out of high school for at least 5 years.

**High-school records requirements:** Official high-school transcript

**High-school records requirements for applicants who completed outside the US:** Original or attested copies of all transcripts, diplomas, mark sheets, and certificates from all secondary and postsecondary schools attended. Documents must be mailed in a sealed envelope directly from the secondary or postsecondary school, examination board, or university. To be evaluated, secondary documents must include 3 consecutive years of completed coursework. In some cases, students may need to send records from junior high.

**Submission requirements for transfer applicants who completed high-school equivalency test:** Official GED results

**College transcript requirements:** Official transcripts from all colleges/universities attended

**Interviews available for transfer applicants:** No information provided.

**Additional requirements for transfers seeking admissions to engineering major:** Transfer students applying to Purdue apply to the major, not the school as a whole. Students should check their desired major for more information on required courses: www.admissions.purdue.edu/majors/index.php

## Costs & Financial Aid

**FAFSA code:** 1825

**CSS Profile code:** N/A

**Are internal school financial aid forms required?** No

**Financial aid deadline for transfer applicants:** 3/1/18

**Costs for the 2017–2018 year:** Tuition & Fees: Indiana resident: $10,002. Non-resident: $28,804. International student: $30,964. Room & Board: $10,030.

**Financial aid for transfer students:** Yes

**Guarantees meeting 100% need for transfer students:** No

**Need-based aid for transfer students:** Yes

**Merit-based financial aid for transfer students:**
No information provided.

**Phi Theta Kappa Scholarship:** Yes. For Indiana residents: $4,000 per year; for non-Indiana residents: $6,500 per year. 3.5 GPA required.

**Reduced or zero tuition fees for low-income students:** No

**Includes loans in financial aid packages:** Yes

**% of all undergraduates receiving financial aid:** 43%

**% of all undergraduates qualifying for Pell Grants:**
No information provided.

**Average financial aid award for all undergraduate students:** $13,849

**Funding available for low-income students to visit:**
No information provided.

**Enrollment deposit can be waived for low-income students:** Yes

## Academics

**GPA range for transfer students accepted in 2016–2017:**
Varies by major

**SAT ranges for all students admitted in 2016:**
Critical Reading: 520–640. Mathematics: 560–690. Writing: 520–630.

**ACT composite score range for all students admitted in 2016:** 25–31

**Type of curriculum:** Gen. Ed. requirements

**Type of academic year:** Semester

**Advisors specifically for transfer students:** No

**Credit policy (in their own words):** Transfer credit is course credit represented on an official transcript from a regionally accredited institution.

Purdue's academic departments determine equivalency to Purdue courses based on comparable learning outcomes.

Only those courses for which you receive C– grades or better will be considered for transfer.

Equivalent courses will count toward degree requirements just like corresponding Purdue courses do. And just like all approved transfer courses, the credit transfers but grades do not.

Purdue completes credit evaluations after admitted students have provided their official college transcripts. Students and their Purdue academic advisors receive credit evaluation reports. Current students can view transfer credit via their myPurdue student portal.

Only credit transfers; grades do not.

Not all courses will transfer and/or satisfy degree requirements for every major. You should consult with your academic advisor for additional information about transferring credit for your major.

Transfer credit that was earned 10 or more years prior to your Purdue entry term will not be accepted, in accordance with Student Regulations regarding degree requirements. Any exceptions to this rule must be approved on a case-by-case basis by an Associate Dean (or approved designee).

Courses listed as 1XXXX, 2XXXX, etc., transfer as "undistributed credit," rather than Purdue course equivalencies. You may consult with your academic advisor to determine how these courses might apply to a plan of study and meet specific degree requirements.

Credit listed as "pass," "satisfactory" or "credit" (no letter grade) will not transfer. For graded coursework, grades must be C– or better.

No credit is granted for military training programs. A minimum of 6 months active duty military service is required to receive credit for military duty. Please submit a copy of your DD-214 (or an LES, if still active duty).

Credit by exam from another institution does not transfer to Purdue. For credit from exams such as AP or CLEP, you must provide official score reports from the testing service; the University does not accept this type of credit from another school's transcript.

The only way to replace grades from Purdue courses is to retake the course at Purdue (or at one of our regional campuses or IUPUI). Course credit from another school does not replace grades for equivalent Purdue courses.

Graduate-level coursework will not transfer to an undergraduate record.

Credit is granted only once for duplicate courses. This does not apply to repeatable courses.

Purdue's School of Nursing does not accept credits from non-baccalaureate nursing programs.

Agriculture and natural resources courses from non-land grant institutions will be sent to the College of Agriculture for evaluation. Courses will be loaded at a later date if approved.

If course credit is awarded by a regionally accredited institution and you provide an official transcript from that institution, Purdue will evaluate the coursework for transfer credit regardless of the method of delivery (including online, dual- or concurrent-credit courses taught in a high school).

**Max number of transfer credits accepted:** Unlimited

**Residency requirement for transfer students:** Yes. Transfer students must earn at least 32 Purdue credits to earn a degree from the University.

**Study abroad available for transfer students:** Yes. Students who transfer to Purdue University must complete at least 1 semester of academic work at Purdue before they can apply to study abroad.

**Free tutoring for all students:** Yes

**Writing center for all students:** Yes

**Career support/access to internships and resume prep for all students:** Yes

**% of undergraduate students hired within 6 months of graduation:** No information provided.

**Additional resources specifically designated for transfer and/or non-traditional students:** Yes. Purdue has a transfer student support class that meets weekly to help transfer students acclimate to being at Purdue and map out a path to success. Purdue also has a transfer student task force that is available to answer any questions that students may have.

## Housing

**Available for transfer students:** Yes

**Available for non-traditional students:** Yes

**Guaranteed for transfer students:** No

**Non-traditional students can reside in housing year-round:** No information provided.

**Family housing available:** Yes

## Non-Traditional Admissions

**Non-traditional student policy (in their own words):** Span Plan provides services to non-traditional students who meet at least 1 of the following criteria: Parent, pregnant, or legal guardian; married or in a domestic partnership; financially emancipated; or coming back to school from a 2+ year break in formal education.

**Name of program:** Span Plan

**Program description:** Span Plan Nontraditional Student Services offers an array of support services for non-traditional undergraduate students at Purdue University. The program, based on the belief that learning is a lifelong endeavor, provides services that positively impact the personal, academic, and career success of adult non-traditional students. Span Plan has provided guidance and support for adult non-traditional students since 1968, and is dedicated to assisting these students achieve their goals.

**Program deadline:** Summer 2018: 4/1/18.

Fall 2018: 7/1/18 (exceptions: vet tech deadline is 2/1/18; computer science and nursing deadline is 5/1/18)

Spring 2019: 11/1/18

**Program admission requirements:** Same as for transfer students.

**Program website:** https://www.purdue.edu/spanplan

**Program contact person:** Peggy Favorite, Director of Span Plan

**Program contact info:** spanplan@purdue.edu, (765) 494-5860

## Military/Veteran Students

**Military/veteran admissions policy (in their own words):** Purdue's Veterans Success Center (VSC) provides an array of resources and support for veteran students and those still serving in the military, as well as their dependents. In addition to providing a physical space in the Purdue Memorial Union where students can gather, the VSC serves as an on-ramp to navigating and accessing military-related education benefits.

Our services are intended to empower veteran and military students at every point in their academic journey, whether they are new to Purdue or seeking to enter the workforce.

**Status considered in admissions:** No

**Special admissions process:** No

**Special financial aid:** Yes. The Yellow Ribbon Program.

**Specific programs/policies to address needs:** Purdue has a Veterans' Success Center that provides a variety of resources and services to veterans at the university. For more information, please see the website: https://www.purdue.edu/veterans/index.html.

## DACA/Undocumented Students

**DACA and undocumented admissions policy (in their own words):** No information provided.

**Admitted:** Yes

**Status considered in admissions:** No

**Special admissions process:** No

**Eligible for institutional financial aid:** No. To be eligible for federal, state of Indiana, and Purdue need-based aid eligibility, a student must be a US citizen or "eligible" non-citizen.

For a noncitizen to be eligible for financial aid consideration, the student must possess a valid Alien Registration Card I-551 or I-151, be classified as a conditional permanent resident with a valid I-151C Registration Card, or have a passport or I-94 (Arrival/Departure Record) showing 1 of the following designations: refugee; asylum granted; indefinite parole and/or humanitarian parole; and Cuban-Haitian Entrant.

International students are eligible for small, merit-based awards.

**Specific programs/policies to address needs:** No information provided.

# RUTGERS UNIVERSITY—NEWARK

**Location:** Newark, New Jersey

**Website:** www.newark.rutgers.edu

**Endowment:** $117 million

**Type of School:** Public/Co-ed, Research University

**# of Undergraduate Students:** 8,170

**# of Graduate Students:** 4,151

**Average Class Size:** No information provided.

**School Mission (in their own words):** The academic mission of Rutgers University in Newark is to provide a first-rate education to an exceptionally diverse community of undergraduates and graduate students. Besides fostering a lively spirit of inclusion and opportunity, our institution commands local and broader influence through its high educational standards, top-ranked faculty, and nationally recognized research in the sciences, the arts, humanities, social sciences, and global affairs, and in the professions of business, criminal justice, law, nursing, social work, and public administration.

## Admissions

**Admissions office mailing address:** 195 University Ave, Newark NJ 07102

**Admissions office phone:** (973) 353-5205

**Admissions office email:** newark@admissions.rutgers.edu

**# of transfer applications:** Fall 2015 admissions: 4,530

**# of transfer students accepted:** Fall 2015: 2,608

**Transfer student acceptance rate (2015–2016 academic year):** 57.6%

**Freshman applications received in Fall 2015:** 11,646

**Freshman applications accepted in Fall 2015:** 7,529

**Acceptance rate for 2016–2017 freshmen:** 64.6%

## Transfer Admissions Process

**Transfer policy (in their own words):** Transfer applicants are students who have completed 12 or more college credits at an accredited postsecondary institution. Read more at https://admissions.newark.rutgers.edu/information-for/transfer-student-applicants.

**Transfer application deadline:** Fall 2018 deadline is 5/15/18. Spring 2019 deadline is 12/23/18.

**Acceptances announced to transfer applicants:** Fall 2018 on rolling basis. Spring 2019 on rolling basis.

**Transfer application on Common App:** No

**Separate application or in addition to the Common App:** Yes

**Fee for separate transfer application:** $65

**Waiver available for separate transfer application fee:** College Board fee waiver application

SAT/ACT required for transfer applicants.

You are not required to submit SAT or ACT scores if:

- You graduated from high school 2 or more years prior to the date you intend to begin classes at Rutgers.
- You finished high school and subsquently completed 12 college credits with final course grades available by the application due date.

You are required to submit official SAT or ACT scores if:

- You graduated from high school fewer than 2 years before beginning classes at Rutgers.
- You are currently in your first semester of college.
- After leaving high school, you will complete fewer than 24 college credits by October 1 for spring term entry or February 1 for fall term entry. Do not include courses taken during high school in this number.

**High-school records requirements:** Official high-school transcript

**High-school records requirements for applicants who completed outside the US:** Submit official high-school/secondary-school transcripts. All records must be official, original documents or certified true copies. Documents not in English must be accompanied by a translation verified by a language professor or professional translator.

**Submission requirements for transfer applicants who completed high-school equivalency test:** GED holders must submit official results and a transcript of any high-school work attempted.

**College transcript requirements:** Submit official college transcripts from each college you have attended including all courses attempted and grades earned through the priority filing date.

**Interviews available for transfer applicants:** No information provided.

## Costs & Financial Aid

**FAFSA code:** 2629

**CSS Profile code:** N/A

**Are internal school financial aid forms required?** Yes

**Financial aid deadlines for transfer applicants:** Fall 2018: 2/1/18

**Costs for the 2017–2018 year:** Tuition & Fees: In-state: $14,633. Out-of-state: $30,274. Room & Board: In-state and out-of-state: $13,910.

**Financial aid for transfer students:** Yes

**Guarantees meeting 100% need for transfer students:** No

**Need-based aid for transfer students:** Yes. Must be US citizens.

**Merit-based financial aid for transfer students:** Yes. Apply to Rutgers by 10/1/18 for PTK and 2/1/18 for all others. Must be a US citizen/permanent resident.

**Phi Theta Kappa Scholarship:** Yes, $8,000. Renewable. Details available at https://admissions.newark.rutgers.edu/paying-for-college/scholarships.

**Reduced or zero tuition fees for low-income students:** Yes

**Includes loans in financial aid packages:** Yes

**% of all undergraduates receiving financial aid:** 78%

**% of all undergraduates qualifying for Pell Grants:** No information provided.

**Average financial aid award for all undergraduate students:** $16,376

**Funding available for low-income students to visit:** No

**Enrollment deposit can be waived for low-income students:** No

## Academics

**GPA range for transfer students accepted in 2016–2017:** No information provided.

**SAT ranges for all students admitted in 2016:** Critical Reading: 450–550. Mathematics: 480–580. Writing: 460–550.

**ACT composite score range for all students admitted in 2016:** No information provided.

**Type of curriculum:** Gen. Ed. requirements

**Type of academic year:** Semester

**Advisors specifically for transfer students:** Yes

**Credit policy (in their own words):** The maximum number of credits transferred from a 2-year college is 60–65 credits. The maximum number of credits transferred from a 4-year college may not exceed 90 credits. For those students who attended both types of institutions, the total number of credits may not exceed 90 credits, 65 of which may be from a 2-year college.

**Max number of transfer credits accepted:** 60

**Residency requirement for transfer students:** Yes. Dependent upon major.

**Study abroad available for transfer students:** Yes. Must fulfill residency requirements.

**Free tutoring for all students:** Yes

**Writing center for all students:** Yes

**Career support/access to internships and resume prep for all students:** Yes

**% of undergraduate students hired within 6 months of graduation:** No information provided.

**Additional resources specifically designated for transfer and/or non-traditional students:** No

## Housing

**Available for transfer students:** Yes

**Available for non-traditional students:** No

**Guaranteed for transfer students:** No information provided.

**Non-traditional students can reside in housing year-round:** Yes, if eligible for family housing

**Family housing available:** Yes

## Non-Traditional Admissions

No non-traditional student policies or programs available.

## Military/Veteran Students

**Military/veteran admissions policy (in their own words):** As a Yellow Ribbon educational institution, we are accredited by the US Department of Veterans Affairs (VA) and provide enrollment certification of education benefits as a core service. If you are a military-affiliated student at Rutgers University—Newark, you will have access to a dedicated office and staff who will help you access and use all the services that Rutgers University—Newark has to offer.

Military/veteran students apply either as freshmen or transfer applicants depending on the amount of credits they have obtained from an accredited postsecondary institution.

Read more at https://admissions.newark.rutgers.edu/information-for/veterans.

**Status considered in admissions:** No

**Special admissions process:** No

**Special financial aid:** Yes. The Yellow Ribbon Program.

**Specific programs/policies to address needs:** Veterans Affairs Office, headed by Paul Lazaro, Assistant Director, (973) 353-5515, lazaro.paul@rutgers.edu.

## DACA/Undocumented Students

**DACA and undocumented admissions policy (in their own words):** Undocumented immigrants are welcome to apply to Rutgers and should follow the same steps for admission as any other applicant. Students should carefully review the Rutgers University application requirements. The Rutgers online admission application does ask for citizen and immigration status of applicants, but provides options for Status Pending (SP) or Deferred Action for Childhood Arrivals (DACA) options.

Read more at http://deanofstudents.rutgers.edu/student-advocacy/undocumented-students-faq.

**Admitted:** Yes

**Status considered in admissions:** No

**Special admissions process:** No

**Eligible for institutional financial aid:** Yes. New Jersey DREAM Act.

The law, now in effect, allows undocumented students who meet certain criteria to qualify for the in-state tuition rates at all of New Jersey's public institutions of higher education. Undocumented students can pay in-state tuition if the student:

- Attended a high school in New Jersey for 3 or more years.
- Graduated from a high school in New Jersey or received the equivalent of a high-school diploma in New Jersey.
- Registers as an entering student or is currently enrolled in a public institution in New Jersey, and
- Files an affidavit with the college or university stating that the student has filed an application to legalize immigration status or will file an application as soon as the student is eligible to do so. Student information submitted in affidavit is a part of the student's record and kept private.

**Specific programs/policies to address needs:** Yes. The Immigrant Rights Clinic through Rutgers Law in Newark serves the immigrant population through a combination of individual client representation and broader advocacy projects. Under faculty supervision, students represent immigrants seeking various forms of relief from removal, including asylum for persecuted individuals; protection for victims of human trafficking; protection for battered immigrants; protection for victims of certain types of crimes; protection for abused, abandoned, or neglected immigrant children; and cancellation of removal.

The Student Legal Services Office at Rutgers University— New Brunswick provides students with access to high-quality and confidential immigration law services to help individuals and families on their path to US citizenship. A staff attorney will provide one-on-one consultations to assess participants' eligibility for legal benefits at no cost to the student. Staff attorneys will then assist students with getting connected to a local immigration attorney for assistance with legal services needed. Legal services through local attorneys are typically provided to students at costs lower than market rate.

# SCRIPPS COLLEGE

**Location:** Claremont, California
**Website:** www.scrippscollege.edu
**Endowment:** $295.8 million
**Type of School:** Private/Single-Sex Female, Liberal Arts
**# of Undergraduate Students:** 1,039
**# of Graduate Students:** 18
**Average Class Size:** 20 students or fewer

**School Mission (in their own words):** To educate women to develop their intellects and talents through active participation in a community of scholars so that as graduates they may contribute to society through public and private lives of leadership, service, integrity, and creativity.

## Admissions

**Admissions office mailing address:** 1030 Columbia Ave, Claremont CA 91711

**Admissions office phone:** (909) 621-8149

**Admissions office email:** admission@scrippscollege.edu

**# of transfer applications:** Fall 2016 admissions: 199

**# of transfer students accepted:** Fall 2016: 44

**Transfer student acceptance rate (2016–2017 academic year):** 22.1%

**Freshman applications received in Fall 2016:** 3,032

**Freshman applications accepted in Fall 2016:** 903

**Acceptance rate for 2016–2017 freshmen:** 29.8%

## Transfer Admissions Process

**Transfer policy (in their own words):** Any student who has graduated from high school has enrolled in a degree-seeking program, and has any transferable credits is considered a transfer student. Scripps welcomes applicants who wish to transfer in at first-year, sophomore, or junior status. Read more at www.scrippscollege.edu/admission/apply/transfer-applicants/faqs.

**Transfer admissions contact person:** Jessica Johnston, Associate Director of Admissions

**Transfer admissions contact info:** jjohnsto@scrippscollege.edu, (909) 621-8149

**Offers transfer-focused admissions events:** N/A

**Transfer application deadline:** Fall 2018 deadline is 4/1/18. Spring 2019 deadline is 11/1/18.

**Acceptances announced to transfer applicants:** Fall 2018 on 6/1/18. Spring 2019 on 1/1/19.

**Transfer application on Common App:** Yes. Common App Fee: $60.

**SAT/ACT required for transfer applicants:** Yes

**High-school records requirements:** Official transcript

**High-school records requirements for applicants who completed outside the US:** Translation of all documents

**Submission requirements for transfer applicants who completed high-school equivalency test:** Official transcript(s) from all secondary schools

**College transcript requirements:** Official transcript from each college attended

**Interviews available for transfer applicants:** Yes. Optional. On and off campus.

## Costs & Financial Aid

**FAFSA code:** 1174

**CSS Profile code:** 4693

**Are internal school financial aid forms required?** No

**Financial aid deadlines for transfer applicants:** Fall 2018: 3/1/18. Spring 2019: 11/15/18.

**Costs for the 2017–2018 year:** Tuition & Fees: $50,766. Room & Board: $15,682.

**Financial aid for transfer students:** Yes

**Guarantees meeting 100% need for transfer students:** Yes

**Need-based aid for transfer students:** Yes

**Merit-based financial aid for transfer students:** No

**Phi Theta Kappa Scholarship:** No

**Reduced or zero tuition fees for low-income students:** No

**Includes loans in financial aid packages:** Yes

**% of all undergraduates receiving financial aid:** 37%

**Average financial aid award for all undergraduate students:** $37,987

**Funding available for low-income students to visit:** No

**Enrollment deposit can be waived for low-income students:** No, but it can be lowered.

## Academics

**GPA range for transfer students accepted in 2016–2017:** No information provided.

**SAT ranges for all students admitted in 2016:** Critical Reading: 660–740. Mathematics: 630–700. Writing: 660–730.

**ACT composite score range for all students admitted in 2016:** 28–32

**Type of curriculum:** Gen. Ed. requirements

**Type of academic year:** Semester

**Advisors specifically for transfer students:** No

**Credit policy (in their own words):** Requirements for graduation: A minimum of 16 courses, evidenced by a minimum of 2 years in regular, full-time attendance at Scripps. The last 8 courses must be registered at Scripps; affiliated off-campus study programs meet residence requirement. Only courses graded C or above (not including C–) will be considered for transfer credit. Pass/fail or credit/no credit grades must be equated to C by the sending institution and will be elective credit only, not meeting any general education, major, or minor degree requirements at Scripps. All transfer credit will be translated into equivalent Scripps course credits. 1 Scripps course is equivalent to 4 semester units or 6 quarter credits. Courses approved as transfer credit may be applied toward general degree requirements and as elective credit upon initial evaluation at admission. They may only be used toward major or minor requirements when approved by faculty in the department of the major or minor as listed on an approval form. Read more at http://catalog.scrippscollege.edu/content.php?catoid=9&navoid=658#Transfer_Credit.

**Max number of transfer credits accepted:** 16 courses

**Residency requirement for transfer students:** Yes. Transfer students must spend the equivalent of 4 full-time semesters at Scripps, completing at least 16 courses, in order to receive the B.A. degree from the College.

**Study abroad available for transfer students:** Yes. Courses and grades completed through Scripps Study Abroad and Global Education programs are considered to be resident credit, will be itemized on the Scripps official transcript, and will be computed in Scripps grade point averages.

**Free tutoring for all students:** Yes

**Writing center for all students:** Yes

**Career support/access to internships and resume prep for all students:** Yes

**% of undergraduate students hired within 6 months of graduation:** When Scripps College seniors graduate, more than 50% begin work full-time within 3 months of graduation.

**Additional resources specifically designated for transfer and/or non-traditional students:** No

## Housing

**Available for transfer students:** Yes

**Available for non-traditional students:** Yes

**Guaranteed for transfer students:** Yes

**Non-traditional students can reside in housing year-round:** Summer housing at Scripps is available to matriculating Scripps students only.

**Family housing available:** No

## Non-Traditional Admissions

**Non-traditional student policy (in their own words):** No specific non-traditional student policy.

**Name of program:** Articulation agreements

**Program description:** Scripps College has collaboratively developed transfer articulation agreements with a few California community colleges for the purpose of identifying courses or sequences of courses at these individual colleges that are comparable to or acceptable in lieu of specific courses toward meeting general education requirements or as elective credit at Scripps.

**Program admission requirements:** Contact office of the registrar.

**Program website:** www.scrippscollege.edu/registrar

## Military/Veteran Students

**Military/veteran admissions policy (in their own words):** Student veterans should follow the same application procedures as other applicants for admission as first-year students or transfer students. Read more important information about military/veteran admissions at www.scrippscollege.edu/admission/apply/veteran-applicants.

**Status considered in admissions:** Yes

**Special admissions process:** No

**Special financial aid:** Yes. The Yellow Ribbon Program. Up to $10,000 per year.

**Specific programs/policies to address needs:** N/A

## DACA/Undocumented Students

DACA/undocumented students are not admitted via the transfer process.

# SMITH COLLEGE

**Location:** Northampton, Massachusetts
**Website:** www.smith.edu
**Endowment:** $1.727 billion
**Type of School:** Single-Sex Female, Liberal Arts
**# of Undergraduate Students:** 2,514
**# of Graduate Students:** 382
**Average Class Size:** 19

**School Mission (in their own words):** Smith College educates women of promise for lives of distinction and purpose. A college of and for the world, Smith links the power of the liberal arts to excellence in research and scholarship, thereby developing engaged global citizens and leaders to address society's challenges.

## Admissions

**Admissions office mailing address:** 10 Elm St, Northampton MA 01063

**Admissions office phone:** (413) 585-2500

**Admissions office email:** admission@smith.edu

**# of transfer applications:** Fall 2016 admissions: 249. Spring 2017 admissions: No information provided.

**# of transfer students accepted:** Fall 2016: 70. Spring 2017: No information provided.

**Transfer student acceptance rate (2016–2017 academic year):** 28.1%

**Freshman applications received in Fall 2016:** 5,254

**Freshman applications accepted in Fall 2016:** 1,956

**Acceptance rate for 2016–2017 freshmen:** 37%

## Transfer Admissions Process

**Transfer policy (in their own words):** While many colleges and universities consider transfer applicants only after the first-year class is selected, Smith reserves a number of places especially for transfers because we believe they enrich our community. Each year, more than 100 transfer students enter Smith either in January or September.

Transfer students must have completed at least 1 semester at any of a variety of institutions, including 4-year private and public colleges and universities, community and junior colleges, and international institutions. Like you, every transfer student has her own reasons for leaving one school for another, but you all share common qualities: an interest in academic excellence, strong motivation and self-discipline, and an adventurous spirit.

Women who are 24 or older, a veteran, or have a dependent other than a spouse are eligible to apply to Smith as Ada Comstock Scholars.

**Transfer admissions contact person:** Sidonia Dalby, Associate Director of Admissions and Ada Comstock Scholar

**Transfer admissions contact info:** sdalby@smith.edu, (413) 585-2523

**Offers transfer-focused admissions events:** Yes

**Transfer application deadline:** 2/1/17 is the usual preferred Fall 2018 deadline; however, materials can be submitted up to 5/15/17. Spring 2019 deadline is 11/15/17.

**Acceptances announced to transfer applicants:** Fall 2018 on 5/1/18. Spring 2019 on 12/15/18.

**Transfer application on Common App:** Yes. Common App Fee: None.

**Separate application or in addition to the Common App:** Yes

**Fee for separate transfer application:** None

**SAT/ACT required for transfer applicants:** No

**High-school records requirements:** Must submit official transcript from all secondary schools attended

**High-school records requirements for applicants who completed outside the US:** Must submit official high school transcripts. Submission requirements for transfer applicants who completed high-school equivalency test: Must submit official scores.

**College transcript requirements:** Must submit official transcripts from all colleges or universities previously attended.

**Interviews available for transfer applicants:** Yes. Recommended. In-person or online.

**Additional requirements for transfers seeking admissions to engineering major:** Yes. Must have taken basic prerequisite classes, such as general physics, calculus, and other courses that general engineering students usually take.

## Costs & Financial Aid

**FAFSA code:** 2209

**CSS Profile code:** 3762

**Are internal school financial aid forms required?** Yes

**Financial aid deadlines for transfer applicants:** Fall 2018: The fall financial aid deadline is usually on or around January 25. Spring 2019: Usually on November 15.

**Costs for the 2017–2018 year:** Tuition & Fees: Tuition: $49,760. Fees: $284. Room & Board: $16,730.

**Financial aid for transfer students:** Yes

**Guarantees meeting 100% need for transfer students:** Yes

**Need-based aid for transfer students:** Yes. Must demonstrate need.

**Merit-based financial aid for transfer students:** Yes. Students are chosen for these scholarships based on recommendations from the Office of Admission.

**Phi Theta Kappa Scholarship:** Yes, $5,000. Renewable.

**Reduced or zero tuition fees for low-income students:** Yes

**Includes loans in financial aid packages:** Yes

**% of all undergraduates receiving financial aid:** 61%

**% of all undergraduates qualifying for Pell Grants:** No information provided.

**Average financial aid award for all undergraduate students:** $48,115

**Funding available for low-income students to visit:** Yes

**Enrollment deposit can be waived for low-income students:** Yes

## Academics

**GPA range for transfer students accepted in 2016–2017:** No information provided.

**SAT ranges for all students admitted in 2016:** Critical Reading: 630–740. Mathematics: 600–740. Writing: 640–730.

**ACT composite score range for all students admitted in 2016:** 29–33

**Recommended completed level of math for transfer applicants:** Pre-calculus or above

**Recommended completed level of English for transfer applicants:** 1 year college English, writing-intensive coursework

**Type of curriculum:** Open

**Type of academic year:** Semester

**Advisors specifically for transfer students:** Yes

**Credit policy (in their own words):** In order to graduate, a student must have: A minimum of 128 credits of academic work. Bachelor of arts: completion of 64 credits of academic work outside the department of the major (64-Credit Rule). Bachelor of science: additional requirements for the bachelor of science degree are listed in the Smith College Course Catalog (under "Engineering") and on the Picker Engineering Program website.

A maximum of 64 transfer credits may be recorded on the Smith transcript. Transfer credit is accepted from accredited institutions of higher education in the United States and abroad. Normally only those courses falling within the scope of Smith's liberal arts curriculum will be approved. Credit is evaluated and transferred on a course-by-course basis with approval from the registrar.

**Max number of transfer credits accepted:** 64

**Residency requirement for transfer students:** Yes. Candidates for the degree must complete at least 4 semesters of academic work and a minimum of 64 credits in academic residence at Smith College in Northampton; 2 of these semesters must be completed during the junior or senior year.

**Study abroad available for transfer students:** Yes. Students are recommended to apply to programs that have been approved by Smith. However, students may submit a petition if they are interested in a non-approved program. Also, a transfer student or Ada Comstock scholar who enters with 64 credits must spend the junior and senior year on campus in Northampton.

**Free tutoring for all students:** Yes

**Writing center for all students:** Yes

**Career support/access to internships and resume prep for all students:** Yes

**% of undergraduate students hired within 6 months of graduation:** No information provided.

**Additional resources specifically designated for transfer and/or non-traditional students:** Yes. There are academic and career advisors that specifically work with these students.

## Housing

**Available for transfer students:** Yes

**Available for non-traditional students:** Yes

**Guaranteed for transfer students:** Yes

**Non-traditional students can reside in housing year round:** Yes

**Family housing available:** Yes

## Non-Traditional Admissions

**Non-traditional student policy (in their own words):** Smith College's Ada Comstock Scholar Program was created to help non-traditional students, including veterans, to complete a bachelor of arts degree either part-time or full-time, with flexible options for reduced course loads, special academic advising, career counseling, and housing.

**Name of program:** Ada Comstock

**Program description:** Ada Comstock Scholars range in age from their 20s to their mid-60s, with varying backgrounds and life paths, whether they chose to begin work, start families, or travel after high school. They have come to Smith from all parts of the US and as far as Asia and Africa. A common denominator for all Ada Comstock Scholars is that they reached a point where they wished to complete their education and fulfill their potential in new and creative ways. They have chosen to pursue a bachelor of arts degree at Smith College precisely because of the Ada Comstock Scholars Program and its innovative approach. Enables women of non-traditional college age to complete a bachelor of arts degree either part-time or full-time, with flexible options for reduced course loads, special academic advising, career counseling, and housing.

**Program deadline:** January entrance: 11/15/18. Fall entrance: 2/1/17.

**Program admission requirements:** Women who are 24 or older*, a veteran, or have a dependent other than a spouse are eligible to apply to Smith as Ada Comstock Scholars. Women who have already earned a bachelor's degree are not eligible to apply.

Candidates are expected to present at least 48 liberal arts credits. On average, admitted students have 50 transfer credits. The maximum number of transfer credits is 64. Contact the Office of the Registrar for what qualifies for transfer credit.

*Women must be at least 24 years by December 31 of the academic year in which they enter Smith (fall or spring). A student entering in January does not qualify as an Ada/ independent student if she will turn 24 during her first term at the college.

The following are required:

- An interview. Applicants must contact the Office of Admission to schedule their appointment. If distance is a problem, a telephone interview can be arranged.
- Autobiographical essay: Your personal statement illustrates how you think and write. Your jobs, activities, and family responsibilities help us learn about what you would contribute to our vibrant community.
- Official college transcripts
- Official high-school transcript or GED certificate
- 2 reference forms (at least 1 from a faculty member who has taught you in a college-level class)
- Resume
- Midterm evaluation form if applicable
- Photocopies of course descriptions for all college courses completed and in progress

**Program website:** www.smith.edu/about-smith/ada-comstock-scholars-program

**Program contact person:** Sidonia Dalby, Associate Director of Admissions

**Program contact info:** (413) 585-2523, sdalby@smith.edu

**Name of program:** Bridge Program

**Program description:** Begun in 1970 as a program for African American students entering Smith, Bridge now welcomes first-year and transfer students of color who demonstrate a commitment to creating and maintaining culturally inclusive communities. Bridge provides opportunities for finding mentors, friends, resources, and a community—all before other students even arrive on campus.

**Program deadline:** Applications for the 2017 program will be available in May. The program dates are Friday, August 25, to Thursday, August 31.

**Program admission requirements:** Bridge is open to first-year and transfer students of color who are residents of the US.

**Program website:** www.smith.edu/about-smith/diversity/programs-services/bridge

**Program contact person:** L'Tanya Richmond, Director of Multicultural Affairs

**Program contact info:** (413) 585-4940, lrichmon@smith.edu

## Military/Veteran Students

**Status considered in admissions:** Yes

**Special admissions process:** Yes. These students are recommended to apply through the Ada Comstock Program (see above).

**Special financial aid:** Yes. Students must meet requirements given by the Dept. of Veteran Affairs.

**Specific programs/policies to address needs:** Yes. The Yellow Ribbon Program.

## DACA/Undocumented Students

**DACA and undocumented admissions policy (in their own words):** Undocumented and Deferred Action for Childhood Arrivals (DACA) students follow the procedures and requirements for first-year or transfer admission. They are evaluated in the same way as US citizens and US permanent residents. Undocumented and DACA students should indicate "Non-citizen" or "Other" in the citizenship field on the Common Application. Because we want to obtain a comprehensive picture of the student's background and experiences in the context of her school and community, we encourage undocumented and DACA applicants to disclose their citizenship status in the application. Undocumented and DACA students may apply under any admission plan, including Early Decision.

**Admitted:** Yes

**Status considered in admissions:** No

**Special admissions process:** No

**Eligible for institutional financial aid:** Yes. Must demonstrate need. Smith meets 100% of the demonstrated need of all admitted students who apply for financial aid by the published deadlines. Because federal financial aid is not available for undocumented and DACA students, Smith provides institutional, need-based financial aid in its place.

**Specific programs/policies to address needs:** Yes. DACA students may talk to advisors who are aware of their situations and who have experience and knowledge dealing with DACA laws.

# Mariana Estrella

**University of Massachusetts Amherst, C'19**
Master's Degree in Education

**Smith College, C'15**
Bachelor's Degree in Sociology

**Hostos Community College, C'12**
Associate's Degree in Paralegal Studies

**Current Employment:** Administrative Assistant for Inclusion, Diversity, and Equity, Smith College

**Bio:** Born and raised in San Juan, Puerto Rico, Mariana lived in NYC for 12 years, where she worked as a legislative aide at the city and state levels. Upon graduating from Smith, her interest in public policy with higher ed led to a career path in leadership theory and the holistic development of students. Her next endeavor is to gain her master's degree in higher education at the University of Massachusetts Amherst.

*"I came to Smith expecting it to change my life. The three years I've spent there have been the hardest, most frustrating, enlightening, and inspiring of my life. If my life had a status update it would be: extremely complicated. Yet the amount of love, support, and encouragement my friends, professors, and allies have provided has felt like hitting the lottery. When I realized the hardest parts were all still up to me, it was the foundation's network and the skills they taught me that grounded me and gave me the strength to carry on.*

*My post-grad plan is to never stop reinventing myself, to rise above all expectations, to continue pursuing things that matter, to love with every fiber in my body, to stand up for the things that I care about, even when that means standing up alone, to not settle nor apologize for who I am, to continue to praise the womyn whom I admire and to remember the light, the fire within me. I look forward to sharing my experiences and to showcase that while this journey was not easy, it was exactly where I needed to be."*

## Leadership Activities

- Member, Phi Theta Kappa International Honor Society of Community Colleges, Hostos Community College
- Hostos Leadership Academy
- Recipient, The Diversity Foundation New York Yankees Scholarship, 2011
- Senator, Student Government Association, Smith College
- Ada Comstock Scholar, Smith College
- Member, Organization Resources Committee, Smith College
- House Representative, Ada Class Cabinet, Smith College
- Diversity Representative, Office of Student Affairs, Smith College
- Legislative Aide, New York State Assembly, Assemblyman Nelson Castro, 86th District
- Intern, Corporate Compliance, New York City Health and Hospitals Corporation
- Director of Community Affairs, New York State Assembly, 78th District
- Constituent Services Liaison, New York City Council, 18th District

# Yolanda Watson

**Smith College, C'17**
Dual Bachelor's Degrees in Africana Studies and English

**Kingsborough Community College, C'15**
Associate's Degree in Liberal Arts with a concentration in English

**Learning Enterprises, C'15**
Nantong, Jiangsu, China

**Bio:** Yolanda would like to combine her love for literature, history, and the performing arts to promote positive change in underrepresented communities like the one she grew up in. She is currently a senior at Smith College, double majoring in Africana Studies for Literature and English for Creative Writing. After graduating from Smith College, Yolanda plans to pursue an MFA in Creative Writing so that she can begin working on her very first book.

*"Transferring to Smith College has given me the opportunity to work with and befriend some of the best and brightest minds. My professors constantly challenge and encourage me to question, explore, and grow through every obstacle. As a low-income, first-generation college student who once believed I would never be able to afford to go to college, I am proud to have come so far (even when I have a million assignments to complete!).*

*As a Smithie, I have explored far beyond my academic interests. When I am not busy with my classwork, I am performing in theater productions, putting on vocal performances, and performing spoken word poetry at campus events. I have grown not only as an intellectual, but also as an artist. I truly believe that after graduating from Smith College, I will be unafraid to pursue my dreams, and will do so with a fierce determination."*

## Leadership Activities

- Member, Phi Theta Kappa International Honor Society of Community Colleges
- Secretary, Board of Directors, Urban Neighborhood Services
- Presidential Scholar, KBCC
- ASAP, KBCC
- Board Member, Urban Neighborhood Services
- Fellow, America Needs You
- Usher, On Stage at Kingsborough
- Spoken Word Poet, Independent Artist
- Member, Blackappella, SC

# SPELMAN COLLEGE

**Location:** Atlanta, Georgia

**Website:** www.spelman.edu

**Endowment:** $346.9 million

**Type of School:** Private/Single-Sex Female, Liberal Arts

**# of Undergraduate Students:** 2,144

**# of Graduate Students:** 0

**Average Class Size:** No information provided.

**School Mission (in their own words):** Spelman College, a historically Black college and a global leader in the education of women of African descent, is dedicated to academic excellence in the liberal arts and sciences and the intellectual, creative, ethical, and leadership development of its students. Spelman empowers the whole person to engage the many cultures of the world and inspires a commitment to positive social change.

## Admissions

**Admissions office mailing address:** 350 Spelman Ln SW, Box 875, Atlanta GA 30314

**Admissions office phone:** (404) 270-5193

**Admissions office email:** admiss@spelman.edu

**# of transfer applications:** Fall 2014 admissions: 170

**# of transfer students accepted:** Fall 2014: 61

**Transfer student acceptance rate (2014–2015 academic year):** 35.9%

**Freshman applications received in Fall 2014:** 4,324

**Freshman applications accepted in Fall 2014:** 2,335

**Acceptance rate for 2016–2017 freshmen:** 41%

## Transfer Admissions Process

**Transfer policy (in their own words):** A transfer applicant has completed a high-school diploma, or its equivalent, and has attended another college for at least 1 term as a degree-seeking student. Transfer admission to Spelman is selective, and students applying must have earned fewer than 60 semester hours or the equivalent at their previous institutions. Limited space is available for transfer students, and some majors may not be available. If you have 31 or more earned credit hours, it is at the discretion of the admissions committee to request test scores and official high-school transcript to assist in rendering a decision. Applicants must be in good standing and eligible to return to their previous institutions. Students with fewer than 1 year of attempted college credits as a full-time student (30 earned semester hours or the equivalent) must meet new first-time applicant eligibility as well as transfer admission requirements. Transfer applicants should specify a major other than undecided.

**Transfer admissions contact person:** Tiffany Nelson, Director

**Transfer admissions contact info:** tnelso15@spelman.edu, (404) 270-5193

**Offers transfer-focused admissions events:** No

**Transfer application deadline:** Fall 2018 deadline is 4/1/18. Spring 2019 deadline is 11/1/18.

**Acceptances announced to transfer applicants:** Fall 2018 on 5/1/18. Spring 2019 on 12/1/18.

**Transfer application on Common App:** Yes. Common App Fee: $35. Transfer students are not eligible for a fee waiver.

**SAT/ACT required for transfer applicants:** Yes, for those transferring with fewer than 30 credits; may be requested at college's discretion for students with 31+ credits.

**High-school records requirements:** Required for those transferring with fewer than 30 credits; may be requested at college's discretion for students with 31+ credits.

**High-school records requirements for applicants who completed outside the US:** Official high-school and/or college transcript(s); if not in English, an official translation is needed.

**Submission requirements for transfer applicants who completed high-school equivalency test:** GED not accepted.

**College transcript requirements:** Required from all colleges/universities attended.

## Costs & Financial Aid

**FAFSA code:** 1594

**CSS Profile code:** N/A

**Are internal school financial aid forms required?** Yes, may be requested.

**Financial aid deadlines for transfer applicants:** Fall 2018: 2/1/18

**Costs for the 2016–2017 year:** Tuition & Fees: $27,314. Room & Board: $12,795.

**Financial aid for transfer students:** Yes

**Guarantees meeting 100% need for transfer students:** No

**Need-based aid for transfer students:** Yes. Institutional scholarships available after 2 semesters at Spelman.

**Merit-based financial aid for transfer students:** No

**Phi Theta Kappa Scholarship:** No

**Reduced or zero tuition fees for low-income students:** No

**Includes loans in financial aid packages:** Yes

**% of all undergraduates receiving financial aid:** 89%

**% of all undergraduates qualifying for Pell Grants:** 48%

**Average financial aid award for all undergraduate students:** No information provided.

**Funding available for low-income students to visit:** No

**Enrollment deposit can be waived for low-income students:** No information provided.

## Academics

**GPA range for transfer students accepted in 2014–2015:** 2.0 and up

**SAT ranges for all students admitted in 2014:** Critical Reading: 460–560. Mathematics: 440–540. Writing: 460–550.

**ACT composite score range for all students admitted in 2014:** 19–24

**Type of curriculum:** Gen. Ed. requirements

**Type of academic year:** Semester

**Advisors specifically for transfer students:** No information provided.

**Credit policy:** A graduating student should have completed a minimum of 120 credit hours in total and have earned a minimum of 60 credit hours at the college.

**Max number of transfer credits accepted:** 30

**Residency requirement for transfer students:** Yes. Students must complete at least 60 credits at Spelman.

**Study abroad available for transfer students:** Yes. Spelman restricts study abroad to junior year.

**Free tutoring for all students:** Yes

**Writing center for all students:** Yes

**Career support/access to internships and resume prep for all students:** Yes

**% of undergraduate students hired within 6 months of graduation:** 30%

**Additional resources specifically designated for transfer and/or non-traditional students:** No

## Housing

No information available on housing for transfer students, non-traditional students, and students with families.

## Non-Traditional Admissions

**Non-traditional student policy (in their own words):** Spelman has a program catered specifically to non-traditional students called the Pauline E. Drake Scholars Program.

**Name of program:** Pauline E. Drake Scholars

**Program description:** The Pauline E. Drake Scholars Program was designed to assist the non-traditional college student, which is defined as an individual who:

- Is at least 25 years old and graduated (or was scheduled to graduate) from high school at least 5 years ago.

- Previously has attended college, but did not complete her degree and is returning to college after time off.
- Graduated from high school, entered the workforce, and is now attending college for the first time. Allows non-traditional students an opportunity to study at Spelman.

**Program deadline:** Fall semester: 3/1/18. Spring semester: 11/1/18.

**Program admission requirements:**

- Completed application for admission through the Common Application
- Official high-school transcript or GED record
- Official transcripts from ALL postsecondary institutions attended
- Resume
- Letters of recommendation from any 2 of the following: college professors or administrators, college or school counselors, supervisors or employers

**Program website:** www.spelman.edu/admissions/pauline-e-drake-scholars

**Program contact person:** Tiffany Nelson, Admissions Director

**Program contact info:** (404) 270-5193, tnelso15@spelman.edu

## Military/Veteran Students

**Military/veteran admissions policy (in their own words):** Military/veteran students follow the same application process as any other students. The amount of credits that they hold will determine if they will apply as first years, transfers, or as Pauline E. Drake Scholars (non-traditional students).

**Status considered in admissions:** No

**Special admissions process:** No

**Special financial aid:** Yes, ROTC scholarships. Scholarship benefits include tuition, book allowance, academic fees, and a monthly stipend. Benefits will depend upon a student's degree plan, but typically not to exceed 4 years without approval for extended benefits.

**Specific programs/policies to address needs:** No

## DACA/Undocumented Students

**DACA and undocumented admissions policy (in their own words):** The admissions process for these students is "blind," meaning that the school does not consider their immigration status.

**Admitted:** Yes

**Status considered in admissions:** No

**Special admissions process:** No

**Eligible for institutional financial aid:** No information provided.

**Specific programs/policies to address needs:** No information provided.

# STANFORD UNIVERSITY

**Location:** Stanford, California

**Website:** www.stanford.edu

**Endowment:** $22.4 billion

**Type of School:** Private/Co-ed, Research University

**# of Undergraduate Students:** 7,034

**# of Graduate Students:** 9,880

**Average Class Size:** No information provided.

**School Mission (in their own words):** Its nature, that of a university with such seminaries of learning as shall make it of the highest grade, including mechanical institutes, museums, galleries of art, laboratories, and conservatories, together with all things necessary for the study of agriculture in all its branches, and for mechanical training, and the studies and exercises directed to the cultivation and enlargement of the mind.

Its object, to qualify its students for personal success, and direct usefulness in life.

And its purposes, to promote the public welfare by exercising an influence in behalf of humanity and civilization, teaching the blessings of liberty regulated by law, and inculcating love and reverence for the great principles of government as derived from the inalienable rights of man to life, liberty, and the pursuit of happiness.

## Admissions

**Admissions office mailing address:** 450 Serra Mall, Stanford CA 94305

**Admissions office phone:** (650) 723-2091

**Admissions office email:** admission@stanford.edu

**# of transfer applications:** Fall 2016 admissions: 1,959

**# of transfer students accepted:** Fall 2016: 42

**Transfer student acceptance rate (2016–2017 academic year):** 2.14%

**Freshman applications received in Fall 2016:** 43,997

**Freshman applications accepted in Fall 2016:** 2,118

**Acceptance rate for 2016–2017 freshmen:** 3.95%

## Transfer Admissions Process

**Transfer policy (in their own words):** Students who have enrolled either full-time or as a degree-seeking student after graduating from high school must apply for transfer admission.

Students who are dual-enrolled in both high school and college programs should apply for freshman admission.

Students must have a high-school diploma or the equivalent in order to enroll at Stanford.

Transfer coursework must be completed at an accredited degree-granting institution; coursework completed in vocational, technical, performance, or professional programs is not considered.

Transfer students are required to complete at least 2 years of full-time enrollment at Stanford in order to attain a bachelor's degree from the University.

Students who have already earned a bachelor's degree are not eligible to apply for undergraduate admission, but they may contact the Graduate Admissions Office at gradadmissions@stanford.edu.

**Offers transfer-focused admissions events:** Yes

**Transfer application deadline:** Fall 2018 deadline is 3/15/18.

**Acceptances announced to transfer applicants:** Fall 2018 on 5/1/18.

**Transfer application on Common App:** Yes. Common App Fee: $90 (fee waiver available).

**SAT/ACT required for transfer applicants:** Yes

**High-school records requirements:** Official high-school transcript

**High-school records requirements for applicants who completed outside the US:** Official high-school transcript or certified copy of final examination results

**Submission requirements for transfer applicants who completed high-school equivalency test:** Must submit official certificate.

**College transcript requirements:** Official transcripts from all colleges and universities attended

**Interviews available for transfer applicants:** No

**Additional requirements for transfers seeking admissions to arts major:** No. Students who wish to highlight their extraordinary talent in the fine or performing arts—art practice, dance, music, and theater—may submit an Arts Portfolio. These materials are entirely optional and will be reviewed at the discretion of the Office of Undergraduate Admission and the fine arts faculty.

## Costs & Financial Aid

**FAFSA code:** 1305

**CSS Profile code:** 4704

**Are internal school financial aid forms required?** No

**Financial aid deadlines for transfer applicants:** Fall 2018: 3/15/18

**Costs for the 2017–2018 year:** Tuition & Fees: $47,940. Room & Board: $14,601.

**Financial aid for transfer students:** Yes

**Guarantees meeting 100% need for transfer students:** Yes

**Need-based aid for transfer students:** Yes

**Merit-based financial aid for transfer students:** No

**Phi Theta Kappa Scholarship:** No

**Reduced or zero tuition fees for low-income students:** Yes

**Includes loans in financial aid packages:** Yes

**% of all undergraduates receiving financial aid:** 70%

**% of all undergraduates qualifying for Pell Grants:**
No information provided.

**Average financial aid award for all undergraduate students:**
$51,614

**Funding available for low-income students to visit:**
No information provided.

**Enrollment deposit can be waived for low-income students:**
No information provided.

## Academics

**GPA range for transfer students accepted in 2016–2017:**
No information provided.

**SAT ranges for all students admitted in 2016:** Critical Reading:
680–780. Mathematics: 700–800. Writing: 690–790.

**ACT composite score range for all students admitted in 2016:**
31–35

**Recommended completed level of math for transfer
applicants:** Pre-calculus or above

**Type of curriculum:** Gen. Ed. requirements

**Type of academic year:** Semester

**Advisors specifically for transfer students:** Yes

**Credit policy (in their own words):** Candidates for a single
bachelor's degree (B.A., B.S., or B.A.S.) must complete a
minimum of 180 units of University work, with a minimum
of 135 units completed at Stanford.

Undergraduates who have completed (or plan to complete)
coursework at a non-Stanford, regionally accredited college
or university may request an evaluation for transfer credit.
External coursework may be considered for transfer credit
if all of the following conditions are met:

- The coursework is completed at a regionally accredited
  institution.
- The coursework is substantially similar to Stanford
  courses.
- The final grade posted for each potential transfer course
  is a C– grade (or better).
- The coursework does not duplicate, overlap, or regress
  previous work.
- The university or college offering the courses allows
  these courses to be used for credit toward its own
  undergraduate degree.
- The coursework did not count toward secondary-school
  diploma and/or graduation requirements.

- No more than 45 (90 for transfer students) quarter units
  of credit for work done elsewhere may be counted toward
  a bachelor's degree at Stanford.
- Transfer work can be used to satisfy a department major
  or minor requirement.
- The transfer work must first be officially accepted into the
  University through the Office of the University Registrar.
  Students should contact their departments directly for
  additional details regarding departmental transfer credit
  policies.

**Max number of transfer credits accepted:** 90

**Residency requirement for transfer students:** Yes. Students
must spend at least 2 years at Stanford and earn 90 credits.

**Study abroad available for transfer students:** Yes. Must fulfill
residency requirements.

**Free tutoring for all students:** Yes

**Writing center for all students:** Yes

**Career support/access to internships and resume prep for
all students:** Yes

**% of undergraduate students hired within 6 months of
graduation:** No information provided.

**Additional resources specifically designated for transfer
and/or non-traditional students:** Yes

## Housing

**Available for transfer students:** Yes

**Available for non-traditional students:** Yes

**Guaranteed for transfer students:** Yes

**Non-traditional students can reside in housing year-round:**
Yes, upon request

**Family housing available:** Yes

## Non-Traditional Admissions

No non-traditional student policies or programs at this time.

## Military/Veteran Students

**Military/veteran admissions policy (in their own words):**
Veteran applicants add a highly valued voice to the
undergraduate community; the life experience that students
bring from previous career paths or military service provides
a unique perspective in discussion seminars, student groups,
and campus activities. We select students with varying
educational histories, and while we uphold a standard of fine
academic preparation and a determined passion for learning,
we also look for personal attributes that contribute unique
qualities to our already broadly diverse class.

Read more important information regarding military/veteran
admissions at https://admission.stanford.edu/application/
veterans/index.html.

**Status considered in admissions:** No

**Special admissions process:** Determine whether you are eligible to apply as a freshman or a transfer. You are considered a transfer applicant if the following applies: You have, at any time, enrolled either full-time or as a degree-seeking student in a college or university after graduating from high school.

**Special financial aid:** Yes. The Yellow Ribbon Program.

**Specific programs/policies to address needs:** The Office of Military-Affiliated Communities in the Student Services Center serves as the first point of contact for veterans.

## DACA/Undocumented Students

**DACA and undocumented admissions policy (in their own words):** Stanford treats undocumented students as domestic students in the admission process.

**Admitted:** Yes

**Status considered in admissions:** No

**Special admissions process:** No

**Eligible for institutional financial aid:** Yes, meets 100% demonstrated financial need.

**Specific programs/policies to address needs:** The Bechtel International Center maintains resources for DACA students.

# Qudus Lawal

**Stanford University, C'16**
Master's Degree in Chemical Engineering

**Stanford University, C'14**
Bachelor's Degree in Chemical Engineering

**Hostos Community College, C'11**
Associate's Degree in Engineering Science

**Current Employment:** Technology Analyst, Clark Street Associates

**Bio:** Growing up in Nigeria, Qudus became aware of the lack of reliable energy sources. He was alarmed by his country's dependence on oil, its damaging effects on the environment, and its contribution to political rifts in the region. Qudus would like to focus on green energy and ensure that developing countries have the technology necessary to tap into the natural resources of the earth without damaging the environment.

*"Stanford changed my view of myself and the world around me in ways that I could have never imagined. The engineering classes were expectedly rigorous and challenging, but my most influential class was not an engineering class. In the spring of my senior year, I took a class called 'Finding Your Own Story,' taught through the Stanford Storytelling Project. The class challenged me to question and evaluate the forces that motivate the way we tell our story and how we define our own success. It did this through a series of short stories like the 'Death of Ivan Ilych' by Tolstoy, books like Siddhartha, and meditative contemplation and introspective writing. It changed my view of success and the motivations behind it.*

*Before the class, I thought I had to obtain a Ph.D.; it was the only way I would be valuable and impactful. Thanks to that class, I was open to other avenues and options. During the last quarter of my master's program, I took a class on the intersection of policy, technology, and business development. I became open to a career path in which I could take part in all areas crucial to not just the success, but also the impact, of a company. Now, I work with a small consulting firm doing business development and government strategy and outreach for a variety of clients, ranging from advanced manufacturing and energy to artificial intelligence. The knowledge I gain from this experience will prepare me to advance renewable energy by fostering the needed synergy between technology, business development, and government policies.*

*It is this holistic approach to educating the mind that makes Stanford a great citadel of learning, and I am proud and lucky to call myself a Stanford Cardinal, all thanks to the assistance of the Kaplan Educational Foundation."*

## Leadership Activities

- Valedictorian, Hostos Community College
- Member, Phi Theta Kappa International Honor Society of Community Colleges
- Ambassador, Hostos Leadership Academy
- Hostos Science Club Scholar
- Certificate of Merit in Service Learning, Natural Science Department, Hostos Community College
- Student Researcher, Stanford University
- Intern/Researcher, Younicos Inc., Germany
- Volunteer, Future Scientist
- Financial Officer, Nigerian Student Association, Stanford University
- Treasurer, Stanford Black Scientists and Engineers
- Dean's List, Stanford University
- Director of Events, Stanford Association of International Development
- Member, American Institute of Chemical Engineers
- Research Assistant, Brookhaven National Laboratory
- Research Assistant, Hunter College
- Research Assistant, Weill Cornell Medical College
- Research Assistant, City College of New York
- Researcher, Louis Stokes Alliance for Minority Participation (LSAMP), Brookhaven National Laboratory
- Germany Study Abroad/Research

# SWARTHMORE COLLEGE

**Location:** Swarthmore, Pennsylvania

**Website:** www.swarthmore.edu

**Endowment:** $1.75 billion

**Type of School:** Private/Co-ed, Liberal Arts

**# of Undergraduate Students:** 1,620

**# of Graduate Students:** 0

**Average Class Size:** No information provided.

**School Mission (in their own words):** Swarthmore students are expected to prepare themselves for full, balanced lives as individuals and as responsible citizens through exacting intellectual study supplemented by a varied program of sports and other extracurricular activities. The purpose of Swarthmore College is to make its students more valuable human beings and more useful members of society. Although it shares this purpose with other educational institutions, each school, college, and university seeks to realize that purpose in its own way. Swarthmore seeks to help its students realize their full intellectual and personal potential combined with a deep sense of ethical and social concern.

## Admissions

**Admissions office mailing address:** 500 College Ave, Swarthmore PA 19081

**Admissions office phone:** (610) 328-8300

**Admissions office email:** admissions@swarthmore.edu

**# of transfer applications:** Fall 2016 admissions: 230

**# of transfer students accepted:** Fall 2016: 27

**Transfer student acceptance rate (2016–2017 academic year):** 11.7%

**Freshman applications received in Fall 2016:** 7,717

**Freshman applications accepted in Fall 2016:** 988

**Acceptance rate for 2016–2017 freshmen:** 12.8%

## Transfer Admissions Process

**Transfer policy (in their own words):** You may apply for transfer admission if you have completed the equivalent of 2 or more semesters of college or university-level coursework by the end of the current academic year. We make admissions decisions on a case-by-case basis for students who have completed less than the equivalent of 2 semesters of college or university-level coursework. We discourage transfer applications from students who have completed the equivalent of 6 or more semesters of college coursework. Students who have already completed a bachelor's degree or higher are not eligible for transfer admission.

**Transfer admissions contact person:** Joseph "J.T." Duck, Director of Admissions

**Transfer admissions contact info:** jduck1@swarthmore.edu, (610) 328-8303

**Offers transfer-focused admissions events:** No information provided.

**Transfer application deadline:** Fall 2018 deadline is 4/1/18.

**Acceptances announced to transfer applicants:** Fall 2018 on 5/15/18.

**Transfer application on Common App:** Yes, with Swarthmore supplement. Common App Fee: $60—fee waiver available (no fee for students currently enrolled in a community or junior college).

**SAT/ACT required for transfer applicants:** Yes

**High-school records requirements:** Official final high-school transcript

**High-school records requirements for applicants who completed outside the US:** Same as for domestic transfer students

**Submission requirements for transfer applicants who completed high-school equivalency test:** Official GED

**College transcript requirements:** Official college transcripts for all colleges/universities attended

**Interviews available for transfer applicants:** Yes. On campus; off campus.

## Costs & Financial Aid

**FAFSA code:** 3370

**CSS Profile code:** 2821

**Are internal school financial aid forms required?** No

**Financial aid deadlines for transfer applicants:** Fall 2018: 4/30/18

**Costs for the 2017–2018 year:** Tuition & Fees: $50,822. Room & Board: $14,952.

**Financial aid for transfer students:** Yes

**Guarantees meeting 100% need for transfer students:** Yes

**Need-based aid for transfer students:** Yes

**Merit-based financial aid for transfer students:** Yes. Finalists are selected from all admitted students who have committed to attend Swarthmore.

**Phi Theta Kappa Scholarship:** No

**Reduced or zero tuition fees for low-income students:** No

**Includes loans in financial aid packages:** No

**% of all undergraduates receiving financial aid:** 60%

**% of all undergraduates qualifying for Pell Grants:**
No information provided.

**Average financial aid award for all undergraduate students:**
$45,907

**Funding available for low-income students to visit:** Yes

**Enrollment deposit can be waived for low-income students:**
No information provided.

## Academics

**GPA range for transfer students accepted in 2016–2017:**
No information provided.

**SAT ranges for all students admitted in 2016:** Critical Reading:
645–760. Mathematics: 660–770. Writing: No information
provided.

**ACT composite score range for all students admitted in 2016:**
30–34

**Type of curriculum:** Gen. Ed. requirements

**Type of academic year:** Semester

**Advisors specifically for transfer students:** No

**Credit policy (in their own words):** A minimum of 32 credits
are required for graduation. Credit for work done elsewhere
is awarded to transfer students by the Swarthmore registrar
according to guidelines approved by the faculty.

Swarthmore evaluates all presented transcripts representing
work done at 2-year or 4-year schools, so long as the work
done was considered transferable to a liberal arts bachelor's
degree program on a case-by-case basis. Official transcripts
from previous schools are required, and, to be considered
for credit at Swarthmore, courses must have been graded
straight C or better. Credit for work done elsewhere is always
done on a course-by-course basis. Course descriptions and
occasionally work done by the student facilitate the credit
award process. The Swarthmore registrar only performs
transfer evaluations for admitted transfer students.

**Max number of transfer credits accepted:** 16

**Residency requirement for transfer students:** Yes. Students
must complete at least half of their credits at Swarthmore.

**Study abroad available for transfer students:** Yes. Must fulfill
residency requirements.

**Free tutoring for all students:** Yes

**Writing center for all students:** Yes

**Career support/access to internships and resume prep for
all students:** Yes

**% of undergraduate students hired within 6 months of
graduation:** No information provided.

**Additional resources specifically designated for transfer
and/or non-traditional students:** No

## Housing

No information available on housing for transfer students,
non-traditional students, and families.

## Non-Traditional Admissions

No non-traditional student policies or programs available.

## Military Students

**Military/veteran admissions policy (in their own words):**
Swarthmore College encourages applications from veterans,
military service members, and their dependents. Our registrar,
Martin Warner, is Swarthmore's point of contact for support
services for veterans, military service members, and their
families. He can be contacted at mwarner1@swarthmore.edu
or (610) 328-8299.

The Registrar's Office processes requests for US Veterans
Affairs (VA) education benefits and communicates with the VA
regarding enrollment certification.

**Status considered in admissions:** Yes

**Special admissions process:** No

**Special financial aid:** Yes. The Yellow Ribbon Program.

## DACA/Undocumented Students

**DACA and undocumented admissions policy (in their own
words):** If you are an undocumented or DACA-eligible student,
you will apply to Swarthmore in the same manner as all US
citizens and permanent residents. We evaluate context and
background, so you are encouraged to share your story with
us through the application process. This policy extends to all
first-year as well as transfer students.

If you need assistance to learn more about Swarthmore
College, the admissions process, or financial aid, you can
contact our Director of Access and Programming, Andrew Moe,
at amoe1@swarthmore.edu or (610) 328-7764.

**Admitted:** Yes

**Status considered in admissions:** No

**Special admissions process:** No

**Eligible for institutional financial aid:** Yes. For undocumented
and DACA students, Swarthmore's admissions process is
need-blind. We do not take your financial need or application
for financial aid into account when making the decision
about whether to admit you to the College. Swarthmore
College is committed to meeting 100% of admitted students'
demonstrated financial need, and our aid awards do not
include loans that need to be repaid. We believe all students
should be able to afford a Swarthmore education regardless
of socioeconomic status or ability to pay.

**Specific programs/policies to address needs:** Swarthmore has
declared itself a sanctuary college.

# SYRACUSE UNIVERSITY

**Location:** Syracuse, New York

**Website:** www.syracuse.edu

**Endowment:** $1.2 billion

**Type of School:** Private/Co-ed, Research University

**# of Undergraduate Students:** 15,218

**# of Graduate Students:** 6,752

**Average Class Size:** No information provided.

**School Mission (in their own words):** As a university with the capacity to attract and engage the best scholars from around the world, yet small enough to support a personalized and academically rigorous student experience, Syracuse University faculty and staff support student success by:

- Encouraging global study, experiential learning, interdisciplinary scholarship, creativity, and entrepreneurial endeavors
- Balancing professional studies with an intensive liberal arts education
- Fostering a richly diverse and inclusive community of learning and opportunity
- Promoting a culture of innovation and discovery
- Supporting faculty, staff, and student collaboration in creative activity and research that address emerging opportunities and societal needs
- Maintaining pride in our location and history as a place of access, engagement, innovation, and impact

## Admissions

**Admissions office mailing address:** 900 South Crouse Ave, Syracuse NY 13244

**Admissions office phone:** (315) 443-3611

**Admissions office email:** orange@syr.edu

**# of transfer applications:** Fall 2016 admissions: 1,754

**# of transfer students accepted:** Fall 2016: 840

**Transfer student acceptance rate (2016–2017 academic year):** 47.9%

**Freshman applications received in Fall 2016:** 31,000

**Freshman applications accepted in Fall 2016:** Not provided.

**Acceptance rate for 2016–2017 freshmen:** Not provided.

## Transfer Admissions Process

**Transfer policy (in their own words):** You're considered a transfer student if you've enrolled in a degree program at another college or university and completed at least 12 credit hours. If you have taken college classes without enrolling in a degree program, or will have less than 12 credits when you plan to enroll, you should apply as a first-year student.

**Transfer application deadline:** Fall 2018 deadline is 7/1/18, but we recommend applying earlier because admissions are rolling. Spring 2019 deadline is 11/15/18.

**Acceptances announced to transfer applicants:** Fall 2018 on rolling basis. Spring 2019 on rolling basis.

**Transfer application on Common App:** Yes. Common App Fee: $75. Fee waiver available.

**SAT/ACT required for transfer applicants:** Yes, if applicant has completed fewer than 30 college-level credits

**High-school records requirements:** Official high-school transcript required for those who have completed fewer than 30 college-level credits.

**High-school records requirements for applicants who completed outside the US:** Official academic credentials as well as English translations of the documents

**Submission requirements for transfer applicants who completed high-school equivalency test:** Required for those who have completed fewer than 30 college-level credits.

**College transcript requirements:** Required for all colleges/universities attended.

**Interviews available for transfer applicants:** Yes. Optional. On campus.

**Additional requirements for transfers seeking admissions to arts major:** Yes. School of Art/School of Design/Department of Transmedia: Portfolio required.

**Additional requirements for transfers seeking admissions to engineering major:** Yes. 4 years of college-preparatory mathematics (including pre-calculus and calculus). Laboratory science (including physics). Please submit at least 1 academic recommendation from a math or science teacher.

## Costs & Financial Aid

**FAFSA code:** 2882

**CSS Profile code:** 2823

**Are internal school financial aid forms required?** No

**Financial aid deadlines for transfer applicants:** Fall 2018: 7/1/18. Spring 2019: 11/15/18.

**Costs for the 2017–2018 year:** Tuition & Fees: $46,755. Room & Board: $15,588.

**Financial aid for transfer students:** Yes

**Guarantees meeting 100% need for transfer students:** No

**Need-based aid for transfer students:** Yes. Applicants are considered for financial aid upon submission of application.

**Merit-based financial aid for transfer students:** Yes. All applicants are considered for scholarships by the admissions committee.

**Phi Theta Kappa Scholarship:** Yes, $2,000. Renewable. Details available at http://financialaid.syr.edu/typesofaid/scholarships/su/#Phi Theta Kappa Scholarships.

**Reduced or zero tuition fees for low-income students:** No

**Includes loans in financial aid packages:** Yes

**% of all undergraduates receiving financial aid:** 75%

**% of all undergraduates qualifying for Pell Grants:** 21%

**Average financial aid award for all undergraduate students:** No information provided.

**Funding available for low-income students to visit:** No

**Enrollment deposit can be waived for low-income students:** No information provided.

## Academics

No information available on GPA or standardized testing results for admitted students.

**Type of curriculum:** Gen. Ed. requirements

**Type of academic year:** Semester

**Advisors specifically for transfer students:** No

**Credit policy (in their own words):** A minimum of 120 credit hours are required for a bachelor's degree. 1 unit usually corresponds to 1 hour of lecture or seminar per week per quarter. A minimum grade of C is required in courses accepted for transfer credit from an accredited institution.

**Max number of transfer credits accepted:** 66 from 2-year colleges; 90 from 4-year colleges

**Residency requirement for transfer students:** Yes. Students must take at least 30 credit hours of coursework at SU to qualify for the degree; in most cases, more than 30 credits will be required in order to fulfill degree requirements.

**Study abroad available for transfer students:** Yes. Must meet residency requirements.

**Free tutoring for all students:** Yes

**Writing center for all students:** Yes

**Career support/access to internships and resume prep for all students:** Yes

**% of undergraduate students hired within 6 months of graduation:** No information provided.

**Additional resources specifically designated for transfer and/or non-traditional students:** No

## Housing

**Available for transfer students:** Yes

**Available for non-traditional students:** No

**Guaranteed for transfer students:** No

**Non-traditional students can reside in housing year-round:** N/A

**Family housing available:** No

## Non-Traditional Admissions

**Non-traditional student policy (in their own words):** Syracuse has the University College, which caters specifically to non-traditional students. Part-time students earning a Syracuse University associate's or bachelor's degree through University College may enroll for 11 or fewer credits each semester. Students have the option of taking day, evening, online, or flexible format classes and have numerous choices in programs of study offered by the academic schools and colleges. Curriculums are the same for both part- and full-time undergraduates.

Begun in Fall 2014 and available only through University College is an innovative career-focused degree program—the Bachelor of Professional Studies (B.P.S.). This non-traditional program of study, available fully online or in blended format, designed specifically for working adults, offers a Syracuse University degree, or a certificate, in either Creative Leadership or Knowledge Management. Both B.P.S. programs are expressly designed to prepare students for the demands of the current workplace and job market. An all-University faculty committee oversees the 2 degree programs, including policies and procedures.

**Minimum requirements for degree:**

- At least 120 credits of coursework are required for the B.P.S. degrees.
- To be eligible for graduation, B.P.S. students must attain a minimum GPA of 2.0 in courses taken at Syracuse University.
- Students must earn a GPA of at least 2.0 in courses counted toward completion of their program of study.

**Name of program:** University College

**Program description:** University College is the point of entry to Syracuse University for non-traditional students. University College offers degree programs, certificates, and noncredit courses in a variety of formats to accommodate the busy schedules of part-time students, many of whom juggle work, family, and community responsibilities along with their educational commitments. Traditional classroom courses are offered in the daytime, evenings, and online. Condensed and accelerated classes are also available. University College offers a variety of degree programs, certificates, and noncredit courses in the daytime, evenings, online, and in condensed and accelerated formats.

**Program deadline:** Rolling

**Program admission requirements:**

- Interview
- High-school transcript/GED if graduated within 5 years
- Official transcripts from all colleges/universities attended
- Personal essay

**Program website:** http://parttime.syr.edu

**Program contact person:** Michael Frasciello, Ph.D., Interim Dean

**Program contact info:** (315) 443-5502, mfrascie@syr.edu

## Military/Veteran Students

**Military/veteran admissions policy (in their own words):**
Syracuse University ranks among the nation's top schools for veterans, including being named the #1 Private School for Veterans by the *Military Times*. The support of military-connected scholars is central to the University's mission, and includes commitments to affordability, academic success, and a comfortable fit within the student body. Syracuse University participates in all veterans' education programs and is a Yellow Ribbon school.

**Status considered in admissions:** Yes

**Special admissions process:** Yes. Military/veteran students must fill out a separate application, and there is no fee for their application.

**Special financial aid:** Yes. The Yellow Ribbon Program.

**Specific programs/policies to address needs:** Syracuse has an Office of Veteran and Military Affairs and a Veterans Resource Center. They also have a Student Veterans Lounge. These resources help veterans navigate financial aid, credit transfers, housing, and more.

## DACA/Undocumented Students

**DACA and undocumented admissions policy (in their own words):** These students have to apply as international students because they hold citizenship in another country. However, they do not have to take the TOEFL like international students. Also, the international financial requirement forms are waived for DACA/undocumented students. Note: Students are advised to be honest in their application and state that they hold DACA status or are undocumented to further assure that the financial requirement forms be waived.

**Admitted:** Yes

**Status considered in admissions:** No

**Special admissions process:** No

**Eligible for institutional financial aid:** Yes

**Specific programs/policies to address needs:** No

# Aaron Hudson

**Syracuse University, C'11**
Bachelor's Degree in Information Management and Technology

**LaGuardia Community College, C'08**
Associate's Degree in Network Systems Administration

**Current Employment:** Project Associate, JP Morgan Chase

**Bio:** A Cleveland native and active Syracuse alum, Aaron is passionate about improving college access and building diverse and thriving work environments. Aaron plans to impact recruitment and retention efforts at JP Morgan Chase and link them with his alma mater.

*"Kaplan is the sole reason I am where I am today in life. My Phi Theta Kappa advisor recognized the opportunity and pointed me in the right direction, and I grabbed it. But it was Kaplan that saw that determination and grit within and said . . . he will thrive!*

*As an older student, I was set in my ways and at times stubborn, but I was always open to new discovery and ideas. Kaplan did not disappoint. As my mind expanded, unimaginable doors were opened and barriers destroyed. Kaplan helped me envision a future for myself and my daughter well beyond anything I thought possible. But this is what Kaplan does: helps scholars dream bigger than anything we could fathom.*

*Before visiting Syracuse, I was unsure where I wanted to continue my four-year education, though I had received multiple acceptances. I always tell the story of how Syracuse rolled out that 'orange carpet' for my visit, as this was the first campus where I truly felt at home. I will forever be indebted to the Foundation for recognizing, more so than I did, that I belonged at Syracuse University. Ideas turned to dreams, dreams turned to reality, and now my reality is brighter than ever. I have excelled as a father, in my career, and as a human being. I owe my current and future successes to Kaplan for selecting me for this program and pushing me to be the best person I am meant to be and will continue to become."*

## Leadership Activities

- Veteran, Sgt. Information Systems Coordinator, United States Marine Corps
- Undergraduate Chapter President, Omega Psi Phi Fraternity
- Founding Host, Underground Poetry Spot
- Vice President, Transitional Experience, Syracuse University
- Transfer Mentor Orientation Leader, Syracuse University
- Vice President of Recruitment, Syracuse Chapter of NAACP
- Vice President, Alpha Theta Phi Chapter of Phi Theta Kappa, International Honor Society of Community Colleges
- College Ambassador, LaGuardia Community College
- Resident Host and Poet, Live Poet Society

# Perez Shaw

**Syracuse University, C'17**
Bachelor's Degree in Sport Management

**Kingsborough Community College, C'15**
Associate's Degree in Applied Science: Physical Education, Recreation, and Recreation Therapy with a concentration in Sport Management

**Bio:** In his younger years, Perez remembers walking into the recreational center by his home and being unable to play basketball because the neighborhood gang members had taken over the court. He also remembers attending an affluent high school on the Upper East Side of Manhattan and being unable to afford the monthly membership at the nearby gym. His ultimate goal is to build recreational facilities in inner-city neighborhoods that will provide a bully-free, affordable environment.

*"While my experience at Kingsborough Community College was great, I knew that I needed to challenge myself more. The Kaplan Leadership Foundation enabled me to pursue my dream of attending a four-year institution by eliminating the financial burden. Making the jump from community college to Syracuse was tough at first, but the advising and support available at Kaplan has allowed me to stay on the right path, as my success is their primary concern.*

*As a young black male, transferring to Syracuse has allowed me to not only even the playing field, but also has given me the skills necessary to jump ahead of my competition and increase my chances of having a successful career in sports management. At Syracuse, I've been able to build a solid network, varying from professors who worked at ESPN for 30+ years to executives at NFL, UFC, NBA, and EA Sports. The Sport Management department at SU is top-notch, and I am forever thankful for what Kaplan has done to help me get here."*

## Leadership Activities

- Member, Phi Theta Kappa International Honor Society of Community Colleges
- ASAP, KBCC
- Dean's List, KBCC
- Basketball, KBCC
- Volunteer, Aviator Sports and Events Center
- Program Intern, Kaplan Educational Foundation
- Member, Sports Management Club, SU

# TRINITY COLLEGE

**Location:** Hartford, Connecticut

**Website:** www.trincoll.edu/Pages/default.aspx

**Endowment:** $524 million

**Type of School:** Private/Co-ed, Liberal Arts

**# of Undergraduate Students:** 2,309 (2015–2016)

**# of Graduate Students:** 21 (2015–2016)

**Average Class Size:** No information provided.

**School Mission (in their own words):** Engage. Connect. Transform.

As the preeminent liberal arts college in an urban setting, Trinity College prepares students to be bold, independent thinkers who lead transformative lives.

We engage. We foster critical, reflective engagement with scholarship and the creative arts as well as with one another and the wider world. Our location in Connecticut's capital offers excellent opportunities for engagement beyond the classroom in internships, student research, and community learning.

We connect. We link students, faculty, and staff to form a diverse community of learning. The connections of Hartford and Trinity College engage students as global citizens in the wider world, and a network of devoted alumni provide lifelong opportunities for Trinity graduates.

We transform. We combine the liberal arts with life in a diverse city, enabling students to learn what they love, to build confidence, and to become leaders and innovators. We support all members of our community in achieving their potential and in moving forward with the skills to navigate and transform a dynamic world.

Trinity College is where the liberal arts meet the real world.

## Admissions

**Admissions office mailing address:** 330 Summit St, Hartford CT 06106

**Admissions office phone:** (860) 297-2180

**Admissions office email:** admissions.office@trincoll.edu

**# of transfer applications:** Fall 2016 admissions: 226. Spring 2017 admissions: No information provided.

**# of transfer students accepted:** Fall 2015: 61. Spring 2016: No information provided.

**Transfer student acceptance rate (2015–2016 academic year):** 27%

**Freshman applications received in Fall 2015:** 7,570

**Freshman applications accepted in Fall 2015:** 2,530

**Acceptance rate for 2016–2017 freshmen:** 33%

## Transfer Admissions Process

**Transfer policy (in their own words):** Trinity is a small, highly selective liberal arts college. We recognize that there should be a place for students who, after enrolling at another college or university, want to transfer to Trinity. Accordingly, Trinity admits a limited number of transfer students both for entrance in the fall and at midyear.

The number of openings for transfers varies somewhat from year to year, and several factors can affect the degree of competition for admission. Generally speaking, we suggest that candidates present a postsecondary cumulative grade point average equivalent to a B or better. The application invites candidates to express their reasons for transfer and to elaborate on any pertinent concerns or circumstances.

Who is considered a transfer applicant?

- Applicants who have matriculated at another collegiate institution, regardless of completed work, are considered transfer candidates.
- Applicants who have not matriculated at another collegiate institution but have accumulated a minimum of 4 completed full-credit courses (or the equivalent) are generally considered transfer candidates.

Please note that students may apply as transfer students as early as their first semester in college; however, we recommend that they complete a full year so we can review their college work.

**Transfer admissions contact person:** James Sargent, Assistant Director of Admissions and Coordinator of Transfer Admissions

**Transfer admissions contact info:** james.sargent@trincoll.edu, (860) 297-2180

**Offers transfer-focused admissions events:** No

**Transfer application deadline:** Fall 2018 deadline is 3/1/15. Spring 2019 deadline is 11/1/18.

**Acceptances announced to transfer applicants:** Fall 2018 on 5/1/18. Spring 2019 on 11/30/18.

**Transfer application on Common App:** Yes. Common App fee: $65.

**SAT/ACT required for transfer applicants:** No

**High-school records requirements:** Final high-school transcript

**High-school records requirements for applicants who completed outside the US:** Trinity requires a diploma from and certification by an accredited secondary school. The academic program should consist of at least 16 academic units, typically including the following minimum number of courses: English (4 years), foreign language (3 years), laboratory science (2 years), algebra (2 years), geometry (1 year), and history (2 years).

**Submission requirements for transfer applicants who completed high-school equivalency test:** Official GED results

**College transcript requirements:** Official college transcripts required for all colleges/universities attended

**Interviews available for transfer applicants:** N/A

## Costs & Financial Aid

**FAFSA code:** 1414

**CSS Profile code:** 3899

**Are internal school financial aid forms required?** No

**Financial aid deadlines for transfer applicants:** Fall 2018: 3/1/18. Spring 2019: 11/1/18.

**Costs for the 2017–2018 year:** Tuition & Fees: $54,770. Room & Board: $14,200.

**Financial aid for transfer students:** Yes

**Guarantees meeting 100% need for transfer students:** Yes

**Need-based aid for transfer students:** Yes

**Merit-based financial aid for transfer students:** Yes. Eligible for PTK.

**Phi Theta Kappa Scholarship:** Yes, for the Individualized Degree Program. Award amount varies. Renewable. Details available at www.trincoll.edu/Academics/IDP/IDPFinAid/Pages/PhiThetaKappa.aspx.

**Reduced or zero tuition fees for low-income students:** No information provided.

**Includes loans in financial aid packages:** Yes

**% of all undergraduates receiving financial aid:** 40%

**% of all undergraduates qualifying for Pell Grants:** 10.6% (2015–2016)

**Average financial aid award for all undergraduate students:** $45,223 (2015–2016)

**Funding available for low-income students to visit:** Yes

**Enrollment deposit can be waived for low-income students:** No information provided.

## Academics

**GPA range for transfer students accepted in 2016–2017:** No information provided.

**SAT ranges for all students admitted in 2016:** Critical Reading: 570–670. Mathematics: 580–670. Writing: 580–670.

**ACT composite score range for all students admitted in 2016:** 27–30

**Type of curriculum:** Gen. Ed. requirements

**Type of academic year:** Semester

**Advisors specifically for transfer students:** Yes

**Credit policy (in their own words):** At least 18 course credits earned at Trinity, for a total of 36 including transfer credits, are required for graduation.

Transfer credit to Trinity College is considered from 2 categories of institutions: 1) regionally accredited US institutions of higher education and 2) the liberal arts universities of other countries that are recognized by their appropriate national educational authorities and have been approved by the Trinity College Office of Study Away. The Office of the Registrar evaluates transfer credit and acts on behalf of the Trinity Curriculum Committee in granting final approval for transfer credits. Students must obtain the signature of their faculty adviser on the application for transfer credit, indicating that the students' proposed study plan has been reviewed and recommended for transfer of credit. However, final approval of each course rests with the Office of the Registrar.

Credit is transferred on a course-by-course basis, not on a semester-by-semester basis. Coursework accepted for transfer must parallel Trinity's own course offerings and/or be liberal arts in nature. Courses that primarily focus on the acquisition of technical skills related to professional training, rather than requiring exposure to the bases in literary, philosophical, interpretive, or scientific understandings fundamental to the liberal arts, will not be granted credit. Examples of non–liberal arts courses that are not transferable include, but are not limited to, business, management, marketing, advertising, public relations, crafts, public speaking, cooking, interior decorating, fashion design, and professionally oriented courses in law and medicine. Examples of other courses that are not transferable to the College include English as a second language, credit by examination, CLEP (College Level Examination Program) credit, internships without a sufficient academic component, ROTC courses, military courses, and correspondence courses. Courses taken online, via Distance Education, Internet, or through other electronic means of delivery are not accepted for transfer. Credit will be removed for any course already transferred if the College becomes aware that it was taken online, via Distance Education, Internet, or other electronic means of delivery.

Coursework that duplicates other work already credited at Trinity may not be transferred. Lower-level courses in mathematics and languages cannot be transferred subsequent to the crediting of higher-level courses in the same discipline.

Credit is not awarded for courses taken to fulfill requirements for either secondary-school graduation or graduate or professional degrees.

Transfer credit will not be entered onto the student's record until all questions concerning particular courses have been resolved. Written notice that transfer credit has been posted will be provided to each student each time credit is posted for him or her by the Office of the Registrar. After credit has been transferred to a student's record at Trinity, such credit may not be removed unless the student later gains credit for a Trinity course that duplicates the earlier credit. The faculty reserves the right to examine a student on any work presented for transfer before allowing credit. A student who wishes to receive credit for work completed through direct enrollment in a foreign college or university for which Trinity approves enrollment only through the sponsorship of an American institution or program must successfully petition the Office of Study Away. Please see the Office of Study Away for further details.

**Max number of transfer credits accepted:** 18

**Residency requirement for transfer students:** Yes. At least 18 credits must be earned at Trinity.

**Study abroad available for transfer students:** Yes. Still need to fulfill residency requirement.

**Free tutoring for all students:** Yes

**Writing center for all students:** Yes

**Career support/access to internships and resume prep for all students:** Yes

**% of undergraduate students hired within 6 months of graduation:** No information provided.

**Additional resources specifically designated for transfer and/or non-traditional students:** No

## Housing

No information provided on housing policies for transfer students, non-traditional students, or students with families.

## Non-Traditional Admissions

**Name of program:** Individualized Degree Program (IDP)

**Program description:** Program that allows adult learners to complete their bachelor's degree. Applicants must meet the following criteria: We welcome all applicants at least 23 years old or self-supporting, and our community of non-traditional students includes veterans, second bachelor's degree candidates, and international students. An outstanding liberal arts and sciences education that will challenge you, excite you, and prepare you for professional advancement, graduate study, and new life directions.

Support and services for adult learners, including full- or part-time study, a flexible timeframe for degree completion, mentoring and advising, IDP-dedicated staff members, and a customized admissions and transfer credit process.

The program is affordable due to 2 key factors: course-based tuition and need-based financial aid that covers both tuition and expenses.

The program has a strong community within IDP and across Trinity. While IDP students are very diverse, they share a common bond and at the same time enjoy mixing with traditional-age students in classes and projects.

The program's alumni pursue many professional fields, including education, financial services, law, government and public policy, information technology, social services, and medical research. A significant proportion go on to graduate study and earn advanced professional or academic degrees.

**Program deadline:** Fall 2018: 4/15/18. Spring 2018: 12/11/18.

**Program admission requirements:** Application, personal essay, official college transcript(s), official high-school transcript or GED, 2 letters of recommendation

**Program website:** www.trincoll.edu/Academics/IDP/Pages/default.aspx

**Program contact person:** Roberta Rogers, IDP Assistant Director

**Program contact info:** roberta.rogers@trincoll.edu, (860) 297-2150

## Military/Veteran Students

**Military/veteran admissions policy (in their own words):** These students apply either as freshmen or transfer students based on the amount of credits they have or if they have attended a higher institution before Trinity.

**Status considered in admissions:** No

**Special admissions process:** Yes. Military/veteran students need to apply through the Individualized Degree Program (see above).

**Special financial aid:** Yes. The Yellow Ribbon Program.

**Specific programs/policies to address needs:** N/A

## DACA/Undocumented Students

**DACA and undocumented admissions policy (in their own words):** These students are considered international students for both the admissions and the financial aid application process.

# TUFTS UNIVERSITY

**Location:** Medford, Massachusetts

**Website:** www.tufts.edu

**Endowment:** $1.6 billion

**Type of School:** Private/Co-ed, Research University

**# of Undergraduate Students:** 5,290

**# of Graduate Students:** 5,847

**Average Class Size:** 20

**School Mission (in their own words):** Tufts is a student-centered research university dedicated to the creation and application of knowledge. We are committed to providing transformative experiences for students and faculty in an inclusive and collaborative environment where creative scholars generate bold ideas, innovate in the face of complex challenges, and distinguish themselves as active citizens of the world.

## Admissions

**Admissions office mailing address:** 419 Boston Ave, Medford MA 02155

**Admissions office phone:** (617) 627-3170

**Admissions office email:** undergraduate.admissions@tufts.edu

**# of transfer applications:** Fall 2016 admissions: 1,009. Spring 2017 admissions: N/A.

**# of transfer students accepted:** Fall 2016: 56. Spring 2017: N/A.

**Transfer student acceptance rate (2016–2017 academic year):** 5.6%

**Freshman applications received in Fall 2016:** 20,223

**Freshman applications accepted in Fall 2016:** 2,889

**Acceptance rate for 2016–2017 freshmen:** 14.3%

## Transfer Admissions Process

**Transfer policy (in their own words):** Tufts welcomes transfer applicants to the School of Arts and Sciences, the School of Engineering, and the School of the Museum of Fine Arts at Tufts who are in good academic and disciplinary standing at accredited 2- and 4-year institutions. To be considered for transfer admission, a candidate needs to have completed at least 1 year of college study by the time he or she plans to enroll at Tufts. Applicants to the School of Engineering must meet a designated level of curriculum completion to be considered for admission.

In order to receive a Tufts degree, students must be fully enrolled members of the Tufts community for at least 2 years. Therefore, students who have already earned more than 2 years' worth of full-time college credit are discouraged from applying to Tufts.

**Transfer admissions contact person:** N/A

**Transfer admissions contact info:** transfer.admissions@ase.tufts.edu

**Offers transfer-focused admissions events:** Yes. Transfer Q&A sessions in December and January.

**Transfer application deadline:** Fall 2018 deadline is 3/15/18.

**Acceptances announced to transfer applicants:** Fall 2018 on 5/15/18.

**Transfer application on Common App:** Yes, with Tufts writing supplement. Common App fee: $75.

**SAT/ACT required for transfer applicants:** Yes

**High-school records requirements:** Official high-school transcript

**High-school records requirements for applicants who completed outside the US:** Same as for transfer students

**Submission requirements for transfer applicants who completed high-school equivalency test:** Official GED results

**College transcript requirements:** Official college transcripts

**Interviews available for transfer applicants:** No

**Additional requirements for transfers seeking admissions to arts major:** Yes. Submit 15–20 images of recent work and/or up to 10 minutes of time-based work. Allowed media types: images (up to 10MB each); video (up to 500MB each); audio (up to 60MB each); PDFs (up to 20MB each); 3D models; external media from YouTube, Vimeo, and SoundCloud.

**Additional requirements for transfers seeking admissions to engineering major:** Yes. For the School of Engineering, applicants for sophomore transfer need at least 2 semesters of calculus or higher level math and 2 semesters of calculus-based physics or chemistry at the time of matriculation. Applicants for junior transfer to the School of Engineering need 2 years of coursework at the time of matriculation that completes the introductory coursework for engineering and must be making progress toward completing the foundation requirements for their intended major.

## Costs & Financial Aid

**FAFSA code:** 2219

**CSS Profile code:** 3901

**Are internal school financial aid forms required?** No

**Financial aid deadlines for transfer applicants:** Fall 2018: 3/1/18

**Costs for the 2017–2018 year:** Tuition & Fees: $54,318. Room & Board: $14,054.

**Financial aid for transfer students:** Yes

**Guarantees meeting 100% need for transfer students:** Yes

**Need-based aid for transfer students:** Yes

**Merit-based financial aid for transfer students:** No

**Phi Theta Kappa Scholarship:** No

**Reduced or zero tuition fees for low-income students:** No

**Includes loans in financial aid packages:** Yes

**% of all undergraduates receiving financial aid:** 43% (2015–2016)

**% of all undergraduates qualifying for Pell Grants:** 12% (2014–2015)

**Average financial aid award for all undergraduate students:** $43,331

**Funding available for low-income students to visit:** No information provided.

**Enrollment deposit can be waived for low-income students:** No

## Academics

**GPA range for transfer students accepted in 2016–2017:** No information provided.

**SAT ranges for all students admitted in 2016:** Critical Reading: 680–750. Mathematics: 690–770. Writing: 680–760.

**ACT composite score range for all students admitted in 2016:** 31–34

**Type of curriculum:** Gen. Ed. requirements

**Type of academic year:** Semester

**Advisors specifically for transfer students:** Yes

**Credit policy (in their own words):** At Tufts, the University's academic departments authorize transfer credit in their particular disciplines. The Office of Undergraduate Admissions does not determine transfer of credit for accepted or enrolling students.

Upon matriculating to Tufts, newly enrolled transfer students petition the necessary academic departments for transfer credit. During each transfer orientation program in September, a transfer of credit meeting is held, allowing enrolling transfer students to meet with faculty from the academic departments to discuss transfer credit. Please be aware that only courses earned with a grade of C– or better are eligible to receive credit from Tufts. You can also submit a request for credit transfer electronically through the student services web center once you have enrolled.

In Tufts's course credit system, each semester-long course equals 1 credit. Students enrolled in the School of Arts and Sciences need 34 semester courses (or credits) to graduate; students in the School of Engineering need 38. Because of the wide variety of academic schedules and course loads at colleges and universities in the United States and abroad, Tufts does not automatically transfer credit on a course-for-course basis. Students may only transfer the equivalent of 17 courses in liberal arts or 19 courses in engineering. Typically, courses similar to those offered at Tufts will receive

transfer credit; however, the actual transfer of credit is the responsibility of the Tufts faculty. If your current institution employs a different credit system, then the number of credits you receive at Tufts may not be equal to the number of credits given at the other institution. Where semester hours are used, 1 3- or 4-semester-hour course equals 1 Tufts credit, and 1 2-semester hour course equals 1/2 Tufts credit. Where quarter hours are used, 1 Tufts credit equals 5.25 quarter hours.

Read more at http://admissions.tufts.edu/apply/transfer-students/transfer-of-credit.

**Max number of transfer credits accepted:** 17 for Arts & Sciences; 19 for School of Engineering

**Residency requirement for transfer students:** Yes. 17 for Arts & Sciences; 19 for School of Engineering.

**Study abroad available for transfer students:** Yes. Must fulfill residency requirements.

**Free tutoring for all students:** Yes

**Writing center for all students:** Yes

**Career support/access to internships and resume prep for all students:** Yes

**% of undergraduate students hired within 6 months of graduation:** No information provided.

**Additional resources specifically designated for transfer and/or non-traditional students:** No

## Housing

**Available for transfer students:** No

**Available for non-traditional students:** No

**Guaranteed for transfer students:** No

**Non-traditional students can reside in housing year-round:** N/A

**Family housing available:** No

## Non-Traditional Admissions

**Non-traditional student policy (in their own words):** Tufts University has a specific program in order to serve these students. The following is the description of the program.

**Name of program:** Resumed Education for Adult Learning (REAL)

**Program description:** The REAL program is designed for individuals who are: 24 years of age or older, parents, married, currently serving in the US Armed Forces, or veterans. The REAL program was established in 1970. Originally designed for women who had not had the opportunity to attend college, or who had interrupted their education to raise families, the program offered these women a chance to advance in their careers through attaining a college degree from a selective university. In 1976, the program broadened to welcome men as well.

At a time when most other programs denied institutional funds for financial aid to adult students, segregated them in special degree programs, and ignored the unique needs of adults returning to or beginning a college education, Tufts provided financial aid, enrolled its adult students in the regular undergraduate program, and provided resources to help meet their academic needs.

Today, the program continues this tradition of serving the needs of adult students. Each of the 60 or so REAL students receives individual attention from admission to graduation.

The power of the REAL program lies in the support its students receive. Beginning with the admissions process and continuing through graduation, REAL students benefit from guidance specifically tailored for adult learners.

The REAL program is open to adults at least 24 years old who are seeking a bachelor's degree. Applicants should have some college experience, including at least 2 courses taken at either a 2- or 4-year institution within the last 5 years.

Read more at https://students.tufts.edu/academic-advice-and-support/real-program.

**Program deadline:** Spring 2018: 11/1/17. Fall 2018: 3/15/18.

**Program admission requirements:** Application, all official college transcripts, and 2 recommendations

**Program website:** http://admissions.tufts.edu/apply/transfer-students/real-application

**Program contact info:** Dean Jean Herbert (617) 627-2000, real.admissions@tufts.edu

## Military/Veteran Students

**Military/veteran admissions policy (in their own words):**
Military/veteran students follow the same application process as other students. The amount of credits that these students have will determine whether they apply as freshmen or transfer students.

Furthermore, in order to support these students, Tufts participates in the Yellow Ribbon Program.

**Status considered in admissions:** No

**Special admissions process:** Yes. Military applicants should apply to the REAL program (see above).

**Special financial aid:** Yes. The Yellow Ribbon Program.

**Specific programs/policies to address needs:** N/A

## DACA/Undocumented Students

**DACA and undocumented admissions policy (in their own words):** Tufts's core values include a commitment to equal opportunity, inclusion, accessibility, and diversity. Therefore, Tufts welcomes all undergraduate applicants regardless of citizenship status. Undocumented students, with or without Deferred Action for Childhood Arrivals (DACA), who apply to Tufts are treated identically to any other US citizen or permanent resident.

Tufts meets 100% of the demonstrated need of all admitted students. While procedures for financial aid vary between domestic and international applicants, undocumented students are considered for domestic, need-based financial aid like any other US citizen or permanent resident. Please note that health insurance is required for all Tufts students, and this can be provided by Tufts as part of your financial aid package.

Read more at http://admissions.tufts.edu/apply/first-year-students/undocumented-students.

**Admitted:** Yes

**Status considered in admissions:** No

**Special admissions process:** No

**Eligible for institutional financial aid:** Yes DACA/undocumented students are considered domestic students. Tufts makes up for any lack of federal/state aid with institutional aid.

**Specific programs/policies to address needs:** Yes. Tufts has a list of academic, community, and legal resources for undocumented students.

# TUSKEGEE UNIVERSITY

**Location:** Tuskegee, Alabama

**Website:** www.tuskegee.edu

**Endowment:** $112 million

**Type of School:** Private/Co-ed, Liberal Arts

**# of Undergraduate Students:** 2,485

**# of Graduate Students:** 510

**Average Class Size:** No information provided.

**School Mission (in their own words):** Tuskegee University is a national, independent, and state-related institution of higher learning that is located in the State of Alabama. The University has distinctive strengths in the sciences, architecture, business, engineering, health, and other professions, all structured on solid foundations in the liberal arts. In addition, the University's programs focus on nurturing the development of high-order intellectual and moral qualities among students and stress the connection between education and the highly trained leadership Americans need in general, especially for the workforce of the 21st century and beyond. The results we seek are students whose technical, scientific, and professional prowess has been not only rigorously honed, but also sensitively oriented in ways that produce public-spirited graduates who are both competent and morally committed to public service with integrity and excellence.

## Admissions

**Admissions office mailing address:** 1200 W Montgomery Rd, Tuskegee AL 36088

**Admissions office phone:** (800) 622-6531

**Admissions office email:** admissions@tuskegee.edu

No information provided on freshman or transfer admissions.

## Transfer Admissions Process

**Transfer policy (in their own words):** A transfer student is a person admitted/applying to Tuskegee University after attending another institution of higher learning. A student who attends summer school immediately after receiving a high-school diploma and before enrolling at Tuskegee University will not be considered a transfer student. If the student expects to transfer college credit hours completed during the summer period prior to enrolling in Tuskegee University, a transcript must be submitted to the registrar by September and the student must also inform their advisor that transfer credit is being requested. Also required are transcripts from various colleges you have attended.

Applications will not be evaluated until the application itself and all required materials are received. A transfer student must indicate on the application for admission all previous colleges or universities attended. A student who has registered in other colleges and/or universities may not disregard their record in such institutions and make application for admission to Tuskegee University solely on the basis of the high-school record. Any student who does so is subject to suspension from the University, and transfer credit will be denied.

**Transfer admissions contact person:** N/A

**Transfer admissions contact info:** admissions@tuskegee.edu

**Offers transfer-focused admissions events:** N/A

**Transfer application deadline:** Fall 2018 deadline is 3/1/18.

**Acceptances announced to transfer applicants:** Fall 2018 on rolling basis.

**Transfer application on Common App:** Yes. Common App fee: $25.

**SAT/ACT required for transfer applicants:** Yes

**High-school records requirements:** Official WES translated high-school transcript(s)

**High-school records requirements for applicants who completed outside the US:** Same as for transfer students

**Submission requirements for transfer applicants who completed high-school equivalency test:** Official GED results

**College transcript requirements:** Official transcripts for all US colleges or universities attended

**Interviews available for transfer applicants:** No

## Costs & Financial Aid

**FAFSA code:** 1050

**CSS Profile code:** N/A

**Are internal school financial aid forms required?** No

**Financial aid deadlines for transfer applicants:** Fall 2018: 3/31/18

**Costs for the 2017–2018 year:** Tuition & Fees: $21,470. Room & Board: $9,104.

**Financial aid for transfer students:** Yes

**Guarantees meeting 100% need for transfer students:** No

**Need-based aid for transfer students:** Yes

**Merit-based financial aid for transfer students:** Yes

**Phi Theta Kappa Scholarship:** No

**Reduced or zero tuition fees for low-income students:** No

**Includes loans in financial aid packages:** Yes

**% of all undergraduates receiving financial aid:** 72

**% of all undergraduates qualifying for Pell Grants:** No information provided.

**Average financial aid award for all undergraduate students:** No information provided.

**Funding available for low-income students to visit:** No

**Enrollment deposit can be waived for low-income students:** No

## Academics

No information provided on GPA or standardized testing.

**Type of curriculum:** Gen. Ed. requirements

**Type of academic year:** Semester

**Advisors specifically for transfer students:** No information provided.

**Credit policy (in their own words):** A student who transfers to Tuskegee University from other colleges and universities is governed by the following specific requirements and procedures:

1. A transfer student must satisfy the general orientation requirement. If the transfer student transfers at least 30 semester hours, only 1 semester of orientation is required; otherwise, 2 semesters of orientation must be taken.

2. A transfer student who has not received transfer credit for mathematics, English, and reading, and who does not present satisfactory records on tests specified by the University, must take Placement Examinations prescribed before enrolling in any courses.

3. A transfer student must satisfy physical education requirements.

4. A transfer student must be eligible to reenter the institution last attended when application for admission to Tuskegee University is submitted.

5. A student desiring to transfer to Tuskegee University must be able to furnish the following:

   a. A letter of good standing from the institution last attended.

   b. A certificate of high-school work covering the Tuskegee University requirements for admission.

   c. An official transcript of the work done in all institutions prior to application for admission to Tuskegee. This transcript should reach the Admissions Office of Tuskegee University at least 1 month before the date the candidate expects to enroll. If possible, a marked catalog showing courses referred to in the transcript presented should be submitted.

   d. A cumulative grade point average that meets at least the minimum academic retention level set by Tuskegee University as defined under the section "Probation, Suspension, and Dismissal" found here: www.tuskegee.edu/admissions-aid/admission-criteria/criteria-for-transfer-students.

6. Credit for courses transferred to Tuskegee University is awarded under the normal conditions prevailing in institutions of higher education:

   a. The courses accepted and the number of hours completed determine the classification of a transfer student.

   b. Transfer credit is given only for courses approved by the dean of the school in which the student applies for admission. Transfer credit will be awarded on a course-by-course basis. Courses in which students earned D grades will not be considered for transfer credit.

   c. Credit toward graduation is given only for courses that have been approved for transfer by the dean. The maximum transfer credit allowed to meet degree requirements will not exceed 80 hours.

   d. Courses taken on a pass/fail basis will not be considered for transfer.

   e. Courses in which credit was not awarded for the degree will not be considered for transfer credit.

7. A student who wishes to apply for financial assistance should request each postsecondary institution attended to forward an official financial aid transcript to the Tuskegee University Office of Financial Aid Services.

**Free tutoring for all students:** Yes

**Writing center for all students:** Yes

**Career support/access to internships and resume prep for all students:** Yes

**% of undergraduate students hired within 6 months of graduation:** No information provided.

**Additional resources specifically designated for transfer and/or non-traditional students:** No

## Housing

**Available for transfer students:** Yes

**Available for non-traditional students:** No information provided.

**Guaranteed for transfer students:** No information provided.

**Non-traditional students can reside in housing year-round:** N/A

**Family housing available:** Yes

## Non-Traditional Admissions

No non-traditional student policies or programs available.

## Military/Veteran Students

**Military/veteran admissions policy (in their own words):** Military/veteran students follow the same application process as other students. The amount of credits that these students have will determine whether they apply as freshmen or transfer students.

**Status considered in admissions:** No

**Special admissions process:** No

**Special financial aid:** Yes. The Yellow Ribbon Program.

**Specific programs/policies to address needs:** The Veterans Affairs Office serves as liaison between veteran students enrolled at Tuskegee University and the Department of Veterans Affairs. Counseling and support services are provided to address unique characteristic needs and problems of veteran students, dependents, and National Guard/reserve members. Newly enrolled veterans, widows of veterans, children of disabled or deceased veterans, and reservists eligible for educational benefits should report to the Office of the Dean of Students, located in the Old Administration Building, Room 100 F.

## DACA/Undocumented Students

No DACA and undocumented student policies or programs available.

# UNION COLLEGE

**Location:** Schenectady, New York

**Website:** www.union.edu

**Endowment:** $385.2 million

**Type of School:** Private/Co-ed, Liberal Arts

**# of Undergraduate Students:** 2,269

**# of Graduate Students:** 0

**Average Class Size:** No information provided.

**School Mission (in their own words):** Union College, founded in 1795, is a scholarly community dedicated to shaping the future and understanding the past. Faculty, staff, and administrators welcome diverse and talented students into our community, work closely with them to provide a broad and deep education, and guide them in finding and cultivating their passions. We do this with a wide range of disciplines and interdisciplinary programs in the liberal arts and engineering, as well as academic, athletic, cultural, and social activities, including opportunities to study abroad and to participate in undergraduate research and community service. We develop in our students the analytic and reflective abilities needed to become engaged, innovative, and ethical contributors to an increasingly diverse, global, and technologically complex society.

## Admissions

**Admissions office mailing address:** 807 Union St, Schenectady NY 12308

**Admissions office phone:** (518) 388-6112

**Admissions office email:** admissions@union.edu

**# of transfer applications:** Fall 2016 admissions: 190. Spring 2017 admissions: N/A.

**# of transfer students accepted:** Fall 2016: 67. Spring 2017: N/A.

**Transfer student acceptance rate (2016–2017 academic year):** 35.3%

**Freshman applications received in Fall 2016:** 6,648

**Freshman applications accepted in Fall 2016:** 2,453

**Acceptance rate for 2016–2017 freshmen:** 36.9%

## Transfer Admissions Process

**Transfer policy (in their own words):** Successful transfer applicants present a 3.0 grade point average (on a 4.0 scale) in at least 1 semester of full-time academic work in courses comparable to those offered at Union College. Consideration is also given to recommendations and personal qualities. In particular, we look for students who can participate enthusiastically and constructively in the life of the College.

Read more at www.union.edu/admissions/apply/transfer.

**Transfer admissions contact person:** Ann Fleming Brown, Director of Admissions

**Transfer admissions contact info:** browna@union.edu, (518) 388-6581

**Offers transfer-focused admissions events:** No

**Transfer application deadline:** Fall 2018 deadline is 4/15/18. Spring 2019 deadline is 11/1/18.

**Acceptances announced to transfer applicants:** Fall 2018 on 5/15/18. Spring 2019 on 12/1/18.

**Transfer application on Common App:** Yes. Common App fee: $0.

**SAT/ACT required for transfer applicants:** No

**High-school records requirements:** Official high-school transcript(s)

**High-school records requirements for applicants who completed outside the US:** Official secondary-school transcript(s) and official exam scores where applicable

**Submission requirements for transfer applicants who completed high-school equivalency test:** Submit directly from the GED testing to the school.

**College transcript requirements:** Official transcripts from all colleges and universities attended

**Interviews available for transfer applicants:** Optional. On campus.

## Costs & Financial Aid

**FAFSA code:** 2889

**CSS Profile code:** 2920

**Are internal school financial aid forms required?** No

**Financial aid deadlines for transfer applicants:** Fall 2018: 4/15/18. Spring 2019: 11/1/18.

**Costs for the 2017–2018 year:** Tuition & Fees: $51,696. Room & Board: $12,678.

**Financial aid for transfer students:** Yes

**Guarantees meeting 100% need for transfer students:** No

**Need-based aid for transfer students:** Yes. Fill out financial aid forms.

**Merit-based financial aid for transfer students:** Yes. All admitted students are considered for merit aid through the admissions process. No separate applications are required. Merit awards are offered to only a select few.

**Phi Theta Kappa Scholarship:** No

**Reduced or zero tuition fees for low-income students:** Yes

**Includes loans in financial aid packages:** Yes

**% of all undergraduates receiving financial aid:** 60%

**% of all undergraduates qualifying for Pell Grants:**
No information provided.

**Average financial aid award for all undergraduate students:**
$41,663

**Funding available for low-income students to visit:** N/A

**Enrollment deposit can be waived for low-income students:**
No information provided.

## Academics

**GPA range for transfer students accepted in 2016–2017:**
At least 3.0

**SAT ranges for all students admitted in 2016:** Critical Reading:
610–680. Mathematics: 630–720. Writing: 600–680.

**ACT composite score range for all students admitted in 2016:**
29–32

**Recommended completed level of math for transfer
applicants:** Pre-calculus

**Recommended completed level of English for transfer
applicants:** Intro to literature

**Type of curriculum:** Gen. Ed. requirements

**Type of academic year:** Semester

**Advisors specifically for transfer students:** No information
provided.

**Credit policy (in their own words):** Transfer credit decisions
are made by the Transfer Coordinators, the Dean of Studies,
and faculty members, who work together to determine which
courses will transfer from other institutions. Courses in
the liberal arts, sciences, and engineering that are roughly
comparable to courses taught at Union are usually awarded
credit. Credit is only given for courses in which a student has
earned a C or better.

Union accepts a maximum of 2 years' worth of credit (about
60 credits from a semester school) or the equivalent of 18
Union College courses. Union also does have a maximum limit
for considering applicants: once a student has completed
more than 4 full years of college-level work, they are no
longer eligible to transfer. Thus, students who already have
a bachelor's degree would not be eligible applicants.

**Max number of transfer credits accepted:** 18

**Residency requirement for transfer students:** Yes. Minimum of
18 credits must be completed at Union College.

**Study abroad available for transfer students:** Yes. Must fulfill
residency requirements.

**Free tutoring for all students:** Yes

**Writing center for all students:** Yes

**Career support/access to internships and resume prep for
all students:** Yes

**% of undergraduate students hired within 6 months of
graduation:** N/A

**Additional resources specifically designated for transfer
and/or non-traditional students:** N/A

## Housing

**Available for transfer students:** Yes

**Available for non-traditional students:** Yes

**Guaranteed for transfer students:** No

**Non-traditional students can reside in housing year-round:**
No

**Family housing available:** Yes

## Non-Traditional Admissions

No non-traditional student policies or programs available.

## Military/Veteran Students

**Military/veteran admissions policy (in their own words):**
Union College is a proud participant in the Yellow Ribbon
Program and its commitment to provide educational
opportunities and resources for US veterans. Congress
passed the Post 9-11 GI Bill to enable affordability for eligible
participants at public and private colleges and universities
as well as other educational programs. In some cases, the
resources provided by the Veterans Administration combined
with the Union College award enable the qualified applicants
to enroll at Union at minimal cost.

As a participant in the Yellow Ribbon program, qualified
applicants must self-identify as Yellow Ribbon eligible on their
admission application. Union College will fund up to 4 Yellow
Ribbon awards for the 2017/18 academic year. These awards
are granted on a first come, first served basis. Qualified
veterans will receive $30,685 (2017/18) in Union Scholarship,
which when combined with the Veterans Administration
assistance, will cover the cost of tuition and fees. Please note
that eligibility for Yellow Ribbon is limited to applicants who
are eligible at the 100% level.

**Status considered in admissions:** Yes

**Special admissions process:** No

**Special financial aid:** Yes. The Yellow Ribbon Program.

**Specific programs/policies to address needs:** N/A

## DACA/Undocumented Students

No DACA and undocumented student policies or programs
available.

# UNITED STATES MILITARY ACADEMY

**Location:** West Point, New York

**Website:** www.westpoint.edu/SitePages/Home.aspx

**Endowment:** $313.8 million (2015)

**Type of School:** Co-ed, Military

**# of Undergraduate Students:** 4,414 (2014–2015)

**# of Graduate Students:** 0

**Average Class Size:** 20 or fewer

**School Mission (in their own words):** To educate, train, and inspire the Corps of Cadets so that each graduate is a commissioned leader of character committed to the values of Duty, Honor, Country and prepared for a career of professional excellence and service to the Nation as an officer in the United States Army.

## Admissions

**Admissions office mailing address:** 606 Thayer Rd, West Point NY 10996

**Admissions office phone:** (845) 938-4041

**Admissions office email:** admissions-info@usma.edu

**Freshman applications received in Fall 2016:** 14,977

**Freshman applications accepted in Fall 2016:** 1,418

**Acceptance rate for 2016–2017 freshmen:** 9.5%

## Transfer Admissions Process

**Transfer policy (in their own words):** Students in college or with previous college credit may apply to West Point if they meet the basic requirements. However, those students still enter West Point as plebes (freshmen) and must complete the 4-year program.

No separate transfer admissions process. All transfers must complete the same admissions process as freshman.

## Costs & Financial Aid

**FAFSA code:** N/A

**CSS Profile code:** N/A

**Are internal school financial aid forms required?** N/A

**Financial aid deadlines for transfer applicants:** Fall 2018: N/A. Spring 2019: N/A.

**Costs for the 2017–2018 year:** Tuition & Fees: $0. Room & Board: $0.

**Financial aid for transfer students:** N/A

**Guarantees meeting 100% need for transfer students:** Yes

**Need-based aid for transfer students:** N/A

**Merit-based financial aid for transfer students:** N/A

**Phi Theta Kappa Scholarship:** N/A

**Reduced or zero tuition fees for low-income students:** Yes

**Includes loans in financial aid packages:** No

**% of all undergraduates receiving financial aid:** 100%

**% of all undergraduates qualifying for Pell Grants:** 0%

**Average financial aid award for all undergraduate students:** Full cost

**Funding available for low-income students to visit:** No

**Enrollment deposit can be waived for low-income students:** No

## Academics

**GPA range for transfer students accepted in 2016–2017:** N/A

**SAT ranges for all students admitted in 2016:** Critical Reading: 570–690. Mathematics: 590–700. Writing: 550–660.

**ACT composite score range for all students admitted in 2016:** 26–31

**Type of curriculum:** Other:
- The Academic Program
- The Physical Program
- The Military Program

**Type of academic year:** Semester

**Advisors specifically for transfer students:** N/A

**Credit policy:** There is no transfer credit policy for this school.

**Max number of transfer credits accepted:** 0

**Residency requirement for transfer students:** Yes. A student must complete all 4 years at West Point. No transfer credit is allowed.

**Study abroad available for transfer students:** Yes

**Free tutoring for all students:** Yes

**Writing center for all students:** Yes

**Career support/access to internships and resume prep for all students:** Yes. Upon graduation, you will be commissioned as a second lieutenant in the Army and serve for 5 years on active duty (if you choose to depart the Army after 5 years, you will be required to serve 3 years in the Inactive Ready Reserve [IRR]).

**% of undergraduate students hired within 6 months of graduation:** 100%

**Additional resources specifically designated for transfer and/or non-traditional students:** No

## Housing

Housing is provided for all students, but West Point does not accept non-traditional students.

## Non-Traditional Admissions

No non-traditional student policies or programs available.

## Military/Veteran Students

**Military/veteran admissions policy:** Soldiers who are currently serving in an Active Duty, Reserve, or National Guard capacity are encouraged to apply to West Point to further their education. West Point is committed to helping qualified soldiers reach their full potentials and secure commissions in the Regular Army.

**Status considered in admissions:** N/A

**Special admissions process:** No. The application steps are the same for soldiers and civilians who apply. However, soldiers can obtain a nomination from their company commanders and are automatically considered for the Preparatory School if not directly admitted to West Point. For more information, see here: www.usma.edu/admissions/SitePages/FAQ_Soldiers.aspx.

**Special financial aid:** N/A

**Specific programs/policies to address needs:** You will receive pay at your current enlistment grade (Regular Army soldiers only). The time at USMAPS counts as time in service, too. At West Point, you receive cadet pay, but your time at West Point is not counted as time in service. Also, every year they work with soldiers who are forward deployed. Many of these areas have education centers and medical facilities. You still can complete the admissions process while deployed. It is imperative to start early and do as much as possible while in garrison.

## DACA/Undocumented Students

No DACA and undocumented student policies or programs available.

# UNITED STATES NAVAL ACADEMY

**Location:** Annapolis, Maryland

**Website:** www.usna.edu/homepage.php

**Endowment:** No information provided.

**Type of School:** Public/Co-ed, Military

**# of Undergraduate Students:** 4,525

**# of Graduate Students:** 0

**Average Class Size:** 20 or less

**School Mission (in their own words):** To develop midshipmen morally, mentally, and physically and to imbue them with the highest ideals of duty, honor, and loyalty in order to graduate leaders who are dedicated to a career of naval service and have potential for future development in mind and character to assume the highest responsibilities of command, citizenship, and government.

## Admissions

**Admissions office mailing address:** 121 Blake Rd, Annapolis MD 21402

**Admissions office phone:** (410) 293-1858

**Admissions office contact page:** www.usna.edu/Admissions/Contact-Admissions-by-Email.php

**Freshman applications received in Fall 2016:** 17,043

**Freshman applications accepted in Fall 2016:** 1,355

**Acceptance rate for 2016–2017 freshmen:** 8%

## Transfer Admissions Process

**Transfer policy (in their own words):** The Academy accepts students from other colleges as long as they meet their age requirements, but they still have to attend the Academy for 4 years.

The Academy's age requirement is as follows: You must be at least 17 years of age and must not have passed your 23rd birthday on July 1 of the year of admission.

No separate transfer admissions process. All transfers must complete the same admissions process as freshman.

## Costs & Financial Aid

**FAFSA code:** N/A

**CSS Profile code:** 0

**Are internal school financial aid forms required?** N/A

**Financial aid deadlines for transfer applicants:** Fall 2018: N/A. Spring 2019: N/A.

**Costs for the 2017–2018 year:** Tuition & Fees: $0. Room & Board: $0.

**Financial aid for transfer students:** N/A

**Guarantees meeting 100% need for transfer students:** Yes

**Need-based aid for transfer students:** N/A

**Merit-based financial aid for transfer students:** N/A

**Phi Theta Kappa Scholarship:** N/A

**Reduced or zero tuition fees for low-income students:** Yes

**Includes loans in financial aid packages:** No

**% of all undergraduates receiving financial aid:** 100%

**% of all undergraduates qualifying for Pell Grants:** 0%

**Average financial aid award for all undergraduate students:** Full cost

**Funding available for low-income students to visit:** No

**Enrollment deposit can be waived for low-income students:** N/A

## Academics

**GPA range for transfer students accepted in 2016–2017:** N/A

**SAT ranges for all students admitted in 2016:** Critical Reading: No information provided. Mathematics: 620–720. Writing: No information provided.

**ACT composite score range for all students admitted in 2016:** No information provided.

**Type of curriculum:** Other:

- Core requirements in engineering, natural sciences, the humanities, and social sciences to assure that graduates are able to think critically, solve increasingly technical problems in a dynamic, global environment, and express conclusions clearly.
- Core academic courses and practical training to teach the leadership and professional skills required of Navy and Marine Corps officers.
- An academic major that permits a midshipman to explore a discipline in some depth and prepare for graduate level work.

**Type of academic year:** Semester

**Advisors specifically for transfer students:** N/A

**Credit policy (in their own words):** There's no transfer credit policy. However, there is information about the credit system for the Academy:

USNA's credit hour policies are consistent with commonly accepted practice in higher education, the federal definition, and MSCHE Credit Hour policy. 1 hour (50 minutes) of classroom or direct faculty instruction is equivalent to 1 credit, and 2 hours of laboratory instruction is equivalent to 1 credit for a 15 week semester. For each credit, 2 hours of out-of-class time is recommended.

**Max number of transfer credits accepted:** 0

**Residency requirement for transfer students:** Yes. A student must complete all 4 years at Annapolis. No transfer credits allowed.

**Study abroad available for transfer students:** Yes

**Free tutoring for all students:** Yes

**Writing center for all students:** Yes

**Career support/access to internships and resume prep for all students:** Yes

**% of undergraduate students hired within 6 months of graduation:** 100%

**Additional resources specifically designated for transfer and/or non-traditional students:** No

## Housing

Housing is provided for all students, but the Naval Academy does not accept non-traditional students.

## Non-Traditional Admissions

No non-traditional student policies or programs available.

## Military Students

**Military/veteran admissions policy:** The United States Naval Academy offers an outstanding opportunity for qualified enlisted members of the regular Navy, Naval Reserves, Marine Corps, and other armed forces to embark on careers as officers in the US Navy or US Marine Corps. Regular and Reserve Navy and Marine Corps service members compete for 170 appointments.

**Status considered in admissions:** Yes

**Special admissions process:** Apply via your Commanding Officer in accordance with OPNAVINST 1420.1 or Marine Corps Order 1530.11 (series); commanding officer's endorsement must accompany application. To receive a SECNAV nomination, a candidate must possess a combined SAT score (verbal and math) of 1050 or ACT equivalent combined score of 46 (English and math).

Teacher recommendations are not required for enlisted applicants who have been out of school for more than 1 year; instead, recommendations are required from 2 officers in the applicant's direct chain of command. In addition to the Secretary of the Navy nomination, applicants are encouraged to apply for congressional nominations.

If offered an appointment to the Naval Academy, candidates must extend their enlistment and/or active duty agreement in order to have a minimum of 24 months of active obligated service remaining as of July 1 of the entering year.

**Special financial aid:** No

## DACA/Undocumented Students

No DACA and undocumented student policies or programs available.

# UNIVERSITY OF CALIFORNIA, BERKELEY

**Location:** Berkeley, California

**Website:** www.berkeley.edu

**Endowment:** $3.91 billion (2014)

**Type of School:** Public/Co-ed, Research University

**# of Undergraduate Students:** 27,496

**# of Graduate Students:** 10,708

**Average Class Size:** 30 students or fewer

**School Mission (in their own words):** The University of California was founded in 1868, born out of a vision in the State Constitution of a university that would "contribute even more than California's gold to the glory and happiness of advancing generations."

## Admissions

**Admissions office mailing address:** 2227 Piedmont Ave, Berkeley CA 94720

**Admissions office phone:** (510) 642-3175

**Admissions office email:** http://admissions.berkeley.edu/ContactUs

**# of transfer applications:** Fall 2016 admissions: 17,251 (2015)

**# of transfer students accepted:** Fall 2016: 3,271 (2015)

**Transfer student acceptance rate (2016–2017 academic year):** 19%

**Freshman applications received in Fall 2016:** 78,924

**Freshman applications accepted in Fall 2016:** 12,048

**Acceptance rate for 2016–2017 freshmen:** 15.3%

## Transfer Admissions Process

Transfer policy (in their own words): You are a transfer student if you have completed coursework during a regular session at a college or university after high school. (The summer session immediately following high-school graduation does not count.) While UC gives California community college students first priority over other transfer applicants, we also accept those from 4-year institutions.

Students who wish to transfer to Berkeley from another UC campus are considered in light of their personal circumstances and the availability of space in their prospective major; these students must apply as junior transfers with a minimum of 60 semester units or 90 quarter units (not to exceed 80 semester units or 120 quarter units). These units must be completed by the end of the spring prior to fall matriculation. Read more at http://admissions.berkeley.edu/transferstudents.

**Transfer admissions contact person:** Lorena Valdez, Director

**Transfer admissions contact info:** lvaldez@berkeley.edu, (510) 642-4257

**Offers transfer-focused admissions events:** Yes

**Transfer application deadline:** Fall 2018 deadline is 11/30/18.

**Acceptances announced to transfer applicants:** Fall 2018 by end of April.

**Transfer application on Common App:** No. Common App fee: N/A.

**Separate application or in addition to the Common App:** Yes

**Fee for separate transfer application:** Yes

**Waiver available for separate transfer application fee:** UC will waive application fees for up to 4 campuses for qualified students who would otherwise be unable to apply for admission. The fee waiver program is for US citizens, permanent residents, and applicants eligible for AB540 benefits.

**SAT/ACT required for transfer applicants:** Yes

**High-school records requirements:** Official high-school transcript

**High-school records requirements for applicants who completed outside the US:** Same as domestic

**Submission requirements for transfer applicants who completed high-school equivalency test:** Official GED results

**College transcript requirements:** Official college transcript

**Interviews available for transfer applicants:** Yes. Optional. Video interview.

**Additional requirements for transfers seeking admissions to business school:** Yes. Microeconomics, macroeconomics, single-variable calculus (1-year sequence), statistics, introduction to business (including finance), financial accounting, managerial accounting, English reading and composition (2 courses)

**Additional requirements for transfers seeking admissions to engineering major:** Yes. Transfer applicants must meet UC admissions requirements, which are detailed online at the University of California's admissions website. In addition, applicants must satisfy the general requirements for admission to Berkeley, as well as the lower-division.

**Additional requirements for transfers seeking admissions to other major:** Selective major requirements are listed here: http://admission.universityofcalifornia.edu/transfer/preparation-paths/index.html.

## Costs & Financial Aid

**FAFSA code:** 1312

**CSS Profile code:** 3107 (School of music is the only one that requires the CSS Profile at Berkeley.)

**Are internal school financial aid forms required?** Yes

**Financial aid deadlines for transfer applicants:** Fall 2018: March 2. Spring 2019: N/A.

**Costs for the 2017–2018 year:** Tuition & Fees: In-state: $8,243.25. Out-of-state: $21,584.25. Room & Board: $15,716.

**Financial aid for transfer students:** Yes

**Guarantees meeting 100% need for transfer students:** No

**Need-based aid for transfer students:** Yes. You are a US citizen, an eligible non-citizen, or a student eligible for Berkeley Undergraduate DREAM Act Aid.

**Merit-based financial aid for transfer students:** Yes. You are a US citizen, an eligible non-citizen, or a student eligible for Berkeley Undergraduate DREAM Act Aid.

**Phi Theta Kappa Scholarship:** No

**Reduced or zero tuition fees for low-income students:** Yes

**Includes loans in financial aid packages:** Yes

**% of all undergraduates receiving financial aid:** 66.7%

**% of all undergraduates qualifying for Pell Grants:** 32%

**Average financial aid award for all undergraduate students:** No information provided.

**Funding available for low-income students to visit:** No

**Enrollment deposit can be waived for low-income students:** Yes

## Academics

**GPA range for transfer students accepted in 2016–2017:** 3.0–4.0

**SAT ranges for all students admitted in 2016:** Critical Reading: 610–730 (2015). Mathematics: 640–770 (2015). Writing: 620–750 (2015).

**ACT composite score range for all students admitted in 2016:** 29–34 (2015)

**Recommended completed level of math for transfer applicants:** Completion of lower division prerequisite courses for the intended major and/or college breadth requirements

**Recommended completed level of English for transfer applicants:** Completion of lower division prerequisite courses for the intended major and/or college breadth requirements

**Recommended courses transfer applicants should have on transcripts:** Completion of lower division prerequisite courses for the intended major and/or college breadth requirements

**Recommended courses transfer applicants interested in STEM should complete before transfer:** Completion of lower division prerequisite courses for the intended major and/or college breadth requirements

**Recommended extracurricular engagement:** No information provided.

**Type of curriculum:** Gen. Ed. requirements

**Type of academic year:** Semester

**Advisors specifically for transfer students:** Yes

**Credit policy (in their own words):** After you have completed 90 units toward the bachelor's degree, you must complete at least 24 of the remaining units in residence in no fewer than 2 semesters in the college or school of the University in which you will take your degree. You must begin these final 24 units in the semester in which you exceed 90 units.

Information taken from University of California (Consortium) Admissions:

> Although UC does not have pre-approved formal agreements on transferable coursework outside of the California community college system, general units or credits from a regionally accredited college or university are transferable if a course is comparable to one offered at a UC campus. If a course is not equivalent to a particular UC course, it must be appropriate for a UC degree in terms of its purpose, scope and depth.

However, some courses are not transferable to UC. The following types of courses, for example, will not garner UC transfer credit:

- Remedial English (composition courses below the first-term college level)
- Mathematics below college algebra (any course for which intermediate algebra is not a prerequisite)
- Instructional/technical how-to courses, such as how to use computer software (e.g., Word, Excel, PowerPoint)

To get an idea of likely transferable courses from 4-year institutions and out-of-state 2-year colleges, refer to the General Catalog for any UC campus or to a transfer course agreement (TCA) that UC has with any California community college.

Read more at http://admission.universityofcalifornia.edu/counselors/transfer/advising/transferring-credits.

**Max number of transfer credits accepted:** 70 semester units of credit

**Residency requirement for transfer students:** Yes

**Study abroad available for transfer students:** Yes. They need to be in-residence their first semester, but can study abroad any semester after that.

**Free tutoring for all students:** Yes

**Writing center for all students:** Yes

**Career support/access to internships and resume prep for all students:** Yes

**% of undergraduate students hired within 6 months of graduation:** No information provided.

**Additional resources specifically designated for transfer and/or non-traditional students:** Yes. Transfer student center, reentry student program, Early Childhood Education Program.

## Housing

**Available for transfer students:** Yes

**Available for non-traditional students:** Yes

**Guaranteed for transfer students:** No

**Non-traditional students can reside in housing year-round:** If they live off campus

**Family housing available:** Yes

## Non-Traditional Admissions

No non-traditional student policies or programs available.

## Military Students

**Military/veteran admissions policy (in their own words):** The UC Berkeley Office of Undergraduate Admissions thanks you for your service to our country. As you begin to consider your educational options, we would like to give you some insight to our admissions requirements.

UC Berkeley's admissions requirements are the same for all prospective students. Applicants have 2 ways of applying for admission to our campus, as a: (1) freshman applicant or (2) transfer applicant. Read more at http://admissions. berkeley.edu/veterans.

**Status considered in admissions:** Yes

**Special admissions process:** No

**Special financial aid:** Yes. Federal Veterans Affairs (VA) educational benefits.

**Specific programs/policies to address needs:** The Cal Veteran Services Center ensures that admitted UC Berkeley students understand how to successfully manage the transition, navigate the research university, and fully engage in the university experience.

## DACA/Undocumented Students

**DACA and undocumented admissions policy (in their own words):** The University of California welcomes and supports students without regard to their immigration status. UC will continue to admit students in a manner consistent with our nondiscrimination policy and without regard to a student's race, color, national origin, religion, citizenship, or other protected characteristic. In other words, undocumented applicants with or without DACA status will be considered for admission on the same basis as any US citizen or other applicant. The University is committed to creating an environment in which all admitted students can successfully matriculate and graduate. Federal law protects student privacy rights, and the California Constitution and statutes provide broad privacy protection to all members of the UC community. University policy provides additional privacy protections. When the University receives requests for information that implicate individual privacy rights, the University will continue its practice of working closely with the Office of General Counsel to protect the privacy of members of the UC community. We will not release immigration status or related information in confidential student records, without permission from a student, to federal agencies or other parties without a judicial warrant, a subpoena, a court order, or as otherwise required by law.

**Admitted:** Yes

**Status considered in admissions:** Yes

**Special admissions process:** No

**Eligible for institutional financial aid:** Yes. The California DREAM Act extends eligibility for certain types of UC and California Financial Aid to students, including undocumented students, who qualify for non-resident tuition exemption under AB540. Read more here: https://undocu.berkeley.edu/financial-aid-for-undocumented-students/.

**Specific programs/policies to address needs:** Yes. Provides academic support through academic counseling, mental health support, the DREAM Lending Library program (provides financial assistance), the summer bridge program (a 6-week rigorous academic residential program that facilitates the transition of students from high school to the university), and research and postgrad opportunities. They also provide legal support, grants, and funding. Read more here: https://undocu.berkeley.edu/.

# UNIVERSITY OF CALIFORNIA, DAVIS

**Location:** Davis, California

**Website:** www.ucdavis.edu

**Endowment:** $985 million

**Type of School:** Public/Co-ed, Research University

**# of Undergraduate Students:** 28,384 (2015)

**# of Graduate Students:** 6,802 (2015)

**Average Class Size:** 20–49

**School Mission (in their own words):** The core purpose of UC Davis as a comprehensive research university is the generation, advancement, dissemination, and application of knowledge. To that end, UC Davis is committed to offering leading programs throughout the academic disciplines and in its professional schools. These programs integrate 3 purposes: teaching students as a partnership between faculty mentors and young scholars; advancing knowledge and pioneering studies through creative research and scholarship; and applying that knowledge to address the needs of the region, state, nation, and globe. UC Davis is committed to the land-grant tradition on which it was founded, which holds that the broad purpose of a university is service to people and society.

UC Davis offers its undergraduates an experience which comprises the central elements of a liberal education—a broad general education with specialization in a scholarly discipline—and opportunities for personal development and academic enrichment through undergraduate research, work-learn experiences, and extracurricular student life. To its post-baccalaureate students, UC Davis offers an array of programs which draw upon its wide range of specialized academic fields. By stimulating cross-disciplinary approaches and using its distinctive graduate groups, UC Davis continues to follow and redefine the mandate of a major research university.

The campus is committed to advancing teaching and scholarly work in the arts, humanities, and social sciences—studies that enrich the life of each person and society as a whole, and infuse the pursuit of careers in education, law, management, and medicine. UC Davis's prominence in the STEM fields, including distinguished programs in agricultural and environmental sciences, makes the campus a leader in solving critical issues in local, state, national, and global health and sustainability.

UC Davis extends service to the region, state, nation, and the world in many forms, such as cooperative extension to agriculture and education; medical services to central California and beyond through the multifaceted UC Davis Health System in Sacramento; University Extension programs that share knowledge with the region; the emerging work of the World Food Center; voluntary contributions of faculty, staff, and students; and athletic and cultural programs for the campus and community at large.

UC Davis is surrounded by vibrant, local communities and its proximity to the state capital gives this outreach urgency and opportunity. Collaborative studies and cooperation between UC Davis and state agencies and the legislature are both a special responsibility and a unique opportunity. UC Davis is characterized by a distinguished faculty, a dedicated and high-achieving staff, and students of great potential and accomplishment. As we move forward, we recognize that our continued excellence is dependent upon our ability to diversify our university community, consonant with the citizenry of California.

## Admissions

**Admissions office mailing address:** 1 Shields Ave, Davis CA 95616

**Admissions office phone:** (530) 752-2971

**Admissions office email:** No specific admissions office email found online, but there is a page where students can enter their questions: https://ucdavis.askadmissions.net/ask.aspx.

**# of transfer applications:** Fall 2016 admissions: 15,355

**# of transfer students accepted:** Fall 2016: 14,419 (2015)

**Transfer student acceptance rate (2016–2017 academic year):** 90.3%

**Freshman applications received in Fall 2016:** 64,510

**Freshman applications accepted in Fall 2016:** 24,614

**Acceptance rate for 2016–2017 freshmen:** 38.2%

## Transfer Admissions Process

**Transfer policy (in their own words):** Transferring to UC Davis from a community college or 4-year institution has become a popular path to obtaining a university degree. We welcome transfer applicants from all schools, though we give priority to transfers from California community colleges. To be considered for transfer admission to UC Davis, you must first ensure that you meet UC transfer admission requirements and any UC Davis major–specific requirements. Applicants must be college juniors, with 60 semester (90 quarter) units—lower-division students may be considered for admission to the College of Agricultural and Environmental Sciences only if space is available.

Read more at www.ucdavis.edu/admissions/undergraduate/transfer.

**Offers transfer-focused admissions events:** Yes

**Transfer application deadline:** Fall 2018 deadline is midnight, 11/30/18. Spring 2019 deadline is N/A.

**Acceptances announced to transfer applicants:** Fall 2018 in late April. Spring 2019 in N/A.

**Transfer application on Common App:** No. Common App Fee: N/A.

**Separate application or in addition to the Common App:** Yes

**Fee for separate transfer application:** Yes

**Waiver available for separate transfer application fee:** Meet eligibility guidelines based on household size and family income.

**SAT/ACT required for transfer applicants:** Required from some.

**High-school record requirements:** Required from some.

**High-school records requirements for applicants who completed outside the US:** You must submit your foreign academic records for evaluation.

**Submission requirements for transfer applicants who completed high-school equivalency test:** Official results

**College transcript requirements:** Official transcripts from all colleges and universities attended

**Interviews available for transfer applicants:** No

**Additional requirements for transfers seeking admissions to engineering major:** Yes. It is strongly recommended that students complete: UC transfer requirements in the areas of English composition (2 courses) and mathematics (1 course) by the end of the fall term prior to enrollment in order to receive priority consideration. Must complete at least 60 semester (90 quarter) transferable units and any required major preparatory courses that are offered at your current college by the close of spring term for fall enrollment at UC Davis; if required courses are not offered at your college, you must complete them after enrolling at UC Davis. You must earn an overall transfer GPA of 3.1 or higher to be a competitive candidate for admission to any engineering major. Applicants must complete all lower-division courses required for their specific engineering major as listed on the ASSIST website under courses "Required for Admission."

**Additional requirements for transfers seeking admissions to other major:** Selective major requirements are listed here: www.ucdavis.edu/admissions/undergraduate/transfer/selective-major-requirements.

## Costs & Financial Aid

**FAFSA code:** 1313

**CSS Profile code:** N/A

**Are internal school financial aid forms required?** Yes

**Financial aid deadlines for transfer applicants:** Fall 2018: March 2. Spring 2019: N/A.

**Costs for the 2017–2018 year:** Tuition & Fees: In-state: $14,383. Out-of-state: $42,397. Room & Board: $16,136.

**Financial aid for transfer students:** Yes

**Guarantees meeting 100% need for transfer students:** No

**Need-based aid for transfer students:** Yes. To qualify for financial aid, you must file either the Free Application for Federal Student Aid (FAFSA) or California DREAM Act Application.

**Merit-based financial aid for transfer students:** Yes. You must earn at least a 2.4 GPA in your UC-transferable classes to meet UC requirements. However, UC Davis requires a minimum 2.8 GPA to be selected for admission, and many of our most popular programs may require a higher GPA. Strive to achieve your highest possible GPA in order to be most competitive. No more than 14 semester (21 quarter) units may be taken Pass/No Pass.

**Phi Theta Kappa Scholarship:** No

**Reduced or zero tuition fees for low-income students:** Yes

**Includes loans in financial aid packages:** Yes

**% of all undergraduates receiving financial aid:** 60.8%

**% of all undergraduates qualifying for Pell Grants:** 41%

**Average financial aid award for all undergraduate students:** $20,360

**Funding available for low-income students to visit:** Yes

**Enrollment deposit can be waived for low-income students:** Yes

## Academics

**GPA range for transfer students accepted in 2016–2017:** 3.92–4.23

**SAT ranges for all students admitted in 2016:** Critical Reading: 550–690. Mathematics: 600–760. Writing: 580–710.

**ACT composite score range for all students admitted in 2016:** 27–32

**Recommended completed level of math for transfer applicants:** You must complete 1 transferable college course (3 semester or 4–5 quarter units) in mathematical concepts or quantitative reasoning. It is strongly recommended that students complete UC transfer requirements in mathematics by the end of fall term prior.

**Recommended completed level of English for transfer applicants:** You must complete 2 transferable college courses (3 semester or 4–5 quarter units) in English composition. It is strongly recommended that students complete UC transfer requirements in mathematics by the end of fall term prior to enrollment, in order to receive priority consideration.

**Recommended courses transfer applicants should have on transcripts:** You must complete the following UC requirements in English and math with grades of C or better: 2 transferable college courses (3 semester or 4–5 quarter units) in English composition. It is strongly recommended that students complete UC transfer requirements in mathematics in the fall term prior to enrollment for priority consideration.

**Recommended courses transfer applicants interested in STEM should complete before transfer:** Depends on major

**Recommended extracurricular engagement:** None

**Type of curriculum:** Gen. Ed. requirements

**Type of academic year:** Semester

**Advisors specifically for transfer students:** Yes

**Credit policy (in their own words):** Academic work at the university is measured by "units of credit." In conjunction with the letter grade you receive from the course instructor, units of credit give a fairly accurate evaluation of the amount of time you have devoted to a given subject. Units of credit also make it possible to anticipate the amount of work involved in a particular course and enable you to transfer from one campus or university to another without undue difficulty. To convert quarter units to semester units, multiply by 0.66; from semester to quarter units, multiply by 1.5.

Coursework from other colleges and universities is considered UC-transferable if the applicant completed the course at an institution that is recognized by the University of California. In addition, the coursework must be comparable to courses and levels offered within the University of California.

A total of 105 quarter (70 semester) UC-transferable units toward a university degree may be earned for lower-division coursework completed at any institution or combination of institutions. Lower- or upper-division units earned at UC (extension, summer, cross/concurrent, UC-EAP, and regular academic year enrollment) are added to the maximum lower-division credits allowed and might put applicants at risk of being denied admission due to excessive units.

You can find information about transferable credit from California community colleges at http://assist.org. Only subject credit will be granted for courses taken in excess of this amount.

If, after applying UC lower-division unit limitations and exclusions, you have completed 120 quarter units (80 semester units) or more of UC-transferable units, your admission is subject to approval by the respective dean for majors in the Colleges of Agricultural and Environmental Sciences, Biological Sciences, and Letters and Science.

Read more at http://catalog.ucdavis.edu/admission/transfer.html.

**Max number of transfer credits accepted:** 70

**Residency requirement for transfer students:** No

**Study abroad available for transfer students:** Yes

**Free tutoring for all students:** Yes

**Writing center for all students:** Yes

**Career support/access to internships and resume prep for all students:** Yes

**% of undergraduate students hired within 6 months of graduation:** 71% (within the year)

**Additional resources specifically designated for transfer and/or non-traditional students:** Yes. The Collective: Transfer & Non-Traditional Student Empowerment program facilitates the retention of transfer, reentry, parent, and all non-traditional UC Davis students by hosting weekly transfer hours, workshops, community mixers, and other events. At these events, students can meet new people, learn about resources on campus, and increase their sense of community. Under the Aggie Transfer Mentorship Program, new transfer students are paired with second-year transfer students based on their major and interests to build a sense of community and support.

## Housing

**Available for transfer students:** Yes

**Available for non-traditional students:** Yes

**Guaranteed for transfer students:** Yes

**Non-traditional students can reside in housing year-round:** Yes

**Family housing available:** Yes

## Non-Traditional Admissions

**Non-traditional student policy (in their own words):** No specific policy available, but there is a student recruitment and retention center that provides both academic and social support to empower transfer, reentry, parent, and all non-traditional students to succeed in higher education. Read more at http://srrc.ucdavis.edu/programs/collective/index.html.

**Name of program:** Transfer Admission Guarantee (TAG)

**Program description:** A UC Davis TAG is a formal written agreement assuring fall admission to UC Davis in your desired major. The online TAG contract will outline the courses you must complete, the GPA you must maintain, and any other admission requirements. The approved contract guarantees your admission as long as you meet the terms of your contract and apply for admission during the UC application filing period. Students that are accepted are guaranteed admissions to the school.

**Program deadline:** Between September 1 and September 30

**Program Admission Requirements:** TAGs are available at all CCCs.

1. TAGs must be submitted online using the UC TAG Application at uctap.universityofcalifornia.edu.
2. Students must submit the UC TAG Application between September 1 and September 30, 2018. Once submitted, UC Davis TAGs are directed to CCC designates for review and authorization.
3. CCC designates receiving the UC Davis TAG must provide a recommendation and submit the TAG to UC Davis by October 15, 2017 (see TAG Counselor Resource section for additional detail).

4. A student with an approved TAG must submit the UC application for undergraduate admission and scholarships during the initial application filing period for the same major and term of the TAG.

   a. Students must use their full legal name throughout the UC TAG and application processes.

   b. Students must thoroughly and consistently report all information, including each college or university of enrollment or attendance, gaps in education, and courses in progress and planned on both the UC TAG and UC undergraduate admission applications. All courses and grades, e.g., D, F, I and W, must be listed as they appear on transcripts. Students must respond to all inquiries in a timely manner and no later than by the specified deadline(s).

5. A student with an authorized TAG must complete the UC Transfer Academic Update (TAU) online, providing grades and course changes as directed, by the specified deadline.

6. TAGs are only accepted for fall quarter admission.

**Program website:** www.ucdavis.edu/admissions/undergraduate/transfer/transfer-admission-guarantee

**Program contact person:** Cindy Bevc, Articulation Officer, TAG Manager

**Program contact info:** (530) 754-7649, cabevc@ucdavis.edu

## Military/Veteran Students

**Military/veteran admissions policy (in their own words):** If you are a veteran, service member, or dependent, the Veterans Success Center (VSC) is your place to file your educational benefits, attend workshops to help you succeed in your educational goals, and engage and network with your veteran community. The VSC serves as a liaison between the Department of Veterans Affairs (VA) and UC Davis student veterans, providing course attendance certification and processing Cal-Vet Fee Waivers. Visit us to learn about benefit eligibility and tutorial assistance, as well as to receive helpful advice about your GI Bill and educational benefits. Upon acceptance to UC Davis, contact our VA Office to initiate a benefit claim and complete the necessary paperwork. Our dedicated staff is here to assist you in making a smooth transition to our university.

Read more about the center at http://success.ucdavis.edu/centers-and-programs/vsc.

**Status considered in admissions:** No

**Special admissions process:** No

**Special financial aid:** Yes. If you are a veteran, service member, or dependent, the Veterans Success Center (VSC) is your place to file your educational benefits, attend workshops to help you succeed in your educational goals, and engage and network with your veteran community.

**Specific programs/policies to address needs:** Upon acceptance to UC Davis, contact our VA Office to initiate a benefit claim and complete the necessary paperwork. Our dedicated staff is here to assist you in making a smooth transition to our university.

## DACA/Undocumented Students

**DACA and undocumented admissions policy (in their own words):** The University of California welcomes and supports students without regard to their immigration status. UC will continue to admit students in a manner consistent with our nondiscrimination policy and without regard to a student's race, color, national origin, religion, citizenship, or other protected characteristic. In other words, undocumented applicants with or without DACA status will be considered for admission on the same basis as any US citizen or other applicant. The University is committed to creating an environment in which all admitted students can successfully matriculate and graduate. Federal law protects student privacy rights, and the California Constitution and statutes provide broad privacy protection to all members of the UC community. University policy provides additional privacy protections. When the University receives requests for information that implicate individual privacy rights, the University will continue its practice of working closely with the Office of General Counsel to protect the privacy of members of the UC community. We will not release immigration status or related information in confidential student records, without permission from a student, to federal agencies or other parties without a judicial warrant, a subpoena, a court order, or as otherwise required by law.

**Admitted:** Yes

**Status considered in admissions:** Yes

**Special admissions process:** No

**Eligible for institutional financial aid:** Yes. The California DREAM Act extends eligibility for certain types of UC and California Financial Aid to students, including undocumented students, who qualify for non-resident tuition exemption under AB540. Read more here: http://financialaid.ucdavis.edu/undergraduate/apply/undocumented.html.

**Specific programs/policies to address needs:** Yes. Campus resources: Community Advising Network, Community Housing Listing, Department of Chicana/o Studies, Educational Opportunity Program, La Raza Pre-Law Student Association, SPEAK, Student Academic Success Center, SASC—Early Academic Outreach Program, SASC—Pre-Graduate/Pre-Professional Advising Office, Student Health and Counseling Services, Student Recruitment and Retention Center, University Library, Legal Resources, and Free Legal Immigration Counseling. Read more here: http://undocumented.ucdavis.edu/.

# UNIVERSITY OF CALIFORNIA, IRVINE

**Location:** Irvine, California

**Website:** https://uci.edu

**Endowment:** $469.7 million (2015)

**Type of School:** Public/Co-ed, Research University

**# of Undergraduate Students:** 27,331

**# of Graduate Students:** 5,423

**Average Class Size:** 20 students or less

**School Mission (in their own words):** In 1965, the University of California, Irvine was founded with a mission to catalyze the community and enhance lives through rigorous academics, cutting-edge research, and dedicated public service. Today, we draw on the unyielding spirit of our pioneering faculty, staff, and students who arrived on campus with a dream to inspire change and generate new ideas. We believe that true progress is made when different perspectives come together to advance our understanding of the world around us. And we enlighten our communities and point the way to a better future. At UCI, we shine brighter.

## Admissions

**Admissions office mailing address:** 260 Aldrich Hall, Irvine CA 92697

**Admissions office phone:** (949) 824-6703

**Admissions office email:** admissions@uci.edu

**# of transfer applications:** Fall 2016 admissions: 19,841

**# of transfer students accepted:** Fall 2016: 9,348

**Transfer student acceptance rate (2016–2017 academic year):** 48%

**Freshman applications received in Fall 2016:** 77,810

**Freshman applications accepted in Fall 2016:** 31,631

**Acceptance rate for 2016–2017 freshmen:** 40.7%

## Transfer Admissions Process

**Transfer policy:** UCI welcomes the distinctive experience transfer students contribute to our campus and gives priority to junior-level students transferring from California Community Colleges. In order to be eligible for admission to our university, you must meet the following requirements:

- Complete 60 semester or 90 quarter UC-transferable units by the end of the spring term prior to the desired fall term admission with a minimum 2.4 GPA; a competitive UCI transfer applicant should have a UC-transferable GPA of 3.0 or above.
- Complete 7 UC-transferable courses with a grade of C or better in each course—2 courses in English composition, 1 course in mathematical concepts and quantitative reasoning, and 4 courses in at least 2 of the following areas: the arts and humanities, the social and behavioral sciences, or the physical and biological sciences.
- If you are a non-California resident, you must have a minimum 2.8 GPA in order to be eligible for the UC System. See the University of California Admissions for additional information. Read more at www.admissions.uci.edu/apply/transfer/index.php.

**Transfer admissions contact person:** N/A

**Transfer admissions contact info:** N/A

**Offers transfer-focused admissions events:** No

**Transfer application deadline:** Fall 2018 deadline is 11/30/18.

**Acceptances announced to transfer applicants:** Fall 2018 in April.

**Transfer application on Common App:** No. Common App fee: N/A.

**Separate application or in addition to the Common App:** Yes

**Fee for separate transfer application:** Yes

**Waiver available for separate transfer application fee:** Meet eligibility guidelines based on household size and family income.

**SAT/ACT required for transfer applicants:** Yes

**High-school records requirements:** Official high-school transcript

**High-school records requirements for applicants who completed outside the US:** Same as for domestic students

**Submission requirements for transfer applicants who completed high-school equivalency test:** Official results

**College transcript requirements:** Official transcripts from all colleges and universities attended

**Interviews available for transfer applicants:** No

**Additional requirements for transfers seeking admissions to all majors:** Yes. Specific course requirements located here: www.admissions.uci.edu/apply/transfer/requirements.php.

## Costs & Financial Aid

**FAFSA code:** 1314

**CSS Profile code:** N/A

**Are internal school financial aid forms required?** Yes

**Financial aid deadline for transfer applicants:** Fall 2018: 3/2/18.

**Costs for the 2017–2018 year:** Tuition & Fees: Resident: $15,026.47. Non-resident: $41,708.47. Room & Board: $6,132.

**Financial aid for transfer students:** Yes

**Guarantees meeting 100% need for transfer students:** No

**Need-based aid for transfer students:** Yes. To qualify for financial aid, you must file either the Free Application for Federal Student Aid (FAFSA) or California DREAM Act Application.

**Merit-based financial aid for transfer students:** Yes. Academic departments and campus organizations offer various scholarship opportunities. Each department has separate processes and criteria for the scholarships they administer.

**Phi Theta Kappa Scholarship:** No

**Reduced or zero tuition fees for low-income students:** Yes

**Includes loans in financial aid packages:** Yes

**% of all undergraduates receiving financial aid:** 73%

**% of all undergraduates qualifying for Pell Grants:** No information provided.

**Average financial aid award for all undergraduate students:** $24,138

**Funding available for low-income students to visit:** No

**Enrollment deposit can be waived for low-income students:** Yes

## Academics

**GPA range for transfer students accepted in 2016–2017:** No information provided.

**SAT ranges for all students admitted in 2016:** Critical Reading: 500–630. Mathematics: 560–700. Writing: 520–630.

**ACT composite score range for all students admitted in 2016:** No information provided.

**Recommended completed level of math for transfer applicants:** Complete at least 2 UC-transferable courses with a grade of C or better in mathematical concepts and quantitative reasoning,

**Recommended completed level of English for transfer applicants:** Complete at least 2 UC-transferable courses with a grade of C or better in English composition.

**Recommended courses transfer applicants should have on transcripts:** Complete 7 UC-transferable courses with a grade of C or better in each course—2 courses in English composition, 1 course in mathematical concepts and quantitative reasoning, and 4 courses in at least 2 of the following areas: the arts and humanities, the social and behavioral sciences, or the physical and biological sciences.

**Recommended courses transfer applicants interested in STEM should complete before transfer:** Depends on major

**Type of curriculum:** Gen. Ed. requirements

**Type of academic year:** Quarter

**Advisors specifically for transfer students:** Yes

**Credit policy (in their own words):** This university utilizes quarter units. A course normally offers 4 quarter units of credit, and a minimum of 180 quarter units is required for graduation.

UCI welcomes the distinctive experience transfer students contribute to our campus and gives priority to junior-level students transferring from California Community Colleges. In order to be eligible for admission to our university, you must meet the following requirements:

- Complete 60 semester or 90 quarter UC-transferable units by the end of the spring term prior to the desired fall term admission with a minimum 2.4 GPA; a competitive UCI transfer applicant should have a UC-transferable GPA of 3.0 or above.

- Complete 7 UC-transferable courses with a grade of C or better in each course—2 courses in English composition, 1 course in mathematical concepts and quantitative reasoning, and 4 courses in at least 2 of the following areas: the arts and humanities, the social and behavioral sciences, or the physical and biological sciences.

- If you are a non-California resident, you must have a minimum 2.8 GPA in order to be eligible for the UC System. See the University of California Admissions for additional information.

- You will be granted up to 70 semester or 105 quarter units of credit for lower-division coursework completed at any institution or any combination of institutions. For units beyond the maximum, subject credit may be granted and used to satisfy requirements.

- Units earned through AP, IB, and/or A-Level examinations are not included in the limitation and do not put applicants at risk of being denied admission.

- Units earned at any UC campus (extension, summer, cross/concurrent, and regular academic year enrollment) are not included in the limitation but are added to the maximum transfer credits allowed and may put applicants at risk of being denied admission due to excessive units.

- No more than 14 semester or 21 quarter units may be taken for Pass/No Pass credit (not major prerequisites).

Read more at www.admissions.uci.edu/apply/transfer/index.php.

**Max number of transfer credits accepted:** 70 semester units

**Residency requirement for transfer students:** No

**Study abroad available for transfer students:** Yes. To be eligible for UCEAP, UCI students must: meet the designated GPA requirement at the time of application (and maintain it through departure), meet any designated class level requirements, meet any designated language requirements, and receive support of UCI EAP.

**Free tutoring for all students:** No

**Writing center for all students:** Yes

**Career support/access to internships and resume prep for all students:** Yes

**% of undergraduate students hired within 6 months of graduation:** 70%

**Additional resources specifically designated for transfer and/or non-traditional students:** Yes. Transfer Student Center: academic, career, commuter, financial, social, and student-parent resources.

## Housing

**Available for transfer students:** Yes

**Available for non-traditional students:** Yes

**Guaranteed for transfer students:** Yes, for the first year

**Non-traditional students can reside in housing year-round:** Yes, in certain places

**Family housing available:** Yes

## Non-Traditional Admissions

**Non-traditional student policy:** No information provided.

**Name of program:** Transfer Admission Guarantee

**Program description:** UCI's Transfer Admission Guarantee (TAG) program guarantees admission to highly qualified students from all California Community Colleges. Admission to most majors at UCI can be guaranteed through TAG for transfer students who meet the eligibility requirements and complete the online TAG application. Students that are accepted are guaranteed admission to the school.

**Program deadline:** To apply to TAG, submit your TAG application between September 1–30 and your UC undergraduate application to UCI between November 1–30.

**Program admission requirements:** Complete 30 semester or 45 quarter UC-transferable units (including AP/IB/A-Level) by the end of the Summer 2017 term for Fall 2018 admission. Earn a minimum GPA of 3.4 in all UC-transferable coursework by the end of the Summer 2017 term for Fall 2018 admission, and maintain a 3.4 GPA in all UC-transferable coursework for all subsequent terms. Complete 1 UC-transferable math course with a grade of C or better by the end of the Summer 2017 term. Complete 1 UC-transferable English course with a grade of C or better by the end of the Summer 2017 term. Complete a second UC-transferable English course with a grade of C or better by the end of the Spring 2018 term. Complete 60 UC-transferable semester units or 90 UC-transferable quarter units by the end of the Spring 2018 term for Fall 2018 admission. Complete all major coursework for your chosen major, including course prerequisites, and maintain minimum course GPA through the end of the Spring 2018 term for Fall 2018 admission. Are in good standing for all colleges attended and satisfy all UC transfer eligibility requirements. Complete the last 30 semester or 45 quarter units at a California community college by the end of the Spring 2018 term for Fall 2018 admission.

**Program website:** www.admissions.uci.edu/apply/transfer/guarantee.php

**Program contact:** Office of Admissions and Relations with Schools

**Program contact info:** (949) 824-6703, admissions@uci.edu

## Military/Veteran Students

**Military/veteran admissions policy (in their own words):** If you have done some college work after high school, then you would be applying as a transfer student. Either way, if you have been out of school for a long period of time, we often advise for you to attend a CA community college for the first 2 years to get back into the swing of things and then apply as a junior transfer student.

Read more at https://veteran.uci.edu/faq.php#Admissions.

**Status considered in admissions:** Yes

**Special admissions process:** No

**Special financial aid:** Yes. The GI Bill provides benefits to veterans, service members, and some dependents of disabled or deceased veterans wishing to pursue an education. The length of time spent on active duty will determine the amount of benefits unless you are currently serving in the reserves or National Guard and have NOT been deployed. In that case, an allotted benefit amount will be issued.

**Specific programs/policies to address needs:** VetNet Ally Program: VetNet Ally is a 4-hour education program increasing campus awareness among UCI faculty and staff about veterans, military culture, and the challenges of transitioning to college and civilian life. Participants learn about the value added to UC Irvine by the veteran population. If you see a VetNet Ally sticker in an office, the faculty or staff member has participated in the program and is committed to being a VetNet Ally. Mentorship Program: Contact Veteran Services to be paired with a UCI faculty or staff member who is either a veteran or actively involved in the military community. Veteran Appreciation Dinner: UCI's annual Veteran Appreciation Dinner held in May recognizes graduating seniors and welcomes newly admitted military students to UCI. The dinner also serves as an avenue to fundraise for the "Bridging the Gap" Military Student Scholarship and Programs Fund.

## DACA/Undocumented Students

**DACA and undocumented admissions policy (in their own words):** The University of California welcomes and supports students without regard to their immigration status. UC will continue to admit students in a manner consistent with our nondiscrimination policy and without regard to a student's race, color, national origin, religion, citizenship, or other protected characteristic. In other words, undocumented applicants with or without DACA status will be considered for admission on the same basis as any US citizen or other applicant. The University is committed to creating an environment in which all admitted students can successfully matriculate and graduate. Federal law protects student privacy rights, and the California Constitution and statutes provide broad privacy protection to all members of the UC community. University policy provides additional privacy protections. When the University receives requests for information that implicate individual privacy rights, the University will continue its practice of working closely with the Office of General Counsel to protect the privacy of members of the UC community. We will not release immigration status or related information in confidential student records, without permission from a student, to federal agencies or other parties without a judicial warrant, a subpoena, a court order, or as otherwise required by law.

**Admitted:** Yes

**Status considered in admissions:** Yes

**Special admissions process:** No

**Eligible for institutional financial aid:** Yes. The California DREAM Act extends eligibility for certain types of UC and California Financial Aid to students, including undocumented students, who qualify for non-resident tuition exemption under AB540. Read more here: http://dreamers.uci.edu/finances/.

**Specific programs/policies to address needs:** Yes. Legal support and referrals, academic consultations, student wellness support and emotional support, housing relocations, and general consultations. Read more here: http://dreamers.uci.edu/.

# UNIVERSITY OF CALIFORNIA, LOS ANGELES

**Location:** Los Angeles, California
**Website:** www.ucla.edu
**Endowment:** $3.6 billion (2015)
**Type of School:** Public/Co-ed, Research University
**# of Undergraduate Students:** 30,873
**# of Graduate Students:** 14,074
**Average Class Size:** 20 or less

**School Mission (in their own words):** UCLA's primary purpose as a public research university is the creation, dissemination, preservation, and application of knowledge for the betterment of our global society.

## Admissions

**Admissions office mailing address:** 1147 Murphy Hall, Los Angeles CA 90095

**Admissions office phone:** (310) 825-3101

**Admissions office contact page:** https://www.admission.ucla.edu/ContactForm/UGADM.aspx

**# of transfer applications:** Fall 2016 admissions: 22,287. Spring 2017 admissions: N/A.

**# of transfer students accepted:** Fall 2016: 5,708

**Transfer student acceptance rate (2016–2017 academic year):** 25.6%

**Freshman applications received in Fall 2016:** 97,121

**Freshman applications accepted in Fall 2016:** 17,474

**Acceptance rate for 2016–2017 freshmen:** 18%

## Transfer Admissions Process

**Transfer policy (in their own words):** Although UCLA is one of the most transfer-friendly campuses in the UC system, competition for transfer openings has increased in recent years. Strong academic preparation and performance are primary elements in our admission decisions. The average GPA of transfer applicants who are admitted to UCLA is more than 3.5 (though GPAs vary by program), and most students who are admitted have completed most or all of the preparatory coursework for their majors. We give highest priority to students who are transferring from California community colleges or other University of California campuses. All schools admit for the fall quarter only.

Read more at www.admission.ucla.edu/prospect/Adm_tr/tradms.htm.

**Transfer admissions contact person:** Gary Clark, Director

**Transfer admissions contact info:** gclark@admission.ucla.edu, (310) 825-5108

**Offers transfer-focused admissions events:** Yes

**Transfer application deadline:** Fall 2018 deadline is 11/30/17.

**Acceptances announced to transfer applicants:** Fall 2018 in April.

**Transfer application on Common App:** No. Common App fee: N/A.

**Separate application or in addition to the Common App:** Yes

**Fee for separate transfer application:** Yes

**Waiver available for separate transfer application fee:** UC will waive application fees for up to 4 campuses for qualified students who would otherwise be unable to apply for admission. The fee waiver program is for US citizens, permanent residents, and applicants eligible for AB540 benefits.

**SAT/ACT required for transfer applicants:** Only for international students

**High-school records requirements:** Official high-school transcripts

**High-school records requirements for applicants who completed outside the US:** Same as domestic students

**Submission requirements for transfer applicants who completed high-school equivalency test:** None

**College transcript requirements:** Junior-level standing (60 semester/90 quarter transferable units completed) by the end of the spring term before you transfer, GPA of 3.2 or higher earned in transferable courses, progress toward completion of major preparation requirements by spring prior to transfer. Should a major not have specific prerequisites, we expect students to demonstrate interest in academic study by completing coursework related to the major and completion of the following course requirements by spring prior to transfer: 2 transferable courses in English composition/critical thinking and writing, 1 transferable math course that has a prerequisite of intermediate algebra or higher, 4 transferable college courses in at least 2 of the following subject areas: arts and humanities, social and behavioral sciences, and physical and biological sciences.

**Interviews available for transfer applicants:** No

**Additional requirements for transfers seeking admissions to arts major:** Yes. Applicants to the school must have a minimum 3.0 GPA at the time of application. In addition to the UC Application, applicants are required to submit supplemental application material (e.g., portfolio or audition, artist statements, and letters of recommendation; additional fees may apply). Specific requirements, deadlines, and procedures for submission must be obtained from each department's website—see individual major sections for more information. Applicants should begin working on the department's supplemental application shortly after submitting the UC Application, as deadlines are strictly enforced.

**Additional requirements for transfers seeking admissions to engineering major:** Yes. Applicants to the Henry Samueli School of Engineering & Applied Science must have a minimum 3.4 GPA at the time of application to be considered for admission and by the time of entrance must have attained junior standing (60 semester/90 quarter units).

## Costs & Financial Aid

**FAFSA code:** 1315

**CSS Profile code:** N/A

**Are internal school financial aid forms required?** Yes

**Financial aid deadlines for transfer applicants:** Fall 2018: 3/2/17

**Costs for the 2017–2018 year:** Tuition & Fees: In-state: $12,918. Out-of-state: $26,682. Room & Board: $15,069.

**Anticipated costs for the 2018–2019 year:** Tuition: $52,000. Fees: $10,500. Room & Board: $4,200.

**Financial aid for transfer students:** Yes

**Guarantees meeting 100% need for transfer students:** No

**Need-based aid for transfer students:** Yes. To qualify for financial aid, you must file either the Free Application for Federal Student Aid (FAFSA) or California DREAM Act Application.

**Merit-based financial aid for transfer students:** Yes. Scholarships are awarded to students who meet the specific criteria established by donors, which may include a variety of factors such as student's academic achievements, ethnicity, volunteer work, and professional interests.

**Phi Theta Kappa Scholarship:** No

**Reduced or zero tuition fees for low-income students:** Yes

**Includes loans in financial aid packages:** Yes

**% of all undergraduates receiving financial aid:** 52%

**% of all undergraduates qualifying for Pell Grants:** 38%

**Average financial aid award for all undergraduate students:** The average need-based scholarship or grant award is $18,966.

**Funding available for low-income students to visit:** No

**Enrollment deposit can be waived for low-income students:** Yes

## Academics

**GPA range for transfer students accepted in 2016–2017:** No information provided.

**SAT ranges for all students admitted in 2016:** Critical Reading: 570–700. Mathematics: 580–740. Writing: 570–720.

**ACT composite score range for all students admitted in 2016:** 25–33

**Recommended completed level of math for transfer applicants:** 1 transferable math course that has a prerequisite of intermediate algebra or higher

**Recommended completed level of English for transfer applicants:** 2 transferable courses in English composition/critical thinking and writing

**Recommended courses transfer applicants should have on transcripts:** 4 transferable college courses in at least 2 of the following subject areas: arts and humanities, social and behavioral sciences, physical and biological sciences

**Recommended courses transfer applicants interested in STEM should complete before transfer:** Depends on major

**Recommended extracurricular engagement:** Depends on major

**Type of curriculum:** Gen. Ed. requirements

**Type of academic year:** Quarter

**Advisors specifically for transfer students:** Yes

**Credit policy (in their own words):** Junior-level standing (60 semester/90 quarter transferable units completed) by the end of the spring term before you transfer. GPA of 3.2 or higher earned in transferable courses. Progress toward completion of major preparation requirements by spring prior to transfer (see below).

There may be additional lower division requirements that students can complete at their current institutions or at UCLA. Should a major not have specific prerequisites, we expect students to demonstrate interest in academic study by completing coursework related to the major.

Completion of the following course requirements by spring prior to transfer:

- 2 transferable courses in English composition/critical thinking and writing
- 1 transferable math course that has a prerequisite of intermediate algebra or higher
- 4 transferable college courses in at least 2 of the following subject areas: arts and humanities, social and behavioral sciences, physical and biological sciences

Read more at www.admission.ucla.edu/prospect/adm_tr/tradms.htm.

**Max number of transfer credits accepted:** 105 quarter units

**Residency requirement for transfer students:** Yes

**Study abroad available for transfer students:** Yes

**Free tutoring for all students:** Yes

**Writing center for all students:** Yes

**Career support/access to internships and resume prep for all students:** Yes

**% of undergraduate students hired within 6 months of graduation:** No information provided.

**Additional resources specifically designated for transfer and/or non-traditional students:** Yes

**Transfer Programs:** Center for Community College Partnerships (CCCP), Community College, Transfer Recruitment (CCTR), Student Transfer Outreach, Mentorship Program (STOMP), Transfer Alliance Program (TAP)

**Non-traditional Students Programs:** Non-Traditional Students Network (NTSN, The Network), Parenting Students at UCLA, Student Veterans Association @ UCLA (SVAUCLA)

## Housing

**Available for transfer students:** Yes

**Available for non-traditional students:** Yes

**Guaranteed for transfer students:** Yes

**Non-traditional students can reside in housing year-round:** Yes

**Family housing available:** Yes

## Non-Traditional Admissions

**Non-traditional student policy (in their own words):** No specific policy available, but UCLA accepts non-traditional students and offers certain resources, such as separate housing and the Non-Traditional Student Network, in order to help these students make the most out of their college experience.

**Name of program:** Transfer Alliance Program

**Program description:** The UCLA Transfer Alliance Program (TAP) gives you the opportunity to enhance your ability to transfer to UCLA at the junior level from a California community college. Students are certified after completing the honors/scholars program at their community college and given priority consideration for admission to UCLA College of Letters and Science. UCLA and California Community Colleges cooperate to assist students in the transfer process.

The TAP Community Colleges offer enriched academic programs and all courses necessary to transfer, including General Education requirements and preparatory courses for majors.

Designated faculty and counselors at the community colleges help students plan academic programs that meet major and general education requirements and honors/scholars certification.

While students are in the community college TAP programs, meaningful linkages with UCLA are provided such as on-campus informational meetings and tours, library privileges, and opportunities to attend selected UCLA cultural and athletic events.

**Program deadline:** No set deadline.

**Program admission requirements:** Must be interested in transferring to UCLA.

**Program website:** www.admission.ucla.edu/prospect/adm_tr/ADM_CCO/tap.htm

**Program contact person:** UCLA Undergraduate Admission Transfer Team

**Program contact info:** (310) 825-3101, transfer@admission.ucla.edu

## Military/Veteran Students

**Military/veteran admissions policy (in their own words):** UCLA admits undergraduate students (seeking bachelor of arts–B.A. or bachelor of science–B.S. degrees) in 2 categories: freshman and junior-level transfer (see below).

Because of the high volume of applications from first-time degree-seeking students, we do not admit students for second bachelor's degrees at UCLA. If you already have a bachelor's degree, UCLA offers many graduate and professional degree programs that may be of interest to you.

If you graduated from high school but have never attempted any coursework at a college or university after graduating, then you would be considered a freshman.

If you have ever enrolled at a college or university, then you must meet the requirements for junior-level transfer admission to UCLA (you cannot disregard college work and apply as a freshman).

Read more at www.admission.ucla.edu/veterans.htm.

**Status considered in admissions:** Yes

**Special admissions process:** No

**Special financial aid:** Yes. GI Bill requirements.

**Specific programs/policies to address needs:** Many different services. The Bruin Resource Center's Veterans Resource Office (VRO) provides caring and personalized support for undergraduate and graduate student veterans in their transition from military service to civilian and college life. We help our student veterans navigate UCLA and provide them with a welcoming space, mentoring from other student veterans, guidance on educational benefits, and tools to succeed academically and personally. We value the skills, assets, and experiences veterans bring to the UCLA community and are committed to helping them achieve their goals and aspirations. The VRO also increases campus awareness of student-veteran issues and fosters a sense of belonging, community, and well-being for all student veterans on campus.

## DACA/Undocumented Students

**DACA and undocumented admissions policy (in their own words):** The University of California welcomes and supports students without regard to their immigration status. UC will continue to admit students in a manner consistent with our nondiscrimination policy and without regard to a student's race, color, national origin, religion, citizenship, or other protected characteristic. In other words, undocumented applicants with or without DACA status will be considered for admission on the same basis as any US citizen or other applicant. The University is committed to creating an environment in which all admitted students can successfully matriculate and graduate. Federal law protects student privacy rights, and the California Constitution and statutes provide broad privacy protection to all members of the UC community. University policy provides additional privacy protections. When the University receives requests for information that implicate individual privacy rights, the University will continue its practice of working closely with the Office of General Counsel to protect the privacy of members of the UC community. We will not release immigration status or related information in confidential student records, without permission from a student, to federal agencies or other parties without a judicial warrant, a subpoena, a court order, or as otherwise required by law.

**Admitted:** Yes

**Status considered in admissions:** Yes

**Special admissions process:** No

**Eligible for institutional financial aid:** Yes. The California DREAM Act extends eligibility for certain types of UC and California Financial Aid to students, including undocumented students, who qualify for non-resident tuition exemption under AB540. Read more here: www.usp.ucla.edu/Resources#183251014-funding.

**Specific programs/policies to address needs:** Yes. Undocumented Student Program supports undocumented students by providing caring, personalized services and resources that enable students to reach their highest potential. Through a variety of programs, workshops, and partnerships with students, campus allies, and community stakeholders, USP strives to support all members of the UndocuBruin community. By advocating for educational equity, empowering students, and fostering a campus environment, USP celebrates the unique contributions of all its members. Read more here: www.usp.ucla.edu/.

# UNIVERSITY OF CALIFORNIA, SAN DIEGO

**Location:** La Jolla, California

**Website:** https://ucsd.edu

**Endowment:** $963.2 million

**Type of School:** Public/Co-ed, Research University

**# of Undergraduate Students:** 26,590 (2015–2016)

**# of Graduate Students:** 5,506 (2015–2016)

**Average Class Size:** 20 or less

**School Mission (in their own words):** In defining our mission, we challenged ourselves to identify what differentiates us from other institutions of higher education and to clarify how we will uniquely contribute in the areas of education, research, and public service.

UC San Diego will transform California and a diverse global society by educating, generating, and disseminating knowledge and creative works and engaging in public service.

## Admissions

**Admissions office mailing address:** 9500 Gilman Dr, La Jolla CA 92093

**Admissions office phone:** (858) 534-4831

**Admissions office contact page:** https://admissions.ucsd.edu/contact/contact-form.html

**# of transfer applications:** Fall 2015: 16,273

**# of transfer students accepted:** Fall 2015: 8,169.

**Transfer student acceptance rate (2015–2016 academic year):** 50.2%

**Freshman applications received in Fall 2015:** 78,056

**Freshman applications accepted in Fall 2015:** 26,509

**Acceptance rate for 2015–2016 freshmen:** 34.2%

## Transfer Admissions Process

**Transfer policy (in their own words):** You are a transfer student if you enrolled in a regular session at a college or university after high school. UC San Diego looks for transfer students at the junior-year level who are well-prepared to succeed in a rigorous and challenging academic setting. Admission is competitive and you must exceed the minimum requirements. Each year about 30% of the new students on the UC San Diego campus are transfer students. To read about all the minimum requirements and other transfer admissions information, refer to the following link: http://admissions.ucsd.edu/transfers.

**Transfer admissions contact person:** Kristina Wong Davis, Director, Undergraduate Admissions

**Transfer admissions contact info:** admissionsdirector@mail.ucsd.edu

**Offers transfer-focused admissions events:** Yes

**Transfer application deadline:** Fall 2018 deadline is 11/30/17; 1/3/18 (extension deadline).

**Acceptances announced to transfer applicants:** Fall 2018 in mid-March–April.

**Transfer application on Common App:** No. Common App fee: N/A.

**Separate application or in addition to the Common App:** Yes

**Fee for separate transfer application:** Yes

**Waiver available for separate transfer application fee:** UC will waive application fees for up to 4 campuses for qualified students who would otherwise be unable to apply for admission. The fee waiver program is for US citizens, permanent residents, and applicants eligible for AB540 benefits.

**SAT/ACT required for transfer applicants:** Only for international students

**High-school records requirements:** Required from some

**High-school records requirements for applicants who completed outside the US:** Official high-school transcript

**Submission requirements for transfer applicants who completed high-school equivalency test:** None

**College transcript requirements:** Official transcripts for all colleges and universities attended

**Interviews available for transfer applicants:** No

**Additional requirements for transfers seeking admissions to engineering major:** Yes. Plan ahead and complete as many courses as possible to prepare for your chosen major. UC San Diego's academic departments specify courses you must take before you transfer to prepare for upper-division study in your major. See the UCSD General Catalog for more information.

## Costs & Financial Aid

**FAFSA code:** 1317

**CSS Profile code:** N/A

**Are internal school financial aid forms required?** Yes

**Financial aid deadlines for transfer applicants:** Fall 2018: 3/2/18

**Costs for the 2017–2018 year:** Tuition & Fees: CA resident: $14,230. Non-CA resident: $42,244. Room & Board: $13,254.

**Financial aid for transfer students:** Yes

**Guarantees meeting 100% need for transfer students:** No

**Need-based aid for transfer students:** Yes. To qualify for financial aid, you must file either the Free Application for Federal Student Aid (FAFSA) or California DREAM Act Application.

**Merit-based financial aid for transfer students:** Yes. Must meet the requirements for the different scholarships.

**Phi Theta Kappa Scholarship:** No

**Reduced or zero tuition fees for low-income students:** Yes

**Includes loans in financial aid packages:** Yes

**% of all undergraduates receiving financial aid:** 68%

**% of all undergraduates qualifying for Pell Grants:** No information provided.

**Average financial aid award for all undergraduate students:** $22,456 (2015–2016)

**Funding available for low-income students to visit:** No

**Enrollment deposit can be waived for low-income students:** Yes

## Academics

**GPA range for transfer students accepted in 2016–2017:** No information provided.

**SAT ranges for all students admitted in 2016:** Critical Reading: 580–680. Mathematics: 630–770. Writing: 590–700.

**ACT composite score range for all students admitted in 2016:** 27–32

**Recommended completed level of math for transfer applicants:** 1 course on mathematical concepts and quantitative reasoning

**Recommended completed level of English for transfer applicants:** 2 English composition courses

**Recommended courses transfer applicants should have on transcripts:** 4 courses from at least 2 of the following: arts and humanities, physical and biological sciences, social and behavioral sciences

**Type of curriculum:** Gen. Ed. requirements

**Type of academic year:** Quarter

**Advisors specifically for transfer students:** Yes

**Credit policy (in their own words):** Most UC San Diego courses carry 4 quarter-units of credit, and a student usually takes 4 courses each quarter. Students will be granted up to 70 semester (105 quarter) units of credit for lower-division coursework completed at any institution (or combination of institutions).

For units beyond the maximum, subject credit for appropriate coursework will be granted and may be used to satisfy requirements. Units earned through AP, IB, and/or A-Level examinations are not included in the limitation (do not put applicants at risk of being denied admission). Units earned at any UC campus in extension, summer, cross/concurrent, and regular academic year enrollment are not included in the limitation but are added to the maximum transfer credit allowed (may put applicants at risk of being denied admission due to excessive units).

Read more at https://admissions.ucsd.edu/transfers/requirements.html.

**Max number of transfer credits accepted:** 105 quarter units

**Residency requirement for transfer students:** No

**Study abroad available for transfer students:** Yes

**Free tutoring for all students:** Most are free, but not all.

**Writing center for all students:** Yes

**Career support/access to internships and resume prep for all students:** Yes

**% of undergraduate students hired within 6 months of graduation:** 56%

**Additional resources specifically designated for transfer and/or non-traditional students:** Yes. For academic experiences, practical experiences, and student involvement.

## Housing

**Available for transfer students:** Yes

**Available for non-traditional students:** Yes

**Guaranteed for transfer students:** Yes

**Non-traditional students can reside in housing year-round:** No

**Family housing available:** Yes

## Non-Traditional Admissions

No non-traditional student policies or programs available.

## Military/Veteran Students

**Military/veteran admissions policy (in their own words):** Veterans follow the application process in the same way as any other student. Once military/veteran students speak to an admissions specialist, they can then decide if they should apply as a freshman or a transfer student. In addition, the application process is done for the entire UC system in 1 application.

The Department of Veterans Affairs (VA), not UCSD, determines your eligibility for veterans education benefits.

The Registrar's Office helps you take full advantage of the programs, services, and benefits available by:

- Processing your paperwork for VA claims so you'll receive your payments on time
- Certifying your student enrollment for the VA
- Preparing the necessary forms for unit or address changes

Read more at https://admissions.ucsd.edu/transfers/veterans.

**Status considered in admissions:** Yes

**Special admissions process:** No

**Special financial aid:** Yes. GI Bill requirements.

**Specific programs/policies to address needs:** Financial aid for veterans and dependents, priority registration for your classes, Welcome Week Orientation, Active Student Veterans Organization, Student Veterans Resource Center

## DACA/Undocumented Students

**DACA and undocumented admissions policy (in their own words):** The University of California welcomes and supports students without regard to their immigration status. UC will continue to admit students in a manner consistent with our nondiscrimination policy and without regard to a student's race, color, national origin, religion, citizenship, or other protected characteristic. In other words, undocumented applicants with or without DACA status will be considered for admission on the same basis as any US citizen or other applicant. The University is committed to creating an environment in which all admitted students can successfully matriculate and graduate. Federal law protects student privacy rights, and the California Constitution and statutes provide broad privacy protection to all members of the UC community. University policy provides additional privacy protections. When the University receives requests for information that implicate individual privacy rights, the University will continue its practice of working closely with the Office of General Counsel to protect the privacy of members of the UC community. We will not release immigration status or related information in confidential student records, without permission from a student, to federal agencies or other parties without a judicial warrant, a subpoena, a court order, or as otherwise required by law.

**Admitted:** Yes

**Status considered in admissions:** Yes

**Special admissions process:** No

**Eligible for institutional financial aid:** Yes. The California DREAM Act extends eligibility for certain types of UC and California Financial Aid to students, including undocumented students, who qualify for non-resident tuition exemption under AB540. Read more here: https://students.ucsd.edu/finances/financial-aid/applying/cadream.html.

**Specific programs/policies to address needs:** Yes. Academic support: Academic Advising, College of Academic Counseling, UCLA Departmental Advisors, Academic Advancement Program, Community Programs Office, Study Abroad, Tutoring, UCLA Libraries, UCLA Undergraduate Writing Center. Read more here: https://students.ucsd.edu/sponsor/undoc/.

# UNIVERSITY OF CALIFORNIA, SANTA BARBARA

**Location:** Santa Barbara, California

**Website:** www.ucsb.edu

**Endowment:** $303 million

**Type of School:** Public/Co-ed, Research University

**# of Undergraduate Students:** 20,607

**# of Graduate Students:** 2,890

**Average Class Size:** 20 students or fewer

**School Mission (in their own words):** The University of California, Santa Barbara is a leading research institution that also provides a comprehensive liberal arts learning experience. Because teaching and research go hand in hand at UC Santa Barbara, our students are full participants in an educational journey of discovery that stimulates independent thought, critical reasoning, and creativity. Our academic community of faculty, students, and staff is characterized by a culture of interdisciplinary collaboration that is responsive to the needs of our multicultural and global society. All of this takes place within a living and learning environment like no other, as we draw inspiration from the beauty and resources of UC Santa Barbara's extraordinary location at the edge of the Pacific Ocean.

## Admissions

**Admissions office mailing address:** 1210 Cheadle Hall, Santa Barbara CA 93106

**Admissions office phone:** (805) 893-2881

**Admissions office email:** admissions@sa.ucsb.edu

**# of transfer applications:** Fall 2016 admissions: 14,808

**# of transfer students accepted:** Fall 2016: 6,946

**Transfer student acceptance rate (2016–2017 academic year):** 47%

**Freshman applications received in Fall 2016:** 70,444

**Freshman applications accepted in Fall 2016:** 23,020

**Acceptance rate for 2016–2017 freshmen:** 32.7%

## Transfer Admissions Process

**Transfer policy (in their own words):** Requirements for admission are explained at the University of California Admissions webpage.

Complete 60 semester or 90 quarter units of transferable college credit with a grade point average of at least 2.4 for California residents and at least 2.8 for non-residents (no more than 14 semester or 21 quarter units may be taken Pass/
Not Pass).

Complete the following 7-course pattern requirement, earning a grade of C or better in each:

- 2 courses in English composition
- 1 course in mathematics beyond intermediate algebra, such as college algebra, pre-calculus, or statistics
- 4 courses from among at least 2 of the following areas:
  - Arts and humanities
  - Behavioral and social sciences
  - Biological and physical sciences

In addition to this course pattern, students are encouraged to complete as much of the lower-division preparation for their intended major as possible. UCSB transfer applicants are required to apply to a specific major. Prospective applicants who have not identified a major are encouraged to take courses that meet general education requirements while researching majors and trying coursework in potential major subject areas. Students attending a California community college are advised to refer to the ASSIST website for major preparation and course articulation.

**Offers transfer-focused admissions events:** Yes

**Transfer application deadline:** Fall 2018 deadline is 11/30/17.

**Acceptances announced to transfer applicants:** Fall 2018 in mid-March–May 1.

**Transfer application on Common App:** No. Common App Fee: N/A.

**Separate application or in addition to the Common App:** Yes

**Fee for separate transfer application:** Yes

**Waiver available for separate transfer application fee:** UC will waive application fees for up to 4 campuses for qualified students who would otherwise be unable to apply for admission. The fee waiver program is for US citizens, permanent residents, and applicants eligible for AB540 benefits.

**SAT/ACT required for transfer applicants:** Yes

**High-school records requirements:** Official high-school transcript

**High-school records requirements for applicants who completed outside the US:** Same as domestic

**Submission requirements for transfer applicants who completed high-school equivalency test:** Official GED results

**College transcript requirements:** Official transcripts for all colleges and universities attended

**Interviews available for transfer applicants:** No

**Additional requirements for transfers seeking admissions to arts major:** Yes. Applicants who apply to UCSB's College of Creative Studies must fill out a supplemental application in addition to the UC application. Applicants are selected on the basis of outstanding academic and personal achievement, special talent, and capacity for excellence in 1 of the 8 available majors.

**Additional requirements for transfers seeking admissions to engineering major:** Yes. Applicants should have a minimum 3.6 GPA in their major preparatory courses—with no individual grade lower than C—to be competitive for admission. Applicants with a GPA between 3.2 and 3.6 will also be considered for admission but will be less competitive.

## Costs & Financial Aid

**FAFSA code:** 1320

**CSS Profile code:** N/A

**Are internal school financial aid forms required?** Yes

**Financial aid deadlines for transfer applicants:** Fall 2018: 3/2/18. Spring 2019: N/A.

**Costs for the 2017–2018 year:** Tuition & Fees: In-state: $17,733. Out-of-state: $45,747. Room & Board: $14,778.

**Financial aid for transfer students:** Yes

**Guarantees meeting 100% need for transfer students:** No

**Need-based aid for transfer students:** Yes. To qualify for financial aid, you must file either the Free Application for Federal Student Aid (FAFSA) or California DREAM Act Application.

**Merit-based financial aid for transfer students:** Yes. New students tell us about their criteria that might meet specific restricted scholarship requirements when they complete the "Scholarship Opportunities" section in Step 2 of the online admissions application or the equivalent section of the paper admissions application. During that process, they are asked to review a list of eligibility characteristics and check off those that apply to them. These characteristics remain part of the students' financial aid application records for future years' scholarship consideration.

**Phi Theta Kappa Scholarship:** No

**Reduced or zero tuition fees for low-income students:** Yes

**Includes loans in financial aid packages:** Yes

**% of all undergraduates receiving financial aid:** 59%

**% of all undergraduates qualifying for Pell Grants:** No information provided.

**Average financial aid award for all undergraduate students:** $18,698

**Funding available for low-income students to visit:** No

**Enrollment deposit can be waived for low-income students:** Yes

## Academics

**GPA range for transfer students accepted in 2016–2017:** No information provided.

**SAT ranges for all students admitted in 2016:** Critical Reading: 550–670. Mathematics: 580–700. Writing: 560–680.

**ACT composite score range for all students admitted in 2016:** 24–30

**Recommended completed level of math for transfer applicants:** 1 course in mathematics beyond intermediate algebra, such as college algebra, precalculus, or statistics.

**Recommended completed level of English for transfer applicants:** 2 courses in English composition

**Recommended courses transfer applicants should have on transcripts:** 4 courses from among at least 2 of the following areas:

- Arts and humanities
- Behavioral and social sciences
- Biological and physical sciences

In addition to this course pattern, students are encouraged to complete as much of the lower-division preparation for their intended major as possible.

**Recommended courses transfer applicants interested in STEM should complete before transfer:** Students are encouraged to complete as much of the lower-division preparation for their intended major as possible.

**Recommended extracurricular engagement:** Depends on major.

**Type of curriculum:** Gen. Ed. requirements

**Type of academic year:** Quarter

**Advisors specifically for transfer students:** Yes

**Credit policy (in their own words):** Credit for academic work at UCSB is expressed in units. Generally, the value assigned to a course is determined at the rate of 1 unit for every 3 hours of student work required each week during a 10-week term. The unit value assigned to a course is determined by the number of class meetings each week and by the student's class preparation time.

**Transfer credit policy:** The Office of Admissions determines transferability of coursework after you present an official transcript of the work. You can contact the College Advising Office or the Office of Admissions for advising and information before enrolling in an outside class, but the final decision rests with the Office of Admissions after your transcript is received.

In other words, you cannot have complete assurance about whether or not your outside coursework will transfer. The following guidelines can help you avoid disappointment:

- Your course must be completed at an accredited college or university and must be reported on an official transcript.
- Your course must cover the same depth and breadth of a subject as UC courses.
- Your course must be listed and described in a college's catalog for the regular year. Note that courses taken through non–University of California extension programs are not always transferable. Within the University of California, UC Extension courses are transferable only if numbered 1–199.
- Credit will not be allowed for any coursework that substantially duplicates a course you already have completed.

- Credit also will not be allowed for any math or foreign language course that is less advanced than those you already have completed.
  - Keep in mind that courses within traditional academic disciplines (e.g., science, literature, and social sciences) generally are transferable.
  - The following types of courses are not transferable: courses that are vocational, technical, or professional in nature (e.g., advertising, real estate, electronics); remedial courses; personal enrichment (e.g., how to use your personal computer).

Read more at www.duels.ucsb.edu/advising/planning/transfer-credit.

**Max number of transfer credits accepted:** 70 semester units

**Residency requirement for transfer students:** Yes. 3 terms in residence at UC Santa Barbara.

20 upper-division units in a major in residence at UC Santa Barbara. This applies to double majors as well. You need 20 separate units in residence in each major.

12 upper-division units in a minor in residence at UC Santa Barbara (if applicable); 27 total upper-division units in the college of the student's major, which includes the 20 above at UC Santa Barbara; 35 of the final 45 units required for graduation in residence at UC Santa Barbara. If you participate in EAP as a senior, this is modified to 35 of the final 90 units.

**Study abroad available for transfer students:** Yes

**Free tutoring for all students:** Yes

**Writing center for all students:** Yes

**Career support/access to internships and resume prep for all students:** Yes

**% of undergraduate students hired within 6 months of graduation:** 66%

**Additional resources specifically designated for transfer and/or non-traditional students:** Yes. Transfer Student Center (academic advising, programs and events, research, and resources) and Non-Traditional Student Resource Center (resources for student parents, 25+ undergrad, and 29+ grads, events, and resources).

## Housing

**Available for transfer students:** Yes.

**Available for non-traditional students:** Yes

**Guaranteed for transfer students:** Yes

**Non-traditional students can reside in housing year-round:** Yes

**Family housing available:** Yes

## Non-Traditional Admissions

**Non-traditional student policy (in their own words):** Non-traditional students include undergraduates over 24 and graduate students over 29 years old, students who are married or in a domestic partnership, and students who are parents or have dependents. The Non-Traditional Student Resource Center on the first floor of the Student Resource Building is available to all non-traditional students, where one-on-one support is also available. Non-traditional students who have school-aged or younger children (and thus have to work around childcare schedules) are approved to receive registration priority. Please self-identify with the Non-Traditional Student Resource Center in order to receive this benefit. If you have children, also see the "Student Parents" section.

Here is the link to the non-traditional student resource center: http://wgse.sa.ucsb.edu/nontrad/home.

**Name of program:** Transfer Admission Guarantee

**Program description:** UCSB has a Transfer Admission Guarantee (TAG) with all California community colleges. TAG offers guaranteed admission to California community college students who meet specific requirements. TAG establishes criteria for guaranteed admission to UCSB for the fall term only. At UCSB, TAGs are available for all majors in the College of Letters and Science except performing arts majors. The TAG is not available for any majors in the College of Engineering or the College of Creative Studies. Students should refer to the ASSIST website under articulation agreements by major between UCSB and their community college for more specific details on articulated courses. Students accepted are guaranteed admission.

**Program deadline:** The filing period for Fall 2018 admission will be September 1–30, 2017.

**Program admission requirements:** Applicants must have completed 30 UC-transferable semester units/45 UC-transferable quarter units (excluding AP/IB/A-Level units) prior to TAG submission and complete the last 30 of 60 or more UC-transferable semester units (45 of 90 quarter units) in residence at a California community college. Earn an overall minimum 3.20 GPA in all UC-transferable coursework

**Program website:** http://admissions.sa.ucsb.edu/applying/transfer/tag

**Program contact person:** Office of Admissions

**Program contact info:** (805) 893-2881, admissions@sa.ucsb.edu.

## Military/Veteran Students

**Military/veteran admissions policy (in their own words):** There are 2 application processes for undergraduates. You can either enter UCSB as a freshman or as a junior-level transfer student. If you have completed any college courses, your only option will be to transfer in as a junior. For information on eligibility and selectivity, visit our Paths to UCSB page.

More important information regarding military/veteran admissions can be found at www.sa.ucsb.edu/veterans/admissions.

**Status considered in admissions:** No

**Special admissions process:** No

**Special financial aid:** Yes. Veteran education benefits are for student veterans, service members, and their families. You can also sometimes get financial aid as well by filling out FAFSA.

**Specific programs/policies to address needs:** Veteran Resource Center, special housing, etc.

## DACA/Undocumented Students

**DACA and undocumented admissions policy (in their own words):** The University of California welcomes and supports students without regard to their immigration status. UC will continue to admit students in a manner consistent with our nondiscrimination policy and without regard to a student's race, color, national origin, religion, citizenship, or other protected characteristics. In other words, undocumented applicants with or without DACA status will be considered for admission on the same basis as any US citizen or other applicant. The University is committed to creating an environment in which all admitted students can successfully matriculate and graduate. Federal law protects student privacy rights, and the California Constitution and statutes provide broad privacy protection to all members of the UC community. University policy provides additional privacy protections. When the University receives requests for information that implicate individual privacy rights, the University will continue its practice of working closely with the Office of General Counsel to protect the privacy of members of the UC community. We will not release immigration status or related information in confidential student records, without permission from a student, to federal agencies or other parties without a judicial warrant, a subpoena, a court order, or as otherwise required by law.

**Admitted:** Yes

**Status considered in admissions:** Yes

**Special admissions process:** No

**Eligible for institutional financial aid:** Yes. The California DREAM Act extends eligibility for certain types of UC and California Financial Aid to students, including undocumented students, who qualify for non-resident tuition exemption under AB540. Read more here: www.finaid.ucsb.edu/scholarships.

**Specific programs/policies to address needs:** Yes. UC Santa Barbara is committed to fostering a safe and supportive environment for students of diverse backgrounds including our DREAM Scholars—undocumented students at UCSB. The University strives to develop an awareness and understanding of the experiences of undocumented students (while maintaining the confidentiality of individual students) and to develop campus responses and processes to address their needs related to persistence, retention, and graduation. Read more here: www.sa.ucsb.edu/dreamscholars/home.

# UNIVERSITY OF CHICAGO

**Location:** Chicago, Illinois
**Website:** www.uchicago.edu
**Endowment:** $7 billion
**Type of School:** Private/Co-ed, Research University
**# of Undergraduate Students:** 5,860
**# of Graduate Students:** 9,866
**Average Class Size:** 20 students or less

**School Mission (in their own words):** The University of Chicago is an urban research university that has driven new ways of thinking since 1890. Our commitment to free and open inquiry draws inspired scholars to our global campuses, where ideas are born that challenge and change the world. We empower individuals to challenge conventional thinking in pursuit of original ideas. Students in the College develop critical, analytic, and writing skills in our rigorous, interdisciplinary core curriculum. Through graduate programs, students test their ideas with UChicago scholars and become the next generation of leaders in academia, industry, nonprofits, and government.

## Admissions

**Admissions office mailing address:** 5801 S Ellis Ave, Chicago IL 60637

**Admissions office phone:** (773) 702-8650

**Admissions office email:** collegeadmissions@uchicago.edu

No information on transfer applications provided.

**Freshman applications received in Fall 2016:** 25,268

**Freshman applications accepted in Fall 2016:** 3,349

**Acceptance rate for 2016–2017 freshmen:** 13.3%

## Transfer Admissions Process

**Transfer policy (in their own words):** If you have completed 1 term as a full-time student in a degree-seeking program at another college or university, you must apply to the University of Chicago as a transfer student. High-school students who have taken college-level courses should apply as first-year applicants.

If you would like to visit the University to study for 1 year or less before returning to another institution, you should apply as a student-at-large. Students who already have a bachelor's degree are not eligible to apply to the undergraduate College at the University of Chicago, as the College does not grant second bachelor's degrees. However, you are welcome to pursue a graduate degree or apply as a graduate-student-at-large through the Graham School of General Studies.

Read more at https://collegeadmissions.uchicago.edu/apply/applicants/transfer.

**Transfer admissions contact person:** Mary Hetlage, Senior Associate Director, Admissions

**Transfer admissions contact info:** mhetlage@uchicago.edu, (773) 702-8658

**Offers transfer-focused admissions events:** N/A

**Transfer application deadline:** Fall 2018 deadline is 3/1/18.

**Acceptances announced to transfer applicants:** Fall 2018 in early May.

**Transfer application on Common App:** Yes. Common App fee: $75.

**SAT/ACT required for transfer applicants:** Yes

**High-school records requirements:** Official transcript

**High-school records requirements for applicants who completed outside the US:** Official score report

**Submission requirements for transfer applicants who completed high-school equivalency test:** Secondary-school report and transcript

**College transcript requirements:** Transcripts must come from the school to be considered an official document.

**Interviews available for transfer applicants:** Yes. Optional. Interview with a current fourth-year student on campus or with a graduate of the University of Chicago near you.

## Costs & Financial Aid

**FAFSA code:** 1774

**CSS Profile code:** 1832

**Are internal school financial aid forms required?** No

**Financial aid deadline for transfer applicants:** N/A

**Costs for the 2017–2018 year:** Tuition & Fees: $50,997. Room & Board: $15,093.

**Financial aid for transfer students:** Yes

**Guarantees meeting 100% need for transfer students:** Yes

**Need-based aid for transfer students:** Yes

**Merit-based financial aid for transfer students:** No

**Phi Theta Kappa Scholarship:** No

**Reduced or zero tuition fees for low-income students:** Yes

**Includes loans in financial aid packages:** No

**% of all undergraduates receiving financial aid:** N/A

**% of all undergraduates qualifying for Pell Grants:** N/A

**Average financial aid award for all undergraduate students:** $45,500

**Funding available for low-income students to visit:** No

**Enrollment deposit can be waived for low-income students:** Yes

## Academics

**GPA range for transfer students accepted in 2016–2017:** N/A

**SAT ranges for all students admitted in 2016:** Combined Reading and Math: 1440–1540

**ACT composite score range for all students admitted in 2016:** 31–34

**Recommended completed level of math for transfer applicants:** Core curriculum classes: Natural and Mathematical Sciences (6 quarters)

**Recommended courses transfer applicants should have on transcripts:**

- Core curriculum classes: humanities, civilization studies, and the arts (6 quarters)
- Natural and mathematical sciences (6 quarters)
- Social sciences (3 quarters)
- Language requirement (can be fulfilled with placement credit)

**Type of curriculum:** Gen. Ed. requirements

**Type of academic year:** Quarter

**Advisors specifically for transfer students:** No

**Credit policy (in their own words):** The course unit is the measure of credit at the University of Chicago. Each 100 unit course is equivalent to 3 1/3 semester hours or 5 quarter hours. Courses of greater or lesser value such as 150 or 050 carry proportionately more or fewer semester or quarter hours of credit.

Read more at https://registrar.uchicago.edu/page/credits.

Transfer credit must be evaluated and approved by the Office of the Dean of Students in the College. If approved, transfer credit is listed on the student's University of Chicago transcript only as the number of credits approved to transfer. Transfer credit does not count toward the University of Chicago GPA, nor do the grades appear on the UChicago transcript. Students participating in University of Chicago–sponsored direct enrollment programs will have their credits vetted by the Study Abroad Office instead of the College Dean of Students Office.

**Minimum requirements for transfer eligibility:**

Courses MUST:

- Be taken at an accredited institution that grants bachelor's degrees, subject to review by the Office of the Dean of Students in the College.
- Confer at least 3 semester hours or 4 quarter hours of credit. For institutions without standard credit hours, contact hours (normally a minimum of 30) may be used.
- Be completed with a grade of C or above (not C– or P). Students in science majors must earn at least a B in science courses.
- Not duplicate credit that students earn or have already earned for college-level coursework. (For instance, a student could not take PLSC 28701 Introduction to Political Theory and also transfer in credit for an Introduction to Political Theory course taken elsewhere.)
- Be in liberal arts subjects similar to those offered at the University of Chicago.

Courses in the following categories are NOT eligible for transfer credit:

- Calculus and pre-calculus (credit may only be earned via accreditation or AP test).
- Foreign language study. Placement level is determined by exam. Advanced literature or topics courses taught in a foreign language may qualify.
- Any kind of online/distance, tutorial, or independent study coursework, including internship credit.
- Professional or technical courses, or coursework otherwise unlike University of Chicago liberal arts courses. This includes such areas as: law, civil/mechanical engineering, speech, education, leadership, first-year writing, and undergraduate courses in business. Courses in media production will only transfer if there is an equivalent course listed in the University of Chicago catalog.

Read more at http://collegecatalog.uchicago.edu/thecollege/transfercredit.

**Max number of transfer credits accepted:** N/A

**Residency requirement for transfer students:** Yes. A student must be in residence at the University of Chicago campus for at least 6 quarters and must successfully complete a minimum of 18 courses while in residence. Please note: Certain College-sponsored study-abroad programs (such as the civilization studies programs) count toward this residency and course requirement.

**Study abroad available for transfer students:** Yes. Must fulfill residency requirements, but some study-abroad programs count toward this requirement.

**Free tutoring for all students:** Yes

**Writing center for all students:** Yes

**Career support/access to internships and resume prep for all students:** Yes

**% of undergraduate students hired within 6 months of graduation:** 100 (2015)

**Additional resources specifically designated for transfer and/or non-traditional students:** No

## Housing

**Available for transfer students:** Yes

**Available for non-traditional students:** Yes

**Guaranteed for transfer students:** Yes

**Non-traditional students can reside in housing year-round:** Yes

**Family housing available:** Yes

## Non-Traditional Admissions

No non-traditional student policies or programs available.

## Military/Veteran Students

**Military/veteran admissions policy (in their own words:** The University of Chicago welcomes veterans of the US armed forces to apply for admission to the College. If you have completed at least 1 term at another college or university in a degree-seeking program, you should apply as a transfer student. If not, you should apply as a first-year applicant.

**No Application Fee:** The University of Chicago does not charge a college application fee to veterans. Upon submitting your application, please email our office and identify yourself as a veteran applicant and your fee will be waived. If you indicate that you intend to apply for need-based financial aid, your application fee will be waived automatically.

**Application for Admission:** When filling out the Application for Admission, please complete sections that do not seem directly relevant to your personal, academic, and military experiences to the best of your ability. For example, the application asks about your extracurricular activities, awards, and honors. Veteran applicants should feel free to include military experiences and distinctions, high-school experiences, and any other postsecondary experiences in these sections. You are also welcome to attach a resume or CV to explain your nonacademic experiences more thoroughly.

**Academic Records:** If for any reason you cannot acquire all your academic records, we will accept whatever documents you can provide. However, the most competitive applicants tend to demonstrate an academic record that is rigorous and engaged in a wide range of subjects.

**Teacher and Other Recommendations:** Although we generally require 2 letters of recommendation from teachers of core academic subjects, we understand the potential difficulty of getting recommendations from high-school or college instructors after service in the military. We highly recommend submitting at least 1 recommendation from a traditional classroom instructor if possible. You may also submit a recommendation from a superior officer to contextualize your military experiences.

**Testing:** We require all applicants to submit either an SAT or ACT score. Veteran applicants are welcome to submit a score from a test date within the last 8 years.

Read more important information regarding veteran admissions at https://collegeadmissions.uchicago.edu/apply/applicants/veterans.

**Status considered in admissions:** Yes

**Special admissions process:** Yes. Veterans do not pay an application fee but must notify Office of Admissions via email introducing themselves as a veteran applicant so their fee can be waived.

**Special financial aid:** Yes. The Yellow Ribbon Program.

**Specific programs/policies to address needs:** Applicants will need to submit the Yellow Ribbon Application Form, Certificate of Eligibility, Veterans Certification Request Form, and DD214 once accepted.

## DACA/Undocumented Students

**DACA and undocumented admissions policy (in their own words):** Recent news and federal legislation have sparked national attention to undocumented student issues. At the University of Chicago, we are committed to creating a diverse campus community. All students who apply, regardless of citizenship, are considered for admission and for every type of private financial aid the University offers.

The University of Chicago has, from its inception, been a place where the best and brightest minds from around the world can gather to shape ideas, produce new knowledge, and contribute to the betterment of human life. Our community has been deliberately inclusive, because it is from the widest possible range of perspectives and viewpoints that the most innovative ideas can be proposed, tested, and debated. We are committed to assembling a community of talented individuals regardless of their backgrounds, financial circumstances, or national origins. This commitment is further discussed in President Zimmer's statement on diversity, posted at diversity.uchicago.edu.

In this context, the University of Chicago considers for admission students from around the world. All students who apply, regardless of citizenship, are considered for admission to the University and for every type of private financial aid that the University offers. In accordance with the law, the University admits and enrolls undocumented students and uses private funds to provide financial aid to support their studies.

Read more at http://inclusion.uchicago.edu/studentsupport/undocumented.

**Admitted:** Yes, as an international student

**Status considered in admissions:** Yes

**Special admissions process:** Apply as an international student. International students are required to have an English proficiency test.

**Eligible for institutional financial aid:** Yes. Students should submit a completed International Student Financial Aid Application (ISFAA).

**Specific programs/policies to address needs:** No

# UNIVERSITY OF FLORIDA

**Location:** Gainesville, Florida
**Website:** www.ufl.edu
**Endowment:** $1.86 billion (2015)
**Type of School:** Public/Co-ed, Research University
**# of Undergraduate Students:** 35,043
**# of Graduate Students:** 17,243
**Average Class Size:** 20 students or fewer

**School Mission (in their own words):** At the University of Florida, we are a people of purpose. We're committed to challenging convention and ourselves. We see things not as they are, but as they could be. And we strive for a greater impact: one measured in people helped and lives improved.

## Admissions

**Admissions office mailing address:** 201 Criser Hall, PO Box 114000, Gainesville FL 32611

**Admissions office phone:** (352) 392-1365

**Admissions office email:** transfer@admissions.ufl.edu

**# of transfer applications:** Fall 2016 admissions: 6,203. Spring 2017 admissions: N/A.

**# of transfer students accepted:** Fall 2016: 2,500. Spring 2017: N/A.

**Transfer student acceptance rate (2016–2017 academic year):** 40.3%

**Freshman applications received in Fall 2016:** 30,118

**Freshman applications accepted in Fall 2016:** 13,835

**Acceptance rate for 2016–2017 freshmen:** 46%

## Transfer Admissions Process

**Transfer policy (in their own words):** A transfer student is a person who changes from one college to another. At UF, an undergraduate transfer is a student who has earned at least 12 semester hours following graduation from high school and has not received a bachelor's degree.

Planning to transfer into UF in advance is strongly advised and will greatly enhance the opportunity for a successful transfer experience. Eligible transfer applicants must have completed an associate of arts degree from a Florida public institution or at least 60 transferable semester credit hours from a regionally accredited institution.

Prospective transfers from Florida public community colleges can refer to the Fla. Virtual Campus (FLVC) Common Prerequisite Manual for state university transfer prerequisite course requirements. Transfer applicants who meet UF minimum admission requirements will be referred to the appropriate UF college for an admission decision. Applicants who exceed minimum requirements are most competitive for admission at the junior level, if space is available.

Transfer applicants should visit the college's website or contact the college to be sure that academic requirements are met and to become familiar with transfer application deadlines.

If you have less than 60 semester credit hours or have already completed a bachelor's degree, you are not eligible for our on-campus program and should consider applying for a UF Online Program or to our graduate, professional, or post-baccalaureate admissions.

**Transfer admissions contact person:** Sergio Rodriguez, Counselor

**Transfer admissions contact info:** transfer@admissions.ufl.edu, (352) 294-0954

**Offers transfer-focused admissions events:** N/A

**Transfer application deadline:** Fall 2018 deadline varies by college. Spring 2019 deadline varies by college.

**Acceptances announced to transfer applicants:** Fall 2018 varies by college. Spring 2019 varies by college.

**Transfer application on Common App:** No. Common App fee: N/A.

**Separate application or in addition to the Common App:** Yes

**Fee for separate transfer application:** $30

**Waiver available for separate transfer application fee:** N/A

**SAT/ACT required for transfer applicants:** Yes, required for sophomore transfers and those applying to teacher certification programs.

**High-school records requirements:** Official transcript, documentation of 2 sequential courses of foreign language in secondary school

**High-school records requirements for applicants who completed outside the US:** Official transcript, documentation of 2 sequential courses of foreign language in secondary school

**Submission requirements for transfer applicants who completed high-school equivalency test:** Official GED results

**College transcript requirements:** Official transcripts from all colleges/universities attended

**Interviews available for transfer applicants:** No

## Costs & Financial Aid

**FAFSA code:** 1535

**CSS Profile code:** N/A

**Are internal school financial aid forms required?** No

**Financial aid deadlines for transfer applicants:** Fall 2018: 10/1/18. Spring 2019: N/A.

**Costs for the 2017–2018 year:** Tuition & Fees: $21,230. Room & Board: $5,440.

**Financial aid for transfer students:** Yes

**Guarantees meeting 100% need for transfer students:** Yes

**Need-based aid for transfer students:** Yes. Submit financial aid documents.

**Merit-based financial aid for transfer students:** Yes. FL residents only.

**Phi Theta Kappa Scholarship:** No

**Reduced or zero tuition fees for low-income students:** Yes

**Includes loans in financial aid packages:** Yes

**% of all undergraduates receiving financial aid:** No information provided.

**% of all undergraduates qualifying for Pell Grants:** No information provided.

**Average financial aid award for all undergraduate students:** $12,494

**Funding available for low-income students to visit:** No

**Enrollment deposit can be waived for low-income students:** Yes, generally, if your UF application fee was waived, you will receive a tuition deposit waiver as well.

## Academics

**GPA range for transfer students accepted in 2016–2017:** 2.0 minimum GPA

**SAT ranges for all students admitted in 2016:** Critical Reading: 580–680. Mathematics: 600–690. Writing: 580–680.

**ACT composite score range for all students admitted in 2016:** 27–31

**Type of curriculum:** Gen. Ed. requirements

**Type of academic year:** Semester

**Advisors specifically for transfer students:** Yes

**Credit policy (in their own words):** To be eligible for transfer, you must have 60 transferable semester hours of college credit and meet all competitive requirements. Please contact the UF college prior to completing an application if you have questions about your major. Your admission to UF as a transfer is determined by the college and major to which you are applying. If you will receive a bachelor's degree prior to attending UF, please review the requirements for graduate, professional, or post-baccalaureate admissions.

Read more at www.admissions.ufl.edu/apply/transfer/transferapp.

**Max number of transfer credits accepted:** 60

**Residency requirement for transfer students:** Yes. Must complete at least 30 semester hours at the university.

**Study abroad available for transfer students:** Yes. Must fulfill the residency requirements.

**Free tutoring for all students:** Yes

**Writing center for all students:** Yes

**Career support/access to internships and resume prep for all students:** Yes

**% of undergraduate students hired within 6 months of graduation:** No information provided.

**Additional resources specifically designated for transfer and/or non-traditional students:** No

## Housing

**Available for transfer students:** Yes

**Available for non-traditional students:** Yes

**Guaranteed for transfer students:** No

**Non-traditional students can reside in housing year-round:** Yes

**Family housing available:** Yes

## Non-Traditional Admissions

No non-traditional student policies or programs available.

## Military/Veteran Students

**Military/veteran admissions policy (in their own words):** The amount of credits that a military/veteran student has will determine if they should apply as a freshman or transfer student. Read more at http://veterans.ufl.edu/benefits/application-checklist.

**Status considered in admissions:** No

**Special admissions process:** No

**Special financial aid:** No

**Specific programs/policies to address needs:** Veterans Affairs Office that helps students with various issues including academic support and scholarships

## DACA/Undocumented Students

**DACA and undocumented admissions policy (in their own words):** No information provided.

**Admitted:** Yes

**Status considered in admissions:** Yes

**Special admissions process:** No

**Eligible for institutional financial aid:** Undocumented students and students with DACA (Deferred Action for Childhood Arrivals) do not qualify for federal or state aid in Florida, including Machen Florida Opportunity Scholarship, Bright Futures, National Merit, and federal loans and grants.

**Specific programs/policies to address needs:** Undocumented students can apply for an out-of-state fee waiver if they:

- Attended a secondary school in Florida for 3 consecutive years immediately before graduating from a high school in this state
- Applied for enrollment in an institute of higher education within 24 months after high-school graduation

Read more about the waiver and scholarship opportunities here: www.sfa.ufl.edu/process/additional-information/undocumented-students.

# UNIVERSITY OF ILLINOIS, URBANA-CHAMPAIGN

**Location:** Champaign, Illinois

**Website:** http://illinois.edu

**Endowment:** $3.2 billion

**Type of School:** Public/Co-ed, Research University

**# of Undergraduate Students:** 32,579

**# of Graduate Students:** 11,024

**Average Class Size:** No information provided.

**School Mission (in their own words):** The University of Illinois at Urbana-Champaign is charged by our state to enhance the lives of citizens in Illinois, across the nation, and around the world through our leadership in learning, discovery, engagement, and economic development.

## Admissions

**Admissions office mailing address:** 300 Turner Student Services Building, 610 E John St, Champaign IL 61820

**Admissions office phone:** (217) 333-0302

**Admissions office email:** admissions@illinois.edu

**# of transfer applications:** Fall 2016 admissions: 4,704 Spring 2017 admissions: No information provided.

**# of transfer students accepted:** Fall 2016: 2,100. Spring 2017: No information provided.

**Transfer student acceptance rate (2016–2017 academic year):** 44.6%

**Freshman applications received in Fall 2016:** 34,721

**Freshman applications accepted in Fall 2016:** 22,468

**Acceptance rate for 2016–2017 freshmen:** 64.7%

## Transfer Admissions Process

**Transfer policy (in their own words):** Transfer requirements vary depending on your credit level and intended program of study. Our handbook is a detailed guide designed to help you determine what you need to do in order to transfer to Illinois, while our requirements directory gives a quick overview of course and GPA requirements. If you took AP, IB, or A-Level exams, you can also review our credit equivalencies.

Read more at https://admissions.illinois.edu/Apply/Transfer/prepare.

**Transfer admissions contact person:** Kristin Smigielski, Coordinator of Transfer Recruitment

**Transfer admissions contact info:** ksmigiel@illinois.edu, (217) 333-9371

**Offers transfer-focused admissions events:** Yes. Transfer Orange and Blue days in the fall and transfer information sessions on select Fridays.

**Transfer application deadline:** Fall 2018 deadline is 3/1/18. Spring 2019 deadline is 10/15/18.

**Acceptances announced to transfer applicants:** Fall 2018 in mid-April. Spring 2019 in mid-December.

**Transfer application on Common App:** No. Common App fee: N/A.

**Separate application or in addition to the Common App:** Yes

**Fee for separate transfer application:** $50

**Waiver available for separate transfer application fee:** If you're a domestic student who qualifies for a fee waiver, your counselor or current institution's financial aid office must submit our fee waiver form. If you're a student at the University of Illinois at Chicago or Springfield, you don't need to submit a fee.

**SAT/ACT required for transfer applicants:** Yes, if the student has fewer than 30 graded transferable semester hours of credit. Strongly recommended for those with 30–59 hours of transferable credit.

**High-school records requirements:** Official high-school transcript

**High-school records requirements for applicants who completed outside the US:** Same as for domestic transfer students

**Submission requirements for transfer applicants who completed high-school equivalency test:** Official GED results

**College transcript requirements:** Official transcripts from all colleges/universities attended

**Interviews available for transfer applicants:** Yes. Dependent upon major. On campus.

**Additional requirements for transfers seeking admissions to arts major:** Yes. Submit a portfolio.

## Costs & Financial Aid

**FAFSA code:** 1775

**CSS Profile code:** N/A

**Are internal school financial aid forms required?** Yes. Undergraduate Scholarship Supplement Form.

**Financial aid deadlines for transfer applicants:** Fall 2018: 3/15/18. Spring 2019: 10/15/18.

**Costs for the 2017–2018 year:** Tuition & Fees: In-state: $15,868. Out-of-state: $31,988. Room & Board: $11,308.

**Financial aid for transfer students:** Yes

**Guarantees meeting 100% need for transfer students:** No

**Need-based aid for transfer students:** Yes

**Merit-based financial aid for transfer students:** Yes. Awarded to first-generation students with 30+ transferable graded hours and demonstrated financial need who are transferring from an Illinois community college.

**Phi Theta Kappa Scholarship:** No

**Reduced or zero tuition fees for low-income students:** No

**Includes loans in financial aid packages:** Yes

**% of all undergraduates receiving financial aid:** 73%

**% of all undergraduates qualifying for Pell Grants:** No information provided.

**Average financial aid award for all undergraduate students:** $15,959

**Funding available for low-income students to visit:** No

**Enrollment deposit can be waived for low-income students:** Yes, if applicant submitted a fee waiver form with their application

## Academics

**GPA range for transfer students accepted in 2016–2017:** No information provided.

**SAT ranges for all students admitted in 2016:** Critical Reading: 570–680. Mathematics: 700–790. Writing: 590–690.

**ACT composite score range for all students admitted in 2016:** 26–31

**Type of curriculum:** Gen. Ed. requirements

**Type of academic year:** Semester

**Advisors specifically for transfer students:** No information provided.

**Credit policy (in their own words):** In addition to specific course and scholastic average requirements, each candidate for a bachelor's degree from the University of Illinois at Urbana-Champaign must earn at least 60 semester hours of Illinois credit, of which as least 21 hours must be 300- or 400-level courses at this campus (Student Code Art 3-801). Consult your admissions/records officer in LAS Student Academic Affairs with questions.

Read more at www.las.illinois.edu/students/requirements/minimum.

**Max number of transfer credits accepted:** N/A

**Residency requirement for transfer students:** No

**Study abroad available for transfer students:** Yes

**Free tutoring for all students:** Yes

**Writing center for all students:** Yes

**Career support/access to internships and resume prep for all students:** Yes

**% of undergraduate students hired within 6 months of graduation:** No information provided.

**Additional resources specifically designated for transfer and/or non-traditional students:** No

## Housing

**Available for transfer students:** Yes

**Available for non-traditional students:** Yes

**Guaranteed for transfer students:** No

**Non-traditional students can reside in housing year-round:** Yes

**Family housing available:** Yes

## Non-Traditional Admissions

No non-traditional student policies or programs available.

## Military/Veteran Students

**Military/veteran admissions policy (in their own words):** Veterans Support Services has created a Getting Started guide to help step you through the application process. As a first step, you can begin preparing to apply as a freshman or transfer student and find more information about the admissions process by visiting the University of Illinois Undergraduate Admissions page or the Graduate Admissions page.

Read more at http://veterans.illinois.edu/admissions/index.asp.

**Status considered in admissions:** No

**Special admissions process:** No

**Special financial aid:** Yes. The Yellow Ribbon Program.

**Specific programs/policies to address needs:** Office of Veteran Students Support Services provides mentoring, family and community resources, career counseling, and more to military veterans.

## DACA/Undocumented Students

**DACA and undocumented admissions policy (in their own words):** All students are welcome to apply to Illinois regardless of citizenship or residency status. Residency status isn't a factor for admission. However, tuition rates differ for in-state and out-of-state residents. Some non-citizens, including undocumented students, may be eligible for in-state tuition. Review our residency information for more information about eligibility.

Read more at http://admissions.illinois.edu/apply/undocumented.

**Admitted:** Yes

**Status considered in admissions:** No

**Special admissions process:** No

**Eligible for institutional financial aid:** No

**Specific programs/policies to address needs:** Yes. Student groups, Office of Diversity, and Centers for Cultural Understanding and Social Change assist students with individualized support and provide referrals to undocumented students seeking information about academics, financial aid, legal referrals, and community resources.

# UNIVERSITY OF MICHIGAN, ANN ARBOR

**Location:** Ann Arbor, Michigan

**Website:** www.umich.edu

**Endowment:** $9.7 billion

**Type of School:** Public/Co-ed, Research University

**# of Undergraduate Students:** 28,983

**# of Graduate Students:** 15,735

**Average Class Size:** Class sizes vary; however, for Fall 2016, 84% of all U-M undergraduate classes had 50 students or less, and only 7% of classes had more than 100 students.

**School Mission (in their own words):** The mission of the University of Michigan is to serve the people of Michigan and the world through preeminence in creating, communicating, preserving, and applying knowledge, art, and academic values, and in developing leaders and citizens who will challenge the present and enrich the future.

## Admissions

**Admissions office mailing address:** 500 S State St, Ann Arbor MI 48109

**Admissions office phone:** (734) 764-7433

**Admissions office email:** There is no general admissions email, but if you are unable to locate the answer to a question you have, you can use the live chat function on their website: https://umich.custhelp.com/app/chat/chat_launch.

**# of transfer applications:** Fall 2016 admissions: 3,988. Spring 2017 admissions: No information provided.

**# of transfer students accepted:** Fall 2016: 1,547. Spring 2017: No information provided.

**Transfer student acceptance rate (2016–2017 academic year):** 38.8%

**Freshman applications received in Fall 2016:** 55,504

**Freshman applications accepted in Fall 2016:** 15,871

**Acceptance rate for 2016–2017 freshmen:** 28.6%

## Transfer Admissions Process

**Transfer policy (in their own words):** Students applying to transfer must be in good standing, both academically and socially, at the institution(s) attended. The University of Michigan considers the college grade point average, the quality and quantity of transferable college credit, TOEFL/MELAB scores (if applicable), and the quality of high-school credentials (including grades, strength of curriculum, and standardized test scores) during the transfer review process. The closer a student is to having 60 transferable credits, the less the student's high-school work will be used in the evaluation.

In addition, there are specific admissions requirements for individual schools and colleges.

Read more at https://admissions.umich.edu/apply/transfer-students.

**Transfer admissions contact person:** Kristin Heinrich, Senior Admissions Counselor (LSA)

**Transfer admissions contact info:** khein@umich.edu, (734) 764-6870

**Offers transfer-focused admissions events:** Yes

**Transfer application deadline:** Fall 2018 deadline is 2/1/18. Spring 2019 deadline is 2/1/18.

**Acceptances announced to transfer applicants:** Fall 2018: Depends on school/college. Spring 2019: Depends on school/college.

**Transfer application on Common App:** Yes. Common App fee: $75.

**SAT/ACT required for transfer applicants:** No, but it is recommended.

**High-school record requirements:** High-school transcripts

**High-school records requirements for applicants who completed outside the US:** Final official high-school/secondary-school record, including 9th–12th grades and graduation date

**Submission requirements for transfer applicants who completed high-school equivalency test:** GED results

**College transcript requirements:** Official transcripts required for all colleges and universities attended.

**Interviews available for transfer applicants:** Yes. Required from some.

**Additional requirements for transfers seeking admissions to business school:** Yes. Complete the equivalent of the University of Michigan's courses in First-Year Writing, Economics 101, and Calculus I, II, or III, each with a grade of C or better, by June 1. AP credit for Calculus I or II (Math 120 or 121) will substitute for the required course in calculus. IB or A-Level credit for Economics 101 and U-M Calculus I, II, or III will substitute for the required courses in economics and calculus. Review the Advance Standing Credit guidelines for AP, IB, and A-Level to see what scores are needed to obtain course credit.

Earn at least 27 credits that will transfer to U-M Ann Arbor, each with a grade of C or better, by June 1.

At least the final 13.5 of these credits must be earned in the US. The Ross BBA program does not accept transfer students directly from institutions located outside the US.

AP, IB, and A-Level credits do not count toward the 27 required credits.

**Additional requirements for transfers seeking admissions to arts major:** Yes. Portfolio and recommenders: 1 counselor, 1 academic teacher, and 1 art/design teacher.

**Additional requirements for transfers seeking admissions to engineering major:** Yes. Students wishing to transfer should complete a series of prerequisite courses. All courses should be taken for a letter grade and not pass/fail. A letter grade of a C or better is required. The prerequisite courses cannot be filled by placement exams.

## Costs & Financial Aid

**FAFSA code:** 2325

**CSS Profile code:** 1839

**Are internal school financial aid forms required?** No

**Financial aid deadlines for transfer applicants:** Fall 2018: April 30. Spring 2019: April 30.

**Costs for the 2017–2018 year:** Tuition & Fees: In-state: $16,218. Out-of-state: $48,598. Room & Board: $10,872.

**Financial aid for transfer students:** Yes

**Guarantees meeting 100% need for transfer students:** Meets demonstrated financial need.

**Need-based aid for transfer students:** Yes. The Office of Financial Aid distributes need-based grant, scholarship, loan, and work-study funds equitably among all eligible applicants who apply for financial aid by established deadline dates. Award amounts are determined by a combination of demonstrated financial need, federal award maximums, available funding, and other factors.

**Merit-based financial aid for transfer students:** Yes. Scholarships are gift funds that are awarded to students based on criteria set by the donor or sponsoring organization.

**Phi Theta Kappa Scholarship:** No.

**Reduced or zero tuition fees for low-income students:** Yes

**Includes loans in financial aid packages:** Yes

**% of all undergraduates receiving financial aid:** About 70% of Michigan resident undergraduates and 50% of non-resident undergraduates on the U-M Ann Arbor campus receive financial aid.

**% of all undergraduates qualifying for Pell Grants:** No information provided.

**Average financial aid award for all undergraduate students:** $15,400

**Funding available for low-income students to visit:** No

**Enrollment deposit can be waived for low-income students:** Yes

## Academics

**GPA range for transfer students accepted in 2016–2017:** No information provided.

**SAT ranges for all students admitted in 2016:** Critical Reading: 640–730. Mathematics: 670–770. Writing: 650–740.

**ACT composite score range for all students admitted in 2016:** 29–33

**Recommended courses transfer applicants should have on transcripts:** Our competitive LSA applicants will have completed coursework in the following disciplines: English composition, natural science, social science, foreign language, humanities, and math.

**Type of curriculum:** Gen. Ed. requirements

**Type of academic year:** Semester

**Advisors specifically for transfer students:** Yes

**Credit policy (in their own words):** To successfully transfer into the University of Michigan, you will have to demonstrate that your course of study is balanced on a foundation of general education courses that fulfill basic requirements and provide grounding in prerequisites or required courses that enable you to focus on a particular major at Michigan.

In order for your coursework to be considered transferable to the University of Michigan, it must meet the following criteria:

- You have completed coursework at an accredited college or university.
- The work that you have completed at your previous/current institution(s) is of similar rigor and content to the course offerings available at Michigan.
- You have earned a grade of C or better while completing it.

When transferring courses, you will typically receive the number of semester hours of credit (i.e., quarter hours converted to semester hours) earned on the campus(es) in which you took them. This is true, regardless of the number of credit hours similar courses may be worth at Michigan. Individual academic units may have limits on the number of transferable credits. Please check with the school or college in which you are interested.

International students should be aware that international credits are converted to U-M credit, and the credit earned may be different from what is listed on the original transcript.

Read more at https://admissions.umich.edu/apply/transfer-students/transfer-credit.

**Max number of transfer credits accepted:** From a 2-year institution: 62. From a 4-year institution: 60.

**Residency requirement for transfer students:** Yes. A minimum of 60 credits toward degree must be completed in residence.

**Study abroad available for transfer students:** Yes. Must meet residency requirements.

**Free tutoring for all students:** With some restrictions

**Writing center for all students:** Yes

**Career support/access to internships and resume prep for all students:** Yes

**% of undergraduate students hired within 6 months of graduation:** No information provided.

**Additional resources specifically designated for transfer and/or non-traditional students:** Yes. Housing, mentoring, childcare, and other services are available.

## Housing

**Available for transfer students:** Yes

**Available for non-traditional students:** Yes

**Guaranteed for transfer students:** No

**Non-traditional students can reside in housing year-round:** No

**Family housing available:** Yes

## Non-Traditional Admissions

**Non-traditional student policy (in their own words):** If you have not attended high school for more than 5 years and have not taken any college courses, you will be applying as a freshman student and will need to complete an admissions application and have your high-school records sent to our institution.

If you have not attended high school for more than 5 years, but have previously completed college courses after graduating from high school, you will be applying as a transfer student. You will need to complete an admissions application and have all transcripts from college and high school sent to our institution.

## Military/Veteran Students

**Military/veteran admissions policy (in their own words):** The majority of our U-M veterans apply as transfer students. A "transfer applicant" is defined as any student who has attended any institution of higher education after high-school graduation on any basis for any period of time. UM-Dearborn and UM-Flint students are considered new transfer students.

If you are a veteran or still serving in the military, you may be eligible for in-state tuition even though you may have been initially classified as an out-of-state student due to your duty station or deployment.

You may qualify for in-state tuition, without regard to your legal residence, by demonstrating any of the following:

- You are serving on active duty in the US Army, Navy, Air Force, Marines, National Guard, Merchant Marine, or Coast Guard.
- You are a reservist in one of those branches.
- You were honorably discharged or received a general discharge under honorable conditions from 1 of those branches or their reserve component.
- You are serving as an officer in the US Public Health Service.
- You are the spouse or dependent child of someone living or stationed in Michigan who is serving in the US Army, Navy, Air Force, Marines, National Guard, Merchant Marine, or Coast Guard, whether on active duty or as a reservist.
- OR you are the spouse or dependent child of someone living or stationed in Michigan who is serving as an officer in the US Public Health Service.

**Status considered in admissions:** No

**Special admissions process:** No

**Special financial aid:** Yes. Unit scholarships, transfer student scholarship, private military scholarships (each have different requirements), and the Yellow Ribbon Program.

**Specific programs/policies to address needs:** Resources for students include medical clinics to keep you healthy, recreational activities to keep you active, academic advising to ensure your academic success, and student clubs and groups to help connect you with peers with similar interests.

## DACA/Undocumented Students

**DACA and undocumented admissions policy (in their own words):** While there is no specific DACA/undocumented admissions policy, there is an FAQ for these students available here: http://publicaffairs.vpcomm.umich.edu/faq-on-undocumented-students.

**Admitted:** Yes

**Status considered in admissions:** No

**Special admissions process:** No

**Eligible for institutional financial aid:** Yes. Limited availability for undocumented/DACA students. The most common category of eligible noncitizen is that of permanent resident (someone with a green card), but there are other categories as well. There are also scholarships available.

**Specific programs/policies to address needs:** Yes. Legal advice, health insurance help, scholarships and financial aid, and community.

# UNIVERSITY OF NORTH CAROLINA, CHAPEL HILL

**Location:** Chapel Hill, North Carolina

**Website:** www.unc.edu

**Endowment:** $4.5 billion

**Type of School:** Public/Co-ed, Research University

**# of Undergraduate Students:** 18,523

**# of Graduate Students:** 10,946

**Average Class Size:** N/A

**School Mission (in their own words):** Our mission is to serve as a center for research, scholarship, and creativity and to teach a diverse community of undergraduate, graduate, and professional students to become the next generation of leaders. Through the efforts of our exceptional faculty and staff, and with generous support from North Carolina's citizens, we invest our knowledge and resources to enhance access to learning and to foster the success and prosperity of each rising generation. We also extend knowledge-based services and other resources of the University to the citizens of North Carolina and their institutions to enhance the quality of life for all people in the State.

## Admissions

**Admissions office mailing address:** Morehead Planetarium Building, 250 E Franklin St, Chapel Hill NC 27599

**Admissions office phone:** (919) 966-3621

**Admissions office email:** No information provided. Students can contact admissions here: http://admissions.unc.edu/contact-us/.

**# of transfer applications:** Fall 2016 admissions: 2,772

**# of transfer students accepted:** Fall 2016: 1,271

**Transfer student acceptance rate (2016–2017 academic year):** 45.9%

**Freshman applications received in Fall 2016:** 34,889

**Freshman applications accepted in Fall 2016:** 9,400

**Acceptance rate for 2016–2017 freshmen:** 26.9%

## Transfer Admissions Process

**Transfer policy (in their own words):** If you've been out of high school for at least 1 year and have taken any college coursework, you should apply as a transfer student. We don't have any specific course requirements for transfers, beyond the minimum course requirements that all enrolling students must meet to be eligible for admission. While we aren't looking for any specific courses on your college transcript, we do recommend that you get a strong foundation in the core academic areas: English, foreign language, math, the social sciences, and the natural sciences. These courses are most likely to transfer, and they're most closely aligned with the type of courses that our students take in their first 2 years.

We receive about 3,000 applications for transfer admission each year, about a third of which we're able to admit. Successful applicants present a strong college record—the average college GPA of enrolling transfer students last year was a 3.7.

Read more at http://admissions.unc.edu/apply/transfer-students.

**Transfer admissions contact person:** Yolanda L. Arroyo, Student Information Specialist

**Transfer admissions contact info:** yarroyo@email.unc.edu, (919) 966-3983

**Offers transfer-focused admissions events:** Yes. "Tar Heels in Your Town" goes to North Carolina community colleges to talk about transfer.

**Transfer application deadline:** Fall 2018 deadline is 2/15/18.

**Acceptances announced to transfer applicants:** Fall 2018 in mid-April.

**Transfer application on Common App:** Yes. Common App fee: $85.

**SAT/ACT required for transfer applicants:** Sophomore applicants (those with less than 60 transferable credit hours) must submit either the SAT or ACT; these scores are optional for junior applicants.

**High-school records requirements:** Official high-school transcript

**High-school records requirements for applicants who completed outside the US:** Official high-school transcript. All transcripts must be translated to English. If your school does not issue English transcripts, students must have an official English translation made and submit this in addition to the official copy from the school.

**Submission requirements for transfer applicants who completed high-school equivalency test:** Complete at least 24 total transferable semester hours from an accredited college or university (excluding hours awarded by dual enrollment, AP, IB, or other credit by exam) OR complete at least 24 total transferable semester hours from an accredited college or university.

**College transcript requirements:** Official transcripts for all colleges and universities attended

**Interviews available for transfer applicants:** No

**Additional requirements for transfers seeking admissions to business school:** Yes. Applicants should apply to the College of Arts and Science first, and then once they have completed a semester, they may apply directly to the Business School.

**Additional requirements for transfers seeking admissions to engineering major:** Yes. Applicants must first complete prerequisite courses listed here: http://bmeundergrad.bme.unc.edu/unc-biomedical-engineering/admission.

## Costs & Financial Aid

**FAFSA code:** 2974

**CSS Profile code:** 5816

**Are internal school financial aid forms required?** No

**Financial aid deadlines for transfer applicants:** Fall 2018: 3/1/18

**Costs for the 2017–2018 year:** Tuition & Fees: In-state: $8,898. Out-of-state: $34,588. Room & Board: $11,556.

**Financial aid for transfer students:** Yes

**Guarantees meeting 100% need for transfer students:** Yes

**Need-based aid for transfer students:** Yes

**Merit-based financial aid for transfer students:** No

**Phi Theta Kappa Scholarship:** No

**Reduced or zero tuition fees for low-income students:** No

**Includes loans in financial aid packages:** Yes

**% of all undergraduates receiving financial aid:** No information provided.

**% of all undergraduates qualifying for Pell Grants:** No information provided.

**Average financial aid award for all undergraduate students:** $19,310

**Funding available for low-income students to visit:** No information provided.

**Enrollment deposit can be waived for low-income students:** Yes

## Academics

**GPA range for transfer students accepted in 2016–2017:** 2.0 minimum

**SAT ranges for all students admitted in 2016:** Critical Reading: 590–700. Mathematics: 600–710. Writing: 580–690.

**ACT composite score range for all students admitted in 2016:** 27–32

**Recommended completed level of math for transfer applicants:** Pre-calculus

**Recommended completed level of English for transfer applicants:** 3 semesters of college-level English

**Type of curriculum:** Gen. Ed. requirements

**Type of academic year:** Semester

**Advisors specifically for transfer students:** Yes

**Credit policy (in their own words):** When submitting a request for transfer credit, please consider the following rules:

- If you have already completed 64 semester hours of credit at UNC-Chapel Hill, or will have 64 hours at the conclusion of the semester in which you plan to dual-enroll at a 2-year school, you cannot transfer additional credit hours for concurrent courses taken at the 2-year institution.

- You may take coursework away from UNC-Chapel Hill provided that your UNC-Chapel Hill grade point average meets the minimum academic eligibility requirement for the semester you plan to reenroll (see UNC-Chapel Hill catalog section entitled "Academic Eligibility"). Grades and quality points earned elsewhere are not computed into your UNC cumulative grade point average. Enrollment elsewhere (other than summer school) will be counted as semesters earned toward computing eligibility requirements.

- For study abroad, please note that you may receive credit only for courses taken through officially sanctioned UNC programs. Contact the Study Abroad Office to learn more.

- A minimum of 45 semester hours of credit must be earned at UNC-Chapel Hill in order to receive a degree from UNC-Chapel Hill.

- Only 6 hours of your last 30 semester hours may be taken at another institution by permission of your dean.

- A minimum of 18 hours of C or higher grades (not C average) in the major is required.

- We do not award more hours to be transferred for approved courses than those earned at the original institution.

- The conversion for quarter hours to semester hours is a 2/3 ratio. For example, a 5-quarter-hour course converted to semester hours is 3.33 semester hours.

- You should only submit a course approval request for the term in which you plan to take and complete the course. Approved courses taken outside of the term for which they were approved will not be honored in the event that a transfer credit update or change is made.

- Self-Paced Courses: Enrolled students are not permitted to take Self-Paced Courses except in unusual circumstances; written consent of the student's dean is required to enroll; thus, if your course is determined to be Self-Paced in nature before or after you complete it, the course will be denied if it does not contain an academic dean's approval.

- After receiving the results of your credit request from the Office of Undergraduate Admissions, please consult with an academic advisor in your school to verify that the approved UNC-Chapel Hill equivalent(s) will fulfill curriculum/degree requirements.

**Max number of transfer credits accepted:** 64

**Residency requirement for transfer students:** Yes. Students may transfer up to 75 semester hours from a 4-year institution, or 64 hours from a 2-year institution. A minimum of 45 semester hours must be earned at UNC-Chapel Hill in order to receive a degree from the University.

**Study abroad available for transfer students:** Yes. Must fulfill the residency requirements.

**Free tutoring for all students:** Yes

**Writing center for all students:** Yes

**Career support/access to internships and resume prep for all students:** Yes

**% of undergraduate students hired within 6 months of graduation:** 72%

**Additional resources specifically designated for transfer and/or non-traditional students:** No

## Housing

**Available for transfer students:** Yes

**Available for non-traditional students:** No

**Guaranteed for transfer students:** No

**Non-traditional students can reside in housing year-round:** N/A

**Family housing available:** Yes

## Non-Traditional Admissions

No non-traditional student policies or programs available.

## Military/Veteran Students

**Military/veteran admissions policy (in their own words):**
If you're a veteran seeking to earn a bachelor's degree, we appreciate your service and welcome you to consider Carolina. Veterans are a small but growing number of students who contribute to the diversity of our student body. These students bring qualities such as curiosity, discipline, kindness, and a clear commitment to public service. We are committed to helping you earn a degree at Carolina that will help you keep growing personally and professionally while you accomplish your goals.

Admission to Carolina is competitive, but we also recognize that students travel many paths to Carolina. Our holistic review considers each application thoroughly, as fairly and as thoughtfully as we can, for excellence in academics, the arts, athletics, leadership, service, citizenship, and character. Your military service is a definite plus, as it demonstrates many of these qualities and more, such as discipline, organization, and patriotism.

We offer a number of benefits at Carolina for active duty military and enrolling veterans. Veterans who are on active duty may qualify for the military tuition benefit, which allows them to attend the University at the in-state tuition rate. We will also waive the application fee for any applicant who is an active-duty member of the US armed forces. If you are eligible for VA benefits, you may apply to the US Veterans Administration for these funds after being admitted to the University. We are also honored to be a participating institution in the Yellow Ribbon Program sponsored by the Veterans Administration. This program is designed to help meet the gap in tuition and fees that exceeds the cost of in-state tuition.

In addition, the University is committed to doing more to support veterans and military-affiliated students, both prospective and current students. The Office of Undergraduate Admissions is proud to have numerous staff who recently participated in the Green Zone Training initiative sponsored by the Office of Dean of Students. The purpose of this program is to teach members of the Carolina community about the issues and concerns faced by military-affiliated students and to identify individuals who are available to assist this population. Please continue to visit this website as new pages and resources are added.

Read more at http://admissions.unc.edu/apply/military-veterans.

**Status considered in admissions:** No

**Special admissions process:** No

**Special financial aid:** Yes, the Yellow Ribbon Program for veterans and in-state tuition for active duty military. The Post-9/11 GI Bill will pay you:

- All resident tuition & fees for a public school
- The lower of the actual tuition & fees or the national maximum per academic year for a private school

Your actual tuition & fees costs may exceed these amounts if you are attending a private school or are attending a public school as a non-resident student.

Degree-granting institutions of higher learning participating in the Post-9/11 GI Bill Yellow Ribbon Program agree to make additional funds available for your education program without an additional charge to your GI Bill entitlement. These institutions voluntarily enter into a Yellow Ribbon Agreement with VA and choose the amount of tuition and fees that will be contributed. VA matches that amount and issues payments directly to the institution.

**Specific programs/policies to address needs:** Veterans Services, through the Dean of Students Office, offers resources and information to help in a successful transition to the Carolina community. Carolina Veterans Organization is a student group for veteran students and their families.

## DACA/Undocumented Students

**DACA and undocumented admissions policy (in their own words):** There is no specific DACA/undocumented admissions policy, but there is a letter written by the school's chancellor stating that due to North Carolina's immigration laws, the school cannot call itself a sanctuary for undocumented students. Here is a link to the letter, which includes links to services DACA/undocumented students can make use of: www.unc.edu/campus-updates/message-university-leadership-response-petition-undocumented-students.

**Admitted:** Yes

**Status considered in admissions:** Yes

**Special admissions process:** No

**Eligible for institutional financial aid:** No

**Specific programs/policies to address needs:** No

# UNIVERSITY OF PENNSYLVANIA

**Location:** Philadelphia, Pennsylvania

**Website:** www.upenn.edu

**Endowment:** $10.7 billion

**Type of School:** Private/Co-ed, Research University

**# of Undergraduate Students:** 9,726

**# of Graduate Students:** 11,669

**Average Class Size:** No information provided.

**School Mission (in their own words):** The College is committed to offering a broad education that will lay a durable foundation for critical and creative thinking. The College's goal is to help students to become knowledgeable about the world and the complexities of today's society; aware of moral, ethical, and social issues; prepared to exercise intellectual leadership; and enlivened by the use of their minds. We believe that students should explore fundamental approaches to the acquisition and interpretation of knowledge through introduction to substantive bodies of current thought in the natural sciences, social sciences, and humanities. Equally important, they should learn to understand and evaluate the sources and methods from which this knowledge derives. In this way, they can be led to appreciate the contingency of all knowledge and to participate in the ongoing excitement of intellectual discovery that is at the heart of the College.

## Admissions

**Admissions office mailing address:** 1 College Hall, Room 100, Philadelphia PA 19104

**Admissions office phone:** (215) 898-1988

**Admissions office email:** info@admissions.upenn.edu

**# of transfer applications:** Fall 2016 admissions: 2,491

**# of transfer students accepted:** Fall 2016: 210

**Transfer student acceptance rate (2016–2017 academic year):** 8.4%

**Freshman applications received in Fall 2016:** 38,918

**Freshman applications accepted in Fall 2016:** 3,674

**Acceptance rate for 2016–2017 freshmen:** 9.4%

## Transfer Admissions Process

**Transfer policy (in their own words):** At least 1 full year of transferable academic coursework (8 courses) must be completed by the close of the spring term prior to the September of anticipated enrollment at Penn. Students who are completing their senior year of high school concurrently with their first year of college, or who are enrolled in a dual-enrollment program taking courses in college while still enrolled in high school, should apply as freshmen.

The University does not admit freshmen or transfers to enroll midyear. Students who leave college at the end of the first term may apply to the freshman class entering in the subsequent September. Once the application has been submitted, a student may not enroll in additional college-level courses.

Penn maintains a 2-year academic enrollment requirement. At least 1/2 of the total number of courses required for the Penn degree must be completed here, regardless of the number of transferable credits completed elsewhere. If you have completed more than 2 years of transferable work at other institutions, you may not be eligible to transfer to Penn. Students who have already completed a bachelor's degree are not eligible to transfer to an undergraduate school at Penn.

**Offers transfer-focused admissions events:** Yes. Transfer information sessions are held on Fridays, from January through March 15, at 1:30 p.m. for 30 minutes.

**Transfer application deadline:** Fall 2018 deadline is 3/15/18.

**Acceptances announced to transfer applicants:** Fall 2018 in mid-May.

**Transfer application on Common App:** Yes, with Penn writing supplement. Common App fee: $75.

**SAT/ACT required for transfer applicants:** Yes

**High-school record requirements:** Official high-school transcript

**High-school records requirements for applicants who completed outside the US:** Official transcript submitted with certified English translations.

**Submission requirements for transfer applicants who completed high-school equivalency test:** Official copy of GED results

**College transcript requirements:** Official transcripts for all colleges and universities attended

**Interviews available for transfer applicants:** No

**Additional requirements for transfers seeking admissions to business school:** Yes. Students are strongly encouraged to transfer after their freshman year to enter for their sophomore year. There are very few spaces available for entering juniors.

Required coursework for transferring after 1 year:

- 1 semester of calculus
- 1 semester of introductory microeconomics
- 1 semester of introductory macroeconomics
- 1 semester of a combined introductory micro and macroeconomics course

Required coursework for transferring after 2 years:

- All required coursework for 1-year transfers
- A 1-semester financial accounting course
- A 1-semester managerial accounting course
- 2 semesters of statistics
- 1 semester of intermediate microeconomics

Recommended that applicants satisfy Wharton's foreign language requirement by the time they enroll at Penn.

**Additional requirements for transfers seeking admissions to arts major:** Yes. The individualized major is available only to students applying to study in their sophomore year at Penn, and whose proposed course of study is approved before their junior year once enrolled at the University. The major in architecture is only an option for students applying as freshmen to study in their sophomore year at Penn. A portfolio is required for transfer applicants to architecture to ensure a fit with the design studio sequence.

**Additional requirements for transfers seeking admissions to engineering major:** Yes. Students transferring into Penn Engineering after 1 year of college should have completed at least:

- 1 course in chemistry
- 1 course in physics (involving the use of calculus)
- 1 course in computer programming
- 2 courses in calculus

Students pursuing a major in bioengineering, computer engineering, mechanical engineering and applied mechanics, materials science and engineering, systems science engineering, electrical engineering, or networked and social systems engineering should also complete a second course in physics.

Depending on their desired discipline, students transferring into Penn Engineering after 2 years of college should have completed:

- A total of 4 courses in math (calculus through differential equations).
- 2 courses in physics (involving the use of calculus).
- 1 course in chemistry.
- 1 course in computer programming.
- 3 or 4 courses in the social sciences and humanities.
- As many engineering and applied science courses as possible (e.g., in mechanics, electrical circuits, materials, or thermodynamics). In addition, computer science, computer engineering, digital media design, and networked and social systems engineering students must take a second computer programming course.
- Prospective junior transfers to the Networked and Social Systems Engineering major should note that only students majoring in computer science at their current institution will be considered for this major.

**Additional requirements for transfers seeking admissions to other major:**

School of Nursing:

Transfer applicants must have completed a minimum of 8 transferable college courses, including the following prerequisites:

- Introduction to Chemistry with lab
- Introduction to Biology with lab
- Introduction to Anatomy and Physiology I with lab or Human Anatomy with lab

The following courses are recommended:

- Introduction to Microbiology with lab
- Introduction to Anatomy and Physiology II with lab or Human Anatomy with lab
- Introduction to Nutrition
- Introduction to Statistics

## Costs & Financial Aid

**FAFSA code:** 3378

**CSS Profile code:** 2933

**Are internal school financial aid forms required?** Yes

**Financial aid deadline for transfer applicants:** Fall 2018: 4/15/18

**Costs for the 2017–2018 year:** Tuition & Fees: $53,534. Room & Board: $15,066.

**Anticipated costs for the 2018–2019 year:** No information provided.

**Financial aid for transfer students:** Yes

**Guarantees meeting 100% need for transfer students:** Yes

**Need-based aid for transfer students:** Yes

**Merit-based financial aid for transfer students:** No

**Phi Theta Kappa Scholarship:** Yes, for the College of Liberal & Professional Studies. Tuition for 2 courses in spring, fall, and summer terms. Details available at www.sas.upenn.edu/lps/undergraduate/ba/tuition/scholarships.

**Reduced or zero tuition fees for low-income students:** No

**Includes loans in financial aid packages:** No

**% of all undergraduates receiving financial aid:** 46%

**% of all undergraduates qualifying for Pell Grants:** No information provided.

**Average financial aid award for all undergraduate students:** $43,542

**Funding available for low-income students to visit:** No information provided.

**Enrollment deposit can be waived for low-income students:** No information provided.

## Academics

**GPA range for transfer students accepted in 2016–2017:** No information provided.

**SAT ranges for all students admitted in 2016:** Critical Reading: 690–790. Mathematics: 710–800. Writing: 700–790.

**ACT composite score range for all students admitted in 2016:** 31–34

**Type of curriculum:** Gen. Ed. requirements

**Type of academic year:** Semester

**Advisors specifically for transfer students:** No information provided.

**Credit policy (in their own words):** The total number of course units (c.u., or credits) needed for graduation varies between 32 and 36 depending on the number of credits required in the major. Each major specifies a certain number of credits that must be completed, but never less than 12. In addition to the major, students must normally complete 20 credits outside the major. No more than 36 credits will be required for graduation. Those whose majors require more than 16 credits may take correspondingly fewer than 20 outside the major. At least 16 of the 20 credits outside the major must be Arts and Sciences courses. (See Policies Governing Non-College Courses.)

Students who are completing more than 1 major must use their largest major to calculate the required graduation credits. For example, a student majoring in English (12 c.u.) and fine arts (16 c.u.) needs at least 36 c.u. to graduate.

Read more at www.college.upenn.edu/credits-needed.

For students to apply as transfers, they must have completed at least 8 transferable academic courses at an accredited institution by the time they enroll at Penn. In addition, we will only accept up to the equivalent of 2 academic years for coursework.

You will contact the advising center in the undergraduate school to which you are enrolling. Please remember that the transfer credit process only happens after a student matriculates and enrolls at Penn.

All students seeking credit for college-level work completed prior to matriculation must use Penn's online system, XCAT. A representative of the appropriate Penn department will need to review all courses before transfer credits will be awarded. A syllabus and other supporting materials may be required.

**Max number of transfer credits accepted:** 16

**Residency requirement for transfer students:** Yes. At least 2 years and 1/2 the credits must be earned at Penn.

**Study abroad available for transfer students:** Yes. Transfer students must complete 1 semester at Penn before applying. They must have completed 2 semesters at Penn before studying abroad and be enrolled at Penn the semester before their departure. Junior transfer students are not eligible to study abroad. Petitioning for an exemption from these policies is an option if there are compelling academic and intellectual reasons.

**Free tutoring for all students:** Yes

**Writing center for all students:** Yes

**Career support/access to internships and resume prep for all students:** Yes

**% of undergraduate students hired within 6 months of graduation:** No information provided.

**Additional resources specifically designated for transfer and/or non-traditional students:** No

## Housing

**Available for transfer students:** Yes

**Available for non-traditional students:** Yes

**Guaranteed for transfer students:** Yes

**Non-traditional students can reside in housing year-round:** No

**Family housing available:** No

## Non-Traditional Admissions

**Non-traditional student policy (in their own words):** The bachelor of arts (B.A.) degree at the College of Liberal and Professional Studies (LPS) is designed for individuals from a variety of backgrounds, and the eligibility requirements reflect our search for applicants who are ready to take advantage of the experiences Penn has to offer. The Admissions Committee considers each applicant's academic potential, intellectual strengths and ability to think independently, and motivation and ability to be a contributing member of the Penn community.

Applicants must be a high-school graduate or have passed the high school equivalency exam or GED (General Educational Development) test with a minimum score of 450. Successful applicants to the bachelor of arts program must possess a minimum 3.0 grade point average in their high school and previous undergraduate studies.

While there are no specific prerequisite courses, and no required number of college-level courses need to be completed prior to applying to the B.A., the majority of admitted applicants have successfully completed at least 6–8 college-level courses in the liberal arts.

Standardized tests, such as the SAT and ACT, are not generally required when applying for the bachelor of arts. However, you may choose to submit standardized test scores in support of your application. Most international applicants are required to demonstrate English proficiency via the Test of English as a Foreign Language (TOEFL) scores.

Students who have been denied admission to any bachelor's degree program at the University of Pennsylvania must wait 1 year before reapplying to the University of Pennsylvania.

**Name of program:** College of Liberal and Professional Studies

**Program description:** Through our programming and our community, the College of Liberal and Professional Studies proudly embodies the University of Pennsylvania's mission to encourage lifelong learning relevant to a changing global society. The College of Liberal and Professional Studies (LPS) is the home of lifelong learning at the University of Pennsylvania. Housed within the School of Arts and Sciences, we offer high-school, undergraduate, post-baccalaureate, graduate, summer, and online studies as well as customizable professional training with courses that span across disciplines.

**Program deadline:** Fall Priority: March 1

**Fall Regular Admission:** July 1

**Spring Priority:** October 1

**Spring Regular Admission:** November 1

**Summer Regular Admission:** April 1

**Program Admission Requirements:** Applicants must be high-school graduates or have passed the high-school equivalency exam or GED (General Educational Development) test with a minimum score of 450. Successful applicants to the bachelor of arts program must possess a minimum 3.0 grade point average in their high school and previous undergraduate studies.

**Program website:** www.sas.upenn.edu/lps

**Program contact person:** Kathy L. Urban, Director, Undergraduate Programs

**Program contact info:** (215) 898-7326, lps@sas.upenn.edu

## Military/Veteran Students

**Military/veteran admissions policy:** No policy information provided, but you can read more at: www.sas.upenn.edu/lps/students/veterans-active-military.

**Status considered in admissions:** No

**Special admissions process:** Yes. Most military students go into the College of Liberal and Professional Studies.

**Special financial aid:** Yes. The Yellow Ribbon Program. Maximum annual award varies by college.

**Specific programs/policies to address needs:** Student Veteran Association; veteran-specific career services; veteran leave of absence policy

## DACA/Undocumented Students

**DACA and undocumented admissions policy (in their own words):** Any student can apply/transfer to the university without being turned away due to lack of US legal immigration status. Students should complete the Common Application and Penn supplement as international applicants. If accepted, students might be asked to provide student visas. Since undocumented students cannot return to their countries of origin in order to acquire such student visas, they need not submit one. Hence, it is okay to disregard reminders to submit such forms. Furthermore, deferred action status is not required upon application to the University of Pennsylvania, but it does affect students' eligibility for work-study in their financial aid packages. The University itself will not provide legal consultation to accepted students aiming to apply for DACA, but there are various community organizations that might be helpful. Read more at www.vpul.upenn.edu/lacasa/files/UndocumentedFAQs.pdf.

**Admitted:** Yes

**Status considered in admissions:** No

**Special admissions process:** No

**Eligible for institutional financial aid:** Yes. They must apply as international students and complete the CSS Profile.

**Specific programs/policies to address needs:** Yes. Penn for Immigrant Rights and UndocuOrientation, an event where self-identified undocumented freshman can meet other undocumented Penn students and ask personalized questions from undocumented upperclassmen.

# UNIVERSITY OF RICHMOND

**Location:** Richmond, Virginia

**Website:** www.richmond.edu

**Endowment:** $2.3 billion

**Type of School:** Private/Co-ed, Liberal Arts

**# Undergraduate Students:** 3,036

**# of Graduate Students:** 534

**Average Class Size:** 16

**School Mission (in their own words):** The mission of the University of Richmond is to educate in an academically challenging, intellectually vibrant, and collaborative community dedicated to the holistic development of students and the production of scholarly and creative work. A Richmond education prepares students for lives of purpose, thoughtful inquiry, and responsible leadership in a diverse world.

## Admissions

**Admissions office mailing address:** 28 Westhampton Way, Richmond VA 23173

**Admissions office phone:** (800) 700-1662

**Admissions office email:** admission@richmond.edu

**# of transfer applications:** Fall 2016 admissions: 304. Spring 2017 admissions: 75.

**# of transfer students accepted:** Fall 2016: 154. Spring 2017: 21.

**Transfer student acceptance rate (2016–2017 academic year):** 46%

**Freshman applications received in Fall 2016:** 10,422

**Freshman applications accepted in Fall 2016:** 3,385

**Acceptance rate for 2016–2017 freshmen:** 32.5%

## Transfer Admissions Process

**Transfer policy (in their own words):** Transfer candidates must have completed a minimum of 6.82 transferable units (equivalent to approximately 24 semester hours) at another college or university to be considered for admission at the University of Richmond. You may submit your application before the minimum requirements have been met, but the coursework must be complete by the time you enroll at Richmond. Transfer students are not accepted in the middle of their first year of college.

Read more at http://admissions.richmond.edu/process/transfer/index.html.

**Transfer admissions contact person:** Nadine Saint, Transfer Coordinator

**Transfer admissions contact info:** nadine.saint@richmond.edu, (804) 289-8640

**Offers transfer-focused admissions events:** No

**Transfer application deadline:** Fall 2018 deadline is 2/15/18. Spring 2019 deadline is 11/1/18.

**Acceptances announced to transfer applicants:** Fall 2018 on 4/15/2018. Spring 2019 on 12/5/18.

**Transfer application on Common App:** Yes. Common App fee: $50.

**SAT/ACT required for transfer applicants:** No

**High-school records requirements:** Official final high-school transcripts

**High-school records requirements for applicants who completed outside the US:** Same as domestic students

**Submission requirements for transfer applicants who completed high-school equivalency test:** Official GED results

**College transcript requirements:** Official transcripts from all colleges and universities attended.

**Interviews available for transfer applicants:** No

**Additional requirements for transfers seeking admissions to engineering major:** Yes, Calculus I—Math 115

## Costs & Financial Aid

**FAFSA code:** 3744

**CSS Profile code:** 5569

**Are internal school financial aid forms required?** No

**Financial aid deadline for transfer applicants:** Fall 2018: 2/15/18. Spring 2019: No information provided.

**Costs for the 2017–2018 year:** Tuition & Fees: $50,910. Room & Board: $11,820.

**Financial aid for transfer students:** Yes

**Guarantees meeting 100% need for transfer students:** Yes

**Need-based aid for transfer students:** Yes. Submit financial aid documents.

**Merit-based financial aid for transfer students:** No

**Phi Theta Kappa Scholarship:** No

**Reduced or zero tuition fees for low-income students:** No

**Includes loans in financial aid packages:** Yes

**% of all undergraduates receiving financial aid:** 66%

**% of all undergraduates qualifying for Pell Grants:** 15%

**Average financial aid award for all undergraduate students:** $36,750

**Funding available for low-income students to visit:** No

**Enrollment deposit can be waived for low-income students:** Yes

## Academics

**GPA range for transfer students accepted in 2016–2017:** 2.0 minimum

**SAT ranges for all students admitted in 2016:** Critical Reading: 600–700. Mathematics: 620–720. Writing: 610–700.

**ACT composite score range for all students admitted in 2016:** 29–32

**Recommended completed level of math for transfer applicants:** Calculus 1

**Recommended completed level of English for transfer applicants:** 2 semesters of college-level English

**Recommended courses transfer applicants should have on transcripts:** 1 social science class and 2 semesters of foreign languages

**Recommended courses transfer applicants interested in STEM should complete before transfer:** 1 laboratory science

**Type of curriculum:** Gen. Ed. requirements

**Type of academic year:** Semester

**Advisors specifically for transfer students:** No

**Credit policy (in their own words):** With your acceptance letter, you should receive a letter from the Registrar's Office detailing how to view how your coursework has come in to Richmond. If you have specific questions regarding your transcript, course transfer equivalencies, or the conversion of your previous work to units, please contact the Registrar's Office. Final transcripts should be received in our Registrar's Office as soon as possible.

The University's curriculum is based on a 35-unit bachelor's degree. 1 Richmond unit is considered to be equivalent to 3.5 semester hours. Therefore, transfer credit from universities under the semester-hour system may not transfer as exactly 1 Richmond unit. Students may transfer a maximum of 5 courses valued at 3 semester hours as 1 unit. After this 5-course maximum has been met, 3 semester hour courses will transfer as 0.86 units. 4 semester hours courses will transfer as 1.14 units.

For more information, see: www.richmond.edu/transfer/coursework.html.

**Max number of transfer credits accepted:** No maximum number of credits

**Residency requirement for transfer students:** Yes. Transfer students must complete a specific number of units at Richmond in order to receive their degree. This depends on how much coursework has been completed prior to transferring and is as follows: If you have completed up to 1 year at another institution, you must complete at least 23 units at Richmond. If you have completed up to 1 1/2 years of study at another institution, you must complete at least 20.5 units at Richmond. If you have completed 2 or more years of study at another institution, you must complete at least 17.5 units at Richmond.

**Study abroad available for transfer students:** Yes. While we encourage all students to take advantage of study abroad, the University requires that a minimum of 17.5 units be completed here at the University of Richmond. However, students who transferred in after 1 1/2 years of study at another institution may apply 1 additional unit earned on an approved study abroad program toward this 17.5 unit residency requirement. Students who transferred in after 2 years of study at another institution may apply up to 4 units earned on an approved study-abroad program toward this 17.5 unit residency requirement.

**Free tutoring for all students:** Yes

**Writing center for all students:** Yes

**Career support/access to internships and resume prep for all students:** Yes

**% of undergraduate students hired within 6 months of graduation:** 96%

**Additional resources specifically designated for transfer and/or non-traditional students:** No

## Housing

**Available for transfer students:** Yes

**Available for non-traditional students:** No

**Guaranteed for transfer students:** No

**Non-traditional students can reside in housing year-round:** N/A

**Family housing available:** No

## Non-Traditional Admissions

**Non-traditional student policy (in their own words):**
As a private university, Richmond can use its resources and independence not only to serve traditional-age college students, but also to provide enriching and meaningful undergraduate and graduate experiences for adult students and working professionals through the School of Professional & Continuing Studies.

Regardless of your educational goals, you'll be part of a vibrant and inspiring campus, 1 of only a few true college campuses in Richmond with dedicated programs for adult students and working professionals. Walk the paths between our Collegiate Gothic buildings, cross the footbridge over our lake, or attend an upcoming Information Session and imagine yourself as a student here.

Whether you're attending class, looking for a quiet study space, researching your next paper, grabbing a bite to eat, or attending a cultural or athletic event, you'll feel like a Spider through and through.

Read more at http://spcs.richmond.edu/degrees/admissions.

**Name of program:** School of Professional and Continuing Studies

**Program description:** At the School of Professional and Continuing Studies, our students are serious about what they do. They have goals in mind and unbelievable drive to achieve them. But sometimes life gets in the way, and that's okay. In any given semester, our students range in age from 20–65. Flexible scheduling, relevant degrees, and convenient admissions.

**Program deadline:** Fall: 7/1/18. Spring: 11/15/18.

**Program admission requirements:** Application, transcripts for all college/university work, and required supporting materials as requested by the specific college/department.

**Program website:** http://spcs.richmond.edu

**Program contact person:** N/A

**Program contact info:** (804) 289-8133, spcs@richmond.edu

## Military/Veteran Students

**Military/veteran admissions policy (in their own words):** Students using veterans' benefits are required to uphold the same standards of progress as all other students enrolled at the University of Richmond. For details regarding academic procedures, graduation, academic standing, and other important policies, read more at http://registrar.richmond.edu/registration/programs/veterans/vet_policies.html.

**Status considered in admissions:** No

**Special admissions process:** No

**Special financial aid:** Yes. The Yellow Ribbon Program.

**Specific programs/policies to address needs:** N/A

## DACA/Undocumented Students

**DACA and undocumented admissions policy (in their own words):** The University of Richmond values a diverse community which brings together students from all backgrounds and experiences in an inclusive and caring community dedicated to personal and intellectual growth.

The University welcomes applications from all students regardless of citizenship or residency. All applications are reviewed holistically, and the unique accomplishments and attributes of each applicant are considered within the context of their educational environment.

We are committed to meeting the full demonstrated need of all students admitted as freshmen to our full-time undergraduate degree programs. Students who are not US citizens or permanent residents should apply for financial aid consideration at the point of their application for admission. All applicants are also eligible to compete for university-funded merit scholarships.

Undocumented and DACA students with questions about the application process should feel free to contact the Office of Admission for a confidential conversation about the opportunities available to them at the University of Richmond.

Read more at http://admissions.richmond.edu/process/international/undocumented-daca.html.

**Admitted:** Yes

**Status considered in admissions:** Yes

**Special admissions process:** No

**Eligible for institutional financial aid:** Yes. For students who are neither US citizens nor US permanent residents—including undocumented, refugee, asylee, and Deferred Action for Childhood Arrival students who graduated from US high schools—the commitment to meeting a student's full demonstrated need means that the University provides financial aid awards that do not include loans. Undocumented students are considered under the need-aware, non-US citizen admission and financial aid processes.

**Specific programs/policies to address needs:** Yes. The Office of Common Ground supports the University's priorities of diversity and inclusion by providing campus-wide resources and programming that foster community across lines of difference. The Office of Multicultural Affairs supports the enrollment and retention of underrepresented students and serves as a vehicle to promote a campus community that embraces difference and values inclusive diversity.

# UNIVERSITY OF ROCHESTER

**Location:** Rochester, New York

**Website:** rochester.edu

**Endowment:** $2.2 billion (2015)

**Type of School:** Private/Co-ed, Research University

**# of Undergraduate Students:** 6,046

**# of Graduate Students:** 3,424

**Average Class Size:** 20 or fewer

**School Mission (in their own words):** Learn, Discover, Heal, Create—and Make the World Ever Better

## Admissions

**Admissions office mailing address:** 500 Joseph C Wilson Blvd, Rochester NY 14627

**Admissions office phone:** (585) 275-3221

**Admissions office email:** admit@rochester.edu

**# of transfer applications:** Fall 2016 admissions: 1,092. Spring 2017 admissions: No information provided.

**# of transfer students accepted:** Fall 2016: 375. Spring 2017: No information provided.

**Transfer student acceptance rate (2016–2017 academic year):** 34%

**Freshman applications received in Fall 2016:** 16,503

**Freshman applications accepted in Fall 2016:** 5,845

**Acceptance rate for 2016–2017 freshmen:** 35%

## Transfer Admissions Process

**Transfer policy (in their own words):** The University of Rochester encourages students who have begun their academic careers at other colleges or universities to continue their educations here on either a full-time or part-time basis. Students who have graduated from high school or earned a high-school equivalence and have earned 8 or more college credits at a college or university following graduation are eligible to apply for transfer admission. Students undertaking college-level coursework as part of their high-school programs, or in order to satisfy high-school diploma requirements, are eligible to enter as freshmen, although they are welcome to request academic credit for their college work.

**Transfer admissions contact person:** Sarah Gerin, Senior Counselor, Humanities and Transfer Representative, Admissions

**Transfer admissions contact info:** sgerin@admissions. rochester.edu

**Offers transfer-focused admissions events:** Yes. Transfer visit days.

**Transfer application deadline:** Fall 2018 deadline is 3/15/18. Spring 2019 deadline is 10/1/18.

**Acceptances announced to transfer applicants:** Fall 2018 on rolling basis (March–July). Spring 2019 on rolling basis (September–December).

**Transfer application on Common App:** Yes. Common App fee: $50.

**SAT/ACT required for transfer applicants:** No, but it is recommended.

**High-school record requirements:** Final high-school transcript

**High-school records requirements for applicants who completed outside the US:** Final high-school transcript

**Submission requirements for transfer applicants who completed high-school equivalency test:** If you have completed at least 1 year of full-time college coursework, you may request that it be waived after applying.

**College transcript requirements:** College transcript(s), college report (optional)

**Interviews available for transfer applicants:** Yes. Optional (recommended). On campus, off campus, Skype, phone.

**Additional requirements for transfers seeking admissions to engineering major:** Students with engineering or computer science interests may transfer into the Hajim School of Engineering and Applied Sciences from other institutions. If they have had the equivalent of the first 2 years of science, mathematics, and pre-engineering, such students may enter the school directly and complete their degree requirements in an additional 2 years. Otherwise, students may transfer into Hajim School of Engineering and Applied Sciences at the University of Rochester at any time, but may find it necessary to satisfy those prerequisites they may be lacking. Course equivalency and credit are determined on a case-by-case basis.

## Costs & Financial Aid

**FAFSA code:** 2894

**CSS Profile code:** 2928

**Are internal school financial aid forms required?** No

**Financial aid deadline for transfer applicants:** Fall 2018: 3/15/18. Spring 2019: 10/1/18.

**Costs for the 2017–2018 year:** Tuition & Fees: $51,750. Room & Board: $9,342.

**Financial aid for transfer students:** Yes

**Guarantees meeting 100% need for transfer students:** No

**Need-based aid for transfer students:** Yes. Same as first-year applicants.

**Merit-based financial aid for transfer students:** Yes. These awards are not based on financial need and are renewable for up to 3 years if the minimum criteria are met. Award amounts remain constant and do not increase with tuition and fee increases. Merit aid is reserved for students with exceptional and distinguished academic qualities.

**Phi Theta Kappa Scholarship:** Yes, $8,000. Renewable. Additional application and 3.5 GPA required.

**Reduced or zero tuition fees for low-income students:** Yes

**Includes loans in financial aid packages:** Yes

**% of all undergraduates receiving financial aid:** 51%

**% of all undergraduates qualifying for Pell Grants:** 18.1%

**Average financial aid award for all undergraduate students:** $44,628

**Funding available for low-income students to visit:** No

**Enrollment deposit can be waived for low-income students:** No

## Academics

**GPA range for transfer students accepted in 2016–2017:** 3.56 median

**SAT ranges for all students admitted in 2016:** Critical Reading: 600–710. Mathematics: 640–760. Writing: 610–710.

**ACT composite score range for all students admitted in 2016:** 29–33

**Type of curriculum:** Gen. Ed. requirements

**Type of academic year:** Semester

**Advisors specifically for transfer students:** Yes

**Credit policy (in their own words):** Degree requirement credit policy:

> 32 4-credit courses or 128 credit hours, with an average grade of C or better. No more than 20 courses from a single department, and no more than 20 credit hours from Naval Science may be counted toward the degree. For students not majoring in music or pursuing simultaneous B.M. degrees at Eastman, no more than 16 credit hours of applied music instruction (e.g., lessons) and 8 credit hours of River Campus ensemble may be counted toward the degree.

Read more at www.rochester.edu/college/ccas/AdviserHandbook/DegreeReq.html.

Transfer credit policy:

> A maximum of 64 credit hours is transferable to the UR degree from 2-year schools, there is no specified limit to the amount of credit that can be earned through online courses. Approved courses that are completed with a grade of C or better will transfer. Please note: Only the credit will transfer. The grades do not transfer and will not affect the GPA, therefore the grades cannot replace grades earned at UR. A Transfer Credit Evaluation will be emailed to the student. The number of transfer credit hours to be granted is determined by comparison of total hours required for graduation; for example, a student who had earned 15 credits at a school requiring 120 credits for the degree would be awarded 16 credits here, based on our degree requirement of 128 hours.

Courses taken while a student was in high school which were sponsored by a college but were taught in the high school are not approved for transfer credit. However, students enrolled in college coursework on a college campus are eligible to receive transfer credit assuming the courses are completed with a grade of C or better and are approved. Students who believe their situations warrant an exception should always speak with a CCAS adviser. A special petition form is available for coursework taught in the high school. It requires a comprehensive letter of support from the appropriate faculty member. The final decision then is made by the Dean of the College.

Students who have taken credit-bearing courses at the University of Rochester while in high school, through the Taste of College program or otherwise, should be aware of the following: Grades for these courses will be factored into the cumulative grade point average, and credit will count toward undergraduate degree requirements. Students have the option of requesting that these courses be treated as if they were transfer courses, in which case the grade will be removed from the average, and credit will be counted toward degree requirements as long as the grade was a C or better. Petitions should be submitted to the College Center for Advising Services.

However, per College policy, the College is not required to provide (or allow the making of) copies of these documents. Transcripts submitted to the University of Rochester for admission or credit transfer become the property of the University of Rochester and cannot be returned to the student or forwarded to other institutions.

Read more at www.rochester.edu/college/ccas/AdviserHandbook/TransferCrdt.html.

**Max number of transfer credits accepted:** 64

**Residency requirement for transfer students:** Yes. The College requires that students complete a minimum of 4 semesters of full-time study in residence or, for part-time students, the equivalent number of credit hours to be eligible for the bachelor's degree.

**Study abroad available for transfer students:** Yes. Complete 1 year at UR, be in good standing, and declare your major.

**Free tutoring for all students:** Yes

**Writing center for all students:** Yes

**Career support/access to internships and resume prep for all students:** Yes

**% of undergraduate students hired within 6 months of graduation:** 39%

Additional resources specifically designated for transfer and/or non-traditional students: Yes. Academic advisers are available to assist transfers with their concerns. Financial aid is available to transfer students.

## Housing

**Available for transfer students:** Yes.

**Available for non-traditional students:** Yes

**Guaranteed for transfer students:** No

**Non-traditional students can reside in housing year-round:** No

**Family housing available:** Yes

## Non-Traditional Admissions

No non-traditional student policies and programs available.

## Military/Veteran Students

**Military/veteran admissions policy (in their own words):**
The University of Rochester encourages and supports past and present military service members and their families as they work toward their higher education goals. Veterans and dependents who choose Rochester pursue their academics at one of the nation's most rigorous, top-tier research universities.

Rochester has been named a Top Military-Friendly College 2 years in a row for its efforts to ensure veterans face minimal barriers in attaining higher education. Rochester also participates in the Yellow Ribbon Program, offers the Rochester Pledge scholarship, and has a Veterans Alliance group. Veterans and their dependents have access to many resources to help navigate any hurdles.

To become a student at the University of Rochester in the undergraduate College of Arts, Sciences, and Engineering, you must apply either as a freshman or a transfer applicant. To apply as a transfer, you must have completed at least 2 college-level courses. The average transfer applicant has completed a year of full-time courses (24–32 credits) before enrolling.

**Status considered in admissions:** No

**Special admissions process:** No

**Special financial aid:** Yes. The Yellow Ribbon Program, the Rochester Pledge scholarship, and Veterans Alliance.

**Specific programs/policies to address needs:** Veterans and their dependents have access to many resources to help navigate any hurdles. You can read more here: https://enrollment.rochester.edu/apply/veterans/.

## DACA/Undocumented Students

**DACA and undocumented admissions policy (in their own words):** Educational institutions in the US, unless restricted by their state law, are permitted to admit and enroll all qualified students, regardless of their immigration status. If admitted to the University of Rochester, undocumented students may accept merit-based scholarships and awards that are not service-based. Additionally, some students may have secured employment authorization under the Deferred Action for Childhood Arrivals program and may, therefore, be eligible to work during their program as a full-time student.

**Admitted:** Yes

**Status considered in admissions:** No

**Special admissions process:** No

**Eligible for institutional financial aid:** Yes

**Specific programs/policies to address needs:** UR DREAMers is a group created in order to provide a support group for students that are either undocumented or have DACA status, so that they can connect with each other. It is also for allies so that together the group can bring awareness for immigration reform.

# UNIVERSITY OF SOUTHERN CALIFORNIA

**Location:** Los Angeles, California

**Website:** www.usc.edu

**Endowment:** $4.6 billion (2015)

**Type of School:** Private/Co-ed, Research University

**# of Undergraduate Students:** 18,810 (2015–2016)

**# of Graduate Students:** 24,591 (2015–2016)

**Average Class Size:** 26

**School Mission (in their own words):** The central mission of the University of Southern California is the development of human beings and society as a whole through the cultivation and enrichment of the human mind and spirit. The principal means by which our mission is accomplished are teaching, research, artistic creation, professional practice, and selected forms of public service.

## Admissions

**Admissions office mailing address:** University Park Campus, Los Angeles CA 90089

**Admissions office phone:** (213) 740-1111

**Admissions office email:** To email the Office of Admission, use the askUSC portal: http://uscesd.custhelp.com/app/ask/.

**# of transfer applications:** Fall 2015 admissions: 8,179

**# of transfer students accepted:** Fall 2015: 2,483

**Transfer student acceptance rate (2015–2016 academic year):** 30.4%

**Freshman applications received in Fall 2015:** 51,924

**Freshman applications accepted in Fall 2015:** 9,181

**Acceptance rate for 2015–2016 freshmen:** 17.7%

## Transfer Admissions Process

**Transfer policy (in their own words):** USC defines a transfer student as anyone who has attended college since finishing high school.

Keep in mind that admission is competitive, and students who have completed all suggested courses might not be offered admission. Successful transfer applicants have generally completed a year of rigorous academic courses.

**Transfer admissions contact person:** Timothy Brunold, Dean of Admission

**Transfer admissions contact info:** admdean@usc.edu, (213) 740-6753

**Offers transfer-focused admissions events:** Yes

**Transfer application deadline:** Fall 2018 deadline is 2/1/18 (some exceptions are in December).

**Acceptances announced to transfer applicants:** Fall 2018 on 6/1/18.

**Transfer application on Common App:** Yes. Common App Fee: $80.

**SAT/ACT required for transfer applicants:** Required from applicants who have completed fewer than 30 semester units of college coursework.

**High-school record requirements:** Official final high-school transcripts with date of graduation

**High-school records requirements for applicants who completed outside the US:** May substitute a copy of a diploma or leaving certificate.

**Submission requirements for transfer applicants who completed high-school equivalency test:** Students who did not finish high school should also submit a copy of their completion certificate (such as a GED) and may also submit a letter of explanation.

**College transcript requirements:** All official college transcripts

**Interviews available for transfer applicants:** No

**Additional requirements for transfers seeking admissions to business school:** Yes. Transfer applicants will be considered for admission once they have completed the prerequisite college writing and business calculus courses. Transfer applicants interested in accounting must apply to Business Administration. A formal request to transfer to the Leventhal School of Accounting can be made once the resident accounting course(s) are successfully completed.

**Additional requirements for transfers seeking admissions to arts major:** Yes. Depends on which art you intend on majoring in. See http://admission.usc.edu/docs/AdditionalCourseworkbyMajor.pdf for more details.

**Additional requirements for transfers seeking admissions to engineering major:** Yes. There are nearly 30 different engineering majors and areas of emphasis with very different curricula in the junior and senior years. However, the following lower-division coursework generally applies: CHEM 105a (General Chemistry I); MATH 125 (Calculus I); MATH 126 (Calculus II); MATH 226 (Calculus III); PHYS 151 (Fundamentals of Physics I: Mechanics and Thermodynamics); PHYS 152 (Fundamentals of Physics II: Electricity and Magnetism). Visit viterbi.usc.edu/transfer for more detailed information and transfer course plans.

## Costs & Financial Aid

**FAFSA code:** 1328

**CSS Profile code:** 4852

**Are internal school financial aid forms required?** No

**Financial aid deadline for transfer applicants:** Fall 2018: 3/2/18.

**Costs for the 2017–2018 year:** Tuition & Fees: $54,323. Room & Board: $14,886.

**Financial aid for transfer students:** Yes

**Guarantees meeting 100% need for transfer students:** Yes

**Need-based aid for transfer students:** Yes

**Merit-based financial aid for transfer students:** Yes

**Phi Theta Kappa Scholarship:** No

**Reduced or zero tuition fees for low-income students:** Yes

**Includes loans in financial aid packages:** Yes

**% of all undergraduates receiving financial aid:** 66.70%

**% of all undergraduates qualifying for Pell Grants:** 24%

**Average financial aid award for all undergraduate students:** $51,311

**Funding available for low-income students to visit:** No

**Enrollment deposit can be waived for low-income students:** Yes

## Academics

**GPA range for transfer students accepted in 2015–2016:** 3.7 average

**SAT ranges for all students admitted in 2015:** Critical Reading: 620–730. Mathematics: 650–770. Writing: 650–750.

**ACT composite score range for all students admitted in 2015:** 30–33

**Recommended completed level of math for transfer applicants:** Minimum math requirement demonstrates a mastery of algebra II in high school, or intermediate algebra in college with a grade of C or better. Many majors require more math.

**Recommended completed level of English for transfer applicants:** Complete the equivalent of USC's lower-division writing requirement, Writing 150.

**Type of curriculum:** Gen. Ed. requirements

**Type of academic year:** Semester

**Advisors specifically for transfer students:** Yes

**Credit policy (in their own words):** Students are required to take a minimum of 128 baccalaureate units at the undergraduate level (of which not more than 4 units may be physical education units). A student may earn a maximum of 16 units for individual instruction in music at the 101/201/301 levels and comparable transfer courses. No more than 8 units of dance technique courses. Students must also complete all upper-division coursework in the major at USC. Some disciplines require more than the minimum requirements. Check individual department listings for specific requirements.

Transfer students must complete a minimum of 64 units in residence at USC (half the units usually required for graduation).

While in residence at USC, you are also expected to:

- Complete all upper-division units in your major and minor.
- Complete WRIT 340, General Education categories IV and VI, and any General Education courses not taken before entering USC.
- Take all your fall- and spring-semester courses for subject or unit credit at USC. Courses for subject or unit credit may be taken at other institutions only during summer sessions.
- Students in the Engineering "3–2" program must complete a minimum of 48 units in residence at USC. 2/3 of any transferable coursework must be completed at one of USC's 4-year partner institutions.
- Bachelor of architecture students must earn at least 80 units at USC. A maximum of 70 of the transferable units for this program may be earned at 2-year colleges.

Read more at http://admission.usc.edu/counselors/transfercredit.html.

**Max number of transfer credits accepted:** 64

**Residency requirement for transfer students:** Yes. Minimum of 64 credits.

**Study abroad available for transfer students:** Yes. Transfer students may study overseas upon completion of 2 semesters at USC.

**Free tutoring for all students:** Yes

**Writing center for all students:** Yes

**Career support/access to internships and resume prep for all students:** Yes

**% of undergraduate students hired within 6 months of graduation:** No information available.

**Additional resources specifically designated for transfer and/or non-traditional students:** Yes. TransferMation Series: a series of 1-hour workshops designed to highlight opportunities for transfer students to maximize their Trojan experience. Topics include career planning and preparation, jobs and internships, undergraduate research, leveraging the Trojan Network, study abroad, USC Progressive Degree Programs, summer coursework, and much more.

## Housing

**Available for transfer students:** Yes

**Available for non-traditional students:** Yes

**Guaranteed for transfer students:** No

**Non-traditional students can reside in housing year-round:** Yes (sometimes)

**Family housing available:** Yes

## Non-Traditional Admissions

No non-traditional student policy provided.

## Military/Veteran Students

**Military/veteran admissions policy (in their own words):**
The University of Southern California has a long history of support for the US military, veterans, and their families. Initially utilized as a training school during WWI and WWII, USC has evolved through peace and wartime years to become a leading institution for innovative military strategies, technologies, academics, training, and support for US military personnel and their families.

The University of Southern California offers a number of services and benefits to military veterans to assist in their transition and overall experience at USC, including the Veterans Resource Center. The center is a collaborative effort between the Division of Student Affairs and the Office of Academic Records and Registrar, and is located in the Tutor Campus Center Suite 330. Contact Jennifer Perdomo, coordinator at the Veterans Resource Center, at vrc@usc.edu and (213) 821-6028, or go to https://campusactivities.usc.edu/veterans/ for more information.

**Status considered in admissions:** No

**Special admissions process:** No

**Special financial aid:** Yes. Federal Need-Based Aid, University Aid, Yellow Ribbon Program. Cal Grants (each have different requirements and funding).

**Specific programs/policies to address needs:** Online programs give students the freedom to take world-class higher education courses with the same level of academic rigor, professors, and opportunities as on-campus classes, and USC works with military students to make sure that they can be successful whether at home or abroad.

## DACA/Undocumented Students

**DACA and undocumented admissions policy (in their own words):** Thanks to the Family Education Rights and Privacy Act, school officials cannot disclose personal information (including immigration status) about students. When applying to USC, use the following guidelines:

- Country of citizenship: Choose the option "Other, Non-US."
- Social Security number: Leave it blank.

Read more at http://usg.usc.edu/resources/undocumented-student-guide.

**Admitted:** Yes

**Status considered in admissions:** No

**Special admissions process:** No

**Eligible for institutional financial aid:** Please note: You will only be eligible for in-state assistance if you are a California resident. Unfortunately, most of the laws and aid do not transfer to students who are not California residents. Furthermore, undocumented students are not eligible for federal work-study, but may receive the DREAM grants if they are from California. Available scholarships include: Educators for Fair Consideration (E4FC) Scholarships, Mexican American Legal Defense and Educational Fund (MALDEF) Scholarships, IDEA's at USC Scholarship List, DREAM Act Application (requirements and funding vary).

**Specific programs/policies to address needs:** Yes. USC Undocumented Student Resource Guide, USC IDEA's Student Organization, Resources for Undocumented Students, advisors, student diversity organizations, external support organizations, on-campus support organizations & communities, cultural centers, housing resources, and legal resources.

# UNIVERSITY OF VIRGINIA

**Location:** Charlottesville, Virginia

**Website:** www.virginia.edu

**Endowment:** $7.6 billion

**Type of School:** Public/Co-ed, Research University

**# of Undergraduate Students:** 16,331

**# of Graduate Students:** 7,567

**Average Class Size:** 20 students or fewer

**School Mission (in their own words):** The University of Virginia is a public institution of higher learning guided by a founding vision of discovery, innovation, and development of the full potential of talented students from all walks of life. It serves the Commonwealth of Virginia, the nation, and the world by developing responsible citizen leaders and professionals; advancing, preserving, and disseminating knowledge; and providing world-class patient care.

## Admissions

**Admissions office mailing address:** PO Box 400160, Charlottesville VA 22904

**Admissions office phone:** (434) 982-3200

**Admissions office email:** undergradadmission@virginia.edu

**# of transfer applications:** Fall 2016 admissions: 2,484. Spring 2017 admissions: No information provided.

**# of transfer students accepted:** Fall 2016: 989. Spring 2017: No information provided.

**Transfer student acceptance rate (2016–2017 academic year):** 39.8%

**Freshman applications accepted in Fall 2016:** 9,668

**Acceptance rate for 2016–2017 freshmen:** 29%

## Transfer Admissions Process

**Transfer policy (in their own words):** Applicants who have completed at least 1 full year (at least 24 semester hours after high-school graduation) of college study before entering the University are considered most competitive by the Committee on Admission. Summer is not considered part of this 1-year minimum. Since the University has no program for "visiting students," successful transfer applicants who enroll at UVA must spend at least 2 full years in residency at the University.

Students who have at any time completed 3 or more years of study at another 4-year college or university are not eligible for transfer admission to the College of Arts and Sciences. This also applies to students who have attempted a full junior year at a 4-year institution after transferring from a community college or another 4-year institution.

Students who already hold bachelor's degrees may apply for a second undergraduate degree only in the School of Engineering and Applied Science (the exception being individuals who have already earned engineering or physics degrees. These students are rarely offered admission as we prefer to give spots to students who have not previously earned the aforementioned degrees.

**Transfer admissions contact person:** Gregory Roberts, Dean of Admission

**Transfer admissions contact info:** gwr2g@virginia.edu

**Offers transfer-focused admissions events:** Yes

**Transfer application deadline:** Fall 2018 deadline is 3/1/18. Spring 2019 deadline is 10/1/18.

**Acceptances announced to transfer applicants:** Fall 2018 by 5/1/18. Spring 2019 by 12/1/18.

**Transfer application on Common App:** Yes. Common App fee: $70.

**SAT/ACT required for transfer applicants:** Fall: No (optional). Spring: Required for Commerce and Education, optional for other schools.

**High-school record requirements:** Transcript only

**High-school records requirements for applicants who completed outside the US:** Official high-school transcript required (official translation required of transcripts not presented in English).

**Submission requirements for transfer applicants who completed high-school equivalency test:** Official GED score required.

**College transcript requirements:** Official transcripts for all colleges and universities attended

**Interviews available for transfer applicants:** No

**Additional requirements for transfers seeking admissions to business school:** Yes. A student must apply directly to the Commerce School as a transfer applicant if applying to enter UVA as a third-year student. If a student is applying to enter UVA as a second-year student, they would apply to the College of Arts and Sciences, not Commerce. A student must have completed 2 full years of general liberal arts work at an accredited college or university. A minimum of 54 semester hours is required for admission. It is strongly recommended, however, that students enter with at least 60 semester hours so that they will be on track for graduation without having to take an overload of courses. The SAT or ACT is required for all applicants. It is recommended that non-native English speaking applicants also take the TOEFL or IELTS to be competitive for admission. Strong preference is given to students who have received or will be receiving their associate's degree from a Virginia Community College prior to the fall term to which they are applying. Candidates for transfer admission should have completed coursework in the following areas:

- Elementary accounting (6 credits)—financial and managerial
- Principles of economics (6)—micro and macro
- English composition (6)
- Mathematics (6)—1 course in statistics (descriptive and inferential) and 1 course in calculus
- Humanities (3)—1 course before enrollment; an additional humanities course prior to graduation can be completed before or after entering McIntire
- Foreign languages—varies; demonstrated proficiency equal to the intermediate level of college instruction (the 202 level)
- Comm 180—introduction to business/computer usage course

**Additional requirements for transfers seeking admissions to arts major:** No. Students are not admitted into a particular major. Admission is offered to the school you've chosen to apply to, and then you meet with advisors and department chairs to determine qualifications for specific majors. Arts supplement with the application is accepted, but not required.

**Additional requirements for transfers seeking admissions to engineering major:** Yes. If you are interested in computer science (CSE), you will want to complete calculus I, II, linear algebra, then choose between calculus III and differential equations.

## Costs & Financial Aid

**FAFSA code:** 3745

**CSS Profile code:** 5820

**Are internal school financial aid forms required?** No

**Financial aid deadlines for transfer applicants:** Fall 2018: 4/1/18. Spring 2019: 11/1/18.

**Costs for the 2017–2018 year:** Tuition & Fees: Virginian: $30,572. Non-Virginian: $60,062. Room & Board: $10,726.

**Financial aid for transfer students:** Yes

**Guarantees meeting 100% need for transfer students:** No

**Need-based aid for transfer students:** Yes

**Merit-based financial aid for transfer students:** Yes. Scholarships are awarded to students with special qualifications, such as academic, athletic, or artistic achievement.

**Phi Theta Kappa Scholarship:** No

**Reduced or zero tuition fees for low-income students:** Yes

**Includes loans in financial aid packages:** Yes

**% of all undergraduates receiving financial aid:** 33%

**% of all undergraduates qualifying for Pell Grants:** 13%

**Average financial aid award for all undergraduate students:** $20,058

**Funding available for low-income students to visit:** No

**Enrollment deposit can be waived for low-income students:** Yes

## Academics

**GPA range for transfer students accepted in 2016–2017:** Average GPA of 3.5

**SAT ranges for all students admitted in 2016:** Critical Reading: 620–720. Mathematics: 620–740. Writing: 610–730.

**ACT composite score range for all students admitted in 2016:** 29–33

**Type of curriculum:** Gen. Ed. requirements

**Type of academic year:** Semester

**Advisors specifically for transfer students:** Yes

**Credit policy (in their own words):** For credits transferred from an American college or university, the College will consider only courses completed at a degree-granting institution of higher education that has been fully accredited by 1 of the 6 regional accrediting agencies (e.g., the Southern Association of Colleges and Schools) or from a program approved prior to study by the Committee on Educational Policy and Curriculum.

Credit is allowed only for those courses in which a grade of C or better has been earned. Some programs may require a grade of B or better. Approval to take courses on a pass/fail basis must also be obtained prior to taking the courses. Courses in which "pass" or "credit" (CR) grades are received must be certified as equivalent to a grade of C or higher to be accepted.

Courses applied toward the major may not be transferred to the University from another institution without special permission of the department.

Students may transfer a maximum of 60 non-UVA credits to the University from a combination of testing programs and academic institutions. Those with fewer non-UVA credits must earn correspondingly more UVA credits. Students receive no more than the number of credits earned at the host institutions and may receive fewer credits.

Read more at http://college.as.virginia.edu/transfer-credit.

**Max number of transfer credits accepted:** 60 semester hours

**Residency requirement for transfer students:** 2 full years at UVA, 60 credits

**Study abroad available for transfer students:** Yes. Students in the College of Arts and Sciences who wish to study abroad must be in academic good standing and have a cumulative 2.5 GPA at the time they apply to study abroad. Before leaving for study abroad, students must complete their first semester of study at the University of Virginia in Charlottesville. All students must complete at least 2 full-time semesters (fall or spring) and earn at least 30 credits at UVA in Charlottesville.

**Free tutoring for all students:** Yes

**Writing center for all students:** Yes

**Career support/access to internships and resume prep for all students:** Yes

**% of undergraduate students hired within 6 months of graduation:** 46.2%

**Additional resources specifically designated for transfer and/or non-traditional students:** Yes. Transfer student support: Career resources, job search and networking tools, UVA student groups and resources, scholarships and funding.

## Housing

**Available for transfer students:** Yes

**Available for non-traditional students:** Yes (but it is not housing exclusively for non-traditional students)

**Guaranteed for transfer students:** No

**Non-traditional students can reside in housing year round:** Only in off-campus housing

**Family housing available:** Yes

## Non-Traditional Admissions

**Non-traditional student policy (in their own words):** No information provided.

**Name of program:** Guaranteed Transfer Admission

**Program description:** Students attending the Virginia Community College System or Richard Bland College may take advantage of guaranteed admission to UVA if they fulfill certain requirements. Community college students of Virginia can learn in depth about the admissions process and have a higher opportunity of being admitted to UVA by visiting https://admission.virginia.edu/vccsguide.

**Program deadline:** No information provided.

**Program admission requirements:** Requirements depend on the major/school that students would like to be a part of at UVA.

**Program contact person:** Undergraduate Admissions Office

**Program contact info:** (434) 982-3200, uvaapplicationinfo@virginia.edu

## Military/Veteran Students

**Military/veteran admissions policy (in their own words):** Our goal is to support active-duty service members, veterans, reservists, guardsmen, and dependents in pursuing their academic and professional goals by assisting them in maximizing the use of their educational benefits at the University. We strive to be a military- and veteran-friendly university.

Read more here: www.virginia.edu/registrar/vabenefits.html.

**Status considered in admissions:** No

**Special admissions process:** No

**Special financial aid:** Yes. Educational benefits are available for veterans, family members of veterans, and active military personnel. These programs have different benefits packages and eligibility requirements.

**Specific programs/policies to address needs:** Educational benefits, discounted active-duty military tuition rate, disability assistance, drop a class during deployment, and other services that help with success

## DACA/Undocumented Students

No DACA and undocumented student policies or programs available.

# UNIVERSITY OF WISCONSIN—MADISON

**Location:** Madison, Wisconsin

**Website:** www.wisc.edu

**Endowment:** $2.4 billion

**Type of School:** Public/Co-ed, Research University

**# of Undergraduate Students:** 31,710

**# of Graduate Students:** 11,626

**Average Class Size:** 29

**School Mission (in their own words):** The primary purpose of the University of Wisconsin—Madison is to provide a learning environment in which faculty, staff, and students can discover, examine critically, preserve, and transmit the knowledge, wisdom, and values that will help ensure the survival of this and future generations and improve the quality of life for all. The university seeks to help students to develop an understanding and appreciation for the complex cultural and physical worlds in which they live and to realize their highest potential of intellectual, physical, and human development.

It also seeks to attract and serve students from diverse social, economic, and ethnic backgrounds and to be sensitive and responsive to those groups which have been underserved by higher education.

## Admissions

**Admissions office mailing address:** 702 W Johnson St, Suite 1101, Madison WI 53715

**Admissions office phone:** (608) 262-3961

**Admissions office email:** onwisconsin@admissions.wisc.edu

**# of transfer applications:** Fall 2016 admissions: 4,352. Spring 2017 admissions: No information provided.

**# of transfer students accepted:** Fall 2016: 2,042. Spring 2017: No information provided.

**Transfer student acceptance rate (2016–2017 academic year):** 46.9%

**Freshman applications received in Fall 2016:** 32,887

**Freshman applications accepted in Fall 2016:** 17,304

**Acceptance rate for 2016–2017 freshmen:** 52.6%

## Transfer Admissions Process

**Transfer policy (in their own words):** A transfer student is anyone who has attended another college or university after graduating from high school and wishes to enroll in an undergraduate degree program at UW—Madison. In order to be eligible for transfer admission, you must have completed at least 24 transferable semester hours of college-level work. AP, A-Level, IB, and CLEP cannot be used toward the 24 transferable credit requirement. We do not admit freshman-level transfer students.

**Offers transfer-focused admissions events:** Yes

**Transfer application deadline:** Fall 2018 deadline is 2/1/18 (priority), 3/6/18 (regular). Spring 2019 deadline is 10/12/18.

**Acceptances announced to transfer applicants:** Fall 2018 by end of March (priority), end of April (regular). Spring 2019 by end of December.

**Transfer application on Common App:** Yes. Common App fee: $60.

**SAT/ACT required for transfer applicants:** Yes

**High-school record requirements:** Official transcripts, which need to be sent by your high school.

**High-school records requirements for applicants who completed outside the US:** All international applicants are required to submit official transcripts, which are the equivalent of grades 9–12, for all schools. They must be in the original language and include an official English translation.

**Submission requirements for transfer applicants who completed high-school equivalency test:** Submit your official GED score report in addition to the high-school transcript.

**College transcript requirements:** Request official transcripts from all postsecondary institutions. The transcripts should include all college-level coursework completed to date, including your current term in progress, and (if applicable) college classes taken while in high school.

**Interviews available for transfer applicants:** No

**Additional requirements for transfers seeking admissions to business school:**

- If currently attending a school in the UW system or Wisconsin technical college system: You are eligible to apply directly to the Wisconsin BBA Program if you complete a minimum of 24 degree credits by the end of the spring semester. You must also complete the pre-business course requirements shown below by the end of the spring semester.

- If currently attending a private college or university in Wisconsin or any college or university outside the state: You are not eligible to apply directly to the Wisconsin BBA Program and should apply for admission to UW—Madison as a first step. While enrolled at UW—Madison, you must complete a minimum of 12 in-residence credits; these can be obtained in the spring semester while you are applying to the Wisconsin School of Business. You must also have a minimum total of 24 degree credits and complete the pre-business course requirements shown below by the end of the spring semester:

- Communications Part A: One of: English 100 (3 credits), Introduction to College Composition, Comm Arts 100 (3 credits), Introduction to Speech Composition, English 118 (3 credits, non-native English speakers only), ESL: Academic Writing II
- Calculus: One of: Math 211 (5 credits), Calculus, Math 217 (5 credits), Calculus with Algebra and Trigonometry II (must complete Math 171 first), Math 221 (5 credits), Calculus and Analytic Geometry
- Economics: One of: Economics 101 (4 credits), Microeconomics, Economics 111 (4 credits, honors course), Principles of Economics—Accelerated Treatment
- Psychology: One of: Psych 201 (4 credits), Introduction to Psychology, Psych 202 (3 credits), Introduction to Psychology, Psych 281 (4 credits, honors course), Introduction to Psychology

**Additional requirements for transfers seeking admissions to arts major:**

- Dance: Choose an audition day, apply to UW—Madison, apply to Dance Department, complete an audition.
- Music: Apply to UW—Madison, apply to the School of Music (submit the following materials: School of Music application, 2 recommendation letters, a music resume in PDF or DOC format (email to admissions@music.wisc.edu), copies of your audition repertoire (for Voice applicants only, see area page), supplementary materials (for Composition applicants only, see area page), complete an audition, take a music theory exam, and audition for piano proficiency (note: not applicable to piano majors).

**Additional requirements for transfers seeking admissions to engineering major:** Math and science courses common to most engineering curricula—such as calculus, chemistry with lab, calculus-based physics with lab, calculus-based statistics, and computer programming. Recommended for strong preparation: at least 3 courses on the list of Core Math and Science Courses in the General College Requirements for Off Campus Transfer Students. An introduction to engineering course is optional but strongly recommended, if available. Engineering courses related to the intended major are recommended as well.

## Costs & Financial Aid

**FAFSA code:** 3895

**CSS Profile code:** 0

**Are internal school financial aid forms required?** No

**Financial aid deadlines for transfer applicants:** Fall 2018: December 1, 2017 (priority deadline). It is possible to apply for aid anytime during the academic year. However, it can often take in excess of 4 weeks to complete the processing of your application in our office; therefore, it is best to apply as early as possible. Spring 2019: It is possible to apply for aid anytime during the academic year. However, it can often take in excess of 4 weeks to complete the processing of your

application in our office; therefore, it is best to apply as early as possible.

**Costs for the 2017–2018 year:** Tuition & Fees: In-state: $10,488. Minnesota resident: $13,761. Out-of-state: $34,738. Room & Board: $10,842.

**Financial aid for transfer students:** Yes

**Guarantees meeting 100% need for transfer students:** No

**Need-based aid for transfer students:** Yes. To be considered for any federal aid, you must be enrolled at least half-time (6 credits for undergraduates, 4 credits for graduates). You must also be a US citizen or an eligible non-citizen. For certain types of funds, there may be other requirements.

**Merit-based financial aid for transfer students:** Yes

**Phi Theta Kappa Scholarship:** Yes, $7,500. Renewable. Additional application required.

**Reduced or zero tuition fees for low-income students:** Yes

**Includes loans in financial aid packages:** Yes

**% of all undergraduates receiving financial aid:** 36%

**% of all undergraduates qualifying for Pell Grants:** 14% of all undergraduates and 18% of Wisconsin resident undergraduates

**Average financial aid award for all undergraduate students:** $10,169

**Funding available for low-income students to visit:** No

**Enrollment deposit can be waived for low-income students:** Yes

## Academics

**GPA range for transfer students accepted in 2016–2017:** 3.3–3.8

**SAT ranges for all students admitted in 2016:** Critical Reading: 570–660. Mathematics: 640–760. Writing: 600–690.

**ACT composite score range for all students admitted in 2016:** 27–31

**Recommended courses transfer applicants should have on transcripts:** Rigorous coursework (appropriate for continued study at UW—Madison and increasing in difficulty), course breadth (showing a combination of English, math, science, literature, social science, and foreign language), required courses, and 2 high-school years or 2 college semesters of a single foreign language.

**Type of curriculum:** Gen. Ed. requirements

**Type of academic year:** Semester

**Advisors specifically for transfer students:** Yes

**Credit policy (in their own words):** Credit is awarded for college-level coursework completed at institutions accredited by a regional or national accrediting organization recognized by the Council for Higher Education Accreditation (CHEA). Foreign institutions must be recognized by the Ministry of Education in that country. Courses must be similar in nature, level, and content to a course in our undergraduate curriculum and applicable to one of our academic programs. Continuing education courses, graduate-level courses, and courses that are remedial, technical, vocational, or doctrinal in nature are not transferable.

**Credit Conversion:** If you have taken courses at an institution that uses quarter credit or units other than semester credits, we will convert your quarter credits/units to semester credits. If you have attended an institution that uses quarter credits, you will not lose credits in the conversion. For example, if you have 40 quarter credits (40 x .666 = 26.64), you will receive 27 semester credits.

Credits completed at an international institution will be converted to UW—Madison credits using the average number of credits taken by a UW—Madison student (15 credits per semester). Total degree credits granted may not equal total course credits due to rounding in the conversion of fractional credits to semester hours.

**Grades:** The grades you received at your previous institution(s) will not be calculated into your UW—Madison grade point average.

**Degree Requirements:** Specific degree requirements differ among the various UW—Madison schools and colleges. Transfer credit applies toward degree requirements appropriately, depending on which major and/or degree you intend to complete. To learn more about degree and major requirements, consult the Undergraduate Catalog or the appropriate undergraduate major.

Read more at www.admissions.wisc.edu/apply/transfer/transfer_credit.php.

**Max number of transfer credits accepted:** Maximum credits from a 2-year institution: 72. Maximum credits from a 4-year institution: 90.

**Residency requirement for transfer students:** Yes. Must complete at least 30 credits at UW—Madison.

**Study abroad available for transfer students:** Yes. If you are a transfer student, you may apply to study abroad your first semester at UW—Madison as long as you meet the program-specific eligibility requirements: A minimum overall GPA requirement; a minimum language course GPA requirement; language course prerequisites; course prerequisites, e.g., English 100; having good academic and disciplinary standing at the time of application; and/or participation (students who are on probation at the time of application or who are put on probation prior to the start date of their program are ineligible to participate); having the required student standing, e.g., freshman, sophomore, junior, senior, graduate.

**Free tutoring for all students:** Yes

**Writing center for all students:** Yes

**Career support/access to internships and resume prep for all students:** Yes

**% of undergraduate students hired within 6 months of graduation:** No information provided.

**Additional resources specifically designated for transfer and/or non-traditional students:** Yes. University Access for Non-traditional Learners (has programs), Transfer Transition Program.

## Housing

**Available for transfer students:** Yes

**Available for non-traditional students:** Yes

**Guaranteed for transfer students:** No

**Non-traditional students can reside in housing year-round:** No information provided.

**Family housing available:** Yes

## Non-Traditional Admissions

**Non-traditional student policy (in their own words):** UW—Madison defines an adult student as someone who is 25 years of age or older. Students who wish to take courses at UW—Madison but are not pursuing a degree should direct their questions to Adult Career and Special Student Services, reachable here: https://continuingstudies.wisc.edu/advising/.

An applicant who wants to pursue an undergraduate degree and has not earned college credits is considered a freshman student. An applicant who previously attended college at either a community college or a different university is considered a transfer student. Someone who was previously enrolled at UW—Madison as an undergraduate, but did not complete a degree, is considered a reentry student.

We encourage applicants who have been away from formal classroom teaching for an extended period to request a letter of recommendation from someone who can speak to their academic potential, such as an employer (preferably a supervisor or manager), a program or departmental trainer, or some other individual in an official instructional capacity.

## Military/Veteran Students

**Military/veteran admissions policy (in their own words):** The University of Wisconsin—Madison assists eligible veterans, active duty service personnel, disabled veterans, reservists, National Guard members, and dependents with state and federal education benefit programs.

We welcome applications from veterans and military personnel and currently have more than 400 student veterans receiving education benefits at UW—Madison.

All veteran applicants must submit a complete application for admission. The application review process parallels that of other freshman and transfer applicants. Ultimately, student veterans are expected to cover required coursework at a level of achievement similar to that noted on our general freshman and transfer admission requirements and expectations webpages.

Applicants can also contact the Veteran Services and Military Assistance Center in the Registrar's Office to receive assistance with questions and paperwork.

**Status considered in admissions:** No

**Special admissions process:** No

**Special financial aid:** Yes. The Yellow Ribbon Program.

Specific programs/policies to address needs: Veteran Services and Military Assistance Center (student support programs, advisors, benefits). Read more here: https://veterans.wisc.edu/.

## DACA/Undocumented Students

**DACA and undocumented admissions policy (in their own words):** There is no federal law that prohibits the admission of undocumented immigrants to US colleges, public or private. All students are welcome to apply to Edgewood College, Madison College, and UW—Madison regardless of their citizenship or residency status. Residency status is not a factor that is considered in admission, but tuition rates are different for students who are from in-state and students who are identified as out-of-state.

Read more at https://msc.wisc.edu/undocumented-student-resources.

**Admitted:** Yes

**Status considered in admissions:** No

**Special admissions process:** No

**Eligible for institutional financial aid:** No information provided.

**Specific programs/policies to address needs:** Yes. In the Multicultural Student Center, there is an Undocumented Support Group. The Undocumented Students Taskforce consists of campus partners, faculty, staff, and community liaisons. The taskforce focuses on awareness and advocacy, student services, research, policy and procedures, and community partnerships in order to better serve DACA/undocumented students at UW—Madison.

# VASSAR COLLEGE

**Location:** Poughkeepsie, New York

**Website:** www.vassar.edu

**Endowment:** $928 million

**Type of School:** Private, Co-ed, Liberal Arts

**# of Undergraduate Students:** 2,435 (Common Data Set 2015–2016)

**# of Graduate Students:** N/A

**Average Class Size:** 17

**School Mission (in their own words):** The mission of Vassar College is to make accessible "the means of a thorough, well-proportioned and liberal education" that inspires each individual to lead a purposeful life. The college makes possible an education that promotes analytical, informed, and independent thinking and sound judgment; encourages articulate expression; and nurtures intellectual curiosity, creativity, respectful debate, and engaged citizenship. Founded in 1861 to provide women an education equal to that once available only to men, the college is now open to all. Vassar supports a high standard of engagement in teaching and learning, scholarship and artistic endeavor; a broad and deep curriculum; a community diverse in background and experience; and a residential campus that fosters a learning community.

## Admissions

**Admissions office mailing address:** 124 Raymond Ave, Poughkeepsie NY 12604

**Admissions office phone:** (845) 437-7300

**Admissions office email:** admissions@vassar.edu

**# of transfer applications:** Fall 2016 admissions: 264. Spring 2017 admissions: 57.

**# of transfer students accepted:** Fall 2016: 34. Spring 2017: 5.

**Transfer student acceptance rate (2016–2017 academic year):** 12.1%

**Freshman applications received in Fall 2016:** 7,306

**Freshman applications accepted in Fall 2016:** 1,964

**Acceptance rate for 2016–2017 freshmen:** 26.9%

## Transfer Admissions Process

**Transfer policy (in their own words):** Any student who has already earned their high-school diploma or GED and has enrolled at a college or university is considered a transfer applicant. There is no minimum credit requirement; students may apply as early as the first semester of their freshman year. (However, students who have completed several semesters are generally more competitive candidates.) For students at 4-year institutions, Vassar does have a maximum limit for considering applicants: once a student has completed more than 4 full semesters of college-level work, they are no longer eligible to transfer. Thus, students who already have a bachelor's degree would not be eligible applicants.

**Transfer admissions contact person:** Kelly Harrington, Assistant Director of Admission and Coordinator of Transfer Admission

**Transfer admissions contact info:** admissions@vassar.edu, (845) 437-7300

**Offers transfer-focused admissions events:** Yes

**Transfer application deadline:** Fall 2018 deadline is 3/15/18. Spring 2019 deadline is 11/1/18.

**Acceptances announced to transfer applicants:** Fall 2018 on 5/10/18. Spring 2019 on 12/15/18.

**Transfer application on Common App:** Yes. Common App fee: $70.

**SAT/ACT required for transfer applicants:** Yes

**High-school record requirements:** Since the transfer admission process is highly competitive, an applicant's entire academic history is considered in the admission process, and Vassar requires high-school records with the application.

**High-school records requirements for applicants who completed outside the US:** Official transcript

**Submission requirements for transfer applicants who completed high-school equivalency test:** The portion of high-school transcript completed along with GED exam

**College transcript requirements:** Official transcripts for all colleges and universities attended

**Interviews available for transfer applicants:** No

**Additional requirements for transfers seeking admissions to engineering major:** Yes. If you are interested in Industrial and Operations Engineering (IOE), you will want to complete calculus I, calculus II, calculus III, and linear algebra.

## Costs & Financial Aid

**FAFSA code:** 2895

**CSS Profile code:** 2956

**Are internal school financial aid forms required?** Yes

**Financial aid deadlines for transfer applicants:** Fall 2018: 3/15/18. Spring 2019: 11/1/18.

**Costs for the 2017–2018 year:** Tuition & Fees: $55,210. Room & Board: $12,900.

**Anticipated costs for the 2018–2019 year:** No information provided.

**Financial aid for transfer students:** Yes, but the school is need-aware for transfers.

**Guarantees meeting 100% need for transfer students:** Yes

**Need-based aid for transfer students:** Yes

**Merit-based financial aid for transfer students:** No

**Phi Theta Kappa Scholarship:** No

**Reduced or zero tuition fees for low-income students:** No information provided.

**Includes loans in financial aid packages:** Yes

**% of all undergraduates receiving financial aid:** 66%

**% of all undergraduates qualifying for Pell Grants:** 22%

**Average financial aid award for all undergraduate students:** $51,257

**Funding available for low-income students to visit:** No information provided.

**Enrollment deposit can be waived for low-income students:** No information provided.

## Academics

**GPA range for transfer students accepted in 2016–2017:** 3.5–4.0

**SAT ranges for all students admitted in 2016:** Critical Reading: 670–750. Mathematics: 660–750. Writing: 660–750.

**ACT composite score range for all students admitted in 2016:** 31–34

**Recommended completed level of math for transfer applicants:** Calculus

**Recommended extracurricular engagement:** We look for student involvement in both high school and at their current college/university.

**Type of curriculum:** Gen. Ed. requirements

**Type of academic year:** Semester

**Advisors specifically for transfer students:** No information provided.

**Credit Policy (in their own words):** Students who are accepted as transfer students have spent a minimum of 1 semester at a school other than Vassar. The work they have completed at their previous institution(s) is considered pre-matriculation coursework and is evaluated for transfer credit. Transfer students may also earn transfer credit once they have matriculated at Vassar. The maximum amount of transfer credit a transfer student may apply to their Vassar transcript is 17.0 units. Transfer students are also able to do summer work, go JYA, or take a domestic leave of absence, provided they have not exceeded their transfer credit limit.

**Max number of transfer credits accepted:** 17 units

**Residency requirement for transfer students:** Yes. 2 years.

**Study abroad available for transfer students:** Yes. Must fulfill the residency requirement.

**Free tutoring for all students:** Yes

**Writing center for all students:** Yes

**Career support/access to internships and resume prep for all students:** Yes

**% of undergraduate students hired within 6 months of graduation:** No information provided.

**Additional resources specifically designated for transfer and/or non-traditional students:** No information provided.

## Housing

**Available for transfer students:** Yes

**Available for non-traditional students:** No information provided.

**Guaranteed for transfer students:** Yes

**Non-traditional students can reside in housing year-round:** No information provided.

**Family housing available:** No

## Non-Traditional Admissions

**Non-traditional student policy (in their own words):** Well-qualified non-traditional students who live within commuting distance of the campus and who wish to study on a part-time basis are encouraged to discuss special-student status and resumption of work with the Advisor to Special Students in the Office of the Dean of Studies, who can be reached at (845) 437-5255.

## Military/Veteran Students

**Military/veteran admissions policy (in their own words):** Actively seeking to enroll qualified men and women who are veterans of the US armed forces, Vassar is a member of the Yellow Ribbon Program and a partner with the Posse Foundation in the Posse Veterans Program, aimed at increasing the enrollment of veterans at selective colleges and universities.

Read more at https://admissions.vassar.edu/apply/veterans.html.

**Status considered in admissions:** No

**Special admissions process:** No

**Special financial aid:** Yes. The Yellow Ribbon Program.

**Specific programs/policies to address needs:** No information provided.

## DACA/Undocumented Students

**DACA and undocumented admissions policy (in their own words):** Vassar only admits DACA/undocumented students as freshman. No transfer DACA students are allowed.

# WAKE FOREST UNIVERSITY

**Location:** Winston-Salem, North Carolina

**Website:** www.wfu.edu

**Endowment:** $1.17 billion (2015)

**Type of School:** Private/Co-ed, Research University

**# of Undergraduate Students:** 4,955

**# of Graduate Students:** 3,013

**School Mission (in their own words):** Wake Forest is a distinctive university that combines a liberal arts core with graduate and professional schools and innovative research programs. The University embraces the teacher-scholar ideal, prizing personal interaction between students and faculty. It is a place where exceptional teaching, fundamental research and discovery, and the engagement of faculty and students in the classroom and the laboratory are paramount.

The University continues to fulfill its ideal of a more diverse learning community, providing students an example of the world they will be called upon to lead. The University sustains a vibrant residential community with a broad-based program of service and extracurricular activities. The University recognizes the benefits of intercollegiate athletics conducted with integrity and at the highest level.

Central to its mission, the University believes in the development of the whole person—intellectual, moral, spiritual, and physical. From its rich religious heritage, Wake Forest is committed to sustaining an environment where vital beliefs and faith traditions can engage secular thought in a climate of academic freedom and an unfettered search for truth. The University embraces the challenges of religious pluralism.

While national in scope, the university has been shaped by a culture that is distinctively North Carolinian. This history provides it with a sense of place and community responsibility. In extending its reach, the University has made a priority of international study and international understanding. Wake Forest seeks to be a place where a vibrant and diverse learning community weds knowledge, experiences, and service that lift the human spirit.

## Admissions

**Admissions office mailing address:** 1834 Wake Forest Rd, Winston-Salem NC 27109

**Admissions office phone:** (336) 758-5255

**Admissions office email:** admissions@wfu.edu

**# of transfer applications:** Fall 2016 admissions: 330. Spring 2017 admissions: No information provided.

**# of transfer students accepted:** Fall 2016: 78. Spring 2017: No information provided.

**Transfer student acceptance rate (2016–2017 academic year):** 23.6%

**Freshman applications received in Fall 2016:** 14,006

**Freshman applications accepted in Fall 2016:** 4,249

**Acceptance rate for 2016–2017 freshmen:** 30.3%

## Transfer Admissions Process

**Transfer policy (in their own words):** We may be just what you're looking for. Wake Forest welcomes the submission of applications from transfer students, and the number of transfer students admitted varies from semester to semester depending on the current enrollment. Traditionally, more students are admitted for the fall semester than the spring semester.

An applicant for admission who has attended another college must have an overall average of at least C on all college work attempted and must either be a graduate of a standard junior college or furnish a certificate of honorable dismissal stating eligibility in all respects to enter the last college attended.

Transfer students are eligible for all Wake Forest need-based financial aid programs. There are no available merit-based scholarships for transfer students. For information on our need-based financial aid programs, visit our financial aid website.

International students should review information found on our International Applicants page for additional information and instructions.

**Transfer admissions contact person:** Arron Marlowe-Rogers, Associate Dean of Admissions

**Transfer admissions contact info:** marlowaa@wfu.edu, (336) 758-4929

**Offers transfer-focused admissions events:** No

**Transfer application deadline:** Fall 2018 deadline is 4/1/18. Spring 2019 deadline is 11/1/18.

**Acceptances announced to transfer applicants:** Fall 2018 on rolling basis. Spring 2019 on rolling basis.

**Transfer application on Common App: Yes. Common App fee: $65.**

**SAT/ACT required for transfer applicants:** No

**High-school record requirements:** Final high-school transcript

**High-school records requirements for applicants who completed outside the US:** Certified transcripts are required from each secondary school, college, or university attended. A record of at least 4 years of schooling is needed in order to evaluate the application.

**Submission requirements for transfer applicants who completed high-school equivalency test:** Official GED results

**College transcript requirements:** Official transcripts from all colleges/universities attended

**Interviews available for transfer applicants:** No

## Costs & Financial Aid

**FAFSA code:** 2978

**CSS Profile code:** 5885

**Are internal school financial aid forms required?** No

**Financial aid deadlines for transfer applicants:** Fall 2018: 2/1/18. Spring 2019: 11/15/18.

**Costs for the 2017–2018 year:** Tuition & Fees: $51,400. Room and Board: $13,926.

**Financial aid for transfer students:** Yes

**Guarantees meeting 100% need for transfer students:** Yes

**Need-based aid for transfer students:** Yes

**Merit-based financial aid for transfer students:** No

**Phi Theta Kappa Scholarship:** No

**Reduced or zero tuition fees for low-income students:** No

**Includes loans in financial aid packages:** Yes

**% of all undergraduates receiving financial aid:** 32%

**% of all undergraduates qualifying for Pell Grants:** No information provided.

**Average financial aid award for all undergraduate students:** 47,288

**Funding available for low-income students to visit:** No

**Enrollment deposit can be waived for low-income students:** No

## Academics

**GPA range for transfer students accepted in 2016–2017:** 2.0 minimum

**SAT ranges for all students admitted in 2016:** Critical Reading: 600–700. Mathematics: 640–740. Writing: 620–710.

**ACT composite score range for all students admitted in 2016:** 28–32.

**Type of curriculum:** Gen. Ed. requirements

**Type of academic year:** Semester

**Advisors specifically for transfer students:** No information provided.

**Credit policy (in their own words):** Degree credit requirements:

- A Wake Forest student must finish 3 requirements for 120 hours of credit: a core set of classes, a course of study related to a major, and electives. The core set of classes includes basic requirements (a first-year seminar, a writing seminar, health and PE classes, and foreign language literature) and divisional requirements (at least 2 classes in each of the humanities, social sciences, and math/natural sciences and at least 1 in the fine arts and literatures).

- Once a student has been accepted as a transfer student by the Admissions Office, their transcript is sent to the Office of the University Registrar and the transfer process begins.

- Wake Forest does not maintain articulation agreements with any other college or university—all decisions are made by the chair of the department where credit is being requested as to whether a course will transfer upon a student's acceptance to the university. The department chair has the right to limit the amount of credit awarded or to stipulate that a higher-level course must be completed here at Wake Forest before a student may receive credit. No evaluations are done prior to a student being admitted. Please refer to specific departmental policies for further information.

- There are also limits to the amount of transfer work you can bring into the major. The general rule is that you must take 1/2 of the major at Wake, but some departments have more stringent rules. You can direct inquiries about this to the appropriate department.

- The Wake Forest departments listed do NOT accept transfer work from a 2-year community or junior college: Accounting, Anthropology, Biology, Business and Enterprise Management, Chemistry, Economics, English, Finance, Philosophy, Physics, Psychology, Sociology, Women's Studies.

- Once you have been admitted to Wake Forest, you will need to submit syllabi for all the courses you took or are taking at your current college or university.

- In all cases, a student must have earned a grade of C or better in order to transfer a course (a C– is not transferable). The grades you earned at your prior institution(s) do not factor into your Wake Forest GPA although they will appear on your transcript. You will be starting with a clean slate as far as your GPA is concerned. All work attempted at another college or university must be reported to the WFU registrar, and all such courses must appear on the Wake Forest transcript. In order to graduate from Wake Forest, you must complete at least half of your degree and half of your major at Wake Forest.

- Once enrolled at Wake Forest, a student may subsequently count, at most, 30 hours of credit from sources other than Wake Forest programs toward the graduation requirement. (Non-Wake study abroad and summer school elsewhere are considered transfer.)

**Max number of transfer credits accepted:** 60

**Residency requirement for transfer students:** Yes. Students must earn at least 60 credits and half the credits of their major/minor at Wake Forest.

**Study abroad available for transfer students:** Yes. Must fulfill residency requirements.

**Free tutoring for all students:** Yes

**Writing center for all students:** Yes

**Career support/access to internships and resume prep for all students:** Yes

**% of undergraduate students hired within 6 months of graduation:** No information provided.

**Additional resources specifically designated for transfer and/or non-traditional students:** No

## Housing

**Available for transfer students:** Yes

**Available for non-traditional students:** No information provided.

**Guaranteed for transfer students:** Yes

**Non-traditional students can reside in housing year-round:** N/A

**Family housing available:** No information provided.

## Non-Traditional Admissions

No non-traditional student policies or programs available.

## Military/Veteran Students

**Military/veteran admissions policy (in their own words):** Students who receive VA Education Benefits are encouraged to apply for need-based aid. Please note: The Undergraduate Schools do not participate in the Yellow Ribbon Program of the Post-9/11 GI Bill, and Wake Forest University does not participate in the US Department of Defense (DoD) federal Tuition Assistance (TA) program.

Read more at http://financialaid.wfu.edu/veterans/.

**Status considered in admissions:** No

**Special admissions process:** No

**Special financial aid:** Yes, but those benefits vary depending on the particular school from the University that the student is applying to. The student must meet service requirements according to the Department of Veteran Affairs. The eligibility requirements for military/veteran aid also vary depending on the school from the University that the student is applying to.

**Specific programs/policies to address needs:** No

## DACA/Undocumented Students

**DACA and undocumented admissions policy (in their own words):** There is not a specific DACA/undocumented student admission policy, but there's a letter of support for these students written by the school. The following excerpt is taken from the letter:

> Many members of the University administration, faculty, and staff are deeply concerned about the fear created by recent political rhetoric and recognize how many in our community feel unsafe, unvalued, or unwelcome because of the current divisive climate. We pledge full support, and that the wonderfully talented staff that are here will help undocumented students get the most from their Wake Forest experience.

The full letter is available here: http://community.wfu.edu/files/2016/11/Support-for-Undocumented-Students_Draft-Points-12-7-16.pdf.

**Admitted:** Yes

**Status considered in admissions:** No

**Special admissions process:** No

**Eligible for institutional financial aid:** Yes. Submit required financial aid forms. Institutional aid replaces federal aid.

**Specific programs/policies to address needs:** No

# WELLESLEY COLLEGE

**Location:** Wellesley, Massachusetts

**Website:** www.wellesley.edu

**Endowment:** $1.8 billion

**Type of School:** Private, Single-Sex Female, Liberal Arts

**# of Undergraduate Students:** 2,300

**# of Graduate Students:** N/A

**Average Class Size:** 17–20 students

**School Mission (in their own words):** To provide an excellent liberal arts education for women who will make a difference in the world.

## Admissions

**Admissions office mailing address:** 106 Central St, Wellesley MA 02481

**Admissions office phone:** (781) 283-2270

**Admissions office email:** admission@wellesley.edu

**# of transfer applications:** Fall 2016 admissions: 257. Spring 2017 admissions: No information provided.

**# of transfer students accepted:** Fall 2016: 11. Spring 2017: No information provided.

**Transfer student acceptance rate (2016–2017 academic year):** 4.28% (Fall 2016)

**Freshman applications received in Fall 2016:** 4,854

**Freshman applications accepted in Fall 2016:** 1,388

**Acceptance rate for 2016–2017 freshmen:** 29%

## Transfer Admissions Process

**Transfer policy (in their own words):** Each year, Wellesley accepts a small number of transfer students for entrance in September or January. In order to receive a Wellesley College degree, a student must complete at least 2 years (16 units) of coursework at the College. Transfer students are integrated into an existing class and enjoy the same opportunities and privileges available to their classmates—including financial aid and guaranteed housing.

**Transfer admissions contact person:** John T. O'Keefe, Dean and Director of Advising and Academic Support

**Transfer admissions contact info:** jokeefe@wellesley.edu, (718) 283-2326

**Offers transfer-focused admissions events:** Yes

**Transfer application deadline:** Fall 2018 deadline is 3/1/18. Spring 2019 deadline is 11/1/18.

**Acceptances announced to transfer applicants:** Fall 2018 in late May. Spring 2019 in mid-December.

**Transfer application on Common App:** Yes. Common App fee: N/A.

**SAT/ACT required for transfer applicants:** Applicants are required to send us their scores if their current school required them. Community college students are not required to submit scores.

**High-school record requirements:** Submit an official final transcript from the high school from which you graduated.

**High-school records requirements for applicants who completed outside the US:** An official transcript is a certified record of the courses you have completed and the marks you received at each marking period in all schools attended during the previous 4 years. We need both the transcript in the original language as well as a translated copy.

**Submission requirements for transfer applicants who completed high-school equivalency test:** If you received a High School Certificate of Equivalency, official GED scores and a high-school transcript for the years you attended are required.

**College transcript requirements:** Submit official transcripts from all colleges and universities you have attended. Transcripts must be sent directly from the college to Wellesley's Board of Admission.

**Interviews available for transfer applicants:** Yes. Recommended. On campus and off campus with an alumna.

**Additional requirements for transfers seeking admissions to arts major:** Yes. If you have a special talent in the arts, you might want to submit an Arts Supplement. Our Art Department, Music Department, and Theatre Studies Department will accept electronic submissions of portfolios, recordings, or presentations. The appropriate department will review your material. Wellesley College does not have a dance department and does not review creative writing materials. Please do NOT submit any dance and/or creative writing supplements as they will not be evaluated.

**Additional requirements for transfers seeking admissions to engineering major:** Yes. If you are interested in Naval Architecture and Marine Engineering (NAME), you are required to complete Calculus I and Calculus II.

## Costs & Financial Aid

**FAFSA code:** 2224

**CSS Profile code:** 3957

**Are internal school financial aid forms required?** Yes (Wellesley College Dependent Student Verification Worksheet)

**Financial aid deadlines for transfer applicants:** Fall 2018: 4/15/18. Spring 2019: 11/15/18.

**Costs for the 2017–2018 year:** Tuition & Fees: $51,148. Room & Board: $15,836.

**Financial aid for transfer students:** Yes

**Guarantees meeting 100% need for transfer students:** Yes

**Need-based aid for transfer students:** Yes

**Merit-based financial aid for transfer students:** No

**Phi Theta Kappa Scholarship:** No

**Reduced or zero tuition fees for low-income students:** No

**Includes loans in financial aid packages:** Yes

**% of all undergraduates receiving financial aid:** 60%

**% of all undergraduates qualifying for Pell Grants:** No information provided.

**Average financial aid award for all undergraduate students:** $47,527

**Funding available for low-income students to visit:** Yes

**Enrollment deposit can be waived for low-income students:** Yes

## Academics

**GPA range for transfer students accepted in 2016–2017:** Not available.

**SAT ranges for all students admitted in 2016:** Critical Reading: 660–750. Mathematics: 650–750. Writing: 660–750.

**ACT composite score range for all students admitted in 2016:** 30–33

**Recommended completed level of math for transfer applicants:** Minimum pre-calculus

**Recommended completed level of English for transfer applicants:** Writing intensive courses beyond English composition

**Recommended courses transfer applicants should have on transcripts:** 1 year of foreign language, math through pre-calculus, science with lab, social science, humanities

**Recommended courses transfer applicants interested in STEM should complete before transfer:** Calculus, natural sciences with lab

**Type of curriculum:** Gen. Ed. requirements

**Type of academic year:** Semester

**Advisors specifically for transfer students:** Yes

**Credit policy (in their own words):** 1 unit of Wellesley College work typically equals 4 semester hours or 6 quarter hours. That means that if you attended an institution where you took 5 courses each semester worth 3 credits each, each course could transfer as .8 or .75 units of Wellesley College work, depending on the total number of credit hours needed for the degree.

Students may transfer in a maximum of 16 units, only 4 units of which may be earned in summer sessions.

Distribution requirements (except for writing) must be fulfilled by taking or transferring in 1 whole unit of coursework.

Read more at www.wellesley.edu/admission/esp/transfer/ credit#SReP6hV28kwOgX8i.99.

**Max number of transfer credits accepted:** 16 units, which means students must obtain at least 2 years' worth of credits from Wellesley.

**Residency requirement for transfer students:** Yes. In order to receive a Wellesley College degree, a student must complete at least 2 years (16 units) of coursework at the College.

**Study abroad available for transfer students:** Yes. A transfer student can study abroad if she transferred with less than 16 units, meaning if she entered Wellesley as a sophomore or second-semester sophomore. However, all transfer students may participate in Winter Session programs, some of which take place abroad. They may take advantage of the many internships Wellesley offers during the academic year, Winter Session, and summer. Most transfer students are also eligible to take courses through Wellesley's cross-registration programs at MIT, Brandeis, Babson, and Olin. Note: One exception is that transfers who bring in 16 credits cannot cross-register.

**Free tutoring for all students:** Yes

**Writing center for all students:** Yes

**Career support/access to internships and resume prep for all students:** Yes

**% of undergraduate students hired within 6 months of graduation:** No information provided.

**Additional resources specifically designated for transfer and/or non-traditional students:** Yes. Transfer orientation, advisors, and Continuing Education House.

## Housing

**Available for transfer students:** Yes

**Available for non-traditional students:** Yes

**Guaranteed for transfer students:** Yes

**Non-traditional students can reside in housing year-round:** Yes

**Family housing available:** No

## Non-Traditional Admissions

**Non-traditional student policy (in their own words):** No information provided.

**Name of program:** Elizabeth Kaiser Davis Degree Program

**Program description:** Designed with the needs of the returning student in mind, the Elisabeth Kaiser Davis Degree program affords women beyond traditional college age who have begun but not completed a bachelor's degree the opportunity to complete their degree at Wellesley. The Davis Degree Program gathers women from diverse backgrounds and life experiences, providing them with a fully engaged college experience in one of the best liberal arts programs available and, in the process, creating an extraordinary community. Davis Scholars take the same classes and meet the same academic degree requirements as all other Wellesley students; they can participate in the same organizations and activities, and they have access to all the resources and supports of the College. They are eligible for financial aid; in addition, the Davis Scholar Lifeline Fund can provide some supplemental financial assistance.

**Program deadline:** Early March

**Program admission requirements:** Applicants that qualify include US veterans, mothers, and any woman who was unable to complete her bachelor's degree during the traditional 18- to 24-year-old period of her life.

To apply to Wellesley as a Davis Degree candidate, you must complete and submit the online Common Application for Transfer Candidates. It's free to do so. Please be sure to identify yourself as a transfer applicant when you register for your Common App account. Must interview and the deadline for requesting an interview is February 15. Also, an updated resume is required.

**Program website:** www.wellesley.edu/admission/esp/davis#0437wyu1ozGUe1T4.97

**Program contact person:** Susan Cohen, Director and Dean of Davis Degree Program

**Program contact info:** (781) 283-2325, scohen@wellesley.edu

## Military/Veteran Students

**Military/veteran admissions policy (in their own words):** There's no specific policy for veteran admissions, but usually many veteran students apply through the Davis Program, which is Wellesley's non-traditional program. See above for details.

**Status considered in admissions:** No

**Special admissions process:** No

**Special financial aid:** Yes. The Yellow Ribbon Program.

**Specific programs/policies to address needs:** Yes

## DACA/Undocumented Students

**DACA and undocumented admissions policy (in their own words):** Wellesley accepts applications from undocumented and DACA students. For financial aid purposes, Wellesley considers undocumented and DACA students as international citizens. Financial assistance is available for a limited number of international citizens, undocumented students, and DACA students. Because of the keen competition for these funds, candidates should apply for them only if family resources cannot adequately meet college expenses.

Wellesley is committed to meeting 100% of demonstrated need for all admitted undocumented and DACA students who apply for financial aid during the admission process. Admitted undocumented and DACA students will receive financial assistance in the form of grant aid. Students will not be expected to borrow (via a student loan) as part of their

aid packages. If students are ineligible to work in the US, students will receive grant aid in place of the typical school year work-study expectation.

**Admitted:** Yes

**Status considered in admissions:** Yes. Considered in the same category as international students, and Wellesley is need-aware for this type of student.

**Special admissions process:** Yes. Must apply as international students.

**Eligible for institutional financial aid:** Yes. The admissions process is need-aware. Once accepted, the school meets 100% financial need and will substitute grants for work-study if the student is unable to work. Must demonstrate need. Average financial aid offered: $58,036.

**Specific programs/policies to address needs:** There are advisors on campus who have experience working with undocumented students and know about DACA laws.

# WESLEYAN UNIVERSITY

**Location:** Middletown, Connecticut

**Website:** wesleyan.edu

**Endowment:** $802.2 million

**Type of School:** Private/Co-ed, Liberal Arts

**# of Undergraduate Students:** 2,971

**# of Graduate Students:** 235

**Average Class Size:** No information provided.

**School Mission (in their own words):** Wesleyan University is dedicated to providing an education in the liberal arts that is characterized by boldness, rigor, and practical idealism. At Wesleyan, distinguished scholar-teachers work closely with students, taking advantage of fluidity among disciplines to explore the world with a variety of tools. The university seeks to build a diverse, energetic community of students, faculty, and staff who think critically and creatively and who value independence of mind and generosity of spirit.

## Admissions

**Admissions office mailing address:** 45 Wyllys Ave, Middletown CT 06459

**Admissions office phone:** (860) 685-3000

**Admissions office email:** admission@wesleyan.edu

**# of transfer applications:** Fall 2016 admissions: 499. Spring 2017 admissions: No information provided.

**# of transfer students accepted:** Fall 2016: 141. Spring 2017: No information provided.

**Transfer student acceptance rate (2016–2017 academic year):** 28.3%

**Freshman applications received in Fall 2016:** 11,928

**Freshman applications accepted in Fall 2016:** 2,129

**Acceptance rate for 2016–2017 freshmen:** 17.8%

## Transfer Admissions Process

**Transfer policy (in their own words):** An applicant is considered a transfer student at Wesleyan if they have completed at least 1 full-time year of college and the equivalent of at least 6 Wesleyan credits by the time they matriculate at Wesleyan. 1 Wesleyan credit is considered equivalent to 4 semester hours or 6 quarter hours. Students who have taken college courses through a high school or part-time only will normally be considered first-year applicants. Applicants, including international students, may not discount academic credits in order to qualify as first-year applicants. Wesleyan does not grant a second bachelor's degree.

**Transfer admissions contact person:** Tara Lindros, Associate Dean of Admissions

**Transfer admissions contact info:** tlindros@wesleyan.edu

**Offers transfer-focused admissions events:** N/A

**Transfer application deadline:** Fall 2018 deadline is 3/15/18. Spring 2019 deadline is 11/1/18.

**Acceptances announced to transfer applicants:** Fall 2018 on 5/15/18. Spring 2019 on 12/11/18.

**Transfer application on Common App:** Yes. Common App fee: $55.

**SAT/ACT required for transfer applicants:** No, test is optional.

**High-school record requirements:** Submit an official final transcript from the high school from which you graduated.

**High-school records requirements for applicants who completed outside the US:** An official transcript is a certified record of the courses you have completed and the marks you received at each marking period in all schools attended during the previous 4 years. We need both the transcript in the original language as well as a translated copy.

**Submission requirements for transfer applicants who completed high-school equivalency test:** If you received a High School Certificate of Equivalency, official GED scores and a high-school transcript for the years you attended are required.

**College transcript requirements:** Official transcripts from all colleges/universities attended

**Interviews available for transfer applicants:** Yes. Required for CT community college students; optional for all other transfers. On campus, off campus.

**Additional requirements for transfers seeking admissions to arts major:** Yes. Applicants may submit supporting materials in music, theatre, visual arts, and scientific research that represent a special accomplishment or reflect an education goal. All supplementary materials must be submitted through SlideRoom, which can be accessed through the Common Application.

## Costs & Financial Aid

**FAFSA code:** 1424

**CSS Profile code:** 3959

**Are internal school financial aid forms required?** No

**Financial aid deadlines for transfer applicants:** Fall 2018: April 1, 2018. Spring 2019: No information provided.

**Costs for the 2017–2018 year:** Tuition & Fees: $50,312. Room & Board: $13,950 (freshman & sophomore years), $15,858 (junior & senior years).

**Financial aid for transfer students:** Yes

**Guarantees meeting 100% need for transfer students:** Yes

**Need-based aid for transfer students:** Yes

**Merit-based financial aid for transfer students:** No

**Phi Theta Kappa Scholarship:** No

**Reduced or zero tuition fees for low-income students:** No

**Includes loans in financial aid packages:** Yes

**% of all undergraduates receiving financial aid:**
No information provided.

**% of all undergraduates qualifying for Pell Grants:**
No information provided.

**Average financial aid award for all undergraduate students:**
$47,077

**Funding available for low-income students to visit:** No

**Enrollment deposit can be waived for low-income students:**
No information provided.

## Academics

**GPA range for transfer students accepted in 2016–2017:**
No information provided.

**SAT ranges for all students admitted in 2016:** Critical Reading: 620–740. Mathematics: 630–740. Writing: 640–750.

**ACT composite score range for all students admitted in 2016:** 30–33

**Type of curriculum:** Gen. Ed. requirements

**Type of academic year:** Semester

**Advisors specifically for transfer students:** No information provided.

**Credit policy (in their own words):** The requirements are (1) satisfaction of requirements for a major; (2) satisfactory completion of 32 course credits, no fewer than 16 of which must be earned at Wesleyan or in Wesleyan-sponsored programs; (3) a cumulative average of 74% or work of equivalent quality; and (4) at least 6 semesters in residence at Wesleyan as full-time students for students entering in their first year (for students entering as sophomore transfers, at least 5 semesters in residence at Wesleyan as full-time students; for students entering as midyear sophomores or junior transfers, at least 4 semesters in residence at Wesleyan as full-time students). A semester in residence is defined as any semester in which a student attends classes on the Wesleyan campus, has attempted at least 3 credits, and received at least 1 grade. If a conversion to semester hours is required, each Wesleyan credit may be assigned a value of 4 semester hours.

All courses taken at Wesleyan will be listed on the student's transcript. However, there are limits on the number of credits students can count toward the total of 32 course credits required for the bachelor of arts. No more than 16 credits in any 1 subject (i.e., course code) can be counted toward the degree requirements. All course credits posted to a student's academic records will be considered for oversubscription including pre-matriculant, study-abroad, and/or transfer credits. A course offered in more than 1 subject designation (i.e., cross-listed) will count in all subjects in which it is offered. A student who exceeds these limits will be

considered oversubscribed, and the additional course credits may not count toward the 32 required for the bachelor of arts.

**Transfer credit policy:** We provide a credit review with the offer of admission, but generally coursework will be creditable and will help to determine transfer admission eligibility if:

- The course was taken on a college campus (not a college-level course taken at high school)
- The course is similar to a course offered by a Wesleyan department or is from a department or program available at Wesleyan
- The course is at the college level (e.g., algebra would not count)
- A grade of C– (B– for a summer course) or better was earned

**Max number of transfer credits accepted:** 16

**Residency requirement for transfer students:** Yes. Must earn at least 16 credits at Wesleyan.

**Study abroad available for transfer students:** Yes. Must complete the residency requirement.

**Free tutoring for all students:** Yes

**Writing center for all students:** Yes

**Career support/access to internships and resume prep for all students:** Yes

**% of undergraduate students hired within 6 months of graduation:** No information provided.

**Additional resources specifically designated for transfer and/or non-traditional students:** No

## Housing

**Available for transfer students:** Yes

**Available for non-traditional students:** Yes, but only for Posse Foundation students/military students.

**Guaranteed for transfer students:** Yes

**Non-traditional students can reside in housing year-round:** No

**Family housing available:** No

## Non-Traditional Admissions

**Non-traditional student policy (in their own words):** Applicants who have significant interruptions in their schooling or who were homeschooled should provide a thorough explanation of their educational situation, background, and chronology in the personal statement or in an additional essay. Competitive applicants will need to have enrolled recently in a full-time course of study to demonstrate a record of success in such a program.

## Military/Veteran Students

**Military/veteran admissions policy:** No information provided.

**Status considered in admissions:** Yes

**Special admissions process:** No

**Special financial aid:** Yes. The Yellow Ribbon Program (maximum $22,679 per year).

**Specific programs/policies to address needs:** No

## DACA/Undocumented Students

**DACA and undocumented admissions policy (in their own words):** Wesleyan has a rich history and tradition of providing access to underrepresented students from all backgrounds and has long been a leader in diversity efforts. The University strives to provide a welcoming community for all students and holds as essential values inclusion, tolerance, and equal opportunity. In that spirit, Wesleyan welcomes all undergraduate applicants regardless of citizenship status. Undocumented students, with or without DACA, who apply to Wesleyan are treated identically to any other US citizen or permanent resident in their high school.

**Admitted:** Yes

**Status considered in admissions:** No

**Special admissions process:** No

**Eligible for institutional financial aid:** Wesleyan meets 100% of demonstrated need for all admitted students. Because DACA/undocumented students are ineligible for federal aid, Wesleyan will meet this demonstrated need with its institutional funding instead.

**Specific programs/policies to address needs:** No

# WILLIAMS COLLEGE

**Location:** Williamstown, Massachusetts
**Website:** www.williams.edu
**Endowment:** $2.3 billion
**Type of School:** Private/Co-ed, Liberal Arts
**# Undergraduate Students:** 2,042
**# of Graduate Students:** 57
**Average Class Size:** No information provided.

**School Mission (in their own words):** Williams seeks to provide the finest possible liberal arts education by nurturing in students the academic and civic virtues, and their related traits of character. Academic virtues include the capacities to explore widely and deeply, think critically, reason empirically, express clearly, and connect ideas creatively. Civic virtues include commitment to engage both the broad public realm and community life, and the skills to do so effectively. These virtues, in turn, have associated traits of character.

For example, free inquiry requires open-mindedness, and commitment to community draws on concern for others.

We are committed to our central endeavor of academic excellence in a community of learning that comprises students, faculty, and staff and draws on the engagement of alumni and parents. We recruit students from among the most able in the country and abroad and select them for the academic and personal attributes they can contribute to the educational enterprise, inside and outside the classroom. Our faculty is a highly talented group of teachers, scholars, and artists committed deeply to the education of our students and to involving them in their efforts to expand human knowledge and understanding through original research, thought, and artistic expression. Dedicated staff enable this teaching and learning to take place at the highest possible level, as do the involvement and support of our extraordinarily loyal parents and alumni.

## Admissions

**Admissions office mailing address:** 880 Main St, Williamstown MA 01267
**Admissions office phone:** (413) 597-3131
**Admissions office email:** admission@williams.edu
**# of transfer applications:** Fall 2016 admissions: 226
**# of transfer students accepted:** Fall 2016: 12
**Transfer student acceptance rate (2016–2017 academic year):** 5.3%
**Freshman applications received in Fall 2016:** 6,985
**Freshman applications accepted in Fall 2016:** 1,230
**Acceptance rate for 2016–2017 freshmen:** 18%

## Transfer Admissions Process

**Transfer policy (in their own words):** Because so few students choose to leave Williams prior to graduating, we have relatively few places available for transfer candidates. Transfer students must enroll at Williams for a minimum of 2 years. Students are not eligible for admission if they have already received a bachelor's degree or if they have completed more than 2 years of full-time college coursework at a 4-year college or university.

**Transfer admissions contact person:** Richard Nesbitt, Director of Admission
**Transfer admissions contact info:** rnesbitt@williams.edu, (413) 597-2214
**Offers transfer-focused admissions events:** No
**Transfer application deadline:** Fall 2018 deadline is 4/1/18.
**Acceptances announced to transfer applicants:** Fall 2018 on 5/15/18.

**Transfer application on Common App:** Yes. Common App fee: $65 (fee waiver available).
**SAT/ACT required for transfer applicants:** Yes
**High-school record requirements:** Final high-school transcript
**High-school records requirements for applicants who completed outside the US:** Same as for domestic students
**Submission requirements for transfer applicants who completed high-school equivalency test:** Official GED results
**College transcript requirements:** College transcript
**Interviews available for transfer applicants:** No

## Costs & Financial Aid

**FAFSA code:** 2229
**CSS Profile code:** 3965
**Are internal school financial aid forms required?** No
**Financial aid deadline for transfer applicants:** Fall 2018: 4/15/18.
**Costs for the 2017–2018 year:** Tuition & Fees: $53,550. Room & Board: $14,150.
**Financial aid for transfer students:** Yes
**Guarantees meeting 100% need for transfer students:** Yes
**Need-based aid for transfer students:** Yes. All admitted students are offered 100% demonstrated need.
**Merit-based financial aid for transfer students:** No
**Phi Theta Kappa Scholarship:** No
**Reduced or zero tuition fees for low-income students:** No
**Includes loans in financial aid packages:** Yes. Maximum loan amount of $4,000/year.
**% of all undergraduates receiving financial aid:** 50%

**% of all undergraduates qualifying for Pell Grants:**
No information provided.

**Average financial aid award for all undergraduate students:**
$51,890.

**Funding available for low-income students to visit:** Yes, for high school students

**Enrollment deposit can be waived for low-income students:**
N/A

## Academics

**GPA range for transfer students accepted in 2016–2017:** N/A

**SAT ranges for all students admitted in 2016:** Critical Reading: 670–770. Mathematics: 660–770. Writing: 670–770.

**ACT composite score range for all students admitted in 2016:** 31–34

**Type of curriculum:** Gen. Ed. requirements

**Type of academic year:** Semester

**Advisors specifically for transfer students:** Yes

**Credit policy (in their own words):** To be eligible for the bachelor of arts degree, a student must pass 32 semester courses (at least 29 of which must be regularly graded A–E, including 19 with grades of C– or better), pass 4 Winter Study Projects, fulfill the 4-part distribution requirement, complete all requirements for the major including an average of C– or higher, and complete the physical education requirement. A student may not repeat a course for which degree credit has been awarded.

Transfer students must enroll at Williams for a minimum of 2 years. Students are not eligible for admission if they have already received a bachelor's degree or if they have completed more than 2 years of full-time college coursework at a 4-year college or university.

**Max number of transfer credits accepted:** 16

**Residency requirement for transfer students:** Yes. Students who begin college at Williams must spend a minimum of 6 semesters in residence at Williams. Students transferring to Williams from other institutions must spend a minimum of 4 semesters in residence at Williams, and those entering as sophomores are expected to spend 6 semesters in residence. Students are considered to be in residence if they are taking a program of study under the direction of the Williams College faculty. Students must be in residence for both semesters of the final year.

The degree requirements must be completed within 8 semesters, including any semesters for which a student receives credit while not in residence at Williams. Thus, semesters spent away on exchange or other approved programs at other colleges are included in the 8 semesters.

**Study abroad available for transfer students:** Yes. Must fulfill the residency requirements.

**Free tutoring for all students:** Yes

**Writing center for all students:** Yes

**Career support/access to internships and resume prep for all students:** Yes

**% of undergraduate students hired within 6 months of graduation:** No information available.

**Additional resources specifically designated for transfer and/or non-traditional students:** No

## Housing

**Available for transfer students:** Yes

**Available for non-traditional students:** No

**Guaranteed for transfer students:** Yes

**Non-traditional students can reside in housing year-round:** No

**Family housing available:** No

## Non-Traditional Admissions

No non-traditional student policies or programs.

## Military/Veteran Students

**Military/veteran admissions policy (in their own words):** Williams encourages applications from qualified men and women who've actively served in the US military. We are also a proud partner with Service to School, a 501(c)(3) nonprofit organization, which provides free application counseling, peer-to-peer guidance, and networking support to all US military service members and veterans. Its mission is to help every transitioning military veteran gain admission to the best college or graduate school possible. These services are provided at no cost to the applicant.

For veterans returning from service, applying to college can sometimes feel overwhelming, and we stand ready to advise and aid throughout the process. Please contact admission counselor Carolina Echenique at carolina.e.echenique@williams.edu to discuss any special circumstances and to help you determine whether Williams might represent the best educational fit for you. If you have a spouse or partner who will need relocation assistance, please reach out to Marybeth Mitts in Human Resources at marybeth.f.mitts@williams.edu.

**Status considered in admissions:** No

**Special admissions process:** No. Williams takes a holistic approach to the admission process and will evaluate each application—including transcripts—in context, taking into account any time that may have elapsed since enrollment.

**Special financial aid:** Yes. The Yellow Ribbon Program. Qualified veterans or their dependents are eligible for unlimited Yellow Ribbon institutional matching funds from the college without limitation on the number of recipients.

**Specific programs/policies to address needs:** No

# DACA/Undocumented Students

**DACA and undocumented admissions policy (in their own words):** Williams welcomes applications from undocumented students and those with Deferred Action for Childhood Arrivals status and evaluates their applications in the domestic applicant pool under a need-blind admission policy.

The college meets 100% of the demonstrated financial need of all undocumented students—as it does for every student admitted to Williams, regardless of country of citizenship or visa status. Undocumented students who qualify for financial aid but are not permitted to work in the US will have the work-study portion of their financial aid package replaced with additional Williams grants.

For more information about the financial aid application process for undocumented and DACA students, please email the financial aid office or visit their website.

If you are an undocumented or DACA student with questions about applying to Williams, please visit our admission website or contact Adrian Castro, Assistant Director of Admission, at rac1@williams.edu.

Williams is committed to supporting undocumented and DACA designated students throughout their time at the College.

**Admitted:** Yes

**Status considered in admissions:** No

**Special admissions process:** No

**Eligible for institutional financial aid:** Williams meets 100% of the demonstrated financial need of all undocumented students—as it does for every student admitted to Williams, regardless of country of citizenship or visa status. Undocumented students who qualify for financial aid but are not permitted to work in the US will have the work-study portion of their financial aid package replaced with additional Williams grants.

**Specific programs/policies to address needs:** The following is a short list of staff members who can provide resources and offer guidance:

- Rosanna Reyes, Associate Dean of the College; serves as the advisor for current undocumented and DACA-designated students.
- Tina Breakell, Director of International Education and Study Away; supports DACA students interested in participating in study away opportunities, advises on support resources available during the Advance Parole application process and financial aid budget process, and works closely with students and their program providers throughout the application and immigration process.
- Ninah Pretto, Assistant Dean of International Student Services; provides support and guidance on how students can seek legal advice from community nonprofit agencies that specialize in immigration assistance or immigration attorneys, and helps students navigate the USCIS website and other resources.
- Molly Magavern, Director of Special Academic Programs; helps students from underrepresented groups, including undocumented students, find opportunities that help them advance their educational goals. For more about the Office of Special Academic Programs and related programs, please visit their website.
- Gary Caster, Catholic Chaplain; the Chaplains' Office is eager to provide emotional and spiritual support and guidance for students as they settle into life at Williams and throughout their years here. Fr. Gary Caster is the primary contact person for undocumented and DACA students (and family members).
- The Davis Center director and staff; work with all students, especially those from historically underrepresented and underserved groups, as they engage with complex issues of identity, history, and culture and in support of their academic and co-curricular interests. For more information about the Davis Center and related programs, please visit their website.
- Michelle Shaw, Associate Director of the Career Center; serves as the primary contact for current undocumented and DACA-designated students.

See https://admission.williams.edu/apply/undocumented-applicants/ for more info.

# XAVIER UNIVERSITY OF LOUISIANA

**Location:** New Orleans, Louisiana

**Website:** www.xula.edu

**Endowment:** $152.5 million

**Type of School:** Private, Co-ed, Liberal Arts

**# Undergraduate Students:** 2,327

**# of Graduate Students:** 670

**Average Class Size:** No information provided.

**School Mission (in their own words):** Xavier University of Louisiana, founded by Saint Katharine Drexel and the Sisters of the Blessed Sacrament, is Catholic and historically Black. The ultimate purpose of the University is to contribute to the promotion of a more just and humane society by preparing its students to assume roles of leadership and service in a global society. This preparation takes place in a diverse learning and teaching environment that incorporates all relevant educational means, including research and community service.

## Admissions

**Admissions office mailing address:** 1 Drexel Dr, New Orleans LA 70125

**Admissions office phone:** (504) 520-7388

**Admissions office email:** apply@xula.edu

**Freshman applications received in Fall 2016:** 6,640

**Freshman applications accepted in Fall 2016:** 4,084

**Acceptance rate for 2016–2017 freshmen:** 61.5%

## Transfer Admissions Process

**Transfer policy (in their own words):** No information provided

**Transfer admissions contact person:** Bryan M. Carraway, Senior Admissions Counselor

**Transfer admissions contact info:** bmcarraw@xula.edu, (504) 520-7576

**Offers transfer-focused admissions events:** No

**Transfer application deadline:** Fall 2018 deadline is 6/1/18. Spring 2019 deadline is 12/1/218.

**Acceptances announced to transfer applicants:** Fall 2018 on rolling basis. Spring 2019 on rolling basis.

**Transfer application on Common App:** No. Common App fee: N/A.

**Separate application or in addition to the Common App:** Yes

**Fee for separate transfer application:** No

**SAT/ACT required for transfer applicants:** Yes, if applicant has fewer than 20 hours of transferrable credit.

**High-school record requirements:** Required if applicant has fewer than 20 hours transferrable credit.

**High-school records requirements for applicants who completed outside the US:** N/A

**Submission requirements for transfer applicants who completed high-school equivalency test:** Official GED results

**College transcript requirements:** Official transcripts from all colleges/universities attended

**Interviews available for transfer applicants:** No

**Additional requirements for transfers seeking admissions to other major:** Pharmacy—transfer students: Xavier University classifies students who apply to the University to complete their pre-pharmacy coursework as transfer students. As such, these students must comply with the requirements for admission to Xavier University. In general, the College of Pharmacy does not accept transfer students from other colleges or schools of pharmacy. However, these students may be considered for admission under exceptional circumstances. Each request for transfer is evaluated on an individual basis.

## Costs & Financial Aid

**FAFSA code:** 2032

**CSS Profile code:** N/A

**Are internal school financial aid forms required?** Yes

**Financial aid deadlines for transfer applicants:** Fall 2018: 4/15/18. Spring 2019: N/A.

**Costs for the 2017–2018 year:** Tuition & Fees: $20,594. Room & Board: $8,528.

**Financial aid for transfer students:** Yes

**Guarantees meeting 100% need for transfer students:** No

**Need-based aid for transfer students:** FAFSA

**Merit-based financial aid for transfer students:** No

**Phi Theta Kappa Scholarship:** No

**Reduced or zero tuition fees for low-income students:** No

**Includes loans in financial aid packages:** Yes

**% of all undergraduates receiving financial aid:** 87%

**% of all undergraduates qualifying for Pell Grants:** 65%

**Average financial aid award for all undergraduate students:** N/A

**Funding available for low-income students to visit:** No

**Enrollment deposit can be waived for low-income students:** N/A

## Academics

**GPA range for transfer students accepted in 2016–2017:** 2.0 minimum

**SAT ranges for all students admitted in 2016:** Critical Reading: 450–560. Mathematics: 430–550. Writing: 410–530.

**ACT composite score range for all students admitted in 2016:** 20–26

**Type of curriculum:** Gen. Ed. requirements

**Type of academic year:** Semester

**Advisors specifically for transfer students:** No

**Credit policy (in their own words):** This school utilizes credits and semester hours.

The University grants transfer credits only for courses in which the student has received a grade of C (2.0/4.0) or better and which are comparable to Xavier courses. Ordinarily, the grades of transfer courses are not computed in the Xavier GPA. Not more than 1/2 of the credits required for the degree may be transferred from a community and/or junior college.

The University will confer a degree only after the applicant has fulfilled the requirement of at least 25% of course credit in residence. 18 hours of the 25% must be in the major with a grade of C or better in each course, and 9 hours must be in the minor. At most, 50% of transfer credit can be fulfilled from community college credits.

**Max number of transfer credits accepted:** 60

**Residency requirement for transfer students:** Yes. The University will confer a degree only after the applicant has fulfilled the requirement of at least 25% of course credit in residence. 18 hours of the 25% must be in the major with a grade of C (2.0/4.0) or better in each course, and 9 hours must be in the minor. At most, 50% of transfer credit can be fulfilled from community college credits.

**Study abroad available for transfer students:** Yes. Students must:

- Be in good standing (academic, disciplinary, financial)
- Earn a minimum cumulative GPA of 2.5 before participating in study abroad
- Successfully complete at least 2 semesters of college-level coursework (or a minimum of 29 semester credit hours) before participating in a program
- Obtain transfer credit and/or course preapproval authorization

**Free tutoring for all students:** Yes

**Writing center for all students:** Yes

**Career support/access to internships and resume prep for all students:** Yes

**% of undergraduate students hired within 6 months of graduation:** 26.6%

**Additional resources specifically designated for transfer and/or non-traditional students:** Yes. Transfer orientation.

## Housing

**Available for transfer students:** Yes

**Available for non-traditional students:** No

**Guaranteed for transfer students:** No

**Non-traditional students can reside in housing year-round:** N/A

**Family housing available:** No

## Non-Traditional Admissions

No non-traditional student policies or programs available.

## Military/Veteran Students

**Military/veteran admissions policy (in their own words):** Xavier University of Louisiana is proud to be a Yellow Ribbon Program school. Only veterans (or dependents under Transfer of Entitlement) at the 100% benefit level qualify. Active-duty members and spouses thereof are not eligible for this program.

Read more at www.xavier.edu/veterans or call (513) 745-3620.

**Status considered in admissions:** No

**Special admissions process:** No

**Special financial aid:** Yes. The Yellow Ribbon Program. Details at www.xula.edu/registrar/documents/XULAYellowRibbonPolicy.pdf.

**Specific programs/policies to address needs:** The Student Veterans Center strives to provide veterans of Xavier University a safe, studious, and recreational setting. Located on campus at the Conaton Learning Commons in room 529, the Student Veterans Center offers veterans a space of their own where they can print out papers, work on assignments, or have a cup of coffee and friendly conversation. More at www.xavier.edu/veterans/About-Us.cfm.

## DACA/Undocumented Students

**DACA and undocumented admissions policy (in their own words):** No information provided.

**Admitted:** Yes

**Status considered in admissions:** Yes

**Special admissions process:** No information provided.

**Eligible for institutional financial aid:** No

**Specific programs/policies to address needs:** No

# YALE UNIVERSITY

**Location:** New Haven, Connecticut

**Website:** www.yale.edu

**Endowment:** $25.41 billion

**Type of School:** Private Co-ed, Research University

**# Undergraduate Students:** 5,453 (2015–2016)

**# of Graduate Students:** 6,859 (2015–2016)

**Average Class Size:** No information provided.

**School Mission (in their own words):** Yale is committed to improving the world today and for future generations through outstanding research and scholarship, education, preservation, and practice. Yale educates aspiring leaders worldwide who serve all sectors of society. We carry out this mission through the free exchange of ideas in an ethical, interdependent, and diverse community of faculty, staff, students, and alumni.

## Admissions

**Admissions office mailing address:** PO Box 208234, New Haven CT 06520

**Admissions office phone:** (203) 432-9300

**Admissions office email:** transfer.admissions@yale.edu

**# of transfer applications:** Fall 2015 admissions: 1,250

**# of transfer students accepted:** Fall 2015: 28

**Transfer student acceptance rate (2015–2016 academic year):** 2.2%

**Freshman applications received in Fall 2015:** 30,236.

**Freshman applications accepted in Fall 2015:** 2,034.

**Acceptance rate for 2015–2016 freshmen:** 6.7%

## Transfer Admissions Process

**Transfer policy (in their own words):** Yale welcomes a small number of transfer students each year. Transfer students begin in either the sophomore or junior year and must enroll at Yale for a minimum of 2 years (4 terms) to qualify for a bachelor's degree. Students may transfer from fully accredited 2- or 4-year institutions. The Admissions Committee meets once a year in the spring to consider all transfer applicants for the coming academic year.

Who is eligible to transfer?

- Students are eligible to transfer if they will have at least 1 year's worth of transferable postsecondary work upon entrance to Yale.
- Transfer students may enroll at sophomore or junior standing.
- Yale does not accept students who have more than 2 years' worth of transferable undergraduate coursework. All Yale students must complete at least 2 years of coursework at Yale.
- Students who are dual-enrolled in both a high-school and a college program should apply as freshmen.
- Any college credits earned prior to high-school graduation will not be evaluated as transferable credit.
- If you will have fewer than 8 transferable credits upon entering Yale, you should apply as a freshman.
- Yale does not accept transfer applicants who already hold a bachelor's degree.

If your college experience was delayed or interrupted at any point for 5 or more years, then you may apply to the Eli Whitney Students Program (EWSP). Keep in mind that freshman and transfer students must attend full-time, but Eli Whitney students have the flexibility to attend on a part- or full-time basis. Undergraduate on-campus housing is not available to Eli Whitney students. Unlike all other undergraduates, tuition costs for Eli Whitney students vary depending on the number of credits taken in any given semester. The maximum amount of Yale Scholarship per semester for Eli Whitney students is capped at the cost of tuition.

**Transfer admissions contact person:** Moira Poe, Senior Associate Director and Director of Transfer Admissions

**Transfer admissions contact info:** moira.poe@yale.edu, (203) 432-9316

**Offers transfer-focused admissions events:** No

**Transfer application deadline:** Fall 2018 deadline is 3/1/18.

**Acceptances announced to transfer applicants:** Fall 2018 in mid-May.

**Transfer application on Common App:** Yes. Common App fee: $80.

**SAT/ACT required for transfer applicants:** Yes. ACT with Writing or SAT with Essay.

**High-school record requirements:** Official high-school transcript

**High-school records requirements for applicants who completed outside the US:** Official high-school transcript with graduation date

**Submission requirements for transfer applicants who completed high-school equivalency test:** Official GED results

**College transcript requirements:** Official transcripts from all colleges/universities attended

**Interviews available for transfer applicants:** No

**Additional requirements for transfers seeking admissions to engineering major:** Physics II—Physics 240 and Physics 241 lab

**Additional requirements for transfers seeking admissions to other major:** Students majoring in Computer Science are advised to complete CPSC 201 (Introduction to Computer Science) and 223 (Data Structures and Programming Techniques) by the end of the sophomore year. This means that a transfer student entering as a junior should have equivalent courses. Students who would like to major in a language and studied it elsewhere must take the language's placement examination before enrolling in any of the language's courses at Yale.

## Costs & Financial Aid

**FAFSA code:** 1426

**CSS Profile code:** 3987

**Are internal school financial aid forms required?** No

**Financial aid deadline for transfer applicants:** Fall 2018: 3/15/18.

**Costs for the 2017–2018 year:** Tuition & Fees: $51,400. Room & Board: $15,500.

**Financial aid for transfer students:** Yes

**Guarantees meeting 100% need for transfer students:** Yes

**Need-based aid for transfer students:** Yes

**Merit-based financial aid for transfer students:** No

**Phi Theta Kappa Scholarship:** No

**Reduced or zero tuition fees for low-income students:** No

**Includes loans in financial aid packages:** No

**% of all undergraduates receiving financial aid:** 50%

**% of all undergraduates qualifying for Pell Grants:** No information provided.

**Average financial aid award for all undergraduate students:** $47,000

**Funding available for low-income students to visit:** No

**Enrollment deposit can be waived for low-income students:** No

## Academics

**GPA range for transfer students accepted in 2016–2017:** No information provided.

**SAT ranges for all students admitted in 2016:** Critical Reading: 720–800. Mathematics: 710–800. Writing: 710–790.

**ACT composite score range for all students admitted in 2016:** 31–35

**Type of curriculum:** Gen. Ed. requirements

**Type of academic year:** Semester

**Advisors specifically for transfer students:** No

**Credit policy (in their own words):** Admitted transfer students may be eligible to transfer up to a maximum of 18 course credits. Most courses at Yale are semester courses that carry 1 course credit. The Yale Dean's Office evaluates transcripts for all admitted transfer students to determine course transferability, once a student has been admitted. College courses that are similar to those available to Yale undergraduates are likely transferable.

Most courses at Yale are term courses that carry 1 course credit if completed with a passing grade.

There are, however, some variations:

- A couple courses at Yale, including intensive language or research courses, award 2 course credits for a single term's work.
- There are a couple yearlong course sequences in which 2 course credits are awarded upon the satisfactory completion of both terms of the sequence; other course sequences, including some research and laboratory courses, give 1 or 4 course credits for the successful completion of the full year's work.
- Some laboratory courses carry no separate credit toward the degree, others carry a full course credit for a term's work, and still others carry 0.5 course credit.
- All courses that carry 0.5 or 1.5 course credits and that are not bound by the credit/year restriction count toward the 36-course-credit requirement for the bachelor's degree.

**Max number of transfer credits accepted:** 18

**Residency requirement for transfer students:** Yes. Minimum of 18 credits earned and 4 semesters spent at Yale.

**Study abroad available for transfer students:** Yes. Must fulfill residency requirements.

**Free tutoring for all students:** Yes

**Writing center for all students:** Yes

**Career support/access to internships and resume prep for all students:** Yes

**% of undergraduate students hired within 6 months of graduation:** No information provided.

**Additional resources specifically designated for transfer and/or non-traditional students:** No

## Housing

**Available for transfer students:** Yes

**Available for non-traditional students:** No

**Guaranteed for transfer students:** Yes. Sophomore transfers.

**Non-traditional students can reside in housing year-round:** No

**Family housing available:** No

## Non-Traditional Admissions

**Non-traditional student policy (in their own words):** Yale welcomes applications from non-traditional students with exceptional backgrounds and aspirations. The Eli Whitney Students Program (EWSP) at Yale is designed for individuals with high academic potential who have had their education interrupted, at some point during their educational careers, for 5 or more years. The program enrolls a small number of non-traditional students who have demonstrated maturity and achievement. These students enrich Yale through their life experience, sense of purpose, and character. Students in the EWSP may enroll on a full- or part-time basis. Eli Whitney students take classes with other Yale undergraduates and earn either a bachelor of arts or a bachelor of science degree from Yale. Need-based financial aid is available to those who qualify.

**Name of program:** Eli Whitney Students Program (EWSP)

**Program description:** The EWSP at Yale is designed for individuals with high academic potential who have had their education interrupted, at some point during their educational careers, for 5 or more years. The program enrolls a small number of non-traditional students who have demonstrated maturity and achievement. These students enrich Yale through their life experience, sense of purpose, and character. The Eli Whitney Students Program presents the non-traditional student with a flexible path to fulfill the standard requirements of a Yale undergraduate degree.

**Program deadline:** 3/15/18

**Program admission requirements:** To be eligible to apply to the EWSP, candidates must hold a high-school or GED diploma and have had their education interrupted for 5 or more years at some point during their educational career. SAT and ACT are not required, but strongly recommended.

**Program website:** https://admissions.yale.edu/eli-whitney

**Program contact person:** Patricia Wei, Director of Admission, Eli Whitney Students Program

**Program contact info:** (203) 432-9316, patricia.wei@yale.edu

## Military/Veteran Students

**Military/veteran admissions policy (in their own words):** Yale welcomes applications from veterans. Most veterans interested in Yale's undergraduate program submit applications to the Eli Whitney Students Program for non-traditional students (see above). A Yale education is very affordable for veterans as Yale is a participant in the Yellow Ribbon Program, a provision of the 9/11 Veterans Education Assistance Act. Yale has also partnered with Service to School's Vetlink Program, which supports veterans in their college search process. In addition, Yale participates in the Marine Corps Leadership Scholar Program.

Approximately 1/3 of current Eli Whitney students have served in the US military. Examples of veterans at Yale include a former USAF cryptologic linguist, USMC corporal, Navy journalist, and Army Ranger. Most of these veterans took college classes while on active duty and/or pursued full-time college study at community colleges after being discharged.

**Status considered in admissions:** No

**Special admissions process:** No

**Special financial aid:** Yes. The Yellow Ribbon Program.

**Specific programs/policies to address needs:** Yale has a veteran liaison who serves as Yale's central point of contact in supporting faculty, students, staff, and alumni who are military veterans. He will assist veterans in accessing services and resources both within and external to Yale. See https://admissions.yale.edu/veterans for more details.

## DACA/Undocumented Students

**DACA and undocumented admissions policy (in their own words):** Yale is proud of its strong commitment to equal opportunity and accessibility to all candidates from any part of the world who show great academic and personal promise. We extend our need-blind admissions policy and holistic application review to all students without regard to citizenship or immigration status.

**Admitted:** Yes

**Status considered in admissions:** No

**Special admissions process:** No

**Eligible for institutional financial aid:** Yes. Same as all admitted students.

**Specific programs/policies to address needs:** Yes. Legal assistance, study-abroad assistance, career and fellowship resources. Read more here: http://oiss.yale.edu/immigration/undocumented-dacamented-students.

# The Language of Transfer

As you look through this guide, there may be some terms you aren't familiar with. If you get lost, just refer to this glossary.

## TYPES OF SCHOOLS

- **Current college:** The pre-transfer school where you are currently enrolled and earning credits. If you are applying to transfer and are not currently enrolled, consider this the most recent college you attended.

- **Previous college:** Any school where you enrolled for classes. Transfer students need to submit transcripts from all colleges they have attended. You will need to submit a transcript for any previous school where you were enrolled even if you did not earn a degree from that institution.

- **Prospective college:** A college that you are thinking about attending in the future. As a transfer applicant, you should develop a list of prospective colleges to apply to based on your interests, skills, and goals, as well as the resources, financial aid, and college experience the prospective colleges can provide.

- **Community college or county college:** A type of postsecondary (after high school) educational institution that typically offers open enrollment. Most offer associate's degrees aimed at preparing students to transfer to a bachelor's degree program or to obtain employment. Community colleges also offer certificates and other nondegree options that provide enrichment for local residents.

- **City or state school:** A college or university that is generally named after the city or state in which it is located and usually funded by state and/or city governments. These schools offer lower tuition for in-state or local students and higher rates for students applying from other areas in the country. As a transfer student, you should consider city or state schools, as they often have agreements with local community colleges to admit their students.

- **Liberal arts college:** These are schools that focus on undergraduate study and giving their students broad general knowledge and intellectual competencies, as opposed to technical skills. Usually, students at these schools will focus on one area of study (their major) but also be exposed to a variety of other subjects to give them a well-rounded education.

- **Research university:** At these schools, all faculty are first and foremost researchers. They recruit some of the most brilliant researchers in the world to teach, meaning students can expect to learn from the top experts in their fields. However, not all world-class researchers are also world-class teachers. These schools are generally very prestigious.

- **Women's college:** A college that only offers admission to women. Traditionally, colleges were only open to men, and women's colleges were founded to provide opportunities for women to pursue higher education.
- **Men's college:** A college that only offers admission to men.
- **HBCU:** Historically black colleges and universities (HBCUs) are US schools established before 1964 that primarily serve African American students, who were historically prevented from attending other educational institutions. However, they now accept students of all races.

## SCHOOL REGIONS

- **New England:** Maine, New Hampshire, Vermont, Massachusetts, Rhode Island, and Connecticut
- **Mid-Atlantic:** New York, Pennsylvania, New Jersey, Delaware, Maryland, and Washington, D.C.
- **The South:** West Virginia, Virginia, North Carolina, South Carolina, Georgia, Florida, Kentucky, Tennessee, Alabama, Mississippi, Louisiana, Arkansas
- **Midwest:** North Dakota, South Dakota, Nebraska, Kansas, Minnesota, Iowa, Missouri, Wisconsin, Illinois, Indiana, Michigan, Ohio
- **Southwest:** Oklahoma, Texas, New Mexico, Arizona
- **The West:** Montana, Wyoming, Colorado, Utah, Idaho, Nevada, Washington, Oregon, California, Hawaii, Alaska

## TYPES OF ADMISSION

- **Open enrollment:** This means that a school allows all applicants who meet basic requirements to attend. Community colleges generally allow all students with a high-school diploma or high-school equivalency to enroll in an associate's degree program.
- **College selectivity:** This is tied to a college or university's overall acceptance rate. Colleges that accept a smaller percentage of students have a higher level of selectivity. Highly selective schools usually have a bigger price tag, but they may also have more money available for financial aid and be able to spend more on their students. As a transfer applicant, you should consider applying to schools with varying levels of selectivity when forming your school list.
- **First-year applicant:** A student who has completed high school and is applying to college as a freshman.
- **Transfer applicant:** A student who has been enrolled in a college, earned college credit, and is seeking transfer to another school to complete their degree. Transfer students usually have different application requirements from first-year applicants. For example, many schools do not require SAT or ACT test scores from transfer applicants. Some schools may have credit or enrollment policies that determine whether a student applies as a freshman or transfer student.
- **Traditional student:** A student who applies to and enrolls in college immediately after high school. These students enter college as freshmen aged 17–19. Colleges generally gear their policies toward traditional-age students. For example, many colleges require underclassmen (freshmen and sophomores) to live on campus in dorms typically located toward the center of campus to ease the transition to independent living for students who have never lived

away from home. As a transfer student, your status as a traditional or non-traditional student will impact the development of your list of prospective schools.

- **Non-traditional student:** A student who does not fit the profile of a traditional college freshman in age, family composition, or other areas. Schools differ in terms of their processes and policies around defining which students are categorized as traditional or non-traditional, which often affects the application process. Schools may also have specific financial aid or housing set aside for students they define as non-traditional.

# TYPES OF DEGREES

- **Associate's degree:** Awarded to students that complete credits equivalent to two years of full-time study (typically 60 credit hours). Community colleges primarily offer associate's degree and certificate programs. Credits earned toward an associate's degree can often be applied toward a bachelor's degree program. Types of associate's degrees include:
  - **A.A.—Associate of arts:** Includes general education requirements and courses related to a specific degree program, usually focused in liberal arts. Includes majors like history, English, psychology, and sociology.
  - **A.S.—Associate of science:** Includes general education requirements and courses typically related to a specific area in science. Includes majors like biology, chemistry, public health, education, and computer science.
  - **A.A.S.—Associate of applied science:** Includes general education requirements and is usually geared toward obtaining a specific job upon graduation. Includes majors like nursing, accounting, paralegal studies, and radiologic technology.
- **Bachelor's degree:** Awarded to a student who earns credits equivalent to four years of full-time study (typically 120 credit hours) toward a major in a specific discipline. As a transfer student, you will be seeking acceptance into a program to earn a bachelor's degree.
  - **B.A.—Bachelor of arts:** Awarded to students who complete the degree requirements for a four-year degree in a field associated with the humanities (e.g., English, foreign language, history, sociology). Some schools use the abbreviation A.B. for the traditional Latin name of *artium baccalaureus*.
  - **B.S.—Bachelor of science:** Awarded to students who complete the degree requirements for a four-year degree in a field associated with the sciences (e.g., biology, chemistry, pharmacology, computer science). Some schools use the abbreviation S.B. for the traditional Latin name of *scientiae baccalaureus*.
- **Master's degree:** Awarded to a student who completes the course of study to earn the credits that satisfy the requirements for a master's degree program, which typically lasts two years and comes after a student has earned a bachelor's degree.
  - **M.A.—Master of arts:** Awarded to students who complete the degree requirements for a graduate degree in a field associated with the humanities (e.g., English, foreign language, history, sociology).
  - **M.S.—Master of science:** Awarded to students who complete the degree requirements for a graduate degree in a field associated with the sciences (e.g., biology, chemistry, pharmacology, computer science).

- **Doctoral degree:** These degrees are also known as terminal degrees as they are the final degrees that can be earned in a subject area. Doctoral degrees require anywhere from four to eight years to complete, depending on the discipline and specialization.
  - **Ph.D.—Doctor of philosophy:** This is typically awarded after a student completes and publishes academic, peer-reviewed research.
  - **M.D.—Doctor of medicine:** This is the highest degree conferred upon an individual in medicine. To practice medicine, people who hold an M.D. must pass state board examinations.
  - **J.D.—Juris doctor:** The terminal degree for law students. Students who have earned their J.D. must first pass their state's bar exam to be able to practice law.
  - **Ed.D.—Doctor of education:** The highest level that can be achieved in the field of education. This degree is often held by people who want to lead administration and policy-making in education.

# SCHOOL OFFICES

- **Admissions:** The first office that a student interacts with when seeking to enroll at a school. This office is tasked with managing the application process, including collecting and reviewing all the documents within the application, answering questions from interested students, conducting interviews, hosting information sessions, and deciding who is admitted.
- **Financial aid:** The office that handles the applications for and disbursement of financial aid funding. As a transfer student, you will likely need financial aid to cover the cost of a bachelor's degree program.
- **Registrar:** The office tasked with maintaining student academic records, including course enrollment and transcripts. As a transfer student, you will need to request copies of your transcript through the registrar's office. At your transfer school, your credit evaluation will be handled through the registrar's office, often with assistance from the department chair of your intended major.
- **Bursar:** Responsible for maintaining student accounts and handling tuition payments. During the transfer process, you may need to go to the bursar's office to request a copy of your financial aid package.
- **Residential life:** Manages housing for students attending the institution. As a transfer student, you may end up enrolling at a school where you live on campus. This office manages the roommate matching process and coordinates events in student housing to help build a sense of community. In building your college list, you may need to contact the office of residential life to confirm whether housing for transfer students is available and whether it is guaranteed for renewal. This office can also assist students in locating off-campus housing if transfer housing is not offered or guaranteed.
- **Dean:** This office manages different administrative and academic areas of the college, including: faculty, students, student affairs, diversity and inclusion, and academic affairs. Deans manage day-to-day operations and deal with any issues that occur in their departments. As a transfer student, you may need to submit a dean's report to confirm that you are in good standing or if you have any honor-code violations on your permanent record.

- **President:** This office directs the overall management of the school's faculty, staff, administrators, and students. The president of a college or university reports to the Board of Trustees, a group of elected prominent leaders tasked with ensuring the success of the institution. The president also represents the school to the nation and develops the policies and strategies that govern the school. As a transfer student, you will need to research schools to determine if they will provide you with an optimal environment to pursue a degree. It is important to read the biographies of school presidents to get an idea of the leadership of the prospective schools on your list. Presidents often host open hours when you can go and speak to them about any questions or concerns after you transfer.

## STUDENT CLASSES

- **Undergraduate students:** Students enrolled in a college or university who are pursuing associate's or bachelor's degrees.
- **Graduate students:** Students who have completed their bachelor's degree and are enrolled in master's or doctoral degree programs.
- **Freshmen:** Students in their first year at an educational institution.
- **Sophomores:** Students in their second year at an educational institution.
- **Juniors:** Students in their third year at an educational institution. During junior year, students are often encouraged to start thinking about their career goals.
- **Seniors:** Students in their fourth or last year at an educational institution.
- **Underclassmen:** Generally used to refer to freshmen and sophomores, who are less senior than upperclassmen.
- **Upperclassmen:** Generally used to refer to the more senior classes at a school: juniors and seniors.

## PEOPLE TO KNOW

- **Teaching assistant (TA):** Support professors by delivering lectures, administering tests and quizzes, and hosting TA sessions for reviewing material for large introductory classes of 30 or more students. In large classes, it may be difficult to access your professor when you have questions about a challenging concept or assignment. Take time to build a good relationship with your TA; they are there to help you succeed in the course.
- **Academic advisor:** Upon enrollment, students are typically assigned academic advisors to assist with course selection to ensure all academic requirements will be met prior to graduation. When students declare a major, they will be reassigned to an academic advisor within that department. Students intending to double major may need academic advisors in both departments.
- **Financial aid counselor:** Tasked with managing students' financial aid applications. During the transfer process, you may need to provide information about your current application package to the schools you are applying to. Building a relationship with your financial aid counselor can be helpful in fully understanding your financial responsibilities, locating documents, and filling out forms. In the event that your financial situation changes (e.g., decrease in your family's ability to pay due to a parent retiring or losing a job), your

financial aid counselor can help you apply for additional funding. If you have received a larger financial aid package from another transfer school, you should make your desired transfer school aware and ask if they are able to match the better package.

- **Residential advisor (RA):** Students employed by the Office of Residential Life to provide on-site support to students living in on-campus housing. If you are a transfer student living on campus, your RA will be an important resource during your first semester for learning the ropes and getting up to speed on navigating your new school. RAs are selected through a rigorous interview process and are provided training to deal with conflict resolution and community engagement.

- **Faculty (professors):** Faculty are the instructors who teach your courses, but it's important to understand that the role they play in your education extends beyond the classroom. It is important to build strong relationships with your professors for each of your classes. When applying for internships and transfer, you will need strong recommendations from professors who can speak to your academic achievements. Take advantage of office hours, or email your professor to schedule times to meet to discuss your progress. Maintaining consistent communication with your professor can help you meet your academic goals by keeping you aware of your performance and ways you can improve your grade.

- **Transfer advisor:** Available to assist you with navigating the transfer process. Many community colleges have a transfer office with advisors ready to help you complete your applications to transfer. While some transfer offices are geared toward helping students transfer to local colleges and universities, they can still help you apply to schools across the nation.

- **Admissions officer:** Tasked with recruiting and selecting students for their school. Some admissions offices will have an officer that is assigned specifically to transfer applicants. Alternatively, admissions officers can be assigned by geographical region or by state. As a transfer student, it is important for you to identify and communicate directly with your assigned admissions officer. They will likely read your application, so it is important for you to interact with them in a professional manner that will provide them with insight into your character beyond what is on the page.

## CALENDAR

- **Academic calendar:** Each school publishes a calendar that details the schedule of events for the coming year. An academic calendar is the most official breakdown of an academic year. It includes important dates and deadlines that affect enrollment, grades, and expected attendance. It offers the official dates for terms, reading periods, observed holidays, the last day to withdraw from classes, and graduation. It is important that you remain aware of all academic deadlines, and you should take the time to mark them in your personal calendar. Failure to meet deadlines can result in additional fees, loss of financial aid, or a derogatory mark (e.g., "W" for a withdrawal or "I" for incomplete) on your transcript.

- **Shopping or add/drop period:** Typically, the first two weeks at the beginning of a semester. During this time frame, students can attend classes without a commitment to complete the course and can add or drop classes from their registration without a penalty. This allows students the chance to get into a class that was initially full during registration. After this period ends, students can only remove themselves from a class through a withdrawal.

- **Withdrawal:** This is a mark a student receives in place of a grade when they decide to drop a class after the add/drop period has closed. While a W will not count against your GPA, admissions committees generally look upon them unfavorably on a transcript. They may indicate poor planning and suggest the student was doing poorly in the class and would otherwise have received a low grade or failed. Avoid receiving withdrawals on your transcript. However, if you do have a W on your transcript, be prepared to provide an explanation for your decision to withdraw from the course.

- **Incomplete:** This mark can be given if a student is currently passing the course but was unable to submit their final assignments prior to the end of the term. This I mark requires permission from the professor, and students often have the option of repeating the course or handing in their work at a later date. If the course is not repeated or if the student fails to hand in their work, an incomplete will be often be converted into an F—with extremely negative consequences for your GPA. If you need to take an I for a course, be diligent in following up to ensure you do not fail the class.

- **Semester:** Schools with semester systems divide the academic year into two required terms. Usually, these schools also offer optional summer sessions that are half as long as their semesters.

- **Trimester:** Schools with trimester systems divide the academic year into three terms, requiring attendance two trimesters per year.

- **Quarter system:** Schools with quarter systems divide the academic year into four terms, one per season, requiring attendance three quarters per year.

- **Intersession:** Refers to the periods of time between traditional semesters (e.g., winter, summer, and spring breaks). Many schools offer classes during intersession periods. As a transfer, you can use intersession classes to catch up on credits to avoid spending an extra semester to take one or two classes that you need in order to graduate.

- **J-term:** Short for January term, this refers to a shortened academic term during which some schools offer classes. Transfer students can use J-term study-abroad opportunities to travel and earn college credit while still fulfilling residency requirements.

## THE TRANSFER PROCESS

- **Credit evaluation:** Used to determine the number of credits that will be accepted toward your degree at your transfer school. The registrar's office is typically responsible for reviewing your transcript and providing your credit evaluation. Credits obtained at a community college typically are a fraction of the cost of credits obtained at a four-year school, so it is helpful and more affordable to select a major and take courses that are likely to transfer. Different schools have different requirements, so save your syllabi and assignments in case you need to submit them for your credit evaluation. Keep in mind, credits that transfer may not be counted toward your major—this is particularly important for science majors.

- **Syllabus:** A document provided by professors at the beginning of their course that outlines objectives, a schedule of all required work, and all policies regarding late work, attendance, and grading. It is imperative that you keep copies of your syllabi in case they are needed during your credit evaluations. Each of your prospective schools will have different requirements. They may even request to see a graded assignment, so keep track of all graded papers as well as syllabi.

- **Articulation agreements:** Formalized written agreements, typically agreed upon between community colleges and four-year schools to outline transfer credit policies. If you transfer to a school that has an articulation agreement with your community college, your credits are guaranteed to transfer as long as they meet the requirements outlined in the agreement, which may include a minimum GPA and good disciplinary standing. These may be limited to specific majors. You should research your community college's articulation agreements when developing your college list.

- **Safety school:** A school that you can safely assume will accept your application and offer you a spot in their enrollment. Generally, safety schools have a lower level of college selectivity and admit a greater percentage of applicants. Your list of prospective schools should include a few safety schools to ensure you have options.

- **Target school:** A school you are likely to be accepted to that has a medium level of selectivity. Schools with greater selectivity tend to offer more financial aid and resources to applicants. Transfer applicants should consider a range of schools both in location and selectivity.

- **Reach school:** A school that is highly selective where you have a shot but are not guaranteed acceptance. Highly selective schools tend to have large endowments and often have special programs that offer additional support and resources for transfer students. It is important that you stretch out of your comfort zone and apply to reach schools that fit your transfer profile.

- **Midsemester report:** A report you must get filled out by each professor you are taking a class with in the semester when you are applying for transfer. This document provides a summary of your academic performance so far in that course.

- **Veteran resources:** Programs and policies put in place to provide veterans with additional support while completing their degrees. Schools may have a veteran affairs office that deals directly with students or participates in the Yellow Ribbon Program.

  - **Yellow Ribbon Program:** According to the Post-9/11 GI Bill, veterans (or their transferees) eligible for the maximum benefit rate, based on their service requirements, can receive additional funding from their transfer school.[13]

  - **Post-9/11 GI Bill:** Provides 100 percent of tuition and fees for in-state public schools and up to $21,084.89 toward private schools, plus a living allowance and money toward books and supplies.[14]

  - **Credit for military training:** Veterans can apply as transfer students and seek academic credit for their military training. They can request a joint services transcript of all military training to be presented for credit evaluation. Keep in mind that accepted credit will typically be applied to general education requirements and not toward major requirements.

- **Residency requirements:** Policies that require transfer students to earn a specific number of credits at their transfer school in order to earn their degree from the institution. For example, many schools will cap the number of transfer credits they receive to a maximum of 60 credits, or two years of study. Schools may also require transfer students to live on campus for at least two semesters.

---

13  Source: www.benefits.va.gov/gibill/yellow_ribbon.asp
14  Source: www.vets.gov/education/gi-bill/post-9-11

- **STEM:** The acronym for Science, Technology, Engineering, and Mathematics. As a transfer applicant, you may be interested in majoring in a STEM field. It is important to learn the requirements for pursuing degrees within STEM (e.g., required level of math, a specific sequence of courses, courses with required labs).

# FINANCIAL AID

- **FAFSA (Free Application for Federal Student Aid):** A form completed by students who wish to apply for federal financial aid. Financial aid awards include federal grants, loans, and work-study. To be eligible, students need to demonstrate financial need (an inability to pay for school on their own) and be an American citizen or have permanent residency.

- **SAR (Student Aid Report):** Filling out the FAFSA generates a Student Aid Report that provides a summary of all the financial information you entered and calculates your EFC, or estimated family contribution.

- **Estimated family contribution (EFC):** The amount you are expected to pay toward your cost of attendance. Your EFC is used to determine the amount of federal aid you are eligible to receive and appears on your SAR after filling out the FAFSA. As a transfer student, your schools will use this information to calculate your financial aid package.

- **Cost of attendance (COA):** The full amount of funding you need to live and study during the academic year. When calculating your financial aid package, schools consider housing and food (often written as *room and board*), books, tuition, fees, travel, and miscellaneous and personal expenses. If you have a family, the costs of housing and caring for your family are considered.

- **Financial need:** This is the amount of financial assistance you will need to meet the costs of attending school. Your school calculates your financial need by subtracting your expected family contribution (EFC) from the cost of attendance (COA). The cost of attendance will vary between your schools, but your EFC is determined annually based on your FAFSA.[15]

- **Financial aid package:** A listing from your prospective school of the total amount of financial funding you will receive toward the cost of attendance at a school where you have been accepted. Your financial aid will detail the federal and/or institutional aid that has been offered to you. As a transfer student, it is important to apply early to maximize your financial aid. Keep in mind that you can petition your top school for more funding if another school offers you more aid.

- **College Scholarship Service (CSS) Profile:** Used to collect financial documentation that certain colleges and universities use in awarding institutional financial aid. This application is completed in addition to the FAFSA and has a fee, but low-income students can apply for a fee waiver. As a transfer, you should not let the CSS Profile deter you from applying to selective schools. This application allows you to be considered for funding beyond the federal support from the FAFSA. Keep in mind you may need financial documentation from your parents to complete this application. Do not wait until the last minute, as you want to have your application in the system for primary consideration. Also, more funding tends to be available in the fall semester, which may inform your decision for which term to apply for transfer to a particular school.

---

15   https://studentaid.ed.gov/sa/glossary

- **Grant:** Financial aid funding that does not need to be paid back under most conditions. But grants may be dependent upon completing your degree or maintaining certain requirements, like a high GPA.
- **Need-based scholarship:** An amount of money given to a student toward their educational expenses based on determining they are unable to pay for school on their own. Students may need to submit an application to be considered for this award.
- **Merit-based scholarship:** An amount of money given to a student toward their educational expenses based on academic achievement and extracurricular engagement.
- **Loan:** Funding you must pay back to the organization that provided you with the funds, plus interest.
  - **Subsidized loan:** This type of loan is determined by financial need, and the federal government agrees to pay the interest while you are in school and during a grace period after graduation.
  - **Unsubsidized loan:** This type of loan starts accruing interest from the moment you receive funding until you finish paying off the loan.
- **Interest:** When you take out a loan, the lender (the organization loaning you the money) charges you over time through an expense called interest. Interest is calculated as a percentage of the principal, the total unpaid amount of the loan.
- **Federal work-study:** A federal student aid program that provides funding that you earn through part-time work at your transfer school. As a transfer student, you will be adapting to a new environment. Consider applying for work-study jobs in quiet locations like offices or libraries where you may be able to fit in some studying.
- **Institutional financial aid:** Funding provided to you from your transfer school to be used to help cover the total cost of attendance. Institutional aid can take the form of a grant or a loan.
- **Transcript:** An official academic record of the classes you have taken, the grades earned in each class, and your overall grade point average (GPA). When applying for transfer, you will need to submit official copies of your transcript to each school you apply to.
- **Common Application (Common App):** An online platform that allows you to apply to multiple colleges at once. This helps cut down on sending the same information separately to different schools. However, as a transfer student you may have different application requirements, from additional essay questions on the Common App to filling out a special transfer application for each prospective school.
- **Recommender:** A person whom you ask to write a recommendation to support your application to your transfer schools. You should pick people who know you well and can provide concrete examples of your positive traits and accomplishments. Options for recommenders include teachers, advisors, mentors, coaches, and bosses.
- **Academic evaluation (Common App):** Recommendation provided by a college academic advisor, professor, dean, or instructor that can speak to your academic performance. The Common App requires at least one of these recommendations for transfer student applications, as opposed to a nonacademic recommendation from an employer.[16]
- **Extracurricular:** An activity or experience that occurs outside of the classroom. Examples of extracurriculars include participation in athletics, art or music groups, hobby groups, community organizations or religious groups, and charitable organizations.

16   Source: Common App

- **SAT:** A standardized college admissions exam required by many competitive schools for application. Please see the standardized test section of Chapter Four: How to Be a Transfer Star for more details.

- **ACT:** A standardized college admissions exam required by many competitive schools for application. Please see the standardized test section of Chapter Four: How to Be a Transfer Star for more details.

- **High-school diploma:** Awarded to students who successfully graduate from high school. Transfer students are required to submit proof of high-school completion. Don't be discouraged from applying to transfer if your high-school performance wasn't great. Use your time at your pre-transfer college to build a new academic record by performing well in your courses to establish a new GPA.

- **High-school equivalency (HSE) diploma:** Earned by taking a test, this document can be used in place of a high-school diploma to enroll in college. Students who dropped out of high school, were home-schooled, or emigrated from another country may choose to obtain an HSE.

## EVENTS AND OPPORTUNITIES

- **Orientation:** For freshmen, orientation occurs at the beginning of the academic year and consists of different events to orient them to the school's landscape and policies, as well as welcome them to campus. Usually, several social events are held to help students feel at home, get into the school spirit, and make new friends. Some universities also have orientation sessions specifically for transfer students. Since transfer students are generally already familiar with college life, their orientation sessions are designed to acquaint them with their new school through campus tours, introductions to advisers and teachers, and social events with other transfer students.

- **Study abroad:** When a student goes to school outside of their home country, it's called studying abroad. In the United States, students who study abroad generally spend one or two semesters in another country. Benefits of study abroad include gaining expertise in other languages, becoming more independent and mature, and getting the opportunity to research, volunteer, and study on the ground in your area of interest. There are many ways to study abroad, and schools have different policies about it, so it's a good idea to look up how it works at schools you are interested in if you are thinking about taking advantage of study-abroad opportunities.

- **Research:** Engaging in research, whether under the guidance of a faculty member or independently, is an important part of some students' college experience. It can be very helpful in supporting students' applications to graduate school, scholarships, fellowships, and awards. It also can help students form relationships with professors who are interested in the same areas of study. Engaging in research projects of any kind can help develop students' talents and prepare them for a career.

- **Internships:** Internships serve as on-the-job training for professional careers. They can be paid or unpaid. When unpaid, a student usually benefits by getting school credit or being able to put the internship on their resume when applying for jobs. They also help form your professional network, get you letters of recommendation, and sometimes even result in a full-time paid job at the company you interned at. Schools have different policies on internships, so make sure you understand how they work at schools you are interested in if you are thinking about internship opportunities.

- **Externships:** Like internships, externships give students practical experience in their field. They tend to be shorter than internships (days or weeks rather than months) and usually consist of shadowing someone on the job rather than performing the work oneself. Most are unpaid and do not result in college credit, but provide students with insight into a field they may be thinking of entering.

# HOUSING

- **On-campus:** Living in an on-campus dorm or residence hall puts you in the middle of campus life and close to facilities like dining halls, laundry rooms, and gyms. Not having to worry about wireless Internet and maintenance of common spaces can make life easier as well, and on-campus housing puts you close to other students who can become lifelong friends. However, dorm life can be distracting and cramped for some people. It's always a good idea to check out on-campus housing amenities, policies, financial costs and aid, and lifestyles as you decide whether to live on- or off-campus.

- **Off-campus:** Living off-campus can mean larger and/or more private spaces in which to live, work, and study. It also gives you more independence and lets you escape the "bubble" of college life. Still, depending upon location, off-campus housing could make you feel more isolated from campus life or give you a longer commute to classes. You will also be more responsible for taking care of bills, maintenance, and cleaning. Some colleges provide financial aid for off-campus housing.

- **Affinity:** Affinity housing allows student organizations, athletic teams, and academic groups to create their own housing communities around their specific needs and interests. These vary significantly from school to school. Some colleges have affinity housing designated for transfer students so they can share their experiences and become engaged in campus life.

CPSIA information can be obtained
at www.ICGtesting.com
Printed in the USA
LVOW04s0117080118
562195LV00006B/83/P